PEARSON   ALWAYS LEARNING

Human Communication in Society

Custom Edition **2**

Jess K. Alberts
Arizona State University

Thomas K. Nakayama
Northeastern University

Judith N. Martin
Arizona State University

Taken from:
Human Communication in Society, Second Edition
by Jess K. Alberts, Thomas K. Nakayama, and Judith N. Martin

Cover Art: Courtesy of EyeWire/Getty Images + Digital Vision/Getty Images + PhotoDisc/Getty Images.

Taken from:

Human Communication in Society, Second Edition
by Jess K. Alberts, Thomas K. Nakayama, and Judith N. Martin
Copyright © 2010, 2007 by Pearson Education, Inc.
Published by Allyn & Bacon
Boston, Massachusetts 02116

This special edition published in cooperation with Pearson Learning Solutions.

All trademarks, service marks, registered trademarks, and registered service marks are the property of their respective owners and are used herein for identification purposes only.

Pearson Learning Solutions, 501 Boylston Street, Suite 900, Boston, MA 02116
A Pearson Education Company
www.pearsoned.com

Printed in the United States of America

14 15 16 17 V011 16 15 14 13

000200010271290898

RG

PEARSON
ISBN 10: 1-256-50921-3
ISBN 13: 978-1-256-50921-9

Contents

9
Small Group Communication 222

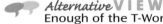

Alternative V I E W

▥ Did You Know?

COMMUNICATION IN SOCIETY

10
Communicating in Organizations 254

▥ Did You Know?

 COMMUNICATION IN SOCIETY

Alternative V I E W

Preface

As experienced researchers and instructors in the field of communication, we continue to be impressed by the breadth and depth of scholarship in our discipline; we also recognize that it presents challenges for students and instructors in the introductory survey course. For example, which research traditions should be covered: the traditional functionalist and psychological perspectives, the interpretive-qualitative perspectives, or the more recent critical and postmodern perspectives? Which subfields should be covered: intercultural communication, communication technologies, nonverbal communication, or rhetorical studies? Should instructors focus primarily on helping students develop communication skills or should they focus primarily on theories and inquiry?

Our struggle to answer these questions led us to write the first edition of this text, which we believe met the goals we established early on: first, to expose beginning students to the breadth and depth of our discipline's scholarship, and second, to provide a balance between theory and application. A third goal was to present a lively overview of the discipline, to meet students "where they live," and to engage them in exploring the implications of communication in their daily lives. Our overarching theme for the first edition was the interaction between the individual and society. In the second edition, we've enhanced the emphasis on this theme, adding new examples, illustrations and margin material that connect the more traditional individual-centered, functionalist approach—that is, "who you are (gender, race, age) affects how you communicate"—with the more contemporary critical approaches, which focus on the impact of societal structures and history on communication outcomes. By highlighting this tension between individual and societal forces, we encourage students to recognize the value of multiple perspectives in understanding communication.

Human Communication in Society, Second Edition, like the first edition, covers the full range of topics addressed in existing textbooks but also introduces some useful innovations. We include coverage of rhetoric and a discussion of the range of paradigmatic approaches in the field. We offer a balance between theory and practice: Chapters 3 through 14 each cover the major theoretical approaches for a given topic and conclude with practical guidelines for applying the material. Ours is the first book to separate coverage of the field of rhetoric (Chapter 11) from public speaking instruction (Chapter 14). Computer-mediated communication (Chapter 13) is covered in addition to media (Chapter 12).

NEW TO THIS EDITION

In this edition, general changes are integrated into each chapter as well as changes specific to each chapter (described in the next section). The general changes include the addition of:

- Chapter objectives to each chapter to help guide student learning and to articulate for the instructor desired outcomes for the chapter.

- "Communication in Society" boxes in each chapter that serve to reinforce for students the connection between the individual and society.

- Discussion questions to the "Did You Know?" boxes in each chapter to stimulate student thought and discussion.

- Updated examples to include contemporary events and trends to help students connect the concepts to their personal experiences.

- More activities and discussion to strengthen students' skills and help them become more effective communicators.

CHAPTER-BY-CHAPTER CHANGES

Human Communication in Society, Second Edition, is divided into three sections:

Section 1

The first section, which comprises Chapters 1–3, provides an overview of the book and outlines its theoretical foundation.

- **Chapter 1** explains the theme of this book—the interaction between the individual and society. This edition **includes a new section explaining how communication differs from other social sciences and an extended introduction to communication ethics.**

- **Chapter 2** provides a brief history of the field from its early rhetorical roots to contemporary multi-paradigmatic traditions. This edition includes **updated examples of contemporary research approaches, and the discussion of the early history of rhetoric has been transferred to Chapter 11.**

- **Chapter 3** explores the relationship between communication and identities. This edition includes **updated examples of contemporary identity issues (e.g., Obama and religion, women and pay) and a new discussion of self-respect.**

Section 2

The second section, consisting of Chapters 4–6, provides the foundation for the study of human communication.

- **Chapter 4** focuses on communication and perception. This edition includes **new discussions on cognitive prototypes and interpretive frames as well as the inclusion of more current examples, such as the effect of perception on the ability to hear mosquito ringtones.**

- **Chapter 5** outlines the elements of verbal communication. This edition includes **a new section on words and power, an extended discussion of pragmatics, and further discussion of the connection between perception and language.**

- **Chapter 6** addresses issues of nonverbal communication. This chapter now focuses more specifically on **the influence of society on nonverbal communication, and vice versa. It discusses the role of power in nonverbal communication and examines how prejudice and discrimination are triggered by and expressed through nonverbal communication.**

Section 3

The third section, which includes Chapters 7–14, explores the various contexts in which human communication occurs.

- **Chapter 7** explores communication across cultures. This edition contains **updated cultural adaptation theories, as well as new examples of how societal forces affect intercultural encounters, for example, the varying reactions toward some immigrant groups after 9/11.**

- **Chapter 8** discusses communication in close relationships. **The discussion on dialectics has been moved to the models of relationship development section, and the information on Rawling's stage models of friendship has been deleted. This edition also includes the social penetration model, as well as a detailed discussion of interpersonal aggression, battering, and situational couple violence.**

- **Chapter 9** explores small group communication. **This edition includes an enhanced discussion of technology and small group communication (effective virtual teamwork), as well as new discussions on shared leadership and servant leadership.**

- **Chapter 10** explores how organizational communication is impacted by societal forces and structures. The new edition includes **more contemporary organizational theories, new material on social influences on organizations, and coworker communication as well as an extensive discussion of the influence of organizations on individuals and society (the new social contract, contingent workers, urgent organizations and the blurred boundaries between work and home).**

- **Chapter 11** covers the area of public communication. In this edition, the **discussion of early history of rhetoric (from Chapter 2) has been transferred to this chapter.** Chapter 11 sets the stage for public speaking skills, which are covered fully in Chapter 14.

- **Chapter 12** discusses communication and mass media. The revised chapter includes **more contemporary studies about media (including the impact of media messages in health campaigns and studies of masculinity).**

- **Chapter 13** covers computer-mediated communication (CMC). This edition **includes updated statistics, a new theoretical framework for the discussion of new media use (media deficit and media augmentation approaches), as well as new discussions on mobile communication technology and social networking sites (SNS).**

- **Chapter 14** offers a mostly skills-based discussion of public speaking. **The new edition includes updated examples that reflect current topics and issues.**

FEATURES

The features in this new edition, like the first, reflect our four goals for this textbook.

ACCESSIBLE PRESENTATION OF COMMUNICATION THEORY. In addition to using a down-to-earth writing style and providing plenty of examples, *Human Communication in Society, Second Edition,* offers specific tools throughout the text to help students understand the theory and key concepts:

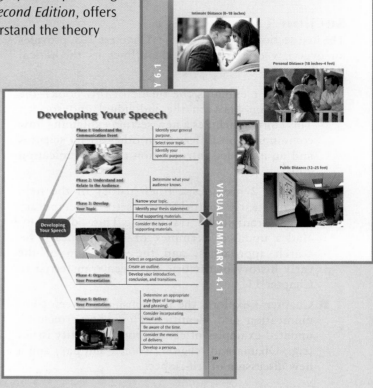

■ **Visual summaries** in every chapter illustrate theories and connections among key concepts.

■ **Key terms** are glossed in the margins of the page where the term is first used and defined, listed at the end of each chapter with the page number where the term and definition can be found, and compiled in a convenient Glossary at the end of the text.

portant role in educational institutions as well. Public speaking was taught regularly to help prepare all male students to operate effectively in a democratic society. (Remember that at this time in the United States, women did not yet have the right to vote.)

Interest in **behaviorism,** the focus on the study of behavior as a science, began to take hold within educational institutions during the nineteenth century. Before exploring that topic further, we would like to point out that by placing the roots of

human nature and its potential

Enlightenment
eighteenth-century belief that science and reason are the pathways to human knowledge

behaviorism
the focus on the study of behavior as a science

■ **Chapter summaries** conclude each chapter.

SUMMARY

Learning about identities and communication is important for at least four reasons: (1) we bring our identities to each communication interaction, (2) we encounter increasing numbers of people whose identities are different from our own, (3) much of our life is organized around specific identities, and (4) identity is a key site in which individual and societal forces come together.

Identities are defined social categories, and each of us is made up of many of them. They may be primary or secondary. Primary identities (race, ethnicity, age) are the focus in this chapter and have the most consistent and enduring impact on our lives; secondary identities, such as occupation and marital status, are more changeable over the life span and from situation to situation. Our identities exist at both the individual and social level, are both fixed and dynamic, and are created through interaction. Furthermore, identities must be understood within larger historical, social, and cultural environments. Important communication processes that influence personal identity development include reflected appraisals, self-concept, and self-fulfilling prophecies.

The primary identity categories—race, nationality, ethnicity, gender, sexuality, age, social class, and religion—are constructed between individual and social forces and what society communicates about those identities. Individuals perform their identities, and these performances are subject to social commentary. Straying too far from social expectations in these performances can lead to disciplinary

EMPHASIS ON ETHICS IN COMMUNICATION.

Each chapter includes one or more detailed sections discussing ethical issues relevant to that chapter's communication topic.

ETHICS AND COMPUTER-MEDIATED COMMUNICATION

One message we hope you take from this chapter is that CMC, in itself, is neither better nor worse than face-to-face communication. It is simply different. However, these differences allow for irresponsible, thoughtless, or even unethical communication online. How can you become an ethical user of CMC? There are at least two areas of ethical consideration. The first concerns presentation of identity online, and the second involves building online relationships.

Ethics and Online Identity

As we discussed earlier, the issue of identity and ethics online is complex, and one can take various positions on these issues. An extreme position would be that one should never misrepresent oneself. On the other hand, CMC clearly offers legitimate opportunities (like MMOGs), where one can take on an entirely new identity. A

OPPORTUNITIES TO APPLY WHAT WAS LEARNED. We advocate a
hands-on approach to the study of communication. For this reason, we've added features throughout the text that will help bring the theory home for students:

■ **Improving Your Communication Skills,** Chapters 3–13 conclude with a section providing practical guidelines for applying chapter material to everyday communication.

IMPROVING YOUR PERCEPTION SKILLS

You probably realize now that perceptions are subject to variance and error because of the variety of steps one goes through in forming them (selection, organization, and interpretation) and the range of factors that influence the perception process (individual characteristics, cognitive complexity, power, culture, historical time period, and social roles). However, certain cognitive and communication behaviors can improve your ability to perceive and understand the world.

First, engage in *mindfulness* to improve perception and understanding. Mindfulness refers to a clear focus on the activity you are engaged in, with attention to as many specifics of the event as you can (Langer, 1978). People tend to be most mindful when they are engaged in a new or unusual activity. Once an activity becomes habitual, we are likely to overlook its details. Mindfulness requires that you

TEST YOUR KNOWLEDGE

1. What are the key concepts in identity development?
2. How do individual and societal forces influence our understanding of identity?
3. What are the primary identity categories? Define each.
4. How is identity performed? Give an example for each primary identity category.
5. What are three key ethical concerns related to identity?

APPLY WHAT YOU KNOW

1. List the identities that are most important to you. Some of these identities may not have been discussed in this chapter. Note some situations in which the identities not discussed in the chapter become most relevant and some situations where other identities dominate.
2. Which of your identities are shared by a majority of people in society? What are some of the stereotypes of those identities? To answer this question, you may need to ask people who do not share that identity.
3. Interview someone who is at least twenty years older than you. Ask the person how her or his identities have changed over the years and what those changes entailed. Then reflect on changes in your own identity as you have grown up. How many of these changes were motivated by individual forces and how many might have been due to social forces?

EXPLORE

1. Go to www.msnbc.com/:d/6666338/ and read the description for purchasing a "Going Canadian" kit. What are the ethics of U.S. Americans pretending to be Canadians? Why would U.S. Americans want to pretend to be Canadians?
2. Read this essay on personal home pages and identity:

erance and identities. Name several groups represented in these exhibits. How were the campaigns of intolerance against them expressed, coordinated, and conducted? What kinds of intolerance are being perpetrated today?
4. Go to Margaret Cho's Web page at www.margaretcho.

■ **Exercises and activities,** including end-of-chapter **Test Your Knowledge** questions, **Apply What You Know** prompts, and **Explore** activities, encourage students to work through challenging concepts.

STUDENT ENGAGEMENT. We like to think that we have translated our commitment to the field and our love of teaching into a text that will engage students. We encourage this involvement with the following pedagogical features:

■ **It Happened to Me** boxes offer real-life accounts of student experiences that provide a "connection" or "hook" to important communication concepts.

Peer Communication.   While the field of availab[...] in work contexts, access to certain kinds of informa[...] relies on CMC. For example, in face-to-face work co[...] son in the next office during meetings and talk with [...] However, if you are communicating with cowor[...] through CMC, you have little information about t[...]

It Happened to Me: Mei-Lin

I sent an urgent email to a colleague requesting information for a report I was writing. He didn't respond, and I became very irritated at his lack of response. A few days later I found out that his child had been in a serious accident, and he had missed work for several days. If we had been located in the same office, I would have known immediately what was wrong, would have responded more appropriately to his absence, and could have gotten the information I needed in some other way.

■ **Alternative View** boxes offer a discussion of perspectives that challenge mainstream thinking on a topic. These features are written to encourage students to think critically about what they have learned.

Alternative **VIEW**
The First Vietnamese American in Congress

2008 was a year of many political "firsts," not the least of which included the election of Barack Obama as the first African American president of the United States. Making waves in New Orleans, however, is Joseph Cao, the first Vietnamese American elected to Congress. This is a brief look into his life.

Anh "Joseph" Cao—the hot new property in Congress, Mr. Upset, the first Vietnamese American elected to the U.S. House or Senate, the first Republican to win Louisiana's 2nd Congressional District since before Louis Armstrong was born—is driving across this Gothic American bayou. He's relating how, as [...]

■ **Communication in Society** boxes, a new feature, serve to reinforce for students the connection between the individual and society.

COMMUNICATION IN SOCIETY
The Smell Report

Have you noticed a difference in sense of smell between the sexes?
Why do you think women typically have a keener sense of smell?

Sex-Differences

On standard tests of smelling ability—including odour detection, discrimination and identification—women consistently score significantly higher than men. One

(It has been shown that other senses such as hearing are more acute around ovulation, when women can also hear slightly higher frequencies than at other times.) These fluctuations may account for some inconsistencies in the findings, although hormone cycles cannot explain why female children score higher than male children.

In an experiment at the Hebrew University, Jerusalem, women without children held an unrelated infant in their arms for one hour and then were tested for infant-smell-recognition. Most were successful. The re-

■ **Reflection questions** in the margins encourage students to reflect on how major concepts connect with their everyday experiences.

■ **The "Did You Know?"** boxes offer examples of chapter-related material that students may find surprising or unfamiliar. This material supplements and reinforces chapter concepts.

What artifacts are important to you in terms of communicating your identity or status? If you had only one means of communicating high status, would you drive an expensive car, wear designer clothes, or live in an upscale

convey i[...] perceived[...] and polic[...] messages[...] tions of t[...] Hall, 200[...] to easily [...]

Indiv[...] jewelry, s[...] personali[...] briefcase[...]

Did You Know?
Famous Twins Just Want to be Individuals
Mary-Kate: "As you get older, you create your own identity;"
Ashley: "It's not like we're forcing our own identities. It's who we are; our own styles are coming through, and other people are just realizing we're two separate people" (Arnold, 2004).
Mary-Kate and Ashley: "If you can respect us as businesswomen, and powerful young ladies, respect us also as individuals" (Aames, 2004).

Most twins strive to differentiate themselves from one another, whether that means dressing differently or pursuing disparate hobbies and careers. However for famous twins, developing separate identities is a greater challenge than for most. Celebrity twins Mary-Kate and Ashley Olsen, James and Oliver Phelps (who play the Weasley twins in the *Harry Potter* movies) and Dylan and Cole Sprouse (of Disney's *The Suite Life of*

A Word About Language

The text's commitment to presenting comprehensive coverage of the complex field of communication carries with it a responsibility to use language thoughtfully. We recognize the fact that, for complex historical and political relations, identity labels carry strong denotative meanings that may vary from person to person and across time. Hence, we have used the most inclusive terms possible to represent the heterogeneity of opinions within various ethnic and racial groups.

For example, the term *Hispanic* was created and used in 1980 by the U.S. government when collecting census statistics but is rejected by many individuals of Spanish descent. They (and we) prefer *Latina/o* (referring to U.S. Americans of Spanish descent from a specific ancestral nation like Argentina, Mexico, or any country in Latin America or Spain). We also use *Mexican American* when referring to individuals coming more directly from Mexico, or *Chicana/o* to designate a more political consciousness among persons of Mexican descent.

Similarly, we use the inclusive term *Asian American*, unless referring to individuals with a specific national origin (e.g., Japan or the Philippines). We use *African American* or *Black* interchangeably, recognizing that some individuals (often those from the Caribbean) prefer the more inclusive term *Black*, whereas others prefer *African American*. We also use *Native American* and *American Indian* interchangeably, recognizing that individuals are divided in their preferences for each of these terms.

We should also note that we use *White*, since this is the term preferred by U.S. Americans of European ancestry, rather than *European American*. We believe that this term appropriately emphasizes the racial distinction that is more important than ethnic distinctions in contemporary U.S. society. At the same time, we recognize that some individuals prefer to emphasize their more specific origins (*Japanese American* rather than *Asian American, Yaqui* rather than *Native American,* or *German American* rather than *White*).

Finally, we are learning to think more internationally in our use of language. Many of our neighbors in Latin and South America, as well as in Canada, find it offensive when we use the term *American* to refer to ourselves. (After all, these people are *Americans* as well.) Therefore, we prefer the term *U.S. American*, in recognition of the fact that we are only one society out of many that make up the continents of North and South America.

ACKNOWLEDGMENTS

We are once again grateful to all the students and instructors who have provided invaluable feedback to us as we wrote the first and second editions of Human Communication in Society. *Unfortunately we are unable to list here all of the students who participated, but we would like to acknowledge the instructors who have helped to shape and define both editions of our book.*

Reviewers (First Edition)

Bob Alexander: University of Louisiana–Monroe
Isolde K. Anderson: Hope College
Jay Baglia: San Jose State University
Cheryl L. Bailey: Western Illinois University
John R. Baldwin: Illinois State University
E. Tristan Booth: Arizona State University
Joseph Bridges: Malone College
Lynn S. Cockett: Juniata College
Elisia L. Cohen: Saint Louis University
Lisa Coutu: University of Washington
Peter A. DeCaro, PhD: California State University–Stanislaus
Aaron Dimock: University of Nebraska–Kearney
Donald G. Ellis: University of Hartford
Larry A. Erbert: University of Texas at El Paso
Marty Feeney, PhD: Central College
Dr. Charles Feldman: George Washington University
Sarah L. Bonewits Feldner: Marquette University
Karen A. Foss: University of New Mexico
Kenneth D. Frandsen: University of New Mexico
John Gareis: University of Pittsburgh
Sonja M. Brown Givens: University of Alabama in Huntsville
Carroll Glynn: Ohio State University
Beryl S. Gutekunst: Chestnut Hill College
Thomas Edward Harkins: New York University
Carla Harrell: Old Dominion University
Brian L. Heisterkamp: California State University, San Bernardino
Dr. Patrick J. Hérbert: University of Louisiana–Monroe
Christine Courtade Hirsch: State University of New York–Oswego
Dr. John Katsion: Hannibal-LaGrange College
Joann Keyton: University of Kansas
Larry J. King: Stephen F. Austin State University
Thomas J. Knutson: California State University, Sacramento
Peter Lah: Saint Louis University
William A. Lancaster: Northeastern University

Sara McKinnon: Arizona State University
Jennifer Mease: Arizona State University
Diane Millette: University of Miami
Todd Norton: University of Utah
Shirley Oakley: Coastal Georgia Community College
Richard K. Olsen, Jr: University of North Carolina–Wilmington
Karen Otto: Florida Community College at Jacksonville–North Campus
Frank G. Pérez: University of Texas at El Paso
Linda Pledger: University of Arkansas–Little Rock
Steven B. Pratt: University of Central Oklahoma
Leanne Stuart Pupchek, PhD: Queens University of Charlotte
John C. Reinard: California State University–Fullerton
Brian Reynolds: State University of New York–Buffalo
Scott J. Robson: Washburn University
Pamela Schultz: Alfred University
Dr. David Schulz: California State University–Stanislaus
Kristina Horn Sheeler: Indiana University Purdue University Indianapolis
Deborah Shelley: University of Houston–Downtown
Nancy J. Street: Texas A&M University
Crispin Thurlow: University of Washington
Sarah Tracy: Arizona State University
April Trees: University of Colorado, Boulder
Kathleen J. Turner: Davidson College
Kyle Tusing: University of Arizona
Sam Wallace: University of Dayton
Toni S. Whitfield: James Madison University
Bill Yousman: University of Hartford

Reviewers (Second Edition)

Marcia S. Berry: Azusa Pacific University
Lynn S. Cockett: Juniata College
Larry A. Erbert: University of Colorado, Denver
Emma K. Gray: Portland Community College
Carla J. Harrell: Old Dominion University
Christine Courtade Hirsch: SUNY Oswego
Heather A. Howley: Cazenovia College
Thomas J. Knutson: Sacramento State University
Joanna Kostides: Holyoke Community College
Tema Milstein: University of New Mexico
Cynthia Ridle: Western Illinois University
Renee Beth Stahle: Aquinas College
Jenny Warren: Collin College

ADDITIONAL ACKNOWLEDGMENTS

We would also like to thank our colleagues and students for their invaluable assistance and moral support: a special thanks to Professor Pauline Cheong for providing foundational ideas for our revised chapter on computer-mediated communication, Professor Clark Olson who generously contributed his knowledge on small-group communication, Professor Karen Ashcraft (University of Utah) for her substantial assistance with the organizational communication chapter, and Professor Angela Trethewey for her support and help throughout this project.

And, of course, we need to thank the many, many students, both at Arizona State University and elsewhere, who have good-naturedly provided invaluable feedback on the first edition, helping us to make the necessary changes in the second edition.

Thanks also to our editorial assistants, Charee Mooney and Patrick McDonald, who spent hours searching for (and finding) the most recent and relevant research articles. They also successfully persuaded fellow graduate student instructors and their students to provide us with updated examples, and contemporary margin material.

We especially appreciate their assistance given that they had their own work to do.

Thanks to the team at Pearson Allyn & Bacon who made it all happen. Thanks to Editor-in-Chief Karon Bowers. We could not have managed without her expertise, patience, and practiced hand guiding us through a rather complicated publishing process. Thanks also to Susan Messer, development editor, for her enthusiasm and hard work on the first edition; and to Kristen Desmond LeFevre, development editor for the second edition for her important guidance and help throughout the work on this revision. We want to acknowledge the work of project managers Karen Mason at Pearson and Assunta Petrone at Preparé, who kept us on track. Thanks, too, to the marketing manager Blair Tuckman, editorial assistant Susan Brilling, development manager David Kear, designer Gina Hagen, photo researcher Katharine Cebik, and supplements editor Corey Kahn.

Finally, to our partners—James LeRoy, David Karbonski, and Ronald Chaldu, who continue to tolerate our frequent absences with good grace. We give them our deepest thanks for their support throughout this and many other projects.

About the Authors

Jess Alberts is President's Professor in the Hugh Downs School of Human Communication at Arizona State University. She is a social scientist who focuses on interpersonal communication and specializes in the study of conflict. **Thomas Nakayama** is chair and professor in the Department of Communication Studies at Northeastern University. He is a critical scholar who focuses on rhetoric and intercultural communication. **Judith Martin** is a professor in the Hugh Downs School of Human Communication at Arizona State University. She is an interpretive scholar whose expertise is in intercultural communication. With their different areas of expertise, the authors have created a comprehensive text with a truly balanced approach to the study of human communication.

Jess Alberts

Thomas Nakayama

Judith Martin

1

Introduction to Human Communication

chapter outline

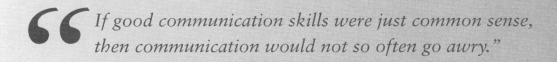

"If good communication skills were just common sense, then communication would not so often go awry."

On her way to class, Charity called her mom to let her know what time she would arrive home for Thanksgiving break; she then text messaged a friend to arrange to meet at lunch. While she waited for class to begin, she checked her email and chatted with classmates. When the professor arrived, she turned off her iPhone and listened attentively as the lecture began.

Most people, like Charity, exist in a sea of communication—they watch television (perhaps too much); attend class lectures; phone, email, and text message their friends and family; and are inundated by messages over loudspeakers as they shop for groceries or use public transportation. Given all of this, it is hard to imagine that only seventy-five years ago most communication occurred either face to face or via "snail" mail. But in fact, throughout much of human history, individuals lived very close to the people they knew. They conducted commerce and maintained relationships primarily with the same small group of people throughout their lives. Today, people maintain relationships with individuals thousands of miles away, and they buy and sell products halfway around the globe on eBay. This instant and widespread access to the world has its benefits, but it also has its costs.

With so many communication options, people need a wider range of communication skills than ever before. Successful communicators must converse effectively face to face; correspond clearly via email; learn text messaging; and absorb the norms and etiquette surrounding cell phones, chat rooms, and video and telephone conferences.

Becoming an effective communicator involves both understanding the components and processes of communication and putting them into practice. As you work in this course to improve your communication skills, you may see positive changes in your relationships, your career, your engagement in civic life, and even in your identity. How many other courses can claim all that?

Once you have read this chapter, you will able to:

- Discuss the importance of studying communication.
- Define *communication*.
- Describe a variety of careers in communication.
- Articulate how verbal and nonverbal messages create meaning.
- Name and explain the six primary components of human communication.
- Identify the four primary models of communication and explain how they differ from one another.
- Understand the ethical responsibilities of speakers and receivers.
- Formulate your own communication ethic.

THE IMPORTANCE OF STUDYING HUMAN COMMUNICATION

As you begin this book, you may wonder exactly how the study of communication differs from other studies of human behavior, such as psychology. Communication differs from other social science disciplines because it focuses exclusively on the exchange of messages to create meaning. Scholars in communication explore what, when, where, and why humans interact (Emanuel, 2007). These studies increase our understanding of how people communicate and help individuals improve their abilities to communicate in a wide variety of contexts. Unlike most social sciences, the study of communication has a long history—reaching back to the classical era in Western civilization when Isocrates, Plato, and Aristotle wrote about the important role of communication in politics, the courts, and in learning (National Communication Association Poole & Walther, 2001). However, the ability to speak effectively and persuasively has been valued since the beginning of recorded history. As early as 3200–2800 B.C., the Precepts of Kagemni and Ptah-Hopte commented on communication (NCA, 2003), and even the Old Testament acknowledges the importance of communication skills, such as when God appoints Aaron as Moses's spokesperson (*New World Encyclopedia*, 2008).

In a typical day, how many forms of communication (telephone, text messaging, face to face) do you use? Which forms do you use most often? Which forms feel most comfortable to you?

You may also wonder why you need to study communication; after all, you have probably been doing a reasonably good job of it thus far. And isn't most communication knowledge just common sense? Unfortunately, it is not. If good communication skills were just common sense, then communication would not so often go awry. We would live in a world where misunderstandings rarely occurred; conflicts were easily resolved; and public speakers were organized, clear, and engaging. Instead, communication is a complex activity influenced by a variety of factors, including cultural differences, cognitive abilities, and social norms.

Good communication is not a cure-all for every relationship or career ill, but it can help you attain your goals, establish relationships, and develop your identity. Every day you use communication to accomplish practical goals such as inviting a friend to see a movie with you, resolving a conflict with a colleague, or persuading the city council to install speed bumps in your neighborhood. Essentially, communication is functional, as it allows you to accomplish the daily tasks of living. For a discussion concerning the role of communication in relationships, refer to *Alternative View: Too Much Talk Can Lead to Problems.*

You rely on communication to meet people, to develop professional and personal relationships, and to terminate dissatisfying ones. Steve Duck, a communication scholar, argues that relationships are primarily communicative (1994). Moreover, the relationships you have with others, including how you think and feel about one another, develop as you communicate. Through your communication interactions, you and your relationship partners develop shared meanings for events, explanations for your past, and a vision of your future together (Alberts, Yoshimura, Rabby, & Loschiavo, 2005; Dixon & Duck, 1993). Thus when you tell your romantic partner, "I have never loved anyone as much as I love you, and I never will," you simultaneously redefine your past romantic relationships, create shared meaning for your present relationship, and project a vision of your future together. Similarly, through your communication with friends, coworkers, and acquaintances, you define and redefine your relationships.

Perhaps most fundamentally, your communication interactions with others allow you to establish who you are

©Kes/www.CartoonStock.com

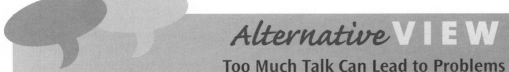

Alternative VIEW
Too Much Talk Can Lead to Problems

A researcher at the University of Missouri–Columbia has found that girls who talk extensively about their problems with friends are likely to become more anxious and depressed.

Talking extensively about problems can cause girls to become anxious and depressed.

The research was conducted by Amanda Rose, associate professor of psychological sciences in the College of Arts and Science. The six-month study, which included boys and girls, examined the effects of co-rumination—excessively talking with friends about problems and concerns. Rose discovered that girls co-ruminate more than boys, especially in adolescence, and that girls who co-ruminated the most in the fall of the school year were most likely to be more depressed and anxious by the spring.

"When girls co-ruminate, they're spending such a high percentage of their time dwelling on problems and concerns that it probably makes them feel sad and more hopeless about the problems because those problems are in the forefront of their minds. Those are symptoms of depression," Rose said. "In terms of anxiety, co-ruminating likely makes them feel more worried about the problems, including about their consequences. Co-rumination also may lead to depression and anxiety because it takes so much time, time that could be used to engage in other, more positive activities that could help distract youth from their problems. This is especially true for problems that girls can't control, such as whether a particular boy likes them, or whether they get invited to a party that all of the popular kids are attending."

Ironically, although co-rumination was related to increased depression and anxiety, Rose also found that co-rumination was associated with positive friendship quality, including feelings of closeness between friends. Boys who co-ruminated also developed closer friendships across the school year but did not develop greater depressive and anxiety symptoms over time.

Rose said adolescents should be encouraged to talk about their problems, but only in moderation and without co-ruminating.

"They also should engage in other activities, like sports, which can help them take their minds off their problems, especially problems that they can't control," she said.

FROM: "Prospective associations of co-rumination with friendship and emotional adjustment," July 16, 2007, New-Medical.Net, www.news-medical.net. Reprinted by permission.

to them (Gergen, 1982; Mead, 1934). As you communicate, you attempt to reveal yourself in a particular light. At work, you may try to establish yourself as someone who is pleasant, hardworking, honest, and/or powerful. With a new roommate, you may want your communication behavior to suggest you are responsible, fun, and easygoing. However, at the same time that your communication creates an image of who you are for others, *their* communication shapes your vision of yourself. For example, if your friends laugh at your jokes, compliment you on your sense of humor, and introduce you to others as a funny person, you probably will see yourself as amusing. Thus, communication helps create both your self-identity and your identity as others perceive it.

Communication has the potential to transform your life—both for the better and for the worse. As many people have discovered, poor or unethical communication can negatively affect lives. How? Communicating poorly during conflict can end relationships, inadequate interviewing skills can result in unemployment, and negative feedback from conversational partners can lessen one's self-esteem. Sometimes communication can have even more significant effects. As you may recall, Martha Stewart was sent to jail not for insider trading but for lying (and thereby obstructing justice) when her case was being investigated. Thus she was imprisoned for a specific unethical (and illegal) communication act.

Fortunately, developing excellent communication skills also can transform your life for the better. Good communication can help you become more effective at work, develop and maintain close relationships, participate in your community, and change the way you see yourself. The three authors of this book have all had students visit months or years after taking our communication classes to tell us what a difference the classes have made in their lives. A student in a public-speaking class reported that, because of her improved presentation skills she received the raise and promotion she had been pursuing for years; another student in a conflict and negotiation class revealed that her marriage, which had been troubled, became more stable once she learned to express her disagreements better. A third student believed he became more confident after he took a persuasion class that taught him how to influence people. To read about one student's transformative experience, see *It Happened to Me: Chelsea.*

Studying human communication may also benefit you by leading you to a new career path. A wide variety of communication careers are available, and a degree in communication can prepare you for many of these. For information on careers in communication, see *Did You Know? Careers in Communication.*

It Happened to Me: Chelsea

When the professor asked us to identify a time when communication was transformative, too many examples came to mind. Finally, I settled on one involving a negative relationship. In high school there's usually one person you just don't get along with. Boyfriend drama, bad mouthing, you name it. I remember dreading seeing this one girl, and I'm sure she felt the same about me. Graduation came and went, and I completely forgot about her. A year later, I came across her Web page online as I was searching for old classmates. As I thought about how petty our arguments were and how cruel we were to each other, I felt smaller and smaller. So I decided to end it. I used email to apologize for my bad behavior, because with email I felt safer. I could compose my thoughts, avoid a direct confrontation, and give her time to respond. A couple days later I received an email from her saying she felt the same way and was also sorry for the way she acted. Sometime next week we're going to have a cup of coffee together to really put the past behind us. Maybe to some people that doesn't seem all that life changing, but after hating this girl for two years, it's an amazing transformation for me.

Did You Know?
Careers in Communication

Careers in Advertising: Including advertising or marketing specialist, copy writer, account executive, sales manager, media planner, media buyer, creative director, media sales representative, and public opinion researcher.

Careers in Communication Education: Including language arts coordinator, high school speech teacher, forensics/debate coach, drama director, college or university professor, and speech communication department chairperson.

Careers in Electronic Media/Radio–Television/Broadcasting: Including broadcasting station manager, director of broadcasting, film/tape librarian, community relations director, unit manager, film editor, news director, news writer, transmitter engineer, technical director, advertising sales coordinator, traffic/continuity specialist, media buyer, market

Did You Know? *(continued)*

researcher, actor, announcer, disc jockey, news anchor, public relations manager, comedy writer, casting director, producer, business manager, researcher, account executive, floor manager, and talk show host.

Careers in Journalism: Including reporter, editor, newscaster, author, copy writer, script writer, publisher, news service researcher, technical writer, acquisitions editor, and media interviewer.

Careers in Public Relations: Including publicity manager, advertising manager, marketing specialist, press agent, lobbyist, corporate public affairs specialist, account executive, development officer, fund raiser, membership recruiter, sales manager, media analyst, media planner, creative director, audience analyst, news writer, and public opinion researcher.

Careers in Theater/Performing Arts/Dramatic Arts: Including performing artist, script writer, producer, director, arts administrator, performing arts educator, costume designer, scenic designer, lighting designer, theater critic, makeup artist, stage manager, model, theater professor, and casting director.

Careers in Fields Related to Communication

Careers in Business and Communication: Including sales representative, executive manager, personnel manager, public information officer, industrial and labor relations representative, negotiator, director of corporate communication, customer service representative, newsletter editor, communication trainer, human resources manager, mediator, and buyer.

Careers in Education: Including teacher (elementary and secondary), school counselor, educational researcher, audiovisual specialist, educational administrator, school/university information specialist, director of college news, director of a collegiate information center, educational tester, development officer, educational fund-raiser, alumni officer, college placement officer, college admissions director, and college recruiter.

Communication and Government/Political–Related Careers: Including public information officer, speech writer, legislative assistant, campaign director, research specialist, program coordinator, negotiator, lobbyist, press secretary, and elected official.

Careers in Health and Communication: Including health educator, school health care administrator, medical grants writer, hospital director of communication, clinic public relations director, health communication analyst, research analyst, medical training supervisor, communications manager for federal health agencies, health personnel educator, medical center publications editor, hospice manager, drug rehabilitationist, health care counselor, activities director, marketing director, and health facility fund-raiser.

Careers in International Relations and Negotiations: Including on-air international broadcasting talent, corporate representative, translator, student tour coordinator, diplomat, foreign relations officer, host/hostess for foreign dignitaries, and foreign correspondent.

Careers in Law and Communication: Including public defender, corporate lawyer, district attorney, public interest lawyer, private practice lawyer, legal researcher, mediation and negotiation specialist, paralegal researcher, legal secretary, legal reporter, and legal educator.

Careers in Social and Human Services: Including public administrator, social worker, recreational supervisor, human rights officer, community affairs liaison, park service public relations specialist, philanthropic representative, religious leader, and mental counselor.

Note: These career titles were derived from a survey of communication graduates from sixteen colleges and universities and has been supplemented with other jobs clearly in the speech communication field.

human communication
a process in which people generate meaning through the exchange of verbal and nonverbal messages

messages
the building blocks of communication events

symbol
something that represents something else and conveys meaning

iconic signs
signs that represent a thing itself and always bear some resemblance to the object to which they refer

WHAT IS HUMAN COMMUNICATION?

Although you have been communicating for your entire life, you probably have not given much thought to the process. You may question why we even need to provide a definition for something so commonplace. Although communication is an everyday occurrence, the term covers a wide variety of behaviors that include talking to friends, broadcasting media messages, and emailing coworkers. Because the term *communication* is complex and can have a variety of definitions, we need to acquaint you with the definition we will use throughout this text.

Broadly speaking, **human communication** can be defined as *a process in which people generate meaning through the exchange of verbal and nonverbal messages.* In this book we emphasize the influence of individual and societal forces and the roles of culture and context more than competing models do. In the following sections, we will illustrate the means by which we arrived at our definition of human communication. We first look at the process of human communication and its components as highlighted in earlier scholars' definitions. Next, we examine the way these components serve as the building blocks of three important models of communication. Finally, we introduce our own model of human communication in society.

The Process of Communication

As we have stated, communication is a process of creating meaning through the exchange of verbal and nonverbal messages. The following sections explain this process in more detail.

An Exchange of Messages

Messages are the building blocks of communication events. When we communicate we exchange two types of messages—verbal and nonverbal—and most are symbolic. A **symbol** is something that represents something else and conveys meaning (Buck & Vanlear, 2002). For example, a Valentine's Day heart symbolizes the physical heart, it represents romantic love, and it conveys feelings of love and romance when given to a relational partner. By the same token, an octagonal-shaped sign represents the command "stop!" Thus, symbols can represent ideas, actions, or objects.

The verbal system is composed of symbols that construct the words and phrases we use to speak. The nonverbal message system is composed of nonlinguistic symbols such as smiles, laughter, winks, vocal tone, and hand gestures.

When we say communication is symbolic, we also are describing the fact that the symbols we use—the words we speak and the gestures we use—are arbitrary, or without any inherent meaning (Dickens, 2003). Rather, their meaning is derived as communicators employ agreed-upon definitions. Thus, an octagonal shape in and of itself would not mean stop unless people in the United States agreed to this meaning, and the word *mother* would not mean a female parent unless speakers of English agreed that it would. Because communicators create meanings, different groups often develop distinct words for the same concept. For instance, the common word for a feline house pet is *cat* in English, but *neko* in Japanese. Thus, there is no intrinsic connection between the animal we call cat and the word itself. This is true for both verbal and nonverbal messages.

Human communication is primarily symbolic, but not all nonverbal communication is symbolic or arbitrary. For example, some signs represent the thing itself (Deacon, 1997), such as a prehistoric image of a bison on a cave wall—which stands for the actual bison. These signs are called **iconic signs,** and they always bear some resemblance to the things to which they refer. Another example of an iconic sign is the "smiley" face [:)] that people use in email to represent an actual smile. In addition, a photograph is an iconic representation of the event it captures, and a dog's bared teeth stand for the actual bite it is threatening to deliver. In each of these cases a direct relationship exists between the sign and the thing it represents.

Which part of this sign is iconic? Which is symbolic?

Indexical signs reveal something beyond the thing itself (Deacon, 1997). For example, by examining animal prints in the snow humans can determine which direction the animal traveled. In this case, the paw prints reveal where the animal went, rather than the animal itself. Similarly, smoke is indexical in that its presence reveals that a fire has ignited. In both cases, the indexical sign is not arbitrary. Thus, while symbolic systems are arbitrary, neither iconic nor indexical systems are arbitrary (Dickens, 2003). (See Figure 1.1.)

Symbolic communication is uniquely human. When animals communicate they typically use iconic and indexical messages, but rarely do they understand symbolic communication, except when taught by humans. For example, a person can teach a dog certain words (*fetch*, *treat*, *walk*), but a dog cannot teach another dog what these words mean (Deacon, 1997). On the other hand, virtually all dogs recognize that bared teeth represent a threat.

Because human communication is predominantly symbolic, humans must agree on the meanings of words. Consequently, words can, and do, change over time. For example, the term *phat* (meaning excellent, cool, or attractive) originally was spelled "fat" and was used mostly by urban African Americans (Trumble & Brown, 2002). Although the word *phat* was first noted in print in 1963, it has come to be used widely only in the past decade, first in hip-hop culture and then more broadly, because users agreed to its meaning and spelling. However, people may have different meanings for specific symbols or words, especially if they come from different ethnic or national cultures. Read about one student's difficulties communicating while on a trip to Europe in *It Happened to Me: Alyssa*, on p. 8.

Just as verbal symbols possess shared meanings, so do nonverbal symbols, such as the "okay" and the "thumbs-up" hand signals familiar to many in the United States and other parts of the world. In the United States, one of the first nonverbal gestures infants learn is to wave "bye-bye," which virtually everyone in the country understands. Just like verbal messages, nonverbal messages can be iconic or indexical. For example, when you pucker your lips and make a smacking noise, your nonverbal message both mimics and stands for a kiss. See *Did You Know? A World of Eloquence in an Upturned Palm,* on p. 8, to learn more about the relationship between verbal and nonverbal messages.

indexical signs
signs that reveal something beyond the thing itself

FIGURE 1.1: Iconic and Indexical Signs

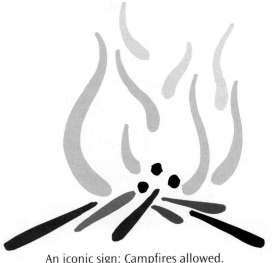

An iconic sign: Campfires allowed.

An indexical sign: Where there's smoke, there's fire.

Although words and gestures are typically symbolic, these symbols can also be material—or have material consequences. In other words, communication messages can have a real impact on the conditions in which we live. During a wedding ceremony, for example, when participants utter the words "I do," they become married under the law, and their material circumstances change. Powerful social symbols—flags, the bald eagle, and the McDonald's logo—also communicate meaning nonverbally. The way we interact with some of these symbols can have material effects in the world as well. For example, in North Korea it is illegal to deface a picture of the country's leader Kim Jong IL. He is believed to be a semideity, and even spilling a cup of coffee on his picture in the newspaper is a punishable offense. This social meaning is so strong that citizens have lost their lives trying to save his picture during catastrophes such as house fires (Koreans die, 2004).

It Happened to Me: *Alyssa*

Over the summer I traveled in Europe with my mom. I had no idea how difficult it was going be to communicate, even in England. We spent the first few days in London and attempted to navigate the city on our own. It was honestly one of the most difficult things to do. Although people were willing to help us, because of differences in word choice and accents we weren't able to fully understand the directions they gave us. After London we went to Germany and Italy. When we broke off from the tour group, it was nearly impossible for us to get around. We had a hard time communicating due to the language barrier. However, I made good use of nonverbal gestures such as pointing, smiling, thumbs-up, and thumbs-down. My experiences really brought home to me how connected language, communication, and culture are.

Did You Know?
A World of Eloquence in an Upturned Palm

Do chimpanzees and apes communicate? Do they have language? What do our similarities to—and differences from—chimpanzees and apes tell us about language and communication?

An orangutan uses the upturned palm to make a request.

The chimpanzees, after spotting the humans at the corner of their compound, came over to us with their arms outstretched and their palms turned upward. This was the chimps' way of asking for a banana—and a lot more.

That simple gesture, the upturned palm, is one of the oldest and most widely understood signals in the world. Chimps and other apes, notably humans, adapted it to ask not just for food, but also for more abstract forms of help, creating a new kind of signal that some researchers believe was the origin of human language.

The palm-up gesture is what the anthropologist David Givens, director of the Center for Nonverbal Studies in Spokane, Washington, calls a "gestural byproduct" of the circuits in the brain and spinal cord that protected vertebrates hundreds of millions of years ago. Confronted with a threat, ancient lizards instinctively bent their spine and limbs to press their bodies closer to the ground, protecting the neck and head and signaling submission to a larger animal. The human remnant of the crouch display is a shrug of the shoulders, which lowers the head and rotates the forearms outwards so that the palms face up.

Many gestures are performed unconsciously, but the palm-up was adapted long ago for conscious gestures by humans and other apes. Chimps and bonobos have been observed using it in the wild and in captivity. Chimps have been observed to use the palm-up gesture to ask other chimps to share food, for help in a fight, for sex or, most frequently, to request a grooming session. Bonobos

Did You Know? *(continued)*

use it most often as an invitation to play. The chimps and bonobos also send signals though vocalizations and facial expressions, but these don't vary much.

"These observations," lead researchers "to speculate that gestures may have served as the steppingstone for easily hominid communication and, possibly, language." Researchers at Emory note that gestures are controlled by the same part of the brain that controls speech. But it is possible, they said, that gestures and speech evolved jointly to create language.

As language evolved, humans used the palm-up for more complex ideas. They could signal, "I don't know," by holding both palms face up—or cradling one upturned palm inside the other, a gesture North Africans use to mean, "I don't understand."

Chimps are not so subtle, but they can understand "Gimme" even when it's coming from nonchimps. Dr. Pollick found that she could get a chimp to give her something by pointing to the object and making the palm-up gesture.

Watching the chimps, I began thinking of the palm-up as a sort of linguistic missing link, and it was comforting to think we still had some way to talk with our relatives. But this gesture has its limits for interspecies communication, as I realized when I tried making the palm-up gesture from the corner of the compound.

None of the chimps responded in any way. That wasn't surprising, if only because they don't normally respond to strangers. But even if they had wanted to, they would have been hard pressed to continue the conversation. They didn't have anything to give me, and they lacked a vital human skill: the ability to counter one palm-up with another.

They didn't know how to helplessly shrug their shoulders and hold out their empty upturned palms to send a sympathetic reply: I'd love to help you, buddy, but I'm all tapped out. Hominids learned to ask for favors early in their evolution. It look longer to figure out how to say a polite no.

FROM: "A World of Eloquence in an Upturned Palm," by John Tierney, *The New York Times*, August 28, 2007. © 2007 *The New York Times*. All rights reserved. Used by permission and protected by the Copyright Laws of the United States. The printing, copying, redistribution, or retransmission of the Material without express written permission is prohibited.

A Creator of Meaning

The goal of exchanging symbols—that is, of communicating—is to create meaning. The messages we send and receive shape meaning beyond the symbols themselves. We also bring to each message a set of experiences, beliefs, and values that help shape meaning. This is why people can hear the same message but understand it differently. For example, Tim told Alice "You were pretty good in the play tonight," which he thought was a compliment. Alice, however, thought it meant that she was only okay in her role, not great. When she responded by being hurt, the couple had to clarify what "pretty good" meant to each of them.

Meaning is made even more complex, because each message carries with it two types of meaning—content meaning and relationship meaning. **Content meaning** includes denotative and connotative meaning. Denotative meaning is the concrete meaning of the message, such as the definition you would find in a dictionary. Connotative meaning describes the meanings suggested by or associated with the message and the emotions triggered by it. For example, denotatively the word *mother* refers to one's female parent, while connotatively it may include meanings such as warmth, nurturance, and intimacy. **Relationship meaning** describes what the message conveys about the relationship between the parties (Robinson-Smith, 2004; Watzlawick, Beavin, & Jackson, 1967). For example, if a colleague at works tells you to "run some copies of this report," you may become irritated, while you likely would not mind if your boss told you to do the same thing. In both cases the relationship message may be understood as "I have the right to tell you what to do," which is probably okay if it comes from your supervisor—but not if it comes from a peer.

What is the connotative meaning of the word *mother*?

content meaning
the concrete meaning of the message, and the meanings suggested by or associated with the message and the emotions triggered by it

relationship meaning
what a message conveys about the relationship between the parties

When you communicate you may assume that the other person understands the meaning you intend. However, given the multiple meanings that a particular message can relay, your assumption may not be accurate. This may be especially true if you and your conversational partner have different cultural backgrounds and experiences. We explore this important issue later in this chapter and throughout this book.

Components of Human Communication

Earlier we stated that communication is a complex process. This is due in part to the variety of factors that compose and influence it. The six basic components of communication are *setting*, *participants*, *message creation*, *channels*, *noise*, and *feedback*. Each of these features influences how a communication interaction unfolds.

Setting

The physical surroundings of a communication event make up its **setting**. Setting includes the location where the communication occurs (in a library versus a bar), environmental conditions (including the temperature, noise, lighting), time of day or day of the week, and proximity of the communicators. Together these factors create the physical setting, which affects the communication interaction. Imagine that you wanted to end your relationship with your romantic partner. What physical setting would you choose for that conversation? A booth at a loud, smoky bar at midnight on a Thursday? Sitting side by side on the couch in your living room in the early evening? The physical setting you select will likely impact the interaction.

Participants

During communication, **participants**—two or more people—interact. The number of participants, as well as their characteristics, influence how the interaction unfolds. Typically, the more characteristics participants share (cultural values, history), the easier they will find it to communicate, because they can rely on their common assumptions about the world. In addition, the smaller a group is, the easier it may be for participants to communicate.

The type of relationship the communicators have and the history they share also affect their communication. Typically, whether the communicators are family members, romantic partners, colleagues, friends, or acquaintances affects how they frame, deliver, and interpret a message. For instance, how might you ask to borrow $100 from a family member? How would that message differ if you needed to ask an acquaintance?

In addition, the moods and emotions that communicators bring to and experience during their interaction influence it. If you are in a good mood because you received a big bonus at work, you may be more polite and cheerful when talking with others; however, if you arrive at work in a good mood but then your boss criticizes you, you may be more irritable or withdrawn when you talk to people later in the day.

Message Creation

Messages transmit the ideas and emotions we experience. Thus, you discuss your spring break plans with your friends or let your parents know that you are happy they are coming to visit. As discussed earlier, **message creation** occurs when we use symbols and signs. Taking ideas and converting them into messages is described as **encoding**, while receiving a message and interpreting its meaning is referred to as **decoding**. If you want to let someone know you are happy to see them, you might encode this idea into a message by saying "I am so glad you could come," while if a friend sees you and pretends not to notice you, you probably decode this nonverbal message as unfriendliness or anger.

setting
the physical surroundings of a communication event

participants
the people interacting during communication

message creation
transmitting ideas and emotions via signs and symbols

encoding
taking ideas and converting them into messages

decoding
receiving a message and interpreting its meaning

Channels

For a message to be transmitted from one participant to another, it must travel through a channel. A **channel** is the means through which a message is transmitted. Face-to-face communication involves two channels—the verbal and the nonverbal. Mediated messages, or those transmitted through technology, can be conveyed through one or more channels, such as radio, television, or newsprint. Technologies such as instant messenger, the telephone, and email are all distinct channels through which messages can be transmitted.

Noise

Noise refers to any stimulus that can interfere with, or degrade, the quality of a message. Noise describes external signals such as loud music or voices, a humming air conditioner, or bizarre dress or hairstyles. Noise can come from internal stimuli, such as hunger or sleepiness, and semantic interference, such as when speakers use words you do not know or use a familiar word in an unfamiliar way. If you have ever tried to have a conversation with someone who used highly technical language in a noisy room while you were sleepy, you have experienced a "perfect storm" of noise. See *It Happened to Me: William*, for an example of how noise impeded one young man's communication efforts.

Text messaging is one channel of communication.

Feedback

The response to a message is called **feedback**. Feedback lets a sender know if the message was received and how the message was interpreted. For example, if a friend tells you a joke and you laugh heartily, your laughter serves as feedback that you heard the joke and found it amusing. Similarly, if you fall asleep during a lecture, you provide feedback to your professor that either you are very tired or you find the lecture boring. Thus your feedback serves as a message to the sender, who then uses the information conveyed to help shape his or her next message.

Models of Human Communication

Over time, scholars have taken the six components just described and shown how they interact in the process of communication. Let's examine 3 models of this process.

It Happened to Me: William

Recently I had an experience that reflected a lot of what we are learning in class. I was on Thanksgiving break when my girlfriend called to talk. I was preoccupied watching the Patriots–Eagles game, though I did not tell her. The game captured more of my attention than the conversation, because I was both watching and listening to the game but only listening to my girlfriend. The game became a significant barrier to my ability to listen to her. Unfortunately, she noticed my lack of attention and became very upset with me. She was trying to have a serious conversation with me, but I was not really participating. I had to divert my attention from the game so I could apologize and restore order in my relationship. To do this I used the informative function of language—to explain why I was not talking as much as I should have been. It really brought home to me how we use concepts from communication class every day, even when we don't realize it.

Linear Models

The earliest models conceived of communication as a linear process that primarily involved the transfer of information from one person to another (Eisenberg & Goodall, 1997; Laswell, 1948; Shannon & Weaver, 1949). These models depicted communication as occurring when a sender encoded a message (put ideas into words and symbols) that was sent to a receiver who decoded (interpreted) it. Then, the process was believed to reverse: The receiver became the sender, and the sender became the receiver (Laswell, 1948).

channel
the means through which a message is transmitted

noise
any stimulus that can interfere with, or degrade, the quality of a message

feedback
the response to a message

FIGURE 1.2: A Linear Model of Communication
An early model of communication.

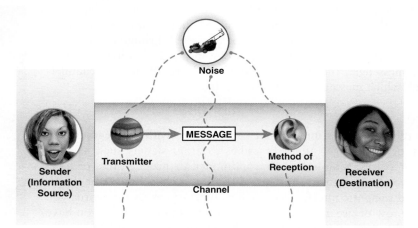

This basic model was later adapted by two engineers, Shannon and Weaver (1949), who added the element of noise. For an example of a typical linear model, see Figure 1.2.

Linear (or information transfer) models stressed the importance of the source and the clarity of the messages sent. Effective communication occurred if the receiver understood the sender's message or meaning. Consequently, efforts to improve communication centered on finding ways to improve the quality of the sender's message through word choice, decreased noise, and accurate nonverbal communication.

Shannon and Weaver originally developed their model to explain how information was transmitted through telephone cables and radio waves. It was later adapted to describe human communication, but eventually scholars realized that the model was too simplistic.

Interactive Models

One problem with linear models was that they assumed communicators played only one role, as either the sender *or* the receiver. This implied that speakers did not listen and receivers did not communicate—even nonverbally. Other important aspects of communication were overlooked as well. Consequently, a scholar named Schramm (1954, 1971; Heinich, Molenda, Russell, & Smaldino, 1996) created an interactive model that acknowledged the dual role of communicators as senders *and* receivers. The model added the components of feedback and **field of experience** (see Figure 1.3). Schramm argued that feedback, or the verbal and nonverbal messages that receivers communicate in response to a message, is an important message element that influences communication. He also argued that each communicator possesses a field of experience (including education, life events, and cultural background) that affects the communication event. Schramm's model accounted for the fact that if your friend looks puzzled (feedback), you alter your message in an effort to make it clearer. It also acknowledged that the participants' background and experience make it either easier or harder to convey meaning. For example, the more two people share a field of experience, the more efficient and effective will be their communication.

Interactive models stressed that communicators both sent and received messages, and they highlighted the fact that receivers convey messages in response to the sender's messages. However, these models still described communication as something that one person created and then transmitted to another; they did not acknowledge that both parties create meaning as they communicate together.

field of experience
the education, life events, and cultural background that a communicator possesses

FIGURE 1.3: An Interactive Model of Communication
Schramm's model added feedback and field of experience.

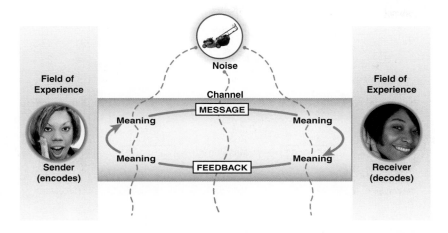

Transactional Models

Although the interactive model depicted communicators as sending *and* receiving messages, it still portrayed them as fulfilling these roles one at a time. In addition, it portrayed meaning as something that one person created and then sent to another.

Describing communication as a transactional process suggests three things: (1) when people communicate, they act together; (2) communication is ongoing; and (3) who people are to each other and the relationships they develop are a result of their interactions (Warren & Yoder, 1998; Watzlawick, Beavin, & Jackson, 1967). *What does this mean?*

First, for a person to communicate, someone else must respond in some way. In face-to-face interactions, the other person usually answers immediately, while an email message may take a few days to elicit a response. However, even a lack of a response might function as response. For example, if you phone or email a friend who doesn't respond for a long time, you may believe your friend is angry at you. This interaction is still communication, because you feel that your friend is angry, even if you do not know exactly why.

Second, when this model describes communication as ongoing, it highlights the fact that it is a process whose specific beginnings and endings can be difficult to discern. All the interactions you have had with individuals in the past influence your communication in the present, just as your current communication affects your expectations for and experiences of future interactions. Suppose that you meet a new colleague at work and the two of you have several enjoyable conversations. You might begin to look forward to seeing your colleague. However, if you have an argument the third time you talk, you may no longer eagerly anticipate your conversations; you may even be less friendly and open the next time you encounter her. As you become less friendly, your colleague may try to avoid you, which may influence you to be even more unfriendly when you do meet. Thus your communication evolves as a continuing process.

Finally, because communication is ongoing and interactive, when you communicate, you and your conversational partner(s) reaffirm or alter your identities and relationships. For example, as you talk, you reveal new aspects of who you are and/or confirm that parts of yourself have not changed (Mabry, 2001; Nussbaum, 1989). You may be most aware of this dimension of communication when you encounter people you have not seen for a long while. You may find yourself asking questions

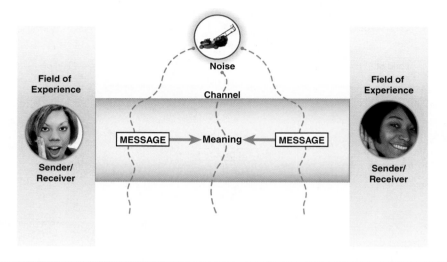

FIGURE 1.4:   A Transactional Model of Communication
Berlo's transaction model captured the fact that meaning is created as people communicate.

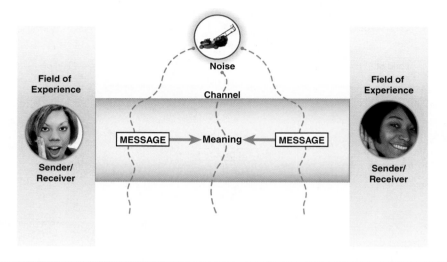

and studying their verbal and nonverbal behavior to see if they are the same. The other person likely will engage in similar behavior. This tendency can make reunions fraught with tension and uncertainty. For example, returning soldiers often comment that although they are thrilled to see their loved ones, they are nervous about how they and others might have changed while they were apart. During their time in Iraq, email and cell phones were very important to soldiers in maintaining their relationships with their families. Small talk (oral, via email, or via text messaging) can be important in this context, serving as an indicator that the individuals and the relationship they share are essentially unchanged (Duck, 1988).

The transactional model captures the fact that (1) each communicator is a sender and receiver *at the same time* and (2) meaning is created as people communicate. The transactional model also reveals that communication is an ongoing process and that previous communication events and relationships influence its meaning. In 1960, David Berlo was one of the first to create a model of communication that stressed the role of the relationship between the source and the receiver as an important variable in the communication process. (See Figure 1.4 for an example of a transactional model.)

The transactional model is the most complicated communication model. It emphasizes communication as an ongoing enterprise in which all the elements are constantly changing, and your ideas about yourself are continuously negotiated or transacted. While the linear, interactive, and transactional models all identify important aspects of the communication process, this book highlights several additional features of human communication, as we explain in the following sections.

Our Approach: Human Communication in Society

Our model of communication is an extension of the transactional model. Like the transactional model, it portrays communication as occurring simultaneously between senders and receivers, with meaning cocreated by all participants. In our model, however, we emphasize the role of individual and societal forces, as well as the influence of culture and context, in the communication process. In the sections that follow, we explain the interaction of these characteristics.

The Influence of Individual and Societal Forces

The individual is a primary focus in communication. Many separate forces contribute to one's identity, and these forces in turn affect our communication. Individual forces include one's demographic characteristics such as age, race, ethnicity, nationality, gender/sex, sexual orientation, regional identity, and socioeconomic class, as well as such factors as personality, experiences, and cognitive and physical ability.

For example, Tiger Woods is in his thirties and describes himself as a Cablasian (i.e., Caucasian, Black, and Asian), as a citizen of the United States, and as an upper-class male. Each of these individual factors influences the way he communicates, as well as the ways others communicate to and about him. Woods's individual experiences and personality also impact his communication with others. For instance, his experiences as a celebrity in the public eye likely cause him to speak less openly about his private life. Similarly, people probably treat him with greater respect and deference (and ask more of him) because he is famous and wealthy.

The combination of these variables is unique for every individual, so we each communicate in a distinctive way. However, every society places limits on the variations that are deemed acceptable. For example, not all men speak assertively, enjoy talking about sports, or "high five" one another. In mainstream U.S. culture, though, many people consider these behaviors as normative for males. Speaking in a more "female" style, such as speaking very quietly or politely, talking about fashion, or using "effeminate" nonverbal gestures typically is considered inappropriate for men and boys. If you veer somewhat from the norm, you may be seen as odd, or you might be shunned, but if you veer too far from the norm, you may be labeled as mentally ill. So while we are each individuals, society places constraints on the range of our individualism, a topic we discuss later.

The Rock's identity is influenced by his Samoan and Canadian Black ethnicity as well as his experiences as a wrestler and actor.

As we suggested earlier, individual differences are not value free. They are arranged in a hierarchy in which some individual characteristics are more highly valued than others. For example, being White is often advantageous in U.S. society, being young has advantages over being old, and being physically able is more advantageous than having a disability. How society evaluates these characteristics affects how we talk to, and about, people who display them.

The political, historical, economic, and social structures of a society influence this value hierarchy and affect how we view specific individual characteristics. Thus, the historical conditions under which many U.S. racial and ethnic groups arrived in the United States continue to affect their identities. For example, many of the earliest Polish immigrants were uneducated, knew little if any English, and were not highly skilled workers. Over the years, the profile of the typical Polish immigrant changed radically; nonetheless, many people still tell "Polish jokes" in which Poles are depicted as slow and incompetent (Drzewiecka & Alberts, 1996). Similarly, even though Barack Obama was elected president the fact that many African Americans came to the United States as slaves continues to impact the ways people think and talk about them.

The values attributed to individual characteristics such as age, sexual orientation, and sex also come from these larger societal forces—whether communicated to us through the media, by our friends and family, or by organizations such as schools, religious institutions, or clubs. For example, the teachings of religious groups shape many people's views on sexual orientation, and because most societies historically have been patriarchal, they continue to value women in the public realm less than they do men.

These hierarchies come from the meanings that societal structures impose on individual characteristics, and communication maintains these hierarchies. For example, cultures that value maleness over femaleness have many more stereotypes and negative terms for women than they do for men. Moreover, these cultures value certain types of communication over others. Thus women in leadership positions may be criticized for not communicating decisively and directly—a style of communication more commonly associated with men and viewed as the superior form for leaders. We will see how these hierarchies work in more detail in Chapter 5 (verbal communication) and Chapter 6 (nonverbal communication).

The Influence of Culture

Communication is embedded in culture. Culture refers to the learned patterns of perceptions, values, and behaviors that a group of people shares. Culture is dynamic and heterogeneous (Martin & Nakayama, 2005), meaning that it changes over time and that despite commonalities, members of cultural groups do not all think and behave alike. You probably belong to many cultures, including those of your gender, ethnicity, occupation, and religion, and each of these cultures will have its own communication patterns.

When you identify yourself as a member of a culture defined by age, ethnicity, or gender, this culture-group identity also becomes one of your individual characteristics. For example, as people move from their teen years into young adulthood, middle age, and old age, they generally transition from one age-related culture to another. Since each cultural group has a unique set of perceptions, values, and behaviors, each also has its own set of communication principles. Thus as you become an adult, you may stop using language you used as a teenager. However, it is important to recognize that while changing your language is an individual decision, it is influenced by cultural and societal expectations as well.

Being gay is both an individual and cultural factor.

Culture affects all or almost all communication interactions (Schirato & Yell, 1996). More specifically, participants bring their beliefs, values, norms, and attitudes to each interaction, and the cultures to which they belong shape each of these factors. Cultural beliefs also affect how we expect others to communicate. For instance, Emily was reared as a Mennonite and was taught to avoid conflict and refrain from directly confronting or disagreeing with others. Her roommate Stephanie was reared by two trial attorneys and was taught to challenge others' comments and to argue vigorously for her beliefs. Both of them found it difficult to live together during their first semester of college. Emily was uncomfortable with Stephanie's aggressive style and avoided Stephanie when she tried to discuss problems and disagreements. On the other hand, Stephanie grew frustrated at Emily's avoidance and became increasingly angry with their inability to talk about their problems. Consequently, they both requested new roommates for the spring semester.

Because the majority culture in the United States is European American, some White communicators assume that all others share their beliefs, values, attitudes, and norms. However, differences in ethnic culture, sexual orientation, or national origin often lead to significant differences in belief as well as differences in communication behavior.

In addition to the participants' cultural backgrounds, the culture in which a communication event takes place impacts how participants communicate. For example, in the United States, politicians routinely mention religion in their public addresses and specifically refer to God; however, in France, because of a stricter separation between church and state, politicians typically avoid mentioning religion or deities in their public communication and would be criticized if they did. Regional culture can also affect participants' expectations for appropriate communication behavior. For instance, Southerners in the United States tend to be more nonverbally demonstrative and thus might hug others more than do Northeasterners (Andersen, Lustig, & Andersen, 1990). Of course, other cultural differences (ethnic background, religious background) might influence these nonverbal behaviors as well.

The Influence of Context

Each communication interaction occurs in a specific context, which influences how it unfolds. For example, you could argue with your close friend in private when just the two of you are present, during a social event when you are part of a group, during a staff meeting at work, over email, on a television talk show about feuding friends, or in the mall. Can you imagine how each of these contexts would influence your communication? You might be more open if the two of you are alone and in private; you may try to get others involved if you are with friends; you could be more subdued at the mall; you might refrain from mentioning anything too negative on television; or you might be more hostile in an email.

The tensions that exist among individual forces, societal forces, cultures, and contexts shape communication and meaning. To help you understand this tension, let's examine a common conversation between romantic partners regarding holiday plans with family. Such conversations are influenced by the context (whether only the partners are talking or if other family members are involved), multiple individual forces (such as each partner's age), and multiple societal forces (such as which holidays each partner's culture celebrates). If the romantic partners are in their fifties, they're speaking in private, they've only been dating a few months, and the holiday is a minor one in their cultures, chances are that neither will be upset if one partner refuses to join the other's family celebration. However, if the partners have the conversation in front of family members, are married, and the holiday is central to at least one partner's culture, then one partner may well feel angry, hurt, and even embarrassed if the other refuses to attend. Thus the context in which the conversation occurs, the cultural importance of the holiday, and the status of the relationship all come together to influence the communication interaction.

Our Definition of Human Communication

Based on our beliefs about the important role of individual and societal forces, contexts, and culture in the communication process, we have developed our own definition and a fourth model of human communication. We define communication as a *transactional process in which people generate meaning through the exchange of verbal and nonverbal messages in specific contexts, influenced by individual and societal forces and embedded in culture.* You can see our model of the communication process in Figure 1.5.

FIGURE 1.5: Our Model of Human Communication in Society
The human communication in society model emphasizes both individual and societal forces.

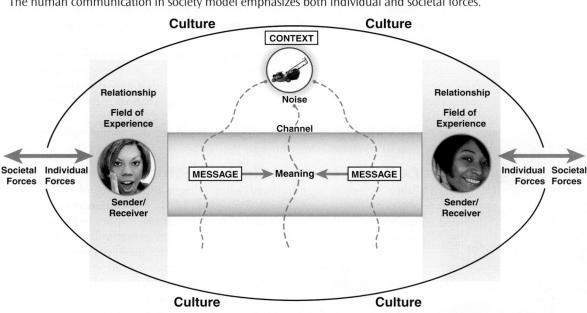

ethics
standards of what is right and wrong, good and bad, moral and immoral

communication ethics
the standards of right and wrong that one applies to messages that are sent and received

This is the definition and model of communication that will guide you as you explore the remainder of this book. After you complete this course, we recommend that you return to this section to assess how your own understanding of the communication process has changed and deepened. You can review all of the models of human communication we discuss in this chapter in *Visual Summary 1.1: Models of Human Communication*, on p. 20.

In this chapter, we have provided you with an overview of the book and a discussion of the basic concepts related to the study of communication. Our goal in doing this is to provide you with a framework that helps organize your reading and understanding of this complex process we call communication. Before moving on, we need to discuss one more essential concept that frames and guides all of your communication efforts—ethics.

A COMMUNICATION ETHIC

In the United States, we appear to be in the midst of a crisis with regard to ethical communication. In the business world, executives at American Insurance Group (AIG) were charged with lying to investors and the public (Verschoor, 2005), and corporate leaders at Global Crossing, WorldCom, Tyco, and Arthur Andersen were investigated or indicted on ethics charges. Unfortunately, ethical communication in the political arena does not appear to be faring much better; recently, Illinois Governor Rod Blagojevich was impeached on ethics charges (Lorg & Pearson, January 30, 2009).

People's personal lives are apparently in a state of ethical disarray as well: Approximately 85 percent of surveyed daters admitted having lied to their partners in the previous two weeks (Tolhuizen, 1990), while 74 percent of students admitted to cheating on exams and 84 percent to cheating on written assignments (McCabe & Trevino, 1996). Some citizens lie on their tax returns, and some salespeople misrepresent the quality or availability of their products. Given examples such as these, one may wonder if a communication ethic still exists.

We strongly believe that it does. Even if unethical communication is widespread, and some people get away with their misbehavior, most people are still held responsible for the messages they create (Barnlund, 1962; Christians & Traber, 1997; Johannesen, 1990). If you spread gossip about your friends, lie to your employer, or withhold information from your family, justifying your behavior by pointing to the ethical failures of others will not excuse you. Those who know you and are close to you still expect you to meet basic standards for ethical communication.

In this section we lay out basic principles of ethical communication. Clearly these guidelines reflect our own communication ethics. We recognize that ethics are a personal code that individuals must develop and that can alter over time. We offer these as guidelines for you to consider as you develop your own communication ethic.

Is it ethical to gossip or share others' secrets?

With these thoughts in mind, we begin the discussion with our definition of *communication ethics*.

Defining Communication Ethics

Ethics refers to standards of what is right and wrong, good and bad, moral and immoral (Jaksa & Pritchard, 1994). **Communication ethics** describes the standards of right and wrong that one applies to messages that are sent and received. When you hear the term *communication ethics*, you might think we are simply referring to whether messages are truthful. Although truthfulness is one of the most fundamental ethical standards, communicating ethically requires much more than simply being truthful. It also involves deciding what information can and should be disclosed or withheld, and assessing the benefit or harm associated with specific messages. Individuals have a responsibility to evaluate the ethics of their own and others' communication efforts. Similarly, organizations ought to weigh the ethics of sharing or withholding information that might affect the value of their stock shares; and broadcasting companies should decide whether it is ethical to report private information about individuals. Let's look at each of these topics more closely.

Truthfulness

Truthfulness plays a fundamental role in ethical communication for two reasons: First, others expect messages to be truthful, and second, messages have consequences. Because people inherently expect speakers to be truthful, we actually may make it easier for them to deceive us (Buller & Burgoon, 1996). If an audience is not suspicious, they probably won't look for cues that the speaker is lying (McCornack & Parks, 1986). However, because of the implicit contract to be honest, discovery of deception can severely damage relationships. The more intimate the relationship, the greater the expectation people have that their partners will be truthful, and the more damaging any deception will be.

As we've implied, messages should be truthful because they have consequences. Your communication can influence the beliefs, attitudes, and behaviors of others. Your communication could persuade a customer to purchase an item, a friend to loan you money, or an acquaintance to become romantically involved with you. The more consequential the outcome of your message, the more you will be held accountable to the truth. For example, you might not be criticized too harshly for exaggerating your salary during a flirtation with a stranger, but an employer probably will consider it unethical if you lie about your salary on a job application.

Sharing or Withholding Information

A related fundamental principle of ethical communication concerns what information should be divulged and what can be withheld. When is withholding information a matter of legitimate privacy, and when is it a matter of inappropriate secrecy? Thus, you have to determine whether to tell your romantic partner the number of sexual partners you have had; news organizations have to decide whether to reveal the names and sexual histories of rape victims; and pharmaceutical companies have to choose how much information to reveal about the side effects of their products. To understand the ramifications of divulging personal information, see *Communication in Society: Employers Scrutinize Facebook Profiles*, on p. 22.

In our view, a message can be considered legitimately private when other parties have no right to expect access to it. Inappropriate secrecy, on the other hand, occurs when other parties might legitimately expect access to a message that is withheld. This distinction is important, because typically, it is ethical to maintain privacy, but it may be unethical to engage in secrecy.

Facebook can be more than just a social networking site.

How does one decide what is private and what is secret? We believe that communicators have an ethical responsibility to share information that other people require to make informed decisions. For example, if you have only dated someone once or twice, you may choose to keep private that you have a sexually transmitted disease. However, if the two of you consider becoming sexually intimate, you have an ethical obligation to reveal the information. Without this information, your partner cannot make an informed decision about whether to engage in sexual contact. What will happen to your relationship if you withhold the information and your partner catches your disease—and finds out later that you withheld the information? Similarly, your friends may not need to know that you were fired from your last job for thievery, but your new boss has a legitimate need for access to this information.

Models of Human Communication

Linear Model

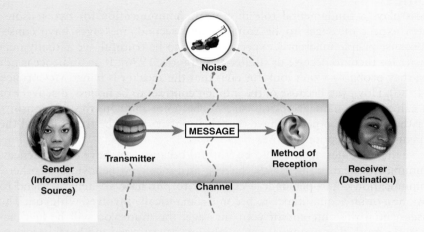

Interactive Model

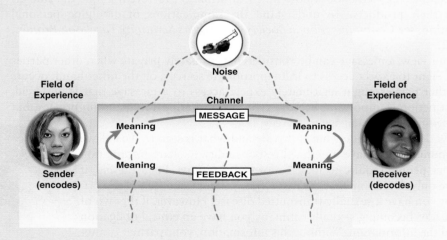

Transactional Model

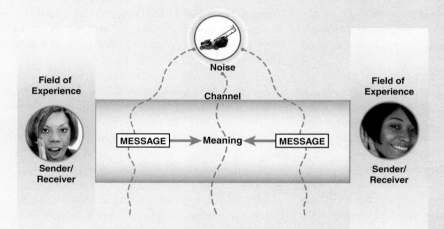

Human Communication in Society

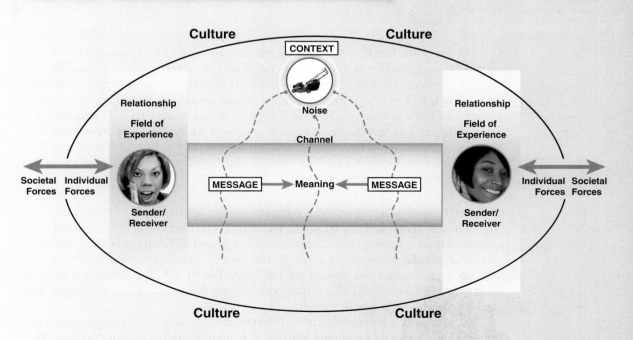

COMMUNICATION IN SOCIETY
Employers Scrutinize Facebook Profiles

Have you ever posted anything online that you wouldn't want a future employer to see? Do you think it is ethical for employers to search the Web to discover future employees' indiscretions? Does the possibility of future employers seeing your MySpace or Facebook site influence what you post on the Web?

College students are now no longer the only people accessing Facebook. Employers are logging on to check up on both current and prospective employees.

Rachel Kearney, director of career services and alumni affairs at Indiana University, reported firsthand experience of employers using Facebook.

"People don't believe this is happening, but it is," she said. "I've seen it."

According to Kearney, in one such incident an outraged government employer who worked closely with IU and hired a number of interns from the university contacted her.

Kearney said the employer used current and former interns to access Facebook, looking into the personal profiles of other interns. Upon finding distasteful information and pictures of a former intern and current IU student, the employer "demanded" its name and the student's internship status be removed from the Facebook profile.

The apologetic student complied, she said.

IU has taken steps to make its students aware of the issue, Kearney said, and other universities are doing the same.

Julia Barlow Sherlock, director of career services at Central Michigan University, said an email was sent to all students warning them that employers are looking at their Facebook accounts to "see the other side of who [they] are."

Administrators at other universities, including the University of Michigan and the University of Minnesota, have noted the growing controversy surrounding the issue and are planning to question employers at their respective spring recruitment rushes. While Kearney said students should be aware of this issue, she doesn't blame employers for using Facebook as a resource.

Not all employers are using Facebook, Nelson noted, but on the other hand, Facebook is certainly not the only means by which employers are checking into potential employees.

He cited Googling as one alternative screening method, and University of Michigan career center assistant director Lynne Sebille-White added criminal and credit checks are also fairly common.

Nelson warns students to protect themselves from possible dangers stemming from personal information displayed in a public domain.

FROM: "Employers scrutinize Facebook profiles," by Kate Maternowski, *The Badger Herald*, February 1, 2006, http://badgerherald.com. Reprinted by permission.

On the other hand, revealing information can sometimes be unethical. For example, if you have agreed to maintain confidentiality about a topic, it could be considered unethical to reveal what you know. However, if you violate a confidence because of a higher ethical principle, most people would likely consider your behavior ethical. For example, if you have a duty of confidentiality to your employer but your company engages in illegal toxic dumping, it likely would be more ethical to break this confidence. Here, the ethics of protecting the public health supersedes the ethics of keeping a confidence. As a communicator, you have to decide which ethical principles are most important to you.

Benefit and Harm of Messages

To determine the most ethical choice, you should consider the benefit or harm associated with your messages. A classic example concerns whether it is right to lie to a potential murderer about the whereabouts of the intended victim. A principle of honesty suggests that you should tell the truth. But in this case, once you evaluate the potential harm of sharing versus withholding the information, you might well decide to withhold the information.

More typically, issues of harm and benefit are less clear. For example, if you discover your best friend's romantic partner is being unfaithful, should you share that information? Will it result in more harm or more benefit? If you know that a relative cheated on her taxes, should you tell the IRS?

Because many communication events are complex and the underlying ethical principles are not definitive, you will gradually develop your own philosophy of ethical communication and apply it on a case-by-case basis. This is one requirement of being an effective communicator. However, just as you develop your own ethical standards and decisions, others will do so as well, which means you and others in your life may not always agree.

Developing Communication Ethics

As a communicator, you will face many ambiguous and difficult choices of both a professional and a personal nature. If you develop your own set of communication ethics you will be better prepared to face these difficult choices. In this section we provide some guidelines to draw on.

Absolutism Versus Relativism

A fundamental decision in communication ethics concerns how **absolute** or **relative** your ethical standards will be. Will you use the same absolute standards for every communication interaction, or will your ethical choices be relative and depend on each situation? The Greek philosopher Plato and the German philosopher Immanuel Kant conceptualized the absolutist perspective (Kant, 1785/1949), and both believed there is a rationally correct, moral standard that holds for everyone, everywhere, every time. Relativists such as French philosopher Jean-Paul Sartre, on the other hand, hold the view that moral behavior varies among individuals, groups, and cultures. They argue that since there is no universal standard of morality, there is no rational way to decide who is correct (Sartre, 1973). (See Figure 1.6.)

If you hold to the absolutist perspective that lying is always wrong, then in the earlier example regarding the murderer you would be obligated to reveal the whereabouts of the intended victim. But if you adhere to a relativistic position regarding truth and deception, you would decide in the moment what the most ethical choice is based on the specific circumstances.

In reality, few people develop an ethical standard that is completely absolute or relative. Instead, absolutism and relativism are the opposite ends of a continuum, and most people's standards lie somewhere along that continuum.

The issue for you is to decide how absolute or relative your ethical standards will be. If you strongly believe that deception is wrong, you may choose the path of deception only when you believe that the truth will cause great harm—a standard that falls toward the absolutist end of the continuum. However, you favor a more relative view if you consider a variety of factors, in addition to harm, as you make your decisions.

Ethics of Language Use

Another important ethical issue related to message creation centers on the types of language you use, particularly language that refers to others. Most of the time, people do not think about the names they use to describe a group of people or an individual as ethical issues. Although we three authors have our own ideas that we'll

absolute
pertaining to the belief that there is a single correct moral standard that holds for everyone, everywhere, every time

relative
pertaining to the belief that moral behavior varies among individuals, groups, and cultures, and across situations

Where do you position your own communication ethics on the absolutism–relativism continuum? Has the placement of your ethics on the continuum changed over time?

FIGURE 1.6: Absolutism Versus Relativism
Where would you place yourself on this ethics continuum?

Absolutism ◄————————————————► Relativism

present about the ethical use of language, you will need to decide how language choices fit within the ethical perspective you are developing.

Some more obvious examples of unethical language include racial and ethnic slurs and sexist and homophobic references, which we will discuss in more detail in Chapter 5. But less obvious examples exist as well. For example, when you refer to a colleague as an "idiot," your enemies as "monsters," or your political opponents as "fascists," you not only denigrate their humanity and their identities, but you shut down open communication and discussion about the salient issues. Unethical language prevents you from engaging in interactions that allow a more complex view both of the issues and of the other person or group.

You may have noticed that some individuals use what might be perceived as negative terms to describe themselves or other members of their group. For example, some gays and lesbians refer to themselves or others as "queer" and "dyke," and some members of ethnic minority groups adopt the ethnic slurs that outsiders have used to demean them. Does this mean that outsiders can use these same terms? Typically, it does not. When members of a group use a negative term, other members of the group usually recognize its intent and know that it is not meant to demean them; however, when an outsider uses the term, group members cannot interpret the intention and, therefore, may take offense (Brewer & Miller, 1996).

Listeners have an ethical responsibility to offer healthy feedback.

Ethical Responsibilities of Receivers

You may not have thought much about your responsibilities as a receiver of communication, in part because receivers typically are thought of as passive members of a communication interaction (Johannesen, 1990). Recall, however, that we view communication as a transactional process in which communicators both send and receive messages. What do your responsibilities as a receiver entail?

Overall, message receivers have a responsibility to listen mindfully (Kruger, 1999), paying close attention to what is being communicated and listening both for what is said and what is left unsaid. This responsibility is particularly great when you must form opinions or make decisions based on information you receive.

Other ethical responsibilities for receivers include **reasoned skepticism** and *healthy feedback* (Johannesen, 1990). *Reasoned skepticism* describes the balance of open-mindedness and critical attitude needed when evaluating others' messages. In order to engage in reasoned skepticism, listeners should ask questions and interrogate speakers to ensure that they have sufficient understanding and information to form an opinion or make a decision. As a corollary, speakers are responsible for listening to their audience and responding accurately to the questions they pose.

Do you see yourself as someone who engages in reasoned skepticism? Most people believe that they form reasoned opinions of current events and controversies based on fact. However, Drew Westen, a professor at Emory University, found otherwise. In a recent study, he examined how people responded to either weak or strong evidence of a soldier's participation in torture at Abu Ghraib prison in Iraq. He found that individuals' opinions regarding the soldier's innocence or guilt was predictable over 80 percent of the time, based not on the strength of the evidence provided but simply on their opinions of the Bush administration, the GOP, the military, or human rights groups. Therefore, the facts had little power to persuade respondents (Westen, 2007).

Healthy feedback refers to the honest and ethical responses receivers provide to the messages of others. For example, if you hear a racist joke, what do you think would count as healthy feedback? If you believe that racist language is unethical, then your responsibility as an ethical listener would be to refuse to laugh at the joke.

reasoned skepticism
the balance of open-mindedness and critical attitude needed when evaluating others' messages

healthy feedback
the honest and ethical responses receivers provide to the messages of others

You may even let the joke teller know that you find the joke and its language offensive.

One caveat: Interactions happen in larger contexts in which communicators and receivers are not equally empowered to speak freely. So, if your boss tells a sexist joke during a meeting, you may feel constrained from providing healthy feedback. In this case, acting as an ethical receiver may not be healthy for your career! On a larger scale, many people have looked back and questioned why observers of certain historical or political events did not "speak up." For example, why didn't more people in Germany speak up or do something to prevent the Holocaust during World War II?

In situations of unequal power relations, less-powerful individuals who speak out are vulnerable. Individuals in these situations must choose between speaking up and suffering the consequences, or remaining quiet and wrestling with their consciences. When ethical people remain quiet, they typically do so because they fear for themselves or others. However, this fear can further empower the powerful, creating a "chilling effect" (Roloff & Cloven, 1990) on the oppressed and vulnerable and on their willingness to ask questions. The more powerful the individual or group is in relation to you, the more difficult it may be for you to protest. Deciding how to communicate in these situations is a serious issue, and individuals have reflected on this topic for centuries. You must decide for yourself how much risk you are willing to bear when speaking out against those in power.

The Ethics of Authentic Communication

Authentic communication is open and free from pretense. Inauthentic communication is closed, attempts to manipulate the interaction or other communicators, and denies those with a legitimate interest in the issue the right to communicate (Deetz, 1990). When a university sets tuition rates, students, parents, and others who help pay those expenses have a legitimate right to participate in the discussion; if the administration refuses to allow these interested parties to have a voice or to participate in the discussion, many observers would label this behavior "inauthentic." Let's look more closely at the elements of inauthentic communication.

Topic Avoidance.   All groups discourage, or even prohibit, communication on specific topics. You may have been told that it is not polite to discuss money, religion, or politics. In a professional context, you probably are aware that discussing emotions is frowned on. When someone does introduce the "forbidden topic," others try to dismiss it or change the subject. They may be direct and say, "Let's not talk about that right now." Alternatively, they may simply ignore the message, or they may use subtle methods, such as transitioning to a different topic. Informally, people today jokingly say, "TMI!" ("Too much information!") when they want to stop discussion on a particular topic.

Topic avoidance is not always unethical, but it can be when the majority group decides some topics are off limits (Deetz, 1990) thereby silencing opposing or minority viewpoints. The movie *Kinsey* provides an excellent example of how the majority group in the United States during the 1950s attempted to prevent scientific, open discussion about human sexual behavior and successfully destroyed the reputation of sex researcher Dr. Alfred Kinsey during his lifetime. Interestingly, when the movie came out in 2004, a group of people again protested the portrayal of this subject; in this instance, however, they were no longer the majority. Political dictators often silence opposing viewpoints as a means of maintaining power. Of course, dictators are not the only ones who attempt to silence disagreement. Historically, politicians, newspaper columnists, and even average citizens have harshly criticized individuals who oppose governmental decisions, and some have done so in an attempt to prevent dissent.

meaning denial
the refusal to acknowledge the intended meaning of a message

disqualification
communication acts that attempt to deny others the right to speak based on their positions or identities

Meaning Denial. As we have discussed, every message contains multiple potential meanings. **Meaning denial** occurs when one meaning is "both present in the interaction and denied as meant" (Deetz, 1990, p. 238). An obvious example of this occurs when your roommate stomps around your apartment, slams doors, sighs loudly, and gives you hostile looks. When you ask what is wrong, she or he replies, "Nothing." Meaning denial also occurs in professional contexts, as when a boss uses sexual innuendo with a subordinate but then denies having done so. Such communication is unethical because it allows speakers to control others without taking responsibility for their messages.

Disqualification. Communication acts that attempt to deny others the right to speak based on their positions or identities are referred to as **disqualification** (Bavelas & Smith, 1982). For example, if a group of students complains that an instructor is unfair, and the university dismisses their claims simply because they are students, the students have been disqualified. In conversation, people's opinions are sometimes disqualified, or viewed as worthless, because they are male, old, Asian, not college educated, or for a whole host of other so-called reasons. An example of disqualification occurred in 2005 in Phoenix, Arizona, when the city council met to decide whether to close a day-workers' center, which is a place where laborers can wait each morning to be hired by local companies or individuals. City council members and people who lived in the neighborhood were invited to speak at the meeting, but no one invited the day workers themselves, even though they would be the ones most dramatically affected by the decision.

At this point you may be asking, "What should I do if I want to ensure that authentic communication occurs?" Avoiding the behaviors just described is crucial. In short, be open to others' communication, take responsibility for what you communicate, and be sensitive to issues of inclusion and exclusion.

Communication Ethics in Practice

In this discussion of ethics we have offered guidelines for creating your own communication ethics. However, in practice, making ethical choices is not always easy or clear-cut. Many situations arise that are ambiguous, complex, and multilayered.

At times you may not see how you can be ethical and accomplish important goals at the same time. For example, if you know that a friend and classmate has plagiarized a paper, what should you do? Should you keep quiet and maintain your friendship, or should you maintain your personal ethics and tell the instructor? Similarly, if you are a salesperson, how do you respond if a potential client asks whether a competitor's product is as good as yours, and you believe it is? Do you tell the truth and thus jeopardize a potential sale? People who tend toward an absolutist view say that you must always tell the truth, so you should only sell a product you truly believe is superior. Others may tell you that no one expects salespeople to be completely truthful in this context; therefore, you are not bound to share your opinion (Diener, 2002; Wokutch & Carson, 1981).

We believe that all communicators need to create an ethical stance based on their own beliefs, values, and moral training. Once you've established your ethical stance, you will be prepared to make thoughtful and deliberate communication choices.

To assist you further in creating your own communication ethic, we include below the National Communication Association's Credo for Ethical Communication (NCA Credo, 2005):

- We endorse freedom of expression, diversity of perspective, and tolerance of dissent to achieve the informed and responsible decision-making fundamental to a civil society.

- We strive to understand and respect other communicators before evaluating and responding to their messages.
- We promote access to communication resources and opportunities as necessary to fulfill human potential and contribute to the well-being of families, communities, and society.
- We promote communication climates of caring and mutual understanding that respect the unique needs and characteristics of individual communicators.
- We condemn communication that degrades individuals and humanity through distortion, intimidation, coercion, and violence, and through the expression of intolerance and hatred.
- We are committed to the courageous expression of personal convictions in pursuit of fairness and justice.
- We advocate sharing information, opinions, and feelings when facing significant choices, while also respecting privacy and confidentiality.
- We accept responsibility for the short- and long-term consequences of our own communication and expect the same of others.

Throughout this book, we will continue to address issues of ethics in communication as they apply in a variety of contexts. This information will help you as you create and/or refine your own communication ethics.

SUMMARY

Studying human communication can enrich and transform your life professionally and personally. To understand how communication occurs, you need to study it.

The *process* of communication between participants involves sending and receiving verbal and nonverbal messages through specific channels in particular settings. Messages are affected by noise and influenced by feedback. As scholars have studied communication in depth, they have moved away from seeing the communication process as a *linear* event that involves transmitting a message from a sender to a receiver. Instead, they began to view it as an *interactive* process in which both senders and receivers communicate—senders through message transmission, and receivers through feedback. More recently, researchers have come to view communication as a transactional process in which each participant is both a receiver and a sender, and each interaction is affected by noise, the participants' relationship, and their fields of experience. The approach taken in this book extends the transactional model by emphasizing that all communication interactions are influenced by the intersection of individual and societal forces, that they are embedded in culture, and that they occur in specific contexts.

The ethics of individual communication choices are another essential feature of communication. This is a topic we will return to throughout the book. Key aspects of communication ethics include truthfulness, decisions regarding sharing or withholding information, and the benefit and harm associated with one's choices. Communicators' ethical choices are affected by their position on the continuum of absolutism versus relativism, which in turn influences their language use, how they receive and respond to others' communication efforts, and their commitment to authentic communication.

With a clear understanding of the material in this chapter, you are now ready to explore the historical development of communication studies.

KEY TERMS

human communication 6
messages 6
symbol 6
iconic signs 6
indexical signs 7
content meaning 9
relationship meaning 9
setting 10

participants 10
message creation 10
encoding 10
decoding 10
channel 11
noise 11
feedback 11
field of experience 12

ethics 18
communication ethics 18
absolute 23
relative 23
reasoned skepticism 24
healthy feedback 24
meaning denial 26
disqualification 26

TEST YOUR KNOWLEDGE

1. What does it mean that communication is a transactional process?

2. How does culture impact the communication process?

3. What are the four primary models of human communication? How are they alike? How do they differ?

4. What is the difference between privacy and secrecy?

5. What are the ethical responsibilities of receivers?

6. What is authentic communication? What can you do to make your communication interactions more authentic?

APPLY WHAT YOU KNOW

1. **Guidelines for Responding to Electronic Communication**
   Much debate has raged over whether it is appropriate to talk on one's cell phone in restaurants, in front of friends, or in the car. The Federal Aviation Administration is considering whether to allow airline passengers to use their cell phones during flights—and many people are already complaining about the possibility. The widespread use of instant text messaging and the ability to access our email almost anywhere have made the issues surrounding the appropriate use of electronic communication even more complex. To focus the discussion and guide your own decisions regarding your responses to these types of electronic communication, develop a list of rules for how, when, and with whom it is appropriate to use communication technologies.

2. **Creating a Communication Ethic**
   Interview three people and ask them to describe the underlying ethic(s) that guide their communication choices. Then write a brief statement that describes your own communication ethic.

3. **Communication Ethics in the Media**
   Watch television for one evening and observe the number of ethical dilemmas related to communication that people and characters confront. Note their response to each dilemma. How many people/characters make ethical choices? How many do not? What justifications or reasons do people/characters give for their choices? What consequences, if any, are portrayed? What conclusions can you draw about the portrayal of communication ethics on television?

EXPLORE

1. Make a list of all of the careers that you believe re-quire good communication skills. Go to the University of North Carolina Wilmington's Career Center page at www.uncw.edu/stuaff/career/Majors/communication.htm to examine the list of careers for which a communication degree prepares students. What careers did you list that are not listed on the University of North Carolina Wilmington site? Why do you think the differences exist? Finally, create a list of careers you would post if you were responsible for creating such a site.

2. Go to the National Communication Association's "Famous People with Degrees in Communication" page at www.natcom.org/NCA/Template?asp?bid=.htm. After reading the page, develop a list of at least ten different careers that famous people have pursued after obtaining degrees in communication.

3. Go to www.hodu.com/authentic.shtml and read the article on "Strategies for More Skillful, Authentic Communication." After reading the article, answer the following questions: When are you most likely to lie? What benefits do you think you will accrue if you lie? What can you do to increase how authentic you are when you communicate with others?

2

Communication Studies:
History and Contemporary Approaches

chapter outline

Because communication seems so . . . well, common, many people are not aware that the study of communication has a substantial history."

As she sat in a coffee shop, Nadia noticed a man sitting at the table next to her. His book caught her eye; it was the autobiography of Andy Warhol, one of her favorite American artists. Nadia was curious about this man's interests in Andy Warhol and wondered if they might have other things in common. She turned toward him and commented that she had always wanted to read the autobiography, and he told her that he was really enjoying it. As Nadia continued to talk to the man, she learned his name, Simon, and that he was also an art student at the same university Nadia attended. The more she talked to Simon, the more she wanted to know about him. Then, Nadia remembered something she had learned in her communication class earlier that week. The professor has discussed *uncertainty reduction theory* (Berger & Calabrese, 1975; Berger & Gudykunst, 1991), which says that a primary motivation for communication is to reduce uncertainty about people you meet—and that uncertainty is reduced through communication with those people. Nadia recognized that striking up a conversation with Simon was a good example of uncertainty reduction in practice. She hoped that this first conversation with Simon would not be their last, because she had enjoyed getting to know him and of their shared interests. To think, she thought, it all started with a book!

Nadia's use of uncertainty reduction theory illustrates how people can use communication theories in their everyday lives. Theories are sets of statements that explain a particular phenomenon. In this case, the uncertainty reduction theory explains what happened as Nadia's uncertainty was reduced. Communication theories are not just academic exercises; they explain and offer insight into one's own and others' communication (Cragan & Shields, 1998).

Uncertainty reduction theory is just one of many communication theories; in fact, there are too many communication theories to include in a single textbook. In writing this book we chose to include theories that would best introduce the student to a broad range of communication theories and would lead to an exploration of the role of societal and individual forces in the communication process.

In this chapter we explain the four major theoretical approaches in the communication discipline: the social science, interpretive, critical, and postmodern perspectives. As you will see, social science and interpretive theories take a more individual approach to the study of communication, while the other two take a more societal approach. To help you understand these four approaches and how they arose, we first explore the long and influential development of the communication discipline.

Once you have read this chapter, you will be able to:

- Describe the two major historical influences in communication studies: rhetoric and behaviorism.
- Identify and describe four contemporary approaches to the study of communication.
- Describe the strengths and limitations of each of these four approaches.
- Understand the role of paradigm, theory, and methods in communication studies.

THE HISTORY OF COMMUNICATION STUDIES

Because communication seems so . . . well, common, many people are not aware that the study of communication has a substantial history. In the United States the communication field traces its origins to the Western intellectual tradition of ancient Greece. Consequently, we begin by exploring these earliest roots and tracing their evolution into the early twentieth century when communication became a formalized discipline. As the final stop on this historical journey, we explore a more recent influence on communication studies: behaviorism.

Strangers can reduce uncertainty by starting a conversation.

The Rhetorical Tradition: The Art of Persuasion

When you hear the word *rhetoric,* what do you think of? If you are like many people, you many think rhetoric refers to empty, meaningless communication, as characterized in the expressions "that's just a bunch of rhetoric" or "that's a rhetorical question" (a question that does not need to be answered). However, rhetoric was not always thought of in this way. Throughout history the study and practice of **rhetoric**, defined as the art of persuasion, were essential parts of an educated person's life.

The rhetorical tradition lies at the heart of the communication discipline, and Chapter 11 covers rhetorical studies in more detail. Here we cover a brief overview of the important role rhetoric played in the development of the communication studies field. The rhetorical tradition flourished in ancient Athens, Greece, in the fifth century B.C.

At that time, rhetoric encompassed the entire discipline of communication studies, and it served a vital role in Greece's thriving democracy. Citizens were required to advocate for themselves in the courts (no lawyers) and to participate fully in their government (no congressional representatives). Consequently, citizens needed strong persuasive skills to advance their arguments in many different public settings. Although citizenship in Athens was restricted to adult males, thus excluding women, the foreign born, and slaves (Crowley & Hawhee, 1999), most historians still refer to Greece as a democracy. They do so because all Greek citizens met together in the Assembly to enact laws and policies and to act as jurors at trials.

Rhetoric flourished for many years, through the rise and fall of the Greek and Roman empires. Even through the early Middle Ages when much of Europe declined (500–1050 A.D.) the rhetorical tradition was kept alive through the Muslim (Moor) rulers who established a library in Toledo, Spain, which included many works of important Greek and Roman rhetoricians and philosophers. During the Middle Ages, the seven liberal arts of the Romans became the curriculum in schools across Europe.

These seven liberal arts included the *trivium* (grammar, rhetoric, logic) and the *quadrivium* (geometry, music, arithmetic, astronomy). As part of the trivium, the study of rhetoric became a traditional academic discipline that has persisted until today. Thus, if you have taken a college course in public speaking, you've participated in an academic tradition that has its roots in the fifth century B.C. (Infante, Rancer, & Womack, 1990).

Thanks to the Arab translators, the writings of early Greek philosophers became firmly established, and some say that these writings stimulated the birth of the **Renaissance**—an era of tremendous intellectual, artistic, and scientific achievements in Europe from the fourteenth to the seventeenth centuries.

The invention of the printing press in about 1450 also had a powerful influence on people's access to information of all kinds. Still, most people living in this era were illiterate and relied heavily on oral communication and oral persuasion.

uncertainty reduction theory
theory that argues that much early interaction is dedicated to reducing uncertainty about others and determining if one wishes to interact with them again

rhetoric
communication that is used to influence the attitudes or behaviors of others; the art of persuasion

Renaissance
an era of tremendous intellectual, artistic, and scientific achievements in Europe spanning the fourteenth to the seventeenth centuries

TABLE 2.1 Major Contributions to the Study of Communication

Rhetorical Tradition	
Ancient Greeks	The power of persuasion
	Guidelines for effective public speaking
Middle Ages	Rhetoric established as liberal art
Renaissance	Humanism and Enlightenment: foundations of behaviorism
Behaviorist Tradition	
Nineteenth Century	Elocution movement: study of proper public speaking
Twentieth Century	Rise of behaviorism
	Establishment of the discipline of communication
	Humanism vs. behaviorism debate

However, over time the written message became the dominant form due to its ability to reach across time and space. See Table 2.1 for a summary of the major rhetorical contributions to the study of communication.

The Renaissance brought together two important new ideas: **humanism**, which celebrated human nature and its potential, and the **Enlightenment**, which held that science and reason were the pathways to human knowledge. These two principles came to characterize diverging strands of learning and offered two approaches to the study of human communication.

Scholars such as Galileo and Isaac Newton, building on rediscovered Greek, Roman, and Muslim knowledge, advanced scientific understanding of the physical world. Sir Francis Bacon (1561–1626), perhaps the first social scientist, used observation to advance the academic study of human gestures—an important aspect of communication. By studying communication as a science, Bacon departed from the earlier rhetoricians who thought that communication should be studied as an art. He laid the foundation for the behaviorist approach described in the next section. [For more information about Bacon's works, go to **www.luminarium.org/sevenlit/bacon/url**]

Not everyone agreed with Bacon's view. Three English scholars continued the traditional, humanistic study of rhetoric during the eighteenth and nineteenth centuries. George Campbell (1776) added a strong *psychological* element to the study of persuasion. He developed a theory suggesting that new knowledge of human nature could explain different types of rhetorical effectiveness. Hugh Blair (1783) emphasized that rhetoric had *artistic* aspects as well as persuasive ones, and he focused on techniques that could increase a speaker's artistry. He noted the importance of outlining, for example, as a precursor to preparing to write or speak. Richard Whately (1828) studied the roles of *reason* and *logic* in persuasive processes. He also helped establish standards by which arguments could be evaluated (Herrick, 2001; Infante, Rancer, & Womack, 1990).

During this same period, educational institutions in the United States became fertile ground for rhetorical theory and practice. At first, the focus was on using rhetoric to train preachers. In the nineteenth century rhetoric came to play an important role in educational institutions as well. Public speaking was taught regularly to help prepare all male students to operate effectively in a democratic society. (Remember that at this time in the United States, women did not yet have the right to vote.)

Interest in **behaviorism**, the focus on the study of behavior as a science, began to take hold within educational institutions during the nineteenth century. Before exploring that topic further, we would like to point out that by placing the roots of

humanism
a system of thought that celebrates human nature and its potential

Enlightenment
eighteenth-century belief that science and reason are the pathways to human knowledge

behaviorism
the focus on the study of behavior as a science

Alternative VIEW
Origins of Classical Rhetoric: Greek or Egyptian?

Where did classical [Western] civilization and rhetoric originate? Martin Bernal, in Black Athena *(1987), shakes the whole foundation of our thinking about this question. He argues that African, specifically Egyptian, culture deeply influenced the Greek and Roman civilizations. He suggests, in fact, that Egypt colonized Greece and that classical Greek culture is essentially Egyptian, but that these influences have been systematically ignored, denied, or suppressed since the eighteenth century—chiefly for racist reasons. Scholar Mark Alford describes one of Bernal's arguments here. What are the consequences for the field of communication when non-European contributors are erased?*

In *Black Athena*, Martin Bernal attacks classicists of the last two centuries for their whitewashing of classical Greece, and alleges that, assuming the racial superiority of Europeans, they ignored the swarthy races of the Western Mediterranean, and looked only at vigorous Northern barbarians as originators of Greek culture.

There are many detailed arguments and observations that Bernal assembles to justify his "Revised Ancient Model" of Greek origins. [For example, he suggests that because] language follows culture, if Classical Greece was indeed founded by invaders and traders from the Levant [Middle East], you would expect to find many of their words left like fossils in the Greek lexicon, just as the Vikings and Normans molded English. And indeed *Black Athena* [is] seeded with fascinating and controversial claims of etymologies for Greek words.

Black Athena's public reception has been extraordinarily varied. . . . However, it is being admitted that nineteenth-century classicists did develop and promulgate a purified picture of classical Greece, ignoring its less noble qualities, and its cultural debt to the high civilizations of antiquity. Perhaps classicists may end up embracing the spirit of *Black Athena*, no matter how many of its explicit claims they reject.

FROM: "Origins of Classical Rhetoric: Greek or Egyptian?" from www.physics.wustl.edu. © 1997 Mark Alford. Reprinted by permission of Mark Alford.

communication studies in ancient Greece, this text assumes that the origin of classical thought, including communication, began in Europe (ancient Greece). Some scholars, however, have challenged this assumption (see *Alternative View: Origins of Classical Rhetoric: Greek or Egyptian?*). Although communication scholars in the United States largely follow the Western model, the study of communication has developed around the world in multiple ways, under different names, to serve differing cultural, social, and political needs.

The Behaviorist Tradition: Communication as Science

The interest in behaviorism led to a new way of thinking about communication—first through the elocution movement and then through more sophisticated communication studies. It eventually led to a vigorous debate between the rhetoricians and behaviorists about how communication should be studied; this debate continues today. Let's look more closely at how these competing studies of communication developed.

The nineteenth century saw the rise of a new approach to the study of communication, foreshadowed by Francis Bacon's scientific study of gestures in the 1600s. The behaviorist tradition based its observations and conclusions on definable, measurable behavior and on experimental methods, rather than concerning itself with the mind or people's thoughts and feelings. This tradition started with the elocution movement of the late 1800s, then strengthened as communication became a formal discipline in the early twentieth century. It later challenged the rhetorical tradition as the primary focus in communication studies.

The Elocution Movement

With the rise of industrialization and the emerging middle classes in England and in the United States in the late nineteenth century, people came to believe they should learn to present themselves properly in society and become more effective communicators. In response, teachers and scholars developed the study of **elocution**. Elocution refers to the mechanics of public speaking, including proper pronunciation, posture, and grammar. Anyone who wanted to function effectively in polite society studied elocution, either in a college course or with a private instructor.

Unlike rhetorical scholars, who believed public speaking was best understood as an art, elocution instructors thought that studying communication as a physical science would prove more useful. They developed comprehensive theories of communication from systematic observations of public speakers, complete with intricate diagrams and definitions (Dues & Brown, 2004). Some of these studies led to unintended and comical results. For example, elocution scholars studied gestures and taught their students which gestures to use when they wanted a specific effect. However, self-conscious speakers sometimes made gestures at inappropriate moments, having failed to grasp that gestures should evolve *naturally* from speech. See the illustration in Figure 2.1.

At the end of the nineteenth century, the study of communication was at a crossroads. The behaviorists had developed their perspective on how communication should be studied and taught, which differed markedly from the approach of the rhetoricians, and it was not clear which approach would prevail.

The Emergence of a Discipline

At the turn of the twentieth century, U.S. and European universities grew rapidly as more and more students enrolled. With this growth, universities organized into smaller departments and colleges. Each department usually represented a single academic discipline. Some universities had departments of rhetoric and oratory or elocution; others created departments of English that concentrated on both oral and written communication. These departments offered two types of courses: elocution courses that taught the mechanics of speech delivery (similar to our public-speaking courses today), and composition courses that were concerned with the substance of communication, including logical thinking, clear use of language, cogent organization, and purposeful discourse—elements that also were included in rhetorical studies (Cohen, 1994).

Professors of rhetoric and elocution soon realized that the English department was not the appropriate home for their academic efforts. Their focus was on spoken communication, while English scholars focused primarily on written communication and the study of literature as a fine art. If communication could not be categorized as

FIGURE 2.1: A Diagram of Elocution
Elocutionists developed comprehensive theories of communication that instructed students in how to gesture and move, as shown in this intricate diagram.

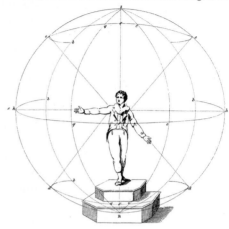

elocution
the mechanics of public speaking, including proper pronunciation, posture, and grammar

What differences do you see between early communication classes (left) and those of today (right)?
Bettmann/Corbis.
All Rights Reserved.

methodology
an accepted set of methods for developing new knowledge about a subject

part of the liberal arts, the other choices were to include it as part of the older, physical sciences (physics, chemistry, biology, astronomy) or with the newer social sciences (psychology, sociology, and anthropology).

For communication to become a separate discipline from English, two requirements had to be met: (1) the content of the proposed discipline had to represent a substantial and separate subject area not covered by any other discipline, and (2) the discipline had to have a distinct **methodology**, or accepted set of methods for developing new knowledge about the subject (Dues & Brown, 2004).

As rhetoric and elocution scholars struggled to define the content and methods of their new discipline, they recognized that a great gulf divided them. The rhetoricians wanted to focus on *speech as the art of public address*. The behaviorists and elocutionists wanted to study the *human behavior of speaking as a social science*. The two approaches differed dramatically in their assumptions about human nature and behavior, the best way to pursue knowledge, and even the nature of reality.

Despite this division, by 1914 scholars began to see speech as a separate discipline from English. The foundation for speech as a discipline already existed. Courses were offered; a professional association was formed (the National Association of Academic Teachers of Public Speaking, today called the National Communication Association or NCA); a body of theoretical knowledge existed; and an academic journal devoted to publishing research in the field was launched (Cohen, 1994). However, within speech, the intellectual gap between the rhetoric and elocution groups was widening. So that you will better understand this gap—and why the divide persists today—we explore these differences next.

Behaviorism Versus Humanism Debate

The two groups of scholars—the rhetoricians (or humanists) and the elocutionists (or behaviorists)—were part of a larger intellectual debate between humanism and behaviorism (Bormann, 1980). Humanistic scholars, including contemporary rhetoricians, emphasize the creative aspect of human nature. They believe that the best way to understand humans is to interpret *individual* behavior. Thus, they study the public-speaking skills of famous speakers in order to determine the most effective public-speaking strategies for specific contexts. However, because one can never repeat a speech in precisely the same way and in precisely the same context, humanists believe that it is only possible to interpret what was and was not effective in a particular speech.

In contrast, the elocutionists' view is that researchers should avoid simple interpretation and critique of speakers' skills. Rather, they believe that by studying speakers' externally observable behavior as well as audience responses, they can come to understand general patterns of behavior that are likely to be effective. In the behaviorist view, human behavior is deterministic, meaning that individuals react in predictable ways to others and their environment. Therefore, behaviorists systematically observe (and collect) data with the goal of identifying universal laws that govern human behavior. The fields of psychology, sociology, and political science influenced this behavioral approach.

Communication scholars also were interested in a topic that psychology researchers pursued—the study of persuasion. This interest sprang from societal forces surrounding the two world wars, when powerful dictators like Stalin, Mussolini, and, later, Hitler were mobilizing people to action. Communication scholars wanted to understand why and how these leaders were able to do this.

In the 1940s a group of Yale University scholars launched a series of studies on the subject. For example, psychologists Carl Hovland and Walter Weiss (1951) found that the credibility of the speaker, the type of message, and how the message was delivered could make it more, or less, persuasive. In addition, the communication channel (spoken or written communication) and the listener played important roles in how persuasive a message was (Hovland, Janis, & Kelly, 1953).

Researchers conducted these behaviorist studies under strictly controlled conditions in laboratories, where they could systematically vary the types of speakers, messages, and channels—a very different approach from the scholarship of rhetoricians. Nevertheless, psychology was becoming a major force in universities, and other psychological studies were taken by this research. The Yale studies and other psychological studies helped move the discipline of communication toward a social science approach, as we describe in the next section (Bormann, 1980).

Psychology's emphasis on individuals and their relationships strongly influenced communication studies. Thus interpersonal communication, group communication, and organizational communication—based primarily on psychological theory and research—became major focuses in the field (Strate, 1998).

Sociology and political science studies also contributed to the young field of communication. Sociologist Paul Lazarsfeld (1944) investigated the influence of media on society, especially on voting behavior. Political scientist Harold Laswell (1948) studied propaganda and mass persuasion in order to explore the influence of communication in shaping world opinion. Laswell also focused on how information was transmitted from one source to a receiver, and he did so at about the same time that communication scholars Claude Shannon and Warren Weaver (1949), along with Wilbur Schramm (1955), developed the linear model of communication described in Chapter 1.

In the 1960s, influenced by societal forces such as the Vietnam War, other communication scholars had "a deep-seated aversion to the manipulative and deceitful aspects of many mass media messages" (Knapp, Daly, Albada, & Miller, 2002, p. 6). Consequently, these scholars emphasized interpersonal relationships. For example, psychologist Paul Watzlawick argued that relationships develop as a result of people's interactions; with his colleagues, he sought to determine how communication could improve these relationships (Watzlawick, Beavin, & Jackson, 1967). In addition, social psychologist Michael Argyle (1969) and communication scholar Dean Barnlund (1968) focused on factors influencing the origin, development, and maintenance of interpersonal relationships.

These behaviorists were not the only ones propelling the development of communication studies. Humanistic rhetoricians also did their part. One early humanistic movement was called public address studies. Scholars involved in this line of research studied rhetorical texts and speeches of people engaged in public debates to gain "insights into the life of an era" (Wrage, 1947, p. 455). By studying the public speeches or public arguments in other eras, they could see why people supported or opposed slavery, or why people wanted to grant or deny women the right to vote. Often these scholars focused on presidential rhetoric, such as that of James Madison (Moore, 1945), as presidents were major voices in setting the public agenda of an era.

Scholars also developed rhetorical criticism, which focuses on interpreting and analyzing rhetorical documents. In 1925, Herbert Wichelns applied the techniques of literary criticism to the analysis of public communication. His efforts helped legitimize the study of public communication based on the criteria of literary criticism. Since then, rhetorical critics have developed a variety of methods to guide their analyses. For example, Robert Ivie studied the use of metaphor in three Cold War speakers (1987); others examined the use of narrative in President Reagan's rhetoric (Lewis, 1987). Rhetorical scholars cannot test their hypotheses with carefully controlled laboratory conditions in the way that behaviorists can. Instead, they compare similar situations, theories, and dialogue with their colleagues, and they exchange analyses in publications and conference presentations. The overall goal of rhetorical criticism is to develop theories about the ways that public communication influences and is influenced by society.

Thus, rhetoricians gained prominence as they focused on the power of rhetoric in social movements like the civil rights movement (Terrill, 2003; Watts, 2001; Wilson, 2003), the women's liberation movement (Borda, 2002; Campbell, 1994; Dow, 2004; Zaeske, 2002), the gay liberation movement (Brookey, 2001; Cloud, 1998;

Gaining the right to vote made public speaking an important communication skill for women in the twentieth century and beyond.

Hasian & Parry-Giles, 1997), and anti-immigration initiatives (Ono & Sloop, 2002). By addressing issues of social change and becoming relevant to important social issues, rhetoric has been rejuvenated.

As you can see, the study of communication during the twentieth century solidified into two approaches: rhetorical studies, emphasizing human choice and the art of public speaking; and behavioral studies, which viewed human behavior as determined and measurable. In the second half of the twentieth century, two additional approaches were added, giving us the four approaches used today. We describe these next.

CONTEMPORARY APPROACHES, THEORIES, AND METHODS

The debate between humanists and behaviorists continues, though the labels have changed. The behaviorist approach has been variously referred to as *positivism,* the *functionalist approach, postpositivism,* and the **social science approach**, the term we have chosen to use here. We include humanistic (rhetorical) study in the **interpretive approach**. In the late twentieth century two other approaches developed: the *critical approach* and the *postmodern approach* (Craig, 1999; Mumby, 1997). Granted, the critical and postmodern approaches at first may seem purely abstract and intellectual. However, like Nadia in our opening story, you will soon see that these approaches address issues that have real relevance in everyday life.

What do we mean by an *approach*? Each approach represents a worldview, much like a religious system or faith does. In the academic world we call these belief systems **paradigms** (Burrell & Morgan, 1988). Moreover, each approach or paradigm carries with it assumptions about knowledge, the nature of reality, and human nature, and these assumptions guide research and theory development. For example, the approach that most social scientists endorse assumes that reality is external to individuals, that it persists across time and groups, and that one can predict future human behavior based on observations of past or present behavior. Therefore, they believe that knowledge can be best acquired through observing the behavior of a group of individuals and generalizing from it. Interpretivists assume that reality is socially constructed and, therefore, is internal to individuals and groups and may not be consistent from group to group. They believe that they can best acquire knowledge by understanding the perspectives and experiences of individuals and groups, although such knowledge may not be generalizable.

As we mentioned at the beginning of the chapter, a **theory** is a set of statements that explains a particular phenomenon. Scholars develop theories in an attempt to explain why people communicate as they do. **Methods** describe the specific ways that scholars collect and analyze data, which they then use to prove or disprove their theories. For example, if you wanted to test the uncertainty reduction theory, your method could be to place strangers in conversational dyads and ask them to interact with each other for a short time. After their interaction, you could create a survey asking the interactants to indicate the degree to which their uncertainty was decreased after the conversation, and whether they had any desire to interact with their conversational partner in the future. Once you surveyed a sufficient number of participants, you could determine whether, on average, reducing uncertainty about a stranger leads to positive feelings and a desire for future interaction. Researchers use surveys to collect information on individuals' beliefs, habits, opinions, and

social science approach
contemporary term for the behaviorist approach

interpretive approach
contemporary term for humanistic (rhetorical) study

paradigm
belief system that represents a particular worldview

theory
a set of statements that explains a particular phenomenon

methods
the specific ways that scholars collect and analyze data which they then use to prove or disprove their theories

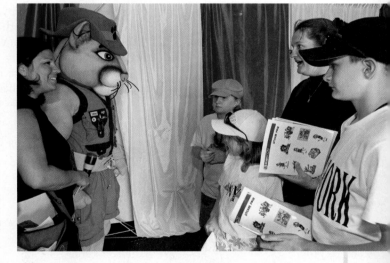

behaviors. Some other types of methods researchers use are interviews, analyses of texts (such as speeches), and observations.

How does a researcher decide which method to use? The method depends on her worldview or approach to the study of human communication. For example, if she believes the best explanations (or theories) of communication behavior come from examining the behavior of a large group of people, a survey would be the most likely method, allowing her to collect information or data from a lot of people. Scholars often disagree about the virtues or faults of a particular paradigm or approach to the study of communication. Thus, some claim that survey studies have limited usefulness, as they can only tell us how *most* people behave, and not much about an individual person. Like religious belief systems, these paradigms also include ethical beliefs about the right (and wrong) ways to study communication.

As a way of understanding the differences among the four contemporary approaches, let us examine how each might view the following communication dilemma. Soon after the terrorist attacks on September 11, 2001, the U.S. government established the Homeland Security Department (HSD). One responsibility of the HSD is to evaluate the level of terrorist threat and then communicate this threat level to the nation. The HSD also provides guidelines for interpreting and responding to these threats.

Many communication questions can be posed about this practice. For example, what principles should guide the government in communicating with us? Should the public be informed about all threats, even when few details are available? Should we only be told about specific threats?

Other questions focus on how the HSD should communicate its messages. For example, the HSD has set up Web sites in English and Spanish that encourage parents and children to discuss the threat level and to help them devise a family emergency plan. There are step-by-step plans and checklists for parents and informational videos for children, to work through and set up their own four-step emergency preparedness plan. A communication scholar might ask what the nature of the communication in these Web sites should be. For example, should the HSD use comforting messages? Or should it use graphic, fear-based messages to inspire people to respond to a particular threat level? [For more information, go to the Homeland Security Department Web site at **www.ready.gov/** in English or **www.listo.gov/** in Spanish.]

Finally, other communication-related questions concern citizen response to the HSD alerts. For example, what is the best way for parents to talk with their children about terrorist threats? Each communication research paradigm has its own way of answering these questions. To explore the characteristics of each paradigm and their contributions and limitations, we next consider how each approach might examine parental communication with children about terrorism.

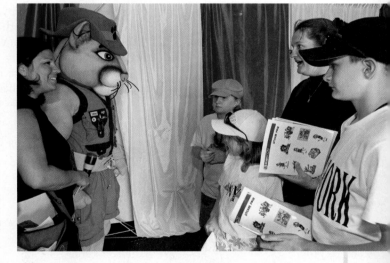

Rex, the HSD mountain lion mascot helps school kids prepare for emergencies.

Before we begin we would like to offer an important caveat. We believe that by clearly differentiating each of these four paradigms from the others, we make it easier for you to understand them. The reality is a bit more complex and fluid. Many communication scholars' work does not fit neatly and precisely into just one of the research paradigms; nor does it follow a single set of research methods. And although these paradigms may have been more clearly differentiated from one another in the early stages of their development, they have evolved. Scholars have borrowed from one another, their understanding of the research process has changed, and the differences among the paradigms have become less clearly defined. Some of the paradigms have more internal variations today than when they were originated. To highlight

naturalistic
relating to everyday, real-life situations, such as a classroom, café, or shopping mall

quantitative methods
methods that convert data to numerical indicators, and then analyze these numbers using statistics to establish relationships among the concepts

the underlying principles of these four paradigms in our discussion, we will focus on their starting points.

The Social Science Approach

Like earlier behavioral studies, the social science approach in communication originally focused on the individual or, more rarely, the dyad. Because this approach grew out of the fields of psychology and sociology, communication scholars typically relied on some of the same research methods used by these social scientists. As shown in the *Visual Summary 2.1: Four Contemporary Approaches to the Study of Communication* on pages 42 and 43, early social science researchers believed the aim of communication research was to describe, predict, and explain human behavior with the ultimate goal of discovering universal laws that apply across situations and contexts. Consequently, these scholars were often described as "behaviorists." They believed predictions were possible because they saw reality as both observable and describable. Let's see how this works.

Methods

Early social science researchers generally focused on causality. Thus they sought to determine what factors influenced communication behavior. They first made predictions (hypotheses) that came from theories, and then they tested these predictions by gathering data through various methods (a practice still followed by scholars working in this tradition). Common methods included observing subjects in either a laboratory or a **naturalistic** setting (that is, in everyday, real-life situations, such as a classroom, café, or shopping mall), using surveys, and conducting focused interviews with participants. When conducting research, social scientists then (and now) abide by a code of ethics dictating that no harm should be done to research participants, that participation in research is voluntary, that participants must be informed about the research they are participating in, and that their privacy and confidentiality be maintained (Martin & Butler, 2001).

Once social science researchers collected their data, they used it to confirm or disconfirm their hypotheses about human communication behavior, most frequently through **quantitative methods**. That is, they converted their data to numerical indicators, and then analyzed these numbers using statistics to establish relationships among the concepts. This approach is still used by many researchers whose work is influenced by the social science paradigm. For example, Jess Alberts (1988) studied the effect of couples' relationship satisfaction on their complaint behavior. In her study, she analyzed the types of complaints that happy and unhappy couples made to each other, such as complaints about behavior and complaints about personal characteristics. She then counted how many of each complaint type happy couples used and how many unhappy couples used. Finally, she applied statistical analyses to the resulting numbers to determine which couple type was more likely to use which complaint type.

Social scientists might manipulate communication behavior to test jealous reactions.

Now, returning to our terrorism-related example, let's suppose that a communication scholar using the social science approach and quantitative methods wanted to discover the best strategies for parents to use in discussing the terrorist threat with their children. The researcher could conduct a controlled experiment, measuring children's anxiety levels before and after discussions in which different types of communication strategies were used. Then, based on their findings, they might predict that one strategy would best reduce children's anxiety.

While we are not aware of any such studies involving children, communication scholars have used the social science approach to conduct similar studies with adults. For example, one group of researchers predicted that angry messages would be more effective than fear-inducing messages in persuading people to support antiterrorist legislation (Nabi, 2002). To test this hypothesis, the researchers used quantitative methods. They gathered two groups of students in a laboratory and gave one group newspaper articles that expressed fear about terrorism; the other group received articles on terrorism that expressed an angry tone. Researchers then asked all students to complete a survey, describing their reactions to the articles and rating their support for antiterrorism legislation using a seven-point scale. After conducting statistical analysis on the data, the researchers confirmed their predictions that angry messages were more persuasive.

A more recent social science study surveyed people around the country and measured their responses to hypothetical news stories about terrorist attacks and other emergencies. The researchers found that responses of anger were related to people's willingness to comply with regulations concerning terror prevention; however, fear reactions were more related to actual planning for emergencies (Cody, Murphy, & Glik, 2007). Staff at the HSD might find it useful to consider these conclusions when developing persuasive messages: Angry messages may be most effective in persuading people to pass legislation and to comply with those regulations, but fearful messages may be more effective in persuading people to plan for future emergencies. In the following chapters, you will see other examples of communication studies from a social science perspective that predict and describe communication behavior.

Although early scholars who used this approach to understanding communication often used quantitative methods (and many still do), contemporary scholars in this tradition also use other methods—including qualitative methods such as conversation analysis.

Strengths and Limitations

You can see that social science research can be useful in identifying and explaining communication patterns and predicting their effects. However, as do all four approaches, this one has its limits. As you probably have realized, human communication is not always predictable, and in particular, predictions based on laboratory research may not hold true outside the lab. Although surveys can provide insight into individuals, beliefs, and attitudes, survey questions cannot fully assess individuals' thoughts and feelings, which are based on a multiplicity of factors and influences, as we described in Chapter 1. In addition, answers to survey questions may be inadequate, particularly for complex issues, because people often provide only short, superficial responses to predetermined questions. One might also argue that when surveys provide a set of answers from which respondents can choose, they are even less likely to tap into their true behaviors, beliefs, and emotions. Critics argue that researchers cannot obtain a full picture if they only measure behavior or if they assess thoughts and feelings only through survey questions.

The social science approach typically has focused on individual forces and their impact on communication without regard for societal forces. For example, social science research can provide useful information about effective strategies for communicating terrorist threat levels, but it tends to ignore the bigger picture, such as whether politicians might communicate terrorist threat levels in order to distract the public from political scandals.

The Interpretive Approach

Scholars who developed the interpretive approach also focused on the individual, but these researchers had goals and assumptions that differed from those who developed the social science paradigm. *Visual Summary 2.1* shows that the goal of

Four Contemporary Approaches to the Study of Communication

	SOCIAL SCIENCE (Behaviorism)	INTERPRETIVE (Humanism)
■ **Goal of Research**	To describe, predict, and explain behavior	To describe, explain, and understand behavior in context
■ **View of Reality**	External and describable	Subjective
■ **View of Human Behavior**	Complex but predictable	Creative and voluntary
■ **Primary Methods**	Quantitative analysis of surveys, **observation**, experiments, focused interviews	Qualitative analysis of rhetorical texts and ethnographic data (such as **participant observation**, observation, interviews)
■ **Contributions**	Identifies communication patterns and associations among variables	Emphasizes in-depth study of communication
■ **Limitations**	Does not focus on the influence of power or societal forces	Limited number of participants; does not focus on power or societal forces

CRITICAL	POSTMODERN
To describe, explain, and understand society in order to affect change	To understand the contemporary human condition
Subjective and material	Subjective
Resistive	Fluid
Textual analysis, **media analysis**	**Textual analysis**, participant observation

Emphasizes power relations in communication interactions; recognizes societal impacts on communication	Challenges assumptions about gender, race, ethnicity, and other social categories
Does not focus on face-to-face communication	Does not focus on face-to-face communication; may be viewed as pessimistic and impractical

qualitative methods
methods in which researchers study naturally occurring communication rather than assembling data and converting it to numbers

ethnographic
relating to studies in which researchers actively engage with participants

rhetorical analysis
used by researchers to examine texts or public speeches as they occur in society with the aim of interpreting textual meaning

interpretive researchers is to understand and describe individual human communication behavior in specific situations, from the perspective of the communicator. Moreover, the emphasis is on the creativity, not the predictability, of human behavior. Interpretive researchers assume that humans construct their own reality and that researchers must tap into these constructions for a full understanding of human communication.

Methods

Interpretive researchers, then and now, generally use **qualitative methods** for rhetorical analysis. Rather than reducing data to numbers as quantitative researchers do, interpretivists use qualitative data and/or tests to understand how communicators and receivers understand a communication event. And rather than manipulating the research situation as one might do in a lab, they tend to study naturally occurring communication. **Ethnographic**, or field study, methods are common in interpretive research. In an ethnographic study, researchers actively engage with participants; methods include participant observations, observations, and ethnographic interviewing. During participant observations the researcher joins the group or community under study. For example, a researcher using this method might join a construction crew in order to understand how construction workers communicate about their roles in the organization. In contrast, during purely observational research, the researcher maintains distance, simply observing participants (for example, construction workers) without actually becoming one. Using the construction-worker illustration, the researcher employing ethnographic interviewing would ask participants open-ended questions about their experiences as construction workers and would then record their responses.

Communication scholar Donal Carbaugh has conducted a number of interpretive studies in which he describes the communication patterns of Finnish people, Blackfeet Indians, and U.S. residents in varying contexts. For example, using in-depth analyses of ethnographic observations and interviews, he describes the role of silence and listening in Blackfeet communication, the tendency of Finns to be reserved in communication, and the emphasis many in the United States place on speaking for themselves. More important is that he shows how these communication patterns are inextricably tied to cultural identities in each community (Carbaugh, 1990; 1999; Carbaugh & Berry, 2001). Ethical issues for interpretive researchers, particularly those doing ethnographic research, go beyond the concern for not harming research participants. Ethnographic researchers strive for equality and reciprocity in their relationships with participants. Other standards include being friendly but at the same time maintaining sufficient scholarly distance, disengaging appropriately from participants after the research is completed, and presenting findings in a way that accurately reflects the views of the participants (González, 2000; Tanno, 1997).

A second interpretive method is **rhetorical analysis**, in which researchers examine and analyze texts or public speeches as they occur in society. The earliest rhetorical scholars were interested in understanding how a speech affected audiences. These researchers sought to determine the best ways for speakers to construct and deliver speeches so they could affect their audiences in particular ways. Modern researchers also focus on interpreting what texts mean in the settings in which they occur. What do we mean by "the settings in which they occur"? We mean the physical space (classroom or place of worship) as well as broader environments (educational versus social; historical versus contemporary) that impact the speech. For example, an analysis of a political speech immediately after 9/11 might examine the setting in which the speech occurred, such as on television from the Oval Office or live at the site of the attacks.

Ethnographers study the communication practice of people in the field.

Researchers who do rhetorical analysis typically do not interact with the speakers or authors of the texts they study, and therefore face different ethical concerns than do ethnographic researchers. Rhetoricians must be especially attentive to accuracy in their depictions of the text and the historical period in which the text occurred.

How might interpretive researchers investigate the communication dilemma of a terrorist threat? In a recent study, researchers interviewed personnel at American Airlines about their communication practices after AA Flight 11 was hijacked and flown into the World Trade Center (Downing, 2004). The researchers also reviewed various internal American Airlines communication messages (phone, email, fax, etc.) that were sent during this time of crisis. As you might imagine, corporate communication demands are intense during and after such a crisis. Employees must manage their own stress while communicating important information to other employees and to the public. As a result of this study, researchers discovered the value and importance of using mediated communication technologies such as email, instant messages, and Web sites. Based on their findings at American Airlines, researchers were able to provide practical suggestions for other corporations. These methods of communication allowed the CEO to quickly relay important messages through management to all employees while maintaining crucial "face time" with the public. In addition, the researchers stressed the importance of the company's "focus on shared emotions" and its messages of hope and renewal—rather than emphasizing blame.

Prior to a study such as this, interpretive researchers would not necessarily assume that their study would help them *predict* the most effective way for airline executives to talk with their employees and the public during a terrorist attack. Rather, they would begin with a general research question, such as, *What did business leaders learn about communication during the recent attack?* and then try to identify patterns of draw conclusions that respond to that question.

Another way to approach the topic of terrorist threats would be through a rhetorical analysis of public speeches on the topic. For example, communication scholars Graham, Kennan, and Dowd (2004) analyzed George W. Bush's (2001) declaration of a war on terror. They showed the similarities in structure, function, and historical significance between this speech and other call-to-arms speeches in Western civilization. Comparing President Bush's speech with those of Pope Urban II (1095), Queen Elizabeth I (1588), and Adolf Hitler (1938), they found that all contained (1) an appeal to a legitimate power source that is external to the speaker and is inherently good; (2) an appeal to the historical importance of the culture under attack; (3) the construction of a thoroughly evil "Other"; and (4) an appeal for unity in the face of attack. Furthermore, the study showed how such speeches typically appear in contexts where the speakers were responding to crises that could undermine their leadership positions.

Joshua Gunn analyzed the significance of this image and how it was used in political discourse after September 11, 2001.

Another rhetorical scholar, Joshua Gunn (2004), analyzed the response to a popular image shot by freelance photographer Mark Phillips after the 9/11 attack. Phillips's photo is of a large plume of smoke coming from one of the Twin Towers, and the smoke appears to contain the face of a demon. The image quickly became available on the Internet, and many people saw evil and demonic power at work in the attacks. According to Gunn, President Bush's speechwriters used this notion of demonic power to mobilize people to fight evil by supporting the war on terror.

Strengths and Limitations

The strengths of the interpretive approach include the in-depth understanding it provides of communication in specific situations and the insight it offers into the purposes of those messages. The limitation is that it usually involves few research

COMMUNICATION IN SOCIETY
On-Air Interpreter for the Deaf Pushes the Boundaries of Interpretation

As you can see, interpreters do not always translate word for word. Sometimes political and social contexts influence their translation. What are potential consequences for this interpreter's communication?

Nataliya Dmytruk was a translator for the deaf on the Ukrainian state-run channel UTI news broadcasts, who became famous for refusing to translate the official script during a live broadcast on November 24, 2004, that announced Viktor Yanukovych as the winner of the presidential election. Dmytruk instead signed to viewers, "Everything you have heard so far is a lie. Yushchenko is our true president." "I am very ashamed to translate these lies," she signed during the broadcast, ". . . and this is probably my last day in this job, so goodbye." Her solo rebellion sparked a stop-work meeting by 250 of her newsroom colleagues who made a broader stand for truth.

SOURCE: "Information about Nataliya Dmytruk." Retrieved March 12, 2009, from www.informationdelight.info/encyclopedia/entry/nataliya_dmytruk

participants—or none—as is the case in rhetorical analyses of texts. From a social science perspective, its utility is limited because researchers cannot generalize conclusions from such small samples. Thus, it does not help us discover broader laws about human behavior. A second limitation is that the researchers often are outsiders to the communities they study, which means that they may not accurately interpret the communication patterns they see. For example, some studies have concluded that the Amish avoid dealing with conflict, whereas an Amish person might explain that they do deal with conflict, but in a different way—by actively strengthening relationships so that they do not reach the point of open conflict (Kraybill, 1989).

The Critical Approach

Visual Summary 2.1 shows that the goal of the **critical approach** is not only to understand human behavior but ultimately to change society. To do this, critical researchers believe that one must understand the societal forces that shape how people come into contact and communicate. The role that power and hierarchy play in these exchanges must be understood as well. For example, a critical scholar might consider the power differences that exist in everyday interactions between the school custodian and the principal, the refugee and the Red Cross worker, the student and the professor. Critical scholars believe that by examining such interactions and writing about how power functions in them, people gain the awareness they need to resist societal forces of power and oppression. Cultural studies is one research approach that arises from the critical paradigm. This approach attempts to reveal the complexities of culture and the ways that people actively participate in their culture and resist its powerful influences. Cultural studies scholars believe such resistance might be expressed in a number of ways. For an example, see *Communication in Society: On-Air Interpreter for the Deaf Pushes the Boundaries of Interpretation*, which discusses the actions of a translator for the deaf who challenged the news reports about the Ukrainian election results in November 2004.

Like interpretivists, critical scholars believe that reality is subjective, or that we each construct our own reality. However, they also stress that these realities have corresponding material, or physical, consequences—meaning that they have real consequences in people's lives. In the United States, we socially construct a reality in which professional athletes are accorded high salaries and power while schoolteachers are not. These social constructions result in real differences in how each group is treated, what each group can buy, and what sacrifices each group must make.

critical approach
an approach used not only to understand human behavior but ultimately to change society

Critical scholars are especially concerned about the way in which they and other scholars present the worldview of others. A key ethical question for them is whether they have the right to study, analyze, and represent other people's views, particularly when crossing racial/ethnic and class boundaries. They point out that many cultural groups—such as Native Americans and the poor—have been exploited and misrepresented by researchers who stood to gain academic rewards. In the meantime, the communities being researched gained little from their participation (Alcoff, 1991/1992).

Methods

Critical scholars generally use qualitative methods in their research including **textual analysis** and observations in the field. They often analyze cultural "products" such as media (TV, movies, journalistic essays) and even speeches (in which case they may be called *critical rhetoricians*). With these analyses critical scholars seek to understand the influence of societal forces such as the economic, government, and cultural institutions that produce, circulate, and profit from these cultural products. In addition, they may use observation to understand how power and privilege affect people's lives. For example, critical scholars might observe people in an organization to understand how management policies and communication practices impact the professional and personal lives of workers. They could examine the nature of the interaction between parole officers and their clients to understand how the relative power of parole officers is expressed and how it impacts their clients' lives.

In one critical study, Elizabeth Suter (2004) explored why, given U.S. women's historical struggle to gain legal and social acceptance, the overwhelming majority of women continue to follow tradition and adopt their husbands' names. (See Chapter 8 for further discussion of this study.) In a similar vein, critical scholars Bernadette Calafell and Fernando Delgado (2004) examined the messages that are communicated about Latino identity in *Americanos*, a published collection of photographs of Latina/Latino life in the United States. We will return to a discussion of this study in Chapter 12.

A critical scholar analyzing communication and the threat of terrorism would examine the consequences of public communication for our society. For example, critical rhetorician Dana Cloud (2003) examines what she calls the often too easy categorization of Iraq and other nations as "evil," as evidenced in current political discourse. She argues that we need to think about good and evil in a more complex way, and she notes that by failing to do so, the U.S. government justified the current war with Iraq, despite the brutal and catastrophic consequences for Iraqi civilians of the first Gulf War (1990–91).

textual analysis
similar to rhetorical analysis; used to analyze cultural "products," such as media and public speeches

We tend to think of everyone as equal and don't consider how power differences may influence communication.

Dana Cloud of the University of Texas at Austin is a critical rhetorician.
Courtesy of Dana Cloud.

Cloud says that any simple understanding of evil is undermined once we look into the history and circumstances of the so-called evildoers and once we understand the perspective of those who render judgment on them. Although she applies this concept to the war in Iraq, we can also use this idea to understand historical uses of the term *evil*. For example, in the 1800s Native Americans were depicted as savages for their attacks on White settlers. An alternative view is that they were simply attempting to defend their homeland. But by characterizing them as savages, White settlers could justify taking their land, and capturing and killing them.

Cloud, like many critical scholars, is not interested in predicting communication or describing communication behavior. Rather, she hopes to educate and illuminate communicators so that, ultimately, they might conduct international relations in more just and equitable ways—a lofty goal for a scholar.

In analyzing government strategies for communicating threat levels, a critical scholar might consider the larger picture, including U.S. policies abroad. As part of this analysis, researchers would examine the social, political, religious, and historical background of 9/11 and the Iraq conflict. Unlike an interpretivist, who might focus on the communication within families who are planning for a terrorist attack, or a social scientist, who might survey residents of the United States who are communicating about emergency plans, a critical scholar explores the communication that contributes to terrorist attacks and to the perceptions of threat.

It Happened to Me: Kenneth

I liked the critical approach because it made me realize that differences in, say, wealth, education, or attractiveness can impact communication between people. I hadn't thought about that before. I tend to think of everybody as equal and didn't consider how inequality can make communication more difficult.

For one of our students, the critical perspective and its focus on uncovering power relations in communication are particularly appealing as you'll see in *It Happened to Me: Kenneth*.

Strengths and Limitations

The strength of the critical approach is its emphasis on the importance of economic, political, and historical forces in communication. These factors are largely ignored by the social science and interpretive approaches. A second strength inherent in the critical approach is its acknowledgment of the role of power in communication encounters.

However, a limitation of this approach is the lack of attention to face-to-face interaction by critical researchers who focus primarily on public and media communication such as film, TV, music videos, and magazine advertisements. So, although critical textual research may help us understand the historical roots of terrorism, our anxieties about it, and how those fears are perpetuated through stereotypical images and speech, it may not help us communicate better about terrorism or comfort our families and children when the need arises.

Like the interpretive approach, the critical approach does not incorporate or rely on quantitative data or generate generalizable conclusions. For example, Calafell and Delgado (2004) did not measure readers' reactions to *Americanos* and then generalize about all readers. Rather, their essay presents their analysis of the photographic images in the book, and the veracity of their conclusions is based only on the strength of their arguments.

The Postmodern Approach

Postmodernism refers to a broad intellectual and social movement of the late twentieth century, and it contrasts sharply with other approaches discussed thus far. Architects were first to use the term as a reaction to and rejection of modern architecture—which celebrated function (use) over form and style (beauty). In the academic world, the term became associated with the movement to reject notions of

postmodernism
a broad intellectual and social movement of the late twentieth century

modernism, or the belief from the eighteenth-century Enlightenment that through rational thinking, humans can advance and discover universal truth. As you might remember (see page 32), these beliefs had an important influence on the development of communication studies. Unlike postmodernism, the previous three approaches (social science, interpretive, and critical) are thoroughly modernist in that they believe in progress and advancement through research (Mumby, 1997).

Postmodern researchers argue that we live in a world fragmented into many cultures with differing systems of truth. They believe that not only is there no universal truth, but that truth and power are interrelated, in that truth is defined by those who have the most power. Thus, they say what we regard as *knowledge* is always "sponsored" by some institutional authority (church, government), which has its own interests to serve. For example, when governments and religions created messages and laws to support the belief that women were weak, nonintellectual, and easily persuaded (Kerber, 1997), such "truths" benefited the men who propagated these truths and laws. In turn, because of the belief that women were childlike, laws were enacted that prevented them from owning or inheriting property. All their resources were owned by their fathers, brothers, or husbands. So, like the critical approach, the postmodern perspective emphasizes the importance of societal forces and power inequalities.

In both the critical and the **postmodern approach,** reality is subjective and power is an important issue. However, unlike the critical approach, which views power as stable and relatively easy to analyze, the postmodern approach views power as slippery and constantly shifting. The postmodern approach assumes that power is built through rhetoric, and, therefore, it asks questions about who controls the rules of rhetoric, how this control is established, and for what purposes (Dues & Brown, 2004; Mumby, 1997).

Communication media, like the telephone and Internet, allow us to present different, even false identities to others. Our identities are not fixed.

A postmodern approach views identities as multiple and fragmented, in part because of the advent of new communication technologies. These technologies allow us to communicate from our many different identities simultaneously. For example, we can email colleagues from work, and chat with a sister on the phone, while engaging in instant messaging with a romantic partner. We will explore the issue of identity and communication technologies in more depth in Chapter 13. All of these identities are who we are, but they are fluid, and postmodernists argue that no one of them is the real us. Psychologist Kenneth Gergen (1991) argues that this is the first time in human history that people have no fixed and stable identity. The goal of scholars in this approach is to understand the human condition in this new postmodern cultural condition.

A recent postmodern study argues that U.S. media sends us many messages about Muslims. However, these messages seem to convey that regardless of Muslims' other identities (whether secular, religious, feminist, gay), they are all people to be mistrusted. This view of Muslims is similar to old colonial notions of non-Western foreign peoples—strange, sometimes exotic, but always inferior to peoples of the West. The researcher suggests that one way to combat these negative messages of Muslims is to "shake up" these notions by presenting students with different views of contemporary Muslims (Khan, 2007). For example, teachers could show videos of the lives of ordinary Muslims, as presented in the HBO film "Baghdad High." This 2007 film shows everyday life in Iraq through the eyes of four Iraqi teenagers during their senior year of high school. The documentary was filmed by the boys themselves, and shows their friendships and family relationships during the entire academic year—as ordinary Iraqi adolescents.

modernism
the belief that through rational thinking, humans can advance and discover universal truth

postmodern approach
an approach in which reality is subjective, and power is an important issue

Because postmodern scholars believe there is no single, objective truth, they face an ethical dilemma when they try to depict or represent others. They recognize that any depiction will be incomplete and provide only one view. Like critical scholars, they are concerned with how others are depicted in communication interactions and the consequences those depictions might have on material, or real, aspects of their lives. Thus, they face a paradox: Any attempt to reveal the postmodern condition of groups ultimately serves some groups' interests and affects other groups' lives.

Methods

Ned Vankevich (2003) takes a postmodern perspective toward analyzing political rhetoric. He argues that since 9/11, a series of shifts has occurred in conventional political categories. Ideological differences that were once clear—namely the distinctions between political liberals and conservatives—have begun to blur. His examples include liberal Michael Walzer, coeditor of *Dissent*, who penned the inflammatory essay "Can There Be a Decent Left?" in 2002, which criticized American liberals who blamed America for the 9/11 attacks. Several months later, he joined a dialogue with conservatives, who would normally support President Bush wholeheartedly, yet now candidly expressed their tormented support for his Iraq War (Packer, 2002).

So how would a postmodern communication scholar approach our communication dilemma involving the terrorist threat level? First, he might study the variety of ways in which those in the United States are responding to the terror threat and to the changes in the threat warning levels. This scholar might find that some in the United States completely ignore the warnings, others have drawn up plans, and still others have Orange-to-Yellow threat parties, go to bars, rent DVDs, or go shopping whenever the threat level changes. Postmodern scholars might look at the ways people do and do not follow the preparation guidelines outlined by the HSD [www.ready.gov] and how those responses reflect the shifting and fluid identities people are constructing in response to terrorism. Postmoderns scholars might also examine contradictory messages from the federal government telling citizens to go shopping to be patriotic, thus denying the ability terrorists have to change our everyday lives—versus telling us to make emergency plans with our families, which means that terrorists *have* changed our everyday lives.

Strengths and Limitations

If our summary of the postmodern approach seems sketchy, it is because postmodernism represents a relatively recent trend in communication studies (Mumby, 1997). A strength of the postmodern approach is its focus on the complex relationship between power and truth and its examination of how those who control communication control "truth" in society. However, critics point out that some forms of postmodernism present a rather depressing view of human behavior and provide little insight into understanding communication (Mumby, 1997). Regardless of this criticism, we think it is important to understand something of this perspective, because of its influence on communication scholarship.

We hope that this review of the four major approaches gives you an idea of the varied viewpoints you will encounter within the field of communication studies. Rather than emphasizing one of the four in this text, we draw from all of them. As shown in *Visual Summary 2.1*, each approach offers a unique way to view communication, even though those views may sometimes conflict with or contradict each other. This is our position: If you only view a sculpture from one perspective, you can never fully appreciate the work. The same goes for the field of communication studies.

To summarize the four perspectives, the social science approach seeks snapshots of certain communication phenomena and from them attempts to find universal laws that explain human communication. In contrast, the interpretive approach takes a more individualized, specific look at human communication. Using intensive textual analyses and field studies in which researchers spend days, months, and sometimes years interacting with a communication community, these researchers often gain great depth of understanding, though they may study only small groups of individuals. Third, the critical perspective seeks to uncover the element of power that exists in every interaction. It is also concerned with societal forces, such as the social, economic, political, and historical, and how they influence communication. Finally, the postmodern approach focuses on the uncertainty of communication, asserting that power is related to truth and not always easy to pin down, and that communication constructs truth, so that there is no externally verifiable truth.

This review of the history of communication studies and research paradigms illustrates the way that these four approaches have guided communication research. Our understanding of the communication process flows from all four research approaches. For example, in our model of communication (see page 17), the focus on societal factors evolved from the critical and postmodern approaches, while our inclusion of individual forces reflects the influence of the social science and interpretive approaches.

Despite differences in the various communication models and research approaches, individual communicators play a key role in all of them. Therefore, to have a complete understanding of communication, you need to understand how individuals' identities influence and are influenced by communication as well as how individual and societal forces act together to affect identity development. Each communicator is unique because of the ways in which individual and social forces together create individual identities. In turn, these identities impact how individuals communicate and how others communicate with them. We explore the question of identity and communication in Chapter 3.

SUMMARY

The history of communication studies includes two primary influences: the rhetorical tradition and the behaviorist tradition. The roots of the rhetorical tradition began with the ancient Greek and Roman philosophers. However, with the invention of the printing press during the Renaissance, the written word came to dominate. Thus, rhetoric, or the art of oral persuasion, slowly declined in importance. In the eighteenth and nineteenth centuries the field was reinvigorated—particularly with the rise of the middle class in England and America and the need for rhetorical skills in the new democracies.

Francis Bacon's scientific study of human gestures in the 1600s foreshadowed the rise of the second tradition in communication studies, behaviorism. It emerged more fully, however, with the rise of the middle class in Europe and the United States at the end of the nineteenth century, when the study of elocution—proper speaking—became important. Elocutionists may be seen as forerunners of the scientific view of communication.

The field of communication became a discipline in the early twentieth century, and the division between the two research approaches—behaviorism and humanism—continued to grow. Behaviorism built on the work of elocution scholars and followed the model of the social sciences, such as psychology and sociology. Humanism built on the rhetorical tradition. Both emphasize the importance of individual forces. As the field evolved, two more approaches that emphasize societal forces emerged, leading to the four current approaches: social science (behaviorism), interpretive (humanism), critical, and postmodern.

KEY TERMS

uncertainty reduction theory 32
rhetoric 32
Renaissance 32
humanism 33
Enlightenment 33
behaviorism 33
elocution 35
methodology 36

social science approach 38
interpretive approach 38
paradigm 38
theory 38
methods 38
naturalistic 40
quantitative methods 40
qualitative methods 44

ethnographic 44
rhetorical analysis 44
critical approach 46
textual analysis 47
postmodernism 48
modernism 49
postmodern approach 49

TEST YOUR KNOWLEDGE

1. How did the Enlightenment influence the development of communication studies?
2. What is *theory*? *Methods*? What is the relationship between them?
3. What is the difference between the humanist and behaviorist approaches to the study of communication?
4. What are the four contemporary approaches to communication? How do they differ from one another?
5. Why is it important to draw from all four research approaches in studying communication?
6. What does each research approach contribute to our understanding of communication?

APPLY WHAT YOU KNOW

1. Find five examples of the word *communication* in popular magazines and newspapers. How is the word being used in those forms? What are some of the different meanings for communication?

2. University communication departments vary as to the communication contexts that they emphasize in their course offerings. Go to the home pages of the communication programs at Arizona State University, Indiana University, Michigan State University, the University of Washington, and your own college or university (if it isn't one of these). Determine the contexts emphasized by each program. What contexts, if any, are consistent across most programs, and which are least frequently represented? What does this tell you about the study of communication in the United States?

3. Locate a journal article and an article in a popular magazine that report on the same communication issue from a social science perspective. How was the issue presented in each? What are the strengths and weaknesses of each article? What are the strengths and weaknesses of a social science approach to this topic? (Hint: Use the information presented in *Visual Summary 2.1: Four Contemporary Approaches to the Study of Communication.*)

EXPLORE

1. www.speechtips.com/ This is a site with free advice on how to prepare and deliver a public speech. What evidence can you see here of the influence of the ancient sophists and rhetoricians?

2. www.luminarium.org/sevenlit/bacon/ This is a site with a compilation of Francis Bacon's works. Click on "Quotes." How many of his famous quotes deal with communication? What aspects of communication was Bacon interested in?

3. www.africa.upenn.edu/Articles_Gen/afrocent_roth.html This site presents an extended discussion of Afrocentricity. It both describes and refutes Bernal's point of view.

4. www.worldagesarchive.com/Individual%20Web%20Pages/BlackAthena.html This site contains various links to arguments for and against Martin Bernal's proposition that the roots of classical civilization and rhetoric are essentially African (Egyptian) and not Greek.

3

Communication and Identities

chapter outline

"We cannot separate our identities—as individuals or as members of society—from our communication experiences."

After goofing off through most of high school, Justin found a major he really liked once he was in college. He became a successful student who tutored other students within his major. However, every time he returns home, his family and friends treat him like the slacker he was in high school. He has begun to wonder if they will ever see the "new" him or if perhaps he really hasn't changed as much as he thinks he has.

When you, like Justin, think about identity, you may be pondering who you "really" are and how you got to be that way. Are you unique or are you inevitably like your parents and siblings? Are you the kind, thoughtful person your parents think you are or are you the wild partier your friends have seen? Can you choose to be whomever you want or do your background and social environment determine who you are? In this chapter we address these identity questions as well as the important role communication plays in them.

As we discussed in Chapter 1, communication is a deeply cultural process. In this chapter we explore how individual characteristics, such as gender and age and the societal meanings associated with them, interact to create cultural identities—and the important role communication plays in that development. Within cultures, communication patterns, habits, values, and practices develop around specific individual characteristics such as race, gender, sexuality, age, social class, and religion. For example, in the United States, people commonly understand that it is not acceptable to curse in front of small children, a communication taboo that also used to apply to women. Although we all possess many cultural identities, some impact our communication experiences more than others. In this chapter we explain which identities are most influential and why. We also examine how societal forces influence identity and discuss ethical issues associated with communication and identities. We conclude by looking at some skills for communicating about identities.

 Once you have read this chapter, you will be able to:

- Identify five reasons identity is important to communication.
- Define *identity*.
- Clarify how reflected appraisals, social comparisons, self-fulfilling prophecies, and self-concept contribute to identity development.
- Describe how identity is performed through communication.
- Articulate how individual identities are influenced by social forces.
- Identify examples of racial, ethnic, national, gender, sexual, age, social class, and religious identities.
- Discuss three ethical considerations for communicating in a sensitive manner to and about others' identities.
- Explain two ways to communicate more effectively about identities.

Our relationships with others help us understand who we are and how others perceive us.

THE IMPORTANCE OF IDENTITY

Identity features in the communication process in several ways. First, because individuals bring their self-images or identities to each communicative encounter, every communication interaction is affected by their identities. For example, when elderly people talk to teenagers, both groups may have to accommodate for differences in their experiences and language use. Second, communication interactions create and shape identities (Hecht, 1993). Returning to our example, if older adults treat young people with respect and admiration during their conversations, these young people may view themselves as more mature and more valuable than they did previously.

Third, identity plays an important role in intercultural communication, which has become increasingly common in our global, technology-based world. For instance, workers in international companies are likely to have contact with people from other cultures. The more familiar they are with the values related to identity in these cultures, the better prepared they will be. In Japan, age is seen as a virtue and older people are treated with great respect (Condon, 1984). In fact, the Japanese have a "respect for the aged" holiday (www.kidlink.org/KIDPROJ/MCC/mcc0294. html). In the United States, on the other hand, people tend to be valued more for their accomplishments than for their age, and youth often is valued over age. Thus if a young person from the United States fails to bestow respect on an older Japanese colleague, the older person may feel insulted and be unwilling to cooperate fully.

Fourth, understanding identity is useful because so much of U.S. life is organized around and geared toward specific identities (Allen, 2004). In the United States we have television stations such as *Black Entertainment Television* and *Telemundo*, and magazines like *Ebony* and *More*, which are targeted to groups based on their race, age, and/or sex. We also have entertainment venues such as Disneyland and Club Med, which are developed specifically for families, romantic couples, and singles. In this identity-based climate, individuals often communicate primarily with others who share their identities. Consequently, learning how to communicate effectively with individuals whose identities vary from yours may require considerable thought and effort.

Finally, identity is a key site where individual and societal forces come together to shape communication experiences. Although we each possess identity characteristics such as social class or nationality, society defines the meanings of those characteristics. Also, we cannot separate our identities—as individuals or as members of society—from our communication experiences. Identity is vital to how meaning is created in communication (Hecht, 1993). We explain this interaction more fully throughout this chapter.

WHAT IS IDENTITY?

Identity is tied closely to identification. *Identity* refers to the social categories you identify yourself with as well as the categories that others identify with you. Society creates social categories such as *middle aged* or *college student*, but they only become part of one's identity when one identifies with them. Thus, although many young people identify with the category *college student* in their late teens and early twenties, a growing number of people in their thirties, forties, and even older are returning to school and now have begun to identify themselves as students. Many social categories exist, and individuals identify with a variety of them during their lifetimes. These various identities may be either *primary* or *secondary identities* (Loden & Rosener, 1991; Ting-Toomey, 1999). Primary identities have the most consistent and enduring impact on our lives, while secondary identities, such as occupation and marital status, are more fluid and more dependent on situation. In this chapter we discuss primary identities, including race, gender, sexuality, age, religion, and nationality.

To help you understand how we define the term **identity**, let's examine its essential characteristics. The first characteristic is that identities exist at the individual and the societal level. Jake Harwood (2006) explains this concept: "At the individual (personal identity) level, we are concerned with our difference from other individuals, and the things that make us unique as people. At the collective (social identity) level, we are concerned with our group's differences from other groups, and the things that make our group unique" (pp. 84–85). For example, your individual identities may include athlete, honor student, and poet, while your social identities might include your ethnicity, nationality, or socioeconomic class.

We should note that identities are not necessarily only individual or social; they can be both, depending on the situation. For example, many readers of this text are U.S. Americans, and their national identity is part of their social identity. Because they are surrounded by others from the U.S., they may not be conscious of this as being part of their individual identity. On the other hand, when they travel abroad, their national identity becomes part of their individual identity, because often this significant characteristic will differentiate them from others.

A second important aspect of identity is that it is both fixed and dynamic. How is this contradiction possible? If you think about it, you will realize that certain aspects of our identities, although stable to some extent, actually do change over time. For instance, a person may be born male, but as he grows from an infant to a boy to a teenager to a young man to a middle-aged man and then to an old man, the meanings of his male identity change. He is still a male and still identifies as a male, but what it means to be male alters as he ages and social expectations change regarding what a man should be (Kimmel, 2005).

A third important characteristic of identity is that individual and social identities are created through interaction with others. The relationships, experiences, and communication interactions you share with others shape how you see yourself. For example, people who travel abroad and then return home may experience stress, but they also experience growth and change—and communication with those they meet as they travel plays a key role in both (Martin & Harrell, 1996). Social identities also can change as people interact with others. In the 1970s, women attended "consciousness raising" groups to alter how they perceived and performed their identities as females. Women in these groups were encouraged to think of themselves not primarily as wives and mothers but as the professional and social equivalents of men. As occurred in this case, women's heightened awareness and dissatisfaction with their social identity prompted them to become involved in a larger social movement. This type of mobilization of women also occurred earlier in history, when they organized to gain the right to vote. It also happened for others who protested against racial discrimination. In these instances a common social identity brought people together into communities, and these communities in turn acted to improve the position of the particular social identity in society.

A fourth consideration is that identities can be understood only in relation to historical, social, and cultural environments. The meaning of any identity is tied to how it has been viewed historically and how people with that identity are situated in a given culture and society (Hecht, Jackson, & Ribeau, 2003; Johnson, 2001). For instance, throughout history, we have had varied notions of what it means to be female (Roth, 2005).

Although Cleopatra was the last Egyptian Pharaoh and Joan of Arc led the French army into battle in the fifteenth century, even in their own times they were significant exceptions to the rule. For much of history, women have been perceived as intellectually inferior, physically delicate, and/or morally weak when compared to men. Because of these beliefs, in many cultures women were denied voting and property rights and even custody of their children in the event of divorce. For example until 1881, upon marriage, English women's legal identities were subsumed by their husbands such that all of their property and wealth transferred to their spouses as well as their right to

identity
who a person is; composed of individual and social categories a person identifies with, as well as the categories that others identify with that person

Your individual identity may include university student or band member while your social identity likely includes your ethnicity, nationality or socioeconomic class.

enter into any contracts. (A. L. Erickson, 1993). In the United States, women didn't win the right to vote until 1920, and it wasn't until 1974 that they were constitutionally guaranteed the right to equal pay for equal work (Imbornoni, 2008).

Contemporary U.S. American women have all of the legal rights of men, yet historical conceptions of women still affect how they are positioned in society today. For example, on average women earn 77 percent of men's pay (see *Did You Know? Women's Pay: Why the Gap Remains a Chasm*), only 16 of 100 U.S. senators and just 74 of 435 representatives are women (Berstein, 2004) and people in many religions remained opposed to women serving as ministers and priests. The situation for women in other cultures can be even more challenging. Although they make up 70 percent of those enrolled in universities, women compose just 5 percent of the workforce in Saudi Arabia; their testimony in court is treated as presumption rather than fact; and they live mostly segregated lives (Azuri, 2006). Thus, a hierarchy exists across cultures in which one identity (male) is preferentially treated over another (female). You can probably think of other examples in which preferential treatment was given—or denied—based on race, sexuality, religion, social class, or age (Allen, 2004).

Did You Know?
Women's Pay: Why the Gap Remains a Chasm

What factors do you believe contribute to the 10 percent of women's pay disparity based on discrimination? Why do you think women continue to be the family members who drop out of the workforce to care for children and the elderly—even though one third of women make more money than their male romantic partners? How does this pattern, and its affect on pay, impact men, women, and children in the long run?

During the heyday of the women's movement more than 30 years ago, "59 cents on the dollar" was an oft-heard rallying cry, referring to how little women earned compared with men. Those concerns seem outdated today, when it's easy to find female doctors, lawyers, pop stars, even Presidential advisers. The progress toward equality in the workplace also shows up in government data on wages, which pegs women's average pay at 77% of men's compensation today.

But there's new evidence that women's advances may not be quite so robust after all. When you look at how much the typical woman actually earns over much of her career, the true figure is more like 44% of what the average man makes. That's the conclusion of a new study by Stephen J. Rose, an economist at Macro International Inc., a consulting firm, and Heidi I. Hartmann, President of the Institute for Women's Policy Research in Washington.

Why the big discrepancy? The Bureau of Labor Statistics (BLS) numbers, published every year, are accurate as far as they go. But they only measure the earnings of those who work full-time for an entire year. Only one-quarter of women, though, achieve this level of participation consistently throughout their working lives. So Rose and Hartmann looked at the pay of all men and women over a 15-year period, including those who worked part-time and dipped in and out of the labor force to care for children or elderly parents. This long-term perspective still shows an arc of progress: The 44%, based on average earnings between 1983 and 1998, jumped from 29% in the prior 15 years. But the more comprehensive view gives a less rosy picture of women's position in the work world.

Outright discrimination against women probably accounts for only about 10 percentage points of the pay gap, according to numerous studies. The bulk of the problem, then, lies with the conflicting needs and norms of society and employers. A majority of men and women still work in largely sex-segregated occupations, Rose and Hartmann's study shows, leaving many women stuck in lower-paying jobs such as cashiers and maids.

FROM: "Women's Pay: Why the Gap Remains a Chasm," by Aaron Bernstein. Reprinted from June 14, 2004 issue of *Business Week*, by special permission, copyright © 2004 by The McGraw-Hill Companies, Inc.

In sum, identity is key to understanding communication, and communication is key to understanding identity. As Abrams, O'Connor, and Giles have stated, "identity and communication are mutually reinforcing" (2002, p. 237).

THE INDIVIDUAL AND IDENTITY

Although it can be tempting to boil a person's identity down to one word—say, *nerd*, *jock*, or *sorority girl*—in reality, everyone is more complex than that. If you had to pick only one word to describe yourself and you had to use it in every situation—personal and professional—what word would you choose? For most people this task is impossible, for we all see ourselves as multidimensional, complex, and unique. People in the United States, especially, are invested in the notion that they are unique. Twins often go to great lengths to assure people that they are *not* the same. Perhaps the most famous example of this is the Olsen twins, Mary-Kate and Ashley (see *Did You Know? Famous Twins Just Want to be Individuals*). Mary-Kate dyed her hair dark so she would look less like her sister, and when the sisters received a star on Hollywood's Walk of Fame, they requested that they be given separate stars (a request that was denied). Like almost everyone, they recognize and value their uniqueness—and they would like others to do so as well.

How is it possible that people who are as much alike as twins can still have distinct identities? It is possible because of the ways in which identities are created and how these identities are "performed" in daily life—the topics we take up in the next section.

Identity Development Through Communication

In communication, our understanding of identity development arises out of a theory called symbolic interactionism (Blumer, 1969; Mead, 1934). According to this theory, individuals' meanings for the objects, actions, and people around them arise out of social, or symbolic, interaction with others. What you define as beautiful, ethical, and even edible is based on what you have heard and experienced during your interactions with others. You likely learned through observing and communicating with

Did You Know?
Famous Twins Just Want to be Individuals

Mary-Kate: "As you get older, you create your own identity;"

Ashley: "It's not like we're forcing our own identities. It's who we are; our own styles are coming through, and other people are just realizing we're two separate people" (Arnold, 2004).

Mary-Kate and Ashley: "If you can respect us as businesswomen, and powerful young ladies, respect us also as individuals" (Aames, 2004).

Most twins strive to differentiate themselves from one another, whether that means dressing differently or pursuing disparate hobbies and careers. However for famous twins, developing separate identities is a greater challenge than for most. Celebrity twins Mary-Kate and Ashley Olsen, James and Oliver Phelps (who play the Weasley twins in the *Harry Potter* movies) and Dylan and Cole Sprouse (of Disney's *The Suite Life of Zack and Cody*) all became famous either playing twins or playing the same character on television and in movies. Because their professional identities are so closely connected, people often forget that they have the same needs as "singletons" to be seen as unique and individual. Consequently, they have to remind us—and remind us again—that they are.

SOURCES: Arnold, T. K. (2004, April 28). Just call them the Olsen "individuals." *USA Today*. Crane, R. (2004, April 30). Interview: Mary-Kate and Ashley from "New York Minute." *Cinema Confidential*, www.cinecon.com/news.php?id=0404301.

Twins often go to great lengths to assure people they are *not* the same.

others that eating lobster is a luxury but that eating bugs is disgusting. We develop and reveal identities through communication interactions in much the same way. In this section we describe three communication processes involved in identity development—*reflected appraisals*, *social comparison*, and *self-fulfilling prophecies*—and explore how they shape one's sense of self, or self-concept.

Reflected Appraisals

A primary influence on identity development is a communication process called **reflected appraisals** (Sullivan, 1953). The term describes the idea that people's self-images arise primarily from the ways that others view them and from the many messages they have received from others about who they are. This concept is also often referred to as the **looking-glass self** (Cooley, 1902; Edwards, 1990), a term that highlights the idea that your self-image results from the images others reflect back to you.

The process of identity development begins at birth. Although newborns do not at first have a sense of self (Manczak, 1999; Rosenblith, 1992), as they interact with others, their identities develop. How others act toward and respond to them influences how infants build their identities. For example, as infants assert their personalities or temperaments, others respond to those characteristics. Parents of a calm and cheerful baby are strongly drawn to hold and play with the infant, and they describe the child to others as a "wonderful" baby. On the other hand, parents who have a tense and irritable baby may feel frustrated if they cannot calm their child, and might respond more negatively to the infant. They may engage in fewer positive interactions with their baby and describe the child as "difficult." These interactions shape the baby's identity for him or herself and for the parents, as well as for others who have contact with the family (Papalia, Olds, & Feldman, 2002).

Children's self-images are affected by their teachers' reflected appraisals.

A study of shy and reticent male toddlers explored the influence that parents can have on their sons' interactions (Phelps, Belsky, & Crnic, 1998). The researchers found that parents who encouraged their sons to interact with others and to take social risks became less reserved over time; when parents did not encourage their sons in this way, however, the children maintained their shy and reticent nature. As this study shows, parental communication influences how children behave and ultimately how they, as well as others, view them.

The reflected appraisal process is repeated with family, friends, teachers, acquaintances, and strangers as the individual grows. If as a child you heard your parents tell their friends that you were gifted, your teachers praised your classroom performance, and acquaintances commented on how verbal you were, you probably came to see yourself those ways. However, if family, friends, and acquaintances commented on how you couldn't "carry a tune in a bucket" and held their ears when you sang, then over time you likely came to view yourself as someone who couldn't sing. Through numerous interactions with other people about your appearance, your abilities, your personality, and your character you developed your identities as a student, friend, male or female, or singer, among others. To read about one student's experiences with reflected appraisals, see *It Happened to Me: Shannon*.

It Happened to Me: Shannon

The section of the course that really has hit home for me is the one that addressed the issue of reflected appraisals. I am a young, hard-working African American woman who does not swear, drink, or do drugs of any type. I come from a very driven and hard-working family with strong morals. But people often treat me as if they assume I come from a dysfunctional family, that I abuse drugs and alcohol, and that I have no goals for my life. The person I see reflected in their eyes is nothing like me! It can be struggle to have to respond to people who do this—and for me to remember that I am *not* who they think I am.

ZITS Partnership. King Features Syndicate

Interaction with two types of "others" influences this process of identity development. George Herbert Mead (1934) described them as *particular others* and the *generalized other*. **Particular others** are the important people in your life whose opinions and behavior influence the various aspects of your identity. Parents, caregivers, siblings, and close friends are obvious particular others who influence your identity. Some particular others may strongly influence just one of your identities or one aspect of an identity. If you perceive that your soccer coach believes you have no talent, then you may see yourself as a poor soccer player even if friends and family tell you otherwise.

Your sense of yourself is also influenced, however, by your understanding of the **generalized other,** or the collection of roles, rules, norms, beliefs, and attitudes endorsed by the community in which you live. You come to understand what is valued and important in your community via your interactions with significant others, strangers, acquaintances, various media such as movies, books, and television, and the social institutions that surround you. For example, if you notice that your family, friends, and even strangers comment on people's appearances, that the media focus on people's attractiveness, that certain characteristics consistently are associated with attractiveness, and that people who look a certain way seem to get lighter sentences in criminal proceedings, get more attention at school, and are hired for the best jobs, then you develop an internalized view of what the generalized other values and rewards with regard to appearance. You then will compare yourself to others within your community to see if you fulfill the norms for attractiveness, which then affects how this aspect of your identity develops.

Gradually, you begin to see yourself in specific ways, which in turn influences your communication behavior, which further shapes others' views of you, and so on. Thus, individual identities are created and re-created by communication interactions throughout one's life. (See *Did You Know? Reflected Appraisals Affect All of Us—Even the Rich and Famous*.)

particular others
the important people in an individual's life whose opinions and behavior influence the various aspects of identity

generalized other
the collection of roles, rules, norms, beliefs, and attitudes endorsed by the community in which a person lives

Did You Know?

Reflected Appraisals Affect All of Us—Even the Rich and Famous

How does the looking-glass self explain successful people's low self-esteem and poor self-concepts? Why do you think their significant success do not change how they feel about themselves? How do the concepts significant other *and* generalized other *apply in the examples discussed in the article below?*

Though it may seem unlikely, many famous, beautiful and/or talented people suffer from negative self-concepts. Kate Winslet has admitted that before going off to a movie shoot, she sometimes thinks, "I'm a fraud, and they're going to fire me . . . I'm fat; I'm ugly . . ." (Eby, 2009). Michael Jackson spoke often in interviews about his poor self-concept, and many people

(continued)

However, reflected appraisals aren't the only type of communication interaction that shapes identity. Each of us also engages in a process called *social comparison*, which influences how we see and value our identities.

Social Comparisons

Not only do we see ourselves as possessing specific characteristics, we also evaluate how desirable those characteristics are. As we discussed, the generalized other becomes the basis for our understanding of which characteristics are valued. For example, Amish children learn through their interactions with family, friends, the church, and their community that aggression is a negative trait that one should minimize or eliminate (Kraybill, 1989). In contrast, in gangs, aggression is valued and encouraged, and community members learn this as well (Sanders, 1994).

Once we understand what characteristics are valued (or disdained) in our communities, we assess whether we individually possess more, or less, of them than do others in our communities. We compare ourselves to others to determine how we measure up, and through this social comparison, we evaluate ourselves. In this way the groups we compare ourselves to—our reference groups—play an important role in shaping how we view ourselves.

We compare ourselves with others in our reference group and decide how we measure up.

We compare ourselves to others in our identity group and decide how we rate. A woman might say, "I look good for my age," comparing herself to others in her reference group, which in this case is other women her age. Similarly, classmates often want to know each other's test scores and grades so that they can decide how to view their own performances. For example, how would you feel if you earned a 78 on an exam and your grade was the highest in the class? What if 78 were the lowest grade in the class? Thus, your evaluation of yourself and your abilities is shaped not only by a specific trait but also by how it compares to the traits of others in your reference group. However, your self-evaluation can vary depending on what you use as a reference group. If you compare your appearance to that of your friends, colleagues, and classmates, you may feel pretty good. However, if you use the idealized images of actors and models in magazines and movies, you may not feel as positively about your attractiveness.

Self-Fulfilling Prophecy

Communication interactions can also influence one's identity through a process known as the **self-fulfilling prophecy**, meaning that when an individual expects something to occur, the expectation increases the likelihood that it will. For example,

self-fulfilling prophecy
when an individual expects something to occur, the expectation increases the likelihood that it will

if you believe you can perform well on an exam, you are likely to study and prepare for the exam, which typically results in your doing well. Others also have expectations for you that can influence your behavior. For example, if your sales manager believes you are a poor salesperson, she may assign you to a territory where you won't have access to big accounts, and she may refuse to send you to sales conferences where your skills could be honed. If you still succeed, she may believe that you just got lucky. However, because you have a poor territory, don't have the opportunity to enhance your sales skills, and receive no rewards for your successes, you probably will not be a very good salesperson.

Thus, the belief in a particular outcome influences people to act and communicate in ways that will make the outcome more likely; in turn, the outcome influences how we perceive ourselves. For example, parents often unwittingly influence how their children perform in math and how their children perceive themselves as mathematicians. If a child hears her mother complain about her own poor math skills and how unlikely it is that her child will do better, the child is unlikely to succeed in math classes. When the child encounters difficulty with math, the messages she heard from her mother may increase the likelihood that she will give up and say, "Well, I'm just not good at math." On the other hand, if a child hears messages that she is good at math, she is more likely to keep trying and work harder when faced with a difficult math problem. This, in turn, will influence her to see herself as a competent mathematician.

Self-fulfilling prophecies can have a powerful effect on an individual's performance, especially when they are grounded in stereotypes of one's identity. For example, stereotypes exist that Asian students excel at math, that African America students are less verbally competent than White students, and that females are worse at math and spatial reasoning than are males. Studies have shown that even subtly or implicitly reminding individuals of these stereotypical expectations can impact their performance, a concept called **stereotype threat**.

In one study, African Americans who were simply reminded of race performed significantly worse on a verbal exam than when the issue of race was not mentioned (Steele & Aronson, 1995); and in another study, Asian American students performed better on a math test when reminded of their race (Shih, Pittinsky & Ambady, 1999). In a similar study, females who were cued to think about gender performed worse on math and spatial ability tests than when the issue of gender was not raised (McGlone & Aronson, 2006). Yet another study found that White male engineering students solved significantly fewer problems when told that they were part of a study to examine why Asian Americans perform better in math than when told it was simply a timed test (Smith & White, 2002).

These studies reveal that individuals' performances can be enhanced or hampered when they are reminded, even implicitly, of expectations related to important identities. This is true not only of sex and gender but also has been shown to be true of socioeconomic status (Croizet & Claire, 1998) and age. These findings remind us that we need to be careful about creating self-fulfilling prophecies for others and allowing others' expectations to become self-fulfilling prophecies for us.

Through repeated communication interactions such as reflected appraisals, social comparisons, and self-fulfilling prophecies, we come to have a sense of who we are. This sense of who we are is referred to as one's *self-concept*.

Self-Concept

As we have suggested, identity generally continues to evolve; at the same time, individuals also have some fairly stable perceptions about themselves. These stable perceptions are referred to as self-concept. **Self-concept** includes your understanding about your unique characteristics as well as your similarities to, and differences from, others. Your self-concept is based on your reflected appraisals and social comparisons. However, reflected appraisals only go so far. When someone describes you in a

stereotype threat
process in which reminding individuals of stereotypical expectations regarding important identities can impact their performance

self-concept
the understanding of one's unique characteristics as well as the similarities to, and differences from, others

Communication plays an important role in how we develop our self-concept.

way that you reject, they have violated your self-concept. For example, if you think of yourself as open and outgoing, and a friend calls you "private," you are likely to think the friend doesn't know you very well. Thus, your self-concept is an internal image you hold of yourself. It affects the external image you project to others, and in turn, your self-concept influences your communication behavior. If you think of yourself as ethical, you may correct others or assert your views when they behave in ways you believe are unethical.

Self-esteem is part of an individual's self-concept. It describes how you evaluate yourself overall. It arises out of how you perceive and interpret reflected appraisals and social comparisons. Like identity, self-esteem can alter over time. It functions as a lens through which we interpret reflected appraisals and social comparisons, which may make it hard to change. For example, if you have relatively high self-esteem, you may discount negative reflected appraisals and overgeneralize positive ones. So, if a student with high self-esteem fails an exam, he may attribute the failure to external factors (the test was unfair), rather than to himself. On the other hand, a person with low self-esteem may see negative reflected appraisals where none exist and may consistently compare herself to unrealistic reference groups. In addition, this person is more likely to attribute a failure to the self (I'm not smart enough) than to external factors.

Because self-esteem is such a powerful lens through which you see the world, your self-concept may not be entirely consistent with how others see you. Several additional factors can create a mismatch between how you see yourself and how others do. First, your self-image and the feedback you receive may be out of synch because others don't want to hurt your feelings or because you respond negatively when faced with information that contradicts your self-image. Few people tell their friends and loved ones that they are not as attractive, talented, smart, or popular as they themselves think they are. Why? They don't want make others feel bad and/or they don't want to deal with the recipient's feelings of anger or sadness.

Second, if you hold onto an image of yourself that is no longer accurate, you may have a distorted self-image—or one that doesn't match how others see you. For example, if you were chubby in grade school, you may still think of yourself as overweight, even if you are now very slim. Similarly, if you were one of the brightest students in your high school, you may continue to see yourself as among the brightest students at your college, even if your GPA slips.

Finally, people may not recognize or accept their positive qualities because of modesty or because they value self-effacement. If your social or cultural group discourages people from viewing themselves as better than others, you may feel uncomfortable hearing praise. In such cases, the individual may only compare himself to exceptionally attractive or talented people or may refuse to acknowledge his strengths in public settings. In Japanese culture the appearance of modesty (*kenkyo*) is highly valued (Davies & Ikeno, 2002). A similar trait of "yieldedness to others" (*glassenheit*) leads the Amish to downplay their accomplishments (Kraybill, 1989). As you can see, both culture and identity are deeply embedded in our communication.

Yet another aspect of self-concept is self-respect. While self-esteem generally refers to feeling good about one's self, **self-respect** describes a person who treats others—and expects themselves to be treated—with respect (Rawls, 1995). Self-respect demands that individuals protest the violation of their rights and that they do so within the boundaries of dignity and respect for others. However, people with high self-esteem may not necessarily have self-respect (Roland & Foxx, 2003). For example, some people with high self-esteem may not treat others with respect or respond to violations of the self with dignity. Many atrocities, such as those committed by

self-esteem
part of one's self-concept; arises out of how one perceives and interprets reflected appraisals and social comparisons

self-respect
treating others, and expecting to be treated, with respect and dignity

Saddam Hussein against his people, have been waged by those who, because of their sense of superiority, thought they had the right to dominate and harm others.

Throughout this discussion of identity development we have focused on four separate concepts—reflected appraisals, social comparison, self-fulfilling prophecy, and self-concept. However, identity development is a circular process in which these concepts are interrelated. For example, reflected appraisals influence your self-concept, which affects your communication behavior, which in turn shapes how others see you, and ultimately, what they reflect back to you. Then the process starts all over again. To view an illustration of this process, see *Visual Summary 3.1: Identity Development Through Communication*, on p. 66. The issue of identity goes beyond this complex process of development, however. In everyday life we enact or "perform" these identities. Let's see how this process works.

Performance of Individual Identity

The **performance of identity** refers to the process or means by which we show the world who we think we are. For example, many Green Bay Packers fans express their identity by wearing team colors, calling themselves Cheeseheads, and wearing plastic cheese wedges on their heads. People also perform their identities in more subtle ways every day—with the type of clothing or jewelry (including wedding rings) that they choose to wear or the name they use. Thus, if Kitty wants to be taken seriously at a job interview, she may wear a business suit, pull her hair back, and carry a briefcase so that she communicates a professional identity. She also may introduce herself as "Kate" and use language appropriate for a business setting. However, Kitty/Kate may have other identities that she performs in different ways at other times, such as "Mother" or "Jewish" or "Canadian."

Communication style is another way people perform, or enact, their identities. For example, do you speak to your mother in the same way that you speak with your friends? If you bring a friend home, do you feel like a different person as he watches you communicate with your family? If so, you're not alone. Most people adapt their communication to the identity they wish to perform in a given context.

In fact, the branch of communication studies called performance studies focuses on the ways people perform, or communicate, their various roles. In other words, people **enact identities** by performing scripts that are proper for those identities. Sometimes we enact family roles; other times we enact occupational roles. The enactment of identity is closely tied to one's movements into and out of different cultural communities and one's expectations regarding particular roles. For example, if parents do not enact appropriate parent roles, children can become confused. Police officers, physicians, and teachers also enact particular roles in performing their occupations. If one of these professionals—say, a teacher—steps out of the appropriate role and tries to be the best friend of her students, problems can arise.

Thus, we perform various roles and communicate with others based on **role expectations**. If you are pulled over for a traffic ticket, you expect the police officer to perform in a particular way. In turn, you communicate with the officer based on a prescribed script. If you do not enact the expected role or if the police officer does not enact the prescribed role, then confusion—or worse—can occur. Everyone carries many scripts with them into all kinds of interactions. For example, the authors of this book are all pet owners. When we speak to our pets, we sometimes repeat communication patterns that our parents used with us when we were children. Pets are not children, yet we often communicate to them as if they were because the script is familiar to us.

As we noted earlier, identities are **mutable** or subject to change. When people change identities, they also change the way they perform them. For example, as people age, if they perform the "grown-up" role appropriately, they hope others will treat them more like adults. If they don't change the way they behave, then they might be told to "stop acting like a child."

performance of identity the process or means by which we show the world who we think we are

enacting identities performing scripts deemed proper for particular identities

role expectations the expectation that one will perform in a particular way because of the social role occupied

mutable subject to change

Identity Development Through Communication

Reflected Appraisal (The Looking-Glass Self)

Social Comparisons

Self-Fulfilling Prophecies

How I see myself is developed through communication with others . . .

- Interactions with parents and others shape our early identity and sense of self.
- The process is repeated with family, friends, teachers, acquaintances, and strangers.
- **Particular others** are important people in our lives who influence aspects of our identity.
- **Generalized others** are the collection of roles, rules, norms, beliefs, and attitudes endorsed by our community.

and how I compare myself to others . . .

- Through our interactions with others, we learn what characteristics are valued (or disdained) by others.
- Then, we assess whether we have more or fewer of those characteristics to determine how we measure up to others in our **identity group**.

each of which affects my evaluation of myself.

affects how I communicate with them and they with me . . .

- When we expect something to occur, that expectation increases the likelihood that it will.
- A belief in a particular outcome influences people to act and communicate in ways that make the outcome more likely.
- Others can also cause their prophecies about us to come true by communicating with us as though they will come true.

Self-Concept

Self-Concept

- Self-concept is composed of the fairly stable perceptions we have of ourselves.
- It includes our understanding of similarities and differences between ourselves and others.
- It is an internal image we have of ourselves and affects the external image we project to others.

- It influences our communication behavior.
- **Self-esteem** is the part of self-concept that is the internal valuation of what we see in the looking glass.
- **Self-respect** the extent to which one feels entitled to regard and respect from self and others.

Because identities are not fixed, sometimes you see mismatches between the performance of identity and any one identity category. Sometimes the difference between identity performance and identity category can be rather benign. For example, if we say that someone is young at heart, we are saying that we perceive that person's identity performance to resemble that of someone much younger in years. Thus, two people may be the same chronological age, but one may listen to contemporary music, watch current films and television shows, and dress according to the latest fashion trends. The other may listen to oldies radio stations and dress as she did years ago.

Sometimes this disconnect is viewed much more negatively. When people enact a gender identity at odds with the cultural identity category, such as when males perform identity scripts that are typically female, they may be ridiculed, ostracized, or worse. Still, how do particular identity categories, or ways of performing them, acquire meaning? How do you know what a particular category is supposed to "look like" or how it is to be performed? The answer has to do with societal forces, the subject we take up next.

When people enact a gender identity at odds with the cultural identity category, they may be ridiculed, ostracized, or worse.

THE INDIVIDUAL, IDENTITY, AND SOCIETY

The development of individual identities is influenced by societal forces. Therefore, you cannot understand yourself or others without understanding how society constructs or defines gender, sexuality, race, religion, social class, and nationality. For example, as a child, you were probably told (some of) the differences between boys and girls. Some messages came from your parents, such as how boys' and girls' clothing differs or how girls should behave as compared with boys. Other messages came from your schoolmates, who may have told you that "they" (either boys or girls) had "cooties." You may also have picked up messages about gender differences, or about any of the identity categories mentioned, from television or other media. By combining messages from these various sources you began to construct images of what is considered normal for each identity category.

Communications scholars are particularly interested in how identities are communicated, and created, through communication. For example, in his work focusing on communication interactions, Donal Carbaugh (2007) is particularly interested in studying intercultural encounters, and he focuses on how communication interaction reveals insights into cultural identities.

Many parents choose clothes that communicate the gender of their babies.

When people enact identities that are contrary to social expectations, they may be pressured to change their performance. Thus, boys and girls who do not perform their gender identities in ways prescribed by society can be called "sissies" or "tomboys." People who do not perform their racial identities in ways that are expected are sometimes called "oreos," "apples," "coconuts," "bananas," or "race traitors." Although the Church of Jesus Christ of Latter Day Saints has banned the use of alcohol, those Mormons who do drink are sometimes called "Jack Mormons." Similarly, a person who does not perform heterosexuality as expected might be seen as gay or lesbian. Calvin Thomas, a professor at Georgia State University, had antigay epithets hurled at him from a passing car. Thomas, who views his sexual identity as heterosexual, is sometimes seen as gay (2000).

Did You Know?
Performing Identity: Calvin Thomas

In this personal narrative, Calvin Thomas describes being mistaken for a gay man. What difference does it make who you think you are and who others think you are?

I am walking in daylight through my neighborhood in Atlanta: Midtown, an area so well known to have a large gay male population that goon squads from the suburbs and hinterlands would often drive through looking for gays to taunt and bash. So it is no surprise when a car pulls up from behind, and slows down, and the chorus sings: "Hey, *queer!*"

I *turned.* . . . Had it been night, I might have had to turn and run, since I am not sure what I might have done to "prove" that they had "the wrong man," had "mistaken" my "identity." After all, I had turned. I was walking in a "gay" neighborhood. I was wearing "gay" clothes: jeans and a shirt. . . . Fortunately for me, the car sped on, with a great squealing of tires on the hot Georgia asphalt, and I was left only with the knowledge that I had turned— a vague knowledge, a recognition, with which I did not exactly know what to do (Thomas, 2000, 33–34).

In *Did You Know? Performing Identity: Calvin Thomas*, Thomas explains that this harassment occurs because his performance of sexual identity does not conform to the usual communication patterns of heterosexual men.

Those who do not conform to expected social communication or performance patterns may become victims of threats, name-calling, violence, and even murder (Sloop, 2004). These aggressive responses are meant to ensure that everyone behaves in ways that clearly communicate appropriate identity categories. For example, after a lengthy lawsuit, Shannon Faulkner became the first woman to enroll at the Citadel, South Carolina's formerly all-male military college. As a result, she received death threats and had to be accompanied by federal marshals (Bennett-Haigney, 1995). Thus, some groups in society have strong feelings regarding how identities should be performed, and they may act to ensure that identities are performed according to societal expectations.

In this section of the chapter we will look at a range of primary identity categories. (See the *Visual Summary 3.2: Dimensions of Self* to review the most salient identity categories for most people.) Note that each is a product of both individual and societal forces. Thus, whatever you think your individual identity might be, you have to negotiate that identity within the larger society and the meanings society ascribes to it.

Racial Identity

Despite its frequent use, the term *race* is difficult to define. Historically, races were distinguished predominantly by physical aspects of appearance that are generally hereditary. A race was defined as a group with gene frequencies differing from those of other groups. However, many physical anthropologists and other scholars now argue that because there is as much genetic variation among the members of any given race as between racial groups, the concept of race has lost its usefulness (Hirschman, 2003). For more on this contemporary view of race, based on the new tools of DNA analysis, refer to *Alternative View: DNA and Racial Identity*, on p. 70, about the PBS series *African American Lives*.

Despite the difficulty in accurately delineating the various races, race is still a relevant concept in most societies, and individuals still align themselves with specific racial groups, which we discuss next.

Racial identity, the identification with a particular racial group, develops as a result of societal forces—because society defines what a race is and what it is called.

racial identity
identification with a particular racial group

Dimensions of Self

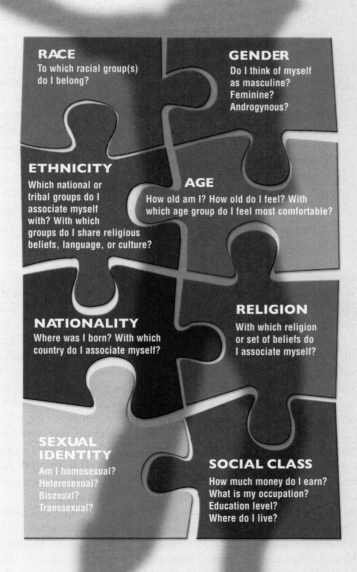

RACE
To which racial group(s) do I belong?

GENDER
Do I think of myself as masculine? Feminine? Androgynous?

ETHNICITY
Which national or tribal groups do I associate myself with? With which groups do I share religious beliefs, language, or culture?

AGE
How old am I? How old do I feel? With which age group do I feel most comfortable?

NATIONALITY
Where was I born? With which country do I associate myself?

RELIGION
With which religion or set of beliefs do I associate myself?

SEXUAL IDENTITY
Am I homosexual? Heterosexual? Bisexual? Transsexual?

SOCIAL CLASS
How much money do I earn? What is my occupation? Education level? Where do I live?

Alternative VIEW
DNA and Racial Identity

"Every year," I once overheard my father say jokingly to a friend, "thousands of Negroes disappear." I remember my 8-year-old imagination going into overdrive, picturing people zapped from their homes in the middle of the night. It was only as I grew older that I realized that the people my father was talking about were *choosing* to disappear, running away from their families, not being taken from them. They were light-skinned blacks who could move into the white world undetected, denying their blackness and the exclusion they suffered in a white-dominated America.

I've been thinking of my father's joke a lot recently. It came back to me last month when scientists reported the discovery of a genetic mutation that led to the first appearance of white skin in humans. Reading about it, I wondered how it is that a minor mutation—just one letter of DNA code out of 3.1 billion letters in the human genome—is so highly prized that it has led scores of people to turn their backs on their families and has served to divide people for generations. Discovery of this mutation, combined with recent findings that all people are more than 99.9 percent genetically identical, has reinforced my belief that race is almost entirely a social demarcation, not a biological one.

Just a month earlier, I'd also recalled my father's joke as I listened to a group of students in a race relations class at Penn State University discuss the results of DNA testing that revealed the complicated strands of their racial backgrounds. Most were surprised by what they learned. African American students expected to find some European ancestry in their DNA, but were surprised at the extent of it. White students, on the other hand, were startled that they had either traces or significant amounts of DNA in common with their African American classmates. According to Mark Shriver, professor of genetics and anthropology at the university, DNA testing reveals that 5 percent of white Americans have some African ancestry and 60 percent of black Americans have white bloodlines.

This type of DNA analysis is becoming increasingly popular among people who do genealogical research, particularly blacks who want to identify their tribal roots in Africa. But I have to wonder: Is it just another manifestation of America's obsession with race? Or can it be used to help us move beyond that obsession?

FROM: "DNA Is Only One Way to Spell Identity," by W. Ralph Eubanks as appeared in *The Washington Post*, January 1, 2006. Reprinted by permission of the author.

This means that racial categories are not necessarily the same from country to country. For example, unlike the United States, the United Kingdom does not include people of Chinese origin in the category it calls Asian. For those in the United Kingdom, only those of Indian, Pakistani, and Bangladeshi origin are considered to be Asian. The Office for National Statistics has established racial categories for England and Wales and posted them on its Web site at **www.ons.gov.uk/about-statistics/classifications/archived/ethnic-interim/presenting-data/index.html**. Even within the United States the categorization of racial groups has varied over time. The category *Hispanic* first appeared on the U.S. Census form as a racial category in 1980. In the 2000 census, however, Hispanic was categorized as an ethnicity, which one could select in addition to selecting a racial identity. Therefore, one could be both *Asian* (a race) and *Hispanic* (an ethnicity), or one could be both *White* (a race) and *Hispanic* (again, an ethnicity). Similarly, as Susan Koshy (2004) has noted, people from India were once labeled "non-White Caucasians," but today are categorized with Asian Americans on the U.S. Census. These categorizations are important because historically they have affected the way people are treated. While discrimination based on race is no longer legal, we continue to live with its consequences. For example, although slavery ended almost 150 years ago in the United States, many churches, schools, and other social institutions remain racially segregated (Hacker, 2003).

Although people often think of racial categories as scientifically or biologically based, the ways they have changed over time and differ across cultures highlight their cultural rather than their biological basis. How cultures describe and define specific races affect who is considered to belong to a given race and, consequently, how those individuals are treated. Moreover, communication is a strong factor in furthering, affecting, or altering racial categories and identities. For example, Guzman and Valdivia (2004) studied the media images of three Latins—Salma Hayek, Frida Kahlo, and Jennifer Lopez—to see how gender and Latinidad are reinforced through the media (see Chapter 11). Face-to-face communication also influences peoples' ideas about racial identities. If individuals have little contact with people of a different racial group, it is especially likely that one or two encounters may lead them to draw conclusions about the entire group.

Beginning with the 2000 census, the U.S. government has allowed people to claim a **multiracial identity** (Jones & Smith, 2001). This category recognizes that some people self-identify as having more than one racial identity. So, how should we categorize Barack Obama? While "there is much to celebrate in seeing Obama's victory as a victory for African Americans," writer Marie Arana (2008) also thinks that "Obama's ascent to the presidency is more than a triumph for blacks." She feels that "Barack Obama is not our first black president. He is our first biracial, bicultural president." What difference does it make if we see Obama as our first African American president, or as our first biracial president? As you think through this issue, you can see the complexities of race and racial politics within a culture.

National Identity

Racial identity can often be confused and conflated with **national identity**. We often misuse the notion of nationality when we ask someone "What's your nationality?" but what we really want to know is their ancestry or ethnic background. *Nationality* or national identity refers to a person's citizenship. In other words, Madonna's nationality is not Italian, but U.S. American, as she holds U.S. citizenship. John F. Kennedy's nationality was not Irish; he was a U.S. citizen. Many U.S. Americans did not actively choose their national identity; they simply acquired it by being born in the United States. Although many of us have not actively chosen our national identity, most of us are content with—or even proud—of it.

Like our other identities, the importance placed on national identity can vary, depending on many factors. In their study of national identity, John Hutcheson et al. (2004) found that U.S. Americans communicated a much stronger sense of national identity after September 11, 2001. Do you remember seeing many U.S. flags flying in your neighborhood after September 11th? This resurgence of national identity was reflected in the media as well.

Because the ability to travel has made the world seem so much smaller and borders seem more permeable, old ideas of national identity may no longer apply. For example, what does it mean to be Irish? In one study, Vera Sheridan (2004) traced the journey of Vietnamese refugees who moved to Ireland to become Irish citizens. Although they may not meet our expectations of what Irish people look like, their nationality is now Irish.

However, as communication scholars Laura Lengel and John T. Warren (2005, p. 5) remind us, "nation does not equal culture or cultural identity; it is merely one facet." Thus, identifying someone's nationality provides a glimpse of only one aspect of their cultural identity, which is both communicated to them, communicated by them, and communicated about them.

Ethnic Identity

Although race and ethnicity are related concepts, the concept of ethnicity is based on the idea of social (rather than genetic) groups. Ethnic groups typically share a national or tribal affiliation, religious beliefs, language, and/or cultural and traditional origins and background. A person's **ethnic identity** comes from identification with a particular group with which they share some or all of these characteristics. Thus, some U.S. citizens say that they are Irish because they feel a close relationship with Irish heritage and custom, even though they are no longer Irish citizens—or perhaps never were. Likewise, in the United States many U.S. Americans think of themselves as Italian, Greek, German, Japanese, Chinese, or Swedish even though they do not hold passports from those countries. Nonetheless, they feel a strong affinity for these

multiracial identity
one who self-identifies as having more than one racial identity

national identity
a person's citizenship

ethnic identity
identification with a particular group with which one shares some or all of these characteristics: national or tribal affiliation, religious beliefs, language, and/or cultural and traditional origins and background

gender identity
how and to what extent one identifies with the social construction of masculinity and femininity

places because of their ancestry. Unlike national identity, ethnic identity does not require that some nation's government recognizes you as a member of its country. It is also unlike racial identity, in that any racial group may contain a number of ethnic identities. For example, people who are categorized racially as White identify with a range of ethnic groups, including Swedish, Polish, Dutch, French, Italian, and Greek.

In other parts of the world, ethnic identities are sometimes called tribal identities. For example, "in Kenya, there are 50 tribes, or ethnic groups, with members sharing similar physical traits and cultural traditions, as well as roughly the same language and economic class" (Wax, 2005, p. 18). Tribal identities are important not only across Africa, but also in many nations around the world, including Afghanistan (Lagarde, 2005). In some societies, tribal or ethnic identity can determine who is elected to office, who is hired for particular jobs, and who is likely to marry whom. In Malaysia the three major ethnic groups are Malay, Indian, and Chinese. Since the Malay are in power and make decisions that influence all three groups, being Malay gives one an important advantage. In the United States, however, the ethnic identities of many White Americans are primarily symbolic, as they have minimal influence in everyday life (Waters, 1990). Even if ethnic identity does not play an important role in your life, it can carry great significance in other parts of the world.

Gender Identity

Similar to race, gender is a concept constructed through communication. *Gender* refers to the cultural differences between masculinity and femininity, while *sex* refers to the biological differences between males and females. Gender describes the set of expectations cultures develop regarding how men and women are expected to look, behave, communicate, and live. For example, in U.S. culture women (who are biologically female) are expected to perform femininity (a cultural construction) through activities such as nurturing, crossing their legs and not taking up too much room when sitting, speaking with vocal variety and expressivity, and wearing makeup. How do people respond to women who cut their hair in a flattop, sit sprawled across the couch, speak in an aggressive manner, and refuse to wear makeup? Often, they call them names or ridicule them; occasionally they even mistake them for males, because these behaviors are so culturally attached to notions of masculinity.

Gender identity refers to how and to what extent one identifies with the social construction of masculinity and femininity. Gender roles and expectations have changed enormously over the centuries, and cultural groups around the world differ in their gender expectations. How do we develop our notions of gender, or what it means to be masculine or feminine? We learn through communication: through the ways that people talk about gender, through the media images we see, and through observing the ways people communicate to males and females. For example, while crying is acceptable for girls, young boys receive many messages that they are not supposed to cry.

A leading scholar on gender, Judith Butler (1990, 1993) was one of the first to argue that gender identity is not biological, but based on performances. She asserted that people's identities flow from the ways they have seen them performed in the past. In other words, a man's performance of male identity rests on previous performances of masculinity. Because the performances of traditional masculinity have been repeated for so long, individuals come to believe that masculine identity and behaviors are natural. However, some people choose to enact their identity in nontraditional ways, and their performances will be interpreted against the backdrop of what is considered acceptable and appropriate.

In many families in the United States, gender roles follow a cultural rule about inside versus outside activities or chores. Those activities that take place inside the house are widely viewed as feminine and, therefore, should be performed by a female. Activities that take place outside are seen as masculine and are expected to be performed by a male.

In many families in the U.S., gender roles follow a cultural rule about inside versus outside activities or chores.

Table 3.1 Statistics on Intersex Births, 2000

People whose chromosomal pattern is neither XX nor XY	1 in 1,666 births
People whose bodies differ from standard male or female	1 in 100 births
People receiving surgery to "normalize" genital appearance	1 or 2 in 1,000 births

Intersex Society of North America (2005). How common is intersex? Retrieved June 12, 2006, from www.isna.org/faq/frequency

Sexual Identity

Sexual identity refers to which of the various categories of sexuality one identifies with. Because our culture is dynamic, it has no set number of sexual identity categories, but perhaps the most prominent are heterosexual, gay or lesbian, and bisexual. Although most people in our culture recognize these categories today, they have not always been acknowledged or viewed in the same ways. In his *History of Sexuality*, French historian and theorist Michel Foucault (1988) notes that over the course of history, notions of sexuality and sexual identities changed. In certain eras and cultures, when children were born with both male and female sexual organs, a condition referred to as *intersexuality*, they were not necessarily operated on or forced to be either male or female. Intersex births are not as rare as you might think, as you can see in Table 3.1.

Many people think of sexuality or sexual identity as private, but it frequently makes its way into the public arena. In everyday life, we often encounter people who will personally introduce us to their husbands or wives, a gesture that shares a particular aspect of their sexual identity. However, our society often exposes an individual's sexual identity to public scrutiny. For example, in 2006, U.S. Representative Mark Foley resigned from Congress amid questions that he sent inappropriate text messages and instant messages to male teenagers who had been congressional pages. The scandal led him to publicly disclose that he was gay (Candiotti et al., 2006). Senator Larry Craig's arrest for solicitation of sex in a men's restroom at the St. Paul–Minneapolis Airport became national news in 2007. Media coverage drew attention to that particular restroom—although by the end of 2008 it began to lose its appeal as a tourist destination (Sen. Craig restroom, 2008). In contrast to Representative Foley, Senator Craig insisted, "Let me be clear: I am not gay. I never have been gay" (Milbank, 2007). Because identity categories are social constructions, there is not always agreement about what they mean. Clearly, in the public arena, people manipulate these identity categories to help retrieve their reputations when their sexual activities become public.

In daily life, a person's sexual identity plays a role in such mundane matters as selecting which magazines to read, television shows and movies to watch, places to socialize, people to associate with, and types of products to purchase. Television shows, magazines, books, Internet sites, and other cultural products are targeted toward particular sexual identities, or they assume a certain level of public knowledge about sexual identities and groups. For example, *Gary Unmarried, Millionaire Matchmaker,* and *Real Housewives of Orange County* presume an understanding of U.S. heterosexual culture. In contrast, Logo cable channel is specifically geared to gay and lesbian viewers. These communication texts can reinforce, confirm, or challenge our notions of various categories of sexual identity.

Age Identity

Age, when thought of strictly as the number of years you've been alive, is an important identity for everyone. But your **age identity** is a combination of how you feel about your age, as well as what others understand that age to mean. How old is "old"? How young is "young"? Have you noticed how your own notions of age have changed over the years? When you were in first grade, did high school students seem old to you? While *age* is a relative term, so are the categories we use for age groups. Today, for example, we use the terms *teenager, senior citizen, adult,* and *minor,* but these terms have meaning only within our social and legal system. For

sexual identity
which of the various categories of sexuality one identifies with

age identity
a combination of self-perception of age along with what others understand that age to mean

social class identity
an informal ranking of people in
a culture based on their income,
occupation, education, dwelling,
child-rearing habits, and other factors

example, the voting age is 18, but people have to wait until they are 21 to buy liquor. Someone who commits a heinous crime can be charged as an adult, even if he or she is not yet 18. Still, whether a person feels like an adult goes beyond what the law decrees and comes from some set of factors that is far more complex.

Other age-related concepts are culturally determined as well. For example, the notion of "teenager" has come into use only relatively recently in the United States, and it is certainly not a universal category (Palladino, 1996). The notion that people have "midlife" crises is not a universal cultural phenomenon either. Moreover, these age categories are relatively fluid, meaning that there are no strict guidelines about where they begin and end, even though they do influence how we think about ourselves (Trethewey, 2001). For example, because people today generally live longer, the span of years thought of as middle age comes later in our lives. These changes all illustrate the dynamic nature of age identity and the categories we have for it.

You probably feel your age identity when you shop for clothes. How do you decide what is "too young" for you? Or what is "too old"? Do you consciously consider the messages your clothing communicates about your age? As you reflect on your shopping experiences, think about the tensions between what you like (the individual forces) and what others might think (societal forces). Here you see the tension that drives all social identities, including age.

Social Class Identity

Social class identity refers to an informal ranking of people in a culture based on their income, occupation, education, dwelling, child-rearing habits, and other factors (Online Glossary, 2005). Examples of social classes in this country include working class, middle class, upper middle class, and upper class. Most people in the United States identify themselves as middle class (Baker, 2003). However, there is no single agreed-upon definition for each of the classes. For example, the Census Bureau describes the middle class as being composed of the 20 percent of the population who earn between $40,000 and $95,000 (Baker, 2003), while the Drum Major Institute for Public Policy (2005) reports that the middle class conventionally has come to include families with incomes between $25,000 and $100,000. However, even 16.8 percent of those with incomes over $110,000 self-identify as middle class (Baker, 2003).

In his work on social class, French sociologist Pierre Bourdieu (1984) found that people of the same social class tended to view the world similarly: They defined art in similar ways and they enjoyed similar sports and other aspects of everyday life. Moreover, based on his study of social class, Paul Fussell (1992) noted that U.S. Americans communicate their social class in a wide variety of ways, some verbal and some nonverbal. For example, middle-class people tend to say "tuxedo," while upper-class people are more apt to say "dinner jacket." In the category of nonverbal elements that express social class identity, he included the clothes we wear, the way we decorate our homes, the magazines we read, the kinds of drinks we imbibe, and the ways we decorate our automobiles. We will discuss more about class and verbal and nonverbal communication in the next two chapters.

Social class identity is an important influence in the ways that people socialize and engage in leisure activities.

Those in occupations such as nursing, teaching, and policing soon may no longer be considered middle class. What other occupations have fallen or might fall from middle-class status? In their study, *The Fragile Middle Class*, Teresa Sullivan and her colleagues noted the increasing numbers of bankruptcy filings (2001), especially among those in occupations that we consider securely middle class, such as teachers, dentists, accountants, and computer engineers.

One reason people in the United States avoid discussing social class is because they tend to believe that their country is based on *meritocracy,* meaning that people succeed or fail based on their own merit. This idea leads to claims such as "anyone can grow up to be president." However, this has not proven to be true. For example, until the election of Barack Obama in 2008, every president in the United States has been White, male, and, all but one, Protestant. Social identity and class have a powerful impact on one's life, as they can determine where you go to school (and what quality of education you receive), where you shop (and what quality of resources you are exposed to), which leisure activities you participate in (on a scale from constructive and enriching to destructive and self-defeating), and who you are most likely to meet and with whom you are mostly likely to socialize. In this way, social class identity reproduces itself. Thus, people who are working class tend to live around other working-class people, make friends with working-class people (who influence their expectations and behavior), and attend schools that reinforce working-class values. As you can see, the social class one is born into often affects the social class one dies in. In an early study that showed how communication was used to perform social class identity in conjunction with gender and race, Gerry Philipsen (1992) noted that men tended to speak much less than women and rarely socialized outside their working-class community that he called "Teamsterville."

Religious Identity

In the United States today, **religious identity** is becoming increasingly important. Religious identity is defined by one's spiritual beliefs. For example, although Jim hasn't been to a Catholic church in decades, he still identifies himself as Catholic due to his upbringing and the impact the religion has had on his outlook. Most researchers and writers agree that "Religion is certainly one of the most complex and powerful cultural discourses in contemporary society, and religion continues to be a source of conflict between nations, among communities, within families, and . . . within one's self" (Corey, 2004, p. 189). While you may believe that your religious identity is part of your private life and irrelevant outside your family, this is not true. For example, in the aftermath of the 2001 September 11 attacks, Muslim identity has been viewed with particular suspicion. A 2004 study done by researchers in the Department of Communication at Cornell University found the following attitudes about Muslim Americans:

> About 27 percent of respondents said that all Muslim Americans should be required to register their location with the federal government, and 26 percent said they think that mosques should be closely monitored by U.S. law enforcement agencies.

How does your own speech reveal your social class background and identity? Can you identify aspects of your family's home, yard, interior decorating, and clothing that reveals social class identity? To reflect further on what social class means to you, see Did You Know? ID Check.

Did You Know?

ID Check

1. What is your social class?
2. How important is your social class to you?
3. What and who have been the primary sources of socialization for you about your social class? Name specific persons. If relevant, identify the organizations or types of organization with which they were affiliated.
4. How, if at all, do you express your social class—through language, communication style, dress, accessories, music?
5. Does your awareness of your social class ever facilitate your communication with others? Explain.
6. Does your awareness of your social class ever hinder your communication with others? Explain.
7. What situations, if any, do you avoid because of apprehensions related to your social class?
8. What situations, if any, do you seek because of your social class?
9. What advantages, if any, do you enjoy based on your social class?
10. Do you know of any stereotypes about your social class? If so, list them.
11. Are you ever aware of stereotypes about your social class as you interact with others? Explain.
12. How do the media tend to depict your social class? Do media depictions correspond with your sense of your social class? Explain.

religious identity
aspect of identity defined by one's spiritual beliefs

Twenty-nine percent agreed that undercover law enforcement agents should infiltrate Muslim civic and volunteer organizations, in order to keep tabs on their activities and fund-raising. About 22 percent said the federal government should profile citizens as potential threats based on the fact that they are Muslim or have Middle Eastern heritage. In all, about 44 percent said they believe that some curtailment of civil liberties is necessary for Muslim Americans. (Cornell University, 2004)

Religious identity also takes on public significance because it correlates with various political views and attitudes (Corey & Nakayama, 2004). For example, the 2004 Cornell study found that Christians who actively attend church were much more likely to support differential treatment of Muslim Americans. In contrast, the nonreligious, or those less active in their churches, were less likely to support restrictions on civil liberties of Muslim Americans.

It Happened to Me: Elizabeth

If I meet someone in a college class, I don't tell them that I'm involved in a church or that I'm a Christian unless they bring it up or it's obvious they are too. I do not want to appear to be a religious nut waiting to shove my belief system down their throat. My belief in Christ is really at the core of who I am though. When I meet people through work who are in churches, I am open with them about my work, my life, and even my challenges. This is because they are my brothers/sisters in Christ, and that's the culture of what we do—care for, and about, one another.

However one responds to other people's religious beliefs, most U.S. Americans feel a very strong need to embrace and enact personal religious identities (Corey & Nakayama, 2004). In 2000, for example, 46 percent of U.S. Americans belonged to religious groups, and approximately 40 percent of U.S. Americans claimed to attend religious services regularly (Taylor, 2005). Thus, in their article on "Religion and Performance," Frederick Corey and Thomas Nakayama (2004) write that individuals feel a "tremendous need to embody religious identities and reinforce those identities through spirited, vernacular performances" (p. 211). To understand how one student's religious identity affects her life, read *It Happened to Me: Elizabeth.*

We've shown throughout this chapter that aspects of our personal identity such as race, nationality, ethnicity, gender, age, social class, and religion develop through the tension between individual and societal forces. While we may assert a particular identity or view of ourselves, these views must be negotiated within the larger society and the meanings that the larger society communicates about that identity. See *Communication in Society: Respecting Religious*

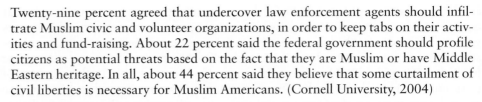

COMMUNICATION IN SOCIETY
Respecting Religious Differences

When any society has multiple religions, difficult issues can arise. As we look back upon the media coverage of the 2008 U.S. presidential election, "much of the coverage related to false yet persistent rumors that Obama is a Muslim" (Pew Forum on Religion and Public Life, 2008). How should we deal with these claims in a society that wants to respect and tolerate different religious beliefs? In response to the claims that Obama is a Muslim, former Secretary of State Colin Powell stated:

"Well, the correct answer is, he is not a Muslim, he's a Christian. He's always been a Christian. But the really right answer is, what if he is? Is there something wrong with being a Muslim in this country? The answer's no, that's not America. Is there something wrong with some 7-year-old Muslim American kid believing that he or she could be president? Yet I have heard senior members of my own party drop the suggestion. 'He's a Muslim and might be associated with terrorists.' This is not the way we should be doing it in America."

SOURCE: Robinson, E. (2007, August 29). The power of Powell's rebuke, *Washington Post*, p. A17. Retrieved December 31, 2000, from www.washingtonpost.com/wp-dyn/content/article/2008/10/20/AR2008102002393.html

Differences for an example of how one individual's is religious identity became a public issue whose meaning was discussed and negotiated within the larger society. In the next section, we discuss the role of ethics in communication about identity.

ETHICS AND IDENTITY

As you are probably aware, a person's sense of identity is central to how he or she functions in the world. Moreover, because identities derive their meanings from society, every identity comes with values attached to it. The ways we communicate may reflect these values. If you wish to be sensitive to other people's identities, you should be aware of at least three key ethical issues that can impact your communication with others.

One issue you might consider is how you communicate with people whose identities are more, or less, valued. What do we mean by more or less valued? You probably already know. In the United States, for example, which of the following identities is more highly valued: White or multiracial? Male or female? Lawyer or school bus driver? Still, these rankings are not necessarily consistent across cultures. In Denmark, for example, work identities do not follow the same hierarchical pattern as those in the United States (Mikkelsen & Einarsen, 2001). Thus, Danes are more likely to view street sweepers and doctors as social equals because they don't place as high a value on the medical profession nor as low a value on service jobs as many U.S. Americans do. In the United States, in contrast, many service workers complain that most of the people they serve either ignore them or treat them rudely—even with contempt. Consequently, you might ask yourself, "Do I communicate more politely and respectfully with high- versus low-status people?" If you find yourself exhibiting more respect when you communicate with your boss than you do with the employees you manage, then you might want to consider the impact of your communication on your subordinates' identities.

How would you describe your religious identity? How do you communicate it to others? Do you ever conceal it? If so, when and why?

The second ethical point to reflect on involves language that denigrates or puts down others based on their identities. Such language debases their humanity and shuts down open communication. Examples of unethical communication and behavior related to identity occur if men yell sexual slurs at women on the street, or straight people harass individuals they believe are gay, or when White people are disrespectful to people of color. Although you probably don't engage in such obvious insults to people's identities, do you denigrate them in other, more subtle ways? For example, have you ever referred to someone as "just a homemaker" or "only a dental assistant"?

Third, think about whether you tend to reduce others to a single identity category. As we pointed out earlier, each of us is composed of multiple identities, and even within a specific identity group, individuals may differ widely from one another. Thus, individuals may be offended when others respond to them based on only one of their identities, especially one that is not relevant to the situation at hand. For example, managers in some organizations will not promote mothers of small children to highly demanding positions. They justify this by claiming the women won't be able to fulfill both their family and their professional roles competently. Although these women may be mothers, their identities as mothers likely are not relevant to their workplace identities and performances—just as men's identities as fathers are rarely seen as relevant to their jobs. Each person is a complex of identities, and each person desires others to recognize his or her multiple identities. You are more likely to communicate ethically if you keep this fact in mind.

SKILLS FOR COMMUNICATING ABOUT IDENTITIES

Related to our discussion about ethical issues, we offer two guidelines for communicating more effectively about identities. The first guideline concerns the self-fulfilling prophecy we discussed earlier: How you communicate *to* someone and *about* someone can influence how they perform their identity or how it develops. If a parent continually communicates with the child as if she were irresponsible, then the child is likely to act irresponsibly. Therefore, you want to be aware of the ways you create self-fulfilling prophecies through your own communication.

Second, there are many ways to perform a particular identity. You can improve your ability to communicate if you are tolerant of the many variations. For example, even if you believe that "real men" should act in certain ways, you are likely to communicate more effectively if you do not impose your beliefs on others. For example, you should not assume that because someone is male, he enjoys watching football, baseball, and other sports; wants to get married and have children; or eats only meat and potatoes. If you do, you are likely to communicate with some men in ways they will find less interesting than you intend.

SUMMARY

Learning about identities and communication is important for at least four reasons: (1) we bring our identities to each communication interaction, (2) we encounter increasing numbers of people whose identities are different from our own, (3) much of our life is organized around specific identities, and (4) identity is a key site in which individual and societal forces come together.

Identities are defined social categories, and each of us is made up of many of them. They may be primary or secondary. Primary identities (race, ethnicity, age) are the focus in this chapter and have the most consistent and enduring impact on our lives; secondary identities, such as occupation and marital status, are more changeable over the life span and from situation to situation. Our identities exist at both the individual and social level, are both fixed and dynamic, and are created through interaction. Furthermore, identities must be understood within larger historical, social, and cultural environments. Important communication processes that influence personal identity development include reflected appraisals, self-concept, and self-fulfilling prophecies.

The primary identity categories—race, nationality, ethnicity, gender, sexuality, age, social class, and religion—are constructed between individual and social forces and what society communicates about those identities. Individuals perform their identities, and these performances are subject to social commentary. Straying too far from social expectations in these performances can lead to disciplinary action.

Ethical concerns center on how people are treated based on their identities. Guidelines to ethical communication include learning to value and respect people within all identity groups, to avoid using denigrating language or reducing people to a single identity category. Guidelines for more effective communication about identities involve being aware of the ways you create self-fulfilling prophecies through your communication and being tolerant of different ways of enacting various identities.

KEY TERMS

identity 57
reflected appraisals 60
looking-glass self 60
particular others 61
generalized other 61
self-fulfilling prophecy 62
stereotype threat 63
self-concept 63

self-esteem 64
self-respect 64
performance of identity 65
enacting identities 65
role expectations 65
mutable 65
racial identity 68
multiracial identity 71

national identity 71
ethnic identity 71
gender identity 72
sexual identity 73
age identity 73
social class identity 74
religious identity 75

TEST YOUR KNOWLEDGE

1. What are the key concepts in identity development?

2. How do individual and societal forces influence our understanding of identity?

3. What are the primary identity categories? Define each.

4. How is identity performed? Give an example for each primary identity category.

5. What are three key ethical concerns related to identity?

APPLY WHAT YOU KNOW

1. List the identities that are most important to you. Some of these identities may not have been discussed in this chapter. Note some situations in which the identities not discussed in the chapter become most relevant and some situations where other identities dominate.

2. Which of your identities are shared by a majority of people in society? What are some of the stereotypes of those identities? To answer this question, you may need to ask people who do not share that identity.

3. Interview someone who is at least twenty years older than you. Ask the person how her or his identities have changed over the years and what those changes entailed. Then reflect on changes in your own identity as you have grown up. How many of these changes were motivated by individual forces and how many might have been due to social forces?

EXPLORE

1. Go to www.msnbc.com/:d/6666338/ and read the description for purchasing a "Going Canadian" kit. What are the ethics of U.S. Americans pretending to be Canadians? Why would U.S. Americans want to pretend to be Canadians?

2. Read this essay on personal home pages and identity: www.aber.ac.uk/media/Documents/short/webident. html. Then scan some home pages and think about the identity that the home page author is constructing. How is someone's identity in everyday life different from his or her identity on a home page?

3. Go to www.ushmm.org/ and explore this Web site of the United States Holocaust Memorial Museum. Explore some of the online exhibits and reflect on intolerance and identities. Name several groups represented in these exhibits. How were the campaigns of intolerance against them expressed, coordinated, and conducted? What kinds of intolerance are being perpetrated today?

4. Go to Margaret Cho's Web page at www.margaretcho.com/ with one caution: If you are offended by vulgar language, you may be bothered by what you find there. Based on your review of her Web site, her performances, and her blog, how do you think she connects performance with social commentary? What are some key elements of her identity? How does understanding these elements help you understand her humor?

Communicating, Perceiving, and Understanding

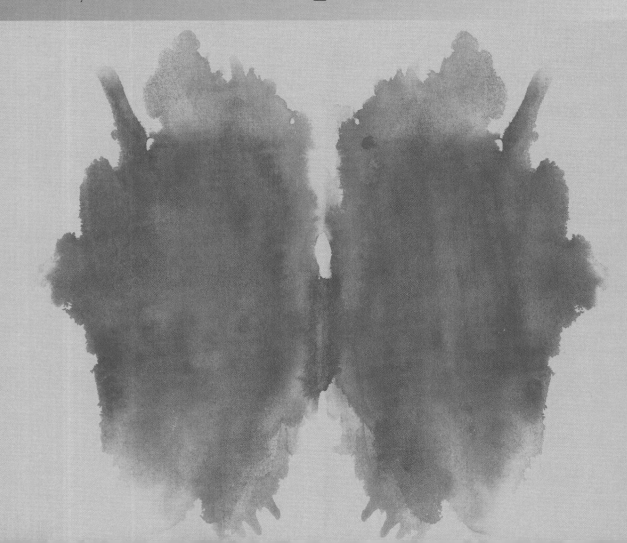

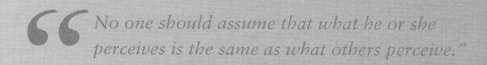

WALID: Wow! Professor Smith sure got angry in class today.

MEREDITH: What do you mean? I didn't notice anything.

WALID: You know, when people kept talking while she was trying to lecture; she turned a little red and glared at us. I was afraid to ask her for help after class because she was so mad at us.

MEREDITH: I talked to her after class and she was perfectly nice.

As Walid and Meredith illustrate, our perceptions strongly influence the ways we respond to and communicate about the world. Our perceptions are affected by individual factors, such as age, gender, genetics, and experience, as well as by societal forces including culture, historical events, and social roles.

For instance, as individuals age, their hearing often becomes less acute; the sounds available to them may be reduced, which can affect their perceptions. But how can societal forces affect perception? One example has to do with smells, and with the different ways that cultures interpret and value them. In the United States, people typically are encouraged to wear deodorant and colognes to mask their natural body odors (Classen, Howes, & Synott, 1994). However, in some cultures natural body odors are considered desirable, and U.S. Americans may be viewed as smelling antiseptic (Danghel, 1996). Thus, a wide range of factors influence what you perceive and how you interpret and evaluate it. In this chapter we will first explore the importance of perception and the perception process. Next we'll examine how individuals' attributes and experiences affect their perception and consider societal influences on perception. We also address ethical issues in perception and will end the chapter with suggestions for sharpening your perception skills.

 Once you have read this chapter, you will be able to:

- Explain why understanding perception is important.
- Discuss the three steps involved in the perception process.
- Define *selection* and name the five features that affect selection.
- Identify the two primary cognitive processes involved in organization.
- Describe the role of frames and attribution in interpretation.
- Name three individual factors that impact one's perceptual processes.
- Understand how power, culture, social comparison, historical time period, and social roles influence perception.
- Articulate three ethical guidelines for perception.
- Offer four ways to improve your perception skills.

Research reveals that when people perceive others as attractive, they treat them better than those viewed as less attractive.

THE IMPORTANCE OF PERCEPTION

How individuals respond to people, objects, and environments depends largely on the perceptions they have about them. For example, when you perceive people as being polite, you are more likely to agree to their requests (Kellerman, 2004). When you communicate, you don't just respond to others' words; you respond to your perceptions of the way they look, sound, smell, and, on occasion, feel. For example, considerable research has established that when people perceive others as attractive, they treat them better than those viewed as less attractive (Chaiken, 1986; Wilson & Nias, 1999)—which may explain why so many people flock to makeover shows like *The Biggest Loser* and *What Not to Wear*. In addition, some research suggests that sexual attraction is based in part on the ways others smell (McCoy & Pitino, 2002; Singh & Bronstad, 2001). So, the next time someone tells you "It's not you; it's me," they may be telling the truth. You just may not smell right to that person! See *Communication in Society: The Smell Report,* on p. 91.

As we noted in Chapter 3, identities play an important role in communication. They also influence and are influenced by perception. That is, primary identities, such as being female or male, may cause you to perceive aspects of your environment in specific ways. For example, because of the frequency of sexual assault in the United States, women may be particularly aware of their environment if it is late at night and they are alone. They may be aware of the level of lighting, who else is around, even small noises. In this case, they focus more on the environment because they are women (and feel more vulnerable); at the same time their focus on the environment reinforces their cultural identity as victims. Secondary identities can also impact one's perception. If you are an artist, for instance, you are more likely to perceive and appreciate color and form in your environment, while if you are an architect you are probably much more aware of how buildings are designed and used.

As you read this chapter, you are receiving considerable sensory input. An air conditioner or heater might be running, cars and people may be moving past you, and the temperature where you sit likely fluctuates over time. In addition, you may feel hungry or tired, you might detect the scent of cleaning products, and the chair you are sitting on could be uncomfortable. How are you able to manage all the information your senses bring to you so that you can focus on your reading? How are you able to make sense of all this sensory input? The answer is that you continuously engage in a variety of processes that limit and structure everything you perceive (Kanizsa, 1979; Morgan, 1977). Let's look at how this works.

WHAT IS PERCEPTION?

Perception refers to the processes of **selection**, **organization**, and **interpretation** of the information we collect through our senses: what we see, hear, taste, smell, and touch. The sensory data we select, the ways we organize it, and the interpretations we assign to it affect the ways we communicate. Although these processes tend to happen concurrently and unconsciously, researchers separate them to better explain how they function. (See *Visual Summary 4.1: Perception Process,* on p. 88.)

Selection

Because people experience more sensory information than they can process, they selectively focus on and remember only part of it. In every interaction, each communicator has a field of perception. In this field some objects, symbols, or words are at the center, while others are on the periphery, and still others are outside the field altogether. Consciously or unconsciously you attend to just a narrow range of the full array of sensory information available and ignore the remainder. This process is called **selective attention**.

selection
the process of choosing which sensory information to focus on

organization
the process by which one recognizes what sensory input represents

interpretation
the act of assigning meaning to sensory information

selective attention
consciously or unconsciously attending to just a narrow range of the full array of sensory information available

Suppose your friend is telling you a very interesting story about a mutual acquaintance while the two of you are seated in a crowded room. Most likely, your friend will have your full attention. Peripherally you may notice that you are hungry and that others are in the room; however, none of this will distract your focus. You probably will not even notice who is sitting at the table next to you, the color of the walls, the type of flooring, or the storm clouds that have gathered outside. Your attention will be devoted to the center of your field.

The sensory input you select, however, is not random (Greenough, Black, & Wallace, 1987). When a wide range of sensory experiences accost you, various factors affect your selection. Such features as intensity, size, contrast, repetition, and movement influence your attention.

Intensity: A loud BANG is audibly more intense than the sound of a soft beep, and thus, is more likely to get your attention. As the number of cell phones around us has increased, their rings have become both louder and more distinctive—so they will capture the owner's attention.

Size: You also tend to be more aware of people and objects that are large. Tall or big people often have an advantage; a teacher is more likely to notice them in a classroom when they wish to speak. However, they may have a hard time blending in with a crowd or withdrawing from others' attention.

Contrast: You are more likely to notice an object or sound that is different from its surroundings. If everyone is wearing a suit, you are likely to notice the person wearing a Hawaiian shirt; similarly, a cough in a quiet room or a sudden silence in a noisy one will draw your attention.

Repetition: You pay more attention when someone repeats a statement or an image. Small children recognize this principle of attention; they are adept at repeating "Mom, Mom, Mom, Mom," until they get a response.

Movement: Sudden movements also may capture attention. The unexpected appearance of someone in your visual field will cause you to pay attention, as may any new or abrupt movement. Consequently, people often walk past or stand close to the people they are interested in, to capture their attention.

In sum, you notice only part of the perceptual field available to you; and what you pay attention to is influenced by the features of the sensory stimuli. Some stimuli are more likely to draw your attention than are others. Thus, objects and people who are intense, large, contrasting, or moving are more likely to be noticed.

People are most likely to pay attention to and remember comments that are negative, violate their expectations, and are made in situations that are important to them (Sui & Finnegan, 2004). When an instructor says, "This will be on the test," students usually pay attention to what the instructor says next. Similarly, when comments violate our expectations, they become more salient and lead people to pay more attention. Thus if you meet someone new and say "How are you?" and the person explains in detail all the misfortunes that have befallen him or her, you not only will be surprised, you will remember the event. You may even decide that this new person is highly negative, or strange, and that you should avoid future interactions.

Aspects of identity also guide our attention. For example, if someone is preaching in front of the campus student union, some students may be drawn to listen and other students may tune it out. The religious identities of these students may influence their selection into or out of this communication event. What you attend to, then, is not random; features of an event and of your identity are influential.

Take a moment to remember the nicest comment anyone has made to you in the past twenty-four hours. Next, recall the unkindest remark anyone has made to you in that time period. Which remark did you find easiest to remember? Was your most memorable comment positive or negative? Did your most memorable comment violate your expectations? What were you doing when you heard the comment?

Is that noise a loose shutter or an intruder? How you organize sensory input influences your response to it.

Organization

After you select the sensory input you will attend to, you need to be able to recognize *what* it represents. To do this, you must organize the information you receive into a recognizable picture that has meaning. If you are awakened in the middle of the night by a loud noise, you will certainly attend to that noise and little else. However, you also must be able to make sense of the sound in order to respond. Is it a mechanical sound or an animal one? Is it human? You can make judgments like these because you possess organizational structures or templates that tell you what information belongs together and how to "read" or understand what you perceive (Kanizsa, 1979). How does this work? In this section we examine two primary cognitive principles—cognitive representation and categorization—which help people organize and respond to their perceptions.

Cognitive Representation

The term **cognitive representation** describes the human ability to form mental models of the world we live in (Levinthal & Gavetti, 2000; Weick, 1995). Think of these models as cognitive maps that humans create and then refer to later when circumstances call for them. For example, you know that a fire alarm communicates danger and know how to respond because you have a cognitive map for alarms. We have fire drills, in fact, to help people create cognitive maps that are familiar and allow them to act more instinctively.

You also develop and use cognitive maps when you communicate. As you grow up, you learn cognitive maps or models for engaging in many types of communication acts, such as complaining, apologizing, and asking for a favor. You probably learned quite early that it is useful to be nice to someone before you ask them for a favor, and this information became part of your map for asking favors. Remember that maps are *representations* of things, not the things themselves. Thus cognitive maps consist of general outlines to guide you; they are not fixed sets of utterances that you memorize.

Three specific types of cognitive representations, or maps, that individuals use to organize their perceptions are schemas, plans, and scripts.

Schemas.　Cognitive structures that represent an individual's understanding of a concept or person are **schemas**. They provide a guide for how one should behave in a particular situation or with a specific person. Schemas are created socially; that is, we develop schemas through routine interactions with others (Lin, Harwood, & Hummert, 2008). Your understanding of people, and how to communicate with them, is strongly influenced by the schemas you have for them. For example, what is your schema for "elderly person"? What type of person do you imagine when you hear this term? If your schema for *elderly person* includes cognitively impaired, infirm, and inactive, you will communicate differently with older adults than if your schema includes wisdom, patience, and kindness.

Communication behavior is strongly influenced by idealized schemas called prototypes. A **prototype** is the most typical or representative example of a person or concept. For example, many people's prototypical idea of a professor is a person who is male, has white hair (and perhaps a beard), and wears a tweed jacket with leather patches. Although a few professors fulfill this prototype, many more do not. (Just look around your campus.) Nonetheless, this prototype persists, in part because of how media depict college instructors.

Prototypes are important because people compare specific individuals to their prototype and then communicate with them based on the degree to which they

cognitive representation
the ability to form mental models of the world

schema
cognitive structure that represents an individual's understanding of a concept or person

prototype
an idealized schema

perceive the individual conforms to that prototype. You likely see this most often when it comes to the issue of gender. People have prototypical ideas of what a "man" or a "woman" is. These prototypes represent idealized versions of masculinity and femininity. The more an individual resembles your prototype, the more likely you are to communicate with that person in a stereotypical (or prototypical) manner. For example, men who are muscular, tall, and who have facial hair are often perceived to be very masculine. Consequently, people tend to communicate with them as if these men embody typical masculine characteristics, such as having an interest in sports, a heterosexual sexual orientation, and a lack of interest in topics such as fashion, interior design, or personal relationships. Similarly, a man who possesses none of those characteristics may be viewed as unmasculine and be communicated with accordingly.

Planning.   When talking with others, you call upon your maps for communication and your schemas for people to plan specific conversations. **Planning** refers to the sequence of actions you develop to attain particular goals (Berger, Karol, & Jordan, 1989, p. 93). For instance, if you want to obtain a bank loan, you likely plan the request. To do that, you call on your general cognitive map for how to ask for a loan. In addition, you will use the schema you have developed for bankers (e.g., how friendly, helpful, and accommodating you believe them to be) to help you adapt your plan or request. However, if you ask for loans frequently, you might even have a specific map for borrowing money.

planning
the sequence of actions one develops to attain particular goals

script
a relatively fixed sequence of events that functions as a guide or template for communication or behavior

You use planning in many types of interpersonal interactions. As the example for borrowing money indicates, persuasion involves considerable planning, as does initiating a conversation with a new person (Berger & Bell, 1988). You may also plan compliments, invitations, and complaints. Because plans can fail, people are capable of developing multiple plans that they can employ sequentially (Berger, Karol, & Jordan, 1989). Good communicators adjust their plans once they determine that one is not working. For example, if you begin inviting a friend to go out with you and she is clearly reluctant, you may switch to a persuasive attempt rather than a straightforward invitation—pointing out all the benefits the outing will bring. As you implement both successful and unsuccessful plans, you learn from your experiences; consequently, you constantly refine your plans.

People who borrow money often may develop a script for how to do so.

Interpersonal Scripts.   When you use a plan repeatedly, it may develop into a script. A **script** is a relatively fixed sequence of events you expect to occur; it functions as a guide or template for how to act in particular situations (Burgoon, Berger, & Waldron, 2000; Pearce, 1994). You develop scripts for activities you engage in frequently. Most people have a script for how to meet a new person. For example, when you first meet someone of interest on campus, you probably approach the person, introduce yourself, and ask a question such as "What is your major?" or "Where is your hometown?" Thus, you follow a routine, of sorts (Douglas, 1990).

We enact scripts because we find them comforting, they are efficient, and they keep us from making too many social mistakes. Although many of the scripts we use will be familiar to others, we also tailor them to fit our own expectations for a situation. Our choice of script or the way we alter a script depends on our perceptions of others. Thus if Kareem perceives that Helene is friendly, attractive, and fun, he may use a different script to initiate a conversation than if he perceives Helene as shy, quiet, and withdrawn.

categorization
a cognitive process used to organize information by placing it into larger groupings of information

label
a name assigned to a category based on one's perception of the category

Communicators also use scripts to reveal their identities. For example, when two men meet for the first time, they may begin their conversation with a discussion of last night's football game. Of course, not every man is a football fan, so this script will not work every time. However, it does fit with the way that masculine gender identity is constructed in our society, so it may allow the two men to become acquainted and to gradually develop more individualized interaction patterns.

As this discussion suggests, cognitive representations help people navigate through the world. Schemas provide guidelines that, when used repeatedly, develop into specific plans that steer our interactions with others. When we use a specific plan very frequently, we may develop an interpersonal script composed of specific choices and sequencing that we rely on to help us accomplish our goals. Thus, schemas are the most general and least specific cognitive representations; plans are somewhat less general and more specific; and scripts are the most specific, detailed, and routinized.

Categorization

Another type of cognitive process we use to organize information is **categorization**. Categorization is inherent to all languages. The linguistic symbols (or words) we use represent the groupings we see around us. Because we have difficulty remembering everything, we use groupings that represent larger categories of information or objects (Lakoff, 1987).

For example, we lump a lot of information under the category of restaurant. What did you think of when you read the word *restaurant*? You probably envisioned a subcategory, such as a café or a pancake house. However, the concept of restaurant has certain features that apply to all subcategories, so that you know what is meant and what to expect when you go to one. You understand that *restaurant* refers to a place to eat and not a place to worship or attend classes. Forming and using categories allows us to understand and store information and makes us more efficient communicators.

Although grouping is a natural cognitive and perceptual process, it also can lead to misperceptions. Categorizing can cause one to reduce complex individuals to a single category or to expect them to behave in ways consistent with the category, regardless of the circumstance. For instance, you might categorize an individual based on your perception that the person is irresponsible, serious, silly, or fun. Once you reduce people to a category, you may communicate with them as if they possess no other characteristics. If you categorize people as serious, you may never joke around with them or allow them to be silly or fun.

When people categorize others they typically also assign them a **label**. The two activities tend to go hand in hand. Thus, once you place people into groups or categories, you probably assign a label to the category. You may have heard groups of people and the individuals within those groups labeled or described as sorority girls, geeks, or gang members. Although labeling others can function as a useful shortcut, it also can lead to negative outcomes (Link & Phelan, 2001). When you label people you tend to view them only through the lens of the label; your expectations, evaluations, and responses to them are influenced by the label(s). Thus labeling can cause problems even when you use positive labels, as you can see was the case in *It Happened to Me: Lin Sue*.

It Happened to Me: Lin Sue

Because I am Chinese American, people often assume that I am some kind of whiz kid in academics. Well, I'm not. I was hit by a car when I was little, and I have residual brain impairment because of it. I have to study hard just to make passing grades. I get both angry and embarrassed when people assume I am this great student and imply that I will surely go to graduate school. I will feel fortunate if I just get out of undergraduate school. I really wish people wouldn't do this to me. They think they are being nice and complimentary, but they are still stereotyping me.

Labels can limit your view of others and even yourself. For example, did your family have a label they used to describe you? Were you the smart one or the well-behaved one or even the goof-up? If you were labeled the goof-up, you may not have been given many opportunities to disprove the label, and your ideas may have been discounted even when they were valid. Gradually, you may have come to discount the value of your own ideas. Of course, sometimes entire groups of people can be labeled in ways that create problems, such as perceiving all Muslims as terrorists.

As you may have guessed, labeling is related to stereotyping. **Stereotyping** occurs when you create schemas that overgeneralize attributes of a group to which others belong (Fiske & Taylor, 1991). You stereotype when you assume that every member of the group possesses certain characteristics. For example, you may assume that most males enjoy talking about sports, as in the discussion about scripts that we presented earlier. So, you initiate a conversation with an unfamiliar man by discussing last night's game. Few characteristics, if any, are true of every single member of a group—and if you use the sports opener with every man you meet, you may eventually get a blank stare in response.

As noted, grouping individuals makes it easy to remember information about them, yet it often leads to inaccurate beliefs and assumptions. When you overgeneralize a group's attributes, you are less able to see the individuality of the people you encounter. Thus, stereotypes can get those who use them into trouble. We will further explore the influence of society and culture on stereotyping later in this chapter.

Interpretation

After you perceive and organize sensory information, you assign meaning to it (Bruner, 1958, 1991). Returning to our earlier example, imagine that you are awakened late at night. You hear a loud noise, which you determine is caused by a banging on your bedroom window. You now have to interpret what this means. Is it a tree branch? A shutter? Is it someone trying to break in?

We all assign meaning to the information we perceive, but we do not all necessarily assign the same meaning to similar information. One of the factors that influences how we interpret information is the *frame* through which we view it.

Frames. Structures that shape how people interpret their perceptions are called **frames.** An individual's understanding of an event depends on the frame used to interpret it (Dijk, 1977). For example, if you frame the world as a dangerous place rife with criminals, you likely interpret that banging on your window as an indication of someone trying to break in. In essence, individuals view the world through interpretive frames that guide how they make sense of events (Fisher, 1997).

Individuals' frames develop over time, based on experience, interaction with others, and innate personality (Neale & Bazerman, 1991; Putnam & Holmer, 1992). Since we cannot perceive every aspect of an experience, frames also direct our attention toward some features of an episode and away from others. A bad mood, for example, directs attention to the negative aspects of an event. Usually, people don't become aware of frames until something happens to force them to replace one frame with another. If a friend points out that you are focusing only on the negative, you will become more aware of how your mood is framing, or focusing, your perceptions and interpretations. Your frame can change, then, as new information is introduced.

How should you use this information about framing? Now that you are aware that interpretations of people, events, and objects are influenced by an individual's specific frames, you should be more critical of your own interpretations. It is helpful to recognize that your interpretations (as well as others') do not necessarily represent the "truth"—but simply represent a particular way of viewing the world.

Frames are important elements of interpretation because they function as lenses that shape how observers understand people and events. But bear in mind,

How do you perceive these two males? Do any stereotypes come to mind?

stereotyping
creating schemas that overgeneralize attributes of a specific group

frame
a structure that shapes how people interpret their perceptions

Perception Process

SELECTION

What do I see?

- Lips pursed
- Nostrils flared
- Eyes squinting
- Skin taut
- Tears

ORGANIZATION

How does all of this fit together?

It looks like he's been crying!

INTERPRETATION

What does it mean?

He must be either sad or mad

Factors include:

- Intensity
- Size
- Contrast
- Repetition
- Movement

- **Cognitive Representation** describes our ability to form mental models of the world.

- **Schemas** are structures that represent an individual's understanding of a concept, person, or event.

- **Planning** is a map of the sequence of actions we develop to attain our goals.

- **Scripts** are relatively fixed sequences of events we expect to occur.

- **Categorization** is the naming of the things we group together (labels and stereotypes, for example).

- **Frames** are structures that shape how people interpret their perceptions.

- **Attribution theory** explain how we judge the behavior of others as well as ourselves.

interpretation involves more than just framing; when individuals interpret events, they also offer explanations for them. When we develop explanations for our own and others' behaviors, we are engaged in making attributions. Let's see how this process works.

Attribution.   How often do you wonder "why did she (or he) do that?" As you observe and interact with others, you probably spend considerable energy attempting to determine the causes of their behavior. For example, if your friend ignores you before class, you try to figure out why. At heart, most of us are amateur psychologists who search for the reasons people behave as they do. **Attribution theory** explains the processes we use to judge our own and others' behavior (Fehr, 1993; Spitzberg, 2001). Fritz Heider (1958), a psychologist and professor, said that attribution is the process of drawing inferences. When individuals observe others, they immediately draw conclusions that go beyond mere sensory information. Imagine that your boss's romantic partner receives a promotion at your organization; what conclusion would you draw? What attribution would you make if you called your romantic partner at 3 A.M., and he or she wasn't home? Although we're constantly being told we shouldn't judge others, attribution theory says we can't help it (Griffin, 1994).

One fundamental attribution we make is whether the cause of an individual's behavior is internal or external. An *internal* cause would be a personality characteristic, while an *external* cause would be situational. Suppose you came home from class one evening and found your roommate in a bad mood. You could attribute the mood to some trait internal to your roommate (she is moody and unpleasant) or to something external (her boss yelled at her).

You are particularly likely to make internal attributions when the behavior is unexpected—that is, when it is something that most other people would not do (Kelley, 1973). For instance, if you laugh during a sad movie, people are more likely to attribute your reaction to something about your personality. But when the behavior fits our expectations, we are likely to attribute it to external causes. Therefore, if you cry during a sad movie, people are likely to attribute your behavior to the movie.

Besides expectations, your attributions may also depend on whether you are the actor or observer of the behavior. You are more likely to attribute your own negative behavior to external causes and your positive actions to internal states (Jong, Koomen, & Mellenbergh, 1988). This is referred to as an **attributional bias.** If you are polite, it is because you have good manners; if you are rude, it is because others mistreated you. These attributions are examples of a **self-serving bias.** Operating under this bias, we tend to give ourselves more credit than is due when good things happen, and we accept too little responsibility for those things that go wrong.

Most individuals are harsher judges of other people's behavior than they are of their own. We tend to attribute others' negative behavior to internal causes (such as their personality), and their positive behavior to external causes (such as the situation). This tendency is referred to as the **fundamental attribution error** (Ross, 1977).

Attributional biases have implications for the way people communicate and conduct relationships. For example, the types of attributions

attribution theory
explanation of the processes we use to judge our own and others' behavior

attributional bias
the tendency to attribute one's own negative behavior to external causes and one's positive actions to internal states

self-serving bias
the tendency to give one's self more credit than is due when good things happen and to accept too little responsibility for those things that go wrong

fundamental attribution error
the tendency to attribute others' negative behavior to internal causes and their positive behaviors to external causes

You are likely to attribute an internal cause to unexpected behavior—such as laughter during a sad movie.

that spouses make are linked to their feelings of marital satisfaction. Unhappy couples tend to see their partner's negative behaviors as enduring: They assume the spouse's negative behaviors are internal, or personality-based, and difficult to change. Unfortunately, they also tend to view their spouse's positive behaviors as situational and therefore transitory (Bradbury & Fincham, 1988). Thus, unhappy spouses often feel helpless to change their partner's negative characteristics. This pessimistic outlook can then increase negative communication within the relationship.

Interestingly, when people make attributions about others, they tend to trust the negative information they hear more than the positive information (Lupfer, Weeks, & Dupuis, 2000). If you hear both positive and negative information about others, you tend to remember and rely on the negative rather than the positive information to formulate your attributions. However, you are not confined to these faulty attributional processes; you can work to overcome them. First, do not assume that you are a mind reader and that the attributions you make are always accurate. Remain aware that your attributions are really just guesses (even if they are educated guesses). You also need to be aware of the self-serving bias and work to minimize it. Recognize that we all have a tendency to attribute our own positive actions to ourselves and others' negative actions to themselves. Look for alternative explanations for your own and others' behavior. Last, avoid overemphasizing the negative. People have a tendency to remember and to highlight the negative, so try to avoid the negative in your own comments and balance the positive against the negative in your evaluations of others.

PERCEPTION AND THE INDIVIDUAL

Thus far we have explained how perceptions are formed: You engage in selective attention, use a variety of organizational processes, and assign meaning to your perceptions. However, a variety of individual factors influence your perceptual processes and affect your selection, organization, and interpretation of sensory input. (See *Visual Summary 4.2: Perception and the Individual,* on p. 94.) These factors generally fall into three categories: physical, cognitive, and personality characteristics. Let's begin with the physical factors.

Physical Differences

Each person's unique physical capabilities affect what they perceive and how they understand it. Some people have more acute hearing than others (see *Did You Know? The Ringtone Adults Cannot Hear*) as you will see in *It Happened to Me:*

Did You Know?
The Ringtone Adults Cannot Hear

Are you familiar with Mosquito Ringtones?

The Mosquito Ringtone is based on technology created by Britain Howard Stapleton who developed a device described as the Mosquito teen repellent. The device emitted a high-pitched frequency tone that adults could not hear but that teenagers found annoying. It was used by shopkeepers to disperse teenagers from public spaces where they congregated.

Later, inventive students converted the same technology into a ringtone that adults could not hear. This allowed them to receive phone calls and text messages while in class without their teachers being aware of it—that is, provided their teachers were old enough.

To test your ability to hear Mosquito Ringtones at different frequency levels, go to www.freemosquitoringtone.org/

COMMUNICATION IN SOCIETY
The Smell Report

Have you noticed a difference in sense of smell between the sexes?

Why do you think women typically have a keener sense of smell?

Sex-Differences

On standard tests of smelling ability—including odour detection, discrimination and identification—women consistently score significantly higher than men. One researcher has claimed that the superior olfactory ability of females is evident even in newborn babies.

One study suggests that sex-difference findings may not be entirely reliable, and that sex differences in olfactory prowess may apply to some odours but not others.

It is also possible, however, that many studies have not taken account of the changes in female sensitivity to smell during the menstrual cycle. It is known that female sensitivity to male pheromones (scented sex hormones), for example, is 10,000 times stronger during ovulation than during menstruation. It may be that female smell-sensitivity is also generally more acute during this phase.

(It has been shown that other senses such as hearing are more acute around ovulation, when women can also hear slightly higher frequencies than at other times.) These fluctuations may account for some inconsistencies in the findings, although hormone cycles cannot explain why female children score higher than male children.

In an experiment at the Hebrew University, Jerusalem, women without children held an unrelated infant in their arms for one hour and then were tested for infant-smell-recognition. Most were successful. The researchers conclude, "This indicates that the ability to identify infants by their odor is a more general human skill than previously realized." But they didn't test men, so it may only be a general female skill. Other tests have shown, however, that both men and women are able to recognise their own children or spouses by scent. In one well-known experiment, women and men were able to distinguish T-shirts worn by their marriage partners, from among dozens of others, by scent alone.

Women are also significantly more likely than men to suffer from "cacosmia"—feeling ill from the smell of common environmental chemicals such as paint and perfume.

FROM: "The Smell Report: Sex Differences," by Kate Fox, Social Issues Research Centre, www.sirc.org. Reprinted by permission.

Danika. Others have more acute sight or taste than others do. For example, professional wine tasters have a very highly developed sense of taste. As mentioned earlier, age can influence perception, and an individual's sex can affect the sensory input they notice. Since women on average have a keener sense of smell than do men, smell may play a more important role in perception for them (Estroff, 2004; Herz & Inzlicht, 2002). Overall, women may be more positively influenced by smells they find attractive and negatively by smells they dislike. For more information on this topic, see *Communication in Society: The Smell Report.*

Synesthesia is another individual physical difference that affects perception, which has only recently been recognized and studied. Synesthesia is a rare cognitive and physical trait that influences people's perception, and to some extent

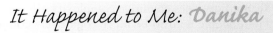

It Happened to Me: Danika

I was at a party recently when I went up to this attractive guy and stood next to him. When he didn't seem to notice me, I introduced myself and tried talking to him. But he completely ignored me! I was so put off that I stomped away and started complaining to my friend Amira. I told her that the guy might be good looking, but he sure was a snob. She looked puzzled. "Oh, were you standing on his left side?" she asked. When I told her yeah, she explained that he was deaf in his left ear and probably hadn't heard me. I felt bad that I had jumped to a negative attribution so quickly. Later, I approached him on his right side and talked to him; I found out he was a really nice guy.

their communication. To learn what synesthesia is (and whether you have it!), refer to *Alternative View: Hearing Colors, Tasting Shapes,* on p. 92.

Alternative VIEW
Hearing Colors, Tasting Shapes

People with synesthesia—those whose senses blend together—provide valuable clues to understanding the organization and functions of the human brain.

What does synesthesia reveal about how the brain affects perception?

How can these differences in perceptual abilities affect how individuals interact with one another?

When Matthew Blakeslee shapes hamburger patties with his hands, he experiences a vivid bitter taste in his mouth. Esmerelda Jones (a pseudonym) sees blue when she listens to the note C sharp played on the piano; other notes evoke different hues—so much so that the piano keys are actually color-coded, making it easier for her to remember and play musical scales. And when Jeff Coleman looks at printed black numbers, he sees them in color, each a different hue. Blakeslee, Jones, and Coleman are among a handful of otherwise normal people who have synesthesia. They experience the ordinary world in extraordinary ways and seem to inhabit a mysterious no-man's-land between fantasy and reality. For them the senses—touch, taste, hearing, vision, and smell—get mixed up instead of remaining separate.

Modern scientists have known about synesthesia since 1880, when Francis Galton, a cousin of Charles Darwin, published a paper in *Nature* on the phenomenon. But most have brushed it aside as fakery, an artifact of drug use (LSD and mescaline can produce similar effects), or a mere curiosity. About four years ago, however, we and others began to uncover brain processes that could account for synesthesia. Along the way, we also found new clues to some of the most mysterious aspects of the human mind, such as the emergence of abstract thought, metaphor, and perhaps even language.

Overview/Synesthesia

- Synesthesia (from the Greek roots *syn*, meaning "together," and *aisthesis*, or "perception") is a condition in which otherwise normal people experience the blending of two or more senses.

- For decades, the phenomenon was often written off as fakery or simply memories, but it has recently been shown to be real. Perhaps it occurs because of cross activation, in which two normally separate areas of the brain elicit activity in each other.

- As scientists explore the mechanisms involved in synesthesia, they are also learning about how the brain in general processes sensory information and uses it to make abstract connections between seemingly unrelated inputs.

Cognitive Complexity

As noted earlier, everyone develops categories to help them organize information. These categories are referred to as **constructs**. **Cognitive complexity** refers to how detailed, involved, or numerous a person's constructs are (Burleson & Caplan, 1998). But how does cognitive complexity affect perception?

First, people tend to be more cognitively complex about—and have more constructs for—those things that interest them or with which they have had experience. If you like music, you have a wide range of constructs, such as rap, hip hop, alternative, progressive, and neocountry, and these are constructs that others may not possess at all. This high number of constructs affects your perceptions of music. As you listen, you can distinguish between multiple forms of music, and you recognize when an artist is employing a specific form or fusing two or more. In addition to these sets of personal constructs that help you interpret the world, you also possess *interpersonal constructs* that you use to make decisions and inferences about other people (Deutsch, Sullivan, Sage, & Basile, 1991).

From an early age, everyone possesses simple constructs that help them explain their perceptions of others. These constructs tend to be bipolar, or based on opposing categories of characteristics, such as funny or serious, warm or cold, or responsible or careless. One's age, intellectual ability, and experiences influence how complex or detailed such constructs are. For example, very young children typically

constructs
categories people develop to help them organize information

cognitive complexity
the degree to which a person's constructs are detailed, involved, or numerous

describe others with only a few constructs, such as nice or mean; most adults, however, have a much more involved set of constructs that allows them to describe others in more varied and specific ways.

In addition, when you have cognitively complex construct systems, you tend to have many ways of explaining and understanding interpersonal interactions. Suppose, for example, that your dinner date was almost an hour late. If you are cognitively complex, you might come up with a number of reasons to explain this behavior: She (a) was in a traffic accident, (b) forgot about the date, (c) was detained by an unforeseen event, (d) decided not to keep the date, and so on. These are all plausible explanations; without further information you will not know which one is correct. The point is that cognitively complex individuals can develop a large set of alternative explanations.

In turn, your degree of cognitive complexity influences your perceptions and thus your communication behavior. For example, if you can only explain your partner's lateness by deciding that she is thoughtless, you will likely perceive her negatively and use a hostile communication style when you meet. Individuals' levels of complexity influence a broad range of communicative issues, such as how many persuasive messages they can generate (Applegate, 1982) and how well they can comfort others (Samter & Burleson, 1984).

Do you wonder how cognitively complex you are? To find out, think of a person you know well. Then for the next sixty seconds, write down as many terms as you can think of to describe that person. How did you do? Typically, the more terms and types of terms you can generate, the more cognitively complex you are believed to be.

Personality Characteristics

Each person's unique mix of personality, temperament, and experience influences how they interpret and respond to sensory information. Elements that make up this mix include emotional state, outlook, and knowledge.

Emotional State

If you are feeling happy or optimistic, you likely will interpret and respond to sensory input differently than if you are feeling depressed, angry, or sad (Planalp, 1993). For instance, if you feel angry you may perceive music, other people's voices, or background noise as irritating. On the other hand, if you are in a positive mood, you may behave more helpfully toward others. In one experiment, researchers tested 800 passersby (Gueguen & De Gail, 2003). In half the cases, researchers smiled at the passerby, and in half they did not. A few seconds after this interaction, the passersby had the opportunity to help another researcher who dropped his or her computer diskettes on the ground. Findings indicated that those who were exposed to the smile in the first encounter were more likely to be helpful in the second. Thus, even a small impact on your emotional state can influence how you communicate and interact with others.

Cognitively complex individuals can develop a large number of explanations for the late arrival of a dinner date.

Outlook

One's outlook refers to a tendency to view and interpret the world in consistent ways. Research shows that people tend to have a natural predisposition to either optimism or pessimism, based on genetics and experience (Seligman, 1998). People who are optimistic by nature may expect more positive experiences and make fewer negative attributions, which influences their behavior—but not always for the best. For example, young people with an optimistic bias tend to believe that they are less likely than others to experience negative consequences from health behaviors. Therefore, they may be more likely than others to engage in sexual risk-taking (Chapin, 2001).

Your emotional state influences how you communicate and interact with others.

Knowledge

People frequently interpret what they perceive based on what they know of an event. If you know that your friend has a big exam coming up, you may interpret his or her irritability as due to nervousness. Our knowledge of specific topics also influences our perceptions,

Perception and the Individual

Which perception factors affect their ability to comunicate with each other?

Individual Perception Factors

PHYSICAL	**COGNITIVE**	**INTERPRETATION**
Differences in:	**Complexity of constructs based on:**	**Elements:**
■ Visual acuity	■ Interests	■ Emotional state
■ Sense of taste	■ Intellectual ability	■ Outlook
■ Sense of smell	■ Experiences	■ Knowledge
■ Hearing acuity		
■ Touch sensitivity		

communication, and decision making. For instance, a study on organ donation revealed that members of families that discussed the subject were twice as likely to donate their organs as were members of other families (Smith, Kopfman, Lindsey, Massi, & Morrison, 2004). The researchers concluded that once people communicate and know more about the topic of organ donation, they perceive it in a more positive light.

Your perceptions strongly shape your communication and your actions. If you encounter someone new who looks physically attractive but whose cologne you dislike, you may choose to terminate your conversation. However, if you meet someone who reminds you of someone you like, you might invest energy in getting to know that person. If you interpret a new friend's teasing as a sign of affection, you may decide to increase your involvement with her. In these ways, your perceptual processes influence your interactions and relationships. In addition, broader societal factors also play a role in what you perceive, how you organize it, and the meanings you attach to it. We discuss these societal influences next.

THE INDIVIDUAL, PERCEPTION, AND SOCIETY

How do societal factors affect perception? As we will explain in this section, the position you hold in society and the cultures in which you live affect what you perceive and how you interpret these perceptions. As you read this section, we encourage you to consider the societal forces that affect your perceptions as well as how they might affect the perceptions of others.

The Role of Power

Every society has a hierarchy, and in a hierarchy some people have more power than others. Your relative position of power or lack of power influences how others perceive you, how you perceive others, and how you interpret events in the world. Moreover, those in power largely determine a society's understandings of reality. For example, in the United States, the dominant perception is that everyone can move up in society through hard work and education ("Middle of the Class," 2005). However, individuals who are born poor and who live in deprived areas with few resources can find it very difficult, no matter how hard they try to follow the path to "success" as defined by mainstream U.S. culture. Thus the perceptual reality of these people will likely differ from the perceptual reality of those higher in the power hierarchy. Nonetheless, a specific view of reality dominates U.S. culture because it is communicated both explicitly and implicitly through media messages, public speeches, schools, and other social institutions.

Your individual experiences within that hierarchy may lead you to accept or reject that dominant perception. For example, middle-class people may believe that if they work hard they will get ahead in society, whereas poor people may perceive that it takes a lot more than hard work and education (Ehrenreich, 2001). Similarly, if you grew up relatively wealthy, you may believe that your admission to a highly selective college is largely due to your intelligence, hard work, and skills, while someone who grew up relatively poor may believe that social connections and family money better explain this achievement (Douthat, 2005).

Your position in the racial hierarchy also influences your perceptions about the reality of racial bias. It is well documented that White Americans and African Americans have very different perceptions regarding the role of race in the United States (Hacker, 2003). A study conducted after Hurricane Katrina devastated the Gulf Coast revealed a broad divergence in perceptions: When asked whether racial inequality remains a major problem, 71 percent of African Americans replied yes, compared to only 32 percent of Whites (Pew Research Center for the People and the Press, 2005).

The Role of Culture

Culture strongly influences individual perception. One way it does so is through its *sensory model*. Every culture has its own sensory model, which means that each culture emphasizes a few of the five senses (Classen, 1990). Moreover, the emphasis placed on one sense over another affects what a culture's members pay attention to. People in the United States, for example, tend to give primacy to the visual; thus, we have sayings such as "seeing is believing," and students almost demand that professors use PowerPoint slides in the classroom. On the other hand, people living in the Andes Mountains of South America tend to place more emphasis on what they hear than on what they see. In their culture, important ideas are transmitted through characters in stories and narrative accounts (Classen, 1990). Knowing this, how do you think students in the Andes prefer to learn? You might imagine that they would prefer oral elaboration of ideas rather than terse visual representations of concepts on slides.

A culture is composed of a set of shared practices, norms, values, and beliefs (Brislin, 2000; Shore, 1996). Due to learning and socialization, these elements shape individuals' thoughts, feelings, perceptions, and behaviors. For example, individuals in East Asian cultures often are highly interdependent and place more emphasis on the group than the individual. For this reason, they discourage self-promotion and encourage greater self-criticism than do European North American cultures. By encouraging self-criticism (and then working on self-improvement), the thinking goes, they are contributing to the overall strength of the group (Heine & Lehman, 2004; Markus, Mullally, & Kitayama, 1997). In the United States, however, the emphasis often is on the individual, and most people are encouraged to distinguish themselves from others. For example, current books on dating and work success teach U.S. Americans how to "brand" themselves like a product. Thus, the dominant culture in the U.S. encourages people to talk about their success and to refrain from self-disparaging rhetoric. As a result, someone from East Asia may see U.S. Americans as braggarts, while a person from the United States may see East Asians as overly self-effacing (Kim, 2002).

Cultural background also influences how people expect communication to occur (Scollon & Wong-Scollon, 1990). In some Native American cultures, individuals perceive strangers as potentially unpredictable, so they may talk little—if at all—until they have established familiarity and trust with the newcomer (Braithwaite, 1990). This approach differs considerably from the customs of some European American cultures in which people view strangers as potential friends and use talk to become acquainted (Krivonos & Knapp, 1975).

Now imagine a Native American and a European American from these different communication cultures meeting for the first time. How is each likely to behave? The Native American may remain relatively quiet while observing the new person. The European American will most likely try to engage in a lively conversation and may ask a number of questions to draw the other person out. Thus the Native American may perceive the European American as pushy and overly familiar, while the European American may perceive the Native American as unfriendly or shy (Braithwaite, 1990). Each perceives or evaluates the other based on expectations that were shaped by his or her own cultural perceptions, values, and the meanings typical for his or her own culture (Scollon & Wong-Scollon, 1990).

Cultural norms, values, and expectations provide a backdrop of familiarity. When we travel or when we meet people from other cultures close to home, we can learn from exposure to our differences. However, sometimes these differences are upsetting, frustrating, or baffling. For example, one of our students, Simone, was taken aback when she was offered *chapulines* (fried grasshoppers) during her trip to Oaxaca, Mexico. Interestingly, most of us not only value the ways of our own culture, we often feel that others' cultural norms are less desirable—or even wrong—an issue we discuss next.

Some travelers become upset when their cultural expectations about what is "food" are not fulfilled.

The Role of Social Comparison

As we discussed earlier, categorizing groups of objects, information, or people is a basic quality of perception. *Social* categorization—or categorizing people—leads us to specific expectations about how others should or should not behave. These social categories and the expectations associated with them typically arise out of our culture and our place within the cultural hierarchy. For example, in the United States, middle- and upper-middle-class people often perceive individuals who receive governmental assistance as people who do not want to work, and they may therefore categorize them as lazy or dependent. However, people who are in the working class or among the working poor may have a different perception, asserting that those who rely on government assistance work hard but are underemployed or have to live on a salary that is not a living wage ("Middle of the Class," 2005; Ehrenreich, 2001). As you can see, the perceptions and categories that we develop tend to be tied to stereotypes and prejudice, which both flow from *ethnocentrism*, the perceptual concept at the core of social comparison.

ethnocentrism
the tendency to view one's own group as the standard against which all other groups are judged

Ethnocentrism

Most people view their own group as the standard against which they evaluate others. Thus, one's own ethnic, regional, or class group is the one that seems right, correct, or normal. This tendency to view one's own group as the standard against which all others are judged is described as **ethnocentrism**. It comes from the Greek words *ethnos*, which means nation, and *kentron*, which refers to the center of a circle (Ting-Toomey, 1999). People behave ethnocentrically when they view their own values, norms, or modes of belief and behavior as better than that of other groups.

While everyone experiences ethnocentrism to some degree, it can lead to polarized thinking and behavior; if *we* are right, correct, normal, and even superior, then *they* must be wrong, incorrect, abnormal, and inferior. Such thinking can seriously interfere with our ability to communicate effectively with those outside our group.

Stereotypes

As noted earlier in the chapter, stereotypes are broad generalizations about an entire class of objects or people, which are based on some knowledge of some aspects of some members of the class (Brislin, 2000; Stephan & Stephan, 1992). When you stereotype computer programmers as smart but socially inept, you likely are basing your beliefs on your interactions with a few programmers—or perhaps on no interactions at all. Stereotypes may be based on what you have read, images in the media, or information you have obtained from others, as you'll see was the case with one college student in *It Happened to Me: Damien*.

If you develop a stereotype, it tends to influence what you expect from the stereotyped group. If you believe that someone is a lesbian, you may also believe she engages in specific types of communication behavior, dress, or interests. When you hold these kinds of beliefs and expectations, they

It Happened to Me: Damien

Shortly after school started, I decided to join a fraternity and began going to parties on the weekends. Often when people heard me mention that I was a part-time computer programmer, they would first look shocked and then crack some kind of joke about it, like, "Bill Gates, Jr., eh?" I guess it surprises people that I don't have glasses, that I venture out into the sunlight once in a while, and that I engage in some social activities! I realize that their preconceived notions about "techies" have come from somewhere, but, since at least half of my fellow "computer geeks" are far from the nerdy stereotype, it would be nice if people would recognize that we aren't all pale, glasses-wearing, socially awkward nerds!

tend to erase the stereotyped person's individual characteristics. In addition, you are likely to communicate with her as if your stereotypes were accurate rather than basing your messages on her actual interests and behavior (Snyder, 1998).

Although stereotyping is an understandable and natural cognitive activity, it can cause trouble. Stereotyping often leads to polarized understandings of the world as "between me and you, us and them, females and males, Blacks and Whites" (Ting-Toomey, 1999, p. 149). In turn, polarized thinking frequently leads to a rigid, intolerant view of certain behavior as correct or incorrect (Ting-Toomey, 1999). For example, do you believe it is more appropriate for adult children to live on their own than with their parents before they marry? People with polarized thinking

prejudice
experiencing aversive or negative feelings toward a group as a whole or toward an individual because she or he belongs to a group

ego-defensive function
the role prejudice plays in protecting individuals' sense of self-worth

value-expressive function
the role played by prejudice in allowing people to view their own values, norms, and cultural practices as appropriate and correct

assume that their own cultural beliefs regarding this issue are right or correct instead of recognizing that cultures differ in what is considered appropriate. If you are interested in this issue, see Chapter 8, where we discuss the Italian view on adult children who live with their parents.

Prejudice

Stereotypes and feelings of ethnocentrism often lead to *prejudice*. **Prejudice** occurs when people experience aversive or negative feelings toward a group as a whole or toward an individual because she or he belongs to a group (Rothenberg, 1992). People can experience prejudice against a person or group because of their physical characteristics, perceived ethnicity, age, national origin, religious practices, and a number of other identity categories.

Given the negative associations most people have with the concept of prejudice, you may wonder why it persists. Researchers believe that prejudice is common and pervasive because it serves specific functions, the two most important of which are *ego-defensive functions* and *value-expressive functions* (Brislin, 2000). Let's explore these concepts.

The **ego-defensive function** of prejudice describes the role it plays in protecting individuals' sense of self-worth. For example, an individual who is not financially successful and whose group members tend not to be financially successful may attribute blame to other groups for hoarding resources and preventing him or her from becoming successful. The less financially successful individual may look down on groups that are even less financially successful as a way to protect his or her own ego. These attitudes may make people feel better, but they also prevent them from analyzing reasons for their own failure and negatively affect the ways they talk to and about the targeted groups. People who look down on groups that are less financially successful may describe them and talk to them as if they were lazy, incompetent, or not very bright.

Prejudice serves its **value-expressive function** by allowing people to view their own values, norms, and cultural practices as appropriate and correct. By devaluing other groups' behavior and beliefs, these people maintain a solid sense that they are right. Unfortunately, this same function causes group members to denigrate the cultural practices of others. You likely have seen many examples of the value expressive function of prejudice, as when individuals engage in uncivil arguments and personal attacks over issues such as men's and women's roles, abortion, and politics.

The Role of Historical Time Period

In addition to a person's place in the power hierarchy, their culture, and their awareness of social comparison, the historical period in which one grows up and lives influences perception and communication (U.S. National Research Council, 1989). For example, this author is writing this chapter on September 11, 2008. Anyone living in the United States who was older than five or six on September 11, 2001, likely has had their perceptions altered by events of that day. They may feel less safe, perceive air travel as riskier, and feel more patriotic than they did before the terrorist attacks on that day. These perceptions may in turn influence how they communicate, for example, with individuals who are Muslim, or how they talk about the United States.

Other historical events have affected the perceptions of individuals who lived through them. For instance, people who lived through the Great Depression may perceive resources as being scarcer than others do; those who were young during the Vietnam War likely believe that collective action can influence political policy; and those who grew up watching *The Real World* and other reality TV programs probably view privacy differently than do prior generations. As you might suspect, these perceptions influence how, and about what, the various generations communicate. Thus those who came of age after 2000 may feel comfortable discussing a wide range of topics previously considered taboo, such as sexual conduct or family dysfunction. Similarly, women who grew up when sexual discrimination was more prevalent might object to the use of "girls" when referring to women.

Social Roles

The roles one plays socially also influence one's perception and, consequently, communication. **Social role** refers to the specific position or positions an individual holds in a society. Social roles include job positions, familial roles (such as mother or father), and positions in society. For example, Teri holds a variety of roles, including mother, religious leader, soccer coach, and community activist. The fact that she holds these social roles affects how people perceive and communicate with her in several ways. First, society defines specific expectations for her various social roles (Kirouac & Hess, 1999). Many people, for example, expect that religious leaders will be especially moral, selfless, and well intentioned. In turn, these expectations affect the ways that religious leaders interact with others. If you expect Teri, as a religious leader, to be highly moral, she may work to communicate with you in ways that fulfill your expectations.

Second, the education, training, and socialization Teri undergoes for her social roles influence her perceptions. In much of U.S. culture it is expected that women will become mothers and that they will behave in specific ways as they fulfill that role. As they grow up, girls are socialized and taught, by both word and example, how mothers are supposed to communicate. Because Teri is a mother, she may perceive different issues as important. For example, she may be more concerned with the quality of schools, the safety of her neighborhood, and the easy availability of health care than a nonparent might. Similarly, when individuals receive education and training to be professors, physicians, or police officers, for example, their perceptions of the world around them are affected. A police officer may perceive the world as populated with more criminals than the average person does because of the way she has been trained.

Each individual's perceptions are unique, based on his or her own roles and characteristics. However, individuals also share certain perceptual realities with others in their power position in society's hierarchy as well as with others in their cultures and social role groups. Because of these differing realities and power positions, your perceptions may lead you into prejudicial and intolerant thinking and communication. In the concluding section of this chapter we suggest strategies for improving your perception processes and communication.

ETHICS AND PERCEPTION

It might seem that ethics play a very small role in perceptual and cognitive processes. However, as we've discussed throughout this chapter, the ways you communicate to and about people are connected to your perceptions and cognitions about them. Thus if you perceive that someone is old and your stereotype of old people is that they are infirm, you may treat that person as if she were a child—a response that we regard as unethical because it stems from stereotypical thinking. This is a common complaint among older adults (Ryan, Bourhis, & Knops, 1991). Similarly, if you categorize people with disabilities as being less than competent, you may choose not to communicate with people you place in that category. In fact, many people with disabilities express frustration that strangers and acquaintances talk to the people who accompany them instead of speaking directly to them, as if they did not exist (Braithwaite & Japp, 2005). As you can see, how you categorize and perceive people strongly influences your communication interaction with them.

social role
the specific position or positions one holds in a society

Perhaps most commonly, speakers who perceive and label other groups of people negatively often use derogatory terms to refer to them. Unfortunately, using such terms can reinforce and even intensify one's own as well as others' negative responses to these groups. In addition, if what you attend to and perceive about people first is their skin color, their sex, or their relative affluence, you may find yourself communicating with them stereotypically and failing to recognize other roles they fulfill. Doing so may lead you to assume and communicate as if all adult women are mothers (or there is something wrong with them if they are not), or you may refer to a physician as nurse, because she happens to be female. Each of these behaviors is unethical in that it denies others their right to legitimate identities.

Although social factors such as power and position can impact many aspects of your life, you have control of, and responsibility for, your perceptions and cognitions. Even though your social circle and your family may engage in unethical perceptual, cognitive, and communicative processes, once you become an adult you are responsible for how you interpret the world. We now provide you with some guidelines to help you become both more effective and more ethical in your perceptual and cognitive processes.

IMPROVING YOUR PERCEPTION SKILLS

You probably realize now that perceptions are subject to variance and error because of the variety of steps one goes through in forming them (selection, organization, and interpretation) and the range of factors that influence the perception process (individual characteristics, cognitive complexity, power, culture, historical time period, and social roles). However, certain cognitive and communication behaviors can improve your ability to perceive and understand the world.

First, engage in *mindfulness* to improve perception and understanding. Mindfulness refers to a clear focus on the activity you are engaged in, with attention to as many specifics of the event as you can (Langer, 1978). People tend to be most mindful when they are engaged in a new or unusual activity. Once an activity becomes habitual, we are likely to overlook its details. Mindfulness requires that you bring the same level of attention and involvement to routine activities as you do to novel ones.

In addition, before you assume *your* perceptions are accurate, ask yourself these questions:

- Have you **failed to notice** any relevant information due to selective attention? For example, did you focus on what the person was wearing rather than what he or she was saying?

- Have you used **faulty organizational patterns**? For example, just because two people are standing next to one another does not mean they are together.

- Have you considered **all possible interpretations** for the information you perceived, using the full range of your cognitive complexity? For example, if you did poorly on a test, was it due to poor test construction, your lack of sleep, the teacher's failure to prepare you, or your own failure to study sufficiently?

- Has your **physical condition** influenced your perceptions? For example, are you tired, hungry, or frightened?

- Has your **cultural background** influenced your perceptions? For example, are you perceiving politeness as deception?

- Has your **social role** influenced your perception? For example, have you begun to perceive all elderly people as infirm because you work in a nursing home?

- Has your **social position** influenced your perception? For example, have you considered how others with different positions might perceive the same issue?

Another way to improve your perception and understanding is to clearly separate *facts* from *inferences*. Facts are truths that are verifiable based on observation. Inferences are conclusions that we draw or interpretations we make based on the facts. Thus, it may be a fact that Southerners speak more slowly than do people from other regions of the United States, but it is an inference if you conclude that their slow speech indicates slow thought processes.

Finally, one communication act in particular will greatly improve your perception skills—perception checking. That is, check with others to determine if their perceptions match yours. If they do not, you may need to alter your perceptions. For example, Rosario once had an extremely negative reaction to a job candidate who interviewed at her company. She perceived him as arrogant and sexist. However, when she talked with her colleagues she discovered that no one else had a similarly strong negative response to the candidate. She decided that her perceptions must have been influenced by something in her own background and that he probably reminded her of someone she had once known who did display those negative traits. In revising her opinion of the candidate, Rosario demonstrated a well-developed sensitivity to the perception side of communication. All of us can benefit from greater awareness of the assumptions and attributions we make.

One communication act that can improve your perception skills is checking with others to see if their perceptions of others is similar to yours.

SUMMARY

Perception plays an important role in everyday communication. People use three perceptual processes to manage the vast array of sensory data in their environments: selection, organization, and interpretation. From all the sounds, sights, smells, tastes, and textures available, people choose only a few to focus on. What they focus on is, in turn, influenced by the distinctive features of the stimuli, such as their intensity, size, contrast, repetition, and movement.

Once you attend to particular sensory information, you have to organize it to make sense of it. Cognitive processes you use to organize information include cognitive representations, such as schemas, planning, and use of interpersonal scripts. Categorization, is also used, which includes framing, labeling, and stereotyping. Finally, after you perceive and organize sensory information, you then assign meaning to it. However, everyone does not necessarily assign the same meaning to similar information. Five factors influence how a person interprets information and makes attributions about it: emotional state, beliefs, expectations, knowledge, and experience.

Furthermore, what you select, how you organize it, and the interpretations you assign are all influenced by your individual characteristics, such as physical abilities and differences, cognitive complexity, and any cognitive disorders. In addition, your perception processes are affected by your position in the power hierarchy, culture, historical events during your lifetime, and your social roles.

Because people vary so much in their perceptions, no one should assume that what he or she perceives is the same as what others perceive. Consequently, we all must carefully check our perceptions on a regular basis and expend energy to overcome errors in processing as well as any attributional biases.

KEY TERMS

selection 82
organization 82
interpretation 82
selective attention 82
cognitive representation 84
schemas 84
prototype 84
planning 85

script 85
categorization 86
label 86
stereotyping 87
frame 87
attribution theory 89
attributional bias 89
self-serving bias 89

fundamental attribution error 89
constructs 92
cognitive complexity 92
ethnocentrism 97
prejudice 98
ego-defensive function 98
value-expressive function 98
social role 99

TEST YOUR KNOWLEDGE

1. How important is the role of interpretation in the perception process? What factors most influence how individuals interpret events?

2. How do cognitive maps, plans, and scripts differ from one another? How are they alike?

3. Why is stereotyping "normal"? When is it helpful? When is it harmful?

4. What is social comparison? How is it related to ethnocentrism and prejudice?

5. What one skill could you develop that would most improve your perception processes?

APPLY WHAT YOU KNOW

1. **Examining Stereotypes**
   For each of the words below, write down your beliefs about the group represented. In other words, provide a list of specific characteristics you believe are typically displayed by members of these groups.

   a. fraternity members
   b. politicians
   c. models
   d. rap stars
   e. body builders
   f. religious leaders

   After you have done so, compare your list to the lists created by other members of your class. What characteristics for each group did you have in common? What characteristics differed? Can you think of at

least one person from each group who does not display the characteristics you listed? How valid do you think your stereotypes are?

2. **Attributional Biases**
   As this chapter explains, people have a tendency to attribute their own positive behavior to internal traits and their negative behavior to external factors. However, they are also more likely to attribute others' positive behavior to external conditions and others' negative behavior to internal traits. In this exercise we want you to indicate how the attributional bias would cause you to describe each of the following behaviors, depending on who had performed it.

   Example: Forgetting to make a phone call
       I'm busy. You're thoughtless.

Example: Earning a good grade

I'm intelligent. You were lucky.

Do the exercise for each of the following behaviors/events

    a. Receiving a raise

    b. Breaking a vase

    c. Arriving late

    d. Winning an award

    e. Burning a meal

    f. Making a group laugh

Compare your responses with others in your class. What terms were used to describe one's own experiences? What terms were used to describe others' experiences?

REMEMBER: Although this is just an exercise, the attributional bias is quite common. Pay attention to your own thoughts and comments the next time something bad happens to you or others.

EXPLORE

1. Go to the Hanover College Sensation and Perception and Tutorials at www.psych.hanover.edu/KRANTZ/ size/constancy/index/html. Click on the size constancy tutorial and complete the activity within the tutorial. Then write a brief paragraph summarizing what you have learned.

2. Go to www.chd.gmu.edu/immersion/knowledgebase/ strategies/cognitivism/gestalt/gestalt.htm and read the material on the Gestalt Laws of Grouping. Select one of the "laws" of perceptions and organization described on the Web site and write a brief summary of

it. Finally, explain how this law of organization can affect your perceptions of and communication with others.

3. Go to the home page of Harvard's Interpersonal Perception and Communication Laboratory at www.wjh.harvard.edu/~na/. Click on one of the links under "Projects" and read a summary of the project that is being conducted. Write a brief paragraph summarizing what this project will explain about perception and communication.

5

Verbal Communication

chapter outline

> *The verbal elements of communication are the foundation on which meaning is created."*

My boyfriend is from Boston, and I'm from California. He has a strong East Coast accent, making it hard for me to understand him sometimes. He also uses slang words that I've never heard before. I continually ask him to repeat himself. It's frustrating for both of us, so our deal is that he will try harder to enunciate, and I will listen more carefully. The most difficult time was when I visited his hometown of Boston and met all his friends and family. It was a big culture shock at first, but eventually I caught on to the slang and pronunciation.

When you think of "communication," you probably most often think about the verbal elements of communication—the words people choose, the accents they speak with, and the meanings they convey through language. You may less frequently consider the ways in which verbal communication assists or hinders relationship development, as illustrated in the opening example, or its effect on the creation of identities.

In this chapter, we explore the verbal elements of communication and how people use verbal communication to accomplish various goals. First, we discuss the importance of verbal communication and its value as a topic of study. We then describe how individuals use verbal communication, including the functions it serves and the components of language that make it possible. Next, we explore individual characteristics, such as gender, age, regionality, ethnicity and race, education and occupation, that influence verbal communication. We investigate the societal forces that influence verbal communication by examining the relationships among language, perception, and power. We then discuss the important role of listening during verbal interaction. Finally, we provide suggestions for communicating more ethically and effectively, both in speaking and listening.

Once you have read this chapter you will be able to:

- Identify three reasons for learning about verbal communication.
- Describe the functions and components of language.
- Identify and give an example of each of the influences on verbal communication.
- Describe the relationship between language and perception.
- Describe the relationship between language and power.
- Identify and give an example of confirming and disconfirming communication.
- Identify and give an example of an "I" statement.
- Discuss ways to improve your own verbal communication skills.

THE IMPORTANCE OF VERBAL COMMUNICATION

Although the nonverbal aspects of communication are important, the verbal elements of communication are the foundation on which meaning is created. If you wonder about the relative importance of the verbal and nonverbal elements of communication, try to convey nonverbally "I failed my exam because I locked my keys in my car and couldn't get my textbook until well after midnight." You probably don't need to conduct this exercise if you have ever traveled in countries where you didn't speak the language; no doubt you already know that nonverbal communication can only get you so far. We will touch on the importance of nonverbal communication here and discuss it in depth in Chapter 6. In this section we propose that to be a highly effective communicator you need to understand the verbal elements of communication.

Verbal communication is also important because of the role it plays in identity and relationship development. As you might remember from our discussion in Chapter 3, individuals develop a sense of self through communication with others. More specifically, the labels used to describe individuals can impact their self-concepts and increase or decrease self-esteem. People's verbal communication practices also can impede or improve their relationships, a topic we will

Children from families who converse and eat meals together on a regular basis have higher self-esteem and interact better with their peers.

discuss further in Chapter 8. Research by two psychology professors at Emory University supports our claims about the relationship between verbal communication and an individual's identity development and relationship skills. These scholars found that families that converse and eat meals together on a regular basis have children who not only are more familiar with their family histories but also tend to have higher self-esteem, interact better with their peers, and are more able to recover from tragedy and negative events (Kurylo, 2005).

In addition, the very language people speak is tied to their identities. Studies of bilingual and multilingual speakers show that their perceptions, behaviors, and even personalities alter when they change languages (Ramírez-Esparza, Gosling, Benet-Martínez, Potter, & Pennebaker, 2006). Why does this occur? The answer is that every language is embedded in a specific cultural context, and when people learn a language, they also learn the beliefs, values, and norms of its culture (Edwards, 2004). So speaking a language evokes its culture as well as who one is within that culture. Thus the language you use to communicate verbally shapes who you are, as you will see in *It Happened to Me: Cristina.*

It Happened to Me: Cristina

I was teaching an adult education class composed primarily of Mexican immigrants when I first noticed that the language people speak affects how they behave. I'm bilingual, so even though we normally spoke English in my class, sometimes we switched to Spanish. Over time, I noticed that several male students were respectful and deferential when we spoke English; however, when we switched to Spanish, they became more flirtatious and seemed less willing to treat me as an authority figure. Now I understand that these differences probably were related to how men and women interact in the two cultures.

WHAT IS VERBAL COMMUNICATION?

Verbal communication generally refers to the written or oral words we exchange; however, as our opening example shows, verbal communication has to do with more than just the words people speak. It includes pronunciation or accent, the meanings of the words used, and a range of variations in the way people speak a language—depending on their regional backgrounds and other factors.

Language, of course, plays a central role in communication. Some argue it is our use of language that makes us human. Unlike other mammals, humans use symbols that they can string together to create new words and with which they can form infinite sets of never-before-heard, -thought, or -read sentences. This ability allows people to be creative and expressive, such as when they coin terms like "googleganger"—nominated by the American Dialect Society as one of the most creative words for 2007—meaning a person with your name who shows up when you google yourself. You can see other words of the year in *Did You Know? Words of the Year*. Even small children, unschooled in grammar, create their own rules of language by using innate linguistic ability together with linguistic information they glean from the people around them. For example, young children often say "mouses" instead of "mice" because they first learn, and apply broadly, the most common rule for pluralizing—adding an *s*.

To help you better understand the role of language in the communication process, the next section explores seven communicative functions of language as well as four components of language use.

Functions of Language

You use language so automatically that you probably don't think about the many roles it plays. However, language helps you do everything from ordering lunch, to giving directions or writing love poems. Moreover, a single utterance can function in a variety of ways. For example, a simple "thank you" not only expresses gratitude, it also can increase feelings of intimacy and liking. Consequently, understanding the ways language functions can help you communicate more effectively. As we discuss next, language can serve at least seven functions: instrumental, regulatory, informative, heuristic, interactional, personal, and imaginative.

- The most basic function of language is **instrumental**. This means you can use it to obtain what you need or desire. For instance, when you invite friends to dinner, the invitation is instrumental in that you want your friends to come to dinner and the invitation helps make that happen.

instrumental
use of language to obtain what you need or desire

Did You Know?

Words of the Year

Each year, the American Dialect Society identifies words that most dominated the national discourse:

2001: 9-11 (dates of simultaneous attacks against major buildings in NYC and D.C.)

2002: WMD (Weapons of mass destruction)

2003: metrosexual (fashion conscious heterosexual male)

2004: red state, blue state, purple states (together, a representation of the American political map)

2005: truthiness (the quality of preferring concepts or facts one wishes to be true, rather than concepts or facts known to be true, popularized by Steven Colbert)

2006: plutoed (to demote or devalue someone or something, as happened to the former planet Pluto when the General Assembly of the International Astronomical Union decided Pluto no longer met its definition of a planet)

2007: subprime (a risky or less than ideal loan, mortgage, or investment)

2008: bailout (rescue by the government of companies on the brink of failure)

Words of the Year reprinted with permission of the American Dialect Society, www.americandialect.org.

regulatory
use of language to control or regulate the behaviors of others

informative
use of language to communicate information or report facts

heuristic
use of language to acquire knowledge and understanding

interactional
use of language to establish and define social relationships

personal language
use of language to express individuality and personality

imaginative
use of language to express oneself artistically or creatively

As a student, which functions of language do you use most frequently? Which do you use most often in your professional life? If you use different functions in each of these roles, why do you think this is true?

- A second (and closely related) language function is **regulatory**, meaning that you can use it to control or regulate the behaviors of others. In your invitation, you may ask your friends to bring a bottle of wine or dessert, as a way of regulating their behavior.

- Another basic function of language is to **inform**—to communicate information or report facts. When you invite your friends to dinner, you usually include the date and time to inform them of when you want them to come.

- You also use language to acquire knowledge and understanding, which is referred to as a **heuristic** use. When you want to invite friends to dinner, you may ask them if they are available at that date and time to learn if your dinner is going to occur as scheduled or if you need to change the date.

- When language is used in an **interactional** fashion, it establishes and defines social relationships in both interpersonal and group settings. Thus, when you invite your friends to dinner, you engage in a behavior that helps maintain your relationship with them as friends.

- **Personal language** expresses individuality and personality and is more common in private than in public settings. When you invite your friends to dinner you might jokingly say, "Don't bring that cheap bottle of wine, like you did last time." In this way, you use language to express your sense of humor.

- A final way you can use language is **imaginatively**. Imaginative language is used to express oneself artistically or creatively, as in drama, poetry, or stories. Thus, if on the cover of your invitation to dinner you wrote "A loaf of bread, a jug of wine, and thou," you would be using the imaginative function of language. For another example of the imaginative use of language, see *Did You Know? A Little Poem Regarding Computer Spell Checkers.*

As our discussion thus far indicates, language has seven basic functions, and speakers use them to accomplish specific goals or tasks. Note that these functions overlap and that one utterance can accomplish more than one function at the same

Did You Know?
A Little Poem Regarding Computer Spell Checkers

Eye halve a spell chequer
It came with my pea sea
It plainly marques four my revue
Miss steaks eye kin knot sea.

Eye strike a key and type a word
And weight four it two say
Weather eye am wrong oar write
It shows me strait a weigh.

As soon as a mist ache is maid
It nose bee fore two long
And eye can put the air or rite
Its rare lea ever wrong.

Eye have run this poem threw it
I am shore your pleased two no
Its letter perfect awl the weigh
My chequer tolled me sew.

SOURCE: Retrieved March 11, 2009, from www.latech.edu/tech/liberal-arts/geography/courses/spellchecker.htm

time. For example, when inviting your friends to dinner, if you jokingly said, "James, our butler, will be serving dinner promptly at eight, so don't be late!" your utterance would both be imaginative (unless you actually have a butler named James) and regulatory. That is, you would be using language creatively while also attempting to regulate your guests' behavior to ensure they arrived on time.

Now that we have summarized the essential functions that language can serve, we next examine the basic components that allow us to use language as a flexible and creative tool of communication.

Components of Language

Scholars describe language use as being composed of four components: *phonology* (sounds), *syntax* (structure or rules), *semantics* (meaning), and *pragmatics* (use), as shown in *Visual Summary 5.1: Components of Language*, on p. 110. In this section, we examine the role each plays in the communication process.

Phonology: Sounds

Phonology is the study of the sounds that compose individual languages and how those sounds communicate meaning. Basic sound units are called phonemes. They include vowels, consonants, and diphthongs (pairs of letters that operate as one, such as *th*). For more information about phonology, see www.langsci.ucl.ac.uk/ipa/ the home page of the International Phonetic Association.

Syntax: Rules

Syntax refers to the rules that govern word order. Due to the English rules of syntax, the sentences "The young boy hit the old man" and "The old man hit the young boy" have very different meanings, even though they contain identical words. Syntax also governs how words of various categories (nouns, adjectives, verbs) are combined into clauses, which in turn combine into sentences. You should recall certain rules about combining words—for example, that the verb and subject in a sentence have to agree, so people say "the pencil *is* on the table," not "the pencil *are* on the table." Because of these rules, people combine words consistently in ways that make sense and make communication possible.

Semantics: Meaning

Semantics is the study of meaning, which is an important component of communication. To illustrate the effect of syntax compared with the effect of meaning, Noam Chomsky (1957), an important scholar in the field of linguistics, devised this famous sentence: "Colorless green ideas sleep furiously" (p. 15). While this sentence is acceptable in terms of syntax and grammar, on the semantic level, it is nonsensical: Ideas logically cannot be either colorless or green (and certainly not both!), ideas don't sleep, and nothing sleeps furiously (does it?).

As you remember from Chapter 1, a central part of our definition of communication is the creation of shared meaning. For any given message, a number of factors contribute to the creation of its meaning. Perhaps most important are the words speakers choose. For example, how would you describe a friend who always has the answer in class, gets excellent grades, and seems to have a wealth of information at his fingertips? Would you describe this friend as *smart, intelligent, clever, wise,* or *brilliant*? Because each word has a slightly different meaning, you try to choose the one that most accurately characterizes your friend. However, in choosing the

phonology
the study of the sounds that compose individual languages and how those sounds communicate meaning

syntax
the rules that govern word order

semantics
the study of meaning

'On no! The dog's eaten the Thesaurus!'

©Robert Thompson/www.CartoonStock.com

While we may recognize that this is a family from a denotative perspective, how you may know connotatively what *family* means may depend upon your experiences.

Components of Language

I Love You

Phonology

ī lŭv yōō

What do the words sound like?

Syntax

I love you

Subject — Verb — Object

How are the words arranged?

Pragmatics

What is really going on here for the people involved? What are the implications of these words for their everyday lives?

Semantics

What do the words mean?

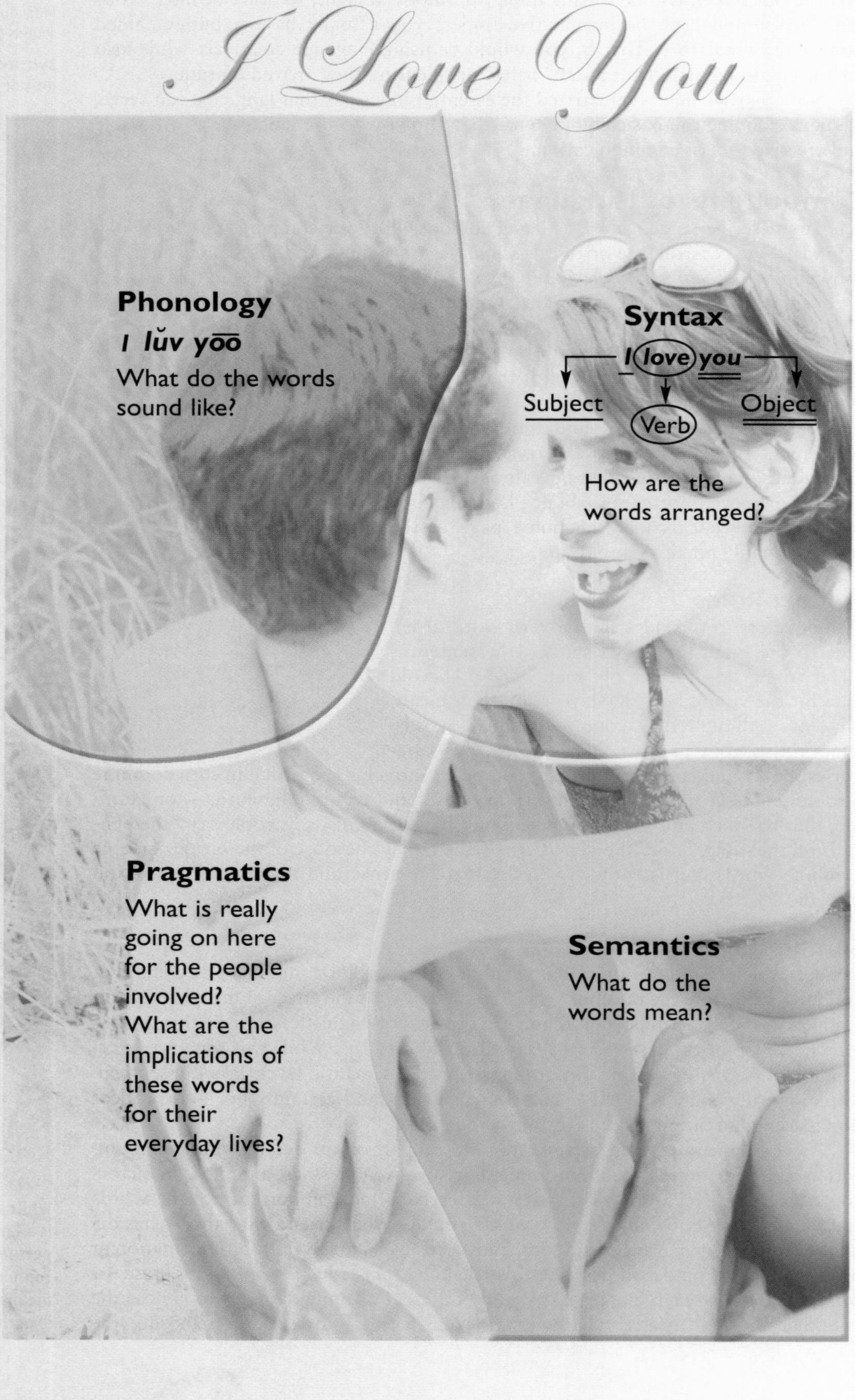

"right" words, you have to consider the two types of meaning that words convey: *denotative* and *connotative*—terms that we also discussed in Chapter 1.

The **denotative meaning** refers to the dictionary, or literal, meaning of a word and is usually the agreed-upon meaning for most speakers of the language. Referring back to our description of your friend: The dictionary defines *wise* as "Having the ability to discern or judge what is true, right, or lasting; sagacious" and *intelligent* as "Showing sound judgment and rationality" (*American Heritage Dictionary*, 2000). Does either word exactly capture how you would describe your friend? If not, which word does?

Words also carry **connotative meanings**, which are the affective or interpretive meanings attached to them. Using the previous example, the connotative meaning of the word *wise* implies an older person with long experience, so it might not be the best choice to describe your young friend.

Pragmatics: Language in Use

Just like phonology, syntax, and semantics, the field of **pragmatics** seeks to identify patterns or rules people follow when they use language appropriately. In the case of pragmatics, however, the emphasis is on how language is used in specific situations to accomplish goals (Nofsinger, 1999). For example, scholars who study pragmatics might seek to understand the rules for communicating appropriately in a sorority, a faculty meeting, or an evangelical church. They would do this by examining communication that is successful and unsuccessful in each setting. The three units of study for scholars of pragmatics are *speech acts*, *conversational rules*, and *contextual rules*. Let's examine what each contributes to communication.

Speech Acts.   One branch of pragmatics, **speech act theory**, looks closely at the seven language functions described previously and suggests that when people communicate, they do not just say things, they also *do* things with their words. For example, speech act theorists argue that when you say, "I bet you ten dollars the Yankees win the World Series," you aren't just saying something, you actually are doing something. That something you are doing is making a bet, or entering into an agreement that will result in an exchange of money.

One common speech act is the request. A recent study examined one type of request that occurs primarily in U.S. family contexts—the common practice of "nagging" (Boxer, 2002). Nagging (repeated requests by one family member to another) often concerns household chores and is usually a source of conflict. The researcher found that nagging requires several sequential acts. First, there is an initial request which is usually given in the form of a command ("Please take out the garbage") or a hedged request ("Do you think you can take out the garbage this evening?"). If the request is not granted, it is repeated as a reminder (after some lapse of time), which often includes an allusion to the first request. ("Did you hear me?" Can you please take out the garbage?") When a reminder is repeated (the third stage), it becomes nagging and usually involves a scolding or a threat, depending on the relationship, for example whether the exchange is between parent/child ("This is the last time I'm going to ask you, take out the garbage!") or between relational partners ("Never mind, I'll do it myself!").

The researcher found that men were rarely involved in nagging, and she suggests that this is because men are perceived as having more power, and are therefore able to successfully request and gain compliance from another family member without resorting to nagging. She also notes that children can have power (if they refuse to comply with a request despite their lack of status) and a parent can lack power despite having status. The researcher also found that nagging mostly occurs in our intimate relationships. She concludes that, by nagging, we lose power—but without power, we are forced into nagging; thus it seems to be a vicious cycle! The study shows that what we *do* with words affects our relationships.

denotative meaning
the dictionary, or literal, meaning of a word

connotative meaning
the affective or interpretive meanings attached to a word

pragmatics
field of study that emphasizes how language is used in specific situations to accomplish goals

speech act theory
branch of pragmatics that suggests that when people communicate, they do not just say things, they also *do* things with their words

Nagging is one common type of speech act that occurs in U. S. family contexts.

Understanding the meaning of various speech acts often requires understanding context and culture (Austin, 1975; Sbisa, 2002). For this reason, people may agree on what is *said* but disagree on what is *meant*. For example, the other day Katy said to her roommate Hiroshi, "I have been so busy I haven't even had time to do the dishes." He replied, "Well, I'm sorry, but I have been busy too." What did he think Katy was "doing" with her utterance? When they discussed this interaction, Katy explained that she was making an excuse, while Hiroshi said he heard a criticism— that because *she* hadn't had time to do the dishes, *he* should have. Thus, messages may have different meanings or "do" different things, from different persons' points of view. This difference lies in the sender's and receiver's interpretation of the statement. Most misunderstandings arise not around what was said—but around what was done or meant.

As we have seen, speech acts may be direct or indirect. That is, speech acts such as requests can be framed more (or less) clearly and directly. Let's suppose that you want your partner to feed the dog. You may directly ask "Would you feed the dog?" Or you could state an order: "Feed the dog!" On the other hand, you may communicate the same information indirectly: "Do you know if the dog was fed?" or "I wonder if the dog was fed?" Finally, you may make your request very indirectly: "It would be nice if someone fed the dog," or "Do you think the dog looks hungry?"

Which do you think is better—to communicate directly or indirectly? This is actually a trick question. The answer is: It depends—on the situation and the cultural context. Although direct requests and questions may be clearer, they also can be less polite. Ordering someone to feed the dog makes one's desire clearly and unequivocally known, but at the same time, it can be seen as rude and domineering.

Recent research shows that U.S. Americans tend to be more indirect in their requests, when compared to Mexicans (Pinto & Raschio, 2007), but probably not as indirect as many Asians (Kim, 2002). However, when expressing disagreement, most U.S. Americans tend to be more direct than most Asians. A recent study investigated how Malaysians handled disagreements in business negotiation and concluded that the Malays' opposition was never direct or on record, but always indirect and implied. Despite their disagreements with the other party, they honored the other, always balancing power with politeness (Paramasivam, 2007). A pragmatic approach reminds us that how language is used always depends on the situation and cultural context. We'll discuss more cross-cultural differences in communication practices further in Chapter 7.

Conversational rules—such as turn-taking—govern the way we communicate and vary somewhat from context to context.

Conversational Rules. Conversational rules govern the ways in which communicators organize conversation. For example, one rule of conversation in U.S. English is that if someone asks you a question, you should provide an answer. If you do not know the answer, others expect you to at least reply, "I don't know" or "Let me think about it." However, in some cultures and languages, answers to questions are not obligatory. Among Warm Spring Indians of Oregon, for example, questions may be answered at a later time (with little reference to the previous conversation) or not answered at all (Philips, 1990).

Perhaps the most researched conversational rules involve turn-taking. The most basic rule for English language speakers, and many others, is that only one person speaks at a time. People may tolerate some overlap between their talk and another's, but typically they expect to be able to have their say without too much interruption (Schegloff, 2000). Still, as a refinement of this point, Susanna Kohonen (2004) found in her cross-cultural study of turn-taking that conversationalists were more tolerant of overlaps in social settings such as at parties or when hanging out with friends.

Other rules for turn-taking determine who is allowed to speak (Sacks, Schegloff, & Jefferson, 1978). For example, if you "have the floor" you can generally continue to speak. When you are finished, you can select someone else. You can do this either by asking a question, "So Sue, what is your opinion?" or by looking at another person as you finish talking. If you don't have the floor but wish to speak, you can begin speaking just as the current speaker completes a turn.

The turn-allocation system works amazingly well most of the time. Occasionally, however, people do not follow these implicit rules. For example, the current speaker could select the next speaker by directing a question to her, but someone else could interrupt and "steal" the floor. Also, some speakers are quicker to grab the talk turn, which allows them more opportunities to speak. Then, speakers who are slower to begin a turn or take the floor have fewer opportunities to contribute to the conversation. They may feel left out or resent the other speakers for monopolizing the conversation.

Contextual Rules. No matter what language or dialect you speak, your use of language varies depending on the communication situation (Mey, 2001). For example, you probably wouldn't discuss the same topics at a funeral that you would at a bar. What would happen if you did? One challenge for pragmatics scholars, then, is uncovering the implicit communication rules that govern different settings. As noted earlier, communication pragmatics also vary by culture. For example, in some houses of worship, appropriate verbal behavior involves talking very quietly or not all, acting subdued, and listening without responding; in others, people applaud and sing exuberantly. Neither set of communication rules is "right"; each is appropriate to its own setting and cultural context.

As you can see, verbal language is far more than the words people use; it also includes the sounds and meanings of those words, and the rules individuals use for arranging words and for communicating in particular settings. Moreover, speakers differ in the ways they use language to communicate. They also differ in the ways they enunciate their words and how they present their ideas. For example, Southerners "drawl" their vowels while New Englanders drop the *r* after theirs; some speakers are extremely direct, while others are not. What accounts for these differences? We explore the answers in the next section.

INFLUENCES ON VERBAL COMMUNICATION

Your communication is influenced by your identity and the various cultures you belong to. In turn, your communication helps shape these identities. When identities influence several aspects of language, we say that speakers have a distinct **dialect**, a variation of a language distinguished by its **lexical choice** (vocabulary), grammar, and pronunciation. In other instances the influence of identity is less dramatic, and speakers vary only in some pronunciations or word choices. In this section we examine how identities related to gender, age, regionality, ethnicity and race, education and occupation shape language use.

Gender

Growing up male or female may influence the way you communicate in some situations, because men and women are socialized to communicate in specific ways. In fact, many people believe that English-speaking men and women in the United States speak different dialects. For example, women's verbal style is often described as supportive, egalitarian, personal, and disclosive, while men's is characterized as instrumental, competitive, and assertive (Mulac, Bradac, & Gibbons, 2001; Wood, 2002). Although these and other studies suggest that men and women do use different language and communication styles, other research refutes this claim. A recent review of studies comparing males and females on a large array of psychological and communication differences, including self-disclosure and interruptions, revealed very few significant differences (Hyde, 2006). In fact, the differences in men's and women's communication patterns are estimated to be as small as 1 percent, or even less (Canary & Hause, 1993).

dialect
a variation of a language distinguished by its vocabulary, grammar, and pronunciation

lexical choice
vocabulary

How can these contradictory findings be explained? To begin, many studies of gender differences ask participants to report on their perceptions or ask them to recall men's and women's conversational styles (e.g., Aylor & Dainton, 2004). This approach can be problematic because people's perceptions are not always accurate. For example, Nancy Burrell and her colleagues (1988) argue that persistent, stereotypical, gender-based expectations likely influence people's perceptions that men and women behave or communicate differently even when few behavioral differences exist. Katherine Knott and Elisabeth Natalle (1997) have found something similar—that "people often communicate and make decisions based on perceptions rather than reality" (p. 525).

How do these faulty perceptions arise about communication differences between men and women? Two important contributors are a person's perceptions of his or her own gendered communication, and media representations of men's and women's communication. Knott and Natalle (1997) and Margaret Baker (1991) explain that individuals who see themselves as being very feminine or masculine tend to view others in the same light, and they tend to have rigid views of the sexes and their communication behavior (Canary & Emmers-Sommer, 1997). The media and popular press also reinforce the belief that the sexes communicate and behave differently. Even scholarly research tends to focus on, and sometimes exaggerate, the importance of sex differences. For example, one team of researchers reviewed how journal articles talked about gender differences in the past fifty years and found that because people are more interested in hearing about differences than similarities, shows and books that emphasize these differences tend to sell better and receive wider recognition (Sagrestano, Heavey, & Christiansen, 1998). In addition, media tend to present stereotypical depictions of men and women (Wood & Dindia, 1998) in magazines, on television, and in movies.

Carol Rose (1995) asserts even more forcefully that gender-based perceptions are hard to change, whether or not the perceptions are true. For example, the negative stereotype of the talkative woman is very persistent. In one recent study, students were shown a videotaped conflict between a heterosexual couple and were asked to rate the couple on likability and competence. The researchers varied how much the man and woman talked in the conflict. Some students were shown the conflict scenario where the woman talked more, others were shown the same conflict, but where the man talked more. As predicted, the couple where the man talked less was rated as less likable than those where the woman talked less. And the man who talked more was rated as most competent (Sellers, Woolsey, & Swan, 2007). Even though this negative stereotype persists, many studies have shown that not only do women generally *not* talk more than men, actually the opposite is true—men tend to be more talkative in many situations (Leaper & Ayres, 2007; Wiest, Abernathy, Obenchain, & Major, 2006). In addition, the stereotype that women are more obliging (or accommodating) continues to exist, despite the fact that some studies have shown that stereotype to be false and that, overall, women are no more likely to oblige and no less likely to dominate than are men. Nonetheless, people act as if the stereotypes are true.

Televisions shows, like Sex and the City tend to present stereotypical depictions of men and women.

Laurie Coltri (2004) also claims that the gender of the communicator heavily influences people's perceptions of her or his communication behavior. In her study of gender stereotypes in mediation, she manipulated transcripts of mediations so that half the time Person A was identified as male and Person B as female, and half the time the reverse occurred. In each case, the person labeled as female was rated more negatively than when that same person was labeled as male. Considering the influence of perception and gender stereotypes, you can see that it can be difficult to objectively evaluate communication differences between the sexes.

Another factor that makes it difficult to assess gender differences in communication is that researchers sometimes overlook the influence of situation and relationship on individuals' language use and communication styles. For example, men and women may communicate differently when they are talking in same-sex groups but similarly in cross-sex groups (Aries, 1996). Thus, they may adapt their communication style to their audience.

When people adapt to a specific audience, they are often adjusting to the communication style of the more powerful members of that audience. Thus, if powerful members of the audience use more direct or task-focused language, so might the speaker. In addition to adapting their communication style, people also often use more deferential or tentative language when communicating with more powerful people. Both men and women adapt to these power differences; thus both groups are more likely to use tentative language with their bosses than with their siblings. Women use language that is more tentative overall because generally they have lower status, and people with lower status are not typically expected to make strong, assertive statements (Reid, Keerie, & Palomares, 2003). Women's use of more "filler words" (such as *like* or *well*) and more conditional words (*would, should, could*) (Mehl & Pennebaker, 2003) probably also is a response to their less powerful status in society.

In a recent study, researchers wanted to see if some gender differences in conversations are a consequence of interacting with a partner who uses a particular style of communication. For example, if you encourage another person to talk by nodding your head in agreement, asking questions, or giving supportive linguistic cues (such as "- [uh-huh]," or "yes . . .,") you are using a facilitative style of communication (Hannah & Murachver, 2007). In the study, male and female partners (who were strangers to each other) met and talked several times. After the first conversation, partners were judged by outside observers to be either facilitative or nonfacilitative; and researchers found that their partners responded to each other in systematic ways, regardless of gender.

Over time, however, in subsequent conversations, women and men shifted their speech toward more stereotypically gendered patterns; that is, the men talked more, for longer times, while women increased their use of minimal responses, reduced the amount they spoke, and asked more questions. In other words, the women increased their facilitative style of speech. The researchers pose the question: Why are women more facilitative in their speech? Why do they talk less when talking with men? Do they feel threatened or insecure? Are they less comfortable in talking more than men? The authors of this research suggest that women may find that dominating the conversation with men has negative social consequences for them and, therefore, they encourage men to do the talking—an explanation that would be confirmed by the earlier study we mentioned, where students negatively evaluated couples where the women talked more than the men. The researchers provide no definitive explanation, but note, as do we, that gender differences are complicated (Hannah & Murachver, 2007).

In conclusion, women and men do show differences in their communication styles, and much of this difference likely is attributable to differences in power, status, and expectations in communication situations.

Age

You may not think of age as affecting language use, but it does, particularly when it comes to word choice. For example, you might have talked about "the cooties" when you were a child, but you probably don't now. Moreover, children have a whole vocabulary to describe "naughty topics," especially related to bodily functions. Yet, most adults do not use those words. Adolescents also develop vocabulary that they use throughout their teenage years and then drop during early adulthood. Adolescents have described highly valued people and things as "cool," "righteous," "bad," "hot," and "phat" depending on the generation and context. This distinct vocabulary helps teenagers feel connected to their peers and separate from their parents and other adults. See *Did You Know? Contemporary Slang*, on p. 116 for other examples of teen slang terms.

Did You Know?

Contemporary Slang

Here are some examples of contemporary slang used by various groups in the United States. Which do you recognize or use?

w'sup: What's Up?

> **Example:** W'sup man?

W.O.S.: the acronym for "walk of shame," which means going to work in the clothes you were wearing the following day due to excessive partying and/or sleeping somewhere you didn't expect.

> **Example:** Did you see? Charlotte did the W.O.S. this morning.

wacked: (adj) Crazy, messed up, stupid, or just doesn't make any sense. Usually when you say wacked, you are completely shocked by what you have just seen or experienced.

> **Example:** Did you see that? He just chugged a gallon of eggnog. That is wacked.

wail: To attack physically or verbally. Variant spelling of *whale*.

> **Example:** You should have seen how those two guys were wailing on each other.

Walken: A disquietingly creepy person or situation. From Christopher Walken characters.

> **Example:** There's Franco over by the bar. Man, that guy can sure walkenize a room.

Wallace and Grommit: To vomit.

> **Example:** Where's Pete? He's out back having a good Wallace and Grommit.

walmart: Inexpensive and readily available but often substandard.

> **Example:** I bought that thing last week at three in the morning and it's broken already; it's so walmart.

warden: Nickname for the parents.

> **Example:** No partying at the house tonight, the warden's home.

ADAPTED FROM: Pseudodictionary.com. Reprinted by permission of H.D. Fowler. Copyright © 2009 H.D. Fowler.

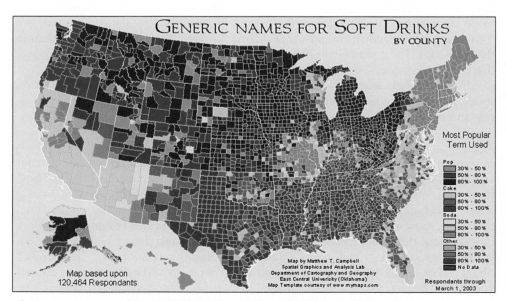

The terms we use to refer to soft drinks also vary by region in the United States. Note these geographical differences on this map.

The era in which you grew up also influences your vocabulary. As you age, you continue to use certain words that were common when you were growing up, even if they have fallen out of use. This is called the **cohort effect** and refers to common denominators of a group that was born and reared in the same general period. For example, your grandparents and their contemporaries may refer to dancing as "cutting a rug," while younger speakers rarely use this term. However, recent research suggests that young girls may be becoming the trendsetters in language use both for their own and other cohorts. Some linguists argue that girls in southern California are influencing young men's—and even older women's—language use; they call it the "northern California vowel shift." For example, "Like, what dew you mean, tha-yt I ha-yvee an accent?" At a recent meeting of a high school club in southern California called Girls for a Change, teen girls gathered to discuss ways to fix cultural ills; they talked about social action as "something important to *dew*." Among different approaches, they considered "*tew-toring*." There is evidence that young men and some older women are beginning to adopt some of the sounds started by teenage girls. As new ways of saying things find their way in the general language, a regional—or even statewide—dialect emerges (Krieger, 2004).

People's communication skills and the meanings they attribute to concepts also vary due to their age. Why? Older people are more cognitively developed and have had more experiences; therefore they tend to view concepts differently than do younger people, especially children (Pennebaker & Stone, 2003). For example, children typically engage in egocentric speech patterns (Piaget, 1952). This means that they cannot adapt their communication to their conversational partners nor understand that others may feel or view the world differently. Children lack the number of constructs adults have. For example, very young children have little concept of future or past time, so understanding what might happen next week or month is difficult for them. Consequently, parents usually adapt their communication when trying to help children understand some event in the future.

Regionality

Geographical location also strongly influences people's language use. The most common influence is on pronunciation. For example, how do you pronounce the word "oil"? In parts of New York it is pronounced somewhat like "earl," while in areas of the South it is pronounced more like "awl," and in the West it is often pronounced "oyl" as in "Olive Oyl." Sometimes regionality affects more than just accent, leading to regional dialects. Why do these differences arise?

Historically, wherever a geographical boundary separated people, whether it was mountains, lakes, rivers, deserts, oceans, or some social boundary, such as race, class, or religion, verbal differences developed (Fromkin & Rodman, 1983). Moreover, people tend to speak similarly to those around them. For example, in the eighteenth century, residents of Australia, North America, and England had relatively little contact with one another; consequently, they developed recognizably different dialects even though they all spoke the same language. Typically, the more isolated a group, the more distinctive their dialect.

In the United States, dialectical differences in English originally arose because two groups of English colonists settled along the East Coast. The colonists who settled in the South, near present-day Virginia, primarily came from Somerset and Gloucestershire—both western counties in England—and they brought with them an accent with strongly voiced *s* sounds and with the *r* strongly pronounced after vowels. In contrast, the colonists who settled in the north, what we now call New England, came from midland counties such as Essex, Kent, and London, and they possessed a dialect that did not pronounce the *r* after vowels, a feature still common to many New England dialects (Crystal, 2003).

Other waves of immigration have occurred over the past four hundred years, increasing dialectical diversity in the United States. Each group of immigrants brings a

cohort effect
the influence of shared characteristics of a group that was born and reared in the same general period

Alternative VIEW
The Great American Vowel Shift

Conventional wisdom says that dialects should be disappearing, due to increasingly transient populations, immigration from other countries, and the influence of pervasive mass media. However, University of Pennsylvania linguist William Labov and his colleagues published a phonological atlas (2005) showing that across the country, regional dialects are stronger than ever. In a radio interview, he described some these specific changes. Do you think that regional accents influence communication between people from different areas of the United States?

The most important differences have developed in this huge area around the Great Lakes region which we call the Inland North, going from Buffalo,

Syracuse, Cleveland, Detroit, Chicago, Milwaukee. Those great cities occupied by about 35 million people are all moving in a very different direction from the rest of the United States.

Now what happens here is the short-*a* becomes "ai" [like in "yeah"] in every single word, so that people have, say, "theaht" and "feahct." In the meantime, the short words spelled with short-*o* like "socks" or "block" or "cot" move into the position that was formerly occupied by "ah." So the man's name [John becomes] "Jahn"—that's man's name, "Jahn." And the girl's name [Jan] becomes "Jain". . . This example of a sound change in the United States called the "Northern Cities Shift."

SOURCES: Voice of America (VOA) radio interview with William Labov on January 12, 2005. Retrieved June 2, 2008, from www.voanews.com/specialenglish/archive/2005-01/a-2005-01-11-5-1.cfm.

Labov, W. (Ed.). (2005). *Atlas of North American English*. New York: Walter De Gruyter, Inc.

distinctive way of speaking and culture-specific communication rules. Some groups, especially those who have remained somewhat isolated since their arrival, maintain much of their original dialect, such as the inhabitants of Tangier Island in the Chesapeake Bay (Crystal, 2003). Other groups' dialects have assimilated with the dialects of their neighbors to form new dialects. Thus, the seventeenth-century "western" English dialect of Virginia has become the southern drawl of the twenty-first century.

Today the world is a global village, so people from all over the country and the world are in contact with one another or have access to similar media. Nonetheless, according to a recent comprehensive study, local dialects are stronger than ever (Labov, 2005; Preston, 2003). This is due in large part to the fact that people tend to talk similarly to the people they live around and hear speak every day. Thus, dialectic differences originally occurred because of patterns of isolation, but they persist because of exposure. As people have increasing contact and access to a range of language models, dialectic differences may become less pronounced, but it will be a long time—if ever—before they completely disappear, as is discussed in *Alternative View: The Great American Vowel Shift*.

Ethnicity and Race

One's ethnicity can influence one's verbal style in a number of ways. In the United States, English is a second or colanguage for many citizens. This, of course, influences syntax, accent, and word choice. For example, if one is Latino/Latina and learns Spanish either before or at the same time as one learns English, one may use the same syntax for both. Thus, Spanish speakers may place adjectives after nouns (*the house little*) when they are speaking English because that is the rule for Spanish. The reverse can also occur: When English speakers speak Spanish, they have a tendency to place adjectives before nouns, which is the rule for English but not for Spanish.

Speakers' ethnicity can also influence their general verbal style. For example, Jewish Americans may engage in a style of talking about problems that non-Jews perceive as complaining (Bowen, 2003); some Native American tribes use teasing as a form of public rebuke (Shutiva, 2004); and some Chinese Americans who live in the southern United States are particularly likely to let other speakers choose conversational topics (Gong, 2004). When two ethnic or racial groups speak the same language but use different syntax, lexical items, or verbal style, one or both of the groups may view the other's verbal style as incorrect, as a failed attempt at proper speech rather than as a dialect with its own rules (Ellis & Beattie, 1986).

These views can have important real-life implications—political and monetary. Take the controversy about **Ebonics**—a version of English that has its roots in West African, Caribbean, and U.S. slave languages. There is no agreed-upon definition. Some linguists emphasize the international nature of the language (as a linguistic consequence of the African slave trade); others stress that is a variety of English (e.g. the equivalent of Black English) or as different from English and viewed as an independent language. For more information on the various definitions of Ebonics see http://en.wikipedia.org/wiki/Ebonics). The controversy over definition has had important real-life consequences. A few years ago the Oakland, California, school board passed a resolution that recognized Ebonics as a separate language, not just a dialect. The resolution instructed teachers to "respect and embrace the language richness of Ebonics." But more important, they required schools to provide English as a second language instruction to students who spoke Ebonics as their first "language." A number of teachers and policymakers viewed Ebonics as simply substandard English, not even a dialect, and were not willing to recognize it as a legitimate language nor provide funds for English language instruction (Wolfram, Adger, & Christian, 1999). This language controversy had far-reaching implications—involving not only the teachers and parents, but linguists and policymakers.

Education and Occupation

We will discuss education and occupation together because they are often mutually influencing. For example, medical doctors speak a similar language because they share a profession, but also because they were educated similarly. Typically, the more educated people are, the more similarly they speak (Hudson, 1983). Thus, larger dialect differences occur between easterners and midwesterners if they have not been to college than if they have doctoral degrees. This does not mean that all lawyers talk the same or that all professors speak similarly; rather, it suggests that differences become less pronounced as people receive more education.

Education affects dialect in part because any given university or college attracts people from different parts of the country. Therefore, college students have contact with a variety of dialects. At the same time, as students attend college they develop similar vocabularies from their shared experiences and learn similar terms in their classes. For example, you may never have used the term *dyad* to refer to two people before you went to college, but this is a term you might encounter in a range of courses, including psychology, sociology, anthropology, and communication.

Your occupation also influences the specialized terms you use to communicate. The specialized terms that develop in many professions are called **jargon**. Professors routinely speak of *tenure*, *refereed journals*, and *student credit hours*. Physicians speak of *contusions* (bruises), *sequelae* (results), and *hemorrhagic stroke* (a stroke where a blood vessel bursts). In fact, most occupations have their own jargon. In addition to influencing your lexical choices, your occupation may also influence your overall communication style—including tone of voice, and some nonverbal behaviors. For example, nursery school

Ebonics
a version of English that has its roots in West African, Caribbean, and U.S. slave languages

jargon
the specialized terms that develop in many professions

Physicians, like members of other professions, develop specialized terms called jargon.

nominalists
those who argue that any idea can be expressed in any language and that the structure and vocabulary of the language do not influence the speaker's perception of the world

relativists
those who argue that language serves not only as a way for us to voice our ideas but "is itself the shaper of ideas, the guide for the individual's mental activity"

Sapir-Whorf hypothesis
idea that the language people speak determines the way they see the world (a relativist perspective)

teachers are often recognizable not only by their vocabulary but also by the rhythm, volume, and expressivity of their communication style.

To sum up, then, various features of language—phonology, syntax, semantics, and pragmatics—contribute to the development of meaning in verbal communication. These features combine with individual influences in language use, such as gender, age, and level of education, to create one's specific communication style. However, we have not yet covered every aspect of verbal communication. We now turn to the influence of societal forces on verbal communication.

THE INDIVIDUAL, VERBAL COMMUNICATION, AND SOCIETY

How do societal forces influence verbal communication? Culture and power are two of the most important influences. Culture impacts verbal communication primarily through its influence on language and perception. Power is connected to verbal communication because within society, some language styles are viewed as more powerful, with consequences for both the powerful and the powerless.

Language and Perception

Scholars have long argued about the influence of language and culture on perception. The central issue they have debated is whether the words a culture has available to it impact how its members see and perceive the world around them. For example, the English language expresses action in the past, present, and future. Thus, English speakers may say "Alan went to the library" (past), "Alan is at the library" (present), or "Alan will be going to the library" (future). In contrast, Japanese makes no distinction between the present and future. Although the verb for "went" is *ikimashita*, the verb used for both "is" and "will be going" is the same, *ikimasu*. Because English and Japanese have two different verb structures, scholars have questioned whether English speakers and Japanese speakers think about present and future actions in different ways. Scholars who have debated this relationship between language and perception generally fall into two camps: the *nominalists* and the *relativists*.

Nominalists claim that any idea can be expressed in any language and that the structure and vocabulary of the language do not influence the speaker's perception of the world. According to nominalists, English and Japanese may express present and future in different ways, but English speakers and Japanese speakers still understand the distinction.

In contrast, the **relativists** argue that language serves not only as a way for us to voice our ideas but "is itself the shaper of ideas, the guide for the individual's mental activity" (Hoijer, 1994, p. 194). This idea is the basis for the **Sapir-Whorf hypothesis**. The Sapir-Whorf hypothesis argues that the language people speak determines the way they see the world. Adherents to this hypothesis believe language is like a prison, as it constrains the ways individuals can perceive the world (Koerner, 2000). According to this hypothesis the distinction between the present and the future is not as clear-cut for Japanese speakers as it is for English speakers. As another example, surfers have many more words for the types of waves in the ocean than do nonsurfers (Scheibel, 1995); the Sapir-Whorf hypothesis argues that, because of this, surfers perceive more types of waves than do others.

Surfers have many more words for the types of waves in the ocean than do nonsurfers.

So how much does language influence perception? The Sapir-Whorf hypothesis position has been challenged by a number of scholars who investigate the connection between language and how we think (Kenneally, 2008). They represent a modified relativist position on the relationship between language and perception. Steven Pinker (2007), a renowned cognitive scientist, for example, cautions against assuming a simplistic connection between language and thought, and rejects the Sapir-Whorf assumption that the particular language we speak compels us to perceive the world in a particular way or prevents us from thinking in different ways. He uses the example of applesauce and pebbles to argue that we naturally categorize (and therefore label) these two substances differently (as "hunk" and "goo"). By looking at language from the perspective of our thoughts, Pinker shows that what may seem like arbitrary aspects of speech, (hunk and goo distinction), aren't arbitrary at all: They are by-products of our evolved mental machinery. In sum, all languages have the formal and expressive power to communicate the ideas, beliefs, and desires of their users. From this vast range of possibilities, human communities select what they want to say and how they want to say it. (Li & Gleitman, 2002, p. 291). This view allows for more freedom than indicated by the Sapir-Whorf hypothesis.

Language and Power

In many ways, language and power are inextricably connected. People in power get to define what languages and communication styles are appropriate. In addition, people who use language and communication according to the rules of the powerful may be able to increase their own power. This view of the relationship between language and power is explained by *cocultural theory*. **Cocultural theory** explores the role of power in daily interactions using the five following assumptions:

1. In each society a hierarchy exists that privileges certain groups of people, and in the United States, these groups include men, European Americans, heterosexuals, the able-bodied, and middle- and upper-class people.

2. Part of the privilege these groups enjoy, often subconsciously, is being able to set norms for what types of communication are acceptable or not acceptable (Orbe, 1998). Consequently, communication patterns of the dominant groups (in the United States, rich, male, White, educated, straight) tend to be more highly valued. For example, the preferred communication practice in many large corporations is still that used by White males—direct, to-the-point, task oriented, and unemotional (Kikoski & Kikoski, 1999).

3. Language maintains and reinforces the power of these dominant groups, again, mostly subconsciously. Thus, people whose speech does not conform to what is valued in society may be excluded and/or negatively stereotyped. As we noted earlier, commentators sometimes characterize women's speech as sounding more tentative than male speech. Because society values male speech styles at work, women in corporate leadership positions often are criticized for not being direct or tough enough, or for being too cooperative or nurturing in their communication practices.

4. In the relationship realm, society tends to value a more female communication style, and men may be critiqued for failing to communicate appropriately with their intimates. Remember that none of these language variations is inherently good or bad, powerful or powerless; it is the societal hierarchies that teach us how to view particular communication practices. Of course, not every White male is direct, to-the-point, and task-oriented, nor does every woman speak tentatively at work. Nor is every woman supportive and self-disclosive, and every man distant and terse in close relationships. These generalizations can help explain communication practices, but they should not solidify into stereotypes.

cocultural theory
explores the role of power in daily interactions

5. These dominant communication structures impede the progress of persons whose communication practices do not conform to the norms. For example, what are the consequences for women who do not conform to "male" communication norms in a corporation? Or for African Americans who do not conform to "White" communication norms of the organizations in which they work? Or for students who do not conform to the "middle-class" communication norms at a university? Most likely they will be labeled negatively ("not serious enough," "soft," "doesn't have what it takes") and marginalized.

We explore these ideas further in Chapter 7. Now, let's look at how these societal hierarchies affect attitudes toward words, accents, and dialects, and how they impact identity labels.

Power and Words

Attitudes about power can be built into language by certain roots or by the very structure of the language. Consider words like *chairman, fireman,* or using "he" as the generic to mean human. While people used to think that it didn't matter whether we used masculine pronouns or words to mean *human,* researchers discovered that people didn't think human when someone mentioned the word *man*—they thought about a man. Similarly, terms such as *Mr.* (not designating marital state) and *Mrs.* (which does) have resulted in changes—like Ms. and he/she.

While some languages, such as Japanese or Korean, are much more gendered (where traditionally, men and women used almost a separate language), English is somewhat gendered—or androcentric. *Androcentrism* is the pairing of maleness with humanity and the consequent attribution of gender difference to females—often to women's disadvantage. Scholars recently reviewed fifty years of psychology articles for androcentric bias. While they found few uses of "he" for *human,* information was still portrayed in a way that emphasized male as the norm. Male data was placed first in tables, and gender differences were often described as female—subconsciously assuming that male is the norm and female is different. Researchers point out that being different is not necessarily harmful but probably reflects some of the underlying stereotypes (and societal hierarchies) we have discussed earlier (Hegarty & Buechel, 2006).

What are the implications for students? We argue that it's not about freedom of speech or being overly politically correct, but rather about audience and awareness. Gender-neutral language has gained support from most major textbook publishers, and from professional and academic groups, as well as major newspapers and law journals. As English professor Carolyn Jacobson (2008) suggests "If you anticipate working within any of these contexts, you will need to be able to express yourself according to their guidelines, and if you wish to write or speak convincingly to people who are influenced by the conventions of these contexts, you need to be conscious of their expectations."

Specific suggestions for avoiding this kind of built-in bias are presented in *Did You Know? Avoiding Bias in Language.*

Did You Know?
Avoiding Bias in Language

The American Psychological Association (APA) provides suggestions for avoiding gender and heterosexual bias in writing. Which view of language is represented here, nominalist or relative? What are the reasons for or against following these suggestions? Which groups of people do you think would be more in favor of these changes, those with or without power in U.S. society? What do you think of the "further alternatives"? Would you use them?

Did You Know? *(continued)*

Using Gender-Neutral Language

- **Use "they" as a singular.** Most people, when writing and speaking informally, rely on singular "they" as a matter of course: "If you love someone, set them free" (Sting). If you pay attention to your own speech, you'll probably catch yourself using the same construction yourself. Some people are annoyed by the incorrect grammar that this solution necessitates, but this construction is used more and more frequently.

- **Use "he" or "she."** Despite the charge of clumsiness, double-pronoun constructions have made a comeback: "To be black in this country is simply too pervasive an experience for any writer to omit from her or his work," wrote Samuel R. Delany. Overuse of this solution can be awkward, however.

- **Use pluralizing.** A writer can often recast material in the plural. For instance, instead of "As he advances in his program, the medical student has increasing opportunities for clinical work," try "As they advance in their program, medical sudents have increasing opportunities for clinical work."

- **Eliminating pronouns.** Avoid having to use pronouns at all; instead of "a first grader can feed and dress himself," you could write, "a first grader can eat and get dressed without assistance."

- **Further alternatives.** "He/she" or "s/he," using "one" instead of he, or using a new generic pronoun (thon, co, E, tey, hesh, hir).

Avoiding Heterosexual Bias in Language

- **Use "sexual orientation" rather than "sexual preference."** The word "preference" suggests a degree of voluntary choice that is not necessarily reported by lesbians and gay men and that has not been demonstrated in psychological research.

- **Use "lesbian" and "gay male"** rather than "homosexual" when used as an adjective referring to specific persons or groups, and lesbians and gay men. The word "homosexual" perpetuates negative stereotypes with its history of pathology and criminal behavior.

- **Such terms as "gay male" are preferable** to "homosexuality" or "male homosexuality" and so are grammatical reconstructions (e. g., "his colleagues knew he was gay" rather than "his colleagues knew about his homosexuality"). The same is true for "lesbian" over "female homosexual," "female homosexuality," or "lesbianism."

- **Bisexual women and men, "bisexual persons," or "bisexual"** as an adjective refer to people who relate sexually and affectionally to women and men. These terms are often omitted in discussions of sexual orientation and thus give the erroneous impression that all people relate exclusively to one gender or another.

- **Use "gender" instead of "sex."** The terms "sex" and "gender" are often used interchangeably. Nevertheless, the term "sex" is often confused with sexual behavior, and this is particularly troublesome when differentiating between sexual orientation and gender.

SOURCES: Some notes on gender-neutral language. Retrieved May 23, 2008, from www.english.upenn.edu/~cjacobso/gender.html

Avoiding heterosexual bias in language. Retrieved May 23, 2008, from www.apastyle.org/sexuality.html

Power and Accent

Where did people learn that an English accent sounds upper crust and educated? Or that English as spoken by an Asian Indian accent is hard to understand? Why do communicators often stereotype Black English as sounding uneducated? While these associations come from many sources, they certainly are prevalent in the media. People have become so accustomed to seeing and hearing these associations that they probably don't even question them. In fact, William Labov, a noted sociolinguist, refers to the practice of associating a dialect with the cultural attitudes toward it as "a borrowed prestige model." For example, until the 1950s, most Americans thought that British English was the correct way to speak English (Labov, 1980); even today, people continue to think that an English accent sounds very refined and educated. On the other hand, Southern drawls and Black English have become stigmatized so that today, people who speak them are often perceived negatively. For similar reasons, people often find the English accent of people from India (where English often is a first language) difficult to understand—as reported by our student in *It Happened to Me: Bart.*

It Happened to Me: Bart

I recently had a course taught by an Asian Indian professor, and it took me some time to understand his accent and form of speaking. Sometimes I thought he was mumbling, and sometimes his speech sounded so fast that I couldn't understand. After a couple of classes, my hearing disciplined itself to understand him better. In the end, I realized he was a fine teacher.

Such language stereotypes can be "set off" in one's head before a person even speaks, when one *thinks,* generally because of the person's appearance, that she or he will not speak Standard English (Ruben, 2003). This is probably what happened to our student, Bart. Once he adjusted to the Indian English accent, he found he could understand his Indian professor just fine. [For examples of accents from many different language backgrounds, go to http://classweb.gmu.edu/accent/]

How does one group become elevated and another denigrated? The answer lies partly in understanding the social forces of history and politics. The positive and negative associations about African American, White, and British English developed during the nineteenth and twentieth centuries when European Americans were establishing themselves as the powerful majority in the United States, while passing legislation that subjugated African Americans and other minority groups. Thus it is not surprising that the languages of these groups were viewed so differently. Similarly, the English spoken by people from India was negatively stereotyped as the aberrant language of the colonized, since England was the colonial power in India until the mid-twentieth century. Similar attitudes can be seen toward immigrant groups today; their accented English is often stigmatized, sometimes leading to language discrimination and lawsuits, as illustrated in *Did You Know? Language Discrimination.*

Did You Know?
Language Discrimination
The American Civil Liberty Union provides the following legal explanation of language discrimination:

What is language discrimination?
Language discrimination occurs when a person is treated differently because of that person's native language or other characteristics of that person's speech. In an employment situation, for example, an employee may be being subjected to language discrimination if he or she is treated less favorably than other employees because he or she speaks English with an accent, or if the employee is told he or she does not qualify for a position because of a lack of English proficiency. Outside the employment context, language discrimination may also occur if a person is denied access to businesses or government services because he or she does not speak English.

Is language discrimination illegal?
Although the law in this area is still developing, many courts and governmental agencies consider language discrimination to be a form of discrimination on the basis of race or national origin, which are prohibited by well-established civil rights laws such as Titles VI and VII of the Civil Rights Act of 1964 (a federal law), and the California Fair Employment and Housing Act (a state law). Other laws, such as the federal Civil Rights Act of 1866, may also apply to such discrimination.

Power and Identity Labels

The language labels that refer to particular identities also communicate important messages about power relations. Members of more powerful groups frequently invoke labels for members of other groups without input from those group members. For example, straight people label gays, but rarely refer to themselves as straight. White people use ethnic and racial labels to refer to others (*people of color*, *African American*, or *Black*), but rarely refer to themselves as White. This power to label seems "normal," so most people don't think twice about specifying that a physician is a "woman doctor" while never describing one as a "male doctor." Or they might identify someone as a gay teacher, but not a White teacher (even if this teacher is both). People usually don't think about the assumptions that reflect societal power relations; in sum, individuals feel the need to mark minority differences, but they tend not to identify majority group membership.

Not only do the more powerful get to label the less powerful—they may also use language labels to stigmatize them. However, the stigma comes from the power relations, not from the words themselves. For example, *Polack* simply means "a man from Poland" in the Polish language, but the stigma associated with the term comes from the severe discrimination practiced against Eastern Europeans in the early twentieth century, which led to jokes and stereotypes that exist to this day. The term *Oriental* originated when Western countries were attempting to colonize, and were at war with, Asian countries—and the connotative meaning was *exotic* and *foreign*. Today, many Asians and Asian Americans resent this label. Read about one of our student's opinions on the topic in *It Happened to Me: Hiroko*.

This resentment can make communication more difficult for Hiroko and those who use this term to refer to her. As this example reveals, understanding the dictionary meanings of words does not always reveal the impact of identity labels. Members of minority communities are the best informants on the communicative power of specific labels.

Not everyone in an identity group has the same denotative meaning for a particular label. For example, some young women do not like to be called "girl"; they find it demeaning. Others are comfortable with this term. Some people view these calls for sensitivity in language as nothing more then unnecessary political correctness, as

Think about labels and terms we have for males and females. Why do you think so many more negative terms exist for females than for males?

It Happened to Me: *Hiroko*

I get really tired of people referring to me as "Oriental." It makes me sound like a rug or a cuisine. I refer to myself as Asian American or Japanese American. I know people probably don't mean anything negative when they use it, but it makes me uncomfortable. If it's somebody I know well, I might ask them not to use that word, but usually I just don't say anything.

Alternative VIEW

Nappy-Headed Ho Tops Politically Incorrect Phrases for 2007

Paul JJ Payack, President and Chief Word Analyst of The Global Language Monitor (GLM) compiled the following list of words nominated by the GLM's "Language Police" (volunteer language observers from the world over), as the most egregious politically incorrect phrases. Which view of language does Payack's essay represent—the nominalist or relativist?

"Nappy-headed Ho," closely followed by "Ho-Ho-Ho" and "Carbon Footprint Stomping" top the list of the most egregious examples of politically incorrect language found in 2007 by the Global Language Monitor in its annual global survey. This year's list includes words and phrases from the U.S., the UK, Australia, and China. "It is no surprise that a 'Nappy-headed Ho' was selected as the Top Politically Incorrect word or phrase for 2007," said Paul JJ Payack, President and Chief Word Analyst of *The Global Language Monitor* (GLM). "A year later that phrase is still ricocheting about the Internet even affecting Christmas-season Santas in Australia."

The Top Politically Incorrect Words and Phrases for 2007:

1. Nappy-headed Hos—Radio personality Don Imus' reference to the women on the Rutgers University championship basketball team. "Nappy" is ultimately derived from the Anglo Saxon hnoppa for the "wooly substance on the surface of cloth." Combined with the word "ho"—a derogratory term for women, Imus' comments led to an uproar in the media and ultimately led to his resignation.

2. Ho-Ho-Ho—Staffing company in Sydney suggesting to prospective Santas to rephrase their traditional greeting of "ho, ho, ho" in favor of "ha, ha, ha" so as not be confused with American urban parlance, a derogatory term for women.

3. Carbon footprint stomping—The movement to flaunt carbon-intensive activities such as driving Hummers and flying private jets; a reaction to the Green movement is the height of political incorrectness.

4. Fire-breathing Dragon—Lindsey Gardiner, a leading British children's author of the popular Lola, Poppy, and Max characters, was instructed to eliminate a fire-breathing dragon from her new book because publishers feared they could be sued under health and safety regulations.

FROM: "'Nappy-Headed Ho' Top Politically inCorrect Phrase for 2007 Closely Followed by 'Ho-Ho-Ho' and 'Carbon Footprint Stomping'", *The Global Language Monitor*, March 21, 2008, www.languagemonitor.com. Reprinted by permission of Paul J. J. Payack, The Global Language Monitor.

seen in *Alternative View*: Nappy-Headed Ho *Tops Politically Incorrect Phrases for 2007*. Moreover, the power of labels can change over time. In an earlier age, many viewed the term *WASP* (White, Anglo-Saxon, Protestant) as a descriptor or even a positive label; now, however, it is seen as rather negative (Martin, Krizek, Nakayama, & Bradford, 1999). The shift probably reflects the changing attitudes of Whites, who are now more aware of their ethnicity and the fact that they are not always the majority. Similarly, the term *Paddy* as in "paddy wagon" (a term for police wagon) originally was a derogatory term. It reflected a stereotype, widely held one hundred years ago, of Irish men as drunks who had to be carted off to jail. Now that discrimination (and stereotyping) against the Irish has all but disappeared, this term has lost much of its impact.

In summary, language, power, and societal forces are closely linked. The societal environment profoundly influences the way people perceive the world and the language choices available to them. Those in power set the language and communication norms, often determining what verbal communication style is deemed appropriate or inappropriate, elegant or uneducated. They frequently get to choose and use identity labels for those who are less powerful. Those whose language does not fit the standard, or who are the recipients of negative labels, may feel marginalized and resentful, leading to difficult communication interactions.

ETHICS AND VERBAL COMMUNICATION

We have already discussed a number of ethical issues related to verbal communication in this book. In Chapter 1 we argued that ethical communicators consider the benefit and/or harm associated with their messages. In this section we examine one specific type of language whose use may harm individuals or relationships.

Confirming and Disconfirming Communication

One type of communication that can be unethical because of the harm it can cause is *disconfirming communication*. **Disconfirming communication** occurs when people make comments that reject or invalidate a self-image, positive or negative, of their conversational partners (Dance & Larson, 1976). Consider the following conversation:

> **Tracey:** Guess what? I earned an A on my midterm.
>
> **Lou:** Gee, it must have been an easy test.

Lou's response is an example of disconfirming communication, because it suggests that Tracey could not have earned her A because of competence or ability. Consequently, his message disconfirms Tracey's image of herself. You can disconfirm people either explicitly ("I've never really thought of you as being smart") or implicitly (as Lou did).

How can messages such as these cause harm? Imagine that you received numerous disconfirming messages from people who are important to you. How might it affect you? Such messages not only can negatively influence your self-image, but they also can impair your relationships with the people who disconfirm you. For instance, Harry Weger, Jr. (2005) and John Caughlin (2002) have found that when couples engage in disconfirming behavior, their marital dissatisfaction increases. Disconfirming messages can harm both individuals and relationships and may be considered unethical as well as ineffective.

If you want to avoid sending disconfirming messages, what should you do instead? You can provide others with confirming messages. Confirming messages validate positive self-images of others, as in the following example of **confirming communication**.

> **Tracey:** Guess what? I earned an A on my midterm.
>
> **Lou:** That's great. I know it's a tough class; you deserve to be proud.

Confirming messages are not only more ethical, they are usually more effective. Most people enjoy communicating with those who encourage them to feel good about themselves. Although engaging in confirming communication will not guarantee that you will be instantly popular, if you are sincere, it will increase the effectiveness of your communication and ensure that you are communicating ethically. If using confirming communication does not come naturally to you, you can practice until it does.

You might be wondering how you can provide negative feedback to people without being disconfirming. We discuss how to do this next.

"I" Statements

One type of disconfirming message involves making negative generalizations about others. Although you recognize that people are complex and variable, have you nevertheless found yourself making negative generalizations such as those listed here?

> "You are so thoughtless."
>
> "You are never on time."

disconfirming communication comments that reject or invalidate a positive or negative self-image of our conversational partners

confirming communication comments that validate positive self-images of others

As you can see, negative generalizations (which also are called "you" statements) are typically disconfirming. But, in the real world everyone lives in, some people *are* thoughtless, and some *are* consistently late. So is there an ethical and effective way to make your dissatisfaction known? Yes. You can use a type of message called an "I" statement. "I" statements allow you to express your feelings (even negative ones) by focusing on your own experiences rather than making negative generalizations (or "you" statements) about others.

"I" statements are conveyed through a three-part message that describes

1. the other person's behavior,
2. your feelings about that behavior, and
3. the consequences the other's behavior has for you.

Taking the examples just given and rewriting them as "I" statements, you could come up with:

"When you criticize my appearance (behavior), I feel unloved (feeling), and I respond by withdrawing from you (consequence)."

"I think I must be unimportant to you (feeling) when you arrive late for dinner (behavior), so I don't feel like cooking for you (consequence)."

Strong verbal statements are likely to trigger defensive reactions from those targeted by the attacks.

"You" statements often lead recipients to feel defensive and/or angry because of the negative evaluation contained in the message, and because the listener resents the speaker's position of passing judgment. "I" statements are useful not only because they arouse less defensiveness, but because they force speakers to explore exactly what they are dissatisfied with, how it makes them feel, and the consequences of the other person's behavior. "I" statements prevent speakers from attacking others in order to vent their feelings. They also are more effective than "you" statements because the receiver is more likely to listen and respond to them (Kubany, Bauer, Muraoka, Richard, & Read, 1995).

While many communication scholars believe in the value of "I" statements, a recent study found that people reacted similarly to *both* "I" and "you" statements involving negative emotions. However, the authors point out that their study involved written hypothetical conflict situations. They admit that their results might have been different if they had studied real-life conflict situations (Bippus & Young, 2005).

Although "I" statements can be very effective in a variety of contexts, this does not mean they are *always* appropriate. Situations may arise where others' behavior so violates what you believe is decent or appropriate that you wish to state your opinions strongly. Thus, if your friend abuses alcohol or takes illicit drugs, you may need to say "You should not drive a car tonight" or "You need to get help for your addiction." The effectiveness of one's verbal communication must always be evaluated in the context of the situation, the relationships one has with others, and one's goal.

IMPROVING YOUR VERBAL COMMUNICATION SKILLS

When considering the ethics of language use, you should think about the effectiveness of your verbal choices. What are some guidelines for engaging in more effective verbal communication? We describe three areas in which you might improve: You can become more aware of the power of language; you can understand the stages, barriers, and approaches to listening; and finally, you can sharpen your listening skills.

COMMUNICATION IN SOCIETY
Mind Your (Terror) Language

This author describes the attempt to use language that is less offensive to Arabs and Muslims when discussing political issues. How important is the language we use in political discourse? What are the reasons for changing our language in the way the author suggests?

Khody Akhavi

From the people who brought you the "war on terror" and the "axis of evil" comes a new verbal tonic for combating that amorphous emotion. Out with pejoratives like "Islamo-fascists," "jihadis" and "mujahideen," and in with "words that work," that is according to a George W. Bush administration memo that was leaked last month to the Associated Press.

The non-binding 14-point guide on counterterrorism communication, prepared by the U.S. National Counterterrorism Center (NCTC), urges U.S. officials to drop language and terminology that may offend Arab and Muslim communities, to use terms such as "violent extremist" or "terrorist" instead of "jihadi," and to shift the discussion away from the dualistic "clash of civilizations" or battle between "Islam and the West," a paradigm that casts Islam as inherently violent.

"A mujahid, a holy warrior, is a positive characterization in the context of a just war. In Arabic, jihad means 'striving in the path of God' and is used in many contexts beyond warfare. Calling our enemies jihadis and their movement a global jihad unintentionally legitimizes their actions," according to the report. "We need to emphasize that terrorists misuse religion as a political tool to harm innocent civilians across the globe."

Other points suggest using the word "totalitarian to describe our enemy" because, according to the report, the term is widely understood in the Muslim world. Keep the focus on the terrorist, not us, it says, and don't ascribe "al-Qaeda and its affiliates motives or goals they have not articulated. Out audiences have more familiarity with the terrorist messages than we do and will immediately spot U.S. government embellishment."

Talking tough on terror has been the main currency of the Republican Party, and the main project of neo-conservative pundits in Washington. . . . The inspiration may have come from Bush confidante and hand-holder Karen Hughes, who acted as an advisor to the administration. . . . Her year-long effort to change the U.S. image abroad did yield a 34-page document that calls for the U.S. to mind its language. "Avoid characterizing people of any faith as 'moderate'—this is a political word which, when extended to the world of faith, can imply these are less devout and faithful. The terms 'mainstream' or 'majority' are preferable," according to Hughes' report.

For U.S.-based Muslim advocacy groups, delinking religious identity from the slippery slope of terror talk is a welcome change. "It is a good step that they at least take these terms into consideration," Ibrahim Hooper, a spokesman for the Council on Islamic American Relations, told Inter Press Service. "What terms are used and what not are a matter of debate. At least, we should all be thinking about this."

FROM: "Mind Your (Terror) Language," by Khody Akhavi, *Asia Times Online*, May 21, 2008. Reprinted by permission of Asia Times Online (www.atimes.com).

Become Aware of the Power of Language

As we noted in Chapter 1, language is a powerful force that has consequences and ethical implications. Wars have been started, relationships have been ruined, and much anger and unhappiness has resulted from intentional and unintentional verbal messages. The old adage "Sticks and stones can break my bones, but words will never hurt me" is not always true. Words *can* hurt, as shown *Communication in Society: Mind Your (Terror) Language* describing language offensive to many Arabs and Muslims.

When a speaker refers to others by negative or offensive identity terms, the speaker not only causes harm, he or she also denies those labeled individuals their identities—even if it isn't intentional. For example, one of our students, Cynthia, told us how bad she felt when she realized that some of her gay coworkers were offended by her use of the term "homosexual" (instead of gay). They explained that "homosexual" was used as a description of a psychiatric disease by the American Psychiatric Association's list of mental disorders until 1973, and has a connotation of this sexual orientation as a cold, clinical "condition." Using her embarrassment as a learning experience, she initiated an enlightening discussion with her coworkers. She learned that often the best way to discover what someone "wants to be called" is to ask. However, a conversation of this nature can only occur in the context of a mutually respectful relationship—one reason to have a diverse group of friends and acquaintances.

Improve Your Receiving (Listening) Skills

Many people value speaking over listening. This is probably due to the strong emphasis on oral communication in U.S. culture. In addition, people receive more rewards for being a good speaker than for being a good listener. Politicians and salespeople are rewarded for how well they make speeches and how well they sell themselves verbally. However, listening is a vital professional communication skill. For example, many of the characteristics of good leaders are the same characteristics as those of good listeners (Bentley, 2000). Listening is an important everyday part of relationships (Alberts, Yoshimura, Rabby, & Loschiavo, 2005; Pecchioni & Halone, 2000). Yet, despite its importance, and despite the existence of many courses and books on how to give successful speeches, people are rarely taught how to listen effectively. (If you want to understand how to be a bad listener, see *Did You Know? Poor Listening Habits*.) So what are the keys to better listening?

Did You Know?
Poor Listening Habits

Experts on listening behavior suggest the following as poor listening habits in two different contexts: listening in social conversation and to public speeches. Have you ever found yourself guilty of any of these? In general, what messages are communicated by these poor listening habits?

- **Interrupting or rushing the speaker, or finishing his/her thoughts.** Sometimes we interrupt or rush because we're excited about the conversation; whatever the reason, it sends a message of disrespect and lack of regard for the speaker, making them feel that they're wasting our time. What we have to say is more valuable. . . .

- **Saying, "Yes, but . . ."** Quick responses like this communicate that the listener has made up his/her mind before actually hearing all that the speaker wants to say.

- **Forgetting what was talked about previously.** Not paying close attention to the speaker can lead us to forget what the speaker has said to us.

- **Deciding quickly that the subject material will not be interesting.** Sometimes we hear a few words from a speaker and decide that the rest is not worth listening to. . . .

- **Pretending attention.** We pretend to listen by giving signals (such as nodding our heads) that would indicate we are listening while, in fact, our minds are focused elsewhere.

- **Yielding to distraction.** The human brain can understand 600 words per minute, however most of us speak at about 120 words per minute. This gives us time to be distracted and not focus on the speaker.

- **Yielding to emotional deaf spots.** There are particular words (specific to each of us) that can trigger negative emotions. As soon we hear one of these words, our ingrained prejudice focuses onto the word and its inferences, and the remainder of the theme is lost. The word has effectively derailed the train of thought.

- **Overanalysis:** Sometimes we hear an argument and begin to mentally compile a list of reasons why it will not work, going over arguments and counterarguments . . . in so doing we have tuned out the speaker and ignored potential useful information and interrupted the chain of communication.

ADAPTED FROM: Nichols, R. G., & Stevens, L. A. (1957). *Are you listening?* Boston: McGraw-Hill. Retrieved March 11, 2009, from http://skills.library.leeds.ac.uk/learnhigherleeds/documents/listening/listening_habits.pptt

First, we must distinguish between two communication processes: hearing and listening. Hearing is the biological act of receiving sounds; listening is an active process of assigning meaning to those sounds. People often presume that if they heard someone, they were listening to what was said. However, when you listen, you not only know what was said; you also understand the emotional content of the conversation and what the person meant by his or her words. To help you become a more effective listener, we will first describe four stages of listening, then identify three barriers to listening, and finally explain three approaches to listening effectively. We will then provide suggestions on how to become a more effective and ethical listner.

Four Stages of Listening

Listening occurs in four stages: *sensing*, *understanding*, *evaluating*, and *responding* (Rosenfeld & Berko, 1990), as shown in *Visual Summary 5.2: Stages of Listening*, on page 132. **Sensing** is the stage most people refer to as "hearing"; it occurs when listeners pick up the sound waves directed toward them. For example, even a "quiet" room has many sounds, such as the hum of heating or ventilation, quiet conversations, or the sounds of a radio. For communication to occur, you must first become aware that information is being directed at you. In other words, you actually have to hear the sounds.

Once you sense that sounds are occurring, you have to interpret the messages associated with the sounds, or **understand** what the sounds mean. For example, you are alone watching a horror movie when you hear a knocking sound. What meaning do you assign it? Is it a friend dropping by to say hello, or a stranger trying to break into your house? The meaning you assign affects how you will respond—both physiologically and communicatively.

After you understand (or at least believe you understand) the message you have received, you **evaluate** the information. When you evaluate a message, you assess your reaction to it. For example, do you believe the story Josie just told? Are you happy your boss recommended you for a promotion? Was the compliment you received sincere? Evaluation is an essential part of the listening process—and your evaluations influence your responses.

Finally, you **respond** to messages. Your response provides the most significant evidence that you are listening to others. Responding means that you show others how you regard their messages. For example, you might respond to a funny story by laughing, to a complaint with an apology, to an apology with forgiveness. Even failing to respond is a type of response! You can respond in numerous ways; however, your response may be influenced by *how* you listen.

Barriers to Listening

People have many reasons for not listening to others, but some typical ones include physical or physiological barriers, psychological barriers, and poor listening habits. (Active Listening, 1999; Nichols, 1995.) Physical barriers include a noisy environment, physical discomforts that make it difficult to concentrate, or hearing impairments. Psychological barriers include boredom, preoccupation, and conflicting listening objectives. Let's explore in more detail how these psychological factors can interfere with effective listening.

A second, related psychological barrier is preoccupation. People often think of other things and, thus, do not listen to what is being said. In addition, people who are feeling strong emotions, such as anger or fear, may be too preoccupied to listen. Emotions also play a significant role in how you understand, evaluate, and react to messages. If you are frustrated or irritable, you are more likely to interpret casual comments as criticism. Thus a wide variety of emotions, from joy to anger to disappointment, can distract you and influence how you listen and respond to communicative interactions.

sensing
the stage of listening most people refer to as "hearing"; when listeners pick up the sound waves directed toward them

understanding
interpreting the messages associated with sounds or what the sounds mean

evaluating
assessing your reaction to a message

responding
showing others how you regard their message

Stages of Listening

STIMULUS

STAGE 1
Sensing
"Michelle is calling."

STAGE 2
Understanding
"She's asking me out."

STAGE 4
Responding
"I'd love to!"

STAGE 3
Evaluating
"I think I like that idea."

Sometimes emotions make people defensive. Defensive listening occurs when someone perceives, anticipates, or experiences a threat (Eadie, 1982; Gibb, 1961). In such cases, the listener often puts up a "wall" for protection. These walls can distort incoming messages, leading to misinterpretation. For example, one of our colleagues described how her emotional reactions to her father hindered her listening to him: "We had such a rotten relationship, and every time he even opened his mouth to speak, I was so defensive, so sure he was going to criticize me or yell at me that I never even heard a word he said." Some people are more defensive than others; their personalities and experiences have influenced them to respond defensively to many messages. However, certain types of messages are more likely to elicit defensive listening. For example, messages that are evaluative, controlling, superior, or dogmatic tend to prompt a defensive reaction.

Possessing preconceived ideas about issues or participants is related to being emotionally defensive. For example, if you expect your sibling to be angry at you, it is likely you will interpret any comment as hostile. By the same token, if you are habitually sarcastic, then others are likely to hear even your compliments as insults. Unfortunately, people often find it difficult to acknowledge their own preconceptions, let alone recognize those of others.

A third and final psychological barrier to listening involves conflicting objectives. How people understand and react to others' communicative attempts depends in part on their objective(s) for the conversation. For example, how do you listen to a lecture when your instructor announces, "This will be on the midterm"? How do you listen when told the material will not be on a test? Your different objectives for these situations likely influence how well you listen.

Sometimes participants to a conversation differ in their objectives for an interaction. For example, during a business meeting Hank's objective was to explain a new procedure for evaluating employees, while Roberta's objective was to get a raise. Consequently, they focused on different aspects of their conversation, assigned different meanings to what occurred, and remembered different aspects of their meeting. Of course, people may have multiple objectives for an interaction, each of which will influence how they listen and respond.

Three Ways of Listening

In addition to overcoming barriers to listening, good listeners engage in a type or style of listening that is appropriate for the situation. Three ways of listening have been identified (Purdy, 2000). *Rational listening*, which is listening as thinking, is the predominant type. In this kind of listening, you evaluate the speaker's verbal and nonverbal cues, trying to figure out what the speaker means based on what is said as well as what is not said. For example, you ask your roommate if he borrowed your car while you were away. When he answers, you not only listen to the content of his reply, you also scrutinize his nonverbal behavior to determine if he's telling the truth.

A second way of listening, *relational listening*, focuses on listening to understand how the other person feels. This type of listening is a key part of relationships (Halone & Pecchioni, 2001). Listening activities that help build better relationships include setting aside time to listen to one another, being open-minded when listening, listening even if one does not want to listen, and just being there to listen to a friend or relational partner who is in need (Alberts et al., 2005; Pecchioni & Halone, 2000). The final type of listening, referred to as *conscious listening*, involves being in tune with the world around you so that you can understand yourself and society. Conscious listening reflects the ability to synthesize rational and relational listening in order to create a comprehensive understanding of others.

Although all listening is interpersonal, not all of it happens in face-to-face encounters. In the twenty-first century, more conversations are occurring asynchronously, which means that the speaker and listener are not engaging in the communication process at the same time, as with email. In these communication situations, issues related to asking questions and giving feedback pose new challenges. Technology also has made synchronous communication, such as via cell phones, more commonplace, making it possible to communicate with more people, more often. These changes mean you may now have to listen even more carefully, since you must take into account where the speaker is, what other activities are distracting him (such as driving, changing baby diapers, grocery shopping), and who else may be listening on the speaker's end. Technology also has made information overload more commonplace, so people may need to be more selective in their listening as they filter out unneeded information (Bentley, 2000). We will address technology and communication in more depth in Chapter 13. In the meantime, here are some suggestions for what you can do to become a more effective and ethical listener.

1. **Talk less.** Most people enjoy talking more than listening. Give the other person a chance to talk.

2. **Keep an open mind.** As we indicated in Chapter 1, receivers have a responsibility to listen critically and openly to what is being said. Listening with an open mind will not only make you a more ethical listener, it will also make you a better listener because you will be focusing on what the other person says rather than using that time to create counterarguments.

3. **Focus on the speaker.** Control distractions; sit so you can comfortably see and hear the speaker. Give your full attention to the speaker. Sit or stand so that you are facing the speaker, making direct eye contact.

4. **Provide nonverbal feedback.** In Chapter 1 we discussed the ethical responsibilities of receivers to provide healthy feedback. Doing so will also make you a better listener. If you are providing feedback, such as nodding your head or saying "I see," you will pay more attention to the speaker's comments.

5. **Provide verbal feedback.** Asking questions will help keep you involved in the conversation because you will be learning something new. Acknowledging the speaker's feelings will let the person know you are listening ("You sound really upset about this"). Paraphrasing or restating the speaker's ideas and waiting for feedback will let you know if you're on track in your understanding. It will also help you to be attentive.

6. **Empathize.** Attempt to understand the speaker's emotions and express your understanding both verbally and nonverbally. Watch for nonverbal cues from the speaker that may signal how he or she is really feeling.

7. **Monitor how you are listening.** Are you trying to second guess what the speaker will say? Do you interrupt the speaker? One way to avoid this is to count to ten after the speaker has stopped talking. This gives the person a chance to continue if she has more to say—and it gives you practice in pausing before speaking.

SUMMARY

Verbal communication plays a significant role in people's lives, assisting in relationship development, creating identities, and accomplishing everyday tasks. Language is the foundation of verbal processes and it functions in at least seven ways: instrumental, regulatory, informative, heuristic, interactional, personal, and imaginative. The four components of language study are phonology, the study of sounds; syntax, the grammar and rules for arranging units of meaning; semantics, the meaning of words; and pragmatics, the rules for appropriate use of language.

Individual influences on language include speakers' memberships in various identity groups (gender, age, regionality, ethnicity and race, education and occupation). When identities influence several aspects of language (vocabulary, grammar, and pronunciation), these speakers have distinct dialects. In other instances identity groups' language variations may be minor, involving only some pronunciation or word choices.

Societal forces affect verbal processes because they shape our perceptions and the power relationships that surround us. The language used in a given society influences its members' perceptions of social reality, while power relationships affect how its members' verbal patterns are evaluated.

Communicating more ethically involves using confirming language and "I" language when expressing dissatisfaction; improving verbal communication skills involves recognizing the power of language and improving listening or receiving skills. Listening is a key element in verbal interaction, but people often overlook its importance. Speakers can improve their listening skills by attending to the three types of listening—rational, relational, and conscious—and by overcoming a range of physical and psychological barriers.

KEY TERMS

instrumental 107
regulatory 108
informative 108
heuristic 108
interactional 108
personal language 108
imaginative 108
phonology 109
syntax 109
semantics 109

denotative meaning 111
connotative meaning 111
pragmatics 111
speech act theory 111
dialect 113
lexical choice 113
cohort effect 117
Ebonics 119
jargon 119
nominalists 120

relativists 120
Sapir-Whorf hypothesis 120
cocultural theory 121
disconfirming communication 127
confirming communication 127
sensing 131
understanding 131
evaluating 131
responding 131

TEST YOUR KNOWLEDGE

1. What are the seven functions of language? Give an example that illustrates how each works.
2. What is phonology? Syntax? Semantics? How do they work together to facilitate effective communication?
3. What do pragmatics scholars study? How do they determine pragmatics in specific communication contexts?
4. What is the difference between connotative and denotative meaning?
5. How do regional dialects develop?
6. How do our gender, age, and ethnicity and race influence the way we speak?
7. What is the difference between the nominalist and relativist perspectives on the relationship between language and perception? Which viewpoint makes more sense to you? Why?

APPLY WHAT YOU KNOW

1. For each scenario, write a paragraph describing a typical communication exchange. For each, think about the various elements of verbal communication: sounds, grammar, meaning (word choice), conversational rules, and contextual rules.

   - an informal family outing
   - a meeting with your advisor
   - a bar, where you are trying to impress potential partners

   Hint: Working in a small group, see whether you and your classmates can come up with some shared contextual rules for communication in these various situations. Give some reasons why you can or cannot come up with shared rules.

2. Take three sheets of paper and write one of the following words on each sheet: *garbage*, *milk*, *mother*. Take the first piece of paper and crumple it up and then stomp on it. Do the same with the second and third pieces. How did you feel crumpling up and stomping on the first piece of paper? The second? The third? What does this say perhaps about the difference between denotative and connotative meanings?

3. Think about two accents or dialects you've heard, either in a personal encounter or on radio or television. For each one, answer the following questions:

   - Do you have a negative or positive association for this dialect/accent?
   - Where did these associations (negative or positive) come from?
   - How might these associations (negative or positive) influence the way you communicate with a person who uses this accent or dialect?

   Share your answers with your classmates. Do you have similar reactions and associations for the same accent or dialect? What does this say about the power of society in influencing perceptions about communication and language use?

4. For each of the examples that follow, create an "I" statement that expresses your feelings about the situation:

   - Once again your roommate has borrowed some of your clothes without asking and has returned them dirty and/or damaged.
   - For the third time this semester, your instructor has changed the date of an exam.
   - Your good friend has developed a habit of canceling plans at the last moment.
   - Your romantic partner embarrasses you by teasing you about personal habits in front of friends.

   Form a group with two or three of your classmates. Take turns reading your "I" statement for each situation. Discuss the strengths and weaknesses of each statement. As a group, develop an "I" statement for each situation above that best expresses the group's feelings without encouraging defensiveness in the receiver.

5. Locate five people who either grew up in different parts of the United States or who grew up in different countries. Try to include both men and women and people of different ages in your sample. Ask each person to answer the following questions:

   - What do you call a carbonated beverage?
   - How do you pronounce "roof"?
   - What expressions do you use that some other people have had trouble understanding?
   - What does the term *feminist* mean?
   - Who do you think talks "different"?

EXPLORE

1. Go to: http://classweb.gmu.edu/accent/, where you can listen to accents from many different language backgrounds, reading the same paragraph. Listen to several recordings. For each recording, answer these questions: What impressions do you have of the speaker? Educated? Uneducated? Clever? Interesting? Someone you'd like to get to know? Think about where your impressions and meanings came from. How might these impressions affect the way you communicate with someone who has this accent?

2. Go to: http://linguistlist.org/topics/ebonics/. This Web site provides an overview of the California Ebonics controversy. It has links to the original and amended resolution passed by the Oakland Unified School district and to a discussion board on this topic. Think about communication between teacher and students in the classroom. How might a teacher communicate with a child who speaks Ebonics if the teacher considers Ebonics (1) a language, or (2) a substandard version of English?

3. Go to: www.arches.uga.edu/~bryan/AAVE/. This is a Web site that provides information on the origin of Ebonics and the distinction between a dialect and a language. After reading this material, do you think Ebonics is a dialect or a language—or neither? How might your view on this influence how you communicate with someone who speaks Ebonics to you?

6
Nonverbal Communication

chapter outline

THE IMPORTANCE OF NONVERBAL COMMUNICATION

WHAT IS NONVERBAL COMMUNICATION?

NONVERBAL COMMUNICATION AND THE INDIVIDUAL
Influences on Nonverbal Communication
Nonverbal Codes
The Functions of Nonverbal Messages

✕ THE INDIVIDUAL, NONVERBAL COMMUNICATION, AND SOCIETY
Nonverbal Communication and Power
Nonverbal Communication, Prejudice, and Discrimination

✕ ETHICS AND NONVERBAL COMMUNICATION

✕ IMPROVING YOUR NONVERBAL COMMUNICATION SKILLS

Recently a colleague took her four-year-old daughter with her to a business meeting. After observing the interaction for a few minutes, her daughter Anna whispered, "When it's your turn to talk, you have to make your mad face."

Even though Anna is only four years old, she is sensitive to the nonverbal behavior of others. She readily reads others' facial expressions and assigns meaning to them. From a very early age, all children learn the basics of nonverbal communication (Boone & Cunningham, 1998); in fact, infants just a few hours old respond to others' nonverbals. For example, when newborns observe caregivers sticking out their tongues, they imitate them and do the same (Als, 1977).

In this chapter, we take a close look at the intricacies of nonverbal communication and the many factors that shape nonverbal messages and their interpretation. First, we describe the importance of nonverbal communication, provide a definition, and explore how it differs from nonverbal behavior. We then give you an overview of the various types of nonverbal codes, and we examine the functions that nonverbal messages serve. We next explore how societal forces intersect with individuals' nonverbal communication. We conclude the chapter by discussing ethical issues in nonverbal communication and providing you with suggestions for improving your nonverbal communication skills.

Once you have read this chapter, you will be able to:

- Explain the important role of nonverbals in the communication process.
- Distinguish between nonverbal behavior and nonverbal communication.
- Identify four factors that influence the meaning of nonverbal communication.
- Define five nonverbal codes.
- Discuss the five functions of nonverbal messages.
- Articulate the role of power in nonverbal communication.
- Understand how prejudice and discrimination are triggered by nonverbal communication and can be expressed through it.
- Discuss six guidelines for ethical nonverbal communication.
- Name five ways to improve your ability to interpret nonverbal.

THE IMPORTANCE OF NONVERBAL COMMUNICATION

We devote an entire chapter to nonverbal communication because of the important role it plays in interaction. Nonverbals help us express and interpret the verbal aspects of communication—such as when a person smiles to indicate her verbal message is intended as a joke. Nonverbals also communicate messages in and of themselves, as when people use the "OK" sign to indicate that they are all right. We also devote a full chapter to this topic because nonverbal communication can be complex and ambiguous—both to convey and to interpret.

If we begin learning nonverbal communication as children, why do we often have difficulty interpreting others' nonverbal communication? Likely it is due to the fact that humans express a wide array of nonverbal behaviors, many of which can be quite subtle. Consequently, understanding nonverbal communication requires knowledge and skill. However, don't rush out to buy a paperback that promises to teach you to "read a person like a book." Unfortunately, no book, not even this one, can give you the ability to interpret every nonverbal behavior in every context.

Why not? Because understanding nonverbal communication requires that you interpret behavior and assign meaning to it, and you don't always have the information you need for that. If you notice a stranger staring at you, what does it mean? Does the person think he knows you? Is he interested in you? Is he being aggressive? Or is the person simply lost in thought and only *appearing* to be looking at you? As you can see, nonverbal cues can be ambiguous. Because a variety of factors, including context, culture, and even intentionality, determine the meaning of a specific nonverbal behavior, interpreting an individual behavior can be tricky. In addition, nonverbal cues are continuous, meaning that people exhibit nonverbal behaviors virtually all the time they are conscious. Therefore, it can be difficult to decide what behaviors are acting in concert to create a given message. For example, Joan was talking to her husband about their need to spend time together to strengthen their marriage. Just when her husband asked what she wanted to do about their marriage, she happened to look over at her computer screen and saw it go blank. In frustration, she threw up her hands and sighed heavily. Even though she was responding to her computer failure, her husband thought she was responding to his question, and his feelings were hurt.

Nonverbal communication also can be difficult to interpret because nonverbal cues are multichanneled; that is, they can be transmitted in a variety of ways simultaneously. Speakers can convey nonverbal messages through their facial expressions, voice qualities, eye gaze, posture, gestures, and by other channels we will discuss throughout this chapter. Moreover, because a variety of cues may occur at the same time, it can be difficult and confusing to keep up with everything (Schwartz, Foa, & Foa, 1983). If, for example, you are focusing on someone's face, you may miss important messages conveyed by the body.

Popular press books on nonverbal communication typically assume that each behavior has one meaning regardless of the context or who is performing it. Such explanations don't distinguish between nonverbal behavior and nonverbal communication; nor do they consider context, culture, individual variations in behavior, or the relationship that exists between the people being observed. All these factors, and more, can influence the meaning of a nonverbal behavior in a specific instance. So don't believe that just because someone has her arms crossed over her body, it means she is closed off to you. It may just mean she needs a sweater.

Nonverbals are not only complex and ambiguous—they are also key components of communication. Understanding nonverbal communication can make you a better *verbal* communicator. In addition, nonverbal communication can help you navigate everyday life. For example, humans rely on nonverbal signals to determine if other humans are a threat. In the television show *Going Tribal,* journalist Bruce Parry visited the remote Suri tribe in Ethiopia. As he approached the first tribal member, Parry carefully observed the tribesman thrust his bow and arrow at him and pace quickly back and forth while averting his eye gaze. Although many

Even young children understand and use nonverbal communication.

Nonverbal communication can highlight or emphasize a verbal message.

of the Suri's nonverbal behaviors communicated belligerence, the fact that he did not stare aggressively influenced Bruce to approach him slowly with a gift of tobacco—which was accepted.

Similarly, on a daily basis people need to be able to read subtle nonverbal behaviors in order to assess how friendly or hostile others may be. This is especially true for individuals whose identities are less valued culturally or whose societal position makes them more vulnerable. Because of this vulnerability, such individuals tend to become quite adept at reading and interpreting nonverbal communication. In a study that compared African Americans' and White Americans' ability to read the nonverbal behaviors of Whites, researchers found that African Americans were far better at detecting prejudicial attitudes as expressed in subtle nonverbal behavior than were Whites (Richeson & Shelton, 2005). Similarly, a study of heterosexual and gay men found that gay men were better able to identify the sexual orientation of unfamiliar men when watching videos of them (Shelp, 2002).

Nonverbal communication also is important because it can affect public policy decisions. For example, more and more schools have begun to institute dress codes. The supporters of this policy argue that school uniforms "help erase cultural and economic differences among students" (Isaacson, 1998) and improve student performance and attendance. This claim rests on the assumption that one form of nonverbal communication, attire, should be regulated because it provides a distraction and disruption. Efforts to ban flag burning in the United States and France's ban on Muslim girls wearing headscarves in school are other examples of public policy attempts to regulate nonverbal expression. Countries would not engage in efforts to control nonverbal expression if it were not so important.

WHAT IS NONVERBAL COMMUNICATION?

The nonverbal components of communication include all the messages that people transmit through means other than words. We communicate nonverbally when we wave hello, blow a kiss, or, like the sorority members pictured, we wear clothing that signals our group membership. Even more frequently, nonverbal and verbal aspects of communication combine to convey messages, as when we indicate anger by turning our backs and saying "I don't want to talk with you right now." However, not all nonverbal behavior is communicative, either intentionally or not. In the discussion that follows, we explain the differences between nonverbal behavior that is communicative and that which is not.

Nonverbal behavior refers to all the nonverbal actions we engage in, from scratching various body parts to moving in time to music. **Nonverbal communication**, in contrast, occurs when nonverbal behavior has symbolic meaning (DeVito & Hecht, 1990). So nonverbal communication stands for something, while nonverbal behavior may not. For example, scratching one's arm usually isn't intended by the scratcher, nor understood by the observer, to convey a particular message. Although it may provide information (that one's arm itches), it doesn't necessarily signal an intentional message. Rather, it is considered an involuntary bodily "output." However, in baseball a manager may scratch his arm to signal that a runner on base should steal home. In this case, scratching the arm is symbolic and therefore, an instance of nonverbal communication.

Of course, many actions exist that generally are not considered communicative but can still convey messages nonverbally. For example, people usually cough because of a scratchy throat or yawn because they are tired, and these behaviors are not communicative. However, when you cough as a signal to capture someone's attention or yawn to indicate you are bored, you are engaging in nonverbal communication. So, how can an observer decide whether a behavior is communicative?

These sorority members signal their group membership nonverbally through their clothing and gestures.

nonverbal behavior
all the nonverbal actions people perform

nonverbal communication
nonverbal behavior that has symbolic meaning

Communication researchers cite three factors. As a rule, they say we can assume nonverbal behavior is communicative when (1) members of a social group *regularly* use it to communicate, (2) the social group typically interprets it as *intentional*, and (3) the members have a *recognized*, agreed-upon interpretation for the behavior (Burgoon, Buller, & Woodall, 1996).

Consider, for example, thumb sucking. Many children suck their thumbs, but we rarely think of it as communicative, because we don't have an agreed-upon meaning for the behavior—nor do children usually do it to send a message. However, if a group of suburban adolescents begin to suck their thumbs to signal someone is behaving childishly, then their behavior *is* communicative. Why? The behavior is symbolic, has an agreed-upon meaning, and is recognized as intentionally relaying a message.

However, some nonverbal communication does lack the element of intentionality. For example, a smile may be understood as an expression of pleasure even if the smiler is unaware that he is smiling. Thus if a behavior typically is used communicatively, then that behavior is understood to be part of our nonverbal "vocabulary" and will be interpreted as such, regardless of one's own conscious use of it (Burgoon, Buller, & Woodall, 1996).

As our discussion thus far suggests, at times it can be difficult to differentiate nonverbal communication from nonverbal behavior. This is another reason that neither we, nor anyone else, can provide you with interpretations for specific nonverbal actions. Because of this difficulty, many people conflate nonverbal behavior and nonverbal communication; therefore, they often overestimate the amount of meaning that nonverbal communication contributes to the overall meaning in an interaction. To see the range of estimates for how much meaning nonverbal components convey in any message, see *Did You Know? How Much Does Nonverbal Communication Contribute to Meaning?*

Did You Know?
How Much Does Nonverbal Communication Contribute to Meaning?

How much of the meaning of a message do you think is conveyed by its nonverbal components? Fifty percent? Seventy-five percent? One of the most common beliefs about communication is that over 90 percent of the meaning of a message is transmitted by its nonverbal elements. However, most scholars now agree that number significantly overstates the true contribution of nonverbal messages.

In 1971, Mehrabian, a researcher, claimed that 93 percent of meaning is conveyed through the nonverbal aspects of communication. Specifically, he argued that 38 percent of meaning is derived from paralinguistic cues and 55 percent from facial expressions, leaving only 7 percent of meaning to be provided by the verbal message. However, a variety of scholars have contradicted this claim. In 1970, anthropologist Ray Birdwhistell argued that only 65 percent of meaning was derived from nonverbal messages. This percentage is now being accepted as closer to accurate, although it is impossible to determine an exact figure.

Mehrabian's analysis exhibited several problems. First, he did not consider the contributions to meaning made by gestures and posture. Second, he tried to estimate the contribution of particular nonverbal behaviors—for example, paralinguistic versus facial expression. In practice, however, no one behavior is particularly useful in determining meaning. So many factors influence each person's body movements that we cannot accurately distinguish which is the most meaningful. Thus, Patterson (1982, 1983) suggests that only correlated groups of behaviors—stance, posture, facial patterns, and arm movements—can combine to provide us with an accurate hypothesis about a person's meaning. In other words, inferences made about the meaning of any given action are not all that reliable, nor are estimates of what percentage of the total message one single gesture communicates.

NONVERBAL COMMUNICATION AND THE INDIVIDUAL

If a smile is viewed as communicating pleasure even when the smiler doesn't intend to do so, then why don't all behaviors that are part of our nonverbal vocabulary always convey the same meaning? The answer is that assigning one simple meaning to a nonverbal behavior ignores the multiple meanings that may exist, depending on the context in which the behavior occurs. For example, you will read in this chapter that when a person leans toward another (called a *forward body lean*), this is often a sign of interest or involvement. Does that mean that the forward body lean always indicates interest? Absolutely not! A person might lean forward for a variety of reasons: her stomach hurts, the back of her chair is hot, or her lower back needs to be stretched.

To understand the meaning of a nonverbal behavior you have to consider the entire behavioral context, including what the person might be communicating verbally (Jones & LeBaron, 2002). Therefore, interpreting others' nonverbal behavior requires that you consider a variety of factors that can influence meaning. To interpret nonverbals, you also need to know the codes, or symbols and rules, that signal various messages. Finally, you will benefit from a familiarity with the variety of ways that nonverbal messages function. These are topics we take up next.

Influences on Nonverbal Communication

Culture is one of the more important factors that influences the meaning of nonverbal communication. In the United States the "thumbs up" signals success, and the "hitchhiker's thumb" asks for a ride, but these nonverbal signs carry potentially vulgar meanings in a variety of other cultures. In East Africa, instead of pointing with fingers, people often point with their lips—a gesture that is completely unfamiliar to most people in the United States. Thus, the meaning of any nonverbal behavior is defined by the cultures of those interacting (Axtell, 1993; Segerstrale & Molnár, 1997). In Chapter 7, we'll discuss in more detail how culture influences communication.

In addition to culture, the relationship between the people interacting affects the meaning of nonverbal behaviors (Manusov, 1995). If a husband takes his wife's hand as they are crossing the street, the meaning is some mixture of care and affection; however, if a boss were to do the same with a subordinate, the meaning is more complex and potentially confusing or troubling.

Third, the meaning we attribute to someone's nonverbal behavior varies based on how well we know the communicator. For example, if you know your best friend tends to smile when she is angry, you will be better at interpreting her nonverbals than will a stranger. Once we know people, we can usually differentiate their nonverbal behavior from nonverbal communication and interpret the associated messages with more accuracy, as Abbad explains in *It Happened to Me: Abbad*.

Finally, we tend to interpret individuals' nonverbal behavior based on their sex. For example, when women toss their hair, the behavior often is read as flirtatious—and therefore communicative. However,

It Happened to Me: Abbad

I am from the Middle East, and I arrived in the United States in 2000 with a couple of my friends. On a school break we decided to travel to Washington D.C. On the road we stopped at a McDonald's to eat and to pray. As Muslims we have to pray five times a day, and during the prayer we cannot talk at all. While in the middle of our prayer, a McDonald's employee approached and asked what we were doing. Since we could not talk, one of my friends used a hand gesture that in our culture means "wait for a minute." This hand gesture is expressed by holding one's fingers together like a pyramid. For some reason the employee understood the gesture as an invitation for a fight. I guess this is what it means in some parts of the United States. That's when the employee called 911. By the time the police officer arrived we were done with our prayer. We explained we were new to this country and that the hand gesture we used means something else in our culture. We apologized to the employee for the misunderstanding and continued on our trip.

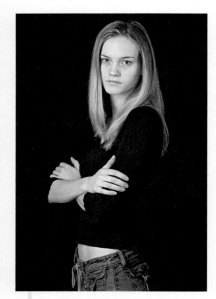

What does this nonverbal behavior mean? Remember that a nonverbal behavior can have multiple meanings—depending on the context.

nonverbal codes
distinct, organized means of expression that consists of symbols and rules for their use

kinesics
nonverbal communication sent by the body, including gestures, posture, movement, facial expressions, and eye behavior

gestures
nonverbal communication made with part of the body, including actions such as pointing, waving, or holding up a hand to direct people's attention

illustrators
signals that accompany speech to clarify or emphasize the verbal messages

emblems
gestures that stand for a specific verbal meaning

adaptors
gestures used to manage emotions

regulators
gestures used to control conversation

immediacy
how close or involved people appear to be with each other

if a man does the same, we are more likely to believe he is just trying to get his hair out of his eyes—a nonverbal behavior that is not communicative. As we discussed in Chapter 3, sex differences in nonverbal and verbal communication are due to biological as well as social and cultural influences.

Nonverbal Codes

Nonverbal codes or signals are distinct, organized means of expression that consist of both symbols and rules for their use (Cicca, Step, & Turkstra, 2003). Although we describe a range of such codes in this section, we do not mean to imply that any one code occurs in isolation. Generally, a set of behaviors and codes together determines the meaning or significance of an action. For our purposes, we isolate a specific kind of behavior for analysis; in the real world, without knowing the context, interpretations about any behavior may be questionable or even wrong (Patterson, 1983). In this section, we'll look at the five aspects of nonverbal codes—*kinesics, paralinguistics, time and space, haptics,* and *appearance and artifacts*—to see how this system of nonverbal codes works.

Kinesics

Kinesics is the term used to describe a system of studying nonverbal communication sent by the body, including gestures, posture, movement, facial expressions, and eye behavior. For clarity we group kinesic communication into two general categories, those behaviors involving the body and those involving the face.

The Body.   Our bodies convey many nonverbal messages. For example, we use **gestures** such as pointing, waving, and holding up our hands to direct people's attention, signal hello, and indicate that we want to be recognized. Communicators use four types of nonverbal gestures: *illustrators, emblems, adaptors,* and *regulators.* **Illustrators** are signals that accompany speech to clarify or emphasize the verbal messages. Thus when people come back from a fishing trip they hold their hands far apart to indicate the size of the fish that got away. **Emblems** are gestures that stand for a specific verbal meaning; for example, raising one's hand in class indicates that one wishes to speak. **Adaptors** are gestures we use to manage our emotions. Many adaptors are nervous gestures such as tapping a pencil, jiggling a leg, or twirling one's hair. Finally, people use **regulators** to control conversation; for example, if you want to prevent someone from interrupting you, you might hold up your hand to indicate that the other person should wait. In contrast, if you wish to interrupt and take the floor, you might raise a finger to signal your desire.

Gestures contribute a lot to our communication efforts; even their frequency can signal meaning. For instance, how frequently a speaker gestures often reveals how involved he is in a conversation. Typically, people who are excited indicate their involvement by using many and varied gestures; those who have little involvement may indicate their lack of interest by their failure to gesture. For an example of how differences in nonverbal gestures can affect communication, see *Communication in Society: Etiquette for the World Traveler.*

We also use our bodies to convey meaning through our posture and our movement. In general, posture is evaluated in two ways: by how *immediate* it is and by how relaxed it appears (Mehrabian, 1971; Richards, Rollerson, & Phillips, 1991). **Immediacy** refers to how close or involved people appear to be with each other. For example, when people like someone they tend to orient their bodies in the other person's direction, lean toward them, and look at them directly when they speak. How do people act when they wish to avoid someone? Typically, they engage in the opposite behavior. They turn their backs or refuse to look at them, and if they are forced to stand or sit near the person they dislike, they lean away from them. To understand this, imagine how you would behave if you were attempting to reject an unwanted amorous advance.

COMMUNICATION IN SOCIETY
Etiquette for the World Traveler

Have you observed travelers from abroad violate a nonverbal norm while visiting the United States? What did they do? How did you respond? After having learned more about nonverbal communication practices around the world, what would be your response now if you observed a similar violation?

To help you prepare for using appropriate nonverbal communication when you travel, the travel Web site Vayama.com offers etiquette tips for the world traveler. Here are 10 tips from the site.

1. In Brazil, don't make the "OK" sign with your hand. It's considered a very rude gesture.
2. In China, don't take the last bit of food on a serving plate. It's considered impolite. Also, leave a little bit of food on your plate when you're full so the hosts know you are done, otherwise they'll bring out even more food!
3. In Denmark, don't be too touchy-feely. It's not appreciated.
4. In Italy, don't pull away or get offended if an Italian associate wishes to hug you. Embrace him or her in return.
5. In Egypt, don't use your left hand to eat.
6. In India, **do** make sure your head is covered when entering a mosque or a Sikh gurdwara.
7. In Iran, do arrive on time. Lateness could be considered rude.
8. In Thailand, don't talk with your hands or put your hands in your pocket while talking to someone.
9. In Nigeria, do understand that Nigerians communicate with a lot of gestures and body language, so you may have to pay attention to nonverbal cues when conversing.
10. In Greece, do be aware of how to indicate "yes" or "no" with body language, as it's different in Greece than in the U.S. "Yes" is a slight downward nod of the head, and "No" is a slight upward nod of the head.

Etiquette for the world traveler. Courtesy Vayama.

Relaxation refers to the degree of tension one's body displays. When you are at home watching TV, for instance, you probably display a relaxed posture: lounging in a chair with your legs stretched out in front of you and your arms resting loosely on the chair's arms. However, if you are waiting at the dentist's office, you may sit hunched forward, your legs pressed tightly together, and your hands tightly grasping the chair arms.

The way you walk or move also can communicate messages to others, particularly about your mood or emotional state. Sometimes you use movement deliberately to communicate a message—such as when you stomp around the apartment to indicate your anger. At other times, your movement is simply a nonverbal behavior—that is, you move naturally and unconsciously without any clear intentionality. Even when your movement is not intentional, observers can and do make judgments about you. One study found that observers could identify when pedestrians were sad, angry, happy, or proud, just from the way they walked (Montepare, Goldstein, & Clausen, 1987). However some emotional states (anger) were easier to identify than others (pride) and some individuals were easier to classify than were others. So although people consciously communicate a great deal with their body movements and gestures and observers interpret others' movements, some messages are more clearly transmitted than others. Many of the same factors discussed earlier, such as culture, context, background knowledge, and gender, affect the ability to interpret kinesic behavior.

This gesture of support for the University of Texas Longhorns might be misinterpreted in Norway, where it is a sign of Satan.

relaxation
the degree of tension displayed by one's body

The Face.   Facial expressions communicate more than perhaps any other nonverbal behavior. They are the primary channels for transmitting emotion, and the eyes, in particular, convey important messages regarding attraction and attention. Some research suggests that facial expressions of happiness, sadness, anger, surprise, fear, and disgust are the same across cultures and, in fact, are innate (Ekman & Friesen, 1969, 1986), although not all scholars agree. Through observations of deaf, blind, and brain-damaged children, researchers have concluded that commonality of facial expressions among humans is not due to observation and learning but rather to genetic programming (Eibl-Eibesfeld, 1972; Ekman, 2003). [To better understand the role of facial expressions in the communication of emotion, go to www.dushkin.com/connectext/psy/ch10/facex.mhtml]

The ability to accurately recognize others' emotions gives individuals' an edge in their interpersonal actions. For example, people with greater emotional recognition accuracy are effective in negotiations and are able to create more value for all parties and to achieve more favorable outcomes (Elfenbein, Maw, White, Tan & Aik, 2007). If you are not very adept at recognizing others' emotions, however, you can improve your ability to do so. A variety of studies show that individuals who are trained in emotion recognition and then receive feedback on their performance can improve their ability to recognize others' emotional expressions, especially if their targets are from different cultures than their own (Elfenbein, 2006).

Of course, people don't display every emotion they feel. Individuals learn through experience and observation to manage their facial expressions, and they learn which expressions are appropriate to reveal in what circumstances. In the United States expectations of appropriateness differ for men and women. Males are often discouraged from showing sadness, while females frequently are criticized for showing anger. In addition, women are routinely instructed to smile, no matter how they feel, while relatively few men receive the same message. Consequently, people learn to manage their facial expressions so they don't reveal emotions that they believe they shouldn't feel or that they don't want others to see.

As mentioned earlier, eye behavior is especially important in conveying messages for humans as well as animals. For example, both humans and dogs use prolonged eye gaze (a stare) to communicate aggression, and they avert their gaze when they want to avoid contact. Furthermore, eye behavior interacts with facial expressions to convey meaning. Thus most people believe a smile is genuine only when the eyes "smile" as well as the lips. Actors such as Julia Roberts and Tom Cruise are particularly gifted at this; they can, at will, express what appears to be a genuine smile.

Like other types of nonverbal communication, context and culture shape the meanings people attach to eye behavior. For example, cultures differ significantly in how long one is supposed to engage in eye contact and how frequently. Many Native Americans such as Cherokee, Navajo, and Hopi engage in minimal eye contact compared to most White U.S. Americans (Chiang, 1993). Swedes tend to gaze infrequently but for longer periods of time, while southern Europeans gaze frequently and extensively (Knapp & Hall, 1992, 2001). Your relationship with others affects how you interpret their eye behavior. Thus you may like a romantic partner to gaze into your eyes but find the same behavior threatening when exhibited by the mail carrier.

Paralinguistics

The vocal aspects of nonverbal communication are referred to as **paralinguistics**, which include rate, volume, pitch, and stress, among others. Paralinguistics are those aspects of language that are *oral* but not *verbal*. That is, paralinguistics describe all aspects of spoken language except the words themselves. For example, typically you recognize other speakers' voices in large part through their paralinguistics, or how they sound, rather than the specific words they say. Thus, callers

The face is the primary channel for conveying emotion.

paralinguistics
all aspects of spoken language except the words themselves; includes rate, volume, pitch, stress

often expect relatives and friends to recognize them just from hearing their voice on the telephone. If a receiver doesn't recognize a caller, the caller may feel hurt or offended, which can turn a simple phone call into an anxiety-producing quiz. Paralinguistics are composed of two types of vocal behavior—*voice qualities* and *vocalizations*.

Voice Qualities.   **Voice qualities** include speed, pitch, rhythm, vocal range, and articulation; these qualities make up the "music" of the human voice. We all know people whose voice qualities are widely recognized. For example former President George W. Bush's vocal qualities are frequently remarked upon. One critic described his vocal style as "a little breathless, and some of the inflections are in the wrong place, like a man who knows that people will listen to him but isn't quite sure what to say" (Segaloff, 2003). To compare the vocal qualities of various presidents, go to www.presidentsusa.net/audiovideo.html and listen to audio and video recordings of many presidents.

Speakers whose voices vary in pitch and rhythm seem more expressive than those whose voices do not. For example, Ben Stein, who appeared in the movie *Ferris Bueller's Day Off* and is a spokesperson for a brand of eyedrops, is well known for his inexpressive, monotone voice, which he uses to comedic effect. Speakers also vary in how they articulate sounds, some pronouncing each word distinctly, and others blurring their words and sounds. We tend not to notice this paralinguistic feature unless someone articulates very precisely or very imprecisely. If you have difficulty understanding a speaker, usually the fault lies not with how fast the person talks but with how clearly he or she articulates. When combined, these voice qualities make your voice distinctive and recognizable to those who know you.

Vocalizations.   **Vocalizations** are the sounds we utter that do not have the structure of language. Tarzan's yell is one famous example. Vocalizations include vocal cues such as laughing, crying, whining, and moaning as well as the intensity or volume of one's speech. Also included are sounds that aren't actual words but that serve as fillers, such as "uh-huh," "uh," "ah," and "er."

The paralinguistic aspects of speech serve a variety of communicative functions. They reveal mood and emotion; they also allow us to emphasize or stress a word or idea, create a distinctive identity, and (along with gestures) regulate conversation.

Time and Space

How people use time and space is so important to communication that researchers have studied their use and developed specialized terms to describe them. **Chronemics**, from the Greek word *chronos*, meaning "time," is the study of the way people use time as a message. It includes issues such as punctuality and the amount of time people spend with each other. **Proxemics** refers to the study of how people use spatial cues, including interpersonal distance, territoriality, and other space relationships. Let's see how these factors influence communication and relationships.

Chronemics.   People often interpret others' use of time as conveying a message, which removes it from the realm of behavior and places it in the realm of communication. For example, if your friend consistently arrives more than an hour late, how do you interpret her behavior? Culture strongly influences how most people answer this question (Hall & Hall, 1987). In the United States, time typically is valued highly; we even have an expression that "time is money." Because of this, most people own numerous clocks and watches, events are scheduled at specific times, and they typically begin "on time." Therefore, in the United States, lateness can communicate thoughtlessness, irresponsibility, or selfishness. A more positive or tolerant view might be that the perpetually late person is carefree.

voice qualities
qualities such as speed, pitch, rhythm, vocal range, and articulation that make up the "music" of the human voice

vocalizations
uttered sounds that do not have the structure of language

chronemics
the study of the way people use time as a message

proxemics
the study of how people use spatial cues, including interpersonal distance, territoriality, and other space relationships, to communicate

Think back to the last time you encountered someone you could tell was truly happy to see you. How could you tell? What nonverbal behaviors communicated the other person's happiness to you?

Not all cultures value time in the same way, however. In some Latin American and Arab cultures, if one arrives thirty minutes or even an hour after an event is scheduled to begin, one is "on time." When people come together from cultures that value time differently, it can lead to conflict and a sense of displacement. This happened when one of our colleagues taught a class in Mexico. On the first class day, she showed up at the school shortly before the class was scheduled to begin. She found the building locked and no one around. And even though she knew that people in Mexico respond to time differently than she did, during her stay she never was comfortable arriving "late," and routinely had to wait outside the building until someone showed up to let her in.

The timing and sequencing of events convey a variety of messages. For example, being asked to lunch carries a different meaning than being asked to dinner, and being asked to dinner on a Monday conveys a different message than being asked to dinner on a Saturday. Also, events tend to unfold in a particular order; so we expect first dates to precede first kisses and small talk to precede task talk. When these expectations are violated, we often attribute meaning to the violations, as shown in *Did You Know? Expectancy Violations.*

In addition, some people use time **monochronically**, while others use it **polychronically**, and the differences can be perceived as transmitting a message (Hall, 1983; Wolburg, 2001). Individuals who use time monochronically engage in one task or behavior at time—one reads *or* participates in a conversation *or* watches a movie. If you engage in multiple activities at the same time, you are using time polychronically. Historically in the United States, people have used time monochronically; however, now that technology is so pervasive, more people are using time polychronically as they listen to their iPods, talk on cell phones, and cruise the Web while they interact with others. Unfortunately, people who use time monochronically may be insulted by those who use it polychronically, leading to comments such as "Put down that iPhone and pay attention to me when I talk to you!"

Did You Know?
Expectancy Violations

Think of a time when someone violated your expectations for nonverbal behavior. How did you interpret the behavior? Did you see it as a positive or negative violation? Why? How did you respond? How can a person use expectancy violation theory to increase liking?

Our expectations are one factor that influences our interpretations of others' nonverbal behavior. *Expectancy violation theory* states that when people violate our expectations, we tend to notice, become aroused, and attribute meaning to the violation, resulting in increased scrutiny and appraisal of the violator's behavior. For example, if you expect a stranger to shake your hand upon being introduced, you likely will search for an explanation if she or he hugs you instead.

However, we don't necessarily interpret and respond to these violations negatively. Judy Burgoon and her colleagues repeatedly have shown that responses to another's violation of our expectations are influenced by how we perceive the violator. In other words, we judge a violation as positive or negative depending largely on whether we view the violator as someone with whom we'd like to interact. Thus if the stranger who hugs you is very attractive and you are single, you may evaluate this violation positively. This judgment shapes your response to the violation; in this case, if you interpret the hug positively, you may respond by hugging back (Burgoon & Hale, 1988; Burgoon & LePoire, 1993).

monochronically
engaging in one task or behavior at a time

polychronically
engaging in multiple activities simultaneously

Whenever an individual's use of time differs from that of others, miscommunication is possible. If you tend to value punctuality more than others do, you may arrive at events earlier than expected and irritate your host, or you may be perceived as too eager. Similarly, if you don't value punctuality, you may discover that others won't schedule activities with you or are frequently angry at you. Relationships and communication benefit when the people involved understand how the others value and use time.

Proxemics. Earlier we touched on *proxemics,* the study of how one uses space, and how this use of space can serve a communicative function. Thus the distance people stand or sit from one another often symbolizes physical and/or psychological closeness. If a longtime friend or partner chooses not to sit next to you at a movie theatre, you probably would be perplexed, perhaps even hurt or angry. Research by Edward T. Hall, a well-known anthropologist, has delineated four spheres or categories of space that humans use (Hall, 1966). Let's take a look at each.

Intimate distance (0 to 18 inches) tends to be reserved for those whom one knows very well. Typically, this distance is used for displaying physical and psychological intimacy, such as lovemaking, cuddling children, comforting someone, or telling secrets. **Personal distance** (18 inches to 4 feet) describes the space we use when interacting with friends and acquaintances. People in the United States often use the nearer distance for friends and the farther one for acquaintances, but cultures and personal preference strongly influence this choice. When others prefer closer distances than you do, you may find their closeness psychologically distressing; Jerry Seinfeld has referred to these people as "close talkers." One of our students details her encounters with such a person in *It Happened to Me: Katarina.*

intimate distance
(0 to 18 inches) the space used when interacting with those with whom one is very close

personal distance
(18 inches to 4 feet) the space used when interacting with friends and acquaintances

social distance
(4 to 12 feet) the distance most U.S. Americans use when they interact with unfamiliar others

public distance
(12 to 25 feet) the distance used for public ceremonies such as lectures and performances

It Happened to Me: Katarina

I have a friend whom I like very much but who makes me really uncomfortable sometimes. She tends to lean in very close when she talks, especially if she has been drinking. One night, we were sitting together at a party. I sat in the corner of a couch while she leaned in to talk with me; I kept trying to pull my face away from hers while she talked until I was almost leaning over the back of the couch.

Social distance (4 to 12 feet) is the distance most U.S. Americans use when they interact with unfamiliar others. Impersonal business with grocery clerks, sales clerks, and coworkers occurs at about 4 to 7 feet, while the greatest distance is used in formal situations such as job interviews. **Public distance** (12 to 25 feet) is most appropriate for public ceremonies such as lectures and performances, though an even greater distance may be maintained between public figures (such as politicians and celebrities) and their audiences. (See *Visual Summary 6.1: Proxemics,* on p. 150.)

One's culture, gender, relationship to others, and personality influence whether one feels most comfortable at the near or far range of each of these spheres. In the United States, two unacquainted women typically sit or stand closer to each other than do two unfamiliar males, while many males are more comfortable sitting or standing closer to unknown females than they are even to men they know (Burgoon and Guerrero, 1994). However, people in other cultures may prefer the closer ranges. Cultural disparities can result in a comedic cross-cultural "dance," where one person tries to get closer to the other, and that person, made uncomfortable by the closeness, moves away.

What does the space between interactants in a given culture reveal? It can communicate intimacy or the lack of it; it also can communicate power and dominance. If person A feels free to enter person B's space without permission but refuses to allow B the same privilege, this lack of reciprocity communicates that A is dominant in the relationship. This situation is common between supervisors and subordinates

Proxemics

Intimate Distance (0–18 inches)

Personal Distance (18 inches–4 feet)

Social Distance (4–12 feet)

Public Distance (12–25 feet)

and may exist in some parent–child relationships as well. On other occasions, violations of your territory just feel intrusive, as described in, *Did You Know? Territoriality: Maintaining Private and Public Spaces.*

All humans, as well as animals, have strong feelings of territoriality. We exhibit territorial behavior when we attempt to claim control over a particular area. A primary way we attempt to claim and maintain control of a space is through personalization or marking, especially by use of artifacts. Thus we alter spaces to make them distinctly our own through activities such as placing a fence around a residence or displaying family photos in an office. These markers are a form of nonverbal communication that specifies territorial ownership or legitimate occupancy (Becker, 1973). Markers function mainly to keep people away, thereby preventing confrontational social encounters.

Did You Know?

Territoriality: Maintaining Private and Public Spaces

Do you have bumper stickers or decals on your car? If so, do you think the research findings below describe you? Do they describe people you know? How do you mark your other personal and public territories? What do you think your markers say about you?

Watch out for cars with bumper stickers.

That's the surprising conclusion of a recent study by social psychologist William Szlemko. Drivers of cars with bumper stickers, window decals, personalized license plates, and other "territorial markers" not only get mad when someone cuts in their lane or is slow to respond to a changed traffic light, but they are far more likely than those who do not personalize their cars to use their vehicles to express rage—by honking, tailgating and other aggressive behavior.

It does not seem to matter whether the messages on the stickers are about peace and love—"Visualize World Peace," "My Kid Is an Honor Student"—or angry and in your face—"Don't Mess With Texas," "My Kid Beat Up Your Honor Student."

Szlemko and his colleagues found that people who personalize their cars acknowledge that they are aggressive drivers, but usually do not realize that they are reporting much higher levels of aggression than people whose cars do not have visible markers on their vehicles.

The more markers a car has, the more aggressively the person tends to drive when provoked," Szlemko said. "Just the presence of territory markers predicts the tendency to be an aggressive driver."

The key to the phenomenon apparently lies in the idea of territoriality. Drivers with road rage tend to think of public streets and highways as "my street" and "my lane"—in other words, they think they "own the road." Why would bumper stickers predict which people are likely to view public roadways as private property?

Social scientists such as Szlemko say that people carry around three kinds of territorial spaces in their heads. One is personal territory—like a home, or a bedroom. The second kind involves space that is temporarily yours—an office cubicle or a gym locker. The third kind is public territory: park benches, walking trails—and roads.

Drivers who individualize their cars using bumper stickers, window decals and personalized license plates, the researchers hypothesized, see their cars in the same way as they see their homes and bedrooms—as deeply personal space, or primary territory.

"If you are in a vehicle that you identify as a primary territory, you would defend that against other people whom you perceive as being disrespectful of your space," Bell added. "What you ignore is that you are on a public roadway—you lose sight of the fact you are in a public area and you don't own the road."

FROM: "Looking to Avoid Aggressive Drivers? Check Those Bumpers." by Shankar Vendantam, *The Washington Post*, June 16, 2008. © 2008 The Washington Post. Reprinted with Permission.

haptics
the study of the communicative function of touch

professional touch
type of touch used by certain workers, such as dentists, hairstylists, and hospice workers, as part of their livelihood; also known as *functional touch*

functional touch
the least intimate type of touch; used by certain workers such as dentists, hairstylists, and hospice workers, as part of their livelihood; also known as *professional touch*

social-polite touch
touch that is part of daily interaction in the United States; it is more intimate than professional touch but is still impersonal

friendship touch
touch that is more intimate than social touch and usually conveys warmth, closeness, and caring

love-intimate touch
the touch most often used with one's romantic partners and family

Primary territories (areas under private control, such as houses and bedrooms) serve as extensions of the owner's sense of identity, so that markers there often include personally meaningful symbols reflecting the owner's style and taste (name plates, art objects, flower gardens). Public territories are less central to our self-concepts and, therefore, we tend to mark them with objects that are less personalized and/or that represent explicit claims to the space (for example, "reserved parking" signs). We may react strongly when someone violates our primary territory, for example, by seeking physical retaliation and legal sanctions. When someone violates public territories, however, we react less vigorously—with verbal retaliation, for example, with the aim of having the violator abandon the territory (Abu-Ghazzeh, 2000).

Haptics

Although researchers in communication know that touch, or **haptics,** is important, it is among the least studied forms of nonverbal communication. Nonetheless, research does indicate that infants and children need to be touched in order to be physically and psychologically healthy (Field, 2002). Also, although people vary considerably in how much or what type of touch they prefer, most enjoy being touched by those they care about. To understand how differences in preferences for touch affect relationships, see *It Happened to Me: Beth.*

Touch can be categorized into several general types (Givens, 2005), but people rarely notice the types unless a discrepancy occurs between their expectations and their experience. **Professional,** or **functional touch** is the least intimate; people who must touch others as part of their livelihood, such as dentists, hairstylists, and hospice workers, use this type of touch. Because touch often conveys intimacy, people who must use professional touch have to be careful of their interaction style; for example, they may adopt a formal or distant verbal communication style to counteract the intimacy of their touch. **Social-polite touch** is part of daily interaction. In the United States, this form of touch is more intimate than professional touch but is still impersonal. For example, many U.S. Americans shake hands when greeting acquaintances and casual friends, though in many European countries, such as France and Italy, hugging and kissing are appropriate forms of social touch. Even within the United States, people have different ideas about what types of touch are appropriate socially.

Friendship touch is more intimate than social touch and usually conveys warmth, closeness, and caring. Although considerable variation in touch may exist among friends, people typically use touch that is more intimate with close friends than with acquaintances or strangers. Examples include brief hugs, a hand on the shoulder, or putting one's arm loosely around another's waist or shoulders. **Love-intimate touch** most often is used with one's romantic partners and family. Examples are the long kisses and extended hugs we tend to reserve for those with whom we are closest.

As is true of other forms of nonverbal communication, sex, culture, and power strongly influence patterns of touch. In the United States, heterosexual males are more likely to reserve hand-holding for their romantic partners and small children, while females touch other women more frequently and hold hands with older children, their close female relatives, and even female friends. In general, women tend to touch other women more frequently than men touch other men, and in cross-sex interactions, men are more likely to initiate touch than do women (Hall & Hall, 1990). However, in cross-sex interactions, the nature of the relationship influences touch behavior more than does the sex of the participants. Across all stages

It Happened to Me: Beth

I grew up in upper Michigan, where people rarely touch unless they know each other very well. Then I started working with a guy from the South. From the beginning, he touched me whenever we talked; he touched my arm, put his hand on my shoulder, or even put his arm on the back of my chair. This infuriated me! I thought he was being condescending and too familiar. Later I realized that he does this with everybody. I understand he doesn't mean anything by it, but I still don't like it.

of heterosexual romantic relationships, partners reciprocate touch, so they do not differ in amount of touch (Guerrero & Andersen, 1991); however, men respond more positively to their partners' touch than do women (Hanzal, Segrin, & Dorros, 2008). In addition, men initiate touch more in casual romantic relationships, while women do so more often in married relationships (Guerrero & Andersen, 1994).

You may have noticed that each form of touch we have discussed has a "positive" quality. Of course, people also use touch to convey negative messages. For example, one study revealed that individuals use aggressive touch and withdrawal of affectionate touch with children to signal their displeasure (Guerrero & Ebesu, 1993). Aggressive touch includes hitting, kicking, and pinching, while withdrawal of affection involves rejecting the touch attempts of others, as when one pushes another's arm away or refuses to hold hands.

Demand touching is often used to establish dominance and power.

Another type of touch that can be perceived negatively is **demand touching**, a type of touch used to establish dominance and power. Demand touching increases in hierarchical settings, such as at work. One significant characteristic of demand touching is that touchers typically have higher status and have more control over encounters than do receivers; this allows them more freedom of movement and more visual contact. An everyday example of demand touch occurs when a supervisor stands behind a subordinate and leans over to provide directions, placing his or her hand on the subordinate's shoulder. The subordinate can't move easily or look directly at the supervisor, and the subordinate may feel both physically and psychologically constrained (Kemmer, 1992).

Appearance and Artifacts

In all cultures, individuals' appearance matters, as do their **artifacts**, or the clothing and other accessories they choose. Let's first consider appearance and how it operates as a nonverbal code.

In general, people's looks are believed to communicate something about them, and people develop expectations based on how others look. Hairstyle, skin color, height, weight, clothing, accessories such as jewelry, and other aspects of appearance all influence how we are perceived and how we perceive others. And in the United States, appearance is seen as especially important (Newport, 1999).

What is considered attractive, however, is influenced by one's culture and the time period in which one lives (Grammer, Fink, Joller, & Thornhill, 2003). Many people find it hard to believe that the Mona Lisa was considered a great beauty in her day, and even more people wonder who could ever have liked the clothes and hairstyles their parents sported in their youth. Although the global village we live in now means the media transmit images that can be seen all over the world, cultures still vary in what they consider most attractive. The current ideal body type for women in the United States, as portrayed in the media, for example, is considered too thin and unfeminine by many African Americans (Duke, 2002). While some American women get collagen injections to achieve full lips, our Japanese students tell us that such thick lips are not considered attractive in Japan. Some Europeans also dislike the defined musculature favored for males in magazines and television ads in the United States.

In the United States, people invest considerable time, money, and energy adapting their appearance to cultural ideals of attractiveness. They diet, color and style their hair, frequent gyms and tanning booths, and even undergo extreme makeovers to be more attractive. People engage in all these efforts because the U.S. culture generally equates beauty with happiness, success, goodness, and desirability.

While people face certain limits in reshaping their bodies and other physical attributes, they also have great flexibility in using clothing and other artifacts to

demand touching
a type of touch used to establish dominance and power

artifacts
clothing and other accessories

What artifacts are important to you in terms of communicating your identity or status? If you had only one means of communicating high status, would you drive an expensive car, wear designer clothes, or live in an upscale neighborhood? What do you think your choice reflects about you?

convey important messages about themselves. In most business contexts a suit is perceived to be authoritative and an indication of status. Nurses, flight attendants, and police officers wear uniforms to help others identify them and to send specific messages about their jobs (Gundersen, 1990). This is especially true of men; evaluations of their status typically are based on their appearance and clothing (Mast & Hall, 2004). Thus, police officers wear paramilitary uniforms not only to allow us to easily identify them but also to reinforce their role in maintaining social order.

Individuals also choose their accessories and artifacts, such as purses, watches, jewelry, sunglasses, and even cars, to communicate specific messages about status, personality, success, and/or group membership. A student who carries a leather briefcase on campus creates a different image than one who carries a canvas backpack. And if you were to visit our campus, you could differentiate the communication professors from the business professors and the engineering students from the theater majors based on their dress and artifacts. We might argue that people in the United States, where it is not considered polite to announce one's status or success, often use artifacts to make those announcements for them (Fussell, 1992).

As you can see, multiple categories of nonverbal behavior influence communication, including kinesics, paralinguistics, chronemics and proxemics, haptics, and appearance and artifacts. These categories are, in turn, influenced by multiple individual and cultural factors. In the next section we explore how these categories work together to influence how we send and interpret messages.

The Functions of Nonverbal Messages

As mentioned earlier, we don't isolate kinesics from haptics or proxemics from appearance when we interpret nonverbal behaviors; rather, we observe an integrated set of behaviors, consider the context and the individual, and then attribute meaning. If you see two people standing closely together in a public place, you wouldn't necessarily assume they were being intimate. Rather, you would examine how relaxed or tense their bodies appeared, evaluate their facial expression and eye gaze, and consider the appropriateness of intimate displays in this public space (for example, a bar versus a church). Only then might you make an attribution about the meaning or function of the couple's behavior.

In general, scholars have determined that nonverbal behaviors serve five functions during interaction (Patterson, 1982, 2003). Those five functions are *communicating information*, *regulating interaction*, *expressing and managing intimacy*, *establishing social control*, and *signaling service-task functions*. The most basic function is to communicate information, and this is the one we examine first.

Communicating Information

Most fundamentally, nonverbal message are used to **communicate information**. From the receiver's point of view, much of a sender's behavior is potentially informative. For example, when you meet someone for the first time you evaluate the pattern of the sender's behavior to assess a variety of factors. First, you might evaluate the sender's general disposition to determine if it is warm and friendly or cool and distant. You likely will also assess her more fleeting nonverbal reactions to help you decide if she seems pleased to meet you or is just being polite. Finally, of course, you evaluate the person's verbal message. For example, does the speaker say, "I've been looking forward to meeting you," or does she say, "I'd love to chat, but I've got to run." You then combine all these pieces of information to ascribe meaning to the encounter.

Nonverbal communication helps individuals convey and interpret verbal messages. They can do this in five ways:

1. By repeating a message (winking while saying "I'm just kidding");
2. By highlighting or emphasizing a message (pointing at the door while saying "Get out!");

communicating information
using nonverbal behaviors to help clarify verbal messages and reveal attitudes and moods

3. By complementing or reinforcing a message (whispering while telling a secret);

4. By contradicting a message (saying "I love your haircut" while speaking in a hostile tone and rolling one's eyes);

5. By substituting for a message (shaking one's head to indicate disagreement).

Effective nonverbal communication can make you a better *verbal* communicator.

Regulating Interaction

Nonverbal communication also is used to **regulate interaction**. That is, people use nonverbal behaviors to manage turn-taking during conversation. Thus, if you want to start talking, you might lean forward, look at the current speaker, and even raise one finger. To reveal that you are finished with your turn, you may drop your volume and pitch, lean back, and look away from and then back toward the person you are "giving" your turn to. The regulating function tends to be the most automatic of the five, and most of us rarely think about it. The behaviors you use in this way include the more stable ones such as interpersonal distance, body orientation, and posture, as well as more fluid behaviors like gaze, facial expression, volume, and pitch, which are important in the smooth sequencing of conversational turns (Capella, 1985).

Expressing and Managing Intimacy

A third function of nonverbal communication, and the most studied, involves **expressing and managing intimacy**. The degree of your nonverbal involvement with another usually reflects the level of intimacy you desire with that person. If you are on a date and notice your partner is leaning toward you, gazing into your eyes, nodding his head, and providing many paralinguistic cues such as "uh huh" as you talk, your date is revealing a high degree of nonverbal involvement, which often signals attraction and interest. Of course, people can manipulate these behaviors to suggest attraction and involvement even if they are not experiencing these feelings. For example, when subordinates talk with their supervisors, they often display fairly high levels of nonverbal involvement, regardless of their true feelings for their bosses.

regulating interaction
using nonverbal behaviors to help manage turn-taking during conversation

expressing and managing intimacy
using nonverbal behaviors to help convey attraction and closeness

establishing social control
using nonverbal behavior to exercise influence over other people

"What bouquet best says 'please don't tell my wife'?"

©RGJ Richard Jolley/www.CartoonStock.com

Establishing Social Control

People also use nonverbal communication to exert or **establish social control,** or to exercise influence over other people. Individuals engage in the social control function when they smile at someone they want to do them a favor or when they glare at noisy patrons in a theater to encourage them to be quiet. You can use either positive or negative behaviors (or both) in your efforts to control others. People who are "charming" or very persuasive typically are extremely gifted at using nonverbal behavior to influence others.

When expressing and managing intimacy people tend to respond in similar, or reciprocal, ways to one another's nonverbals. On the other hand, when engaging in social control, people tend to respond in complementary ways to one another's nonverbals. To better understand the role of these responses in nonverbal interactions, see *Alternative View: Nonverbal Reciprocity or Nonverbal Complementarity?*, on p. 156.

Massage therapists use nonverbal communication that has a service-task function.

*Alternative*VIEW
Nonverbal Reciprocity or Nonverbal Complementarity?

Which of the following explanations seems more accurate to you?

In what situations do you believe people are more likely to engage in nonverbal reciprocity? In nonverbal complementarity?

Nonverbal Reciprocity

Numerous studies provide evidence that many people unconsciously mimic their partner's postures, gestures, and other movements in social settings. Furthermore, this mimicry, or reciprocity, seems to increase liking and rapport between speakers. In turn, increased liking and rapport lead to more frequent mimicry. However, status or dominance affects who is likely to mimic whom. Lower status individuals are more likely to reciprocate the behaviors of higher status people, which may be unconsciously designed to increase liking and rapport (Chartrand & Bargh, 1999; Dijksterhuis & Smith, 2005).

Nonverbal Complementarity

A set of studies found that people respond to another's nonverbal power moves with complementary responses;

that is, they respond to dominant behaviors with submissive ones and submissive behaviors with dominant ones (Tiedens & Fragale, 2003). Thus, if one person stares aggressively at another (a dominant behavior), the recipient of the stare is likely to look away (a submissive behavior). Furthermore, participants reported feeling comfortable with complementarity.

These studies specifically examined how people negotiate status in relationships with no prior hierarchy. Thus in groups and relationships in which everyone is on equal footing, the first dominant or submissive display by an individual may result from a random movement or a tactical strategy. Whatever the cause of the display, a hierarchical relationship can then result if an observer responds in a complementary fashion. Moreover, since people prefer to complement dominance with submissiveness, and vice versa, they are likely to promote that differentiation. Thus nonverbal complementarity and the comfort associated with it may encourage hierarchical relationships and help maintain them. This phenomenon, then, may be one reason why hierarchies are so common and widespread.

---

service-task functions
using nonverbal behavior to signal close involvement between people in impersonal relationships and contexts

Signaling Service-Task Functions

Finally, nonverbal communication has a **service-task function**. Behaviors of this kind typically signal close involvement between people in impersonal relationships and contexts. For example, physicians frequently engage in very intimate touch as a part of their profession, as do manicurists, tailors, and massage therapists. In each of these cases, however, the behavior is appropriate, necessary, and merely a means to a (professional) end.

Accurately interpreting nonverbal messages is a complex endeavor, requiring awareness of a number of elements—factors that influence individuals' communication patterns, nonverbal communication codes and signals, and communicative functions that nonverbals fulfill. However, in some senses, we have only shown you one piece of the picture, as we have thus far focused primarily on nonverbal communication as performed by individuals. In the next section we expand the frame to explore how societal forces influence both the performance and interpretation of nonverbal messages and behavior.

 ## THE INDIVIDUAL, NONVERBAL COMMUNICATION, AND SOCIETY

Nonverbal communication, like all communication, is heavily influenced by societal forces and occurs within a hierarchical system of meanings. One's status and position within the societal hierarchy, as well as one's identity, are all expressed nonverbally. However, the more powerful elements in society often regulate these expressions. In addition, nonverbal communication can trigger and express prejudice and discrimination. Let's see how this operates.

Nonverbal Communication and Power

Nonverbal communication and power are intricately related—especially via the nonverbal codes of appearance and artifacts. In the United States, power is primarily based on an individual's access to economic resources and the freedom to make decisions that affect others. Economic resources typically are revealed or expressed through nonverbal codes. Thus people display wealth through the clothing they wear, the quality of their haircuts, and the value of their homes and cars. Whether one has the money to pay $100 for a haircut or goes regularly to Great Clips communicates clearly one's social class and power. English professor Paul Fussell (1992) provides an extensive description of how nonverbal messages communicated in our everyday lives reveal class standing. Consider, for example, the messages communicated by one's home. Fussell notes that the longer the driveway, the less obvious the garage, and the more manicured the grounds, the higher is one's socioeconomic class.

The NBA issued rules governing NBA players' off-court dress to help shape the images they present to the public.

People use nonverbals to communicate their own status and identities, and to evaluate and interpret others' status and identities. Based on these interpretations, people—consciously and unconsciously—include and exclude others, and approve or disapprove of others. For example, in wealthy communities, people who don't look affluent may be stopped and questioned about their presence or even be asked to leave. More overtly, gated communities offer clear nonverbal messages about who belongs and who does not belong to a community. Of course, it isn't just the wealthy who use artifacts to convey their identity and belonging. Gang members, NASCAR fans, football fans, and many others also use attire as well as gestures to signal their individual and group identities. In these ways, nonverbal communication reproduces—or re-creates—the society, and social classes, we live in.

Although all groups use nonverbal communication to convey identity, more powerful segments of society typically define what is allowed. For example, corporations typically have rules that regulate nonverbal expression of even men's facial hair. Recently the NBA issued rules governing the off-court dress of NBA players: They are to dress in "business casual" whenever engaged in team or league business, and they are specifically excluded from wearing sleeveless shirts, shorts, t-shirts, headgear of any kind, chains, pendants, and sunglasses while indoors. See www.nba.com/news/player_dress_code_051017.html for more information on this topic.

Through these dictums, the organization is attempting to regulate not only the players' clothing, but their expression of their identities as well. Of course, not all players support these regulations (Wise, 2005). Some NBA players feel that the ban on chains and other jewelry was racially motivated. In short, this new policy "called attention to a generational chasm between modern professional athletes, many of whom are black, and their mostly white paying customers" (Wise, 2005, p. A01). Many corporations and other organizations have instituted dress codes to communicate a particular professional image to the public. The military and many police organizations have policies on tattoos as well, and they are starting to enforce them (Zezima, 2005). Because these organizations are hierarchical, the decisions made by those in power in the organization must be followed by those who wish employment there.

The number and range of dress codes and regulations on appearance underscore the powerful impact that nonverbals can have. The more powerful segments of society also define what is most desirable and attractive in our culture. For example, cosmetic corporations spend $231 billion annually to develop beauty products in order to persuade consumers to buy them. The largest cosmetic companies have recently expanded to China where the nation's 451 million women are of great interest to the cosmetic market—which has doubled in the last five years to $8 billion (Carvajal, 2006). The media broadly communicate to us the definitions of beauty. This is why many U.S. Americans believe that blonde hair is better than brown, thin is better than fat, large breasts are better than small, and young is better than old—beliefs that are not shared universally. Messages promoting a specific type of youth and beauty might seem rather harmless, until one considers the consequences for those who are not thin and blonde, especially those who have no

What male and female celebrities do you believe best capture U.S. American standards of beauty? How do you feel about yourself when you see pictures of these people? How do you feel about the appearance of your romantic partner, if you have one?

possibility of meeting the dominant standards of beauty. How does this hierarchy of attractiveness affect their communication with others? Do people respond to them negatively because of their appearance? Might they feel marginalized and resentful—even before they interact with others who more clearly meet the dominant standards?

Nonverbal expressions also are an important part of cultural rituals involving societal expectations. For example, in U.S. culture it is not acceptable to wear white to a wedding, unless one is the bride, and black or other dark colors are appropriate to wear to funerals. Aspects of dress are very important in the United States at other cultural events, particularly for women. The outfits worn to the Academy Awards and Golden Globe ceremonies are reviewed and evaluated and are a topic of great interest for many people. Similarly, what the president's wife wears on Inauguration Day and at subsequent parties is a subject of conversation; in fact, people everyday discuss and refer to Michelle Obama's clothing on TV, in blogs, and in magazines. The interest (and evaluation) of these nonverbal expressions, like clothing, is driven by societal forces. In all of these cases, women know that their nonverbal messages will be carefully scrutinized and evaluated.

Nonverbal Communication, Prejudice, and Discrimination

At the intersection of societal forces and nonverbal communication are prejudice and discrimination. Both can be triggered by nonverbal behavior and are also expressed through nonverbal behavior. Let's look at how this works. First, one's race and ethnicity, body shape, age, or style of dress—all of which are communicated nonverbally—can prompt prejudgment or negative stereotypes. How often do people make a snap judgment or generalization based on appearance? Second, prejudice and discrimination are expressed nonverbally. In some extreme cases, nonverbal signals have even triggered and perpetrated hate crimes. For example, one night in Phoenix, Arizona, Avtar (Singh) Chiera, a small-business owner and a Sikh, waited outside his business for his son to pick him up. Two White men pulled up in a small red pickup truck, yelled at him, and then opened fire on him. Because of anger over the events of 9/11, the two men likely targeted him as an Arab because of his turban and beard, even though Sikhs are neither Arab nor Muslim (Parasuram, 2003). In this encounter, nonverbal messages were the most important; the words spoken (if any) were of minimal impact.

While the example just given is extreme, there are many other more subtle ways that prejudice can be communicated nonverbally—for instance, averting one's gaze, or a smile that is not given. It can be as subtle as shifting your gaze, leaning your body away, or editing your speech. Sociologist A. G. Johnson (2001, pp. 58–59) gives a list of specific nonverbal behaviors that can be interpreted as prejudicial. These are mostly noticed only by the person experiencing them and often happen unconsciously and unintentionally:

Not looking at people when we talk with them;

Not smiling at people when they walk into the room or staring as if to say "What are you doing here," or stopping the conversation with a hush they have to wade through to be included in the smallest way;

Not acknowledging people's presence or making them wait as if they weren't there;

Not touching their skin when we give them something;

Watching them closely to see what they're up to;

Avoiding someone walking down the street, giving them wide berth or even crossing to the other side.

Given the potential consequences of nonverbal communication, you may find it helpful to consider how your nonverbal communication reflects your own ethical stance. To guide you in making appropriate and ethical choices, in the next section we explore the ethics of nonverbal communication.

ETHICS AND NONVERBAL COMMUNICATION

The ethics of nonverbal communication are actually quite similar to the ethics of communication in general. When people engage in unethical behavior, such as deceiving or threatening others or name-calling, their nonverbal behavior typically plays a central role in their messages. For instance, liars use nonverbal behavior to avoid "leaking" the deception, and they may also use it to convey the deceptive message. Moreover, deceivers may feel that lying nonverbally, for example, by remaining silent, is less "wrong" than lying with words. In the Old Testament, Joseph's brothers were very jealous of their father's affection for him, so they sold Joseph into slavery. When they returned without him, however, they didn't "tell" their father what happened; instead they gave him Joseph's bloody coat and let their father draw the conclusion that an animal had killed him. In this way, they deceived their father without actually speaking a lie—behavior that was just as unethical as if they had lied verbally.

Communicators also can behave unethically when they use nonverbals that ridicule, derogate, or otherwise demean others. If you speak in a patronizing vocal tone, if you scream at the less powerful, or if you touch people inappropriately, you are engaging in unethical nonverbal communication. Similarly, if you respond to others' communication in a way that misrepresents how you actually feel, you are being unethical. Thus if you laugh at a racist or sexist joke even though you dislike it, your behavior is unethical both because it derogates others, and because it misrepresents your true reaction to the joke.

Here are some guidelines for ethical nonverbal communication: Consider whether

your nonverbal behaviors reflect your real attitudes, beliefs, and feelings;

your nonverbal behaviors contradict the verbal message you are sending;

your nonverbal behaviors insult, ridicule, or demean others;

you are using your nonverbal behavior to intimidate, coerce, or silence someone;

you would want anyone to observe your nonverbal behavior;

you would want this nonverbal behavior directed to you or a loved one.

This antigroping sign from Japan illustrates a common problem in many parts of the world. What are the ethical issues in this nonverbal behavior?

If you remember that you are just as responsible for your nonverbal communication as you are for your verbal communication, you will make better, more ethical choices.

IMPROVING YOUR NONVERBAL COMMUNICATION SKILLS

By now you may be wondering how to decide what a set of behaviors means. How do you decide, for example, if a physician's touch is appropriately intimate (service-task) or just intimate? How can you determine if your subordinate genuinely likes you and your ideas (nonverbal involvement) or is trying to flatter you (social control)?

One important way of assessing nonverbal communication is to examine how it interacts with the verbal messages you receive (Jones & LeBaron, 2002). That is, how congruent (similar) are the two sets of messages? When the two types of messages are **congruent**, you can be more confident that they are "real." For example, a positive verbal message (I like you) combined with a positive nonverbal message (smile, forward body lean, relaxed posture) conveys a more convincing positive message. Of course, verbal and nonverbal messages can also **contradict** one another. When using sarcasm, people intentionally combine a positive verbal message (I like your new hairstyle) with a contradictory or negative nonverbal message (a hostile tone). However, at other times people offer contradictory messages unintentionally or carelessly. Caretakers often confuse children (and encourage misbehavior) by telling a child to stop a particular behavior while smiling or laughing. How does a child interpret this message? Most will accept the nonverbal aspect of the message and ignore the verbal (Eskritt & Lee, 2003.)

In addition to assessing the congruence of the verbal and nonverbal components of a message, you improve your comprehension of nonverbal messages by analyzing the context, your knowledge of the other person, and your own experiences. For example, if you are playing basketball and a teammate slaps you on the rear and says "good going," the message may be clear. Given the context, you may read it as a compliment and perhaps a sign of affection or intimacy. But what if the slap on the rear occurs at work after an effective presentation? Given that such behavior generally is inappropriate in a business context, you probably will (and should) more closely assess its meaning. You might ask yourself whether this person simply lacks social skills and frequently engages in inappropriate behavior. If so, the message may be inappropriate but still be meant in a positive fashion. In contrast, if the person knows better and has touched you inappropriately at other times, the behavior may be intentionally designed to express inappropriate intimacy or social control.

Here are a few more suggestions to keep in mind:

■ Recognize that others' nonverbal messages don't always mean the same as yours.

■ Be aware of individual, contextual, and cultural factors that influence meaning.

■ Ask for additional information if you don't understand a nonverbal message or if you perceive a contradiction between the verbal and nonverbal messages.

■ Remember that not every nonverbal behavior is intended to be communicative.

■ Don't place too much emphasis on fleeting nonverbal behaviors such as facial expression or vocal tone; rather, examine the entire set of nonverbal behaviors.

congruent
verbal and nonverbal messages that express the same meaning

contradicting
verbal and nonverbal messages that send conflicting messages

SUMMARY

Nonverbals are an important component of communication. They help you interpret and understand verbal messages and, in doing so, help you more effectively navigate your everyday life. Studying nonverbals is particularly important because they are complex and ambiguous. Without sufficient understanding of how the various nonverbal codes work together in specific contexts, cultures, and relationships, one can easily misunderstand others' nonverbal messages or assume meaning where none exists.

Nonverbal communication is defined as all the messages that people transmit through means other than words, and it occurs when nonverbal behavior has symbolic meaning. To understand the meaning of a nonverbal behavior you have to consider the entire behavioral context, including culture, relationship type, background knowledge, and gender. Nonverbal communication occurs through five codes or types of signals: kinesics, paralinguistics (vocal qualities), chronemics (time) and proxemics (space), haptics (touch), and appearance and artifacts. These codes can combine to serve one of five functions, such as communicating information, regulating interaction, expressing and managing intimacy, exerting social control, and performing service-task functions.

As we've shown, nonverbal communication is not performed in a vacuum; rather, power relationships as well as societal norms and rules influence the range of nonverbal behaviors we are allowed to perform and how those behaviors are interpreted. In addition, everyone needs to be aware that nonverbal communication can trigger and express prejudice and discrimination. Thus nonverbal communication has ethical aspects. Ethical considerations for nonverbal communication involve nonverbal "deception" and nonverbal behaviors that ridicule, derogate, or otherwise demean others.

You can become more effective in interpreting others' nonverbal communication by assessing the congruence of the verbal and nonverbal components of a message; analyzing the context, your knowledge of the other person, and your own experiences; recognizing that others' nonverbal messages don't always mean the same as yours do; asking for additional information if you don't understand a nonverbal message; and remembering that not every nonverbal behavior is intended to be communicative.

KEY TERMS

nonverbal behavior 141	emblems 144	voice qualities 147
nonverbal communication 141	adaptors 144	vocalizations 147
nonverbal codes 144	regulators 144	chronemics 147
kinesics 144	immediacy 144	proxemics 147
gestures 144	relaxation 145	monochronically 148
illustrators 144	paralinguistics 146	polychronically 148

TEST YOUR KNOWLEDGE

1. How does nonverbal communication differ from non-verbal behavior that is not communicative? Provide an example of each.

2. How does one's relationship with another person influence one's interpretation of that person's nonverbal communication?

3. What are kinesics? What are two general categories of kinesics?

4. What is nonverbal immediacy? How does liking typically affect one's nonverbal immediacy behaviors?

5. What is the difference between using time mono-chronically and polychronically?

6. What are artifacts, and how do they communicate status or class?

APPLY WHAT YOU KNOW

1. **Waiting Times**
   How long is the "appropriate" amount of time you should wait in each of the following situations? Specifically, after how long a period would you begin to feel angry or put out?

   Estimate waiting times for:
   a. your dentist
   b. a checkout line in a department store
   c. a movie line
   d. a friend at lunch
   e. a friend at dinner
   f. being on hold on the telephone
   g. your professor to arrive at class
   h. a stop light
   i. your romantic partner at a bar
   j. your professor during office hours.

   Do you see any patterns in your expectations for waiting times? What influences your expectations most—your relationship with the other party? The comfort of the waiting area? Your ability to control events? Compare your waiting times with others' to see how similar or different they are.

2. **Violating Norms for Proximity**
   For this exercise we would like you to violate some of the norms for spacing in your culture. Try standing slightly closer to a friend or family member than you normally would, then note how they react. If you have a romantic partner or very close friend, sit much farther from them than you normally would. For example, in a theater, sit one seat away from him or her, or sit at the opposite end of the couch if you would typically sit closer. Pay attention to the reactions you elicit. Finally, when talking with an acquaintance, increase the distance between you each time the other person tries to decrease it and see how the other person responds. What do these responses to your space violations reveal to you regarding the importance of spacing norms in the United States?

   NOTE: Be careful in your selection of people with whom you violate norms of space, and be prepared to explain why you are behaving so "oddly."

3. **Cultural Differences in Nonverbal Communication**
   Go to a search engine such as Google, and look for a Web site that explains the rules for nonverbal communication and behavior in a culture outside the United States with which you are not familiar. What rules surprised you? What rules were similar to the ones you use? What do you think would happen if you used your "normal" rules for nonverbal behavior in this culture?

EXPLORE

1. www.presidentsusa.net/audiovideo.html Go to this Web site and compare the vocal qualities of four presidents—two presidents who served prior to the widespread use of television and two who have served since. What role do you think vocal versus visual cues played in the popularity of each president? Are there presidents whose appearance you find more appealing than their vocal qualities? Are there presidents whose vocal qualities you find more appealing than their appearance?

2. www.dushkin.com/connectext/psy/ch10/facex.mhtml The study of facial expressions of emotion is complex. However, we do typically associate some general features with particular emotions. Go to this Web site and perform the exercise described there. You will be asked to select the eyes and the mouth expression that go with a particular emotion. You can click on the components until you get the combination you are comfortable with. How accurate were you? Did you find one or more of the expressions easier to create than the others?

Communication Across Cultures

7

chapter outline

Many, if not most, of your daily interactions are intercultural in nature."

In my first semester in the United States, I lived in the dorm and made many friends from different countries. One day I was eating lunch when my Korean and Turkish friends started arguing loudly. The issue was the value of our school. The Turkish girl didn't like our school and was thinking of transferring. The Korean student defended our school vehemently.

The Korean and Turkish students wouldn't talk to each other after the argument, and the conflict created a very uncomfortable climate. I was concerned about both of them because we were all friends. So I asked some of my American friends what they thought about the issue. They said, "It's not your problem, Kaori. It's their problem. Stay away from it." I was shocked that my American friends didn't seem to care about the conflict and its negative influence, and it took me a while to understand what the phrase "it's their problem" actually means in this highly individualistic American society. I've been in the States seven years, and now I use the phrase myself. Do I think it's good? I don't know. At least, I know I am adapting better to American culture. Do I like it? I don't know. It's just how it is here. But I know that I would never ever say that to my family or friends in Japan.

Kaori's story illustrates a number of points about intercultural communication. First, intercultural contact is a fact of life in today's world, and second, as Kaori's story shows, while intercultural contact can be enriching, it also can bring conflict and misunderstandings. In Kaori's case, the clash between her American friends' individualistic belief and her more collectivistic orientation led her to believe that Americans did not value friendships as much as she did. Finally, the story illustrates that it is very common now for individuals, like Kaori, to live "on the border"—between two cultures—and like Kaori, to have to negotiate conflicting sets of cultural values.

Also like Kaori, you have many opportunities to meet people from different cultures. You may sit in classes with students who are culturally different from you in many ways—in nationality, ethnicity, race, gender, age, religion, and sexual orientation. In addition, via travel and communication technology, you have many opportunities for intercultural encounters beyond the classroom. Given the current global political situation, however, you might be skeptical about the ability of people from different cultures to coexist peacefully. Interethnic violence in the Darfur region of Sudan in Africa and in the former Middle East, clashes between Buddhists and Hindus in India and between Catholics and Protestants in Northern Ireland, and tension in the United States between African Americans and Whites may lead people to believe that cultural differences necessarily lead to insurmountable problems. However, we believe that increased awareness of intercultural communication can help prevent or reduce the severity of problems that arise due to cultural differences.

In this chapter we'll first explore the importance of *intercultural communication* and define what we mean when we use this term. Next, we will describe the increasingly common experience of individuals who must negotiate different cultural realities in their everyday lives. Then we'll examine how culture influences our communication and present a dialectical perspective on intercultural communication. Finally, we'll discuss how society affects communication outcomes in intercultural interactions and provide suggestions for how one can become a more ethical and effective intercultural communicator.

Once you have read this chapter, you will be able to:

- Identify four reasons for learning about intercultural communication.
- Define *intercultural communication*.
- Give an example of each of six cultural values that influence communication.
- Describe the dialectical approach to intercultural communication.
- Understand the role of power and privilege in communication between people from different cultural backgrounds.
- Give three guidelines for communicating more ethically with people whose cultural backgrounds differ from your own.
- Discuss three ways to improve your own intercultural communication skills.

THE IMPORTANCE OF INTERCULTURAL COMMUNICATION

You can probably think of many reasons for studying intercultural communication. Most likely, you have more opportunities than ever before for intercultural contact, both domestically and internationally, and you will communicate better in these situations if you know something about intercultural communication. In addition, increased knowledge and skill in intercultural communication can improve your business effectiveness, intergroup relations, and self-awareness. Let's look at each of these reasons more closely.

Increased Opportunities for Intercultural Contact

Experts estimate that twenty-five people cross national borders every second—one billion journeys per year (Numbers, 2008). Increasing numbers of people travel for pleasure, some 800 million in 2006 (*Tourism Highlights*, 2007). Many people, like our student Kaori, also travel for study. According to the Institute of International Education, approximately 600,000 international students study in the United States each year and approximately 200,000 U.S. students study overseas (IIE, 2007a, 2007b). Many students study abroad because of the exciting opportunities that exist for intercultural encounters, as exchange student Allison describes in *Did You Know? Meeting Other Travelers Adds Depth to Argentina Visit*.

Another source of increased opportunity for intercultural contact exists because of the increasing cultural diversity in the United States. The 2000 Census revealed a dramatic increase in ethnic and racial diversity, and this trend is expected to continue, as shown in Figure 7.1 (Passel & Cohn, 2008). The Hispanic population will triple in size and constitute approximately 30 percent of the population by 2050; in the same time period, the Asian American population will double in size and will constitute about 10 percent of the total population. African Americans will remain approximately the same in numbers and compose 13 percent of the population; Whites will continue to be a smaller majority as minority populations increase in number.

The nation's elderly population will more than double in size from 2005 through 2050, as the baby-boom generation enters the traditional retirement years. The number of working-age Americans and children will grow more slowly than the elderly population, and will shrink as a share of the total population (Passel & Cohn, 2008).

Of course, the Internet also provides increased opportunity for intercultural encounters. You could play chess with someone in Russia through the Internet, discuss the intricacies of mountain climbing with people anywhere in the world on a sports

Did You Know?

Meeting Other Travelers Adds Depth to Argentina Visit

Allison, from the United States, is an exchange student in Argentina. Here's an excerpt from her travel blog:

Argentina has absolutely EVERYTHING—huge national glacier parks with penguins, and walruses and skiing, deserts and mountains and beautiful plains and they've even got the east coast beach! We went to the North West last week; four of us stayed in a youth hostel there. It was absolutely one of the most fun experiences of my life. I felt like I had discovered a secret that had been hidden from me all my life. I IMMEDIATELY felt at home. It was just a bunch of kids all traveling from all parts of the world just hanging out and meeting people and sharing all their stories. Our first friends we met were two Canadian kids who had been backpacking through South America the past two months. We spent a lot of time with them drinking mate (the traditional Argentine tea) and chatting about all their experiences in South America. There was a Venezuelan girl and a Japanese girl. It was a pleasure sharing a room with them. In talking to everyone I became even more aware of how misinformed about international news we are in America and how uncommon it is for us to actually be interested enough to really be concerned about what's going on in the rest of the world.

I had a really intriguing conversation with an Israeli soldier who had been traveling through South America during his time off. Hearing his stories was absolutely heartbreaking . . . all that he was forced to see and to do was absolutely awful! No one of any age should have to endure those things, and he's been doing it since he was 18. I guess that's how it is for people that live in countries where that's just their reality. They become accustomed to falling asleep with gun shots outside their window and getting up to go to work not having any idea what their day will hold and whether or not they'll die. It's awful and such a foreign concept to us; maybe we should make it more of a reality. . . .

Allison Nafziger Travel Blog. Reprinted by permission of Allison Nafziger.

FIGURE 7.1:   Population by Race and Ethnicity, Actual and Projected: 1960, 2005, and 2050 (percentage of total)

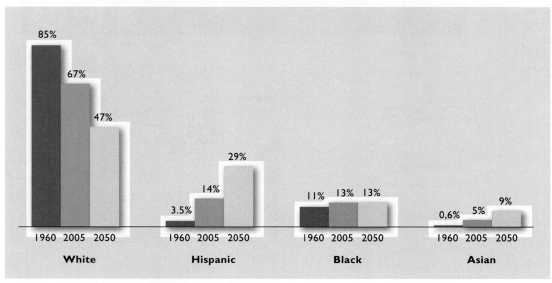

Note: All races modified and not Hispanic; American Indian/Alaska Native not shown.
From: "U. S. Populations Projections: 2005–2050," by J. S. Passel and D. V. Cohn, Washington, DC: Pew Hispanic Center. p. 9, www.pewhispanic.org. Reprinted by permission.

listserv, or collaborate with students from around the country for a virtual team project in one of your classes. In the next sections of this chapter we will discuss the opportunities that these types of contacts offer—and the benefits to be had from learning more about the intricacies of intercultural communication.

Enhanced Business Effectiveness

Studying intercultural communication can lead to greater success in both domestic and international business contexts. In the domestic context, the U.S. workforce is becoming increasingly diverse. Furthermore, businesses the world over are expanding beyond national borders—often to former colonies where the colonizer's language is firmly established but wages are lower. For example, British and U.S. businesses are outsourcing services to the former English colonies of Ireland and India. Likewise, French businesses are sending jobs to Tunisia and Morocco (Blanco, Farrell, & Labaye, 2005).

People in different cultures often hold differing values and attitudes regarding work and leisure.

Despite this trend toward outsourcing, a primary cause for international business failures is lack of attention to cultural factors (Riddle, 2000). For example, when Disney Corporation established its Euro Disney outside Paris in the early 1990s, the venture almost failed, in part because Disney executives mistakenly assumed they could transfer their U.S. cultural practices lock, stock, and barrel to the French context. However, the French workers rebelled at the Disney dress code that mandated their hair and fingernail length; they also rebelled at being told they had to smile and act enthusiastic (also part of Disney code), and eventually they took their displeasure to court (Schneider & Barsoux, 2003).

What cultural differences prompted this displeasure? According to intercultural communication experts, the Disney policies went against French people's fundamental distrust of conformity and disrespect for mandated procedure (Hall & Hall, 1990, p. 106). Also, the notion of smiling constantly at work offended the French—contrary to the U.S. service industry's expectation for workers. Also, the French resented the idea that management and workers could be friends—reflecting a distrust of an egalitarian approach to management (Jarvis, 1995). While the company overcame many of its cross-cultural difficulties, including becoming more multilingual, it continues to struggle financially (Norris, 2007).

On this Web page (www.pstalker.com/migration/mg_map.htm) you can explore some of the global migration patterns of humans and some of the reasons why people move from their homelands.

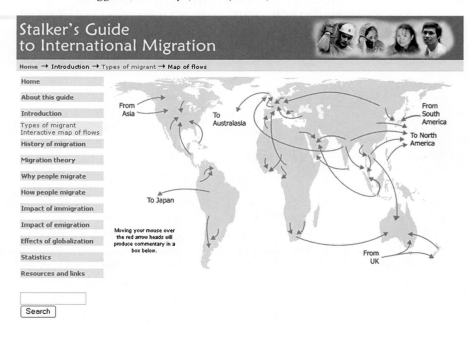

Improved Intergroup Relations

While we cannot reduce all the political problems of the world to ineffective intercultural communication, the need for better communication and understanding between countries and ethnic groups is clear. A case that is particularly important to U.S. citizens is the rise in anti-American sentiment around the globe, especially in the Middle East. Many experts think that to reverse this tide the United States should establish meaningful contact with the silent majority in the Muslim world, in ways other than through military force or traditional diplomacy. One way to do this is to acquire intercultural knowledge and skills through learning the language, culture, and history of a country or region and being able to listen (Finn, 2003). U.S.-sponsored programs such as the Peace Corps and the Fulbright scholarship were designed with this kind of intercultural exchange and understanding in mind.

mediation
peaceful third-party intervention

Intercultural communication expertise also can facilitate interethnic relations, which have increasingly involved conflict. Consider the ethnic/religious strife between Muslims and the Western world; the ethnic struggles in Bosnia and the former Soviet Union; the war between Hutus and Tusis in Rwanda (Africa); the continued unrest in the Middle East; and the racial and ethnic struggles and tensions in neighborhoods in Boston, Los Angeles, and other U.S. cities. These conflicts often call for sophisticated skills of intercultural communication and **mediation,** or peaceful third-party intervention (Bercovitch & Derouen, 2004). For example, communication scholar Benjamin Broome (1997) has successfully facilitated interethnic relations in Cyprus, one of the most heavily fortified regions in the world. Through his efforts, small groups of Greek and Turkish Cypriots have worked together to identify communication barriers and propose suggestions for improved relations between their two groups. It should be noted that even with mediation, miscommunication and intercultural conflicts can persist. Witness the long-standing conflicts in the Middle East, as well as the historical rifts between the world's largest religious groups. In some cases, people are not motivated to resolve intergroup conflict. We must admit that there is no easy cure-all for intercultural tensions and misunderstandings.

Through vacation, study abroad, and professional travel, people have more opportunities than ever before for intercultural contact.

Enhanced Self-Awareness

The final reason for studying intercultural communication is to increase self-awareness. This may seem like a contradiction, but it is not. Psychologist Peter Adler (1975) says that intercultural exploration begins as a journey into the cultures of others but often results in increased self-knowledge and understanding. People often learn more about themselves and their own cultural background and identities by coming into contact with people whose cultural backgrounds differ from their own, as our student discovered during her stay in South Africa (see *It Happened to Me: Susan*).

With these reasons for studying intercultural communication in mind, we need to define precisely what we mean by intercultural communication and culture, which is the subject we turn to next.

It Happened to Me: Susan

I rarely ever thought about being White or an American until my family and I spent a year in South Africa. Then, I thought about both every day, especially about my being White. The official language of South Africa is English, but even though we technically spoke the same language as the South Africans, my family and I had problems. It started when we were to be picked up from the airport in a *combie*, but I didn't know what that was. It turned out to be a van! Small pick-up trucks were *bakkies*, traffic signals were *robots*, and friends wanted to collect my *contact details*, which meant that they simply wanted the number of my *mobile*, better known as a cell phone, and our address. I felt that every time I opened my mouth, everyone *knew* I was American. The Black/White thing was even more pronounced. When we went down to the flea market or to the Zulu mass at the church we attended, we stood out like "five white golf balls on a black fairway" as my husband liked to say. I wondered if the self-consciousness I felt being White was the same as an African American has walking down the street in America.

WHAT IS INTERCULTURAL COMMUNICATION?

Generally speaking, **intercultural communication** refers to communication that occurs in interactions between people who are culturally different. This contrasts with most communication studies, which focus on communicators in the same culture. Still, in practice, intercultural communication occurs on a continuum, with communication between people who are relatively similar in cultural backgrounds on one end and people who are extremely different culturally on the other. For example, your conversations with your parents would represent a low degree of "interculturalness" because while you and your parents belong to two different cultural (age) groups, you probably have much in common—nationality, religion, and language. On the other hand, an interaction with a foreign teaching assistant who has a different nationality, language, religion, age, socioeconomic status, and gender would represent a high degree of interculturalness. While these two examples represent different ends on the continuum, they are both intercultural interactions. So you can see that many, if not most, of your daily interactions are intercultural in nature.

The two essential components of intercultural communication are, of course, culture and communication. Having read this far in your text, you should have a good understanding of communication. However, we think it is worthwhile to review our definition of **culture**. In Chapter 1, we defined culture as *learned patterns of perceptions, values, and behaviors shared by a group of people*. As we also mentioned, culture is dynamic (it changes), **heterogeneous** (diverse), and operates within societal power structures (Martin & Nakayama, 2008, p. 28). Next we explore how these features of culture impact individuals' intercultural interactions.

INTERCULTURAL COMMUNICATION AND THE INDIVIDUAL

While almost everyone communicates daily with people who are different from themselves in some ways, not all cultural differences have equal impact on one's interactions. For example, age differences would be less likely to impact one's interactions with others than would ethnic and/or national differences. Here we will examine some of the cultural differences that affect individuals' interactions with one another. We begin by exploring three types of intercultural interactions that can occur when individuals from different cultures coexist. We then explore specific cultural values that shape individuals' communication experiences, and we conclude this section by examining the ways that individuals within a culture can be both similar to and different from one another.

Intercultural Communication on the Borders

Because of increased opportunities for cultural contact, more people find themselves living a multicultural life. Travelers, racial/ethnic groups that live in proximity, immigrants, and people whose intimate partners come from other cultural backgrounds are only some of the groups that live between cultures, or as **border dwellers**. Here we refer to people who live on cultural borders as border dwellers because they often experience contradictory cultural patterns; thus, they may have to move between ethnicities, races, religions, languages, socioeconomic classes, or sexual orientations. One can become a border dweller in one of three ways: through travel, through socialization (cocultural groups), and through participation in an intercultural relationship. Let's look at each in turn.

Border Dwellers Through Travel

Individuals travel between cultures both voluntarily and involuntarily, and for both long and short periods. **Voluntary short-term travelers** include study-abroad students, corporate personnel, missionaries, and military people. **Voluntary long-term**

intercultural communication
communication that occurs in interactions between people who are culturally different

culture
learned patterns of perceptions, values, and behaviors shared by a group of people

heterogeneous
diverse

border dwellers
people who live between cultures and often experience contradictory cultural patterns

voluntary short-term travelers
people who are border dwellers by choice and for a limited time, such as study-abroad students or corporate personnel

voluntary long-term travelers
people who are border dwellers by choice and for an extended time, such as immigrants

travelers include immigrants who settle in other locations, usually seeking what they perceive is a better life, as is the case for many immigrants who come to the United States. **Involuntary short-term travelers** include refugees forced into cultural migration because of war, famine, or unbearable economic hardship. For example, many people fled Iraq during Saddam Hussein's rule and continue to leave because of the war. **Involuntary long-term travelers** are those who are forced to permanently immigrate to a new location, including many who fled Kosovo during the war in the 1990s. For an illustration, see *Visual Summary 7.1: Border Dwellers Through Travel*, on p. 172.

When people think of traveling or living in a new culture, they tend to think that learning the language is key to effective intercultural interaction; however, intercultural communication involves much more than language issues. People must also adapt to a new environment and deal with an entirely new way of thinking and living.

Travelers who enter another culture voluntarily for a defined period usually experience *culture shock*. **Culture shock** is a feeling of disorientation and discomfort due to the unfamiliarity of surroundings and the lack of familiar cues in the environment. When short-term travelers return home to their own country they may experience similar feelings, known as **reverse culture shock** or **reentry shock**—a sort of culture shock in one's own country. After being gone for a significant amount of time, aspects of one's own culture may seem somewhat foreign, as our student discovered on his return home to Pakistan after living in the United States for four years (see *It Happened to Me: Maham*).

Most travelers eventually adapt to the foreign culture to some extent if they stay long enough and if the hosts are welcoming. This is often the case for northern Europeans who visit or settle in the United States. Sometimes people even experience culture shock when they move from one region of the United States to another, such as someone who moves from Boston to Birmingham or from Honolulu to Minneapolis. The evacuation of tens of thousands of African American southerners from New Orleans after Hurricane Katrina highlighted this experience. Some of the evacuees were sent to stay in the mostly White state of Utah; a number of them said that Utah was so different from what they were used to that the experience seemed unreal.

For many travelers, the most stressful time in their sojourn is the beginning; they may experience anxiety even before leaving their home. International students may worry about finding a place to live, whether they can meet the challenges of navigating a foreign university, surviving without the support of family and loved ones, and whether they will have enough money; tourists may be anxious about transportation and negotiating a new language (Lin, 2006). Once in the new culture, most sojourners find there are two types of challenges: (1) dealing with the psychological stress of being in an unfamiliar environment (feeling somewhat uncertain and anxious) and (2) learning how to behave appropriately in the new culture, both verbally (e.g., learning a new language) and nonverbally (e.g., bowing instead of shaking hands in Japan) (Kim, 2005).

involuntary short-term travelers
people who are border dwellers not by choice and only for a limited time, such as refugees forced to move

involuntary long-term travelers
people who are border dwellers permanently but not by choice, such as those who relocate to escape war

culture shock
a feeling of disorientation and discomfort due to the lack of familiar environmental cues

reverse culture shock/reentry shock
culture shock experienced by travelers upon returning to their home country

Many Katrina evacuees experienced culture shock when they were relocated to regions in the U.S. that were unfamiliar to them.

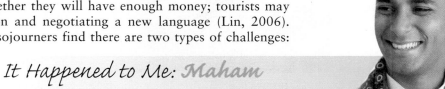

It Happened to Me: Maham

I would say that I experienced culture (reentry) shock when I visited Pakistan after moving away from there four years ago. In those four years I had basically forgotten the language and became very unfamiliar with the culture back home. Even though I enjoyed my visit to Pakistan a lot, I had problems adjusting to some of the ways of life. I was not familiar with the bargaining system . . . where people can go to the store and bargain for prices. I felt very out of place. . . . As I spent more time there, I got adjusted and used to how people did things there.

Border Dwellers Through Travel

Voluntary

Involuntary

Short Term

Tourists, Missionaries, Study Abroad Students

Temporay Refugees from War, Famine, or Economic Hardship

Long Term

Immigrants

Permanent Refugees from War, Famine, or Economic Hardship

Alternative VIEW
Language Issues for Immigrants

Many people think that immigrant families in the United States do not learn English. However, recent studies by the Pew Hispanic Center find that while many immigrants do not speak English, their children and grandchildren do. Why is learning English important for immigrants in the United States? How could immigrants learn English more quickly?

Nearly all Hispanic adults born in the United States of immigrant parents report they are fluent in English. By contrast, only a small minority of their parents describe themselves as skilled English speakers. This finding of a dramatic increase in English-language ability from one generation of Hispanics to the next emerges from a new analysis of six Pew Hispanic Center surveys conducted this decade among a total of more than 14,000 Latino adults. The surveys show that fewer than one-in-four (23 percent) Latino immigrants reports being able to speak English very well. However, fully 88 percent of their U.S.-born adult children report that they speak English very well. Among later generations of Hispanic adults, the figure rises to 94 percent. Reading ability in English shows a similar trend. As fluency in English increases across generations, so, too, does the regular use of English by Hispanics, both at home and at work. For most immigrants, English in not the primary language they use in either setting. But for their grown children, it is.

FROM: *English usage Among Hispanics in the United States*, by S. Hakimzadeh & D. Cohn, 2007, Washington, DC: Pew Hispanic Center, www.pewhispanic.org. Reprinted by permission.

See *Alternative View: Language Issues for Immigrants*. There are many reasons why an individual may be more, or less, successful at adapting to a new culture. Younger people who have had some previous traveling experience seem to be more successful. On the other hand, if the environment is hostile or the move is involuntary, adaptation may be especially difficult and the culture shock especially intense. For example, many evacuees from Hurricane Katrina were forced to relocate. In some instances, they were greeted with great sympathy and hospitality in the new locations; in other instances they were subjected to considerable racism (Rabbi: My radio, 2005). Asian, African, and Latino students in the United States tend to have a more difficult adaptation due to experiences of discrimination and hostility based on their race/ethnicity (Jung, Hecht, & Wadsworth 2007; Lee & Rice, 2007).

One thing that can ease culture shock and make cultural adaptation easier is having a social support network. This can come from organizations like an International Student Office or a Tourist Bureau that can assist with housing, transportation, and so forth. Close relationships with other travelers or host-country aquaintances can also provide support in the form of a sympathetic ear; through these relationships sojourners can relieve stress, discuss, problem-solve, acquire new knowledge, or just have fun (Kashima & Loh, 2006; Lin, 2006).

The role of social support is even more crucial for long-term travelers, such as immigrants. If there is little social support or the receiving environment is hostile, immigrants may choose to separate from the majority or host culture, or they may be forced into separation (Berry, 2005). Another option for immigrants is to adapt in *some* ways to the new culture, which means accepting some aspects, such as dress and outward behavior, while retaining aspects of the old/home culture. For many recent immigrants to the United States, this has been a preferred option, and seems to lead to less stress. For example, Asian Indians constitute one of the largest immigrant groups in the United States. Many have successfully adapted to U.S. life both professionally and socially. Still many retain viable aspects of their Indian culture in their personal and family lives—continuing to celebrate ethnic or religious holidays and adhering to traditional values and beliefs (Hegde, 2000). However, this integration of two cultures is not always easy, as we'll see in the next section. Families can be divided on the issues of how much to adapt, with children often wanting to be more "American" and parents wanting to hold on to their native language and cultural practices (Ward, 2008).

Border Dwellers Through Socialization

The second group of border dwellers is composed of people who grow up living on the borders between cultural groups. Examples include ethnic groups, such as Latinos, Asian Americans, and African Americans, who live in the predominantly White United States, as well as people who grow up negotiating multiple sexual orientations or religions. In addition to those who must negotiate the two cultures they live within, the United States has increasing numbers of multiracial people who often grow up negotiating *multiple* cultural realities. The 2000 Census form was the first that allowed people to designate more than two races—and since then, the group of people who choose to categorize themselves as multiracial has grown faster than any other (Jones & Smith, 2001).

Probably the best known multiracial American is President Barack Obama—his father was an exchange student from Kenya and his mother a U.S. American Student. Other famous multiracial Americans include Vin Diesel, who is Black and Italian American; Dwayne Johnson, also known as the "Rock," who is Black and Samoan; and Tiger Woods who is African American, European American and Thai. British geneticist Spencer Wells (2002) makes the point that Tiger Woods is a person who could only have been born in the twentieth century. His complex web of ancestors, originating on opposite sides of the world, could have encountered each other in the United States only within the past 100 years (p. 193).

Typically, cultural minorities are socialized to the norms and values of both the dominant culture and their own; nonetheless, they often prefer to enact those of their own. They may be pressured to assimilate to the dominant culture and embrace its values, yet those in the dominant culture may still be reluctant to accept them as they try to do so (Berry, 2005). For example, a German woman whose family came from Turkey encountered teachers in Germany who perceived her to be part of a Turkish minority and thus had low expectations for her performance (Ewing, 2004). And members of minority groups sometimes find themselves in a kind of cultural limbo—not "gay" enough for gay friends, not "straight" enough for the majority; not Black enough or White enough.

All of the multiracial Americans we discuss above have had to, at some point, respond to criticism that they did not sufficiently aligned themselves with one or another of their racial groups. During the 2008 presidential campaign, President Obama was criticized for being "too white." Vin Diesel has been criticized for refusing to discuss his Black racial heritage while Dwayne Johnson originally was condemned for not recognizing his Black heritage but later was praised for attending the Black Entertainment Television awards. Tiger Woods also was subjected to considerable pressure to identify as Black and finally issued a press release on the topic in which he stated that he was "EQUALLY PROUD, to be both African-American and Asian!" (Tiger Woods on race, n.d.).

Border Dwellers Through Relationships

Finally, many people live on cultural borders because they have intimate partners whose cultural background differs from their own. Within the United States increasing numbers of people cross borders of nationality, race, and ethnicity in this way, creating a "quiet revolution" (Root, 2001). Overall, partners in interethnic and interracial romantic relationships have faced greater challenges than those establishing relationships across religions, nationalities, and class groups. Many people do not realize that, until 1967, it was illegal for African Americans and Whites to marry within the United States (Root, 2001). However, attitudes toward intercultural relationships have changed significantly in the past decades, particularly attitudes toward interracial relations (Taylor, Funk, & Craighill, 2006). According to the most recent census information, interracial marriages have increased tenfold from 1970 to 2000. Latinos, American Indians, and Hawaiians are most likely to enter interracial marriages, while African Americans and Whites have the lowest rates (Lee & Edmonston, 2005).

Multiracial people, like Tiger Woods, are the fastest growing ethnic/racial group in the United States.

However, such relationships are not without their challenges, as described in *Did You Know? Sobering Advice for Anyone Contemplating a Cross-Cultural Marriage.* The most common challenges involve negotiating how to live on the border between two religions, ethnicities, races, languages, and sometimes, value systems. For example, Whites in close relationships with African Americans learn firsthand about racism from their partners and must learn to function in both White and Black social circles—which often do not overlap (Rosenblatt, Karis, & Powell, 1996).

Did You Know?
Sobering Advice for Anyone Contemplating a Cross-Cultural Marriage

This hard-won advice is intended only for those couples who are truly considering entering into a cross-cultural marital situation. Simply marrying someone whose ancestry is different from your own is not quite the same thing.

My personal experience centers around the relationship between a Japanese female and an American male, although I'd like to think that the basic ideas could be applied to any cross-cultural situation.

Rule #1: *Don't assume that your interest in your partner's culture will last, or that it will somehow prevent conflicts from occurring.* Never underestimate the depth of the roots of your own upbringing. Your beliefs, your emotions, your priorities, in short, your whole approach to life, are shaped by the culture in which you were brought up.

Rule #2: *Don't assume that the other person will change significantly just because of the relationship or because of your charming influence.* The best thing you can do for each other is to acknowledge the fact that conflicts will occur and will often occur for the simplest and most unexpected reasons.

Rule #3: *Don't assume anything. Make sure you discuss with your partner every aspect of your future life together.* Also, don't assume that when your partner says something is unimportant that it does not have to be discussed. Those areas are often the *most* important things to discuss.

Rule #4: *Make it a point to talk about some tough topics (like money, raising children, where to live, etc.) before making those wedding arrangements.* Start an argument or two. Find out what it's like to fight by your partner's rules. You might as well know whether you will be able to work together toward a solution when the inevitable crisis comes up.

Rule #5: *Make sure that between the two of you, there is at least one language in which you are both fluent.* As a test, try taking some very subtle feeling or belief and explain it to your potential mate. Have him or her explain it back. If there is not a substantial understanding of what you explained, wait a while until one or the other of you is able to achieve a good degree of fluency in the other's language.

Rule #6: *Examine your own motives.* Is this someone you would hook up with even if you were safe and happy in your own country? If you are the partner who is trying to live in another culture, remember this: Culture shock can do funny things to a normally rational mind. First get yourself comfortable with your surroundings. Disarm the "convenience" in the relationship and then see what you think. Learn more about the subtle parts of your partner's culture and then decide if you can tolerate, work with, and actually love that person because they are different and not *despite* those differences.

Rule #7: *Don't underestimate the importance of keeping good relations with your partner's parents.* This is especially true if your partner is the one from Japan (or some other non-Western culture). It seems that we in the US (and I can hardly speak for any other Western cultures) have developed a great deal of independence from our families. However, the same is not

(continued)

Did You Know? *(continued)*

true in Japan. There is still a great deal of synergy between parent and offspring, even well after they have left the nest and formed families of their own. If you can't get their active support, then at least settle for passive acceptance. Anything less should be a sign of trouble ahead.

Rule #8:   *Be ready to help your partner through the inevitable rough spots.* Well, okay, this is sound advice for any couple. But just remember that you both will be setting out on an adventure—a full-time first-hand learning experience in the other person's cultural labyrinth. None of us, I am convinced, ever really appreciates how many things we learn about life when we are young and that we take for granted every day. We consider many of these things just plain "common sense" but they're only common if you and your partner have common backgrounds. Expect the unexpected. Then you won't be disappointed.

FROM: Larabell, J. (2003). Sobering advice for anyone contemplating a cross-cultural marriage. Retrieved October 16, 2005, from www.larabell.org/cross.html.

The balancing act between cultures can be especially challenging when friends, family, and society disapprove (Fiebert, Nugent, Hershberger, & Kasdan, 2004). A Jewish professor who married a Muslim woman reflects on how people would react if he decided to convert to Islam:

> What a scandalous action! My family would be outraged and my friends startled. What would they say? How would I be treated? What would colleagues at the university do if I brought a prayer rug to the office and, say, during a committee meeting, or at a reception for a visiting scholar, insisted on taking a break to do my ritual prayers? (Rosenstone, 2005, p. 235)

These challenges can be even more pronounced for women, since parents often play an important role in whom they date and marry. A recent study found that women were much more likely than men to mention pressure from family members as a reason that interethnic dating would be difficult (Clark-Ibanez & Felmlee, 2004).

Negotiating Cultural Tensions on the Borders

How do people negotiate the tensions between often-contradictory systems of values, language, and nonverbal behavior of two or more cultures? The answer depends on many factors, such as one's reason for being on the border, length of stay or involvement, receptivity of the dominant culture, and personality characteristics of the individuals (Kim, 2005).

In most cases, people in such situations can feel caught between two systems; this experience has been described as feeling as if one were swinging on a trapeze, a metaphor that captures the immigrant's experience of vacillating between the cultural patterns of the homeland and the new country (Hegde, 1998). Writer Gloria Anzaldúa (1999), who is Chicana, gay, and female, stresses that living successfully on the border requires significant flexibility and an active approach to negotiating multiple cultural backgrounds. She struggles to balance her Indian and Spanish heritage, as well as her patriarchal Catholic upbringing, with her spiritual and sexual identity. The result, she says, is the *mestiza*—a person who has actively confronted and managed the negative aspects of living on the border.

Similarly, Communication scholar Lisa Flores (1996) shows how Chicana feminist writers and artists acknowledge negative stereotypes of Mexican and Mexican-American women—illiterate Spanglish-speaking laborers, passive sex objects, servants of men and children—and transform them into images of strength. In their descriptions and images, Chicana artists are strong, clever bilinguals, reveling in their dual Anglo-Mexican heritage. In so doing, they create a kind of positive identity "home" where they are the center. In addition, they gain strength by reaching out to other women (women of color and immigrant women), and together strive to achieve more justice and recognition for women who live "in the middle" between cultural worlds.

Managing these tensions while living on the border and being multicultural can be both rewarding and challenging. Based on data from interviews she conducted, Janet Bennett (1998) described two types of border dwellers, or, as she labeled them, "marginal individuals": *encapsulated marginal people* and *constructive marginal people.*

Encapsulated marginal people feel disintegrated by having to shift cultures. They have difficulty making decisions and feel extreme pressure from both groups. They try to assimilate but never feel comfortable or at home.

In contrast, **constructive marginal people** thrive in their "border" life and, at the same time, recognize its tremendous challenges, as Gloria Anzaldúa described. They see themselves as choice makers. They recognize the significance of being "in between," and they continuously negotiate and explore this identity.

To summarize, people can find themselves living on cultural borders for many reasons: travel, socialization, or involvement in an intercultural relationship. While border dwelling can be challenging and frustrating, it also can lead to cultural insights and agility in navigating intercultural encounters.

The Influence of Cultural Values on Communication

In Chapters 5 and 6, we described how culture influences verbal and nonverbal communication. You might think that these differences would be key to understanding intercultural communication. Just as important is understanding **cultural values,** which are the beliefs that are so central to a cultural group that they are never questioned. Cultural values prescribe what *should* be. Understanding cultural values is essential because they so powerfully influence people's behavior, including their communication. Intercultural interaction often involves confronting and responding to an entirely different set of cultural values. Let's see how this works.

About fifty years ago, anthropologists Florence Kluckhohn and Fred Strodtbeck (1961) conducted a study that identified the contrasting values of three cultural groups in the United States: Latinos, Anglos, and American Indians. Later, social psychologist Geert Hofstede (1997, 1998, 2001) and his colleagues extended this analysis in a massive study, collecting 116,000 surveys about people's value preferences in approximately eighty countries around the world. Psychologist Michael Bond and his colleagues conducted a similar, though smaller, study in Asia (Chinese Culture Connection, 1987). Together, these studies identified cultural values preferred by people in a number of countries, six of which are listed in *Visual Summary 7.2: Cultural Values and Communication*, on p. 178, and discussed in the following sections. While these value preferences may apply most directly to national cultural groups, they can also apply to ethnic/racial groups, socioeconomic class groups, and gender groups.

As you read about these cultural value orientations, please keep three points in mind. These guidelines reflect a common dilemma for intercultural communication scholars—the desire to describe and understand communication and behavior patterns within a cultural group and the fear of making rigid categories that can lead to stereotyping:

1. The following discussion describes the *predominant* values preferred by various cultural groups, not the values held by *every person* in the cultural group. Think of cultural values as occurring on a bell curve: Most people may be in the middle, holding a particular value orientation, but many people can be found on each end of the curve; these are the people who *do not go along* with the majority.

2. The following discussion refers to values on the cultural level, not on the individual level. Thus, if you read that most Chinese tend to prefer an indirect way of speaking, you cannot assume that every Chinese person you meet will speak in an indirect way in every situation.

encapsulated marginal people
people who feel disintegrated by having to shift cultures

constructive marginal people
people who thrive in a border-dweller life, while recognizing its tremendous challenges

cultural values
beliefs that are so central to a cultural group that they are never questioned

Cultural Values and Communication

Individualistic/Collectivistic

Highly Individualistic ←——————————————————→ Highly Collectivistic

- North American
- Northern European

- South American
- Asian
- Hispanic and Asian Americans in the United States

Preferred Personality

More Important "to Do" ←——————————————————→ More Important "to Be"

- European Americans
- Asian Americans
- African Americans

- African Americans
- Latinos

View of Human Nature

Humans Are Fundamentally Evil ←——————————————————→ Humans Are Fundamentally Good

- United States

- Middle East
- United States

Human–Nature Value

Humans Intended to Rule Nature ←——————— Harmony ———————→ Nature Intended to Rule Humans

- United States

- American Indians
- Asians

- Middle East
- United States

Power Distribution

Equal Distribution of Power ←——————————————————→ Unequal Distribution of Power

- Denmark
- Israel
- New Zealand

- Mexico
- Philippines
- India

Long-Term Versus Short-Term Orientation

Short-Term Orientation ←——————————————————→ Long-Term Orientation

- Judaism
- Christianity
- Islam
- (monotheistic religions)

- Confucianism
- Hinduism
- Buddhism
- Shintoism
- (polytheistic religions)

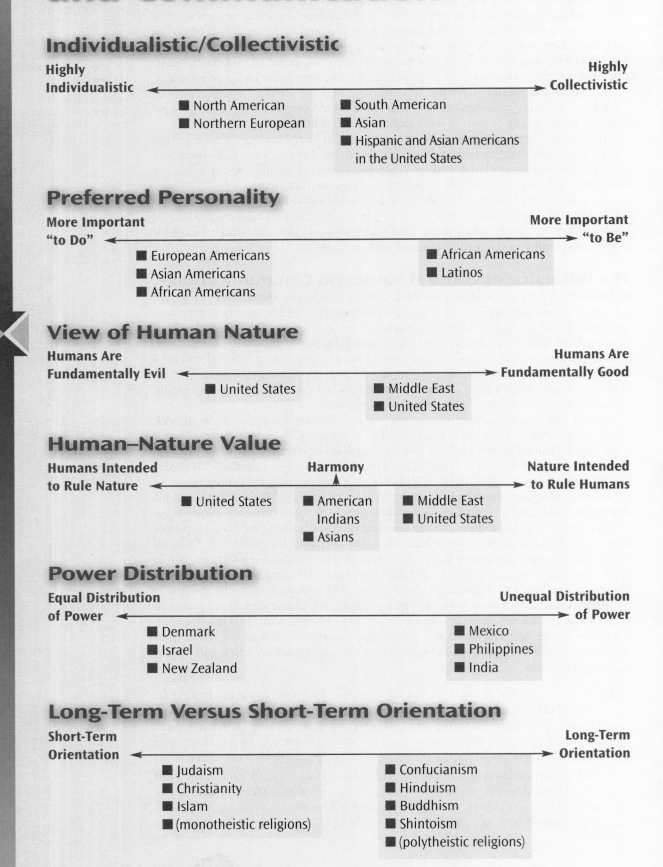

3. The only way to understand what a particular individual believes is to get to know the person. You can't predict how any one person will communicate. The real challenge is to understand the full range of cultural values and then learn to communicate effectively with others who hold differing value orientations, regardless of their cultural background.

Now that you understand the basic ground rules, let's look at six key aspects of cultural values.

Individualism and Collectivism

One of the most central value orientations identified in this research addresses whether a culture emphasizes the rights and needs of the individual or that of the group. For example, many North American and northern European cultural groups, particularly U.S. Whites, value individualism and independence, believing that one's primary responsibility is to one's self (Bellah, Madsen, Sullivan, Swidler, & Tipton, 1996; Hofstede, 2001; Kikoski & Kikoski, 1999). In relationships, as Kaori discovered in our opening vignette, those with this **individualist orientation** respect autonomy and independence, and they do not meddle in another's problems unless invited. For example, in cultures where individualism prevails, many children are raised to be autonomous and to live on their own by late adolescence (although they may return home for short periods after this). Their parents are expected to take care of themselves and not "be a burden" on their children when they age (Triandis, 1995).

In contrast, many cultures in South America and Asia hold a more **collectivistic orientation** that stresses the needs of the group (Hofstede, 2001; Triandis, 1995), as do some Hispanic and Asian Americans in the United States (Ho, 1987). Some argue that working-class people tend to be more collectivistic than those in the middle or upper class (Dunbar, 1997). For collectivists, the primary responsibility is to relationships with others; interdependence in family, work, and personal relationships is viewed positively. Collectivists value working toward relationship and group harmony over remaining independent and self-sufficient. For example, giving money to a needy cousin, uncle, or aunt might be preferable to spending it on oneself. In many collectivist cultures, too, children often defer to parents when making important decisions (McGoldrick, Giordano, & Pearce, 1996). As a U.S. American software consultant in India observed, "At the core of many Indians is a respect for parents that results in involving them in decisions. I have done hundreds of interviews with software professionals in Bangalore, India, and I am amazed to find how often parents are consulted before a job decision is made" (Budelman, 2006).

As noted earlier, however, not all Japanese or all Indians are collectivistic. In fact, generational differences may exist within countries where collectivism is strong. For example, some Japanese college students show a strong preference for individualism while their parents hold a more collectivistic orientation—which sometimes leads to intercultural conflict (Matsumoto, 2002). Young people in many Asian countries (Korea, Vietnam) are increasingly influenced by Western capitalism and individualism and are now making their own decisions regarding marriage and career, rather than following their family's wishes—a practice unheard of fifty years ago (Shim, Kim, & Martin, 2008). In addition, not all cultures are as individualistic as U.S. culture or as collectivistic as Japanese culture. Rather, cultures can be arranged along an individualism–collectivism continuum (Gudykunst & Lee, 2002) based on their specific orientations to the needs of the individual and the group.

individualist orientation
a value orientation that respects the autonomy and independence of individuals

collectivistic orientation
a value orientation that stresses the needs of the group

Cultural values of individualism and collectivism are often expressed through family traditions and relationships.

As you were growing up, in what ways were you reared to be individualistic? Collectivistic? Which orientation was the predominant cultural value of your family?

Preferred Personality

In addition to differing on the individualism–collectivism spectrum, cultural groups may differ over the idea of the **preferred personality**, or whether it is more important to "do" or to "be" (Kluckhohn & Strodtbeck, 1961). In the United States, researchers have found that *doing* is the preferred value for many people (Stewart & Bennett, 1991), including European Americans, Asian Americans, and African Americans (Ting-Toomey, 1999). In general, the "doing mode" means working hard to achieve material gain, even if it means sacrificing time with family and friends (Kohls, 2001). Other cultural groups, for example, many Latinos, prefer the *being* mode—which emphasizes the importance of experiencing life and the people around them fully and "working to live" rather than "living to work" (Hecht, Sedano, & Ribeau, 1993).

What kinds of communication problems do you think occur when members of a diverse work team hold different value orientations toward being and doing? How might someone who prefers a being orientation view someone with a doing orientation and vice versa?

Some scholars suggest that many African Americans express both a doing value (fighting actively against racism through social activity for the good of the community) as well as a being mode—valuing a sense of vitality and open expression of feeling (Hecht, Jackson, & Ribeau, 2002). Cultural differences in this value orientation can lead to communication challenges. For example, many Latinos believe that Anglos place too much emphasis on accomplishing tasks and earning money and not enough emphasis on spending time with friends and family or enjoying the moment (Kikoski & Kikoski, 1999).

View of Human Nature

A third value difference concerns the **view of human nature**—in particular, whether humans are considered fundamentally good, evil, or a mixture. The United States, for example, was founded by the Puritans who believed that human nature was fundamentally evil (Hulse, 1996). In the years since the founding of the country, a shift occurred in this view, as evidenced in the U.S. legal and justice systems. It emphasizes rehabilitation, suggesting a view of humans as potentially good. In addition, the fact that the U.S. justice system assumes people are innocent until proven guilty indicates that people are viewed as basically good (Kohls, 2001).

In contrast, cultural groups that view humans as essentially evil, such as some fundamentalist religions, emphasize punishment over rehabilitation. Some evidence indicates that U.S. Americans in general are moving again toward this view of human nature. For example, recent laws such as the "three strikes rule" emphasize punishment over rehabilitation by automatically sending to prison anyone who is convicted three times. Also, incarceration rates in the United States have increased by more than 500 percent since the early 1970s, and among developed countries, the United States now has the highest percentage of incarcerated individuals (Shelden, 2004). As you might imagine, people who differ on the question of human nature can have serious disagreements on public policies concerning crime and justice.

Human–Nature Value

A fourth value that varies from culture to culture is the perceived relationship between humans and nature, or the **human–nature value orientation**. At one end of this value continuum is the view that humans are intended to rule nature. At the other extreme, nature is seen as ruling humans. In a third option, the two exist in harmony. Unsurprisingly, the predominant value in the United States has been one of humans ruling over nature, as evidenced in the proliferation of controlled environments. Phoenix, Arizona, for example, which is in a desert, has over 200 golf courses—reflecting the fact that Arizonans have changed the natural environment to suit their living and leisure interests. In other parts of the United States, people make snow for skiing, seed clouds when rain is needed, dam and reroute rivers, and/or use fertilizer to enhance agricultural production. Such interventions generally reflect a belief in human control over nature (Trompenaars & Hampden-Turner, 1997).

preferred personality
a value orientation that expresses whether it is more important for a person to "do" or to "be"

view of human nature
a value orientation that expresses whether humans are fundamentally good, evil, or a mixture

human–nature value orientation
the perceived relationship between humans and nature

In contrast, many in the Middle East view nature as having predominance over humans. This belief that one's fate is held by nature is reflected in the common Arabic saying "*Enchallah*" ("Allah willing"), suggesting that nature will (and should) determine, for example, how crops will grow. A comparable Christian saying is "as the Lord wills it," reflecting perhaps a similar fatalistic tendency in Christianity.

Many American Indians and Asians value harmony with nature. People who hold this cultural orientation believe that humans and nature are one and that nature enriches human life. For many traditional American Indians, certain animals such as buffalo and eagles are important presences in human activity (Porter, 2002). For example, a yearly "Good Buffalo Festival" is held in Kyle, South Dakota, to educate young Indians about the importance of the buffalo in Lakota culture (Melmer, 2004). Many native cultures believe eagles carry messages to the Creator, and they use eagle feathers in sacred ceremonies, as described in *Did You Know? Zuni Eagle Aviary Is a Beautiful Sign.*

In the United States, differences arise between real estate developers, who believe that humans take precedence over nature, and environmentalists and many Native American groups, who believe that nature is as important as humans. This conflict has surfaced in disagreements over water rights in Oregon (Hemmingsen, 2002), and over the proposed eight million acre habitat for the endangered spotted owl in the southwestern United States (McKinnon, 2004).

Power Distance

Power distance, the fifth value orientation, refers to the extent to which less powerful members of institutions and organizations within a culture expect and accept an unequal distribution of power (Hofstede, 2001). In Denmark, Israel, and New Zealand many people value small power distances. Thus, most people in those countries believe that inequality, while inevitable, should be minimized, and that the best

power distance
a value orientation that refers to the extent to which less powerful members of institutions and organizations within a culture expect and accept an unequal distribution of power

Did You Know?
Zuni Eagle Aviary Is a Beautiful Sign

In this editorial, the author explains the importance of the eagle and eagle feathers for many Native American tribes today.

The Zuni Eagle Aviary is home to nine bald eagles and 12 golden eagles. All the birds are injured birds. They are cared for by the tribe and treated with dignity. . . . Each bird drops or molts a couple of feathers a day. These are gathered ceremonially and passed on to tribal members and sometimes other tribes. School children often visit the Aviary, which is used for lectures and teaching workshops.

The use of eagle and other bird feathers in ceremony is highly serious [indicating] . . . utmost respect for the animal and for the spirit. . . . There are many ceremonies at this time of the year, including many sundances on the Great Plains and other ceremonies elsewhere in the hemisphere. The use of feathers is completely integrated into the sundance, the Pipe Ways. A fallen feather stops the dance. Special music, special people only can pick it up. In most places, this requires veterans. In other places, this is done by eagle clan matrons, headmen and holy people. . . . When an eagle appears over a prayer or ceremony, the sign is always greeted with awe and thankfulness. The eagle flies highest and can disappear into the clear blue sky. They say this is the moment a prayer is heard.

FROM: "Zuni Eagle Aviary Is a Beautiful Sign". This editorial first appeared in *Indian Country Today*, July 31, 2002, http://indiancountry.com. Reprinted by permission.

Eagle feathers play an important role in many American Indian ceremonies.

leaders emphasize equality and informality in interactions with subordinates. In many situations, subordinates are expected to speak up and contribute.

Societies that value large power distance—for example, Mexico, the Philippines, and India—are structured more around a hierarchy in which each person has a rightful place, and interactions between supervisors and subordinates are more formal (Hofstede, 2001). Seniority, age, rank, and titles are emphasized more in these societies than in small power distance societies.

People who are used to large power distances may be uncomfortable in settings where hierarchy is unclear or ambiguous. For example, international students who come from countries where a large power distance value predominates may initially be very uncomfortable in U.S. college classrooms, where relations between students and teachers are informal and characterized by equality, a situation you will read about in *It Happened to Me: Nagesh*.

It Happened to Me: Nagesh

I was amazed when I first saw American classrooms. The students seemed very disrespectful toward the teacher. They had their feet on the desks and interrupted the teacher while he was talking if they didn't understand something. In my country, students would never behave this way toward a teacher. I found it difficult to speak up in this kind of classroom situation.

In contrast, U.S. Americans abroad often offend locals when they treat subordinates at work or home too informally—calling them by first name, treating them as if they were friends. For example, when former President Bush visited Europe, he referred to the Belgian Prime Minister by his first name, Guy, which surprised and amused many Belgians—who are accustomed to more formality.

Note that value orientations represent what should be, not what is. While many Americans say they desire small power distance, the truth is that rigid social and economic hierarchies exist and most people are born into and live within the same socioeconomic class for their whole lives (Herbert, 2005).

Long-Term Versus Short-Term Orientation

The research identifying the five values we've described has been criticized for its predominately western European bias. In response to this criticism, a group of Chinese researchers developed and administered a similar, but more Asian-oriented, questionnaire to people in twenty-two countries around the world (Chinese Culture Connection, 1987). They then compared their findings to previous research on value orientations and found considerable overlap, especially on the dimensions of individualism versus collectivism and power distance. These researchers did identify one additional value dimension that earlier researchers hadn't seen—**long-term versus short-term orientation**.

This dimension reflects a society's attitude toward virtue or truth. A **short-term orientation** characterizes cultures in which people are concerned with possessing one fundamental truth, as reflected in the **monotheistic** (belief in one god) religions of Judaism, Christianity, and Islam. Other qualities identified in the research and associated with a short-term orientation include an emphasis on quick results, individualism, and personal security and safety (Hofstede, 1997).

In contrast, a **long-term orientation** tends to respect the demands of virtue, reflected in Eastern religions such as Confucianism, Hinduism, Buddhism, and Shintoism, which are all **polytheistic** religions (belief in more than one god). Other qualities associated with a long-term orientation include thrift, perseverance and tenacity in whatever one attempts, and a willingness to subordinate oneself for a purpose (Bond, 1991, 1996).

While knowing about these value differences can help you identify and understand problems that arise in intercultural interactions, you might be concerned that this approach to the study of intercultural communication leads to generalizing and stereotyping. The next section presents an approach that helps counteract this tendency to think in simplistic terms about intercultural communication.

long-term versus short-term orientation
the dimension of a society's value orientation that reflects its attitude toward virtue or truth

short-term orientation
a value orientation that stresses the importance of possessing one fundamental truth

monotheistic
belief in one god

long-term orientation
a value orientation in which people stress the importance of virtue

polytheistic
belief in more than one god

A Dialectic Approach

Dialectics has long existed as a concept in philosophical thought and logic. In this book we introduce it as a way to emphasize simultaneous contradictory truths. Thus, a **dialectic approach** helps people respond to the complexities of intercultural communication and to override any tendencies to stereotype people based on cultural patterns. The notion is difficult to understand, because it is contrary to most formal education in the United States, which emphasizes **dichotomous thinking**, in which things are "either/or"—good or bad, big or small, right or wrong. However, a dialectic approach recognizes that things may be both/and. For example, a palm tree may be weak *and* strong. Its branches look fragile and weak, and yet in a hurricane it remains strong because the "weak" fronds can bend without breaking. Similar dialectics exist in intercultural communication; for example, Didier may be a Frenchman who shares many cultural characteristics of other French people, but he also is an individual who possesses characteristics that make him unique. So, he is both similar to and different from other French people. A dialectic approach emphasizes the fluid, complex, and contradictory nature of intercultural interactions. Dialectics exist in other communication contexts such as relationships, which we explore in Chapter 8. Six dialectics that can assist you in communicating more effectively in intercultural interactions are discussed next.

dialectic approach
recognizes that things need not be perceived as either/or, but may be seen as both/and

dichotomous thinking
thinking in which things are perceived as "either/or"—for example, good or bad, big or small, right or wrong

Cultural–Individual

This dialectic emphasizes that some behaviors, such as ways of relating to others, are determined by our culture, while others are simply idiosyncratic, or particular to us as individuals. For example, Robin twists her hair while she talks. This idiosyncratic personal preference should not be mistaken for a cultural norm. She doesn't do it because she is female, or young, or Protestant, or African American. Although it isn't always easy to tell whether a behavior is culturally or individually based, taking a dialectic approach means that one does not immediately assume that someone's behavior is culturally based.

Personal–Contextual

This dialectic focuses on the importance of context or situation in intercultural communication. In any intercultural encounter, both the individual and the situation are simultaneously important. Let's take the example of a French and an American student striking up a conversation in a bar. The immediate situation has an important impact on their communication, so their conversation would probably differ dramatically if it occurred at a synagogue, mosque, or church. The larger situation, including political and historical forces, also plays a role. In the build-up to the Iraq War of 2003, for example, some French students encountered anti-French sentiment in the United States. At the same time, the characteristics of the specific individuals also affect the exchange. Some students would ignore the immediate or larger situation and reject the anti-French sentiment—especially if they were opposed to the war themselves. Others would attach great importance to the larger context and view the French students negatively. The point is that reducing an interaction to a mere meeting of two individuals means viewing intercultural communication too simplistically.

Differences–Similarities

Real, important differences exist between cultural groups; we've identified some of these in this chapter. However, important commonalities exist as well. One of our students summed up this point nicely in *It Happened to Me: Angelina*.

It Happened to Me: Angelina

In my first year of college I had the most memorable friendship with a person from the Middle East. Through this friendship I learned a lot about the way people from the Middle East communicate with friends, family, and authority. My new friend and I differed in many ways—in religion, culture, nationality, race, and language. However, we were both female college students, the same age, and we shared many interests. She dressed like I did and styled her hair similarly, and we shared many ideas about the future and concerns about the world.

Static–Dynamic

While some cultural patterns remain relatively stable and static for years, they also can undergo dynamic change. For example, many people get their information about Indians from popular films like *Pocahontas* or *The Indian in the Cupboard*, which portray Indians living the rural life they lived centuries ago, even though the majority of Indians today live in urban areas (Alexie, 2003). A static–dynamic dialectic requires that you recognize both traditional and contemporary realities of a culture.

History/Past–Present/Future

An additional dialectic in intercultural communication focuses on the present and the past. For example, one cannot fully understand contemporary relations between Arabs and Jews, or Muslims and Christians without knowing something of their history. At the same time, people cannot ignore current events. For example, the conflict over where Yasser Arafat was to be buried in the autumn of 2004 flowed from a complex of historical and contemporary relations. His family had resided for generations in Jerusalem and wanted him laid to rest there. Israel, having current control of Jerusalem and viewing Arafat as a terrorist leader of attacks against Israel, refused.

Privilege–Disadvantage

In intercultural interactions, people can be simultaneously privileged and disadvantaged (Johnson, 2001). This can become quite clear when one travels to developing countries. While U.S. Americans may be privileged in having more money and the luxury of travel, they can also feel vulnerable in foreign countries if they are ignorant of the local languages and customs. Poor Whites in the United States can be simultaneously privileged because they are White and disadvantaged due to their economic plight. As a student, you may feel privileged (compared to others) in that you are acquiring a high level of education, but you may also feel economically disadvantaged because of the high cost of education.

This dialectic approach helps us resist making quick, stereotypical judgments about others and their communication behavior. A single person can have individualistic and collectivistic tendencies, can be both culturally similar and different from us, and can be culturally privileged in some situations and culturally disadvantaged in others. All these elements affect communication in both business and personal relationships.

This woman is begging for money near the Spanish Steps in Rome, Italy. While many people may think of the Spanish Steps as a famous destination for privileged travelers, it is also the site for begging for those who are less privileged. As you encounter others, keep these dialectical tensions in mind.

THE INDIVIDUAL, INTERCULTURAL COMMUNICATION, AND SOCIETY

As you likely have gathered by now, intercultural communication never occurs in a vacuum, but must be understood in the context of larger societal forces. In this section we first focus on social, political, and historical forces; second, we turn our attention to the role of power in intercultural communication.

Political and Historical Forces

That societal forces can affect intercultural encounters is exemplified by the varying reactions toward some immigrant groups after the attacks of September 11. Scholar Sunil Bhatia (2008) found, through interviews with Asian Indian-Americans, that these immigrants experienced reactions from others that caused them to question their "American" identity. Before 9/11 they considered themselves well-adapted to American culture. However, after 9/11 people treated them differently. Their neighbors, who knew them well, were much friendlier and sympathetic. However, some strangers were more hostile to them (sometimes mistaking them for Muslims).

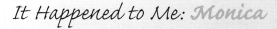

Thus, they were reminded that they were different; they were not completely accepted as Americans, by the American majority. One of our students recounts how the events of 9/11 influenced her relationship with a college friend from Jordan in *It Happened to Me: Monica.*

Historical forces also can influence contemporary intercultural interaction, as we noted earlier in our discussion of dialectics. For example, while slavery is long gone in the United States, one could not understand contemporary Black–White relations in this country without acknowledging its effect. Author James Loewen (1995) describes the twin legacies of slavery that are still with us: (1) social and economic inferiority for Blacks brought on by specific economic and political policies from 1885 to 1965 that led to inferior educational institutions and exclusion from labor unions, voting rights, and the advantage of government mortgages; (2) cultural racism instilled in Whites. These legacies, in turn, affect interracial dialogues, which some have characterized as uneasy, unequal encounters with few authentic conversations (Houston, 2004; Kivel, 1996).

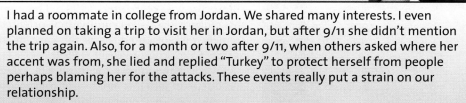

It Happened to Me: Monica

I had a roommate in college from Jordan. We shared many interests. I even planned on taking a trip to visit her in Jordan, but after 9/11 she didn't mention the trip again. Also, for a month or two after 9/11, when others asked where her accent was from, she lied and replied "Turkey" to protect herself from people perhaps blaming her for the attacks. These events really put a strain on our relationship.

As a society, which institutions or contexts now promote the best opportunities for interracial contact? Neighborhoods? Educational institutions? Churches, synagogues, and other places of worship? The workplace? Neighborhoods and workplaces do not seem to provide opportunities for the *type* of contact (intimate, friendly, equal-status interaction) that facilitates intercultural relationships (Johnson & Jacobson, 2005). On the other hand, it appears that *integrated* religious institutions and educational institutions provide the best opportunities for intercultural friendships and the best environment to improve interracial attitudes (Johnson & Jacobson, 2005). For example, a study of six California State University campuses found that the students on these campuses interacted equally, in interracial and intraracial encounters (Cowan, 2005). These campuses are very diverse, no single ethnic or racial group is a majority. However, a more recent study cautions that sometimes students in multicultural campus assume that they have intercultural relationships just by virtue of being surrounded by cultural diversity, and may not make the effort to actually pursue intercultural friendships (Halualani, 2008).

Intercultural Communication and Power

As we noted in Chapter 5 (Verbal Communication), the more powerful groups in society establish the rules for communication, and others usually follow these rules or violate them at their peril (Orbe, 1998). A number of factors influence who is considered powerful in a culture. For example, being White in the United States has more privilege attached to it than being Latino (Bahk & Jandt, 2004). While most Whites do not notice this privilege and dominance, most minority group members do (Bahk & Jandt, 2004). Being male also has historically been more valued than being female (Johnson, 2001), and being wealthy is more valued than being poor. Further, being able-bodied is traditionally more valued than being physically disabled (Allen, 2003; Johnson, 2001). Every society, regardless of power distance values, has these kinds of traditional hierarchies of power. While the hierarchy is never entirely fixed, it does constrain and influence communication among cultural groups.

How do power differences affect intercultural interaction? They do so primarily by determining whose cultural values will be respected and followed. For example,

Wahoo, the Cleveland Indians mascot, is a controversial figure. Some people are ardent Cleveland Indians fans, while others see racism in this mascot. Would we be likely to respond well to a caricature similar to this of African Americans or White Americans?

faculty, staff, and students in most U.S. universities adhere to the values and communication norms set by the White, male-dominant groups. These values and communication norms emphasize individualism (Kikoski & Kikoski, 1999). Thus, while group work is common in many courses, professors usually try to figure out how to give individual grades for it, and most students are encouraged to be responsible for their own work. Moreover, the university is run on monochronic time (see Chapter 6), with great emphasis placed on keeping schedules and meeting deadlines—and these deadlines sometimes take precedence over family and other personal responsibilities (Blair, Brown, & Baxter, 1994). The communication style most valued in this culture also is very individual-oriented, direct and to the point, and extremely task-oriented, as is the case in many organizations in the United States (Kikoski & Kikoski, 1999).

What is the impact for those who come from other cultural backgrounds and do not fit into this mold—say, for those who have collectivistic backgrounds and value personal relationships over tasks and homework assignments? Or for those whose preferred communication style is more indirect? They may experience culture shock; they also may be sanctioned or marginalized—for example, with bad grades for not participating more in class, for not completing tasks on time, or for getting too much help from others on assignments.

To more fully consider these problems we need to introduce the concept of the **cocultural group**, meaning significant minority groups within a dominant majority that do not share dominant group values or communication patterns. Examples include some Native American, Mexican American, and Asian American individuals who choose not to assimilate to the dominant, White U.S. culture. Researcher Mark Orbe (1998) suggests that cocultural group members have several choices as to how they can relate to the dominant culture: They can assimilate, they can accommodate, or they can remain separate. He cautions that each strategy has benefits and limitations. For example, when women try to assimilate and "act like men" in a male-oriented organization, they may score points for being professional, but they also may be criticized for being too masculine. When African Americans try to accommodate in a largely White management, they may satisfy White colleagues and bosses, but earn the label "oreo" from other African Americans. In contrast, resisting and remaining apart may result in isolation, marginalization, and exclusion from the discussions where important decisions are made.

Recently, these three strategies emerged, in reality shows of all places, as described in *Communication in Society: TV Reality Not Often Spoken of: Race*.

ETHICS AND INTERCULTURAL COMMUNICATION

How can you communicate more ethically across cultures? Unfortunately, no easy answers exist, but a few guidelines may be helpful.

First, remember that everyone, including you, is enmeshed in a culture and thus communicating through a cultural lens. Recognizing your own cultural attitudes, values, and beliefs will make you more sensitive to others' cultures and less likely to impose your own cultural attitudes on their communication patterns. While you may feel most comfortable living in your own culture and following its communication patterns, you should not conclude that your culture and communication style are best or should be the standard for all other cultures. Such a position is called ethnocentrism, which you learned about in Chapter 4.

Second, as you learn about other cultural groups, be aware of their humanity and avoid the temptation to view them as an exotic "other." Communication scholar Bradford Hall has cautioned about this tendency, which is called the zoo approach:

cocultural group
a significant minority group within a dominant majority that does not share dominant group values or communication patterns

COMMUNICATION IN SOCIETY

TV Reality Not Often Spoken of: Race

This author shows the challenges minority members face in interactions with majority/White contexts. How could majority individuals adapt their communication to facilitate better working relationships?

The subject was the Sept. 23, 2004, edition of NBC's reality TV game show *The Apprentice*, which many fans rightly anticipated would feature the firing of one of the show's two black contestants—the volatile Stacie "Stacie J." Upchurch. Was Stacie a victim of gender-based racism? *Entertainment Weekly* certainly thought so, concluding in its Oct. 8 issue that her ejection—by a group of white female teammates who fearfully questioned her sanity—was "about the perpetuation of an ugly reality TV stereotype: the Angry/Crazy Black Woman."

But I think reality shows such as *The Apprentice* and CBS's *Survivor* reveal a deeper truth about the personal politics of race in America. What they really portray, in sometimes agonizing detail, is the saga of the assimilated minority vs. the nonassimilated one—not just in racial matters but in a lot of places where outsiders are looking in.

It's a simple story. Adept at fitting in among their white counterparts, the assimilated minority blends in, making few waves and earning loads of friends. In contrast, the unassimilated person sticks out like a burr on a silk-covered bed, constantly conflicting with the larger group until they are isolated, demonized and eventually ejected. What's surprising is how often this cautionary tale plays out on two of TV's most popular reality shows, *The Apprentice* and *Survivor*. . . . Often on these shows, there are two people of color among the contestants. And when they are both black people, one person usually finds fitting into the majority culture a much easier task than the other.

This season, Wharton-educated Kevin Allen has hung in there, while Upchurch took a bullet in the show's third episode. In most cases, the dynamics are striking. The unassimilated person begins to separate from the larger group quickly, usually as a result of personal clashes that lead to hard feelings and harsh assumptions on both sides.

To the unassimilated person, the group seems to be overreacting to their difference, which leads to suspicions of racism. To the group, the isolated person is overreacting to differences rooted in personality and is using race to justify personal friction. It's a sadly familiar pattern for those who study how black people often struggle to fit into corporate culture or white society.

"Corporate America is part of an assimilation culture . . . they expect you to change to fit in," said Gerald D. Jaynes, a professor of economics and African-American studies at Yale University. "For black people, if you misunderstand the social cues, you become more alienated from your co-workers and your work environment, and it only gets worse."

The minority can be "hypervisible," basking in the way their differences may set them apart from the crowd. Or they can be "invisible," minimizing their differences with the majority to the point that they blend in. Both approaches present dangers: The hypervisible person tends to spark conflicts with the majority group, which often doesn't understand why the minority member holds himself apart. And the invisible person has so little impact on the group, she might as well actually be transparent. . . .

After interviewing a wide range of black executives at a financial services company, University of Pennsylvania sociology professor Elijah Anderson divided them into two kinds: those who chose to assimilate and those who didn't. Among the assimilated group, Anderson found that black executives didn't mind close personal relationships with their white co-workers, including friendships outside of work. Their comfort with the dominant culture usually resulted in higher-status jobs, though they risked identifying too much with the corporation. But those who didn't assimilate were reluctant to trust their white co-workers. Exhausted by the effort of navigating white culture at work, they remained certain that most white people in their lives would eventually betray them.

FROM: "TV Reality Not Often Spoke of: Race," by Eric Deggans, *St. Petersburg Times*, October 24, 2004. Reprinted by permission of St. Petersburg Times.

When using such an approach we view the study of culture as if we were walking through a zoo admiring, gasping and chuckling at the various exotic animals we observe. One may discover amazing, interesting and valuable information by using such a perspective and even develop a real fondness of these exotic people, but miss the point that we are as culturally "caged" as others and that they are culturally as "free" as we are (1997, p. 14).

From an ethical perspective, the zoo approach denies the humanity of other cultural groups. For example, the view of African cultures as primitive and incapable led Whites to justify colonizing Africa and exploiting its rich resources in the nineteenth century.

Third, you will be more ethical in your intercultural interactions if you are open to other ways of viewing the world. The ways that you were taught about the world and history may not be the same as what others were taught. People cannot engage in meaningful communication if they are unwilling to suspend or reexamine their assumptions about the world. For example, some Europeans believe that the United States became involved in the Middle East so it could control its oil interests, while many U.S. Americans believe that concern over weapons of mass destruction and human rights was the motivation. If neither group will consider the opinion of the other, they will be unlikely to sustain a mutually satisfying conversation.

✖ IMPROVING YOUR INTERCULTURAL COMMUNICATION SKILLS

How can you communicate more effectively across cultures? As with ethics, no magic formula exists but here are several suggestions.

Increase Motivation

Perhaps the most important component is *motivation*. Without the motivation to be an effective communicator, no other skills will be relevant. Part of the problem in long-standing interethnic or interreligious conflicts—for example, between the Israelis and the Palestinians—is the lack of interest, on both sides, in communicating more effectively. Some parties on both sides may even have an interest in prolonging conflict. Therefore, a strong desire to improve one's skills is necessary.

Increase Your Knowledge of Self and Others

In addition to being motivated, you become a more effective intercultural communicator if you educate yourself about intercultural communication. Having some knowledge about the history, background, and values of people from other cultures can help you communicate better. When you demonstrate this type of knowledge to people from other cultures, you communicate that you're interested in them and you affirm their sense of identity. Obviously, no one can know everything about all cultures; nonetheless, some general information can be helpful, as can an awareness of the importance of context and a dialectical perspective.

Self-knowledge also is very important. If you were socialized to be very individualistic you may initially have a hard time understanding collectivistic tendencies. Once you become aware of these differences, however, you can more easily communicate with someone who holds a different perspective. Growing up in a middle-class family may also influence your perceptions. Many middle-class people assume that anyone can become middle class through hard work. But this view overlooks the discrimination faced by people of color and gays and lesbians. How can you increase your cultural self-awareness? Perhaps the best way is to cultivate intercultural encounters and relationships.

Developing facility in intercultural communication occurs through a cyclical process. The more one interacts across cultures, the more one learns about oneself, and then the more prepared one is to interact interculturally, and so on. However, increased exposure and understanding do not happen automatically. Being aware of the influence of culture on oneself and others is essential to increasing one's intercultural experience and competence (Ting-Toomey, 1999).

How multicultural is your circle of friends? How many of your friends differ from you in nationality, religion, class, gender, age, sexual orientation, or physical ability?

Where should you start? You can begin by examining your current friendships and reach out from there. Research shows that individuals generally become friends with people with whom they live, work, and worship. So your opportunities for intercultural interaction and self-awareness are largely determined by the type of people and contexts you encounter in your daily routine.

Avoid Stereotypes

Cultural differences may lead to stereotyping and prejudices. As we discussed in Chapter 4, normal cognitive patterns of generalizing make our world more manageable. However, when these generalizations become rigid, they lead to stereotyping and prejudices. Furthermore, stereotyping can become self-fulfilling (Snyder, 2001). That is, if you stereotype people and treat them in a prejudiced or negative manner, they may react in ways that reinforce your stereotype.

On the other hand, we must note, overreacting by being very "sweet" can be equally off-putting. African Americans sometimes complain about being "niced" to death by White people (Yamato, 2001). The guideline here is to be mindful that you might be stereotyping. For example, if you are White, do you only notice bad behavior when exhibited by a person of color? Communicating effectively across cultural boundaries is a challenge—but one we hope you will take up.

SUMMARY

Four reasons for learning about intercultural communication are increased opportunity, increased business effectiveness, improved intergroup relations, and enhanced self-awareness. Intercultural communication is defined as communication between people from different cultural backgrounds, and culture is defined as learned patterns of perceptions, values, and behaviors shared by a group of people. Culture is dynamic and heterogeneous, and it operates largely out of our awareness within power structures. Increasing numbers of individuals today live on cultural borders—through travel, socialization, or relationships. Being a "border dweller" involves both benefits and challenges.

Six core cultural values differentiate various cultural groups, and these value differences have implications for intercultural communication. A dialectical approach to intercultural communication can help individuals avoid quick generalizations and stereotyping. There are at least six intercultural communication dialectics: cultural–individual, personal–contextual, differences–similarities, static–dynamic, history/past–present/future, and privilege–disadvantage.

Society plays an important role in intercultural communication because intercultural encounters never occur in a vacuum. Societal forces, including political and historical structures, always influence communication. Power is often an important element in that those who hold more powerful positions in society set the rules and norms for communication. Those individuals who do not conform to the rules because of differing cultural backgrounds and preferences may be marginalized. To ensure that you are communicating ethically during intercultural interactions, attend to the following: avoid ethnocentric thinking, recognize the humanity of others, and remain open to other ways of understanding the world. Finally, you can become a more effective intercultural communicator in at least three ways: by increasing your motivation, acquiring knowledge about self and others, and avoiding stereotyping.

KEY TERMS

mediation 169
intercultural communication 170
culture 170
heterogeneous 170
border dwellers 170
voluntary short-term travelers 170
voluntary long-term travelers 170
involuntary short-term travelers 171
involuntary long-term travelers 171
culture shock 171

reverse culture shock/reentry
   shock 171
encapsulated marginal people 177
constructive marginal people 177
cultural values 177
individualist orientation 179
collectivistic orientation 179
preferred personality 180
view of human nature 180
human–nature value orientation 180

power distance 181
long-term versus short-term
   orientation 182
short-term orientation 182
monotheistic 182
long-term orientation 182
polytheistic 182
dialectic approach 183
dichotomous thinking 183
cocultural group 186

TEST YOUR KNOWLEDGE

1. What are the reasons for studying intercultural communication? Which do you think are most important?

2. How do individuals come to live on cultural borders? What are some benefits and challenges to border dwelling?

3. Identify six common core values that differentiate various cultural groups. How might these values influence intercultural communication?

4. How does adopting a dialectical perspective help us avoid stereotyping and prejudice?

5. What are three suggestions for communicating more effectively across cultures? Which do you think is the most important? Why?

APPLY WHAT YOU KNOW

1. **Cultural Profile**
   List all the cultural groups you belong to. Which groups are most important to you when you're at college? When you're at home? Which groups would be easiest to leave? Why?

2. **Intercultural Conflict Analysis**
   Identify a current intercultural conflict in the media. It can be conflict between nations, ethnic groups, or gender. Read at least three sources that give background and information about the conflict. Conduct an analysis of this conflict, answering the following questions:

   - What do you think are the sources of the conflict?
   - Are there value differences?
   - Power differences?
   - What role do you think various contexts (historical, social, political) play in the conflict?

3. **Intercultural Relationship Exercise**
   Make a list of people you consider to be your close friends. For each, identify ways that they are culturally similar and different from you. Then form groups of four to six students and answer the following questions. Select a recorder for your discussion so you can share your answers with the rest of the class.

   - Do people generally have more friends who are culturally similar or different from themselves?
   - What are some of the benefits of forming intercultural friendships?
   - In what ways are intercultural friendships different or similar to friendship with people from the same cultures?
   - What are some reasons people might have for not forming intercultural friendships?

EXPLORE

1. Go to: www.census.gov/population/cen2000/atlas/censr01-1.pdf This Web site is a U.S. government report on demographic diversity in the United States taken from the 2000 Census. On page 21 of this report, a U.S. map shows the country's racial and ethnic diversity. How diverse are the areas you've lived in? Did the diversity of the population influence your opportunities for intercultural encounters?

2. How high is your intercultural intelligence? Take the "Intercultural Competence Self-Assessment" at www.racerelations.about.com/od/skillbuildingresources/a/selfassessment.htm to find out.

3. Go to: www.online-communicator.com/maskinfo.html The designer of this Web site describes why he removed an image of a Native American mask from his Web site. He had been contacted by an Iroquois Indian who requested that he remove the image because it is sacred and "should not be disseminated among non–Indians." According to this Web site, what other popular images of Native Americans are offensive or inaccurate?

Communicating in Close Relationships

chapter outline

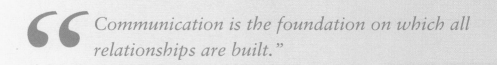

Julia and her friend Cristina were at a club one weekend when Julia spotted a man who had "hit" on her earlier in the evening. As he walked toward the two women, Julia leaned over to Cristina and said, "There's that jerk I was telling you about." Eighteen months later Cristina and the "jerk" were married.

How is it that one person's jerk is another person's ideal mate? On more than one occasion, you may have wondered why your friends pick the romantic partners they do. Or perhaps you even have questioned your own choices. Though relationship researchers haven't unraveled all the mysteries of love and friendship, they have made considerable progress in explaining how and why relationships develop, are maintained, and sometimes fail—and the role communication plays at each stage.

To help you understand communication in close relationships, we begin by describing the importance of these relationships and providing a definition for them. Next, we address the role of the individual in close relationships and explore the factors that increase the likelihood that you will become involved with another person. We then examine four models that explain how communication influences relationship development between friends and romantic partners. We conclude our focus on individuals in relationships by discussing problems that can occur in friendship and romance, such as aversive communication, jealousy, aggression, and sexual coercion. Finally, we explore the societal forces that influence relationships and the communication within them and present you with guidelines for communicating more ethically and effectively in your own relationships.

 Once you have read this chapter, you will be able to:

- Identify the three factors that influence relationship initiation.
- Describe four models of relationship development.
- Identify a wide range of tactics for initiating friendships and romantic relationships.
- Articulate the strategies romantic couples and friends use to maintain their relationships.
- Explain the reasons why individuals terminate romantic relationships and friendships, as well as the communication strategies they use to terminate them.
- Discuss how aversive communication behaviors, deception, jealousy, interpersonal violence, and sexual coercion arise—and describe their impact on relationships and the communication skills you can use to respond to them.
- Understand the role that society plays in the formation and maintenance of interpersonal relationships.
- Describe the role of authentic communication in ethical interpersonal communication.
- Recognize the behavioral characteristics of a batterer.

Close relationships can be a source of happiness, comfort, even distress.

CLOSE RELATIONSHIPS AND THE INDIVIDUAL

Friends play an important role in people's lives, as is illustrated in *It Happened to Me: Olivia*. Close relationships are a source of much happiness (and some distress) and serve as a significant context within which a person's interactions take place (Donaghue & Fallon, 2003). Relationships with friends, lovers, and family members not only provide emotional and physical support, as Olivia did for her friend, but they also offer a sense of belonging, help alleviate loneliness, and are central to psychological and physical health.

Loneliness, or a lack of close relationships, is associated with psychological disorders such as depression and anxiety (Miller, 2002). People with even a few close relationships experience greater well-being than those who are lonely (Gierveld & Tilburg, 1995). People with satisfying relationships also experience greater physical health. For example, a study of longevity determined that the joint effects of having a relatively high number of social relationships, not smoking, and having above average income resulted in an eighteen-fold reduction in mortality. Similarly, studies of marital relationships reveal that people in happy marriages are less likely to experience high blood pressure and serious heart episodes (Holt-Lunstad, Birmingham, & Jones, 2008). Thus, close relationships can improve the quality of one's life.

The relationships you develop with friends, family, and romantic partners are qualitatively different from other types of interpersonal relationships, such as those you develop with your mail carrier or dry-cleaner attendant (LaFollette, 1996). Close relationships are distinguished by their frequency, intensity, and diversity of contact (Kelley et al., 1983) as well as their level of intimacy, importance, and satisfaction (Berg & Piner, 1990).

It Happened to Me: Olivia

I was at a friend's house, eating junk food and watching TV when someone knocked on the door. Standing there in the rain, with tears running down her face, and sobbing, was one of our friends. She told us that her mom had hit her and thrown her things out her bedroom window. We sat with her for ages until she calmed down; then, we asked her to stay the night. Without us, she would have had nowhere to go and no one to talk to.

Typically, people in close relationships see each other as unique and irreplaceable, and high disclosure and openness mark their communication (Janz, 2000). In addition, people in close relationships expect their relationships to endure over time because they are committed to them (Wright, 1999). On the other hand, casual relationships are perceived as interchangeable because they are usually role-based, as between a salesperson and a customer, and involve little disclosure or affection (Janz, 2000). Therefore, although you might like your mail carrier and would miss seeing her if she quit her job, you likely would be content to receive your mail from someone new. But if your fiancé or best friend terminated your relationship, you probably would not be content with a substitute.

Influences on Relationship Development

For any romantic or platonic relationship to develop, you must first notice that a particular person exists and be interested enough to initiate contact. Sara still remembers meeting her husband, Luis, fifteen years ago when she was a doctoral student. A mutual friend introduced them, and she became very interested when she saw him (tall, good looking, and muscular!) and learned that he was finishing his doctorate. She spent most of the evening talking to him, even though thirty other people were at the party.

The three factors that most influence one's attraction to another—*proximity*, *physical attractiveness*, and *similarity*—were all operating the evening Sara and Luis met. They were students at the same university, they found each other physically attractive, and they discovered that they had similar career goals.

Of course, proximity, attractiveness, and similarity don't guarantee a lasting friendship or romance, but they do set the stage for relationships to develop. Next we explore how these three factors influence relational development and the role that communication plays in each.

Proximity

Most people are not aware of it, but **proximity**—how close you are to others—plays an important role in relationship development. Historically, proximity referred to physical closeness between people. Thus people typically became friends with or dated those who lived in their apartment complexes, neighborhoods, or dorms; those who were in their classes; or those with whom they worked (Sias & Cahill, 1998; Sprecher, 1998). Now, however, technologies such as email, text messaging, and cell phones have made it easier for people to create the feeling of proximity even with individuals who are not physically nearby.

Proximity has a strong impact on your interactions and relationships. It provides the opportunity for you to notice others' attractive qualities, learn about your similarities, and develop a relationship (Berscheid & Reis, 1998). Usually, the easier it is to interact with someone, the easier it will be to develop and sustain a relationship. A slang term exists for people who are not physically proximate and therefore harder to sustain a relationship with—*GUD*, or geographically undesirable. Of course, some people do develop and maintain long-distance relationships, but they may need to make more effort to sustain their relationships than those in more proximate relationships (Rindfuss & Stephen, 1990). If you are in a long-distance relationship and want ideas for maintaining it, go to www.sblake.com/index.phtml for some suggestions.

Attractiveness

Obviously, proximity is not enough to launch a relationship. Most of us have daily contact with dozens of people. How is it that you connect with some and not others? One of the more obvious answers is **attractiveness**. While most of us are attracted to those we find physically appealing (Buss, Shackelford, Kirkpatrick, & Larsen, 2001), we also tend to develop relationships with people who are approximately as attractive as we are. This tendency is called the **matching hypothesis**. Interestingly, the matching hypothesis applies to friendships (Cash & Derlega, 1978), romantic relationships (White, 1980), marriage (Hinsz, 1989), and even roommates (Kurt & Sherker, 2003).

Fortunately, attractiveness is a broad concept. People are attracted to others not only because of their physical appearance but also for their wonderful personalities and/or charming ways. Most of these qualities are revealed through communication—thus individuals with good communication skills are often perceived as more attractive than they might be otherwise (Burleson & Samter, 1996). Therefore, improving your communication skills can increase others' desire to form relationships with you.

Similarity

It may be equally obvious that most people are attracted by **similarity**—they like people who are like them, who enjoy the things they enjoy, value what they value, and with whom they share a similar background (Byrne, 1997). In many cases opposites *do* attract, but when it comes to background, values, and attitudes, "birds of a feather [more often] flock together." For example, Buss (1985) found that the more similar the participants in their study were, the more likely they were to report

proximity
how close one is to others

attractiveness
the appeal one person has for another, based on physical appearance, personalities, and/or behavior

matching hypothesis
the tendency to develop relationships with people who are approximately as attractive as we are

similarity
degree to which people share the same values, interests, and background

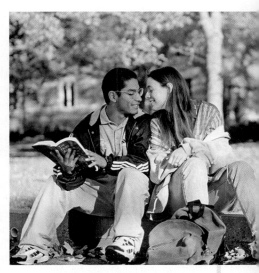

People tend to develop relationships with others who are approximately as attractive as they are.

increased levels of attraction. This makes sense. If you like to socialize, enjoy the outdoors, and are involved in a religious community, you may find it difficult to develop a relationship with someone who is introverted, prefers to stay home to read and listen to music, and avoids organized religion. However open-minded you are, you probably view your orientation to the world as preferable, especially concerning values such as religion, politics, and morals.

You may wonder how individuals determine whether they are similar in values, attitudes, and background. Generally, they discover this during the early stages of conversational interaction (Berger & Calabrese, 1975; Berger & Kellerman, 1994). And according to a communication theory called uncertainty reduction theory (Berger & Calabrese, 1975), which we discussed in Chapter Two, much early interaction is dedicated to reducing uncertainty about others and determining if one wishes to interact with them again. Thus, communication is the foundation on which all relationships are built. With this in mind, let's look next at how researchers view the development of relationships.

Models of Relationship Development

Because relationship development is an important aspect of life and because sometimes the process goes awry—for example, 43 percent of first marriages end within fifteen years (Bramlett & Mosher, 2002)—scholars have devoted considerable effort toward creating models to explain it. Although no model can exactly represent how human relationships evolve, four approaches offer insight into how relationships develop and change over time as people communicate with one another—social penetration theory, stage models, the turning point approach, and dialectical theory.

Social Penetration Theory

Social penetration theory (Altman & Taylor, 1973; 1987) is based on the premise that communication, specifically self-disclosure, is key to relationship development. According to this theory, people gradually increase their self-disclosure as they get to know one another and, through a process of reciprocal disclosure, strangers become friends or lovers. The authors propose that self-disclosure occurs across three dimensions: breadth, depth, and frequency.

Breadth describes the number of different topics dyads willingly discuss. For example, you probably discuss only a few general topics with strangers, such as movies, what you do for a living, or hobbies; however, as you become more intimate with others you likely discuss a wider range of topics, including how you feel about the people in your life or dreams you have for the future. At the same time, the depth of your conversations also increases as the two of you learn more about each other. *Depth* refers to how deep or personal communication exchanges are; people tend to provide superficial disclosures to strangers (e.g., I like Thai food) and reserve more personal revelations for their intimates (e.g., I am disgusted if the different foods on my plate touch each other). *Frequency* is how often self-disclosure occurs; individuals usually share more disclosures with people with whom they are close.

Altman and Taylor propose that through increases in communication breadth, depth, and frequency people become more familiar with and trusting of one another, and as they become closer, they feel comfortable revealing more of themselves. Through this circular process, relationships of increasing intimacy are developed. However, not all dyads engage in increasingly intimate disclosure and closeness. Some, such as romantic couples who repeatedly break up and reconcile, move back and forth between stages of increasing and decreasing disclosure and intimacy.

To help explain in greater detail how relationships develop, Altman and Taylor developed a four-stage model. They label these four stages **orientation, exploratory affective exchange, affective exchange**, and **stable exchange.**

The orientation stage includes a couple's first meeting, or perhaps their first few encounters, especially if some of the initial meetings are brief. During the orientation stage, individuals' interactions tend to display low breadth of topics and

social penetration theory
a theory that proposes relationships develop through increases in self-disclosure

orientation
the stage in which people first meet and engage in superficial communication

exploratory affective exchange
stage in which people increase the breadth of their communication

affective exchange
stage in which people increase the breadth, depth, and frequency of their self-disclosure

stable exchange
stage in which relational partners engage in the greatest breadth and depth of self-disclosure

depth of disclosure as people "feel each other out" to see if they are compatible (Guerrero, Andersen, & Afifi, 2007). These encounters tend to be superficial and positive, since most of the time people want to make a good first impression.

The second, or exploratory affective stage, describes encounters that occur between acquaintances and those engaged in casual dating or friendships. Some dyads stay at this stage (such as is often true of relationships with one's friends' friends) while others move beyond this stage to form a personal and intimate relationship. During this phase, individuals tend to increase the breadth of their interactions but maintain relatively low depth of disclosure.

Relationships that move to the third stage, affective exchange, are marked by an increase in the breadth, depth, and frequency of their self-disclosure. At this stage, people describe each other as good friends or romantic partners. They trust each other more and develop a sense of closeness and connection. Participants may still feel some topics are off limits and fail to share everything they know or feel (Guerrero, Andersen, & Afifi, 2007). However, because they do experience increased trust in each other and the relationship, individuals in the affective exchange stage more willingly share negative disclosures about themselves and their relational partners. Thus, their interactions may be either positive or negative in tone.

Altman and Taylor's fourth and final stage is stable exchange, which involves the greatest breadth and depth of self-disclosure; although even at this stage it is unlikely that anyone reveals everything to their best friends and relational partners (Vangelisti, 1994). In addition, committed relational partners typically cycle back and forth between high and low levels of self-disclosure. They are more likely to share most private and intimate thoughts and feelings but, at the same time, they know each other so well that they may have less new information to share. Nonetheless, the potential for high levels of disclosure is always present (Guerrero, Andersen, & Afifi, 2007).

Knapp's Stage Model

The best-known stage model was developed in 1978 by Mark Knapp, a communication scholar (Knapp, 1978; Knapp & Vangelisti, 1997). As shown in Figure 8.1, **Knapp's stage model** conceptualizes relationship development as a staircase. The staircase depicts relationship development as being composed of five steps that lead upward toward commitment: **initiating, experimenting, intensifying, integrating,** and **bonding**. It also portrays relationship dissolution as occurring in five steps that lead downward: **differentiating, circumscribing, stagnating, avoiding,** and **terminating**. In this model, couples at the relationship maintenance level of development move up and down the staircase as they move toward and away from commitment due to the fluctuation of their relationships.

Knapp's stage model
model of relationship development that views relationships as occurring in "stages" and that focuses on how people communicate as relationships develop and decline

initiating
stage of romantic relational development in which both people behave so as to appear pleasant and likeable

experimenting
stage of romantic relational development in which both people seek to learn about each other

intensifying
stage of romantic relational development in which both people seek to increase intimacy and connectedness

integrating
stage of romantic relational development in which both people portray themselves as a couple

bonding
stage of romantic relational development characterized by public commitment

differentiating
stage of romantic relational dissolution in which couples increase their interpersonal distance

circumscribing
stage of romantic relational dissolution in which couples discuss safe topics

stagnating
stage of romantic relational dissolution in which couples try to prevent change

avoiding
stage of romantic relational dissolution in which couples try not to interact with each other

terminating
stage of romantic relational dissolution in which couples end the relationship

FIGURE 8.1: Knapp and Vangelisti's Stages of Relational Development
Stage models conceptualize relationship development as occurring in a stair-step fashion, with some stages leading toward commitment and other stages leading toward dissolution.

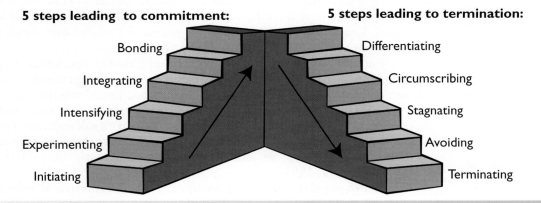

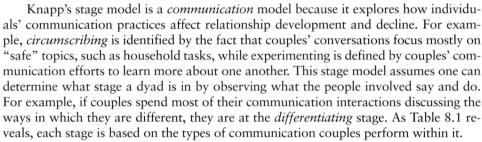

TABLE 8.1	Knapp's Stages of Romantic Relational Development	
Stage	**Goal**	**Example**
Initiating	Appear pleasant, likeable	"Hi! I sure like your car."
Experimenting	Learn about each other	"Do you like to travel?"
Intensifying	Increase intimacy, connectedness	"I can't imagine being with anyone else."
Integrating	Establish dyad as a couple	"I love you. I feel like you are a part of me."
Bonding	Public commitment	"Will you marry me?"
Differentiating	Increase interpersonal distance	"I'm going; you can come if you want to."
Circumscribing	Discuss safe topics	"Did you pick up the dry cleaning?"
Stagnating	Prevent change	"Let's not talk about it right now, okay?"
Avoiding	Decline to interact with partner	"I'm too busy now. I'll get back to you later."
Terminating	Ending the relationship	"It's over."

From: Knapp, M. L., & Vangelisti, A. L., *Interpersonal Communication And Human Relationships, 2/e.* Published by Allyn and Bacon/Merrill Education, Boston, MA. Copyright © 1992 by Pearson Education. Adapted by permission of the publisher.

Knapp's stage model is a *communication* model because it explores how individuals' communication practices affect relationship development and decline. For example, *circumscribing* is identified by the fact that couples' conversations focus mostly on "safe" topics, such as household tasks, while experimenting is defined by couples' communication efforts to learn more about one another. This stage model assumes one can determine what stage a dyad is in by observing what the people involved say and do. For example, if couples spend most of their communication interactions discussing the ways in which they are different, they are at the *differentiating* stage. As Table 8.1 reveals, each stage is based on the types of communication couples perform within it.

As you might have noticed, Knapp's model includes a *termination* stage. This does not suggest that all relationships end, but it does recognize that many relationships do (Weber, 1998). Relationships that end are often treated as "failures," and the people who experience them often feel that they have done something wrong. But, in fact, as people grow and mature, it is not unusual for them to change their social networks (Dainton, Zelley, & Langan, 2003). This is not to suggest that you won't have long-lasting or permanent relationships, but not every relationship termination should be viewed as a mistake.

The models we have discussed thus far are stage models; they help us organize events so we can better understand how relationships develop; however, stage models tend to be linear. They assume that people move from one stage to another in a fairly orderly progression. Knapp has responded to this critique by arguing that dyads can skip stages but that they have to go back at some point and move through the skipped stages. For example, when couples engage in a "one-night stand," they may move from initiation to integration in a matter of hours. However, if they stay together they will have to go back and experience the experimenting and intensifying stages. Knapp also argues that over the course of a relationship, dyads move up and down the staircase as people and events change.

According to the turning point of model of relationship development, becoming engaged is a turning point that increases commitment.

relational trajectory models relationship development models that view relationship development as more variable than do stage models

turning point model a model of relationship development in which couples move both toward and away from commitment over the course of their relationship

As you read about the stage models of relationship development, you may have thought that these models don't describe your own experiences very well. If so, you are not alone. A number of researchers questioned whether all dyads follow sequentially organized stages. Instead, they believed that relationships can follow a number of paths: Some may be fairly straight like a sidewalk, (see Figure 8.2), while others may be like winding mountain paths. **Relational trajectory models** view relationship development as more variable than previously thought (Baxter & Bullis, 1986; Surra, 1987).

The most popular model that emerged from this research is referred to as the **turning point model** (Baxter & Bullis, 1986). It is a nonlinear model that best captures the fact that relationship development can be bidirectional—that is, that couples move both toward and away from commitment over the course of their relationship, as shown in Figure 8.3. This model proposes that couples engage in approximately fourteen types of "turning points" that influence the direction of their relationship trajectory (see Table 8.2). For example, the turning point "passion" (first kiss or saying "I love you") tends to be an event that increases couples' commitment to their relationship, while the turning point "external competition" (such as a rival lover) decreases commitment to the relationship. (For a more controversial, and biological, take on romantic relationship development, see *Alternative View: An Evolutionary Model of Relationship Development*, on p. 200.)

A turning point model of friendship also has been developed, with different turning points than in the romance-based model (Baxter & Bullis, 1986). For example, turning points most often associated with increased closeness between friends included participating in activities together, taking a trip together, sharing living quarters, self-disclosing, hanging out with mutual friends, and sharing common interests.

FIGURE 8.2: An Early Trajectory Model
Early trajectory models were based on social penetration theory and assumed that relationships become closer the more that the partners communicate with each other.

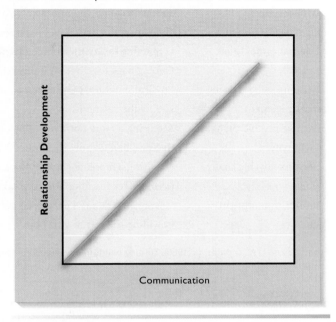

FIGURE 8.3: Turning Point Model
The turning point model captures the fact that relationship development can be bidirectional—that is, that couples move both toward and away from commitment over the course of their relationship.

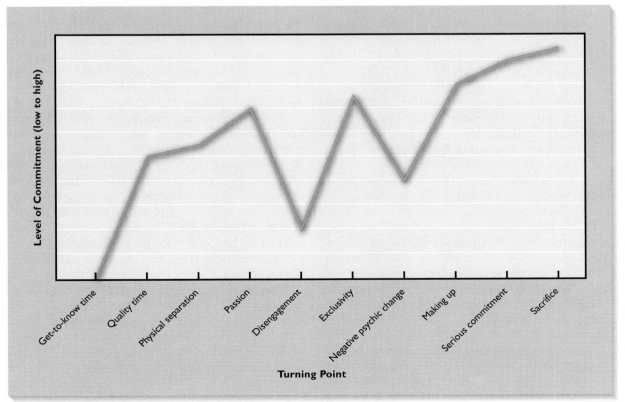

TABLE 8.2	Turning Points in Developing Relationships	
Turning Point	**Description**	**Effect on Relationship**
Get-to-know time	Events and time spent together learning about one another	Increases commitment
Quality time	Special occasions for appreciating the other and/or the relationship	Increases commitment
Physical separation	Time apart due to school breaks, etc.	Little effect on commitment
External competition	Competing for partner's time/attention due to others or events	Decreases commitment
Reunion	Coming back together after physical separation	Increases commitment
Passion	Physical/emotional expression of affection	Increases commitment
Disengagement	Ending the relationship	Decreases commitment
Positive psychic change	Acquiring a more positive outlook on partner/relationship	Increases commitment
Exclusivity	Decision to date only each other	Increases commitment
Negative psychic change	Acquiring a more negative outlook on partner/relationship	Decreases commitment
Making up	Getting back together after a breakup	Increases commitment
Serious commitment	Moving in with one's partner or getting married	Increases commitment
Sacrifice	Providing support or gifts to one's partner	Increases commitment

From: Baxter, L. A., & Bullis, C. (1986). Turning points in developing romantic relationships. *Human Communication Research, 12,* 469–493.

Alternative VIEW

An Evolutionary Model of Relationship Development

What courtship behaviors does the evolutionary model of relationships explain well? What courtship behaviors does it fail to explain? How would an evolutionary model explain the phenomenon of "hooking up"—or could it?

Evolutionary models of relationship development come to us from studies in anthropology and social psychology. These models assume that the primary (though unconscious) motivating factor for most species, including humans, is to reproduce. They also argue that since males and females make different contributions to reproduction, they behave differently during relationship development (Kenrick, Sadalla, Groth, & Trost, 1990; Kenrick & Trost, 1996).

To better understand this theory, consider the amount of time and energy each parent invests in his or her offspring. The mother's investment is inherently greater than the father's. Women generally need to invest at least two years (nine months for gestation and the remainder of the time to nurture the young child), while men must invest only a short time to father a child.

The evolutionary model argues that each sex uses certain behaviors to equalize opportunity and investment in child bearing and rearing. For example, because women do have a greater investment in each child, they tend to be more selective in choosing a mate. Alternatively, males, who can father many children in a short time, may try to engage in coitus more quickly and require less commitment because they have less investment in any one offspring (Trost & Kenrick, 1993).

This model suggests that females and males communicate and behave during relationship development in ways designed to aid them in achieving their goals and maximizing their outcomes. The female's goal is generally to attract a mate who is reliable, trustworthy, and committed to the relationship since she will need help rearing her children. The male's goal may be to have a number of relationships (since his parental investment is less) or to find one mate he can trust, because he does not want to invest time and energy in a child who is not his own.

This model of relationship development also suggests that because motherhood is always certain while fatherhood is not, men and women behave differently in relationships. For example, this view is used to explain men's greater expressions of jealousy and lesser willingness to forgive acts of infidelity.

Decreased closeness most often occurred when friends stopped living together, had conflicts, experienced interference from one person's romantic partner, moved so that they no longer lived near one another, or underwent change (Johnson, Wittenberg, Haigh, & Wigley, 2004).

Communication professor Leslie Baxter and her colleagues have examined relationship dialectics to explain how dyads develop relationships. As you may remember from Chapter 7, *dialectic* is a term that is used in many areas of study, such as philosophy, psychology, and communication (Altman, Vinsel, & Brown, 1981; Baxter, 1988). It refers to the tension people experience when they have two seemingly contradictory but connected needs. As you will see, developing close relationships is associated with the ability to manage these contradictory but connected desires.

Have you experienced any of the following: You feel lonely when you are separated from your romantic partner, but you sometimes feel suffocated when you're together? You want to be able to tell your best friend anything, but you sometimes feel the need for privacy? You want your friends to be predictable—but not so predictable that they're boring? These types of feelings arise when you experience a dialectical tension, and they are common in all types of relationships. How you respond to and manage these tensions impacts how successfully you can develop and maintain relationships.

Three primary dialectical tensions exist in relationships: *autonomy/connection*, *expressiveness/privacy*, and *change/predictability* (Baxter, 1988). **Autonomy/connection** refers to one's need to connect with others and the simultaneous need to feel independent or autonomous. For example, early in relationships people typically have a high need to feel connected to their romantic partners and can barely tolerate being separated from them. But as the relationship develops, most people need time away from their partners so they don't feel stifled or overwhelmed. The openness/closedness tension is more prevalent during the initial stages of relationship development, and the extent to which dyads can effectively manage this tension influences their ability to successfully develop a relationship. If they insist on too much autonomy, the relationship may cease; if they have too much connection, one person may feel overwhelmed and withdraw from the relationship. An example of the dialectical tension between autonomy and connection can be found in *It Happened to Me: Laurel*.

autonomy/connection
a dialectical tension in relationships that refers to one's need to connect with others and the simultaneous need to feel independent or autonomous

expressiveness/privacy
a dialectical tension in relationships that describes the need to be open and to self-disclose while also maintaining some sense of privacy

It Happened to Me: Laurel

I started seeing this guy a few weeks ago, and finally I understand why I've been feeling the way I do. Although I enjoy being with him, I have started to feel smothered. He wants to talk on the phone several times a day, texts me constantly when we are apart, and he wants to spend more evenings together than I do. I enjoy hanging out with my friends and being alone; he wants to be with me all the time. I was beginning to think there was something wrong with him, then I read Baxter's article on relationship dialectics. Now I think we just have different needs for autonomy. However, I don't know if we will be able to manage this so that we'll both be happy.

The second tension, **expressiveness/privacy**, describes the need to be open and to self-disclose while also maintaining some sense of privacy. For example, while Warren may reveal his feelings about his romantic partner to his closest friend, he may not disclose that he was fired from his first job. To maintain their relationships, dyads need to manage this tension effectively. If you reveal too much information too early, others may find your communication behavior inappropriate and may shy away from you. On the other hand, if you fail to open up and express yourself, others may perceive you as aloof or cold and may not continue the relationship. Thus, this dialectical tension is important to relationships in the initiating stage of development as well as during the development and maintenance stages.

COMMUNICATION IN SOCIETY
Friends with Benefits

In the following excerpt, Dr. Paul Mongeau, Dr. Artemio Ramirez, and Dr. Matthew Vorell introduce the idea of friends with benefits, a relationship type they argue is prevalent on college campuses.

Based on what you have observed and experienced in college, do you agree that college norms include considerable casual sex? Why or why not? What function do you think friends with benefits serve for women and men?

Friends with benefits relationships (FWBRs) appear to be a relational hybrid distinguishable from other casual sex practices such as hookups (Paul et al., 2000; Paul & Hayes, 2002) and sex between cross-sex friends (Afifi & Faulkner, 2000). First, Paul et al. (2002) defined "hookups" as "a sexual encounter, usually lasting only one night, between two people who are strangers or brief acquaintances" (p. 76). FWBRs differ from hookups, first, because hookups occur between strangers or brief acquaintances while FWBRs occur between previously acquainted friends. A second important difference is that a vast majority of hookups are one-time sexual encounters (Paul et al., 2000; Paul & Hayes, 2002) while sex in FWBRs occurs multiple times (Marquardt & Glenn, 2001).

FWBRs align more closely to Afifi and Faulkner's (2000) sex with cross-sex friends. Although over one-half of their participants reported engaging in sexual activity with a friend, 21 percent of the study's entire sample indicated that they had engaged in sexual activity with the same friend *on multiple occasions.* . . . Collectively, these studies indicate that modern college norms include considerable casual sex.

FROM: Mongeau, P., Ramirez, A., & Vorell, M. (2003). *Sexual cross-sex friendship: Friends with benefits relationships.* Paper presented to the Western States Communication Association, Salt Lake City, UT. Reprinted by permission of the authors.

change/predictability
a dialectical tension in relationships that describes the human desire for events that are new, spontaneous, and unplanned while simultaneously needing some aspects of life to be stable and predictable

Finally, the **change/predictability** tension delineates the human desire for events that are new, spontaneous, and unplanned while simultaneously needing some aspects of life to be stable and predictable. For example, you probably want your partner's affection for you to be stable and predictable, but you might like your partner to surprise you occasionally with a new activity or self-disclosure. This tension exists at all stages of relationship development but may be most prevalent during the maintenance phase. Relationships that are completely predictable may become boring but those that are totally spontaneous are unsettling; either extreme may render the relationship difficult to sustain.

Dialectics are constantly in process. Each day, couples and friends manage their individual and relationship needs for autonomy/connection, expressiveness/privacy, and change/predictability; the manner in which they manage these tensions influences the continuance of their relationships. Understanding dialectical tensions is useful because it can help you respond to the competing feelings you may experience in relationships.

While we know more about heterosexual relationships than we do about gay and lesbian relationships, what we do know suggests that these two types of relationships may follow different paths. In heterosexual relationships, friendship and romantic sexual involvement traditionally have been mutually exclusive; therefore, the termination of romantic intimacy usually meant the end of the friendship as well (Nardi, 1992). In contrast, gay friendships often start with sexual attraction and involvement but evolve into friendship with no sexual/romantic involvement (Nardi, 1992). However, this difference appears to be less true than it once was, as more heterosexual young people appear to be combining the categories of friendship and sexual involvement. For a closer look at this trend, see *Communication in Society: Friends with Benefits.*

Next, we will examine the specific communication processes that individuals use to develop, maintain, and terminate their relationships.

Communicating in Friendships and Romantic Relationships

In the following, Jeff describes the difference between friendship and romantic relationships:

> You're more likely to let your friends see you warts and all. There's no fear of rejection, for me anyway. . . . In a romantic relationship, you don't want them to see you at your worst. . . . You want them to think you're very well adjusted. And your friends know that's a total crock so there's no use even pretending. (Reeder, 1996)

As Jeff's description illustrates, friendships can differ markedly from romances in how much we reveal, especially in the early stages. But other differences exist as well. For example, we typically expect exclusivity from our romantic partners, but not from our friends. Also, people often have higher expectations about romantic partners, especially with regard to physical attractiveness, social status, and a pleasing personality (Sprecher & Regan, 2002). And we may require greater expressions of commitment and caring from romantic partners than from friends (Goodwin & Tang, 1991). In the following sections we explore in more detail the similarities and differences between friendships and romances.

Initiating Relationships

An individual's ability to begin a conversation is essential to the development of any relationship. While many people disparage small talk, there can be no "big talk" if small talk does not precede it. But even before you engage in small talk, you need to be able to signal your interest to others.

Initiating Romantic Relationships. Meeting romantic partners and establishing relationships can be a problem for many people. Dating anxiety is pervasive among adolescents and young adults (Essau, Conradt, & Petermann, 1999) and even among adults who have previously been married (Segrin & Givertz, 2003). Recent research suggests that locating sexual partners may be easier for young adults than initiating and developing long-term relationships (Mongeau, Ramirez, & Vorell, 2003).

Although men in heterosexual relationships traditionally initiate romantic relationships, waiting for a man to make the first move does not seem to be an effective strategy for women. When men were asked if they would pursue a relationship with a woman who didn't at least hint at her interest and availability, most said no (Muehlenhard & McFalls, 1981; Muehlenhard & Miller, 1988). Thus, in order for men to initiate interaction, they need women to send cues that they are interested and available. How does one do this? Frequently, potential romantic partners "test the water" by flirting. Considerable research has been conducted on flirting in heterosexual relationships, both because of its crucial role in the initiation of romantic relationships and because of its ambiguity. Unfortunately, we know much less about flirting during gay and lesbian courtship, so the discussion that follows refers primarily to heterosexual relationships.

Much flirting (though not all) is nonverbal, because nonverbal communication entails less risk. For example, if the other person does not respond, you can pretend you weren't flirting after all.

When initiating a potential romantic/sexual relationship, women are more active than men. In fact, women use more eye contact, smiles, brief touches, and grooming behavior to signal interest and attraction. Although men do use gazing, smiling, and grooming behaviors, the only behavior they engage in more than women do is intimate touching (hugging, hand holding). Thus, women engage in more flirtation at the onset of the interaction; then, men tend to escalate the relationship through touch (McCormick & Jones, 1989). Visit the Web site for the

Think back to the last time you were aware that someone was interested in you romantically. How did you know? What verbal and nonverbal behaviors suggested that romance was a possibility?

Most flirting, though not all, is nonverbal.

A strong association exists between peoples' communication skills and their satisfaction with their relationships.

Social Issues Research Center at www.sirc.org/publik/flirt.html if you would like to learn more about the "science of flirting."

Once couples successfully convey their interest and initiate a conversation, if their interest continues they may begin dating. Unfortunately, this is not always easy. People often lack confidence in their social and communication skills (Essau, Conradt, & Petermann, 1999). Many people aren't sure how or where to approach others, and they worry about being rejected.

In general, successful dating appears to be related to effective communication skills. For example, individuals who self-disclose a little as they initiate relationships are more successful than those who disclose a lot or none at all. Competent daters know that one should disclose primarily positive information early in relationships. They also act interested in what others have to say, help others out, and are polite and positive. Finally, those who successfully initiate relationships are more able to plan and ask for dates.

Unfortunately, many individuals haven't learned the skills needed to initiate dating relationships (Essau, Conradt, & Petermann, 1999; Galassi & Galassi, 1979). Some people even display conversational behaviors that have been found to be *unsuccessful* in dating situations. These behaviors include trying too hard to make an impression, disclosing too much information too soon, being passive (waiting for the other person to initiate conversation and activities), and acting too self-effacing (or modest) (Young, 1981).

At times, initiating a dating relationship may seem like a rather complicated dance. Each person has a part, but the dance steps vary from one couple to the next. Fortunately, initiating friendship can seem a bit more straightforward.

Initiating Friendships. Initiating a conversation is perhaps the most crucial communication skill in developing friendships. However, saying hello and initiating conversation can be difficult. Why? Just like in courtship situations, people may fear rejection. In fact, many people assume that the other person's failure to initiate a conversation is due to lack of interest (Vorauer & Ratner, 1996). If everyone felt this way, however, no relationship would ever begin! Therefore, you may need to begin the conversation if you wish to meet new people.

What is the best way to approach a new person? Typically, a nonthreatening comment works, such as, "This sure is an interesting class," as does an impersonal question, such as, "Are you a communication major?" If the other person is receptive, you will feel more comfortable continuing the conversation. And if the person isn't responsive, you can easily walk away.

Once you begin the conversation, you can keep it going by asking a broad, open-ended question. For example, you could ask, "Why did you choose this university?" or "What do you enjoy doing when you're not working?" You want to be sure to ask questions that can't be answered with a yes or no or with only a brief response. Your goal is to get the other person talking and to learn more about him or her.

Maintaining Relationships

Effective communication is, of course, essential to developing and maintaining relationships. In fact, a strong association exists between peoples' communication skills and their satisfaction with their relationships, particularly romantic ones (Emmers-Sommers, 2004; Noller & Fitzpatrick, 1990). As romantic relationships become more intimate and move toward greater commitment, couples' ratings of their communication satisfaction increases. In contrast, as dating relationships move toward dissolution, couples' satisfaction with their communication decreases (Guerrero, Eloy, & Wabnik, 1993). It appears that effective communication and relationship satisfaction operate in a circular process in which effective communication increases couples' happiness with their relationships, and satisfaction with the relationship leads to more effective communication. Communication also is essential to developing friendships. Most of the important functions that friends serve—providing companionship and a sense of belonging, offering emotional and physical support as well as reassurance, and giving feedback on self-disclosures—are communication-based (Duck, 1991).

Though initiating friendships and romances can be anxiety-producing, it can also be exhilarating and fun. When relationships are new, we tend to focus on their more positive aspects. However, as relationships endure, we have a harder time ignoring their shortcomings. Consequently, maintaining relationships over time can be challenging.

Couples maintain their relationships through routine as well as strategic behaviors.

Maintaining Romantic Relationships through Communication. Only in the past twenty years have communication scholars really begun to focus on how romantic couples maintain their relationships communicatively. Communication researchers Dan Canary and Laura Stafford conducted some of the earliest studies of how couples keep their relationships satisfying. Based on their research, they created a typology of **relational maintenance** behaviors that heterosexual, gay, and lesbian couples use (Canary & Stafford, 1994; Haas & Stafford, 1998) (see Table 8.3).

More recently, scholars have examined the nonstrategic, routine behaviors couples perform that help maintain their relationships. Alberts, Yoshimura, Rabby, and Loschiavo (2005) studied heterosexual and gay couples to see what types of communication they engaged in day to day. They determined that couples use twelve types of conversational behaviors as they live their lives together, including humor/joking, self-report (or self-disclosure), positivity (attempts to make interactions pleasant), and talking about television (see Table 8.4). Moreover, they found that on the weekend couples tend to engage in more conflict, humor, household task talk, and planning.

relational maintenance
behaviors that couples perform that help maintain their relationships

TABLE 8.3   Couples' Maintenance Behaviors

Behavior	Examples
Positivity	Act nice and cheerful; make interactions enjoyable
Openness	Encourage partner to disclose thoughts and feelings; discuss relationship
Assurances	Stress commitment to partner; imply relationship has a future
Social networks	Spend time with the other's friends; focus on common friends; show willingness to spend time with the other's friends and family
Sharing tasks	Help equally with tasks; perform household tasks
Joint activities	Spend time hanging out; engage in activities together
Mediated communication	Write letters; use email or phone to keep in touch
Avoidance/antisocial	Be less than completely honest; avoid the other; act badly
Humor	Tease; be sarcastic in a funny way; use funny nicknames

From: *Maintaining Relationships Through Communication: Relational, Contextual, and Cultural Variations* by D. Canary & M. Dainton. Copyright 2002 by Taylor & Francis Group LLC–Books. Reproduced with permission of Taylor & Francis Group LLC–Books in the format Textbook and Other Book via Copyright Clearance Center.

TABLE 8.4	Typology of Couples' Everyday Maintenance Conversations
Positivity	Compliments, polite behaviors, thanks, affectional expressions. Example: "Good job, honey!"
Observation	Random comments or questions, often about the environment. Example: "That clock is slow."
Plans	Planning and discussing the future. Example: "What do you want to do this weekend?"
Household task talk	Discussion of tasks that need to be done, such as taking care of housework, cooking, child care, pets, dry cleaning; focused on the present or near future. Example: "Would you empty the dishwasher?"
TV talk	Comments about television programs. Examples: "Is that the woman we saw in that movie last night?"
Other-report	Comments about known others or what known others have said/done. Example: "Ryan is thinking about changing jobs."
Humor	A statement delivered in a humorous style (often with laughter) and/or responded to with laughter or humorous commentary. Example: "Oh, no. A rotten old fish!" (laughs). "That's funny."
Self-report	Description of one's past or current experiences; information not known unless revealed by speaker. Example: "I thought about you today."
Partner's experiences	Questions or comments about partner's experiences or internal states. Example: "How was your day?"
Narratives	Recounting of stories or activities from TV, books, movies, and life. Example: "They said she got sick from drinking that tea."
Conflict	Statements of complaint, criticism, or dissatisfaction. Example: "Why can't you ever take anything seriously?"
Back-channel communication	Verbal fillers that indicate involvement, interest, or that one is listening. Example: "oh," "uhm," and "yeah."

From: Alberts, J., Yoshimura, C., Rabby, M., & Loschiavo, R. (2005). "Mapping the topography of couples' everyday interaction", *Journal of Social and Personal Relationships, 22*, 299–322.

In general, studies of relationship maintenance indicate that specific communication patterns such as joking, spending time talking about one's day, encouraging self-disclosure, and expressing commitment to the relationship may help couples maintain their relationships.

Communication is key to maintaining friendships.

Maintaining Friendships through Communication. Conversation plays an important role in friendship as well. One study determined that many conversations with friends last only about three minutes and that these conversations were mostly small talk. Nonetheless, people rated these conversations as highly significant (Duck, 1991). Thus intimate disclosures may be important, but so are daily, routine interactions, which connect friends and reaffirm or maintain their relationships.

Interestingly, scholars have found that friends are most satisfied with each other when they possess similar levels of communication skills (Burleson & Samter, 1996). That is, it is not how skillful friends are overall that predicts their satisfaction with each other but whether they possess "similar or different degrees of communication skill (or lack of skill)" (Dainton et al., 2003, p. 85).

Scholars also have studied the maintenance behaviors friends use to keep their relationships alive. For example, Canary, Stafford, Hause, and Wallace (1993) found that friends use assurances (indicating the importance of the friendship), positivity, open discussion, and listening, though less often than do romantic partners. Several researchers have found that simply spending time together is an important maintenance strategy for friends (Fehr, 2000; Messman, Canary, & Hause, 2000). More specifically, they discovered that shared activities and ongoing interaction are necessary to sustain a relationship and that absence of interaction is often given as the reason for a friendship ending (Dainton et al., 2003). Other communication researchers argue that good conflict management skills are vital for enduring friendships (Burleson & Samter, 1996), and several point out that the use of telephone calls and email are essential to long-distance ones (Johnson, 2000).

As you can see, communication is essential to both friendship and romantic relationship maintenance. However, sometimes we find ourselves unable, or unwilling, to invest energy in maintaining previously valued friendships or romances.

Ending Relationships

Not all relationships endure. When couples consistently engage in behaviors that are not satisfying, one or both partners likely will exit the relationship. Some courtship relationships end after the first date, while others end after months or years. Friendships end as well. Relatively few people retain all the friends they make over the course of their lives (Rawlins, 1992). Despite this, relationship termination can be an awkward stage—both to experience and to study.

People generally are much more willing to answer questionnaires and speak with researchers about developing or maintaining a relationship than about ending one. Studying this process is also difficult because relationship de-escalation and termination typically occur over an extended period, with no easy way to say when exactly the process began. Some relationships do end abruptly and decisively, however. The two basic trajectories for ending romantic relationships as well as friendships are called *sudden death* and *passing away* (Duck, 1982; Hays, 1988).

Sudden death refers to relationships that end without prior warning (at least for one participant). Some people are shocked to discover their partners are leaving. Though unexpected for the one partner, the other may have been thinking about his or her departure for some time. Regardless of who has been thinking what, and for how long, occasionally an event occurs, such as infidelity or betrayal, that so damages the relationship that the partners terminate the relationship relatively quickly.

More typically, relationships **pass away**, or decline over time, and the partners are aware that problems remain unresolved. During this period, the partners may vacillate between attempts to improve the relationship and efforts to de-escalate it. Over months or even years, romantic couples may seek counseling, take trips together, or try other methods to improve the relationship, while friends may sporadically try to renew their friendship. At the same time, they may develop outside interests or friends as they withdraw from the relationship. It can be a difficult period, especially for romantic couples.

sudden death
the process by which relationships end without prior warning for at least one participant

passing away
the process by which relationships decline over time

"Susan! ...are you trying to tell me we have an interface problem?"

©Noel Ford/www.CartoonStock.com

To help you understand this often-confusing stage of relationship development, we next explore the reasons that relationships end and the strategies people use to terminate them.

Reasons for Courtship Dissolution.   When asked why their relationship terminated, gay and heterosexual couples provide very similar reasons (Baxter, 1991; Kurdek, 1991). The most frequent explanations were lack of autonomy, lack of similarity/compatibility, lack of supportiveness, and infidelity. Heterosexual couples also indicated that insufficient shared time, inequity, and the absence of romance contributed to the demise of their relationships.

People also terminate relationships because characteristics they thought they liked in a partner become less appealing over time. One study determined that in almost one-third of the courtship relationships examined, the qualities individuals initially found attractive became the qualities that led to the end of the relationship (Felmlee, 1995), a concept called *fatal attractions*. For example, one woman liked her relational partner because he had a "don't-care" attitude and liked to have fun, but later she found him irresponsible. (Felmlee, 1995).

When relationships end, everyone looks for explanations. People blame themselves, they blame the other person, they may even blame people outside the relationship. Sometimes no one is to blame (Duck, 1991). For example, relationships may end because the partners live too far apart or the timing is wrong. You might meet Ms. or Mr. Right, but if you meet immediately following a painful breakup or just as you are beginning a new and demanding job, you won't have the emotional stability or time needed to develop a successful relationship.

In sum, relationship termination is normal, though it can be difficult. If you would like more information on how to terminate a romance, or how to recover from one that has ended, you can find a directory of sites at **www.google.com/Top/Society/Relationships/Dating/Advice** that offer advice on ending romantic relationships.

Romance Termination Strategies.   Researchers have identified five general categories of disengagement strategies for dissolving romantic relationships (Cody, 1982). Surprisingly (or perhaps not), the most frequent strategy romantic couples use to end their relationships is negative identity management, which means communicating in ways that arouse negative emotions in order to make the other person upset enough to agree to break off the relationship. When using this strategy, one might criticize one's romantic partner or convey indifference to his or her feelings and desires.

De-escalation strategies were used next most often. De-escalation covers a broad range of strategies, from promising some continued closeness (we can still be friends) to suggesting that the couple might reconcile in the future. De-escalation strategies are characterized by an attempt to reframe or change the definition of the relationship.

Justification strategies occurred third most frequently. As the label implies, justification strategies attempt to provide a reason or excuse for why the relationship has failed and should end. In this case, one partner might explain the positive consequences of ending the relationship (we can devote more time to our careers) or the negative consequences of not ending the relationship (we will come to hate each other). Positive tone strategies, on the other hand, address the feelings and concerns of the partner and try to make her or him feel better; for example, a partner might say, "I care for you, but you deserve someone who can commit to you."

Though difficult, relationship termination is normal.

Behavioral de-escalation strategies occurred least frequently. These strategies involved avoiding the partner. Behavioral de-escalation strategies likely are the least common because it is difficult to avoid a person with whom you have a romantic relationship. If Richard doesn't return Rob's phone calls or avoids the classes they have together, Rob most likely will track him down to find out why.

Reasons for Friendship Dissolution.   Why do friendships end? Friendships are particularly vulnerable to termination because few societal pressures encourage their continuance (Blieszner & Adams, 1992) and because friends may not expect to have consistent contact. Some friendships decline without either person being aware of it. Once the friends recognize the decline, it may no longer be possible for the relationship to recover (Rose, 1984). Thus friendships, unlike romantic relationships, can end without either person being dissatisfied with the relationship.

Friendships end for a range of reasons, based on how close the friendship was. Casual friends are more likely to report that their relationships ended due to lack of proximity, while close and best friends more often state that their relationships terminated because of decreased affection. In addition, best and close friends report that their friendships dissolved due to interference from other relationships, such as one person's romantic partner (Johnson et al., 2004).

Scholars have identified five specific factors that can contribute to the termination of a friendship: lack of communication skills, rule-breaking, deception, boredom, and other reasons (Duck, 1988). With regard to the first factor, if you wish to maintain relationships you must display appropriate communication skills. We know that poor conversationalists tend to be lonely (Duck, 1988) and that lonely people are not perceived to be competent communicators (Canary & Spitzberg, 1985).

Friendships also end because one or both members violate fundamental, often unspoken rules of the relationship that have been established over the course of the friendship (Argyle & Henderson, 1984; Bowker, 2004). For example, most friends believe that good friends don't gossip about each other, flirt with each other's romantic partners, or lie to each other. Successful relationship partners discern the rules of the relationship and adhere to them.

Friends' Termination Strategies.   Because friendships are less formal, their endings may be more subtle and less obvious than those endured by romantic couples (Hayes, 1988). For example, a friend's permission is not required to end a friendship, and one can simply cut off contact abruptly, which happens only rarely in romantic relationships.

When friends desire relationship dissolution, they are likely to use one or more of the following disengagement strategies: withdrawal/avoidance, Machiavellian tactics, positive tone, and openness (Baxter, 1982). As with behavioral de-escalation among romantic couples, when friends engage in **withdrawal/avoidance** they spend less time together, don't return phone calls, and avoid places where they are likely to see the other. **Machiavellian tactics** involve having a third party convey your unhappiness about the relationship and your desire to de-escalate or end it. Positive tone strategies, like those used by romantic couples, express concern for the rejected friend and try to make the person feel better. Thus, you might tell a friend that you wish to end your friendship because school and work take up too much time, rather than admitting you do not enjoy his company any more. Finally, openness means that you straightforwardly explain to your friend why the relationship is ending.

Although this section has focused on how and why friendships and romances end, relationship termination isn't the only difficulty friends and romantic partners face. Individuals face relationship problems at all stages. In the next section we discuss some of the more frequent problems that can emerge: negative communication behaviors, deception, jealousy, and sexual coercion.

What rules do you have for close friendships? That is, what could a friend do that would be such a significant violation of your expectations that you would terminate your friendship?

withdrawal/avoidance
a friendship termination strategy in which friends spend less time together, don't return phone calls, and avoid places where they are likely to see each other

Machiavellian tactics
having a third party convey one's unhappiness about a relationship

Confronting Relationship Challenges

Although relationships can provide love, companionship, and joy, they also can be the source of some of our greatest suffering. Once we open ourselves to intimacy and commitment, we also open ourselves to the possibility of hurt and betrayal. Not all communication behaviors are associated with successful or satisfying relationships; some have negative effects on relationships, the topic we discuss next.

Aversive Communication Behaviors.   Close relationships are often marked by the presence of aversive, or negative, behaviors. According to Miller (1997), 44 percent of us are likely to be annoyed by a relational partner on any given day, and young adults have 8.7 annoying experiences with their romantic partners weekly. In the context of our close relationships, we "criticize, nag, betray, lie, disappoint, ostracize, embarrass, and tease one another, to name just a few behaviors" (Kowalski, Valentine, Wilkinson, Queen, & Sharpe, 2003, p. 473). Whatever the intention of the perpetrator, these negative actions are likely to hurt their victims. In turn, victims often respond with even more negative behaviors, which can lead to a cycle of blame and criticism (Kowalski, 2003). Fortunately, close relationships tend to be resilient and most of them bounce back from these interactions. However, if these behaviors occur too frequently or the cycle escalates, they can devastate close relationships.

Deception.   Some types of **deception** can impair relationships, though not all. For example, a person may withhold information because it is too private to share or because it might cause pain. ("Dinner was wonderful; it didn't taste burned at all.") The importance of the information lied about best predicts the effect the deception will have on the relationship. Individuals who discover they've been deceived about an important issue become resentful, disappointed, and suspicious (Bok, 1978; Sagarin, Rhoads, & Cialdini, 1998).

While relationship partners consider deception to be a rare occurrence, research indicates that concealment and distortion of information are integral to many conversations (Turner, Edgley, & Olmstead, 1975). One study revealed that 85.7 percent of respondents had deceived their dating partners within the previous two weeks (Tolhuizen, 1990), while in another, 92 percent of individuals admitted having lied to their romantic partners (Knox, Schacht, Holt, & Turner, 1993). The most frequent issue individuals deceived their partners about was competing relationships.

The findings about deception in dating relationships are especially interesting for two reasons: First, research has established that people are not very good at detecting deception (Burgoon, Buller, Ebesu, & Rockwell, 1994); and second, most people assume those they love tell the truth (Buller & Burgoon, 1996). This tendency to not suspect our intimates is called the **truth bias**, and it is especially strong in romantic relationships. For example, research shows that people generally do not look for cues that a partner is deceiving them (McCornack & Parks, 1986). However, other research suggests that once suspicion has been introduced, romantic partners' deception detection improves (Stiff, Kim, & Ramesh, 1989). Thus, you probably have a fairly good chance of deceiving your partner *unless* she or he is suspicious; in that case, you are more likely to get caught.

Lying can be just as devastating between friends as between romantic partners. College students have reported being as distressed by a friend's betrayal of their confidences as by a romantic partner's infidelity (Cauffman, Feldman, Jensen, & Arnett, 2000). Some people expect their friends to be even more honest and open with them than are their romantic partners, and, as we previously mentioned, deception is one of the primary reasons friends give for terminating their friendships.

deception
concealment, distortion, or lying in communication

truth bias
the tendency to not suspect one's intimates of deception

Jealousy.   Given the findings about deception, it is not surprising that one of the more problematic types of communication for dating couples is the expression of jealousy. **Jealousy** is a complex and often painful emotion that frequently leads to ineffective communication. The feeling combines anger, sadness, worry, embarrassment, and disappointment (Guerrero & Andersen, 1998). Jealousy occurs when a person perceives a threat to an existing relationship. Of course, one can perceive a threat to a relationship and not feel jealous. Jealousy seems to flow from feelings of insecurity about the relationship and/or the ability to cope with a change in it (Cano & O'Leary, 1997).

Men and women often differ in the ways they express and manage jealousy. Men are more likely to consider leaving the relationship and to become involved with other women in an attempt to repair their self-esteem; women are more likely to focus on repairing the relationship (Buss, 1988; White & Mullen, 1989).

Jealousy often arises because one partner has little trust in the relationship.

One problematic aspect of jealousy concerns the manner in which couples communicate about their jealous feelings (Guerrero & Afifi, 1999). Communication researchers have discovered that how couples deal with and communicate about jealousy has a stronger impact on the relationship than the jealous feelings themselves (Andersen, Eloy, Guerrero, & Spitzberg, 1995). Paradoxically, jealous people tend to seek proof to justify their feelings. In some relationships an individual can dispel the partner's fears, but this requires trust. Unfortunately, jealousy often arises because one partner has little trust in the relationship. Thus jealous people may reject all assurances and even escalate their accusations (White & Mullen, 1989).

Regrettably, some communication interactions about jealousy lead to physical violence (Cano & O'Leary, 1997). A study of 138 jealous subjects determined that almost 80 percent had acted aggressively because of their jealousy, and over 50 percent had actually assaulted their partners (Mullen & Maack, 1985). What types of communication are more likely to escalate interactions about jealousy to these dangerous levels?

Overt rejection or the expression of disdain by an accused partner during an argument can precipitate relationship violence (Psarska, 1970). For example, a partner accused of infidelity may angrily reply, "I've never been involved with anyone else, but who knows why, since you are such a lousy partner." The feelings of jealousy themselves give rise to strong passions, but the hostile response of the loved one may cause expressions of jealousy to explode into violence (White & Mullen, 1989).

Although jealousy may be more common in romantic relationships, it does exist within friendships (Aune & Comstock, 1991). For example, if a person is becoming close to a second friend and fails to include his first friend in their joint activities, the first may feel the relationship is threatened and experience jealousy.

Individuals are often jealous of their friends' romantic partners as well. When people fall in love, they often focus intently on their romantic partners, to the detriment of their friendships (Roth & Parker, 2001). However, the friend who communicates those feelings of insecurity and jealousy poorly can damage the friendship. Criticizing the third party, engaging in aggression toward the third party, or complaining repeatedly to the friend can lead to increased conflict and rejection (Grotpeter & Crick, 1996).

Interpersonal Violence.   **Interpersonal violence**—physical violence against a partner or child—is a serious problem in the United States. By the most conservative estimate, 1 million women suffer nonfatal violence by an intimate each year (Bureau of Justice Statistics, 1995); by other estimates, 4 million American women experience a serious assault by an intimate partner during an average 12-month period (American Psychological Association, 1996). Nearly one-third of American women (31 percent) report being physically or sexually abused by a husband or boyfriend at some point in

jealousy
a complex and often painful emotion that occurs when a person perceives a threat to an existing relationship

interpersonal violence
physical violence against a partner or child

their lives (Commonwealth Fund Survey, 1998). The statistics on violence against men are less consistent and may be underreported, due to men's reluctance to admit being battered by their partners. Current estimates suggest that relational aggression against men comprises 8 to 18 percent of all interpersonal violence (Rennison & Welchans, May 2000). Lest you think you are safe because you are not married, know that even in high school, one in five couples reported violence in their relationships. Thus physical aggression is relatively common in romantic relationships.

Two types of interpersonal aggression can occur in romantic relationships: battering and situational couple violence. *Battering* describes relationships in which one individual uses violence as a way to control and dominate his or her partner (though most batterers are male). During these couples' violent episodes there is a clear perpetrator and a clear victim. The factors that contribute to battering syndrome are many and complex; therefore, just improving one's communication skills is not believed to be effective in redressing the situation, and creating change can be challenging. Therefore, it is very helpful for individuals to be able to recognize the behavioral characteristics of batterers before their relationships solidify. For information on how to recognize a batterer, see *Did You Know? Recognizing a Potential Batterer.*

Situational couple violence is characterized by less intense forms of violence and tends to be more mutual in its performance, although this does not mean that men and women engage in acts of equal severity. Even in these instances, women usually suffer more serious injuries than do men. Among these couples often it is not clear who the perpetrator is and who the victim is. Ineffective communication patterns are common with these couples, so improving communication skills may reduce interpersonal violence in their relationships.

Did You Know?
Recognizing a Potential Batterer

A batterer may display any of these symptoms. However, these are warning signs and you should use judgment before making any sort of accusations or decisions.

Has he or she ever hit you?

Has he or she ever hit former girlfriends/boyfriends, spouses, or brag about previous physical fights with anyone?

What does he or she do when angry?

Is he or she cruel to animals or violent with others?

Does he or she threaten to hurt you, break things, no matter how trivial the disagreement?

Does he or she get angry very fast, very easily, very violently, very often?

Does he or she attempt to keep you and your life under strict control?

Is he or she pathologically jealous?

Does he or she have two personalities?

Does he or she blame you for problems in the relationship—including the violence?

How does he or she react to your success?

Does he or she get violent when drinking?

Is he or she unable to empathize?

Does he or she use sex as a means of apologizing?

Does he or she have trouble with authority figures?

Has he or she had prior trouble with the authorities—been in jail or kicked out of school?

ADAPTED FROM: Recognizing a potential batterer. Estronaut: *A Forum for Women's Health.* Retrieved, October 27, 2008, from www.estronaut.com/a/recognizing_potential_batterer.htm

Research reveals that couples who engage in situational couple violence lack fundamental communication and problem-solving skills. Unfortunately, they also tend to engage in more conflict discussions. They appear unable to let even small matters slide (Lloyd, 1990), and when they do discuss their differences they are unable to present and defend their positions on issues without becoming hostile (Infante, Chandler, & Rudd, 1989; Lloyd, 1999).

During conflict, these couples are more likely than nonabusive couples to attack each other's character, curse, and to threaten their partners (Sabourin, 1996). They also make few attempts to de-escalate the conflict or facilitate their conversations calmly (Cordova, Jacobsen, Gottman, Rushe, & Cox, 1993). In addition, husbands in aggressive relationships attribute hostile intent to their wives' communication and behavior and respond negatively when their wives attempt to influence them (Anglin & Holtzworth-Munroe, 1997). Thus the communication of couples who engage in situational violence appears to contribute significantly to their hostility and abuse.

Situational violence is also present in friendship and peer relationships, although it is a topic that is understudied. Aggressive behavior among friends can be demonstrated in different forms: physical aggression, verbal aggression, and indirect aggression. Physical aggression includes such behaviors as pushing, shoving, or hitting. Verbal aggression includes threatening and intimidating others, and engaging in malicious teasing, taunting, and name-calling. Indirect aggression includes behaviors such as gossiping, spreading cruel rumors, and encouraging others to reject or exclude someone. More than one in three high school students say they have been in a physical fight in the past year (Centers for Disease Control and Prevention, 2002); however, it is not clear how many of these violent conflicts involve friends specifically. What information is available suggests that aggression among friends tends to be more verbal and indirect than physical.

Sexual Coercion.   Date rape is another type of negative, possibly violent, interaction in which the participants' communication is of central importance (Willan & Pollard, 2003). People often find it difficult to discuss date rape. Part of the problem arises from lack of clarity on what date rape is. Legally, the definition of rape is sexual activity that is "against the victim's will/without the victim's consent" and includes some "degree of force or threat" as well as "penetration" (Spitzberg, 1998, p. 181).

Individuals often use the term *date rape* to describe unwanted sex. Unwanted sexual relations occur when one person does not want to have sexual relations but does so without the offender exerting physical force or threats (Spitzberg, 1998). Sometimes people engage in unwanted sex because of concern for the relationship, verbal pressure or harassment, or real concern for personal safety, even though they have not been physically threatened. This situation has been described as **sexual coercion** (Spitzberg, 1998).

One contributor to unwanted sex is the fact that men and women experience cross-sex interaction differently. Behaviors that women call friendly, men are more likely to label *sexy*, and men are more likely than women to believe that women's behavior communicates sexual interest and intent (Abbey, 1987; Muehlenhard, 1989). This difference in perception can lead to differing expectations about sexual contact and misunderstandings regarding sexual consent (Lim & Roloff, 1999). Some research suggests that such misperceptions can contribute to the likelihood of date rape (Abbey, 1988). Some female college students admit to using *token resistance* (saying no; then giving in) (Muehlenhard & Hollabough, 1988), while some males acknowledge that they have discounted their partners' refusals, and persisted in making unwanted sexual advances (Lloyd & Emery, 2000). These patterns can make communicating and interpreting sexual consent more difficult. And if these communication behaviors occur when one or both parties are drinking, as is frequently the case (Muehlenhard & Linton, 1987), ambiguity and miscommunication are even more likely.

Have you ever engaged in physical intimacy when you really didn't want to? Why? What communication could you have used to change the outcome?

sexual coercion
physically nonviolent pressure to engage in unwanted sex

Did You Know?
Preventing Sexual Coercion

The various explanations for date rape and sexual coercion all suggest several cautions. Based on the research concerning date rape, we recommend:

1. Don't drink on a date or in a group unless you are already involved in a positive sexual relationship with your partner. You will not be as effective in communicating your wishes and desires, nor in understanding your partner's, if you are under the influence of alcohol.
2. Do not assume you know what your partner desires. Instead, ask! Reading another's verbal and nonverbal cues can be difficult, especially if you do not have experience with each other in this area.
3. *Always* assume a no is a "real" no.
4. A corollary of number three: Do not use token resistance. If you do, how can your partner differentiate a "token" no from a "real" one?
5. Communicate your desires and expectations clearly. If you don't want to engage in sexual activity, say so firmly, clearly, and unequivocally. Sometimes in trying to be polite, people end up being indirect and unclear about what they want. For example, instead of saying, "I find you very attractive, but I think I'd rather do this another time" say, "I don't want to have sex with you tonight."

For advice on how to minimize the likelihood that you will become involved in coercive sexual contact, see *Did You Know? Preventing Sexual Coercion.* If you would like additional information, the health clinics and security departments of most colleges and universities can provide pamphlets, books, and other resources.

Individuals, of course, are at the center of relationships, and what they say and do affects their relationships at every stage. However, societal norms and pressures shape relationships as well. In the next section, we examine relationships within this broader frame.

THE INDIVIDUAL, RELATIONSHIP COMMUNICATION, AND SOCIETY

Many people think that relationships are an individual matter, that our decision to befriend or become intimate with another person is a matter of choice, and that how we communicate and behave within relationships is strictly a matter of preference. However, society wields strong influences on our choices and behavior. Sometimes these influences are explicit and a matter of law, as in restrictions against marriage between underage teenagers. Other societal influences are more subtle. For example, why is it that 95 percent of all marriages are racially homogenous (U.S. Bureau of the Census, 1998)? Similarly, why do most couples who marry have a wedding ceremony, and why are people expected to tell their romantic partners "I love you"? The reasons lie in powerful, sometimes unrecognized societal norms. These laws and norms determine to a large extent whom we find desirable as romantic partners and friends and how we communicate with them.

Society, Power, Courtship, and Marriage

Most heterosexuals are unaware of the effect of cultural norms on their romance choices (O'Brien & Foley, 1999) or on how they express affection and commitment in them. Until 50 years ago, partners of different races could not legally have intimate relationships in the United States; until the year 2000, Alabama still had a law against interracial marriages (Root 2001; Sollors, 2000). Not surprisingly, the vast majority of marriages in the United States are still racially homogenous. Moreover, they occur primarily between people of similar religious backgrounds (Shehan, Bock, & Lee, 1990), economic status (Kalmijin, 1994), age (Atkinson & Glass, 1985), education (Mare, 1991), weight (Schafer & Keith, 1990), and appearance (Chambers, Christiansen, & Kunz, 1983). Such a high degree of similarity, or **homogeneity**, suggests individual preference is not the only factor influencing our choices.

homogeneity
a high degree of similarity

Commonly held stereotypes also influence choices about whom one should or should not date and marry. In intercultural couples, certain combinations are more common than others. In 75 percent of Black–White marriages, the husband is Black, and in 75 percent of White–Asian couples the husband is White (Sailer, 2003). The frequency of these pairings reflects strong societal norms about who is attractive (and who is not) as well as common stereotypes about what type of woman makes a good wife.

Just as societies have norms for mate selection and behavior, they also have norms for communication in the context of romantic relationships. For example, who do you think should say "I love you" first or propose marriage? Many people believe males in heterosexual relationships should take the lead (Owen, 1987). In some cultures romantic couples rarely express their feelings or only express them in private. In Japan, couples rarely touch or express emotion in public. Although young couples may hold hands, spouses virtually never kiss in public (Times Square Travels, 2004). Other cultures prohibit public expressions of affection, as in Indonesia, where it is illegal to kiss in public (MSNBC News, 2004), or in Kuwait, where homosexuality is illegal, as is any public display of affection between men and women (World Travels, 2004). Thus every relationship is situated within a set of societal and cultural norms and expectations, and what occurs within that relationship is likely to be affected by those norms.

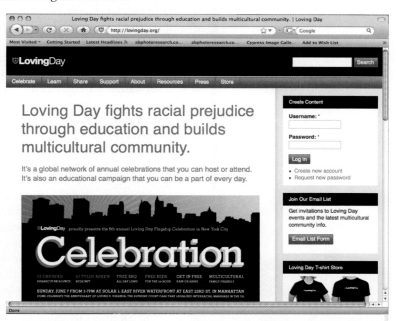

Loving Day is meant to celebrate interracial relationships in remembrance of *Loving v. Virginia,* the Supreme Court ruling that outlawed bans on interracial marriage.

Because of the national debate concerning gay and lesbian marriage, most people recognize that through laws, society in most parts of the United States limits the sex of the person one can choose to marry. However, many heterosexuals fail to consider how strongly social norms and laws affect the ways in which gays and lesbians can communicate with and about their romantic partners. Regardless of one's position on the desirability of gay and lesbian romances and marriage, the impact of legal and normative restrictions on gay relationships merits consideration. Gay people often can't express affection in public without fear of negative, even violent, responses. In many instances they don't even feel safe recognizing their partners or referring to them. For this reason they may refer to their lovers as "friends" or "roommates" or attempt to conceal their romantic partner's sex by never using pronouns such as *him* or *her.*

Having to alter one's verbal and nonverbal behavior to conform to society's norms may seem a small matter if you are heterosexual. But imagine what life would be like if in many contexts you could never acknowledge your partner, you had to pretend that you were "just friends," and you had to be continuously on guard to avoid revealing this "secret"? Not only would this be exhausting, it would significantly inhibit your ability to be close to others. Unfortunately, this is the life that many gays and lesbians live. Visit the Web site **www.geocities.com/WestHollywood/ Heights/5883/debunking.html** to learn more about the experiences of gays and lesbians in U.S. culture.

In addition to the social norms that affect how we develop and communicate within romantic and courtship relationships, the practices of specific institutions impact our communication and relationships. For example, many faiths have long prescribed whom their members should marry, how many spouses they could have, and even if they should date. For example, the Mormon faith once permitted men to have more than one wife (although it no longer does); Muslim men are instructed to marry Muslim women; and Hindus often discourage young people from dating and selecting their own marital partners.

Although over time religions can and do alter their positions on these issues (for example, the Church of Jesus Christ of Latter Day Saints' position on polygamy), they may be slower to change than other social institutions. For example, Penny Edgell (2003) surveyed 125 churches and discovered that 83 percent of them still maintained an organization and theology based on the idea of the nuclear family in which the father works, the mother stays at home, and the couple has children. She further points out that a number of churches are not receptive to gay and lesbian couples, who then have difficulty practicing their faith. In these ways, religious institutions influence how we view relationships as well as how we act within them and communicate about our relationships.

Similarly, business organizations create policies and practices that affect the types of relationships and communication practices their employees can have. Many organizations prohibit coworkers from establishing "affectional relationships" while others (such as the military) ban fraternization—relationships that cross the organizational hierarchy. Corporations also develop policies to limit nepotism—hiring one's family members—or express their views on same-sex relationships by providing, or not providing, domestic-partner benefits. Organizations often create rules that attempt to control and influence employees' communication, through sexual harassment policies, secrecy clauses, and dictates on what can be communicated to others outside the organization.

Societal institutions such as churches influence our communication and relationships.

In addition to shaping relationships in the ways already discussed, societal factors influence negative aspects of romantic relationships, such as violence and rape. For example, most talk about violence in romantic relationships focuses on the behavior of individual aggressors rather than on the social structures that allow abuse (Lloyd & Emery, 2000). Most people assume that men and women experience equity in their relationships (Ferraro, 1996; Lloyd & Emery, 2000) and that men are not abused by their partners. However, the facts are that women typically earn less money than men, are more responsible for children than men, and often are physically weaker than men. These factors seriously compromise how equal women can be in heterosexual relationships and likely account for the fact that far more women are severely injured and murdered by their partners than vice versa (Ferraro, 1996). At the same time, little conversation occurs about violence against men; in fact, men who are abused are often ridiculed and stigmatized so that they have few places to turn for help and support (Kimmel, 2002).

In addition, the ways we talk about romance can encourage acceptance of aggression in relationships. For example, U.S. media frequently portray male aggression as normal and acceptable, as in romance novels, where male aggression is often a central, and recurrent, plot point (Kramer & Moore, 2001), and women often interpret that aggression as a sign of love. The popular image that men have urgent and difficult-to-control sexual drives implies that women are responsible for controlling sexual contact. Thus, more attention is paid to how *women* behave during unwanted sexual encounters than how men behave.

Finally, people frequently blame the victim. For example, people often ask "What was she doing out late at night by herself?" When we blame victims, we ask what they could have done to prevent the violence rather than focusing on what we should do as a culture to minimize relational aggression. Lloyd and Emery argue that how we define aggression is important; when we make statements such as "He just slapped her around a bit," we diminish the real emotional and physical trauma associated with assault. Overall, these researchers propose that if we truly wish to reduce the violence in relationships, we must examine and alter the ways we talk about relational aggression.

Society, Power, and Friendship

Unlike marriage, friendships are not governed by laws and institutions. However, social norms still affect our choice of friends or our behavior within friendships. Take a moment to think about your closest friends over the past five years. How similar are they to you? Do you have any friends who are decades older than you? How many of your friends are from a different ethnic group than you are? Clearly some people do have friends who differ from themselves on demographic factors such as race, age, income, and education, but this is more often the exception than the rule (Aboud & Mendelson, 1996). As we discussed in Chapter 7, these multicultural relationships, though potentially very rewarding, sometimes take more "care and feeding" than relationships in which two people are very similar. Intercultural friends may receive pressure from others, particularly from majority group members, to stick with people who are similar to them (Pogrebin, 1992).

Thus friendship is not only an individual matter; it also is a social event that occurs in contexts that exert a powerful influence on its development (Allan, 1977). In the United States it is understood that friendships play an extremely important role in the lives of adolescents. In this culture, parents are encouraged to understand that their adolescent children will turn away from talking and spending time with them (Rawlins, 1992). On the other hand, married adults are expected to place their romance partners and families before their friends (Dainton et al., 2003).

ETHICS AND CLOSE RELATIONSHIPS

Although communicating ethically is important in all contexts and relationships, it is nowhere more important than in the context of close relationships. If you communicate unethically with your friends, family, and romantic partner, the consequences may be severe. Certainly relationships have ended due to deception, secrecy, and even the truth, too harshly expressed. All the ethical considerations we have discussed throughout this book are important in close relationships, but here we will focus on authentic communication.

As you may recall from Chapter 1, authentic communication refers to communication that is open and free from pretense. *Inauthentic communication* refers to attempts to manipulate the interaction or the other person for personal goals; it denies the right to communicate to those with a legitimate interest in the issue. Authentic communication is particularly important in close relationships for two reasons: We expect our closest friends and family members to be authentic, or "real," with us, and authentic communication is connected to intimacy.

For most people, intimacy is based on the feeling that one knows and is known by another. When we feel intimate with others we believe that we are connecting with their "true" selves and that we are able to be our truest selves in the relationship. However, when people are not authentic in their communication with those close to them or deny them the right to communicate authentically, it can decrease intimacy and even lead to termination of the relationship. And if we discover that an intimate friend or partner was being inauthentic and manipulative, we will feel not only deceived but betrayed. For example, if you discover that your friend has been pretending to like your romantic partner while making negative remarks about her on the sly, you probably will feel angry and betrayed. In addition, if you want to continue the relationship, you now have to deal not only with your friend's feelings about your romantic partner but also with your friend's deceit.

How can you ensure that your interactions with close others are authentic? You can do so by being open to others' communication efforts, being open in your own communication, taking responsibility for what you say, and respecting the rights of others to speak. In effect, we are suggesting that you need to avoid the three "pitfalls" of inauthentic communication: topic avoidance, meaning denial, and disqualification.

 To maintain an authentic relationship, you need to confront issues that are important to the relationship.

To maintain an authentic relationship with another you need to confront issues that are important to the relationship and to the other party. If one or both of you prohibit the other from discussing issues that are important to either of you, you are engaging in inauthentic communication. For example, if your good friend wishes to discuss his or her sexual identity and you refuse to do so, you are shutting down communication and likely damaging your intimacy with the other person.

In addition, authentic relationships require that you take responsibility for what you say and mean. If you are angry and tease your friend harshly because of it, it is inauthentic to deny that you are angry and trying to be hurtful. Even worse, if you put the onus on your friend for being "too sensitive," you are compounding the problem of your inauthenticity. Repeated interactions such as this can undermine trust and intimacy.

Finally, authentic communicators allow others to speak regardless of their own position or experience. If your single friend attempts to give you relationship support and advice, you disqualify him or her if you refuse to listen because your friend isn't married. You can also disqualify a romantic partner by denying him or her the right to speak on a topic because of his or her sex or because you perceive yourself to be more expert on the topic. If you find yourself saying, "What could you know about this?" then chances are you are disqualifying the other party, and you are engaging in inauthentic communication.

Engaging in authentic communication can help you develop and maintain your relationships more effectively. To help you begin the process, we conclude this chapter with suggestions for how you can more effectively engage in an important type of relationship communication—conflict management.

◢ IMPROVING YOUR CONFLICT SKILLS

If you are in a relationship where conflict escalates to the point of verbal or physical aggression, implementing the suggestions below can help you de-escalate your conflicts and reduce incidences of interpersonal violence. Even if you are not in an aggressive relationship, these strategies can provide you with more effective ways to respond to angry relatives, coworkers, and even strangers. Learning these strategies requires, at least initially, that you become more aware of your own thoughts, feelings, and communication.

In the midst of a heat conflicted or if confronted by an enraged person, often the best approach you can take it to try defuse the interaction. We next discuss strategies to de-escalate interpersonal conflict.

De-Escalate Your Own Anger

In the brain, emotion has a privileged position of influence. Our brains are set up so that self-protective emotions are able hijack the conscious mind (Atkinson, 2005). However, you can develop the ability to shift away from critical and defensive positions and toward more conscious, thoughtful choices. You do so by monitoring the negative messages you send yourself and then changing them—because those message affect how you feel and respond. You can minimize your anger by avoiding name-calling (even that directed toward yourself) and by refusing to focus on how unfairly or inappropriately the other person is behaving. Instead, it helps if you realize that most anger is grounded in fear—fear of losing face, fear of losing something desired, or even fear of losing the argument. Also recognize that most people's anger and dissatisfaction is about *them,* not about you. The colleague who yells at you in a meeting likely is fearful, insecure, and unable to communicate effectively.

Listening to Understand

During conflict, most people listen only so they can respond, defend, judge, or persuade. Consequently, one reason people become so loud during a fight is that they don't feel heard (Lenski, 2006). To help de-escalate the conflict and bring down the noise level, for two minutes set aside your desire to defend yourself or fix things and just listen—both to what is being said and what is not being said. If you listen carefully you will better understand the other party—who is likely to calm down since she/he no longer has to fight to be heard over your comments.

Empathizing

It can be very difficult to feel empathy for someone who is arguing with you or behaving badly. However, empathy—along with vulnerability, tenderness, and a desire for connection—is hardwired into our brains (Atkinson, 2005). If you focus on and listen to the other person so you can recognize and feel their fear and vulnerability, you are likely to have an automatic empathetic response. Once you feel it, express it. Say "I see how upset this makes you." or "I can tell you really care about the decision we are making," or even, "It makes me sad to see you so angry." However, making these statements if you don't really empathize can make the conflict even worse because the other party will think you are being manipulative.

Taking Time Out

If nothing else has helped, take a time-out. Removing yourself from the conflict really can help you and the other party calm down so you can better address your differences. However, you must not use your time away to ruminate on the negative aspects of your partner or the conflict—it will just make you angrier (Lenski, 2006). Instead, become involved in something that will draw your attention elsewhere and distract you—such as watching TV, listening to music, or reading a book. Also be sure to communicate that you are not being dismissive and that you will return to the conversation later. You can say "I am feeling pretty emotional right now and it seems you are too. Why don't we take a break to calm down and discuss this again in an hour?"

Trying Again

Once you and your partner are calmer, return to the conversation and enact these tips again. It takes time to learn to use these strategies—but repetition will help you get there.

SUMMARY

Close relationships are worth studying because of the significant impact they have on our health and emotional well-being. Close relationships are those in which the participants see each other as unique and irreplaceable and in which communication is marked by high disclosure and openness. In addition, people in close relationships are committed to their relationships and expect them to endure.

The three factors that most influence one's attraction to another—proximity, physical attractiveness, and similarity—all strongly influence or are influenced by the communication interactions we have. Once people are attracted to one another, they use communication to engage in a process of relational development. This process has been explained using two types of models: stage models, which divide the process of relationship development into phases leading to growth and decline; and trajectory models, which examine the events that lead individuals to move toward and away from commitment.

Communication behaviors are connected with three basic stages of relationship development: initiation, maintenance, and termination. Strategies for initiating relationships include opening with impersonal questions, listening attentively, being polite, expressing approval, and asking open-ended follow-up questions. Strategies and routine behaviors that friends and lovers use to maintain their relationships include being open, expressing positivity, and offering assurances, among others. Because many relationships end, researchers have examined the reasons individuals give for ending them and the strategies they use to do so, which include negative identity management, positive tone strategies, justification, and de-escalation strategies.

Problematic communication events can arise even in close relationships. Specifically, aversive communication, deception, relational aggression, jealousy, and sexual coercion all can affect, and potentially damage, relationships.

Finally, societal laws and norms influence the development of friendships and romances and the communication that occurs within them; these societal elements may determine whom we marry and/or befriend, how we communicate with relational partners, and how we communicate with the rest of the world about these relationships.

KEY TERMS

proximity 195
attractiveness 195
matching hypothesis 195
similarity 195
social penetration theory 196
orientation 196
exploratory affective exchange 196
affective exchange 196
stable exchange 196
Knapp's stage model 197
initiating 197
experimenting 197

intensifying 197
integrating 197
bonding 197
differentiating 197
circumscribing 197
stagnating 197
avoiding 197
terminating 197
relational trajectory models 198
turning point model 198
autonomy/connection 201
expressiveness/privacy 201

change/predictability 202
relational maintenance 205
sudden death 207
passing away 207
withdrawal/avoidance 209
Machiavellian tactics 209
deception 210
truth bias 210
jealousy 211
interpersonal violence 211
sexual coercion 213
homogeneity 215

TEST YOUR KNOWLEDGE

1. What are the four models of relationship development discussed in this chapter? How are they alike? How are they different?

2. What strategies do women use to initiate a relationship through flirting? How do men and women compare in their understanding and interpretation of women's flirting communication?

3. What is a dialectic? What are the three most common dialectics in close relationships?

4. What strategies do romantic partners use to terminate their relationships? Which strategies do friends also use to end their relationships?

5. How do men and women differ in their reactions to jealousy?

APPLY WHAT YOU KNOW

1. **Understanding the Role of New Technologies in Relationship Development**
   In this chapter we discuss the three factors that influence relationship development, including proximity, physical attractiveness, and similarity. Traditionally, proximity referred to how physically close potential friends and romantic partners were to one another. However, with the advent of email, the proliferation of cell phones and the use of texting, Twitter and Facebook, proximity has taken on new meanings. Read at least three articles on the impact of new technologies on relationship development and maintenance, then write a one-page summary of your findings.

2. **Maintaining Friendships and Romantic Relationships**
   Interview two people and ask them how they maintain their closest friendship. What conscious, deliberate strategies do they use to ensure they will stay close with their good friends? Also, what routine behaviors do they use to maintain closeness (for example, using nicknames, emailing funny stories)?

   Then interview two people and ask them the same questions about how they maintain their current romantic relationship.

   Finally, compare the four sets of responses. Do your interviewees use similar or different strategies for maintaining their friendships and their romances?

3. **Societal Influences on Relationships**
   Choose six popular magazines from your local grocery store. Be sure to select a wide range of magazines, including those directed toward men and women as well as some focused on political, social, and health issues. Skim through the magazines first looking at the advertisements. What can you tell about the way friendships and romances are viewed in the United States? As you look through the magazines, ask yourself these questions:

   a. To what degree do the people in the ads "match" by ethnicity, age, attractiveness, height and weight, and other factors?

   b. How many of the romantic couples are gay or lesbian?

   c. How many of the friendship pairs depicted are female? Male?

   d. In the ads depicting friends, what are female friends doing? What are male friends doing?

   e. How many ads picture people who are "overweight"? Physically unattractive? What products are they advertising?

   f. What population of readers does the magazine target?

   After answering these questions, look for patterns that exist within magazines by their target audience. What does this reveal about society's views of friendships and romantic relationships?

EXPLORE

1. Go to www.psychologytoday.com/pto/self_tests.php?cat=Relationships on the *Psychology Today* Web site, and take the jealousy quiz. Choose the quiz that describes your sexual orientation and gender (straight female, gay male, etc.) and complete it. Do your results agree with how you view yourself? What scenarios made you feel most jealous? If you rated high in jealousy, what can you do to moderate your feelings?

2. Go to www.gottman.com/marriage/self_help/, a Web site for the Gottman Institute. Dr. Gottman is the foremost researcher on marital and relationship stability. Read through his "Marriage Tips 101" and then compare them to the strategies listed in Tables 8.3 and 8.4. How are the lists alike? How are they different? Which of the various strategies and recommendations would you find most helpful? Most realistic? What can you do to maintain your romantic relationship (if you have one) more effectively?

9

Small Group Communication

chapter outline

> " *The quality of a group depends on the contributions of individual members.* "

My most interesting group experience happened last year in my Family Communication class. We were a group of five students, and each of us was supposed to write one part of the research paper. It was fun because we had the chance to be creative and write about any subject related to family communication. However, one member never emailed his work on time, didn't do a good, thoughtful job, and didn't show up for group meetings. The four of us met often, became friends, and always knew what the others were doing. The fifth member never knew what was going on because he never communicated with us. That part was frustrating even though we tried to work around him.

The group experience described by our student Dawn is typical and illustrates many of the issues we will discuss in this chapter. As she reports, group work can be productive and fun when group members are motivated and get along. However, poor communication or, as in Dawn's case, the lack of participation by one or more group members can diminish the final product.

In this chapter, we begin by discussing reasons for studying small group communication; we explain what a small group is and define small group communication. We then identify the benefits and challenges of small group work and discuss the various communication roles that group members can assume. Next, we turn to a discussion of group leadership and a description of the group communication process in decision-making and in problem-solving groups. Finally, we discuss the impact of society on small group communication, addressing the issues of power, cultural diversity, and technology in small group communication. We conclude the chapter with suggestions for how you can communicate more effectively and ethically in small groups.

Once you have read this chapter you will be able to:

- Identify four reasons for learning about small group communication.
- Define *small group communication*.
- Identify and give an example of task, relational, and individual small group roles.
- Describe five theories of group leadership.
- Describe the five steps in the problem-solving agenda.
- Describe the characteristics of communication that occur during the four phases of small group decision making.
- Discuss how diversity influences small group processes.
- Give three guidelines for communicating more ethically in your small group communication.
- Discuss ways to improve your own small group communication skills.

grouphate
the distaste and aversion that people feel toward working in groups

primary groups
groups that provide members with a sense of belonging and affection

secondary groups
groups that meet principally to solve problems

THE IMPORTANCE OF SMALL GROUP COMMUNICATION

Small groups seem to be an integral part of life. You probably belong to a number of groups—social groups, course project groups, work teams at your job, or perhaps support or interest groups in your community. However, you might be surprised to discover that learning how to communicate better in groups can actually enhance your academic and professional achievements. Let's see why this is so.

Reasons to Study Small Group Communication

There are at least four reasons to study small group communication: small groups are a fact of life, they enhance college performance, they enhance your career success, and they can enhance your personal life.

A Fact of Life

Some people say they hate working in small groups, and they are not alone. A term actually exists, **grouphate**, which describes the distaste and aversion that people feel toward working in groups (Sorenson, 1981). As one of our students told us, "I would rather just do the whole group project myself than try to get together with a group of students I don't know and might not trust to do a good job." A recent study found that students (in a small group communication course) who reported an active dislike for working in groups (grouphate) also reported experiencing less group cohesion, consensus, and relational satisfaction in their group work (Myers & Goodboy, 2005). It is possible that this active aversion to group work may negatively influence how one experiences working with a group.

Whether you love working in groups or hate it, groups are everywhere. Most of the groups we belong to are either primary or secondary groups (Poole, 1999). **Primary groups** are those that provide us with a sense of belonging and affection, the most common being family or social groups. While these groups are essential, this chapter's focus is on **secondary groups**—those that meet principally to solve problems, such as support groups or work groups. Secondary groups can involve long-term commitments, as in support groups that meet regularly for months or even years, or can be standing committees in an organization. Probably most common are the short-term project groups that students belong to in various classes. Increasingly this type of group work is supported by technologies such as email, electronic bulletin boards, and chat rooms, which we'll discuss later in the chapter.

"To improve our legal team teamwork, only three of the parachutes will open."

Enhanced College Performance

Learning about small group communication can help you in college and later in your career. Considerable research indicates that college students who study in small groups perform at higher intellectual levels, learn better, and have better attitudes toward subject matter than those who study alone (Allen & Plax, 2002). This is probably because you encounter different interpretations and ideas when studying with others; and, as we'll see in the next section, group work in general leads to higher quality thinking and decision making. Thus, learning how to interact more effectively in groups and seeking out learning groups to participate in can lead to enhanced college performance.

Enhanced Career Success

Effective communication in small groups also is essential to career success. According to a recent *Wall Street Journal* survey, when corporate recruiters rate the most important attributes of job candidates for business jobs, "Topping the list are communication, interpersonal skills and the ability to work well in teams" (Alsop, 2003, p. 11). Whether you are in business or another profession, organizations tend to hire those who have proven they can work well with others (Hughes, 2003). Thus your career advancement prospects could very well depend on your success in a collaborative work environment.

Enhanced Personal Life

Most people also participate in at least some small groups outside work—serving on committees in religious organizations as well as in nonprofit and community organizations. In addition, increasing numbers of people join support groups in order to deal with crises, life transitions, or chronic health conditions. So learning how to communicate better in small group settings can serve you personally, academically, and professionally. Despite their prevalence and importance, participation in group work has both advantages and disadvantages, as you'll see in the next section.

Advantages and Disadvantages of Group Work

Working in small groups brings many advantages in addition to those already described. Research shows that groups often make higher quality decisions than do individuals. This occurs for at least two reasons. First, a group can produce more innovative ideas than can an individual working alone. The small group discussion itself actually stimulates creativity (Moore, 2000). This creativity may be due to the **social facilitation** aspect of group work, meaning that "the mere presence of people is arousing and enhances the performance of dominant responses" (Kent, 1994, p. 81). Scholars speculate that the social facilitation response may be innate because, ultimately, we depend on others to survive; or it may result from awareness that others can reward or punish us. In any case, research shows that people often tend to work harder and do better when others are around, particularly if others may be evaluating their performance (Gagné & Zuckerman, 1999). As the scholar Mensch (1993) describes it: "Teamwork is an essential ingredient for successful innovation and transformation. Time and time again, studies of successful innovations have emphasized the need for and importance of close cooperation by members of multifunctional groups" (p. 262).

Second, some evidence indicates that small group work can promote critical thinking, leading to better decisions. A group of people offers more collective information, experience, and expertise than any single person can (Propp, 1999), and through interaction all members can benefit from these collective contributions. Also, because group members have to justify their opinions and judgments to other group members, each opinion is subject to careful scrutiny. This scrutiny can lead members to recognize the flaws in their own and others' arguments and encourage the group to think more critically (Gokhale, 1995).

Of course, group work also has disadvantages. For example, groups usually take more time to make decisions than do individuals. Group discussion can be less than satisfying when some group members dominate or withdraw, as happened with Dawn's group in our opening vignette. Such communication behaviors can cause frustration and conflict, preventing members from working productively (Adams &

Think about all the groups you belong to. Which could help you be more successful personally? Academically? Professionally?

social facilitation
the tendency for people to work harder and do better when others are around

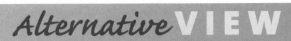

Alternative VIEW
Enough of the T-Word

Business writer Richard Reeves provides an alternative view on the popular concept of teamwork.

Are you a team player or more of an individual performer?

"NATP" is the ultimate contemporary workplace putdown: 'Not A Team Player'. All performance management systems contain a section on 'ability to work in a team'. Team days, team-building and bonding, team dynamics; the T-word is ubiquitous. I team, therefore I am. Businesses are in the grip of a team tyranny. . . . Guff such as 'there's no "I" in team!' surrounds us.

In team sports we expect the hero of the hour—say, David Beckham after a final-minute match-winning free kick—to say: 'It wasn't about me, you know. The lads all worked really hard. It was a team effort.' This is the case even when it is clear that the 'team' has had a terrible game and only the genius of the individual in question saved the day.

Even in literature, by definition one of the most individual art forms, authors now feel the need to spend the first few pages thanking everyone they've ever met, and claiming that the errors are their own. . . . It is enough to make you long for someone to write: 'I wrote this despite the constant nagging of my wife, inane interventions of my editor and obstructionism from certain key people. If it's any good, it is because I am.'

No, no—of course we don't want a world of pompous prima donnas, although it would certainly be more fun than the false modesty that currently besets us. But it is

necessary to keep the teamwork bug at bay. One of the reasons we need managers is precisely that envy, suspicion, rivalry and long-standing grudges mean that many 'teams' are constantly on the verge of civil war. . . . It is more helpful to think of teams as short-term groupings of people assembled to work on specific projects than as fixed families within the corporate world.

Part of the historical dynamic behind the reverence for teams comes from the discovery in the 1980s that Japanese manufacturing was outperforming US and European factories by adopting 'quality circles' and involving teams of workers in decision-making. And by comparison to the stultifying philosophy of the production line, the new philosophy was progressive. But most of us work in services now, where the danger is of too much teamness rather than too little. And it is worth noting that Asian societies are significantly more collective in psychological and social orientation than western ones, which have a consistently more individualistic ethos, and so there may be limits to the degree of importation possible.

We have to strike a balance between individual and collective success, and allow ourselves to celebrate both. Marianne Williamson, in her poem "Our Deepest Fear"—made famous by Nelson Mandela—writes: 'There's nothing enlightened about shrinking/so that other people/won't feel insecure around you. . . . And as we let our own light shine/we unconsciously give other people/ permission to do the same.'

P.S.: My section editor had some ideas for this column, but all the best ones were mine.

This is a condensed version of "Enough of the T-word," by Richard Reeves as first published in *Management Today*, March 2004. Reproduced from *Management Today* magazine with permission of the copyright owner, Haymarket Business Publications Limited.

Galanes, 2003) and cohesively. Finally, teamwork has limits, as author Richard Reeves cautions in *Alternative View: Enough of the T-Word*.

Given that most of us need to work in small groups from time to time and that learning how to communicate better in small groups can enhance academic and professional success, what do you need to know to be a successful group member? In order to answer this question we first must clarify what we mean by *small group communication*.

WHAT IS SMALL GROUP COMMUNICATION?

You might think that a small group is simply a collection of individuals, but we (and most communication scholars) have a more specific definition for small groups. To acquire a clear idea of what we'll be discussing in this chapter, let's consider two types of groups: (1) a group of people waiting in line for a movie and (2) a group of students working on a semester-long research project. The first type of group is not the focus of this chapter, while the second is. We will explain why as we articulate our definition of small group communication.

We define **small group communication** as "communication among a small number of people who share a common purpose or goal, who feel connected to each other, and coordinate their behavior" (Arrow, McGrath, & Berdahl, 2000, p. 34). Let's look more closely at who the small group in this definition is.

small group communication communication among a small number of people who share a common purpose or goal, who feel connected to each other, and who coordinate their behavior

A Small Number of People

Most experts agree that three is the fewest number of people that can constitute a small group and that five to seven people is the optimum upper limit for working groups. This general guideline may vary depending on whether the small group is working face to face or in virtual teams. In general, small groups of three (whether working in direct contact or virtually) experience better communication in terms of openness and accuracy than do larger groups of six. Communication becomes more difficult as group size increases; people may feel more anonymous, and discussions can become unwieldy and unfocused as members tend to break into small groups. However, a recent study found that although group size does decrease the quality of communication in face-to-face groups, group size has less impact on groups that are working virtually (Lowry, Roberts, Romano, Cheney, & Hightower, 2006). Under this portion of our definition, people waiting in line for a movie would not likely be considered a small group since any number of people can wait for a movie.

Research shows that groups often make higher quality decisions than do individuals.

A Common Purpose

While a group of people waiting for a movie fulfills the second requirement of our definition—they share a purpose—that purpose is rather limited. Here we focus on communication in small groups that are working toward a common purpose. Sometimes the purpose may be assigned by an instructor or employer—a semester-long course project, completing a marketing research study for a client, or working together to recommend a candidate for a job. Sometimes groups from many organizations meet to solve a specific problem, such as when a task force is assembled to study the state's disaster preparedness. Having a clear purpose or goal is important and is directly (positively) related to group productivity and increased team performance (Crown, 2007).

A Connection with Each Other

Again, to compare our two kinds of groups, people waiting for the movie need not feel connected to each another. However, work groups need to experience a group identity and recognize their interdependence, because when members do not feel a part of the group, as in Dawn's experience, the group won't function as it should. The challenge for the small group is to find ways to create a sense of group identity for all members, and communication is often key to making this happen.

An Influence on Each Other

Members of small groups need to coordinate their behavior, and in doing so, they may exert influence on each other. People waiting for a movie need not exert influence on each other, whereas members of a work group do. This influence can be positive or negative, and each group member contributes to the success or failure of the whole group. Most groups aren't successful without the positive contribution

Think about a small group experience you've had recently. What did other group members say that made you (and others) feel a part of the group? What was said that made you (and others) feel excluded from the group?

of all members. In Dawn's experience, for instance, the negative influence of one member undermined the success for all.

In sum, a collection of people waiting in line for a movie rarely constitutes a "small group" because they typically don't influence one another, they don't feel connected to each other or develop a shared identity, and they share a common purpose only in the most limited way. With these features of small groups in mind, let's look at individual communication in small groups.

SMALL GROUP COMMUNICATION AND THE INDIVIDUAL

The quality of a group depends on the contributions of individual members, and one reason for ineffective groups is the poor communication skills of individual members (Li, 2007; Oetzel, 2005). Lack of communication among group members can even be disastrous. For example, a British medical journal reported that poor communication among medical team members resulted in a number of deaths in British hospitals.

As communication scholar Lawrence Frey (1994) states: "Communication is the lifeblood that flows through the veins of groups" (p. x). To better understand communication processes in small groups, it is helpful to think of its two primary dimensions: task communication and relational communication. Task communication is the more obvious of the two. It focuses on getting the job done and solving the problem at hand—for example, requesting information or asking for clarification—whereas relational communication focuses on group maintenance and interpersonal relationships, such as offering encouragement or mediating disagreement. These two types of communication are thoroughly mixed during group interaction; in fact, one statement can fill both functions. In addition, for task communication to succeed, group members must be effective relational communicators. Achieving group goals becomes much more difficult, even impossible, when relationships are an overriding concern in the group. In fact, relationship difficulties can more negatively impact group goals than can task-related problems (Keyton, 1999). However, very recent research shows that too much social talk can have a negative impact on group effectiveness in two ways: It may reduce the time that should be used to complete the task, and it also distracts from the task focus that is critical for group effectiveness (Li, 2007).

To help you understand how individuals can contribute to (or detract from) the performance of task and relationship communication, we next explore the various communication roles that members of small groups perform. We then explore another important ingredient of small groups—leadership; and in so doing, we present several important theories of leadership. Finally, we'll look at principles and processes that can make small groups effective.

Types of Communication Roles

Every group member plays a variety of roles within a group. **Group roles** describe the shared expectations group members have regarding each individual's communication behavior in the group. These roles can involve either task or relational communication, and of course, they may have elements of both. If you join an established group you learn these expectations through communication with current members. If all members are new to the group, they rely on their perceptions and beliefs, as well as their group skills and previous group experience, as they work out various role behaviors (Riddle, Anderson, & Martin, 2000).

For example, Mitchell works for a software company. Although the employees of this company are scattered across the country and primarily work at home, they must work together to design software that meets a client's specific needs. Because Mitchell is the expert at writing software programs, he assumes that role. He is

group roles
the shared expectations group members have regarding each individual's communication behavior in the group

careful not to overstep his role, even if he feels that Giuliana, the design person, is not putting the "buttons" where he would put them or the frames where he thinks they would look best. Similarly, Mitchell and Giuliana make sure to follow the advice of the market researcher who has studied the client's market needs. In this case, each group member knows his or her roles; they have developed this understanding based on their individual and collective experiences in groups. The owner of Mitchell's company flies everyone out to Los Angeles periodically so they can work together and build relationships. Mitchell flies in from Providence, Rhode Island, while others travel from Minneapolis, Atlanta, Miami, Seattle, Phoenix, and Milwaukee. Others simply drive in from nearby Orange County, Santa Barbara, or San Diego. These face-to-face meetings build work relationships and a sense of cohesion.

When people work together in virtual teams, periodic face-to-face meetings are important to build trust and cohesion.

Although group roles often evolve as the team works together, sometimes roles are assigned as part of a job description. For example, LaKresha, the chair of her university's Animal Welfare League, always leads the group's discussions, because this is one of her responsibilities as chair. Kristie, as secretary of the organization, always takes notes because that is her role. Effective group members contribute by filling roles that are of interest to them and compatible with their skills, but they also fill roles that the group needs at a particular time. Thus successful small group work depends on task and relational communication, which in turn depends on individuals' effective performance of task and relational roles (Benne & Sheats, 1948). In addition, small group members may perform a third, less productive type of role, referred to as an individual role. Let's look at these three types of roles and how they contribute to, or detract from, effective group communication.

Task

Task roles, a list of which is provided in Table 9.1, are directly related to the accomplishment of group goals; they include behaviors such as leading the discussion and taking notes. These communication roles often involve seeking, processing, and evaluating information.

Let's explore how these roles function within a group using a case study. Lenore and Jaime are part of a campus task force that is working to improve campus safety. Their small group of seven members met twice a month for several months and discussed the problem and possible solutions. During the discussions, group members filled the various task roles, depending on their particular strengths and interests and the needs of the group, changing roles as needed. For example, Karin tended to serve as initiator–contributor, proposing new ideas and suggesting that the group look at several dimensions of the problem, such as personal security and the protection of private property. Information seekers, in particular John and Ralph, often asked for clarification of facts or information. Opinion seekers, such as Eliza and Wen Shu, asked how other group members felt about various proposals—say, the potential expense that would be incurred by implementing suggested solutions. In addition, opinion givers responded by sharing how they felt about the expense.

As information givers, several members provided statistics about the security problem so that the group could know the extent of the problem. They also provided information on how other campuses had solved similar problems—by increasing numbers of campus police, installing better lighting, and having volunteer "security teams" patrol campus. Serving as elaborator, Lenore told about having her bike stolen and suggested that having an increased number of campus police might have prevented the theft. Jaime often served as coordinator and orientor, showing how various

task roles
roles that are directly related to the accomplishment of group goals

TABLE 9.1 Small Group Task Roles

Task Role	Description	Example
Initiator–contributor	Proposes new ideas or approaches to group problem solving	"How about if we look at campus safety as issues of personal security *and* protection of private property?"
Information seeker	Asks for information or clarification	"How many instances of theft occur on our campus each year?"
Opinion seeker	Asks for opinions from others	"How do you feel about charging students a fee that would pay for extra police protection?"
Information giver	Provides facts, examples, and other relevant evidence	"My research showed that other campuses have solved similar problems by increasing numbers of campus police and improving lighting."
Opinion giver	Offers beliefs or opinions	"I'm often concerned about my personal safety when I walk to certain campus parking lots at night."
Elaborator	Explains ideas, offers examples to clarify ideas	"If the university had increased security patrols, my bike might not have been stolen last month."
Coordinator	Shows relationships among ideas presented	"Installing new light fixtures might improve personal safety and reduce thefts on campus."
Orienter	Summarizes what has been discussed and keeps group focused	"We've now discussed several aspects of personal safety; maybe it's time to turn our attention to issues of protection of private property."
Evaluator–critic	Judges evidence and conclusions of group	"I think we may be overestimating the problem of theft."
Energizer	Motivates group members to greater productivity	"Wow! We've gotten a lot accomplished this evening, and we have only have a few more points to discuss."
Procedural technician	Performs logistical tasks—distributing paper, arranging seating, etc.	
Recorder	Keeps a record of group activities and progress	

Based on: Benne, K. D. & Sheats, P. (1948). Functional roles of group members. *Journal of Social Issues, 4,* 41–49.

ideas related to each other, while other members filled the role of evaluator–critic, carefully evaluating various ideas. The procedural technician made sure that everyone had paper and pens, while a designated recorder took notes so that at the end of each meeting, members knew what they had covered. One member often served as the energizer, infusing interest into the group when attention and focus lagged.

Not every group has members who can fill each of these roles, and certainly not with the same level of skill. But, the more effectively these roles are filled, the better the group will function and the more likely it is that goals will be met.

Relational

In contrast with task roles, **relational roles** help establish a group's social atmosphere (see Table 9.2). For example, members who encourage others to talk or mediate disagreements are filling relational roles. Group members can fill both task and relational roles, depending on the needs of the group. For example, in Lenore and Jaime's group, one member sent out emails to get the group organized (task role), and he also sent congratulatory emails after the group did a presentation to the student governing council (relational role).

During their discussion of campus safety, some members served as encouragers (praising and accepting others' ideas). Others served as harmonizers (mediating disagreement) or compromisers (attempting to find solutions to disagreements).

relational roles
roles that help establish a group's social atmosphere

TABLE 9.2   Small Group Relational Roles

Role	Description	Example
Encourager	Offers praise and acceptance of others' ideas	"That's a great idea; tell us more about it."
Harmonizer	Mediates disagreement among group members	"I think you and Ron are seeing two sides of the same coin."
Compromiser	Attempts to resolve conflicts by trying to find an acceptable solution to disagreements	"I think both of you have great ideas. Let's see how we can combine them."
Gatekeeper	Encourages less talkative group members to participate	"Maria, you haven't said much about this idea. How do you feel about it?"
Expediter	Tries to limit lengthy contributions of other group members	"Martin, you've told us what you think about most of the ideas. Why don't we hear from some of the other members?"
Standard setter	Helps to set standards and goals for the group	"I think our goal should be to submit a comprehensive plan for campus safety to the dean by the end of this semester."
Group observer	Keeps records of the group's process and uses the information that is gathered to evaluate the group's procedures	
Follower	Goes along with the suggestions and ideas of group members; serves as an audience in group discussion and decision making	"I like that idea. That's a really good point."

Based on: Benne, K. D. & Sheets, P. (1948). Functional roles of group members. *Journal of Social Issues, 4*, 41–49.

As communication majors, Lenore and Jaime paid close attention to how the discussion was going and, when necessary, served as gatekeepers, encouraging participation from less talkative members, or as expediters, gently limiting the contributions of more talkative members. One group member served as standard setter, periodically reminding his colleagues of the group's standards, while others served as observers, gathering information that could be used to evaluate group performance. In this group, most members served as followers from time to time, simply listening to others' contributions. Overall, the group met its goal of addressing the problems of campus security partly because members effectively filled both task and relational roles as needed.

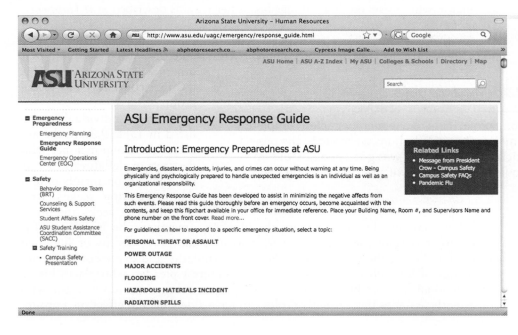

A small group focusing on campus security might be part of a larger program such as this one at Arizona State University focusing on general campus safety.

© 2009 Arizona Board of Regents. Used with permission.

TABLE 9.3   Small Group Individual Roles

Role	Description	Example
Aggressor	Attacks other group members, tries to take credit for someone else's contribution	"That's a stupid idea. It would never work."
Blocker	Is generally negative and stubborn for no apparent reason	"This whole task is pointless. I don't see why we have to do it."
Recognition seeker	Calls excessive attention to his/her personal achievements	"This is how we dealt with campus security when I was at Harvard."
Self-confessor	Uses the group as an audience to report non-group-related personal feelings	"I'm so upset at my boyfriend. We had a big fight last night."
Joker	Lacks involvement in the group's process, distracts others by telling stories and jokes	"Hey did you hear the one about . . .?"
Dominator	Asserts control by manipulating group members or tries to take over group; may use flattery or assertive behavior to dominate the conversation	"I know my plan will work because I was a police officer."
Help seeker	Tries to gain unwarranted sympathy from group; often expresses insecurity or feelings of low self-worth	"You probably won't like this idea either, but I think we should consider contracting out our campus security."
Special-interest pleader	Works to serve an individual need, rather than focusing on group interests	"Since I only have daycare on Wednesdays, can we meet on Wednesday afternoons?"

Based on: Benne, K. D. & Sheats, P. (1948). Functional roles of group members. *Journal of Social Issues, 4,* 41–49.

Individual

The **individual role** tends to be dysfunctional to the group process. Group members serving in individual roles focus more on their own interests and needs than on those of the group. Thus they tend to be uninvolved, negative, aggressive, or constantly joking. A common individual role that blocks effectiveness in student projects is the dominator, who insists on doing things his or her way, as described in *It Happened to Me: James.*

Another common role is the joker. When another member contributes, the joker always has to "one up" the comment with a joke or a story, assuming that others will be interested. This member constantly moves the group off-task.

Other individual roles listed in Table 9.3 are the aggressor, a group member who destroys or deflates the status of other group members and the recognition seeker, who continuously seeks the spotlight. You may also be familiar with the blocker, a member who is negative for no apparent reason; the self-confessor, who uses the group as his or her own personal audience; the help seeker, who seeks sympathy and expresses insecurity or feelings of low self-worth; and the special-interest pleader, who places his or her individual need or biases above group goal or focus. A group member who consistently assumes these negative roles can have a detrimental effect on a group.

It Happened to Me: James

I had an experience in one group project where one member acted completely superior to the rest of us. No matter the contributions we made to the project, he always found a way to criticize them. Nothing was good enough for him. Eventually, no one felt they could satisfy him, so we all stopped trying to do our best.

individual roles
roles that focus more on individuals' own interests and needs than on those of the group

This person can undermine the group's commitment to goals and its sense of cohesion—ultimately resulting in decreased group performance and productivity (Wellen & Neale, 2006).

Any group member may serve in any of these roles at any time. In a successful group, like Jaime and Lenore's task force, members play various roles as needed, with minimal indulgence in the individual roles. Some group members play only to their strengths and consistently serve in one or two particular roles. This is fine as long as all the needed roles are being filled.

Visual Summary 9.1: Roles in Groups, illustrates several roles that may be at work in small groups.

Think about group experiences you've had. Which task communication roles do you tend to fill? Which relational communication roles? Which communication roles would you like to fill? How flexible have you been in your ability to fill various task and relational roles?

Roles in Groups

Scene from *The Office* (television sitcom)

VISUAL SUMMARY 9.1

Theories of Leadership

Most small groups have a leader. Some are designated or appointed, and some emerge during group interaction. In either case, a good leader can be the key to successful communication in a small group. Consequently, researchers have attempted to determine the qualities a small group leader should possess. They have examined questions such as, *Are leaders born or made?* and *Do small groups need a leader?* This research has resulted in five theories that explain effective leaders: trait theory, functional theory, style theory, transformational leadership theory, and servant leadership theory.

Trait Theory

Probably the oldest theory concerning leadership in the communication field is **trait theory** (Stogdill, 1974). Trait theory suggests that leaders are born. Some of the traits associated with effective leadership are physical and include being male, tall, and good looking. For example, not since 1896 have U.S. citizens elected a president whose height was below average, and even today, people associate height with leadership ability (Judge & Cable, 2004).

Other studies have examined the relationship of leadership to personality traits. For example, leaders seem to be more extroverted, open to experience, agreeable, and conscientious than nonleaders (Judge, Bono, Ilies, & Gerhardt, 2002; Stogdill, 1974). Moreover, they seem to be smarter than other people as measured by standard IQ tests (Judge, Colbert, & Ilies, 2004). While one might assume that leaders are better communicators (Cragan & Wright, 1999, p. 166), communication researchers have not confirmed this (Pavitt, 1999).

Despite the correlation between leaders and particular traits, one cannot ignore the role of society in forming our judgments about who we think makes a good leader. For example, early business writings suggested that the function of the business leader was to "fit in" with others in the workplace. Requirements for fitting in were shared "education, experience, age, sex, race, nationality, faith, politics, and such very specific personal traits as manners, speech, personal appearance" (Barnard, 1938, p. 224). Of course, in 1938, fitting in was only possible for White males of a certain background and education. In addition, the trait approach may reinforce the notion that only people born with certain qualities can achieve leadership, ignoring the fact that only those who have the most status and power in the society also possess these qualities.

Many examples challenge the trait approach to leadership. In recent years a number of people have developed leadership qualities out of a tragedy or a deep motivation to make the world a better place. Candy Lightner, who founded MADD (Mothers Against Drunk Driving) when her own child was killed by a drunk driver, is one of these. Judy Shepard, mother of Matthew Shepard, a gay student who was severely beaten and murdered, became an outspoken leader and advocate for tolerance and justice (Groutage, 1999). Neither woman was a "born leader," but both took on leadership roles when the situation demanded it.

Perhaps you know of college students who have been motivated to take on similar leadership roles. For instance, undergraduate Sindhura Citineni felt determined to make a difference when confronted by the appalling statistics of world hunger she found while researching on the Internet. Citineni worked out a deal with her university to sell several simple food items in the cafeteria where part of the revenue went to hunger-relief work—called Hunger Lunch. She then led a group of students who expanded that project into Nourish International, now a nonprofit organization that connects college students from universities around the nation to development projects abroad (**http://nourishinternational.org**).

Functional Theory

A second approach to analyzing leadership, the **functional (situational) theory**, stands in direct contrast to the trait approach. Unlike trait theory, which assumes leadership is innate, this theory assumes that leadership behaviors can be learned, even by group members who are not "leadership types." Functional theory assumes

As an undergraduate, Sindhura Citineni started a campus project to combat world hunger and later led a group of students to form Nourish International, a worldwide non-profit organization.

trait theory
leadership theory that suggests that leaders are born

functional (situational) theory
a theory that assumes leadership behaviors can be learned

that whatever the group needs at a particular time can be supplied by a set of behaviors any group member can contribute (Barnlund & Haiman, 1960; Benne & Sheats, 1948; Pavitt, 1999). Thus this theory argues that the leader can change from time to time, depending on the changing needs of the group.

According to this theory a group does not need a designated leader; rather, any group member can serve as leader at any particular time by filling the required role. For example, the leader can fill task roles when the group needs direction, whereas she steps into relational roles when group members understand the task but need encouragement. Occasionally, no leadership is needed, such as when the short- and long-term purpose is clear and group members are working well independently.

As we noted earlier, group success does not depend on the number of task or relational behaviors that group members engage in, but rather, on whether they exhibit the required role behavior when needed. For example, too much emphasis on task can lead to negative outcomes if the task is already clearly defined and understood by all group members. Too much relational leadership is distracting if members view it as getting in the way of completing the group task (Rauch & Behling, 1984). Thus if a group has almost completed its task and discussion is going smoothly, constant encourager behavior may be distracting and unnecessary.

How might the functional notion of leadership work in a small group? Recently, a humanities council designed and implemented a statewide book festival to promote reading and the humanities. Initially they decided to research how other state humanities councils had approached similar projects. The best leader for this task was the person who knew how to energize the group to contact other state councils and divide the work, which was an organizational task. When the group met again with the information gathered, the leader shifted functions. He helped the group generate ideas for possible activities for the book festival. As the discussion proceeded, the leader needed to help the group weigh the advantages and disadvantages of some suggestions. Then he had to become a decision maker and accept some ideas, discard others, and postpone still others for next year's book festival. Finally, the leader analyzed the strengths and weaknesses of the group members and assigned tasks that fit their expertise. Tasks included corporate fundraising, securing the date and locations of the festival, and selecting authors and arranging for them to read from their books. Throughout this process, the leader shifted roles to help the group succeed in planning the festival.

A related notion is **shared leadership**, also called *collaborative or distributed leadership*. Here the functional leadership approach is extended to an organizational level where team relationships become more of a partnership in an organization (MacNeil & McClanahan, 2005). The requirements for this kind of leadership are a balance of power where: all members are equal partners; all share a common purpose or goal; all share responsibility for the work of the group (take an active role and are accountable for completing their individual contribution); all have respect for the person—and skills and ideas that each brings to the team; and all work together in complex, real-world situations. Recent studies show that shared leadership can be effective for many types of organizations, including police work, education, and nonprofit groups. For example, police teams who practice collaborative or shared leadership (e.g., those having an employee steering committee) have much better labor–management relations, better relations with the community, and an improvement in police perceptions of their working conditions (Steinheider & Wuestewald, 2008). A similar study found that shared leadership is particularly effective in schools, where teachers, administration, and community members need to work together. Under the shared leadership model, the vision for a school is for students, parents, teachers, and principals to all become school leaders in some way. The main job of the administrator, then, is to enhance individual skills, promote productive relationships among members, and create a common culture of expectations (MacNeil & McCanahan, 2005). A final study examined leadership of 12 of the most successful nonprofit organizations in the United States and found that all of the 12 groups used the shared leadership model throughout their organization (Grant & Crutchfield, 2008).

shared (collaborative or distributed) leadership
a type of leadership style where functional leadership is extended to an organizational level; all members are equal partners and share responsibility for the work of the group

Style Theory

A third approach to analyzing leadership asserts that a leader's manner or **style** of leading a group determines her or his success. Further, this theory describes three common styles of leadership summarized in *Visual Summary 9.2: Leadership Styles.*

Authoritarian. An **authoritarian leader** takes charge and has a high level of intellect and expertise (Lewin, Lippit, & White, 1939). The authoritarian leader makes all the decisions and dictates strategies and work tasks. This type of leadership is appropriate in military, sports, or crisis situations. For example, military organizations have a highly authoritarian structure, and the chain of command must be rigorously followed. In battle there is no time for discussion and little room for trial and error. This is also true of sports-team leadership. For example, when 25 seconds are left in a basketball game and the score is tied, only one person—the coach—can tell the team members how to execute the next play.

Authoritarian leadership is also appropriate in crises. Medical teams in an emergency room generally follow authoritarian leadership—one person, the doctor, directs the others in what needs to be done. This style of leadership may also be followed when time for discussion is short or when the stakes are very high (Meade, 1985).

Democratic. This is the style we are most familiar with and that seems to work best in many group situations. The **democratic leader** style is characterized by a great deal of input from group members; the qualities of this leader are best summarized by Lao-tse (550 B.C.): "A good leader is one who talks little; when his work is done, his aim fulfilled, they will all say 'We did this ourselves'" (cited in Foels, Driskell, Mullen, & Salas, 2000, p. 677).

In this style, group discussion determines all policies, strategies, and division of labor. Members are free to assume a variety of roles, to contribute when appropriate, and to share leadership. Further, research supports the idea that most groups are more satisfied with a democratic leader than an authoritarian one (Foels et al., 2000; Gastil, 1994). However, as noted in the examples above, different situations call for different leadership styles.

Laissez-faire. Some small group situations call for a **laissez-faire** style. This style is characterized by complete freedom for the group in making decisions. The leader participates minimally, and may supply materials and information when asked, but she makes no attempt to evaluate or influence the discussion. This style may work when little is at stake, as in some social groups or reading groups (Barge, 1989).

Transformational Leadership Theory

A relatively new theory, **transformational leadership** theory, emphasizes the importance of relationships in leadership. The role of the transformational leader is to empower group members to work independently from the leader by encouraging collaboration between members and group cohesion. Research shows there to be at least four general characteristics shared by transformational leaders. First, they have high moral and ethical standards that engender high regard and loyalty from followers. Second they have a strong vision for the future, which stimulates enthusiasm and builds confidence among followers. Third, they challenge the status quo and encourage innovation in an organization; and last, they recognize unique strengths and capabilities of followers and coach and consult with them to help them develop their full potential (Bono & Judge, 2004). While researchers have attempted to identify very specific personality traits, like agreeableness, conscientiousness, or openness as characteristic of transformational leaders, only one quality seems to be consistent— extraversion—which includes the ability to convey positive emotions and project optimism and enthusiasm (Bono & Judge, 2004).

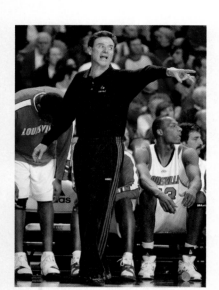

Rick Pitino is the first coach in NCAA history to lead three different basketball teams to the Final Four (Providence, Kentucky, and Louisville). As a leader, he has to make split-second decisions during basketball games.

style theory
theory that asserts that a leader's manner or style determines his or her success

authoritarian leader
leader who takes charge, makes all the decisions, and dictates strategies and work tasks

democratic leader
leader whose style is characterized by considerable input from group members

laissez-faire
a leadership style characterized by complete freedom for the group in making decisions

transformational leadership
a leadership style that empowers group members to work independently from the leader by encouraging group cohesion

Leadership Styles

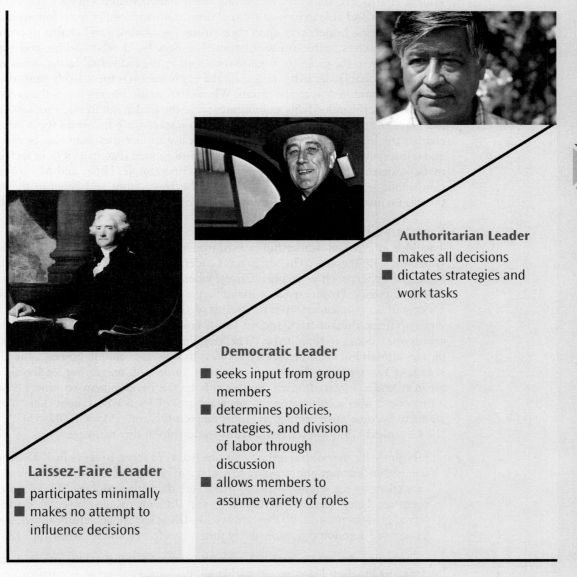

Degree of the Control Exercised by the Leader

Authoritarian Leader
■ makes all decisions
■ dictates strategies and work tasks

Democratic Leader
■ seeks input from group members
■ determines policies, strategies, and division of labor through discussion
■ allows members to assume variety of roles

Laissez-Faire Leader
■ participates minimally
■ makes no attempt to influence decisions

Degree of the Participation of the Leader

237

charismatic leadership
a leadership style in which extremely self-confident leaders inspire unusual dedication to themselves by relying upon their strong personalities and charm

servant leadership
a leadership style that seeks to ensure that other people's highest priority needs are being served in order to increase teamwork and personal involvement

Transformational leaders are especially effective when they can motivate followers to perform beyond standard expectations, often by inspiring them to put the collective needs of the group above their own individual needs. When this occurs, groups are empowered, cohesive, and effective (Jung & Sosik, 2002).

A very recent study of workers in European health-care facilities compared several different types of leadership (authoritarian, laissez-faire, transformational) to discover which, if any, could lead to better employee involvement and better teamwork, all which have been shown to reduce stress levels in an often stressful work environment, such as a hospital. The study found that transformational leadership was the most effective in inspiring individual employee involvement (Savič & Pagon, 2008).

Transformational leadership is sometimes confused with **charismatic leadership**, a notion from political science and religious studies scholarship. Like transformational leaders, charismatic leaders have a strong belief in their vision. They are also extremely self-confident and able to inspire unusual dedication and loyalty from followers. However, charismatic leaders rely upon their strong personalities and charm to create loyalty to themselves, while transformational leaders build relationships and strive to create loyalty to the group or organization, not to the individual leader. Thus when a transformational leader exits the group, the organization is more likely to thrive, since member commitment is to the group. When charismatic leaders leave, the group may falter because the individuals' commitment is to the leader, not to one another. And unlike transformational leaders who manage to inspire their followers for a long time, charismatic leadership may be relatively short-lived, since they may also be autocratic and self-serving, and followers may become disillusioned (Pavitt, 1999). In fact, charismatic leadership can have disastrous results. For example, Hitler and Mussolini were charismatic leaders. While such leaders inspire trust, faith, and belief in themselves, there is no guarantee that their vision or mission will be correct, ethical, or successful.

Servant Leadership Theory

The idea of **servant leadership** was introduced to organizations through Robert Greenleaf's 1970 essay, "The Servant as Leader." The concept was further popularized by recent writers such as Stephen Covey, whose 1989 best seller *The Seven Habits of Highly Effective People*, made a major impact in the business world. However, the concept of servant leadership is thousands of years old. Chanakya or Kautilya, the famous strategic thinker from ancient India, wrote about servant leadership in his 4th century B.C. book, *Arthashastra*: "The king [leader] shall consider as good, not what pleases himself but what pleases his subjects [followers]," and in 600 B.C., the Chinese sage Lao Tzu wrote in *The Tao Te Ching*, a guidebook on servant leadership: "The greatest leader forgets himself and attends to the development of others." Servant leadership is also a cornerstone of the teachings of Jesus who taught that "Whoever wants to become great among you must be your servant" (Mark 10:42–45).

Greenleaf (1977) described servant leadership in this manner:

> It begins with the natural feeling that one wants to serve, to serve first. Then conscious choice brings one to aspire to lead. . . . The difference manifests itself in the care taken by the servant—first to make sure that other people's highest priority needs are being served. The best test, and difficult to administer, is: do those served grow as persons, do they grow while being served, become healthier, wiser, freer, more autonomous, more likely themselves to become servants? (pp. 13–14)

There are ten characteristics—mostly communication skills—that a servant leader must excel at: listening, empathizing, healing, awareness, persuasion, conceptualization, foresight, stewardship, commitment to the growth of others, and building community. Servant leadership emphasizes collaboration, trust, and the ethical use of power. The theory proposes that at heart, the individual is a servant first, and makes a conscious decision to lead in order to better serve others, not to increase his or her own power. The objective is to enhance the growth of individuals in the organization and to increase teamwork and personal involvement (Greenleaf, 1991, 2002).

Effective Small Group Communication

Effective groups maintain a balance of task and relational communication, and the sequence of each appears to be more important than the relative amount of each. For example, after an intense period of task talk, group members might defuse their tension with positive social, or relational, talk and then return to task talk (Pavitt, 1999).

What types of communication lead to effective sequencing of task and relational communication? In a series of studies, communication scholar John Oetzel (1998, 2001, 2005) found that the following communication processes lead to task effectiveness and member satisfaction (relational effectiveness) in small groups in many situations.

1. *Equal participation*: All group members contribute at relatively equal levels, taking approximately the same number of turns speaking.
2. *A consensus decision-making style*: All members participate in and agree with the decisions made by the group.
3. *A cooperative conflict style*: The group manages conflict by integrating all parties' interests—a win–win approach.
4. *A respectful communication style*: Group members demonstrate that other members are valued and important.

Given these principles, when the primary goal of a small group is to solve a particular problem, where do the members begin? One of the great communication challenges for groups is to access the problem and all its possible solutions. In this section, we'll first describe a five-step agenda that problem-solving groups have found useful. Second, we'll examine how decision making occurs in small groups including a negative group process—*groupthink*. Finally, we'll describe the characteristics of discussions in small groups that function at a distance.

Problem-Solving Agenda

Jumping immediately to a solution can be a danger in problem-solving groups. One useful tool for avoiding a premature and incomplete solution is to develop and follow a sequence or agenda. In fact, early research surveying hundreds of small group participants identified lack of strong procedural guidelines as one of the primary barriers to effective problem solving (Broome & Fulbright, 1995). While many agendas exist, perhaps the best known are variations of educator John Dewey's five-step procedure (Cragan & Wright, 1999, p. 97). Two points are central to using an agenda effectively, and at first they may sound contradictory. First, researchers have found that most problem-solving groups have less conflict and a more consistent focus when they follow formal procedures (Sunwolf & Seibold, 1999). Second, successful groups do not necessarily solve all problems in strict sequential order; they may take a variety of paths (Schultz, 1999). In general, then, groups benefit from keeping the agenda in mind, but members should realize that they may have to cycle back and forth between phases before reaching a solution.

Let's return to our earlier example of the campus security problem and see how that group might follow the five-step problem-solving agenda and the recommendations for effective communication at each step.

STEP 1. *Define and Delineate the Problem.* The first step in solving a problem is to make sure that everyone in the group understands it in the same way. After all, the problem can't be solved unless group members know what it is (and is not). On the campus security task force case study, the group members were successful in part because they agreed on the definition of the problem. They decided their problem was twofold: (1) the personal security of students in dorms and while walking on campus and (2) the protection of students' personal property. They decided that they would not address the security of classroom and office equipment, since they were primarily a student group. This helped them narrow the focus and set limits for the discussion of solutions.

STEP 2. *Analyze the Problem.*   In some ways, this is the most important phase of the agenda because it determines the direction of potential solutions (Hirokawa & Salazar, 1999). Group members must look at all sides of the problem. To do so, they answer questions like *Who is affected by the problem? How widespread is it?* In the case of the campus security team, the group had to gather data on the exact nature of security problems—the frequency of burglaries, rapes, assaults, and robberies on campus; where and when these incidents were occurring; and what consequences the incidents had.

However, a word of caution is in order. In some cases, too much analysis can result in **analysis paralysis** and prevent a group from moving toward a solution. (Rothwell, 1995). Our campus security group, for example, could continue to gather statistics, interview people about the problem, and discuss the problems, and never move on to possible solutions.

STEP 3. *Identify Alternative Solutions.*   As noted earlier, one challenge at this stage is to consider several possibilities and not rush to premature solutions. One way to make sure that many solutions are considered is to **brainstorm**, generating as many ideas as possible without critiquing them. By brainstorming, the campus security group put forth a wide range of possible solutions, including putting up more lighting, increasing the number of campus police, and helping students to register their private property (bikes, computers, stereo equipment, etc.) so that stolen property could be traced. Some solutions were more unusual, including suggestions to eliminate foliage where assailants could hide, to sell wristband tracking devices to students, to place guard dogs in dormitories, and to have 24/7 volunteer security details in the dorms.

STEP 4. *Evaluate Proposed Solutions.*   Evaluating proposed solutions involves establishing evaluation criteria. The campus security task force, for example, identified three criteria for its solutions: They had to be economically feasible, logistically feasible, and likely to solve the problem of campus security. With these criteria in mind, the task force had a basis for evaluating each solution. This stage is critical, but it can be difficult; if members are tired or frustrated by all the work they've already done, they may jump to conclusions. However, if they keep to the agenda and carefully consider each alternative, they will quickly reject some solutions and find others attractive. According to one study, a strong positive relationship exists between a group's decision-making performance and members' satisfaction with alternatives chosen (Hirokawa & Salazar, 1999).

STEP 5. *Choose the Best Solution.*   While this step may seem redundant, choosing the best solution(s) is not the same as evaluating all proposed solutions. Here it is especially important that everyone participates and buys into the solution, and decision-making procedures are most critical.

The problem-solving agenda is a specific format or set of guidelines that task groups can follow to ensure high-quality solutions. As groups progress through the stages, however, they will need to make multiple decisions. For example, during stage four, the evaluation stage, the group will need to decide what the appropriate criteria are for evaluating proposed solutions, whether they will evaluate all or just some of the proposed solutions, and how they will manage differences of opinion regarding the value of proposed solutions. To help you understand the decision-making process that occurs throughout the problem-solving agenda, in the next section we explore the *process* of decision making.

Decision-Making Phases

Several years ago, communication scholar B. Aubrey Fisher (1980) identified four phases of any **decision-making process**: orientation, conflict, emergence, and reinforcement. He showed that the way group members talked and interacted with each other followed a unique pattern as they went through these four phases. Another

analysis paralysis
potential pitfall in small group interaction; occurs when excessive analysis prevents a group from moving toward a solution

brainstorm
to generate as many ideas as possible without critiquing them

decision-making process
the four-phase process used by a group to evaluate information and arrive at a decision or solution

communication scholar, Ernest Bormann (1975), studied how group members dealt with conflict and tension in decision making. The research of these two scholars led to the phases we describe next.

While current research supports the phases articulated by Fisher and Bormann (Wheelan, Davidson, & Tilin, 2003), communication scholars have shown that most groups do not proceed through these phases in an orderly, linear fashion. Rather, they may cycle through the orientation phase twice before moving to the conflict phase, or they may revert back to the conflict phase after reaching the emergence phase (Bormann, 1975; Poole, 1983). With these thoughts in mind, let's look at the four phases individually.

PHASE 1. *Orientation and Primary Tension.* During this phase of decision making, group members usually orient themselves to the problem and to each other (if they have just met). Uncertainty at this stage is common and is referred to as **primary tension.** For example, as a group member, you might wonder how the

primary tension
the uncertainty commonly felt in the beginning phase of decision making

secondary (recurring) tension
conflict or tension found in the second or conflict phase of the decision-making process

group is going to function. You may have questions about the relational aspect of the group processes: Are you going to like the other members? Will you all get along, or will you clash? One of our students described a relational problem that emerged at the beginning of her group project, which contributed to the tension the group felt as they began their talk. Read about her experience in *It Happened to Me: Kirstin.*

It Happened to Me: *Kirstin*

Being the only communication major in our group, I immediately noticed some problems. The nonverbal cues from two members contradicted their verbal messages. They rolled their eyes or turned their bodies away from the group when they were asked to do a task. When someone asked what was wrong, those two replied "nothing." I knew this did not bode well for the group, so I shared some of my communication skills and knowledge. I encouraged the two nonparticipating members to contribute, and asked them if anything was wrong. They told us they were worried because they'd had a bad experience in an earlier group project. We talked about how we all needed to pull together. I was kind of a cheerleader for the group. So we got through this, and the group arrived at a decision and completed the task without any major conflict.

During this phase, you may also experience uncertainty about the task you are to undertake: Will everyone contribute equally? Will the work get done efficiently and on time?

Communication at this phase is generally polite, tentative, and focused on reducing uncertainty and ambiguity through clarification and agreement. The importance of the orientation phase is that many relational and task norms are set for the future. Fortunately for Kirstin's group, she realized the importance of group communication and got the group off to a good start.

Regardless of norms that they establish, groups often experience recurring primary tension if they meet over an extended period. For example, at the beginning of each meeting, group members may need to spend time reconnecting and reviewing their views on the task.

PHASE 2. *Conflict and Secondary Tension.* The conflict phase in decision making is characterized by **secondary (recurring) tension.** This phase usually occurs after group members become acquainted, after some norms and expectations are set, and when decision alternatives are to be addressed.

As members become more relaxed, this phase of their communication becomes more animated and honest. Members may interrupt each other, talk loudly, and try on group roles. Some may try to dominate, push their own agendas, and form coalitions in an effort to increase their influence; others may engage in side conversations as they lose their focus on the decision at hand. It is especially important at this time to follow the suggestions for effective group communication mentioned earlier: equal participation, consensus decision making, and respectful communication (see page 239).

If you were a member of this problem-solving group, what communication roles would you use to improve the group's effectiveness?

If the group plans to meet frequently over a period of weeks or months, this is the time to discuss expectations and establish group norms, especially norms for handling conflict. For example, in a small group working on a course project, members might tell each other what grade they expect in the course and discuss their strengths and weaknesses with respect to the project. One group member may be very good at conducting Internet research. Another might be skillful at integrating material that others have collected. Someone else might be good at keeping members on task. Articulating these expectations and strengths verbally is more useful than communicating interests or commitment (or lack thereof) nonverbally, by simply not showing up or not participating in discussions or work sessions.

Of course, all groups experience some conflict, and a certain amount of conflict can be both healthy and functional, because it can increase member involvement (Klocke, 2007). The most productive way to handle group conflict is through using a "win–win" approach—a cooperative conflict style that integrates all members' interests (Oetzl, 2005). If tensions become very high, the strategies outlined in *Did You Know? How to Handle Conflicts in Meetings* might help manage the conflict.

PHASE 3. *Emergence.*   In the **emergence phase**, the group has worked through the primary and secondary tensions, and members express a cooperative attitude. In successful groups, coalitions dissipate, and group members are less tenacious about holding their positions. Comments become more favorable as members compromise to reach consensus, discuss their problem at length, consider possible alternatives, and eventually generate a group decision (Fisher, 1970, cited in Littlejohn, 2002). This is the longest phase. For some suggestions to facilitate group decision-making see *Did You Know? Procedures That Help Groups Agree.*

Recurring and sustained bouts of secondary tension or conflict can be problematic. In response, members can fill relational roles that promote trust (assuring members that they can rely on each other to put forward their best effort) and cohesion (expressing a desire to remain in the group). Members also can reduce tension by articulating a positive attitude or feeling about their group, the task, or other members (Carwright, 1968), and by emphasizing group identity and pride in the group's effort. In short, strong relational bonds within a group promote high-quality decisions and problem solving (Keyton, 1999, 2000), and groups with high trust have fewer relationship conflicts (Peterson & Behfar, 2003).

PHASE 4. *Reinforcement.*   During the **reinforcement phase**, members reach consensus, the decision solidifies, and members feel a sense of accomplishment

Did You Know?
How to Handle Conflicts in Meetings

Conflicts in group meetings can be very disruptive, but they can also be helpful. Remember, conflicts are disagreements. If the person who is disagreeing with you is raising valid questions, the group may benefit by addressing the issues he or she is presenting. In fact, by listening, you may gain valuable insight into what is and is not working within your group. When conflict takes precedence over problem solving, here are a few principles to keep in mind:

- Clarify what the conflict is about.
- Affirm the validity of all viewpoints.
- Frame the conflict in terms of a problem to be solved.
- Create space for problem solving to occur.
- Help participants save face.
- Discuss what happens if no agreement is reached.
- Ask if the group can proceed with what they do agree on and hold back on areas of disagreement.

ADAPTED FROM: Duncan, M. *Effective meeting facilitation: The sine qua non of planning.* Retrieved June 16, 2006, from www.nea.gov/resources/Lessons/DUNCAN1.HTML

Did You Know?

Procedures That Help Groups Agree

- *Voting:* simultaneous (raised hands, vocal), sequential (round robin), or secret (written)
- *Decision rule:* predetermined level of support needed to reach agreement (for example, two-thirds majority, simple majority, or unanimity)
- *Straw poll:* nonbinding voting method that allows the group to get a sense of members' preferences while still allowing them to change preferences
- *Concession:* agreement to eventually agree, in spite of individual preferences
- *Problem-centered leadership:* procedure in which the leader acts as facilitator, guiding group toward agreement
- *Negotiating:* reaching agreement through series of trade-offs

ADAPTED FROM: Sunwolf & Seibold, D. R. (1999). The impact of formal procedure on group processes, members, and task outcomes. In L. R. Frey, D. S. Gouran, & M. S. Poole (Eds.), *Handbook of group communication theory and research* (p. 401). Thousand Oaks, CA: Sage.

and satisfaction. If a small majority makes the decision, they spend phase four convincing other members of its value. In successful groups, members unify and stand behind the solution. Comments are almost uniformly positive.

While coming to a decision easily with lots of group cohesion may seem like the ideal situation, it may actually reflect a negative group process—**groupthink**. Groupthink occurs when members arrive at a consensus before all alternatives have been realistically assessed. This occurs when group members feel a pressure to conform; they reject new information and may have a negative perception of individuals outside the group who may volunteer information that contradicts the group decisions. In addition, the group members have an illusion of invulnerability and unanimity. These symptoms produce pressure on group members to go along with the favored group position, assuming not only that the group preferences will be successful but also just and right (Henningsen & Henningsen, 2006). This phenomenon can have disastrous consequences. The term was coined in an analysis of several foreign policy fiascoes, such as the Bay of Pigs Invasion in 1961 and the escalation of the Vietnam War (Janis, 1982).

A more recent example of the disastrous consequences of groupthink was the *Challenger* space shuttle explosion 73 seconds into its launch on January 28, 1986. Within days, President Reagan appointed a commission of experts who discovered that the primary cause of the accident was a mechanical failure in one of the joints of the right solid rocket booster. The commission concluded that the contributing cause was a flawed decision-making process at NASA. Several NASA personnel had warned of potential problems with the launch, and numerous opportunities arose to postpone it. However, on each occasion, one or more of the following influences surfaced and reduced the chances for preventing the disaster:

- the unwillingness of individuals to step outside their roles and question those in authority;
- questionable patterns of reasoning by key managers;
- ambiguous and misleading language that minimized the perception of risk;
- failure to ask important questions relevant to the final decision.

In this case, poor communication skills and an unwillingness to explore possible problems and to risk disagreement led to an event that ultimately undermined the respect for and prior achievements of the space agency (Gouran, Hirokawa, & Martz, 1986).

Groupthink is not confined to high-level organizational groups. It can occur in any group. For example, Murphy is part of a student advocacy group that works to protest tuition hikes at his college. The group voted quickly to protest tuition hikes, without investigating all the various expenses that could legitimately cause tuition to be increased. They discovered, after organizing a major protest in front of the president's of-

groupthink
a negative, and potentially disastrous, group process characterized by "excessive concurrence thinking"

Groupthink can be very powerful, as evidenced by the history of the House Un-American Activities Committee.

George Tames/The *New York Times*

fice, that a significant portion of the tuition hikes were related to improving technological services (wireless Internet, more student-access computers), which most students would support. The result of their groupthink was that they had to revisit their initial decision and gather more information to understand exactly the causes of tuition hikes, and ultimately decide what—if any—portion of the tuition hike should be protested.

What causes people to engage in groupthink? One reason may be a high level of cohesiveness. While usually viewed as a positive thing, too much group cohesion can lead to premature agreement. Other reasons may be insulation—when groups have very tight boundaries and are not open to new relevant information (Putnam & Stohl, 1996). Leadership can also promote groupthink: either very strong leadership, where one dominating person promotes only one idea—or the opposite—a lack of leadership, meaning that the group has no direction. Groupthink can also result from a failure to set norms for decision making or from a failure to follow a problem-solving agenda. Finally, extreme homogeneity in the backgrounds of group members may also lead to rushed solutions rather than careful examination of alternatives (Henningsen & Henningsen, 2006).

Groupthink can be prevented in several ways. For example, following an established procedure and making sure adequate time is spent in discussion before reaching a decision are both helpful. Perhaps even more important, group members should be aware of the causes and consequences of groupthink and encourage critical evaluation (at the appropriate time) of ideas to prevent premature decisions.

Technology and Group Communication

Technology is playing an increased role in group work, a topic we will address in more detail in Chapter 13. Some researchers assert that technology enhances positive outcomes in a diverse workforce, as communication technologies reduce the cues that often lead to stereotypes and prejudice. For example, in virtual teams, members cannot see the gender, skin color, or age of their colleagues, which may equalize contributions and facilitate discussion (Scott, 1999).

For example, Marek, one of our students, works for an international pharmaceutical company and often collaborates on projects with group members whom he has never met. Members of his team are scattered around the globe in multiple time zones. Thus he may be online with Luc in Montreal, Caroline in London, Liana in Buenos Aires, Ahmed in Riyadh, Setsuko in Osaka, and Giles in Melbourne. Although he may not have met his group members face to face, their tasks are well defined, and thus, the group completes their projects with few problems. Moreover, their diverse cultural backgrounds enhance the group's ideas and produce a stronger product.

A variety of technologies supports work for teams like these that are separated by time or distance. Some are immediate and synchronous, like audio and teleconferencing technologies that allow members to see and hear each other from remote locations. Another technology is Group Support Software (GSS), a computer-aided program that supports real-time discussion between members regardless of physical location; with GSS, each participant sits at a computer terminal and the discussion is facilitated by the software program. The best known of these programs is Group Decision Support Software (GDSS) (Broome & Chen, 1992).

Recent research has found that in order to be effective, GDSS users must perceive there to be an advantage of using this technology over non-technology-enabled groups and it must be compatible with the way the group already works . . . so in order to conduct a successful meeting, one must begin by "marketing the technology, thereby ensuring a greater likelihood of a successful decision-making process. Secondly, group cohesion is the second most important factor—cohesion is the primary driver of GDSS success" (Schwarz & Schwarz, 2007, p. 222).

Some initial research indicates that GSS can lead to group outcomes that are superior to results from those relying solely on face-to-face meetings. This may be because

GSS can manage and organize simultaneous contributions, leading to improved group performance in brainstorming tasks. However, other research has found that GSS did not lead to more effective group functioning (Dennis & Wixom, 2001–2002; Schwarz & Schwarz, 2007). It looks like GSS works well for generating ideas in large groups, but probably less well for decision-making purposes. Perhaps the best use of GSS in group processes would be to have a team use GSS to generate ideas and discuss issues, but to bring team members together for face-to-face or audio or video conferencing when they need to make important decisions (Dennis & Wixom, 2001–2002). Although some misunderstandings and conflict may inevitably arise, groups using GSS don't appear to have more conflict overall than face-to-face groups (Hobman, Bordia, Irmer, & Chang, 2002).

GSS software ensures that every group member has an equal chance to participate, since anyone can submit a comment at any time.

An additional trend involves combining several technologies such as live videoconferences, text-based document exchange, audio connections, and electronically shared whiteboards on which participants in one location can write and associates in other locations can see what has been written. An increasing number of people are working in virtual (or distributed) work teams; in fact, nearly two-thirds of U.S. employees have participated in virtual work (Connaughton & Shuffler, 2007). A virtual work team is a group of people identified as a team by their organization. The members are responsible for making decisions important to their organization, but unlike in-house teams, they may be culturally diverse and geographically dispersed. And as virtual work team members, they are likely to communicate electronically more often than they do face to face. A new kind of virtual team phenomena is changing the way people and businesses develop ideas using Internet collaboration. (See *Communication in Society: Is Collaboration the Future of Invention?*, on p. 246.)

The challenges faced by virtual teams include distance, geography, and available technology. Some experts say that the communication problems between virtual team members are related to the number of time zones that separate them (Smith, 2001). If only a few time zones away, members can come to work earlier or later and still have overlapping workdays. If members are separated by many time zones, it becomes a much bigger challenge, particularly on Fridays and Mondays. However, other experts say that distance is not necessarily a big problem, and that teams find a way to work with the geographical distance and time differences (Connaughton & Shuffler, 2007). For example, one company with team members in the United States and Australia (a 15–time zone difference) has a policy that members from each country take turns getting up at 2 A.M. once a month for videoconferencing with members from the other country. The rest of the time, they rely on voice mail and email.

How can virtual teams work together most effectively? There seem to be two guidelines. One recommendation is for members to communicate frequently, which seems to reduce conflict and build trust, and the second is to choose the most appropriate communication technology for the task at hand (Maznevski & Chudoba, 2000; Schiller & Mandviwalla, 2007). Each technology works best in its niche. Telephone and video conferences provide high-quality and faster communication, but when dealing with large time differences, email is probably better. Some experts suggest that face-to-face communication, particularly at the beginning of a group project, enhances the effectiveness of virtual teams (Connaughton & Shuffler, 2007).

A recent study compared the effectiveness of face-to-face and virtual student groups. The groups being studied were all working on the same final class project. In this project, students were presented with a survival scenario where they had to work together to decide what they would need to survive after a plane crash in northern Canada. After the task was completed, the researchers asked the students to assess their group's performance in terms of task and relational procedures (e.g., cohesion, process satisfaction, satisfaction with outcomes) as well as the quality of their communication. Independent observers also rated the groups' interactions and

COMMUNICATION IN SOCIETY
Is Collaboration the Future of Invention?

In this article, the author describes a new kind of virtual team phenomenon that is changing the way people and businesses develop ideas—through collaboration on the Internet. What are the communication challenges of working in these types of virtual teams compared to the face-to-face teams?

Paul Willis

(CNN)—A question. What connects Facebook enthusiasts in China busy translating the social networking site into Mandarin and a community of orthopaedic surgeons swapping ideas on how to treat spinal injuries? The answer. They're both examples of a worldwide phenomenon that is changing the way people—and ultimately businesses—develop ideas. Collaborative Innovation Networks (COINs) are online communities of like-minded people working together to create innovations. Author and scientist Peter Gloor originated the term. He describes it as a "cyberteam of self-motivated people with a collective vision." These cyberteams are cropping up everywhere, unified not only by their "collective vision" but by the giant tentacles of the Internet. In the case of Facebook, they are the Chinese users of the site who are helping to translate it into their native language. Elsewhere, they are the surgeons collaborating on SpineConnect, an online community where experts from around the world can exchange ideas for innovations in the treatment of spinal injuries.

The potential of all this pooling of ideas is enormous, says Gloor. If you're not convinced, he says, take a look at what COINs have already accomplished—the creation of the World Wide Web itself is the most obvious example. "It was developed by a network of people based all over the world working as a COIN," says Gloor, who ought to know since he was there for part of its inception.

Gloor was a researcher at the Massachusetts Institute of Technology (MIT) in Boston 15 years ago at the same time as British scientist Tim Berners-Lee—the man credited with inventing the Web. ... "I had the benefit of watching him work close up for a few months, and I saw that his real genius lay in his ability to co-ordinate and incorporate the ideas of all these hundreds of other people based around the world." Since then COINs have helped create much of our online landscape. The Web-based encyclopaedia Wikipedia and the Internet browser Mozilla Firefox are just two of the products whose development relies upon the contribution of a community of online

users. Gloor says: "I have a saying: 'Don't be a star, be a galaxy.' If you embed yourself in a galaxy you can go so much further." But Gloor, who is from Switzerland, is not simply a delighted observer of the phenomenon. He was part of the network that helped develop hypertext—online text that links to other text. He worked with a hardcore of around 100 people worldwide, most of whom he never met and who worked on the project in their own time, and for little or no reward. "Most of the innovation that you see on the Internet today was given away for nothing," he says. "People did it for the sheer love of it." This fraternal, almost unworldly attitude is a common feature of many COINs. For the network to be successful, contributors have to operate transparently and be willing to share their knowledge.

This philanthropic, non-hierarchical approach to innovation sounds radical in an era when the theft of ideas by unscrupulous corporations is well documented. . . . it is an approach that the business world has found hard to come to terms with. Gloor says the rigid structure of many big corporations makes this free exchange of ideas difficult to achieve. "In order to gain control, one has to give up control. But the one thing managers don't like doing is giving up control." A case in point is the failure of Xerox to take advantage of the myriad of innovations produced at the company's research facility in the 1970s and early 1980s. The R&D centre known as Xerox PARC and located in Palo Alto, California, was responsible for inventing laser printing and the Ethernet, and for pioneering the use of the computer mouse. Xerox executives failed to grasp the potential of many of PARC's inventions and it was left to other firms to develop them fully, and enjoy the profits. Not all firms have been quite so sluggish. Procter and Gamble, the world's biggest maker of household goods, made a commitment in 2001 to source half of all new innovations from outside of the company. It set up 'Connect + Develop', an initiative that allows people to submit new innovations online. The venture has been so successful that P&G now gets 42 percent of all its new technologies from outside sources.

As a medium for exchanging ideas, the Internet seems almost without peer. Chris Seth, managing director of the social networking site Piczo, says the collaborative potential of the Web has yet to be fully realized, however. "If Web 2.0 was about sharing collective knowledge or publication, then collective action—making decisions en masse—will typify Web 3.0," he says.

EXCERPTED FROM: "Is Collaboration the Future of Invention?" by Willis, P. for CNN.com, April 7, 2008. Reprinted by permission.

outcomes. Who do you think performed better, the virtual group or the students who were working face to face? In fact, each type of team was effective in some ways. The virtual teams performed somewhat higher quality task behaviors but took more time to complete tasks than did the face-to-face groups. The face-to-face groups were better at performing relational role behaviors—that is, they engaged in more social talk, but did not necessarily have better group outcomes (Li, 2007). Remember out earlier caution that too much social talk can divert teams from their task?

In sum, it seems that virtual teams may be most useful for tasks that do not require quick decisions and their work can be enhanced by frequent communication and even face-to-face meetings when possible. We'll discuss computer-mediated communication further in Chapter 13.

THE INDIVIDUAL, SMALL GROUP COMMUNICATION, AND SOCIETY

Small group communication, like all communication, is influenced by societal forces. The world outside influences this form of communication in two important respects: (1) the way power is used inside and outside groups, and (2) the role cultural diversity plays.

Power and Group Communication

Small groups function within the constraints and influences of the societal forces we have discussed throughout this book: political, economic, and historical. People communicating in small groups bring with them their identities and the hierarchical meanings associated with those identities (see Chapter 3). Those group members who hold the values and follow the communication rules of the dominant group in society may more easily contribute to the group and dominate it, which may cause resentment among those who feel marginalized in society more generally (Oetzel, 2005).

Groups also establish a power structure. For example, a group member may be elected or appointed to lead a group, which allows that person to wield *legitimate* power (French & Raven, 1959). These power arrangements come with benefits and drawbacks. On the one hand, productive uses of power can facilitate group processes (Sell, Lovaglia, Mannix, Samuelson, & Wilson, 2004). On the other hand, leaders or group members may turn legitimate power into *coercive* power, or threats, to get others to do what they want. Much of an individual's power is derived from her society/social status and standing. For example, when an individual is appointed to lead a group, this usually occurs because of her position within the social hierarchy of the organization.

Group members may also wield coercive power; they may threaten to withdraw or undermine the process if group members don't do what they want, as experienced by one of our students in *It Happened to Me: Sarah*.

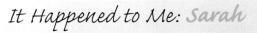

It Happened to Me: Sarah

We had one girl in our group who was headstrong, but very nice. She wanted to do the project "her way." She insisted that we follow her suggestions. If we didn't, she refused to participate and made comments that undermined the group work. If we did listen to her, then she was sweet and cooperative, and everything went fine. Some members wanted to try to please her; others resented her manipulation, and this situation caused a lot of conflict in the group.

The use of coercive power is usually unproductive because, as you can see in Sarah's experience, group members resent the threats and may reciprocate by using coercive power when they get the chance. Thus, too much power or a struggle for power can lead to resentment and poor decision making (Broome & Fulbright, 1995). In contrast, researchers find that groups whose members share power equally exhibit higher quality communication. Social hierarchies are often reproduced in the small group situation because members bring their identities and experiences to the group. Thus members' cultural identities, which fall along a power hierarchy, can impact small group work. Let's examine how this happens.

Cultural Diversity and Small Group Communication

Given the changing demographics in the United States and abroad, small groups will increasingly include members whose backgrounds differ. As we discussed in Chapter 7, cultural backgrounds influence communication patterns, and small group communication is no exception (Broome & Fulbright, 1995). For example, people from countries where a collectivistic orientation dominates may be most concerned with maintaining harmony in the group, whereas members with an individualistic orientation may be more assertive and competitive in groups (Oetzel, 1998). These differences can lead to challenges in accomplishing group goals (Crown, 2007).

How does cultural diversity affect small group processes? Does it result in poor communication, more conflict, lower productivity, and less satisfaction? Or can diverse groups, with their various viewpoints, make better, more effective, and more creative decisions?

Research indicates that even though interactions might be more complex, especially in the early stages of group work, diversity can lead to positive and productive outcomes. Let's look at how diversity influences four aspects of group communication: innovation, efficacy, group processes, and group enjoyment.

Innovation

Several researchers have found that groups with a diverse membership are more innovative than homogeneous groups (King & Anderson, 1990). In one study, ethnically diverse groups produced higher quality ideas in brainstorming tasks (McLeod, Lobel, & Cox, 1996). In a study of *Fortune* 500 teams, racially diverse groups came up with a greater number of innovative ideas than did homogeneous groups (Cady & Valentine, 1999).

This makes sense, because having different perspectives means also having a variety of information sources to apply to a problem or issue (Salazar, 1997). This variety of information broadens people's views and their ability to evaluate. So, ultimately, a diverse workforce operating in a rapidly changing world is better able to monitor, identify, and respond quickly and innovatively to external problems than a homogeneous one (Haslett & Ruebush, 1999).

Performance (Efficacy)

Some research studies report that diverse groups work more effectively (Bowers, Pharmer, & Salas, 2000), while other studies report the opposite (van Knippenberg, De Dreu, & Homan, 2004). This isn't surprising, given the many types of diversity and the fact that each group develops communication and processes that may help or hinder their performance. Communication in diverse groups may be more challenging at the onset, so that cultural differences in attitudes and communication styles may lead to early conflict. However, if group members handle these differences well, the outcome may be as good as or better than in homogeneous groups (Oetzel, 2005).

In one study, researchers placed college students in work groups, with some being racially and ethnically diverse and others being more homogeneous. Their task was to complete a class project—an analysis of an organization of their choice. The students all completed their projects and then filled out a questionnaire that included four statements about their group's cohesion (for example, "I really like my group"), and several questions about their group's effectiveness (such as how high they expected their project grade to be).

Diverse groups reported higher *efficacy*, or effectiveness, in completing their projects than did less diverse groups. Not surprisingly, both groups ranked their group cohesion as very important to their performance. The groups reporting the highest effectiveness were those that were highly cohesive and racially and ethnically diverse. The lowest performing groups were those that were less cohesive and less diverse (Sargent & Sue-Chan, 2001). The researchers concluded that (1) high levels of cohesiveness *and* diversity may weaken barriers that inhibit communication, and that (2) "differences and 'otherness' [are] not experienced as a deficiency among groups of university students" (p. 442). A number of other scholars suggest that building early group cohesion in diverse groups smoothes the way to managing differences in later discussions (Bantz, 1993; Oetzel, 2005; Polzer, Milton, & Swann, 2002). Having a group goal seems to be very important for bringing groups together and reducing conflict in heterogeneous groups (Crown, 2007).

Group Processes

As we discussed in Chapter 7, one way that individuals differ across cultures is in their preference for individualism or collectivism, and these preferences impact **group processes**. To understand these preferences, one group of researchers randomly assigned students to task groups so that each group had varying degrees of age, gender, and ethnic diversity. Their group task was a course assignment in which they analyzed conversations using various theories presented in class. The students then filled out a questionnaire measuring their own communication in the group (competence and style), their individualistic–collectivist tendencies, and their satisfaction with the group work (Oetzel, 1998).

> **group processes**
> the methods, including communication, by which a group accomplishes a task

You may find it interesting that ethnic, gender, and age diversity in this study had very little effect on the communication process, but those who preferred more interdependent or collectivistic interaction participated more and cooperated more in the group, thus having a more positive impact on group processes. Group members who convey respect and participate in a cooperative manner are also likely to put forth substantial effort toward completing a task and to encourage the contributions of others. Why? Effective communication by some may reduce isolation and encourage effort of all group members. Not surprisingly, those members who participated more were more satisfied with the group outcome.

A recent related study examined the effect of diversity on group member relationships both inside the group and outside the group (Valenti & Rockett, 2008). The researchers hypothesized that demographic differences may influence team members' relationships with others in their group and those outside their work group. They hypothesized that when one or more members of the group are demographically different (gender, age, race, ethnicity), they may communicate less with others in their work group and may even develop negative feelings about the group and distance themselves, not forming close relationships. In order to test their hypotheses, they surveyed employees of a national consulting firm about their communication practices and attitudes toward work relationships. The researchers found that while employees with the same demographic characteristics did tend to talk with each other about personal issues, how much they communicated with others on work-related issues was not affected by their demographic characteristics. The findings conclude that diversity did not hamper the formation of friendship within work groups, and that this is good news for management: "A worker's contribution to his or her team does not appear to be hampered by potential harmful feelings toward group membership" based on demographics (p. 194).

These studies show that groups that are diverse in terms of race, ethnicity, and gender don't necessarily experience more difficult processes. Moreover, because people are diverse and different in so many ways, one can't make assumptions about any collection of individuals based on physical attributes like age, race, or gender.

They also indicate that team leaders can implement team-building exercises to increase interdependence, promote an open communication climate, and help establish group cohesion. This kind of leadership in turn enhances cooperation, participation, satisfaction, and effort (Oetzel, 2001).

Group Enjoyment

While diverse groups may be more innovative and effective, are they more enjoyable? To explore this question, another study examined the experience of college students who worked in groups that were composed of either (1) mostly Whites or (2) mostly ethnic minorities (Asians, Asian Americans, African Americans, Hispanics, and others of mixed ethnicity). The researchers found that minorities and White students all preferred minority-dominated teams to White-dominated teams. How to explain these findings? The researchers suggest that some level of collectivism may have been working in the minority-oriented groups, and whether or not it was, members of these groups were more attentive to relational harmony (Paletz, Peng, Erez, & Masclach, 2004).

What are the implications to be drawn from all these studies that have examined the effect of diversity on group work? First, it seems there are two types of diversity: demographic diversity (age, gender, ethnicity, and race) and deeper cultural differences in attitudes and values (individualism and collectivism preferences) that also play an important role (Crown, 2007). Some research shows that demographic differences may influence group processes early in a group's history, while value differences may have more of an impact later on (Ilgen, Hollenbeck, Johnson, & Jundt, 2005). Culturally diverse groups *may* produce more innovative ideas, *may* be more enjoyable, and can be as productive as homogeneous groups. However, as Oetzel's study (2005) points out, enjoyment and productivity do not occur automatically in these groups; they depend largely on the communication skills of the group members, which do not always come naturally. "Many people believe that good communication skills are 'common sense.' Contrary to expectations, the problem with common sense is that it is not all that common" (p. 366). He suggests that leaders of culturally diverse groups need to focus on skill training—to help all team members, including reticent ones, learn to participate fully, and to communicate respectfully in a way that promotes collaboration and consensus building.

These findings suggest that organizations need to develop policies and programs allowing for and valuing the unique characteristics of each group (Cady & Valentine, 1999). Further, with proper education and development, diverse teams have the potential to experience higher levels of satisfaction and lower turnover (Cox, 1994, cited in Cady & Valentine). Supporting this idea is the finding that groups with high diversity but without proper education in group process are associated with high turnover (Sargent & Sue-Chan, 2001).

Diverse groups can outperform homogeneous groups. Seek out opportunities to work with people who are different from you.

To summarize, communicating in groups, like all other communication, occurs within societal structures. These social structures establish power relations and status hierarchies that in turn come into play in group interaction. The cultural backgrounds of group members also influence group communication, and if handled well, cultural diversity can enhance group innovation, performance, communication processes, and enjoyment. However, the bottom line is that effective group work flows from effective and ethical communication skills, the topics we turn to next.

ETHICS AND SMALL GROUP COMMUNICATION

Ethical communication in small groups is especially important because the success of the group and the task depend on it. One might argue that being in a group carries additional ethical responsibilities because one's individual actions can affect how people think about and react to other members of the group and their ideas. In short, in groups, you are no longer responsible only for yourself but for other members as well.

It might be helpful to think about the ethical guidelines discussed in Chapter 1 and consider how they might apply to a small group context. Being truthful in your communication is particularly important, as you are making contributions that affect larger collective decisions (Hargrove, 1998). Truthfulness also includes being accurate and avoiding exaggeration. For example, if you were reporting facts about crime on campus, you would offer statistics, not just say "I found out that crime is really a huge problem."

While you should strive for accuracy and honesty in your language, there may be times when you should not say everything you know—for example, when you should respect the confidentiality of others, including group members. If your friend has been raped and you know this information might be helpful to your group discussion about campus security, you should ask for your friend's permission before divulging this information. Similarly, group members may disclose personal information in the group discussion that they may not wish repeated outside the group.

Group members also should work toward communicating authentically, as discussed in Chapter 1. As we noted earlier, group cohesion and trust are important to the performance and success of groups. Authentic communication that is open and free from pretense, and language that is inclusive and not hurtful to others, go a long way in promoting the kind of group relationships necessary for group effectiveness.

Finally, as a receiver, you must listen with an open mind while also evaluating others' contributions. Doing so will enhance the quality of discussions and help prevent groupthink, in which groups jump to premature conclusions and decisions.

IMPROVING YOUR SMALL GROUP COMMUNICATION SKILLS

While no strategies will work in every group communication situation, two strategies can help you be more effective in many of them.

First, cultivate an interdependent or collectivist attitude. This means that you must sacrifice some of your personal ambition, needs, and wants in favor of the group's needs. People who are extremely individualistic may find this difficult. Yet, those with a more collectivist attitude can influence group processes toward more effective communication, more participation, and more satisfaction of all members (Oetzel, 2005).

In addition to cultivating an interdependent attitude, striving for cohesion also is very important in successful small group relationships and task accomplishment. Cohesion occurs when team members trust each other. Further, group success depends on the participation of each member, but members are unlikely to give their best to the group if they can't trust other members to do the same. Trust is particularly important in virtual teams, where members have less face-to-face interaction which might otherwise provide important cues to the intent or attitude of fellow group members. Several strategies build trust and cohesion:

- Focus on the strengths of all group members, and recognize their contributions to group goals. Be sure to acknowledge all group achievements.

- Remind the group of common interests and background experiences. Doing this can help build cohesion, prevent unnecessary conflict, and strengthen group identity.

- Be observant and notice when a member might be feeling unappreciated or uninvolved in the group. Encourage that person to participate. People gain trust and become more trusting as they participate, especially if their participation is encouraged. Fortunately, more trust leads to more cohesion and stronger group identity, which in turn leads to better communication, more satisfaction, and more cohesion.

In sum, the effectiveness of a small group depends in large part on the communication and the relationships established among the members. As a group member, you can promote (or inhibit) the productive communication needed. We believe that using the tools discussed in this chapter will not only make your small group work more effectively, they will make it more enjoyable.

SUMMARY

Small group communication is a fact of life, and learning to be a better small group communicator can enhance your academic performance, your career achievement, and your personal success. Small group members share a common purpose, are interdependent, and exert influence on each other. The primary benefit of small groups is that they are more productive and creative than individuals working alone. The disadvantages are that decisions take longer, and relational problems and conflicts can make the experience less than satisfying.

Communication is the "lifeblood that flows through the veins of the small group." Thirteen task and eight relational roles are required for effective group work. In effective groups, individuals fill these roles as needed at any given time during group work. Eight individual roles also exist that group members may fill; these roles, however, tend to be dysfunctional and unproductive. Finally, five theories of leadership—trait, style, functional, transformational, and servant explain leadership effectiveness.

The most common type of small group is the problem-solving group, which often follows a five-stage agenda: (1) defining the problem, (2) analyzing the problem, (3) identifying alternative solutions, (4) evaluating the proposed solutions, and (5) choosing the best solution. Related to the five-stage agenda are the four phases of decision making that most groups complete in every stage of the problem-solving agenda: orientation and primary tension, conflict and secondary tension, emergence, and reinforcement. Technology plays an increasing role in small group work, as we touched on here. We'll discuss it in more depth in Chapter 13.

Societal forces impact small group processes via the role of power in small group work and through cultural diversity. While cultural diversity can present challenges for group processes, it can also produce innovative, efficient, and enjoyable group experiences if handled appropriately. Building cohesion and trust in early stages of group work is particularly important in diverse groups. Ethical guidelines for small group communication include being truthful and accurate, respecting confidentiality, and striving for authentic and open communication. Skills for achieving effective group communication include cultivating an interdependent attitude and striving for trust and cohesion.

KEY TERMS

grouphate 224
primary groups 224
secondary groups 224
social facilitation 225
small group communication 227
group roles 228
task roles 229
relational roles 230
individual roles 232
trait theory 234

functional (situational) theory 234
shared (collaborative or distributed)
    leadership 235
style theory 236
authoritarian leader 236
democratic leader 236
laissez-faire 236
transformational leadership 236
charismatic leadership 238
servant leadership 238

analysis paralysis 240
brainstorm 240
decision-making process 240
primary tension 241
secondary (recurring) tension 241
emergence phase 242
reinforcement phase 242
groupthink 243
group processes 249

TEST YOUR KNOWLEDGE

1. How does a small group, as defined in this chapter, differ from a group of individuals waiting in line at a bank?
2. What is the difference between task and relational role behaviors in small group communication? How are they related to each other?
3. What are five theories of leadership? Give an example to support each theory.
4. What is groupthink? What are the primary causes of groupthink?
5. Why do many successful problem-solving groups follow an agenda?
6. What are the four phases of decision making? Do most groups follow these phases in a linear or a more circular fashion?
7. How does a collectivist perspective enhance small group work?

APPLY WHAT YOU KNOW

1. **Group Roles Activity**
   Think of a recent group experience you've had. Look at the lists of task, relational, and individual role behaviors in Tables 9.1 through 9.3. Record all behaviors and roles that you filled. Which behaviors (if any) were missing in your group? Which other roles might you have filled?

2. **Group Problem-Solving Activity**
   This activity can be assigned either as an individual or small group experience. Identify a problem you have encountered recently on your campus. Come up with a viable solution to this problem by following the problem-solving agenda. Which steps of the agenda were relatively easy? Which were more difficult? Why?

3. **Groupthink Exercise**
   Consider experiences you've had in group work. Answer the following questions concerning groupthink. After answering the questions, meet with several classmates and compare answers. Then, as a group, come up with suggestions for ensuring against groupthink.

- Have you ever felt so secure about a group decision that you ignored all the warning signs that the decision was wrong? Why?
- Have you ever applied undue pressure to members who disagreed in order to get them to agree with the will of the group?
- Have you ever participated in a "we-versus-they" feeling—that is, depicting those in the group who are opposed to you in simplistic, stereotyped ways?
- Have you ever served as a "mind guard"—that is, have you ever attempted to preserve your group's cohesiveness by preventing disturbing outside ideas or opinions from becoming known to other group members?
- Have you ever assumed that the silence of the other group members implied agreement?

ADAPTED FROM: Meade, L. (2003). Small group home page. *The message: A communication website*. Retrieved June 19, 2006, from http://lynn_meade.tripod.com/id62.htm

EXPLORE

1. Go to www.wilderdom.com/research.html This Web site of the Outdoor Education Research and Evaluation Center contains useful information about group norms, leadership development, and cultural diversity in groups, as well as group games and activities. This section of the Web site lists strategies for providing support in group settings. What role does communication play in each of these strategies?

2. Go to http://lynn_meade.tripod.com/id62.htm This is another good resource page about group work. It gives examples of groupthink, including the 1986 *Challenger* disaster. Read the descriptions of groupthink. In what ways might the search for weapons of mass destruction in Iraq have been a result of groupthink?

Communicating in Organizations

chapter outline

Lauro's first assignment in his organizational communication class was to list all the organizations he interacted with for one day and to identify the communication purpose of each interaction. At first he thought he would have trouble completing the assignment. Then, as he went through his day, buying a cup of coffee at Starbucks, interviewing for a job on campus, listening to lectures in his classes, ordering lunch at Burger King, and tutoring English language learners at a local community center, he had a realization. Almost every interaction he had that day either occurred with representatives of organizations or within organizations.

We live in a society of organizations. Even if you don't think of yourself as a member of any organizations, they shape your life, in more and less obvious ways. For example, legislative bodies and law enforcement agencies implement formal codes—like traffic laws—that constrain your daily behavior. Educational institutions shape what counts as knowledge, such as when schools determine whether evolutionary theory, intelligent design, or both, will be taught in science classes. In addition, religious groups influence popular moral beliefs about issues such as gay marriage or abortion rights, and various cultural agencies, ranging from museums to textbook publishers, guide our perceptions of "important" history and "legitimate" art.

Business corporations also are major players in shaping our society. Some argue that because they control vast economic resources, huge transnational corporations have become even more powerful than governments, and thus heavily influence government personnel and policy, educational content and practices, and international relations (Deetz, 1992). Corporations also affect our lifestyle desires and choices. For instance, why do consumers want and purchase new, "improved" cell phones, iPods, and computers even when their current ones work perfectly well? At a more subtle level, consider how many people around you make major life decisions—such as what college to attend, where to buy a home with the greatest resale potential, and even when to have children—that are influenced by corporate advertising and policies (Deetz, 1992).

Even though organizations cast a strong influence on individuals, individuals also affect organizations. Certainly, CEOs and managers affect their organizations, but so do you—as a consumer, as a supporter and participant in religious and civic institutions, as a voter, and as an individual who works for, or against, specific organizations. Although living in an organizational society generally means you can't escape the influence of organizations, you can have a profound effect on them, just as they do on you. Your ability to have this effect depends on your understanding of organizations and your skills communicating with and within them.

In this chapter we explain what we mean by *organizational communication* and explore the types of communication that commonly occur within organizations.

On a typical day, what types of organizations do you interact with? Which ones do you believe most strongly influence the choices you make?

First we look at how individuals communicate within organizations. Then we broaden the discussion to examine the ways that society impacts the interaction between individuals and organizations as well as how organizations influence society and individuals. We wrap up this chapter with a discussion of ethical issues associated with communication in and by organizations and offer ways to improve your ability to communicate effectively within organizations.

⊠ Once you have read this chapter, you will be able to:

- ■ Define organizations from a communication perspective.
- ■ Explain the communication functions and structures of *organizations*.
- ■ Identify the different types of organizations.
- ■ Discuss the four types of communication that are integral to organizations.
- ■ Understand the types of communication that occur among coworkers and explain their functions.
- ■ Explain the four types of organizational dilemmas.
- ■ Articulate the influence of historical forces on the study of organizations.
- ■ Clarify the role of power in organizations and on organizational communication.
- ■ Distinguish between individual and communal perspectives on organizational ethics.

Business corporations play a major role in shaping our society.

THE IMPORTANCE OF ORGANIZATIONAL COMMUNICATION

Because you participate in organizations regularly, you will benefit from understanding how to communicate more effectively with and within them. Doing so will enhance your professional success, allow you to ask more informed questions about everyday organizational practices, and help you decide what organizations you wish to frequent and support.

Much of your success within organizations is connected to your communication abilities. For example, if you want an organization to hire you, you must first display good interviewing skills. If you want a promotion, understanding your boss's goals and beliefs, and demonstrating your agreement with them, may be essential (Eisenberg, Monge, & Farace, 1984). Finally, if you seek public or civic office, you must have strong public-speaking and social-influence skills to gain support from your political party and endorsements from influential organizations.

In addition to enhancing your professional success, understanding organizational communication will help you ask more informed questions about everyday organizational practices, such as how the corporation you work for determines pay raises, how a nonprofit charity you support can become a United Way organization, or how you can influence legislation in your community. Knowing what questions to ask and how to ask them will improve your ability to accomplish your goals. Finally, given that a wide variety of religious, corporate, and community organizations exist, there is a limit to how many you can support. Understanding how to question organizations and how to interpret their responses and policies can help you make informed choices regarding which ones to embrace. For example, you might decide not to purchase products or services from for-profit organizations that force their employees to work mandatory overtime at the expense of their home lives. Or you might decide that you are better off working for an organization whose goals and beliefs you support strongly, since your agreement with those goals likely will influence your career success.

In sum, organizational communication is central to a person's ability to navigate successfully the myriad legal, educational, religious, corporate, and civic organizations one confronts across a lifetime.

organizations
the set of interactions that members of groups use to accomplish their individual and common goals

DEFINING ORGANIZATIONAL COMMUNICATION

Next we define what we mean when we say *organization*, and we explain the role communication plays in it. As part of this definition, we focus on two aspects common to all organizing efforts: communication functions and structures. Then we review types of organizations, especially those that organizational communication scholars have emphasized. We then conclude this section by examining the role of communication in establishing organizational cultures.

Organizations from a Communication Perspective

Scholars from a variety of fields including sociology, economics, psychology, and business management are interested in understanding organizational life. However, communication scholars bring a particular focus to the study of organizations. From their perspective, communication is not just another variable of organizational life. Thus, it is not merely the oil that lubricates other parts of the machine or the glue that binds parts together. Put bluntly, without communication, they argue, there are no "parts"; there is no "machine."

Consider the organization of a college classroom, for instance. Communication scholars argue that it is in the *process of interacting* as student and teacher—giving and listening to lectures, taking and grading exams—that the meaning of these abstract roles becomes real. In this view, then, communication is the process that calls organizations into being. Thus communication scholars argue that *communication constitutes organizations*. It enables or creates them.

From this perspective, then, **organizations** are defined as the set of interactions that members of groups use to accomplish their individual and common goals (Taylor & Van Every, 1993). Two parts of this definition are important: That organizations are composed of group members' interactions, and that organizational members pursue goals.

In Chapter 8 we explained how dyads create and maintain their relationships through communication; this same process occurs within organizations. As individuals in organizations maintain, or alter, their communication practices, they influence the organization itself. For example, the new superintendent of a local school district promised to provide "better customer service" to parents, students, and community members. Over time, he communicated this goal to employees of his school district and the public. Consequently, staff members began to see their positions differently and started to communicate differently with the public. In turn, the public developed different expectations regarding how the school district should treat them (*Arizona Republic*, 2005, Dec. 26).

Individuals join organizations such as Habitat for Humanity because they can accomplish their goals more effectively if they work with others.

Through his communication interactions with people throughout the school district, and their interactions with each other, this superintendent affected how his organization operates.

In addition to being composed of communication interactions, our definition indicates that organizations are purposeful. Organizations are not random groupings of people; organizational members come together to accomplish individual and collective goals. For example, organizations such as Greenpeace, Doctors Without Borders, and Habitat for Humanity exist because their individual members want to make positive changes in the world, and they can do so more effectively if they work together.

Communication Function and Structure

Organizational communication is interaction that organizes purposeful groups and it generally exhibits several properties—two of which are especially relevant here. The first we will call **function**, by which we mean the goals and effects of communication. Traditionally, scholars recognized three major functions of organizational communication (Daniels, Spiker, & Papa, 1996). **Production** refers to communication that coordinates activity toward accomplishing tasks. For example, when a manager creates a set of store opening and closing procedures, informs employees of monthly sales goals, or develops a standardized process for assembling products, she allows employees to accomplish various tasks. The **maintenance** function of organizational communication preserves the stability of existing systems. Consider, for example, awarding an employee-of-the-month plaque, conducting a performance review, and clarifying a vague set of work-flow procedures—all of which enforce the status quo and keep the system running smoothly. A third function is **innovation**, which involves communication that facilitates system change. Examples might include suggestion boxes, restructuring and retraining, policy revisions, and the like.

You may have noticed that in the most of these examples the three traditional functions overlap considerably. Let's take performance reviews as an illustration. As a manager, you may hope to reinforce the status quo (maintenance) by providing an employee with positive feedback, but you may also hope to instigate change (innovation) in that employee's behavior by offering suggestions for improvement. Also, most performance reviews involve other goals not adequately captured by the three-function model, such as negotiating trust, flexing egos, and so forth. With closer examination, you may see that at least some of these performance-review goals are at odds with one another. In fact, most organizational communication serves multiple, even competing, functions.

The second major property of organizational communication is **structure**. Traditionally, communication structure referred to lines of communication, or a system of pathways through which messages flow. Such a conduit model of communication emphasizes *direction*: **downward communication** (with subordinates), **upward communication** (with superiors), and **horizontal communication** (with peers) (Putnam, Phillips, & Chapman, 1996). Note that direction-based metaphors presume **hierarchy**, a kind of power structure in which some members exercise authority over others. A more contemporary way to define structure is as *recurring patterns of interaction among members*. Rather than treating messages as literal objects moving through conduits, this newer definition points to communication networks that emerge among members. It recognizes that such networks may be hierarchical, though other possibilities exist.

Another important distinction exists between **formal structure** and **informal structure**. Formal structure refers to the officially designated channels of communication, whereas informal structure refers to unspoken but understood channels (Blau & Meyer, 1987; Roy, 1995). As an analogy, think of sidewalks on your campus as the official walkway (formal structure), while footprints worn in the grass represent the shortcuts and detours people take from the path they are given (informal

function
the goals and effects of communication

production
a function of organizational communication in which activity is coordinated toward accomplishing tasks

maintenance
a function of organizational communication in which the stability of existing systems is preserved

innovation
a function of organizational communication by means of which systems are changed

structure
lines of communication, or a system of pathways through which messages flow

downward communication
in a traditional conduit model of communication, communication with subordinates

upward communication
in a traditional conduit model of communication, communication with superiors

horizontal communication
in a traditional conduit model of communication, communication with peers

hierarchy
a power structure in which some members exercise authority over others

formal structure
officially designated channels of communication, reflecting explicit or desired patterns of interaction

informal structure
unspoken but understood channels of communication, reflecting patterns that develop spontaneously

structure). Thus, formal structures are explicit or desired patterns of interaction (that is, what the organization suggests we do). Informal structures are patterns of interaction that develop spontaneously. Most organizational members use both formal and informal structures, for example, following formal corporate procedures for requesting a leave of absence (formal), and asking a friend in a position of power to recommend their leave request to the boss (informal).

Of the many features of organizational communication we might choose to discuss, we want to highlight function and structure because they have surfaced continually in scholarly visions of organizational communication.

Types of Organizations

Thus far we have emphasized elements that are shared by organizations of all types. Yet across academic studies and in everyday talk we recognize different types of organizations. We might distinguish one organization from the next in a number of ways, and it is important to admit from the outset that all such efforts are inevitably partial and flawed, revealing some important intentions while concealing others. Our goal in offering any categorization is not to advocate one model, but to indicate briefly the rich array of possible types and to show how organizational communication scholars have, nonetheless, devoted most of their attention to one type of organization.

We might differentiate organizations by such factors as size, industry, market share, developmental phase, or governance structure. One classification of particular use to our discussion is **societal role**, or social function (Tompkins, 1982). For instance, some organizations serve **integration roles**—their primary mission is to manage potentially chaotic social conflicts or problems. You might place law enforcement agencies, medical facilities, and certain nonprofit organizations like shelters for domestic violence victims or people without housing in this category.

Other organizations primarily serve **political roles**, in that they generate and distribute valued resources and, thus, power. Political parties, government intelligence, and military agencies illustrate this category. Meanwhile, domestic violence shelters and many other nonprofit agencies demonstrate overlap across the first two categories because they aim not only to treat a social ill but also to transform the unequal relations of power that they believe cause the ill. Organizations that serve **pattern maintenance roles** perform learning and expressive functions, while also establishing and perpetuating certain social and cultural norms. You might think of educational institutions, museums, religious organizations, and families in this category.

Despite this range of organizational roles, organizational scholars in and beyond the field of communication studies have overwhelmingly emphasized another role of organizations: **economic production**, or the delivery of products or services in such a way as to maximize profit. If you consider this category in light of our earlier discussion of business corporations and their political influence, the overlap across categories becomes apparent once again. Yet, there are notable exceptions (e.g., Deetz, 1992). Economic production organizations are rarely considered in terms of their political influence or social maintenance roles. Instead, for over a hundred years, scholars have focused primarily on questions relating to the effective management of these organizations. In this context, "effective" typically describes labor productivity and the organization's capacity to turn a profit. However, it more generally applies to management's ability to achieve all organizational goals, including improving public relations, increasing diversity, or creating products and offering services that improve people's lives. Nonetheless, because research has centered on the economic role of for-profit organizations, much of our upcoming discussion will focus on communication as it occurs in the context of businesses and corporations.

societal role
social function

integration role
organizational function in which potentially chaotic social conflicts or problems are managed

political role
organizational function in which valued resources and, thus, power are generated and distributed

pattern maintenance role
organizational role in which learning and expressive functions are performed, while also establishing and perpetuating social and cultural norms

economic production role
organizational role in which the delivery of products or services maximizes profit

organizational culture
a pattern of shared beliefs, values, and behaviors

Organizational Culture

In addition to structure, function, and social role, each organization also develops a distinct organizational culture. **Organizational culture** refers to a pattern of shared beliefs, values, and behaviors, or "the system of meanings and behaviors that construct the reality of a social community" (Cheney, Christensen, Zorn, & Ganesh, 2004, p. 76). More informally, organizational culture can be thought of as the "personality" of an organization (McNamara, 2008). As these definitions suggest, organizational cultures are created as people act and interact with one another.

Organizational cultures are composed of the languages, habits, rituals, ceremonies, stories, beliefs, attitudes, and artifacts performed by members of that group. For example, universities and colleges usually have specific names for their student unions, nicknames for buildings, rituals that occur around graduation and/or sporting events, and beliefs about what constitutes a good education. As newcomers, students, faculty, and staff become familiar with and integrated into the organization as they learn the specific languages, attitudes, stories, and so on, enacted by that organization.

Organizational cultures develop as a result of organizations' attempts to integrate, or assimilate, new members and as they respond to internal and external feedback. Thus, organizational culture is not static but changes over time. Two recent television shows, *Mad Men* and *Life on Mars* are engaging, in part, for their depiction of specific organizational cultures that no longer exist—an ad agency in the 1960s and a police station in the 1970s. As these shows reveal, organizational culture reflects larger cultural values as well as the beliefs, attitudes, and practices of the specific organizations, which can and do change over time.

Organizational cultures are made up of both the stated and the unstated. That is, organizations articulate both explicit and implicit values, beliefs, and expectations. For example, a company may say it is "family friendly" and offer work–life policies designed to enhance employees' lives, but at the same time it will fail to promote people who refuse to work on weekends or who actually use work–life policies on maternity or paternity leave (Kirby and Krone, 2002).

Each organization develops its own internal culture, even if it is of a similar type or serves a similar function as other organizations. For example, although they are all restaurants, the organizational cultures of McDonald's, Applebee's, and Hooters differ. If you were to assess their cultural differences, you might think about who the employees are, the type of clothing employees wear, how they greet guests, how they interact with patrons and each other, and how they talk about their work experiences. Even a brief visit to these establishments quickly reveals cultural differences.

However, in addition to the corporate culture, groups within organizations develop their own subcultures (Martin, 2002). In law firms for example, support staff, law clerks, and the firm's law team likely each develop their own unique subculture. The lawyers may even develop separate subcultures—for example, one for partners and one for associates. Each group may have its own style of dress, its own values and stories, and its own practices for celebrating birthdays, promotions, or weddings. This illustration also suggests that the subcultures within such an organization likely differ in their power and interests (Howard-Grenville, 2006). Thus, they likely impact the corporate culture to varying degrees, with the more powerful groups having a stronger overall influence.

Now that you have been introduced to the basic features of organizations, in the following section we discuss how individuals become members of organizations and the important role communication serves in supervisor–subordinate and coworker relationships.

The television show *Mad Men* is engaging, in part, because it depicts the organizational culture of an advertising agency in the 1960s.

ORGANIZATIONAL COMMUNICATION AND THE INDIVIDUAL

If you wish to influence the organizations you interact with, you need to understand some of the basic types of communication that help create organizations and organizational life. It is important to be familiar with guidelines for how you might perform these types of communication most successfully. Although all the communication skills and abilities we examine in this book will definitely make you a better communicator in organizational contexts, here we focus on three types of communication that are integral to organizations: assimilation, supervisor–subordinate communication, and coworker communication. We also explore three types of organizational dilemmas or tensions that employees must manage.

Assimilation

In the organizational context, **assimilation** refers to the communicative, behavioral, and cognitive processes that influence individuals to join, identify with, become integrated into, and (occasionally) exit an organization (Jablin & Krone, 1987). When you join an organization, you usually don't become an accepted member of the group automatically, nor do you immediately identify with the organization and its members. Instead, over time you go through a process in which you and others begin to see you as an integral and accepted part of the organization. The pledge process for sororities and fraternities is one highly ritualized form of assimilation.

Assimilation is a common experience for individuals who join any type of organization, whether it is a business, a religious group, or a social group. However, you probably most often think of assimilation as occurring when you begin a new job. Assimilation is similar to the process of cultural adaptation experienced when individuals enter a new culture, as we discussed in Chapter 7.

Organizational identification is a stage of assimilation that occurs when an employee's values overlap with the organization's values (Bullis & Tompkins, 1989). For example, Arizona Public Service (a utility company) values community involvement, encourages its employees to volunteer, and even provides time off for workers to do so. Some new hires, however, may not inherently value volunteerism, and others may even resist the corporation's attempt to influence their behavior outside work. However, over time, some of these new hires will begin to identify more strongly with the organization and its values, and their attitudes will change. Those who had not given much thought to volunteering may now see it as a corporate responsibility, and those who were opposed may come to see time off for community service as a benefit.

Of course, not every new employee experiences organizational identification. Some employees never come to accept their organization's values. For instance, if an employee values an environment where coworkers become friends and socialize frequently, he or she likely will never identify with a highly competitive sales organization in which employees work independently and socialize only rarely. Such employees often leave their jobs, or if they remain, they never come to see themselves as part of the organization.

Over time, most people do identify with the organizations they join, and they become increasingly integrated. If they leave such organizations, they go through a process of decoupling their identities from the organization and move from being seen as insiders to once again being viewed as outsiders. This leaving process can be difficult, especially if one does not have a new

assimilation
the communicative, behavioral, and cognitive processes that influence individuals to join, identify with, become integrated into, and (occasionally) exit an organization

organizational identification
the stage of assimilation that occurs when an employee's values overlap with the organization's values

When these soldiers joined the U.S. Army, they were not immediately integrated. As they learned about the organizational culture and its rules, they became assimilated.

Students and their families take campus tours that help them assimilate to the culture of the college or university.

Mary Haggerty/The *New York Times*

identity and organizational affiliation. For example, people who retire often feel sad and disconnected because they have lost an important identity.

To help you understand how members assimilate to organizational cultures, we next examine the three stages of organizational assimilation and some of the important communication processes that occur during each (Jablin, 1979, 2001). (For a summary, see *Visual Summary 10.1: Communication Processes in the Stages of Organizational Assimilation.*)

Anticipatory Socialization

Anticipatory socialization describes activities and experiences that occur before an individual enters an organization but that later assist in the assimilation process. Such activities include attending college or training programs where one learns the general norms and practices of one's future career. Medical students, for example, learn the medical profession's hierarchy—for instance, that surgeons typically have the most status and prestige—as well as the code of ethics. Anticipatory socialization also includes activities one engages in before being hired by a specific organization, such as conducting research on the organization, listening to media messages about it, asking current employees about its practices and environment (Jablin, 2001), and even going to job interviews. Job interviews are such an important aspect of both socialization and organizational success that we will now explore the interview process in detail.

The employment interview is the most common way business or corporate organizations recruit, screen, and hire new employees. Although organizations such as social and civic groups typically don't have employment interviews, they may have some type of selection process involving an interview. However, here we will focus on the employment interview.

Large corporations spend considerable resources developing effective interview techniques, training their interviewers, and assessing the quality of the job candidates they select. Because of this, potential job candidates benefit if they become familiar with the types of interview questions and interview formats that employers use. Many interviewers use an "inverted funnel" structure for their questioning: They begin with closed-ended questions (for example, *What was your major?*) and progress toward more open-ended questions throughout the interview (such as *What are your career goals for the next five years?*). In addition, they often use follow-up or probing questions to seek greater clarity and specificity—for example, *You mentioned that you would like to go into management in the next five years. What do you think are the essential communication skills for a manager?* To review twenty typical questions asked during job interviews, see *Did You Know? Twenty Typical Interview Questions.*

The behavioral interview is another type of format. The primary purpose of behavior-based interviews is to identify past work behaviors and/or assess how job candidates are likely to respond to specific situations in the future (Harris, 1989). In this format the interviewer asks questions regarding common work scenarios. For example, potential math instructors might be asked to describe the types of enrichment activities they have used or would use in their classrooms. Candidates for management positions may be asked to explain how they would deliver a negative staff evaluation or describe how they handled a conflict with a coworker. Interviewees can prepare for these interviews by reflecting on the types of behaviors that are most relevant to their potential job positions and then rehearsing their responses.

Strong listening skills also can help interviewees succeed. If you listen carefully, you may notice that your interviewer suggests the "correct" answer by using directed

anticipatory socialization
activities and experiences that occur before an individual enters an organization but that later assist in the assimilation process

Communication Processes in the Stages of Organizational Assimilation

STAGE 3: Metamorphosis

Communication Activities

- Become familiar with others
- Acculturate
- Gain recognition
- Get involved
- Increase job competency
- Negotiate roles

STAGE 2: Encounter

Communication Activities

- Seek information using
  - passive strategies
  - active strategies
  - interactive strategies

STAGE 1: Anticipatory Socialization

Communication Activities

- Attend programs to learn about the career field
- Do research on organizations
- Participate in job interviews

Did You Know?

Twenty Typical Interview Questions

1. How would you describe yourself?
2. What specific goals, including those related to your occupation, have you established for your life?
3. How has your college experience prepared you for a business career?
4. Please describe the ideal job for you following graduation.
5. What influenced you to choose this career?
6. At what point did you choose this career?
7. What specific goals have you established for your career?
8. What will it take to attain your goals, and what steps have you taken toward attaining them?
9. What do you think it takes to be successful in this career?
10. How do you determine or evaluate success? Give me an example of one of your successful accomplishments.
11. Do you have the qualifications and personal characteristics necessary for success in your chosen career?
12. What has been your most rewarding accomplishment?
13. If you could do so, how would you plan your college career differently?
14. Are you more energized by working with data or by collaborating with other individuals?
15. How would you describe yourself in terms of your ability to work as a member of a team?
16. What motivates you to put forth your greatest effort?
17. Given the investment our company will make in hiring and training you, can you give us a reason to hire you?
18. Would you describe yourself as goal-driven?
19. Describe what you've accomplished toward reaching a recent goal for yourself.
20. What short-term goals and objectives have you established for yourself?

FROM: "150 Typical Job Interview Questions," copyright by Quintessential Careers. The original article can be found at www.quintcareers.com/interview_question_database/interview_questions.html. Reprinted with permission.

or leading questions. If an interviewer asks, "You would be willing to relocate, wouldn't you?" the question is phrased to suggest that you should say yes. Listening carefully also can help potential employees gather information about the organization. Noting the types of questions that are asked, how informal or formal the interview process is, how friendly or distant the interviewer's style is, and whether high-ranking employees are called by their first or last names all provide important clues as to what the organization is like. This information can help you determine whether you believe the organization is one in which you will feel comfortable and enjoy working.

Successful interviewing also requires that you understand the basic stages of the interviewing process and that you plan for each one. This process includes a preparatory stage, an introductory stage, the formal interviewing stage, and a concluding stage. The preparatory stage describes the work you do prior to attending the interview. This includes conducting research on the organization and the specific job position for which you are applying, reviewing frequently asked interview questions, practicing answers to them, and planning your wardrobe.

Once you arrive (on time!) for your interview, the introductory stage begins. This includes everything—how you approach the building as well as how you interact with receptionists and other staff you meet before you encounter the interviewer. During this stage of the interview you want to create a favorable first impression, which includes displaying a pleasant demeanor, greeting the interviewer and introducing yourself, and sitting in a relaxed but professional manner.

During the formal interviewing stage you should be prepared to both answer and ask questions. You should answer the interviewer's questions completely, with sufficient detail and examples. However, you should keep your answers focused and not allow yourself to wander off topic. On average your answers should last about one to two minutes. In addition, most interviewers will give you the opportunity to ask questions. Failing to do so may suggest that you lack interest or haven't prepared sufficiently.

Finally, you will want to end by leaving a positive impression of yourself and your abilities. Thank the interviewer for his or her time, express your interest in the position, and leave in a timely manner. If the interviewer has to invite you to leave or indicates that he or she has another pressing appointment, you have stayed too long. When you get home, follow up the interview with a brief note thanking the interviewer again for taking the time to meet with you.

You may think of the employment interview as having only one function: for the employer to select or screen out job applicants. Although this is an important purpose, employment interviews also provide important information for applicants, and these interviews can begin the assimilation process for those who later are hired by the organization.

Interviews can provide initial information on organizational norms, rules, and expectations. For example, some organizations, such as law firms, strongly encourage employees to spend many more than forty hours a week on the job. Other organizations encourage their workers to strive for a balance between their jobs and their lives away from the job. In addition, organizations have expectations regarding how employees should dress, when they should arrive for work, how much they should socialize outside work, and much more. The interviewer can help job candidates assimilate to these practices both explicitly, by talking about them, and implicitly, by modeling the desired behaviors.

Job interviews can begin the assimilation process for individuals hired by the organization.

The Encounter Stage

Once an individual joins an organization, she or he enters the encounter stage. During the **encounter stage**, individuals learn the norms, expectations, and practices of the organization and begin to accept and adapt to them. The communication process most central to this stage is information seeking, a reciprocal process in which individuals seek out information that helps them adapt to the organization, and the organization attempts to convey information that will assist in this process. Two organizational communication scholars, Vernon Miller and Fred Jablin (1991), developed a typology of the information-seeking tactics that newcomers use to ascertain organizational roles, rules, and norms. These strategies take the same forms as other types of uncertainty-reduction techniques (see Chapter 2) and include active, passive, and interactive strategies (Berger, 1979).

The passive strategies new members use include observation and surveillance. These strategies involve watching others' communication and behavior or interpreting stories about past communication and behavior so that one can infer the rules and norms of the organization. For example, if you wonder what time employees typically arrive for work, you could go to work quite early one day and observe who arrives at what time, or you might attend to stories about people who arrived consistently late to work and what happened to them.

Active strategies include overt questioning, indirect questioning, disguising conversations, and questioning third parties. In these instances, the employee tries to discern organizational expectations by acquiring information from others. For example, a new

encounter stage
stage in the assimilation process during which individuals learn the norms, expectations, and practices of the organization and begin to accept and adapt to them

Think about your most recent job. Which of the above strategies did you rely on most as you assimilated to your new organization? Which strategies provided you with the most information?

employee might directly ask a more experienced coworker, "Are we expected to stay after 5 P.M.?" or she might pose the question more indirectly by saying, "How often do most employees stay past 5 P.M.?" Or she could engage in a disguising conversation by complaining about how late she had to stay in her previous job, to see how her colleague responds. In addition, she might ask a third party (a secretary) rather than a primary source (her supervisor) whether employees at her level are expected to stay past five o'clock.

Finally, new employees seek information through the interactive strategy of "testing limits." A newcomer tests limits by seeing how far he or she can push specific boundaries. For instance, an employee might determine whether leaving at 5 P.M. is acceptable by leaving consistently at that time and then noting how people respond.

Metamorphosis

Metamorphosis is the final stage of the assimilation process. It describes the period during which employees come to see themselves as members of the organization, and colleagues see them this way as well. The communication processes that occur during metamorphosis include familiarity with others, organizational acculturation, recognition, involvement, job competency, and role negotiation (Myers, 2005; Myers & Oetzel, 2003).

Familiarity with others occurs when the new hire becomes acquainted with employees in the organization. Generally, people feel more positive toward their organizations and a greater sense of belonging as they get to know and feel accepted by their colleagues. A second process, *organizational acculturation,* happens when new employees accept and integrate into their own lives the norms, values, and expectations of their organizations. When this occurs they no longer feel constrained by the organization's formal and informal policies but embrace them.

Recognition describes employees' feelings that they contribute to their organization and that those contributions are recognized and valued by their colleagues and the organization. *Involvement* captures the feelings of being an active participant in the organization and of being willing to go beyond what is required. *Job competency* reflects employees' feelings that they can accomplish their jobs successfully, and *role negotiation* is the process through which they adapt to the requirements of their role(s) within the organization while at the same time placing limits on the degree to which they will adapt.

Supervisor–Subordinate Communication

In addition to assimilation and the multiple processes within it, a second general category of communication within organizations is that between supervisors and subordinates. Supervisor–subordinate communication occurs when one person has the formal authority to regulate the behavior of another. In hierarchical organizations, virtually all employees engage in supervisor–subordinate communication, even CEOs—who must report upward to boards of directors (their supervisors) and downward to other organizational members (their subordinates).

When organizational hierarchies exist, subordinates frequently attempt to please their supervisors to keep their jobs, receive raises and promotions, or perhaps even to become supervisors themselves someday. By the same token, successful supervisors must motivate and manage their subordinates. These sets of needs impact how supervisors and subordinates communicate. Next we explore several dimensions of supervisor–subordinate communication that impact their relationships with each other and their success within the organization. These include semantic-information distance, perceptual co-orientation, and successful communication strategies.

Semantic-Information Distance

Although most supervisors and subordinates communicate frequently, they often have very different perceptions of the organization and their communication with each other (Jablin, 1979). For example, supervisors and subordinates often disagree

metamorphosis
the final stage of the socialization process during which employees come to see themselves as members of the organization, and colleagues see them this way as well

on how decisions are made, how frequently they communicate, and the persuasive abilities of subordinates.

These perceptual differences are called semantic-information distance. **Semantic-information distance** describes the gap in information and understanding between supervisors and subordinates on specific issues (Dansereau & Markham, 1987). What causes this gap? Behaviors of both subordinates and supervisors contribute, but we'll look at the subordinate side first. See *It Happened to Me: Yoshi* for an employee's views on this communication gap.

When subordinates are hesitant to communicate negative news and present information in a more positive light than is warranted, they engage in a behavior called **upward distortion** (Dansereau & Markham, 1987). Why do subordinates do this? Employees naturally edit the information they send upward, because not everything is relevant to their bosses and because they can manage many issues without the supervisor's intervention. However, when workers withhold or alter important information, supervisors may be making decisions based on distorted and inadequate information. This can impact their ability to perform their own jobs successfully. For example, if an

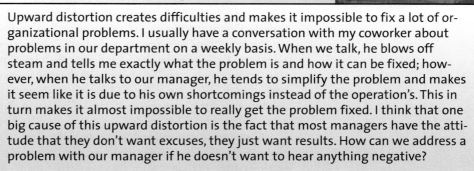

It Happened to Me: Yoshi

Upward distortion creates difficulties and makes it impossible to fix a lot of organizational problems. I usually have a conversation with my coworker about problems in our department on a weekly basis. When we talk, he blows off steam and tells me exactly what the problem is and how it can be fixed; however, when he talks to our manager, he tends to simplify the problem and makes it seem like it is due to his own shortcomings instead of the operation's. This in turn makes it almost impossible to really get the problem fixed. I think that one big cause of this upward distortion is the fact that most managers have the attitude that they don't want excuses, they just want results. How can we address a problem with our manager if he doesn't want to hear anything negative?

employee knows that an important production deadline is looming, he or she may be reluctant to tell the supervisor that the deadline can't be met, for fear of reprisals or blame. Fear of negative repercussions is probably the most important reason that employees distort information as they communicate with their supervisors.

Supervisors, too, may communicate a more positive image than they actually perceive. Why? They do so in part because they need to motivate employees and to create and maintain employee satisfaction with the organization. Employee satisfaction is central to the supervisor–subordinate relationship and, ultimately, to the supervisor's ability to influence subordinates and impact their performance. For example, employee satisfaction has been linked to decreased absenteeism and decreased turnover as well as increased productivity (Richmond, McCroskey, & Davis, 1986).

Although the reasons for it make intuitive sense, semantic-information distance can cause problems in supervisor–subordinate relationships. Supervisors need accurate, honest information to perform successfully. Therefore, when they become aware that employees have been distorting information, they are unlikely to trust or reward those employees. Of course, supervisors also need to communicate clearly so subordinates have the information they need to perform their jobs competently. When supervisors and subordinates share accurate information, they are more likely to experience perceptual co-orientation, the topic we discuss next.

Perceptual Co-Orientation

Perceptual co-orientation describes occasions when two people share similar perceptions and recognize that their perceptions agree (Farace, Monge, & Russell, 1977). Supervisors and subordinates who share perceptions, especially the perception that they agree, evaluate their relationship more positively (Eisenberg, Monge, & Farace, 1984).

Supervisors and subordinates need to establish open and trusting relationships to achieve perceptual co-orientation. Employees who feel secure in their positions, who trust their supervisors, and who are willing to take responsibility for their own actions are better able, and more likely, to convey accurate information to their bosses. In addition, subordinates who are able to communicate their perceptual

semantic-information distance
describes the gap in information and understanding between supervisors and subordinates on specific issues

upward distortion
occurs when subordinates are hesitant to communicate negative news and present information to superiors in a more positive light than is warranted

perceptual co-orientation
a state in which two people share similar perceptions and recognize that their perceptions agree

openness
a state in which communicators are willing to share their ideas as well as listen to others in a way that avoids conveying negative or disconfirming feedback

supportiveness
refers to supervisors who provide their subordinates with access to information and resources

motivation
feeling personally invested in accomplishing a specific activity or goal

empowerment
employees' feelings of self-efficacy

co-orientation to their supervisors tend to get along with their bosses better and are more successful (James, 2007, Mar. 8). Other communication processes between supervisors and subordinates enhance and build on the benefits of co-orientation, and we discuss these next.

Successful Supervisor–Subordinate Communication

A supervisor's communication with her subordinates largely determines how she is perceived and responded to. The supervisor who is liked and has developed a positive relationship with subordinates is more likely to experience job satisfaction and to have subordinates who are satisfied with her supervision. Although many communication strategies contribute to supervisor success, we highlight four: openness, supportiveness, motivation, and empowerment.

Openness occurs when communicators are willing to share their ideas and listen to others in a way that avoids conveying negative or disconfirming feedback (Cheney, 1995; Jablin, 1979). When supervisors are open, they create an environment of trust that decreases the likelihood that upward communication will be distorted.

Even though openness is a desirable characteristic, one can engage in *too much* openness. For example, if an employee is on leave to undergo rehabilitation for addiction, a supervisor typically should not share that information directly, or even indirectly, with others, as doing so would be inappropriate. In addition, sometimes supervisors need to shield their employees from information. For example, informing subordinates of a possible layoff before the decision is final could cause unnecessary stress and panic.

Supportive supervisors provide their subordinates with access to information and resources. Thus, supportive supervisors explain roles, responsibilities, and tasks to those they manage; they also take the time to answer employees' questions. Further, managers are supportive when they give their subordinates the tools, skills, education, and time they need to be successful. Overall, supervisors who help their employees solve problems, listen actively, provide feedback, and offer encouragement not only are supportive, they are successful (Whetton & Cameron, 2002).

Productive and successful supervisors are able to motivate their subordinates. Workers experience **motivation** when they feel personally invested in accomplishing a specific activity or goal (Kreps, 1991). Many U.S. American supervisors and organizations focus on creating extrinsic or external motivators, such as pay raises, bonuses, promotions, titles, and benefits. However, supervisors who can instill intrinsic motivation in their subordinates are more successful. Intrinsic motivation occurs when people experience satisfaction in performing their jobs well, find their jobs to be enriching and are, therefore, dedicated to their organizations or professions (Cheney et al., 2004).

Supervisors can create intrinsic motivation by setting clear and specific goals that are challenging but attainable, and by engaging workers in the creation of those goals. In addition, they need to provide frequent and specific feedback, including praise, recognition, and corrections. Positive feedback is especially important, because it encourages job satisfaction, organizational identification, and commitment (Larson, 1989). Finally, intrinsic motivation thrives in a positive work environment that stresses camaraderie.

Empowerment, the fourth characteristic that improves communication, relates to the supervisor's ability to increase employees' feelings of self-efficacy. They do this by instilling the feeling that the subordinate is capable of performing the job and has the authority to decide how to perform it well (Chiles & Zorn, 1995). In general, supervisors who empower their subordinates function more like coaches than traditional managers. They encourage employees to be involved in decision making, to take responsibility for their tasks, and to provide suggestions for improving their own and the organization's performance. Employees who feel empowered are more likely to develop intrinsic motivation and to communicate openly with their supervisors.

Communication is also central to subordinates' success on the job. Subordinates who get along with their supervisors are much more likely to be satisfied and successful. Consequently, subordinates use a variety of means to manage and maintain

Think about supervisors you have had. What was it about their communication strategies that you liked or disliked? Which of the strategies we've mentioned here did they use?

the quality of their relationships with their supervisors. Studies of subordinate communication tactics determined that employees who use three specific upward communication tactics—ingratiation, assertiveness, and rationality—were most likely to positively affect their manager's perceptions of them (Dockery & Steiner, 1990; Wayne & Ferris, 1990).

Ingratiation refers to behavior and communication designed to increase liking. It includes friendliness and making one's boss feel important. Of course, one can be too ingratiating and come off as being insincere, but genuine respect and rapport can be effective. **Assertive** subordinates who can express their opinions forcefully without offending or challenging their bosses also tend to engender liking and approval. In addition, subordinates who can argue **rationally**—meaning that they communicate with their bosses through reasoning, bargaining, coalition building, and assertiveness—are often adept at managing their supervisors. Finally, employees who understand their bosses' professional and personal goals as well as their strengths and weaknesses, and who can adapt to their preferred communication styles, can create positive working relationships.

Communicating with Coworkers

Along with assimilation and supervisor–subordinate communication, communication with coworkers is fundamental to organizations and their employees. Sometimes the communication that occurs among coworkers or peers is described as *horizontal*, because it is directed neither upward (to superiors) nor downward (to subordinates). No matter how they are described, workplace relationships are distinctive interpersonal relationships that influence both the individuals within them and the organization as a whole (Sias, 2005).

Employees become friends with their colleagues for many of the same reasons they develop other types of interpersonal relationships—proximity, attraction, and similarity. Some people, especially those who live alone, may spend more time with their colleagues than they do with anyone else. Even people who live with others may spend as much—or more—time with coworkers as they do with their families or housemates. However, unlike other interpersonal relationships, friendship development at work is affected by an additional dimension—how supervisors treat individual employees. If supervisors are perceived to treat some employees more favorably and this treatment is perceived as undeserved, coworkers may dislike and distrust favored employees. On the other hand, if a manager is seen as treating a subordinate more negatively than others and the treatment is perceived as unwarranted, it can increase employee interaction and cohesiveness (Graen & Graen, 2006; Sias & Jablin, 1995).

Coworkers in organizations engage in both formal–professional and informal–personal interactions. The formal–professional category includes communication about tasks, solving problems, making plans, and influencing one another's beliefs and decisions (Kram & Isabella, 1985). In addition, coworkers engage in considerable informal, or personal, interaction. In fact, adults draw many of their friends from the pool of people at work, and approximately 50 percent of employees state that they have engaged in a romance at work (Vault, 2003). Coworkers also can serve as an important source of emotional and social support (Rawlins, 1994).

The professional and the personal aspects of coworker communication and relationships are not distinct. Rather, professional interactions influence coworkers' personal relationships, and vice versa.

ingratiation
behavior and communication designed to increase liking

assertiveness
expressing one's opinions forcefully without offending others

rationality
the ability to communicate through reasoning, bargaining, coalition building, and assertiveness

In the movie *Office Space,* these coworkers engage in considerable informal and personal interactions, including launching a plan to take revenge on the company for its planned layoffs.

Sias and Cahill (1998) found that more talk about more topics among coworkers not only resulted from increased closeness in their relationships but also contributed to it. Thus, coworkers who also are friends tend to communicate more intimately and about more topics, both professionally and personally, than those who are not (Sias, Smith, & Avdeyeva, 2003). They also tend to be both less careful and more open in their communication with each other (Sias & Jablin, 1995). Therefore, they are likely to provide increased and more useful task-related information to each other.

As you might expect, being isolated from employee networks can result in isolation from quality work-related information (in addition to loneliness) and cause one to be at an information disadvantage relative to one's colleagues (Sias, 2005). Research indicates that this information disadvantage has important consequences. Poor coworker communication and lack of access to information have been found to predict lower job satisfaction and commitment.

The presence of friendly relationships among coworkers has positive consequences for individuals and organizations. When employees feel connected to their colleagues, they provide each other with support and assistance that can increase their success. Such relationships also intensify workers' loyalty to the company and increase job satisfaction and organizational identification, which can help minimize job turnover (Kram & Isabella, 1985).

Despite the ease, attractiveness, and advantages of forming close relationships at work, such relationships can require careful navigation. Friendship, by its nature, is egalitarian, but power differences often occur among coworkers. Even employees at the same level in the organization may have different levels of informal power, and the situation can become increasingly problematic if one of them receives a promotion and thereby acquires greater formal power in the organization. In addition, coworkers may find themselves torn between their loyalty to the organization and their loyalty to a friend. For example, how should one respond if a friend engages in unethical behavior at work, decides to become a whistleblower, or quits in protest over a denied promotion? It can be difficult for individuals to decide how to respond in a way that protects their own as well as their friend's interests. Finally, it can be more difficult to be objective with a friend, to withhold confidential information, and to provide honest feedback.

In addition, other employees can develop negative perceptions and interpretations of the friendships and courtship relationships of their colleagues. Coworkers may question the motives of the partners, may believe that the individuals involved are conspiring to affect corporate policy, or may perceive that the relationship partners treat others unfairly in comparison. For instance, if two salespeople become close, their coworkers may perceive that they are sharing information or client lists that permit them to be more successful than those outside the relationship. In addition, because of the potential for trouble and bad feelings, some organizations have explicit policies that discourage "affectional" relationships, which may include friendships but most certainly include romance. For suggestions on how supervisors can encourage good coworker communication, see *Did You Know? Encouraging Effective Coworker Communication*.

Organizational Dilemmas

Although organizations can provide many benefits to an individual, including status, money, a sense of belonging, and even a significant part of one's identity, they also can create physical and psychological distress. Thus in addition to being proficient at the three key types of organizational communication, members of organizations may have to communicatively manage and respond to three types of organizational dilemmas: emotion labor, stress and burnout, and work-life conflict. These dilemmas tend to surface when individuals work in organizations engaged in economic production.

Did You Know?

Encouraging Effective Coworker Communication

- **Communicate your vision.** If you're the team leader, your job is really about communicating clearly. By choosing words that connect with different learning styles and personality types, you can paint a picture of the end goal everyone can get excited about.

- **Make sure your expectations are clear.** Team members won't be able to be successful if they don't know what's expected of them. Make sure that everyone knows what they need to do to be successful—this creates a collaborative environment that is more open and trusting and ultimately more supportive and productive.

- **Be definitive about a time frame.** Let others know specifically when you need what you're requesting of them. If the time frame spans a long period, establish checkpoints (one week, two weeks) where you can check in to find out how things are going. This keeps a big project from going horribly wrong when the writers have been holed up in an office for three weeks playing video games and suffering from writers' block.

- **Invite feedback and questions.** The "open door" policy may be a myth in some offices, but listening nondefensively—to questions, concerns, and criticism—is a huge part of building honest communication with others. This shows that everyone has a voice in the success of the project and helps create the openness for creativity and trust to emerge.

- **Encourage and support good communication.** To show others that improving teamwork is important, you might host a series of lunches, invite a speaker in to give an afternoon seminar on communications skills, or hire a consultant to help with team relations. The most important way to encourage good communication is to model it yourself—to make mistakes, to honestly explain what happened, and to try again, all in the name of moving toward better communication with your peers.

FROM: "Improve Staff Communications," by Katherine Murray, www.revisionsplus.com/February article.doc. Reprinted by permission of the author.

Emotion Labor

As we discussed earlier, employees learn a variety of norms for organizational behavior during assimilation. Some of these norms pertain to emotion display rules (Scott & Myers, 2005). Emotion display rules are the explicit or implicit rules that organizations have for what emotions can be appropriately displayed and how those emotions should be communicated. For example, firefighters learn early in the assimilation process that they should not express strong negative emotions such as fear, disgust, and panic (Scott & Myers, 2005). Instead, they learn to speak in calm tones, to offer verbal assurances, and to suppress any comments that might distress the public. Similarly, the employees at our local grocery store have learned to show cheerfulness and helpfulness toward customers, even if they actually feel irritation, anger, or frustration. Consequently, no matter how their day is going, they greet customers with a friendly hello, offer assistance, and wish customers a good day as they leave the store.

When the organization expects or requires workers to display particular feelings, employees are engaging in emotion labor (Hochschild, 1983). Typically, organizations ask employees to alter their emotional behavior in three ways. First, they may ask employees to heighten or increase their expressions of joy (i.e., cruise ship and other tourism employees), to appear mean or indifferent (debt collectors and

law officers, on occasion), or to convey "a vaguely pleasant professional demeanor" (nurses and receptionists) (Cheney et al., 2004, p. 68). (For one student's experience with emotion labor, see *It Happened to Me: Sonya.*)

Some scholars believe that performing emotion labor benefits employees. They argue that when workers perform emotions they do not actually feel, they can better cope with stress (Conrad & Witte, 1994), and they are more able to interact in emotionally satisfying ways with their clients (Shuler & Sypher, 2000). These scholars suggest that social workers, emergency medical personnel, and other employees in the social services find their work easier and more meaningful when they perform emotion labor.

It Happened to Me: Sonya

For a year, I worked on a cruise line as an assistant cruise director. My job was to organize activities and help entertain the passengers. I helped with bingo games, organized costume contests, and participated in various games with the passengers. In addition, I was expected to dance with the passengers in the evening at the nightclub. Unfortunately, I often had to deal with passengers who had had a few drinks and wanted to "get friendly" or invite me back to their rooms. No matter how the passenger behaved, I was expected to be polite, pleasant, and friendly without, of course, ever actually becoming involved with one! It was really difficult sometimes. I would be so angry, upset, or embarrassed at how a passenger behaved, but I could never show it. This is one of the major reasons I did not sign up again after my first year on the ship.

Others believe it can be harmful (Tracy, 2000; Waldron, 1994), especially when it is required and when it benefits the organization but not the employee. For example, Sarah Tracy (2005), an organizational communication scholar, studied correctional officers' emotion labor and its consequences. She found that the officers often were expected to manage contradictory emotional displays—for example, showing respect for inmates but not trusting them, or nurturing them while also being tough. She discovered that performing these contradictory emotions led some of the officers to experience withdrawal, paranoia, stress, and burnout. Thus consistently having to perform emotion labor, especially when the requirements are ambiguous and contradictory, can cause psychological and physical harm to some workers.

Stress and Burnout

As you just read, correctional officers often experience stress and burnout. But they are not the only employees who suffer in this way; stress and burnout have become widespread in the American workplace, and the term has become common in everyday speech. However, **burnout** includes a very specific set of characteristics, including exhaustion, cynicism, and ineffectiveness (Maslach & Leiter, 1997; Maslach, 2003). It is a chronic condition that results from the accumulation of daily stress, where stress is defined as a common reponse to important and consequential demands, constraints, or opportunities to which one feels unable to respond (McGrath, 1976).

Exhaustion, which is a core characteristic of burnout, can include physical, emotional, or mental exhaustion. It expresses itself as physical fatigue, loss of affect (or emotion), and an aversion to one's job. Employees who are emotionally exhausted may try to reduce the emotional stress of working with others by detaching from them, a behavior called depersonalization, which is related to the second characteristic of burnout—cynicism. Cynicism is manifested as an indifferent attitude toward others. A person with a cynical attitude may view others as objects or numbers, and may also express hostility and harsh criticism toward them. Employees might feel ineffective, the third characteristic of burnout, which occurs when workers negatively evaluate their own performance. Ineffectiveness may result in absenteeism, decreased effort, and withdrawal (Richardsen & Martinussen, 2004).

Burnout arises due to a combination of personality factors (for example, how well one manages ambiguity and stress) and organizational stressors. Organizational stressors are aspects of one's job that create strain. Some of the more significant

burnout
a chronic condition that results from the accumulation of daily stress, which manifests itself in a very specific set of characteristics, including exhaustion, cynicism, and ineffectiveness

organizational stressors include work overload; confusion, conflict, and ambiguity related to job roles; being undermined by a supervisor (Westman & Etzion, 2005); and low levels of social support (Koniarek & Dudek, 1996).

Workload refers to the amount of work an individual is expected to perform. Work overload occurs when employees feel they have more work than they can accomplish, and this is a major contributor to feelings of exhaustion. Despite expectations that technology, and especially computer technology, would lessen the burden for workers in the United States, people today are working longer hours and dealing with heavier workloads than before the advent of these technologies. In addition, workers frequently find that now they are never "away" from the job, since they are instantly and constantly available through cell phones, BlackBerries, and pagers. The resulting work pressures are having an increasingly negative effect on individuals, families, and organizations (Glisson & Durick, 1988).

Work overload also is related to our second major organizational stressor—role confusion, conflict, and ambiguity. Role ambiguity occurs when employees do not understand what is expected of them. This is most likely to occur when one begins a new job, but it also occurs when organizations undergo change (Chambers, Moore, & Bachtel, 1998). Because today's workers are faced with continual change due to budget cuts, reorganizations, and new technologies, they frequently experience role ambiguity (Chambers et al., 1998).

To give some perspective on the role ambiguity and confusion play as work stressors, consider this. As recently as twenty years ago, newly hired engineers primarily needed to communicate with other engineers, most of whom were born in the United States and were native speakers of English. Since that time however, U.S. companies have hired more engineers from other countries and have expanded their operations around the world. Consequently, many engineers now need to communicate with and supervise others who do not share their native culture and background. They have been required to develop intercultural communication skills they never expected would be necessary and to become conversant with cultures outside the United States. Some long-term employees are unsure of their ability to respond appropriately. Employees in many industries face similar challenges as organizations respond to changing market conditions, globalization, and new technology. Unfortunately, uncertainty about one's job duties and one's ability to perform those duties creates considerable stress for workers.

Role conflict arises when employees find it difficult to meet conflicting or incompatible job demands (Igbaria & Guimaraes, 1993). For example, the correctional officers we mentioned in our discussion of emotion labor experienced considerable role conflict. On the one hand, they were expected to act like social workers whose job it was to treat prisoners with respect, to nurture them, and to facilitate their well-being and rehabilitation; on the other hand, they were expected to function as paramilitary agents whose job it was to maintain order and safety, to mistrust the prisoners, and to be tough. Similarly, when managers are told to treat their employees fairly and humanely but also to meet tight production deadlines, they suffer from role conflict. Research indicates that being asked to perform such incompatible tasks on the job gives rise to considerable stress and ill effects (Rizzo, House, & Lirtzman, 1970). For example, role conflict and ambiguity can cycle into burnout, leading workers to experience feelings of ineffectiveness in their jobs.

To complete our discussion of organizational stressors and burnout we focus squarely on communication issues. When employees feel undermined by their supervisors, whether through having information withheld, being denied the resources they need to do their jobs, or being treated unfairly, they are more likely to experience cynicism and a lack of efficacy (Maslach & Leiter, 1997). They may feel they cannot accomplish their work because they lack the resources to do so, and they may believe that even if they do perform well, they will not be rewarded.

Communication with coworkers can contribute to burnout when one's colleagues are unable to provide the social support one needs to cope with organizational stressors. Feelings of burnout then may spread from one employee to his or her colleagues. This fact, combined with the faster pace of most organizations, can lead to a breakdown of community within the organization and disconnect coworkers from one another (Maslach & Leiter, 1997).

Interestingly, research has established that communication itself can be an important moderator of employee burnout. Findings show that supervisor communication that includes active listening, effective feedback, participative decision making, and supportiveness can decrease the severity of subordinate burnout (Casey, 1998; Golembiewski, Boudreau, Sun, & Luo, 1998). Similarly, communication with coworkers that conveys warmth and support and reaffirms the meaning of one's work can help employees cope with burnout (Casey, 1998).

If you would like to see if you are experiencing burnout, go to **www.mindtools. com/pages/article/newTCS_08.htm** and take the Burnout Self-Test.

Work–Life Conflict

A third type of organizational dilemma that workers face is work–life conflict, defined by the difficulties individuals and families face as they try to balance job and home responsibilities. Since the 1990s, work–family balance has become an issue of concern and another type of role conflict, especially for dual-career couples (Kirby & Krone, 2002). As more women have entered the workforce, and more families have become reliant on two incomes, people are finding it difficult to manage their competing demands. The pervasiveness of communication technologies such as email, cell phones, instant messaging, and pagers, has made it difficult for some workers to ever get away from work and focus on the other aspects of their lives.

In response to these concerns, organizations began to develop family-friendly policies, such as flextime, family leave, and dependent-care benefits (Morgan & Milliken, 1992). However, studies have shown that many employees do not take advantage of these benefits (Kirby & Krone, 2002; Rapoport & Bailyn, 1996). The reality is, researchers have found, that some employees are discouraged from taking advantage of these benefits, or are not informed about their existence. For example, managers may indirectly communicate that employees should not use the available benefits because it causes problems for them, their departments, and the organization (Rapoport & Bailyn, 1996).

Many U.S. workers must deal with work–life conflict.

A study of Corning, Xerox, and Tandem Computers determined that employees who used such benefits experienced negative career consequences (Rapoport & Bailyn, 1996). Once employees discovered that their coworkers suffered when they used the company's family leave or flextime benefits, they simply stopped requesting them. Kirby and Krone (2002) conducted another study whose title aptly describes this organizational policy: "The Policy Exists, But You Can't Really Use It." The irony is that some organizations receive credit for being family friendly while not having to actually implement their policies (Jenner, 1994; Solomon, 1994). However, when workers are not able to balance the many demands in their lives, they, their families, and society at large suffer the consequences.

To summarize, communication is central to an individual's life within an organization, and individuals face many communication-related issues as they navigate organizations. Such challenges involve assimilation as well as communication with supervisors, subordinates, and coworkers. Inevitably, conflicts arise, as do a variety of potential organizational dilemmas, including emotion labor, stress and burnout, and work–life conflict. Thus, successful individuals are those who are able to communicate effectively as they negotiate the challenges, conflicts, and dilemmas of organizational life. However, as you've seen throughout this book, if you only consider individual forces or factors, you can't understand the whole picture. Individuals and organizations both are subject to numerous societal forces, the topic we turn to next.

THE INDIVIDUAL, ORGANIZATIONAL COMMUNICATION, AND SOCIETY

In this section we explore how organizations and the societies in which they are located exert influence upon each other and the individuals within them. First we examine two of the most significant societal forces that impact organizational communication—history and globalization. Next we discuss four of the important recent organizational practices that influence individuals and society, including the development of a new social contract between organizations and employees, the increase in organizations' use of contingent workers, the rise of urgent organizations, and the blurring of boundaries between home and work. Finally, we examine power relations within organizations and their impact on employees. We address these topics to explicate how each has influenced beliefs about organizational communication and its performance.

Societal Influences on Organizations

Organizations are shaped in part by the societies in which they are located. As societies change over time, so do the organizations within them. In addition, as organizations spread their operations into new cultures, they must change and adapt to those cultures to be successful. In the next section, we focus on these two societal influences on organizations: (1) social change and its impact on organizations and the communication within them, and (2) globalization and it effects on organizations and organizational communication.

Historical Forces

Prevailing beliefs about work, individuals, and knowledge creation have influenced the very ways that organizational communication is studied and the resulting recommendations for how people in organizations should communicate. For example, until the early 1900s, popular talk about organizational techniques took a moral tone. Journalists, novelists, clergy, and other prominent figures often described business owners as men of superior character, which they were obligated to model for the betterment of the lower, working class (Barley & Kunda, 1992). During this time, managers' and owners' opinions and communication were considered important while those of the working classes were not.

The early 1900s saw a sharp turn from moralizing toward scientific techniques. This change occurred because of important advances in how goods were produced. For example, Henry Ford's development of the assembly line for his auto plant resulted in a new focus on efficiency and mass production. As a result, organizational experts focused on efficiency in the production of goods. A consultant named Frederick Taylor (1911) was one of the strongest advocates for the **scientific management** approach, a technique that rested on several principles. First, he believed there was one best way to complete any task and that rigorous study would help him find it. Taylor thus developed **time and motion studies**, which involve repeated measurements of detailed task variables to determine the most efficient combination. Using this research, he determined that a steel worker of a certain build was at his most efficient when he was lifting a certain amount of ore a certain number of times per hour. Taylor also urged a clear division of labor, so that managers were responsible for planning, and workers were responsible for implementing plans. Consequently, organizations that adhered to his principles encouraged downward communication but discouraged upward communication: Managers were encouraged to express their ideas, and workers were discouraged from doing so. Communication among workers was seen as an impediment to efficiency, so it, too, was discouraged.

In the 1930s, another major change in thinking about organization and communication occurred. Mary Parker Follett (1942) was among the most progressive management thinkers of her time. In an age when few questioned the absolute right of managers to command and control employees, she proposed a focus on **human relations**, meaning

scientific management
approach to management advocated by Frederick Taylor, who believed there was a best way to complete any task and that rigorous study would help him find it

time and motion studies
repeated measurements of detailed task variables to determine their most efficient combination

human relations
approach to management that holds that the job of management is actually to educate, interact, and integrate

human resources
approach to management that holds that workers are not only economically motivated but that they also bring personal histories and emotional needs to work with them

general systems theory
theory that organizations are a system composed of many subsystems and embedded in larger systems, and that organizations should develop communication strategies that serve both

that management is actually about education (teaching and persuading), interaction (seeking input), and integration (synthesizing input). She advocated collaboration as an effective conflict-resolution strategy. Organizational conflict should not be addressed from the point of view of power *over*, she said, but about power *with*. Thus, for the first time, organizational theorists and managers came to believe that workers needed to have a voice in the organization.

A continued emphasis on the rights of workers led to the **human resources** movement. Proponents of this perspective argued that workers are not only economically motivated but that they also bring personal histories and emotional needs to work with them. Good managers, therefore, encouraged open communication, listened to employee perspectives, sympathized with them, and engaged in persuasive efforts rather than force (Roethlisberger, 1968).

A variety of developments around the 1960s prompted another shift in thinking about organizations and communication (Barley & Kunda, 1992), toward what we might call a *systems mentality*. Military operations research began to find a home in industry, and the rise of computers fostered interest in organizational communication processes. Across many academic disciplines, researchers began a quest for general, even universal, theoretical principles. Biologist Ludwig von Bertalanffy (1968), for instance, developed a highly influential **general systems theory** that, he believed, applied as well to the social sciences as it did to the life and physical sciences. Many organization scholars agreed. They saw organizations as systems not only comprised of many subsystems but also embedded in larger systems. Hence, they sought to develop strategies for communication that occur within the units or subsystems of the organization as well for communication that occurs between the organization and its environment.

Today, many organizational researchers focus on what they see as increasingly subtle forms of power within organizations, a perspective that often is called the critical approach, as discussed in Chapter 2. These scholars seek to help workers reflect on their work relationships and the consequences of these relationships for their lives. Two central premises of this approach are as follows:

- Organizational structures and practices are inherently political. In other words, organizational communication inevitably produces and reproduces relationships of power.

- Power relations in organizations are neither arbitrary nor neutral. They predictably support dominant groups and work to the disadvantage of subordinate groups—for example, managers over workers, men over women, and so on.

An illustration of this approach to organizations comes from feminist perspectives on organization. The first key assumptions of this view is that organizing, as well as theory about it, is "gendered" in ways that routinely privilege men and masculinity. Second, feminists argue that such inequalities are unethical, impractical, and changeable. In other words, they argue, it is morally indefensible to limit organizational opportunities to one gender. It is also a poor business decision, because women comprise nearly half the available workforce. Finally, they suggest that gender inequalities in organizations are not natural, though they may appear to be so. Hence, the goal of feminist organizational communication studies is to expose how gender inequality works and thereby improve the working lives of women and men.

What does it mean to say that organizations are gendered? Simply put, it means that organizations are biased toward, and even built around, a particular model of gender identity and relations. Acker (1990) uses the case of bureaucracy to explain. Acker contends that the problem begins with bureaucracy's rigid split of public from private life. Think first of *what* we associate with the

©Jim Sizemore/www.CartoonStock.com

"Mr. Bigmeister says you may come in, but *only* if you promise to respect the present hierarchy of dominance."

private sphere—domestic and family life, emotions, and sexuality, among other things. Now ask yourself with *whom* we tend to associate these elements of the private sphere. Historically, women have borne primary responsibility for domestic and family life. Emotions and sexuality are typically associated with femininity as well. Arguably, then, bureaucracy subtly privileges men and masculinity with its quest for impersonal relations and its reliance on members who can devote most of their time to work.

Moreover, bureaucracy invites suspicion of women and things associated with femininity by relying heavily on the suppression of private life. For example, as we noted in Chapter 5, emotional or relational communication styles may be viewed as weak, while certain physical displays (pregnant bellies, visible breasts) are likely to be seen as unprofessional.

For many women, looking and sounding professional means imitating a style associated with masculinity. Yet women may also be criticized for not living up to expectations for femininity, which makes it difficult for them to enact a style that is both "authoritative" (masculine) and "appropriate" (feminine) (Ashcraft & Allen, 2003). Recently though, more organizations have begun to advocate transformational leadership models (as we discussed in Chapter 9) that adopt more traditionally feminine or socioemotional forms of communication. As this practice spreads, women may find it easier to manifest the leadership and communication styles favored by organizations.

Globalization

In the past twenty years, one of the most important societal factors to impact organizations, and the individuals who work within them is globalization. **Globalization** refers to the increasing connectedness of the world in economic, political, and cultural realms (Cheney et al., 2004). Although we typically think of globalization in economic terms, it also describes the ways in which political and cultural events affect people around the world. For example, terrorist attacks in Europe and the Middle East influence tourists' travel plans as well as governments' political alliances. From an economic perspective, conflict in the Middle East leads both to fears that oil production will suffer and to higher energy costs in the United States and other countries reliant on this source of oil. One of the more controversial aspects of globalization in the United States is outsourcing. For example, India is now a major site for outsourcing software and other technology needs because of its highly educated workforce and low labor costs. Because of globalization, people in the United States are connected intimately to other parts of the world; as a result, decisions and events in far-removed places can affect them.

What are the communication implications of globalization? First, it means that more people and businesses have intercultural contact and that they need to learn how to communicate more effectively across cultures, as we noted in Chapter 7. Many categories of individuals need to interact with support personnel around the world, even in their nonwork lives, and increasingly workers in multinational organizations must communicate and work with people from diverse cultures. Second, global forces such as market deregulation may have leveling or homogenizing effects on organizational practices all over the world. For an amusing take on globalization, see *Communication in Society: My Outsourced Life*.

Influence of Organizations on Individuals and Society

Not only are organizations influenced by society and cultures, they influence them and the individuals who compose them. In this section we explore four trends in contemporary organizations and the ways in which they impact society and individuals' lives. These trends include the new social contract, contingent workforces, urgent organizations, and blurred boundaries between work and life.

The New Social Contract

Over the past 20 years, a fundamental change has occurred in the relationship between individuals and their employers (Chilton & Weidenbaum, 1994; Jablin & Sias, 2001). Until recently, employees expected to spend years, if not their entire working

globalization
the increasing connectedness of the world in economic, political, and cultural realms

COMMUNICATION IN SOCIETY
Hollywood to Script Outsourcing Saga

Chidanand Rajghatta

Hollywood will take stab at the practice of outsourcing to India as seen through the eyes of an American writer. Universal Pictures has just bought the film rights to an Esquire article titled "My Outsourced Life" by A. J. Jacobs, a scribe whose off the wall feats include reading the 33-volume, 44-million word Encylopoedia Britannica end-to-end.

"Jacobs, Esquire's editor-at-large, wrote the outsourcing article after he discovered that he could farm out almost everything in his life to India, from ordering his food to fighting with his wife."

"I got the idea while reading Tom Friedman's *The World Is Flat*," he explained in an interview to this correspondent on Wednesday.

"I divided up my work life and home life and sent out the tasks to two Bangalore-based companies. It was just wonderful."

Jacobs' aides in this outsourcing saga were Honey K. Balani of the firm Brickworks, who handled his professional needs such as fixing appointments and researching for his articles, and Asha of Your Man in India (YMII), who handled personal tasks.

To begin with they answered his e-mails, fixed his appointments, ordered his groceries and bought his movie tickets, Jacobs said.

By the end of the month-long exercise, they were making weekly calls to his parents and reading his son bedtime stories. Honey Balani was even giving him story ideas for Esquire.

In one particularly capricious episode, Jacobs, after a domestic quarrel, outsourced a complaint against his wife to Asha.

Asha e-mails Julie on behalf of Jacobs: "Julie, I do understand your anger that I forgot to pick up the cash at the ATM.

I have been forgetful and I am sorry about that, but it does not change the fact that I love you very much." Asha also sends Julie an e-card with hugging teddy bears.

How does Julie feel about this? "I thought it was totally pathetic. AJ, who does not like confrontation whatsoever, was now using a woman 4,000 miles away to handle my confrontation skills," she told ABC's Good Morning America, forgetting that she too could have outsourced her gripe against Jacobs to India.

"I thought Asha was more diplomatic than I could be," Jacobs told Times News Network.

The result of all these outsourcing escapades is a hilarious piece in the September issue of Esquire that is now being made into a movie. Unfortunately for Bangalore—and Bollywood—the making of the movie itself is not being outsourced, although this correspondent could do the screenplay at cut-rate prices.

The comedy will be sized up for Universal by Jay Roach, who directed and co-wrote such blockbuster hits as Meet the Parents and Meet the Fockers.

Jacobs is the author of "The Know-It-All: One Man's Humble Quest to Become the Smartest Person in the World," a chronicle of his reading the entire 44-million word Britannica and his resultant mastery over trivia. That story is also being made into a movie by Barry Sonnenfeld, who made Men in Black.

(Asked what trivia he could recall about India from his encyclopediac excursions, Jacobs said it was the first country to do cosmetic surgery; noses cut off as punishments were often replaced with grafting from cheek in ancient India.)

Earlier this year, Jacobs also sold to Paramount Pictures a story called "The Year of Living Biblically," in which he spends a year living by the literal rules of the Old and New Testament. He begins that ordeal next week.

Jacobs is not the first write to treat the outsourcing issue in a funny vein. Humorist Dave Barry and cartoonist Scott Adams of Dilbert fame, among others, have picked on the topic and made Americans laugh with spoofs about everything from the functioning of the US Congress to the working of the White House being outsourced to India.

But the Jacobs saga will be the first to make it to celluloid outside minor sketches and skits.

lives, with a single company and to be rewarded for their service and loyalty with job security and good retirement benefits (Eisenberg, Goodall, & Trethewey, 2007). This is no longer the case. Along with globalization, an increase in organizations' willingness to lay off workers during economic downturns and corporate restructuring has led to a **new social contract** between employers and employees. Under this "new social contract," loyalty is not expected by workers or organizations and job security rarely exists (Eisenberg, Goodall & Trethewey, 2007). This means that if it is deemed profitable, companies are quick to sell or merge with other corporations, and employees are willing to jump ship if the right opportunity arises. This change in

new social contract
assumes that loyalty is not expected by workers or organizations and that job security is unlikely

employee–employer relationship has led to an increase in job and career shifting as well as to an increase in the employment of contingent workers—workers who do not have a long-term commitment to their organizations nor their employers to them.

Contingent Workers

Contingent employees work in temporary positions, part-time or as subcontractors (Belous, 1989; Jablin & Sias, 2001). Based on this definition, experts estimate that as many as one-third of U.S. employees are contingent workers (United States General Accounting Office, 2000).

Proponents of the trend toward the increased use of contingent workers argue that this practice is a productive response to the forces of a global marketplace. They point out that contingent work offers flexibility both to management and to workers. Firms can use contingent arrangements to maximize workforce flexibility in the face of seasonal and cyclical forces and the demands of just-in-time production. This same flexibility, they say, helps some workers balance the demands of family and work (U.S. Dept. of Labor, 2008). In addition, working in different organizations is believed to help contingent workers develop a wide set of skills that can lead to innovation (Jablin & Sias, 2001). Some commentators claim that these changes have led to the lowest unemployment rate in the United States and has allowed people to obtain better jobs than in the past.

On the other hand, detractors argue that companies often hire contingent workers simply to reduce employee wages, even though these employees perform the same amount and value of work (Conrad & Poole, 2005). They also point out that current tax, labor, and employment laws increase the likelihood of this practice by giving employers incentives to create contingent employment positions merely to sidestep their legal financial obligations to employees and to society. For certain types of contingent workers such as contractors, for example, employers do not have to make contributions to Social Security, unemployment insurance, workers' compensation, and health insurance; they also can save the administrative expense of withholding, and they are relieved of responsibility to the worker under labor and employment laws. At least one study has confirmed that such practices are fairly widespread; a 1989 General Accounting Office (GAO) study found that 38 percent of the employers examined misclassified employees as independent contractors (U.S. Dept. of Labor, 2008).

Although some employees voluntarily choose contingent work to evade their own tax obligations, to provide flexibility, or to supplement retirement income, a large percentage of workers who hold part-time or temporary positions do so involuntarily. Many have been forced into temporary or part-time work due to organizational mergers, layoffs, restructuring, and downsizing (Miller, 2003) or because they have limited choices. A significant portion of contingent workers is drawn from the most vulnerable sectors of the workforce—the young, female, and/or Hispanic.

Overall, contingent employees are more likely than traditional full-time workers to have low family incomes and are less likely to receive health insurance and pension benefits through their employers. The expansion of contingent work has contributed to the increasing gap between high- and low-wage workers and to the increasing sense of insecurity among workers (U.S. Dept. of Labor, 2008). The rise in the number of contingent workers has raised concerns that the United States is moving toward a two-tiered system in which more highly educated and trained employees are supported by lower paid part-time and temporary workers (Jablin & Sias, 2001). Experts worry that this division of workers may result in a caste system whereby permanent employees look down on and denigrate temporary or part-time workers.

Miller (2003) argues that a "disposable workforce" may not be good for organizations either. Contingent employees are aware of the organizations' lack of commitment to them—especially during economic downturns, when they are the first to be let go; this decreases their loyalty to the organization and their commitment to its goals. Also, because organizations are less likely to invest time and money in socializing contingent workers and providing them with the support needed to be successful (Jablin & Sias, 2001), such employees are likely to feel disconnected from the organization and less

contingent employees
individuals who work in temporary positions, part-time or as subcontractors

likely to buy into its organizational culture. In turn, employees' lack of identification with the organization likely decreases job satisfaction and increases job turnover.

In addition, working alongside a contingent workforce can encourage traditional employees to question the value of organizational commitment and loyalty (Gossett, 2001; Miller, 2003). These traditional employees also may be less likely to form relationships and support networks with employees they see as transitory, which can negatively impact all employees' performance and the organization's productivity.

However, the increased use of a contingent workforce is, in part, a response to the competitive demands that U.S. companies face, the topic we take up next.

Competitiveness and Urgent Organizations

Another significant change is the rise of **urgent organizations**. Urgent organizations are companies that attempt to "shorten the time in which they develop new products and respond to customer demands" (Eisenberg, Goodall, & Trethewey, 2007, p. 17). Urgent organizations occur because of the intense time pressures related to global competition and the subsequent consumer demand for innovation and immediate fulfillment of wants and needs. Apple and other technology companies manifest many of the behaviors typical of urgent organizations. For example, the first iPhone was sold to the public in June 2007, and then just 10 weeks later its price

Apple and other technology companies manifest many of the behaviors typical of urgent organizations.

was dropped $200 in response to customer demand (though doing so infuriated those "early adopters" who bought the phone in June and July). In July 2008, just one year later, the new and improved iPhone 3G was released, with the price once again reduced, this time by half. Similarly, Walmart attempts to compete globally by requiring all of its suppliers to abide by a policy that requires every vendor to either lower the price or increase the quality of each product every year (Fishman, 2006).

Urgent companies evolve and thrive because they are successful. Speed and quick response time provides them with an edge; companies that release products first tend to attract the most media and consumer attention, and clients and consumers are more likely to patronize companies that respond quickly to their requests for services and products.

Of course, when organizations increase the speed of innovation and delivery of services, it means that the employees of those organizations also are under time pressures to increase productivity and response time. This development has led to the issue we discuss next, the blurring of boundaries between work and home.

Blurred Boundaries Between Home and Work

The time pressures associated with urgent organizations have led to a blurring of the boundaries between individuals' work and nonwork lives. These pressures in conjunction with the advent of new communication technologies have increased organizations' ability to intrude into what has traditionally been one's nonwork life. The widespread use of email, cell phones, text messaging, and instant messaging has made it possible, and in some instances mandatory, that employees respond to organizations' demands at almost any hour of the day or night, during weekends as well as weekdays, and even when on vacation. Interestingly, just as the use of contingent workers has had a more profound impact on low-wage earners, the blurring of boundaries has had a stronger effect on high-wage earners, leading to positions that are now described as "extreme jobs" (Hewlitt, 2007; Schor, 1992). To read about one group of employees' effort to fight this trend, see *Communication in Society: Technology and Work/Life Balance.*

Extreme jobs are those held by well-paid employees who are required to work more than sixty hours per week (often many more) as well as being subjected to unpredictable work flow, tight deadlines, responsibilities that amount to more than one job, expectations of work performance outside regular work hours, client availability

urgent organizations
companies that try to shorten the time it takes to develop new products and respond to customer demands

COMMUNICATION IN SOCIETY
Technology and Work/Life Balance

Do you think new technologies compromise workers' abilities to balance their work and nonwork lives? Do you think they increase employees' workloads? If you were the supervisor in this department, how would you have responded to employees' concerns?

A federal government department [in Australia] stalled the distribution of a new fleet of BlackBerries following fears the devices would have a negative impact on the work/life balance of staff.

The BlackBerries were purchased for the Minister for Environment, Water, Heritage and Arts, Peter Garrett, as well as 40 other executives including senior departmental staff.

However, access to the new devices was delayed after concerns were expressed about the BlackBerries infringing on the work/life balance of staff.

Staff expressed fears about BlackBerries contributing to a longer working day and felt it was going a step too far because mobile phones are adequate for out-of-office contact.

Not everyone agreed, however, with some senior executives claiming a BlackBerry can contribute to work/life balance by facilitating telecommuting and more flexible schedules.

According to the source, debate became so heated there was talk of completely withdrawing the devices. However, a spokesperson for the department confirmed they will not be withdrawn but confirmed the recent purchase of 40 BlackBerries.

It isn't the first time mobile devices have been at the centre of workplace debate . . . a survey released in early 2007 [showed] one-third of respondents believe[d] a mobile device can increase workloads. Released by the Solutions Research Group, the survey was undertaken by users of BlackBerries, Palm Treos and other PDAs and smart phones.

FROM: "Blackberry rollout stalled over work/life balance debate," by Darren Pauli, *Computerworld*, December 13, 2007, www.pcworld.idg.com.au. Published by IDG Communications. Reprinted by permission of Copyright Agency Limited.

---

twenty-four/seven, extensive travel, many direct reports and/or physical presence at the workplace ten or more hours per day. Jobs with such extreme requirements often negatively affect employees' personal and family lives as well as their ability to contribute to their communities. To see how extreme jobs can even end a life, see *Did You Know? You Can Work Yourself to Death*, on p. 282.

Even employees who don't have extreme jobs find that organizations are expecting longer hours, more "face time" in the organization, and increased responsiveness outside of traditional work hours. These demands are believed to be associated with poorer health outcomes for individuals (Cummings & Kreiss, 2008), increased family stress (Hewlitt, 2003, 2007), and loss of leisure (Schor, 1992).

As our discussion of blurred boundaries—as well as the three other organizational trends described earlier—suggests, many organizational changes occurring over the past twenty years negatively impact the individuals who work in them. However, trend watchers predict that younger generations who are entering the workplace or who will enter the workforce soon will begin to push back against the extreme demands of contemporary organizations. If so, it is likely that we will continue to see new ways that individuals and organizations influence one another.

One persistent trend throughout the history of profit-oriented organizations is that organizations have had more power than the employees they hire. Next we discuss some of the possible consequences that can occur when organizations wield more power than their workers.

Organizations, Communication, and Power

Organizations in the United States historically have been hierarchical, meaning that power, decision-making authority, and control have been held by a relatively small percentage of people within the organization, including managers, vice presidents, presidents, and chief executive officers (CEOs). To a great extent this is still true today. Although a hierarchical structure seems natural and normal to most of us, it can lead to power differences and to communication behavior that negatively affects

Did You Know?

You Can Work Yourself to Death

According to the Associated Press (AP), last week a court in Japan ordered the Toyota Motor Corporation to pay compensation to a woman who argued that her husband died from overwork.

According to the woman's lawyer, Kenichi Uchino (the departed) had been working overtime as a middle manager at a Toyota factory when he suddenly collapsed and died in February 2002. He was just 30 years old.

Before dying, Mr. Uchino had logged 80 hours of overtime a month for a sustained period of six months, and had logged 114 extra hours the month he died.

Sadly, Mr. Uchino is anything but an isolated case. In fact, the Japanese even have a word for punching the clock until you drop. Working yourself to death is known in Japanese as **karōshi** (過労死), which directly translates to "death from overwork."

Known in medical circles as occupational sudden death, the major medical causes of karōshi are believed to be stress-induced heart attack and stroke.

The Japanese Ministry of Health, Welfare and Labour also reports that the leading cause of karōshi is the practice of voluntary undocumented unpaid overtime, which is known as **sabisu-zangyo**. Just to clarify, that means that workers are choosing to work longer hours without documenting their time or seeking compensation.

FROM: *Big in Japan: Man works himself to death, company compensates wife*, by M. Firestone, December 6, 2007, www.gadling.com. Reprinted by permission of Matthew D. Firestone.

those workers who hold little or no power. In the discussion that follows, we examine three of the communication problems that can result from power differences.

Bullying

Organizational **bullying** refers to repeated, hostile behaviors that occur in the workplace over an extended period and that are intended, or are perceived as intended, to harm one or more parties who are unable to defend themselves (Lutgen-Sandvik, Tracy, & Alberts, 2005). Although interpersonal conflict is common in organizations, and perhaps necessary, bullying is not necessary. Bullying differs from conflict in that conflict can be constructive and positive. In addition, intent to harm may not be present in typical interpersonal conflict, and the parties in an interpersonal conflict often are relatively equal in power. However, in bullying, the intent to harm is a defining element, and power differences are key. Bully targets lack the ability to defend themselves and have limited strategies with which to respond. During interpersonal conflict, participants both act and are acted upon. In contrast, in bullying interactions, one party (or group) is the actor or perpetrator, and one (or more) person(s) is the target.

You may wonder why we bring up the issue of bullying, since it may not seem like a prevalent problem. However, it probably is more common than you think. A recent study (Lutgen-Sandvik et al., 2005) found that 30 percent of over 400 respondents claimed that they had been bullied at some point in their careers. Eleven percent revealed that they had been bullied in just the past year. These statistics are similar to reports from workers in Great Britain, though somewhat higher than those reported in Scandinavia. In addition, bullying is important because, fundamentally, it is a communication issue (Alberts, Lutgen-Sandvik, & Tracy, 2005). Of the twenty-two behaviors used to enact bullying, seventeen of them involved verbal interaction, such as ridicule, rumors, false allegations, insults, and threats of violence (Alberts, Lutgen-Sandvik, & Tracy, 2005).

Because bullying does occur regularly and is related to one's power in the organization, scholars have sought to determine strategies that can help targets respond. However, because targets typically have low power in the organization, their options are limited. For example, a problem-solving approach involves discussing the issue

bullying
repeated hostile behaviors that are or appear to be intended to harm parties unable to defend themselves

and seeking resolution. It requires that all parties be able to participate openly. This is rarely true for the target of bullying. Similarly, compromising can occur only if one has leverage within the organization, meaning that each party must be able to offer something in return for a change in the other's behavior, which a low-power person may not possess. Obliging, or accommodating to the bully's demands, may be the only strategy if one wishes to remain in the organization. Withdrawing may be an option if one is willing to leave, and targets report that leaving the organization was the most effective, and often only, solution to the problem. Competing typically is not a useful strategy; it only intensifies the bully's abusive behavior. For a student's account of organizational bullying, see *It Happened to Me: Bob*.

Sexual Harassment

Sexual harassment describes unwanted sexual attention that interferes with an individual's ability to do his or her job and/or behavior that ties sexual favors to continued employment or success within the organization (Equal Employment Opportunity Commission, 1980). Federal law recognizes two types of sexual harassment, quid pro quo and hostile work environment (Roberts & Mann, 2000). **Quid pro quo** is the request for sexual favors as a condition of getting or keeping a job or benefit. ("You do what I ask, and I'll help you advance in the organization.") A **hostile work environment** results when a coworker or supervisor engages in unwelcome and inappropriate sexually based behavior and creates an intimidating, hostile, or offensive atmosphere. Indulging in inappropriate verbal and nonverbal behaviors; repeatedly asking someone for a date; calling coworkers or subordinates by affectionate names (e.g., honey, sweetie); touching, patting, and stroking; and displaying posters and objects of a sexual nature can all constitute acts of sexual harassment.

Even with this list of criteria, however, people could differ over what constitutes a hostile work environment. As a guideline, the U.S. Court of Appeals (Aeberhard-Hodges, 1996) ruled that sexual harassment should be examined from the perspective of what a "reasonable woman," not a "reasonable person," would find offensive. This led some to this central question: If a reasonable woman standard prevailed, would men, even "reasonable men," ever be sure how to behave? The court's ruling, however, rests on the understanding that women are the most frequent targets of sexual harassment and that their experiences in the workplace and around issues of sexuality often differ markedly from men's.

At this point you might be wondering how bullying differs from sexual harassment. We see sexual harassment as a specific type of bullying behavior, because it contains many of the same elements: It is rooted in power differences, the target typically is unable to defend him or herself, and the target perceives it as hostile and intentional.

As you can see, sexual harassment primarily is a communicative behavior. Because of this, researchers have typically explored how targets can use communication to respond effectively. The typical strategies recommended include confronting the harasser and stating that the behavior must stop, complaining to one's boss or the human relations department, suing, or leaving the organization (Sigal, Braden-Maguire, Pat, Goodrich, & Perrino, 2003).

However, the majority of female targets of sexual harassment (in fact 95 percent or more) do not respond assertively by confronting the harasser or reporting the harasser to a supervisor or the organization (Gruber & Smith, 1995; Rudman,

It Happened to Me: Bob

I still can't believe it happened to me. About a year ago I was transferred to a new branch of my credit union. Within a few months, my supervisor began to criticize everything I did and make sarcastic and mean comments about me in front of other people. I tried to talk to her about it, but she just told me I was too thin-skinned. I don't know if it is because I am one of only a few males in the office or what. Finally, it got so bad that I asked for a meeting with my supervisor and her supervisor. During our meeting, I became so upset that I started having chest pains. I thought I was having a heart attack and had to go to the hospital by ambulance. It turns out it was a panic attack. When I got back to work a few days later, my supervisor started ridiculing me for having a panic attack. I have asked for a transfer, but I am also looking for another job.

quid pro quo
requests for sexual favors as a condition of getting or keeping a job or benefit; one of two types of sexual harassment recognized by federal law

hostile work environment
an intimidating, hostile, or offensive workplace atmosphere created by unwelcome and inappropriate sexually based behavior; one of two types of sexual harassment recognized by federal law

Sexual harassment is primarily a communicative behavior.

Borgida, & Robertson, 1995). Why not? Sexual harassment typically occurs between people of unequal power, so confronting the harasser may not be an option. Targets risk losing their jobs, seeing the harassment intensify, or losing out on promotions and raises.

Complaining to a third party does sometimes work, particularly in organizations that have a clearly articulated sexual harassment policy and in which the human resources department has been empowered to handle sexual harassment cases effectively. However, some organizations do not wish to deal with these issues, or do not see them as important, so complaining to a third party does not always result in a benefit. Of course, suing the harasser and the organization that allows harassment is possible, but not every case is settled to the target's satisfaction, and the process can be long, painful, and ultimately unrewarding.

Finally, although leaving the organization does tend to resolve some aspects of the problem, some employees lack the option of leaving or find that leaving takes considerable time and effort. In addition, leaving one's job may resolve the physical/behavioral aspect of the harassment, but it does not help targets manage the long-term physical or psychological effects of harassment, does not address the impact of the harassment on the target's career, and does not result in changes in the perpetrator or the organization.

None of this means that targets should tolerate inappropriate behavior, but it does mean that they should carefully consider their options before committing to a response strategy. Targets should consider what response will be most effective in their specific situations. To do so, targets of sexual harassment (or bullying) might consider the following options. First, a target should consider responding assertively the first time the harassment occurs. This strategy is most likely to be successful when the perpetrator and target have equal power or a relationship of trust. If direct confrontation does not seem to be an option or has not been successful, then the target should consider approaching his or her supervisor, human resources department, or an organizational ombudsperson. Many organizations want to and will respond to such complaints, recognizing that the organization as a whole is harmed by such behavior.

If confrontation and appealing to authorities have not succeeded, targets must assess their needs and options carefully. They might consider seeking social support from family and friends, seeking assistance from a counselor or therapist to help them manage the emotional distress, developing strategies to avoid the perpetrator (if possible), and/or requesting a transfer or another job.

Unfortunately, the most common strategy targets select is to do nothing. This is not a response that, in the long run, benefits the individual *or* the organization. Moreover, doing nothing is especially problematic if the target has not even determined what other options exist. Too often, targets assume their efforts will be unsuccessful before they even make an attempt. If you do become a target, we encourage you not to make this assumption.

Employee Privacy and Monitoring

Monitoring employees electronically and in other ways is a growing part of the way American companies do business (American Management Association, 2005). According to the survey, 76 percent of employers monitor workers' Web connections, while 50 percent store and monitor employees' computer files. Workers are exposed to many other types of privacy-invasive monitoring as well. These include drug testing, closed-circuit video monitoring, email monitoring, instant message monitoring, phone monitoring, location monitoring, personality and psychological testing, and keystroke logging.

Although employers do have an interest in monitoring employees in order to address security risks, sexual harassment, and acceptable performance of work duties, these activities may diminish employee morale and dignity as well as increase worker stress (Ditecco, Cwitco, Arsenault, & Andre, 1992). To better understand the complexities of this issue, read *It Happened to Me: Nichole*. In addition, monitoring may interfere with employee productivity. A study of 134 corporate employees examined the effects of monitoring and found that productivity diminished when people believed they were being monitored for quality (Stanton & Julian, 2002). Nonetheless, employers and employees can develop policies that meet the needs of both parties. Both sides must have a voice in developing the policies, and the process itself must be transparent (Trethewey & Corman, 2001).

In conclusion, organizations experience significant impact from the society and historical time period in which they exist. Three societal factors currently influencing corporations in the United States are critical analyses of organizations, globalization and changing power relations in the workplace. Globalization has meant that many jobs have been transferred from the

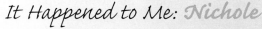

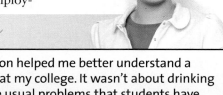

The chapter on organizational communication helped me better understand a problem I encountered with Residential Life at my college. It wasn't about drinking or drugs, or letting in strangers, or any of the usual problems that students have with the dorm; it was about my Resident Assistant, who now is my boyfriend.

Just to clarify, there were no rules stated that I could not date my RA, and he was never told he couldn't date his residents. Plus, there is actual love involved, not just random friends-with-benefits hookups and we really feel as though we have met the right person. But, Residential Life has a huge problem with our relationship, and they called us into a meeting. We both felt as though it was a violation of our privacy. We had the meeting, he quit his job, and we are still dating, ten months strong!

Now, though, when I look at the relationship through the eyes of the school, I can see their problems with it. What would have happened if an employee of the college got me pregnant? Also, he lived in my hall and his duty was to keep us in line, but there was huge preferential treatment going on. I mean, would my boyfriend really write me up for anything? So now I see that they had a point. But I don't understand why nothing was ever said about this practice being against the rules.

United States to other countries, and both consumers and employees now must increase their contact with workers around the world. This change has been accompanied by a more critical approach to studying and understanding organizations engaged in economic production. In turn, critical analyses have increased the focus on power relationships at work and their impact on employees. This tendency to critique organizations has also led to more discussion of organizational ethics, which we examine next.

ETHICS AND ORGANIZATIONAL COMMUNICATION

From debates over drug tests, affirmative action, and the high salaries of CEOs who lead failing companies, to outrage over business scandals in corporations such as AIG and Madoff Investment Securities, U.S. Americans are paying more attention to business ethics than perhaps ever before. However, observers don't agree on where responsibility for ethical behavior rests within the organization. When attempting to determine what ethical choices and decisions organizations should make, people usually view the process either from the *individual perspective* or the *communal perspective* (Brown, 1989).

Many U.S. Americans take an individualistic perspective, viewing ethical failures as resting on the shoulders of individuals within the organization. From this outlook, each person in the corporation is responsible for his own behavior. In the communal view, however, individuals are considered to be members of communities that are all partially responsible for the behavior of their members. Thus, changing an individual's behavior requires a change in the community to which he belongs.

When ethics is discussed in organizational contexts, the focus typically is on the rights of the individual—such as the rights to free speech or privacy—and policies and behaviors that infringe on these rights are seen as unethical. However, a communal approach focuses on the "common good," or what is in the best

AlternativeVIEW
Individual and Communal Approaches to Affirmative Action

Which do you value more—individual justice or social justice? Do you think it is more important to take an individual or a communal approach to ethics? Can you think of a situation in which you favor an individual over a communal approach—or vice versa?

At times, our willingness to consider both the good of the individual and the good of the community leaves us in a dilemma, and we are forced to choose between competing moral claims. Affirmative Action Programs, for example, bring concern over individual justice into conflict with concerns over social justice. When women and minorities are given preferential treatment over white males, individuals are not treated equally, which is unjust. On the other hand, when we consider what these programs are trying to accomplish, a more just society, and also acknowledge that minorities and women continue to be shut out of positions (especially in top management), then these programs are, in fact, indispensable for achieving social justice. Dropping preferential treatment programs might put an end to the injustice of treating individuals unequally, but to do so would maintain an unjust society. In this case, many argue that a communal approach should take moral priority over the good of the individual.

FROM: Brown, M. (Winter 1989). "Ethics in organizations." *Issues in Ethics*, 2(1). Santa Clara University: Markkula Center for Applied Ethics. Reprinted with permission of The Markkula Center for Applied Ethics at Santa Clara University, wwww.scu.edu/ethics

interests of the entire community. Thus, the morality of an action is assessed based on its consequences for the group. In an individualistic approach, discussions regarding drug abuse in the workplace usually center on whether organizations should be allowed to infringe on the employee's right to privacy. From a communal approach, the discussion would revolve around what types of drug policies are most likely to promote the good of the community, the employer, and the employee. To better understand the perspectives of these approaches, see *Alternative View: Individual and Communal Approaches to Affirmative Action.*

However, when we view corporations in the communal way and hold them responsible for their unethical practices (such as dumping toxic waste), no individual may be held accountable or liable. Consequently, those responsible for the decision to engage in unethical and often illegal practices may not suffer any consequences—and may be free to continue these practices.

How should we balance these two approaches? Most likely, we need to hold both the community and the individuals who lead them responsible for their practices—just as political leaders are tried in war courts for crimes against humanity, even though their subordinates performed the atrocities. At the same time, corporate leaders need to consider the impacts of their decisions on both individuals and society.

How is communication a factor in organizational ethics? Communication figures in organizational ethics in two ways (Cheney et al., 2004). First, many of the ethical issues in organizations revolve around communication. For example, organizations have to decide when to tell employees of impending layoffs, they develop advertising campaigns that communicate the identity of their corporation and its products to consumers, and they must decide how to communicate information regarding their profits and losses to shareholders and Wall Street. Second, the ways in which an organization defines, communicates about, and responds to ethical and unethical behavior shape how individuals within the organization behave. If corporate policy and organizational leaders are vague on the issue of ethics, or worse yet, fail to address it, employees may believe that ethics is not a central concern of the organization and may behave accordingly. For example, in 2005, *Esquire* magazine published an article about the alleged ethical violations of military recruiters. The military personnel interviewed for the article claimed that despite written policies that encouraged ethical behavior, their communication with their superiors revolved only around their success or failure at meeting their recruitment goals and never about *how* they met those goals.

Thus, they concluded that recruiting ethically was a secondary, or perhaps even an unnecessary, consideration.

IMPROVING YOUR ORGANIZATIONAL COMMUNICATION SKILLS

One of the most useful communication skills that you can develop is the ability to negotiate effectively. People who negotiate their salaries can earn up to one million more dollars in their lifetimes (Babcock & Laschever, 2003), and these skills can make it easier for you to achieve all your goals in organizational contexts, from work assignments, to professional leave, to promotions.

Effective bargaining begins with the decision to negotiate for what you want. Many people don't even think to negotiate, or hesitate to do so. Consequently, first you must commit to negotiating. Once you have decided to do so, you need to prepare and practice.

To prepare, you should follow four key steps (Fischer & Ury, 1981):

- **Create a best-case scenario.** This step requires that you detail all the items you would like to address and decide exactly what you want. For example, if you are negotiating for a new position, you should decide what issues you want to discuss (salary, vacation, moving expenses, review and raise schedule) and decide what you would like to receive (a salary of $65,000 per year, three weeks of vacation, $10,000 in moving expenses, and a semiannual review schedule). At this stage, you attempt to develop a scenario that is realistic (which may require that you conduct research) but that you would find very satisfying.

- **Create a fallback position.** A fallback position is a second scenario that details what you need to be satisfied with the negotiation, even if it isn't ideal. Using the previous example, you might decide that you would accept a salary of at least $54,000, two weeks vacation, $5,000 in moving expenses, and at least an annual review.

- **Create a BATNA** (Best Alternative to a Negotiated Agreement). In this step you decide what you can or will do if you cannot reach a satisfying negotiated agreement. Consider what other options exist for you, such as another job offer, returning to school, or continuing your job search. Having alternatives provides you with greater leverage during your negotiation and gives you increased confidence.

- **Decide on a walk-away point.** Finally, at which point will you leave the negotiation and not accept the offer? For example, working with the earlier scenario you might decide that your walk-away point is a salary of less than $50,000, less two weeks vacation, and less than $5,000 moving expenses. Knowing your walk-away point prevents you from accepting a negotiated agreement that will leave you dissatisfied and regretful in the end.

After you have prepared to negotiate by following the above-mentioned steps and conducting any necessary research, you should practice negotiating. Begin with issues that are smaller and less consequential than negotiating for a new job or promotion. For example, negotiate an upgrade to your hotel room, a discount on a rental car, or reimbursement for job training from your organization.

Improving your negotiation skills can help you transform your work life. It can help you feel more in control, achieve more of your goals, and increase your overall confidence. A number of excellent books exist that can help you improve your negotiating skills, including Fischer & Ury's (1981) *Getting to Yes*, and Babcock and Lashever's (2003) *Women Don't Ask: Negotiation and the Gender Divide*.

SUMMARY

Organizations have a powerful influence on individuals' lives; consequently, it is important to learn how to communicate effectively in organizational contexts. Doing so can enhance professional success, allow one to ask more informed questions about everyday organizational practices, and help individuals decide what organizations they wish to frequent and support.

Organizations are composed of interactions that members use to accomplish their individual and common goals. The two fundamental properties of organizations are function, or the goals and effects of communication, and structure, or the lines of communication through which messages flow. In addition, organizations may be categorized based on their social roles or functions, including integration roles, political roles, pattern maintenance roles, and economic production roles.

In organizations focused on economic production, some of the basic types of communication that occur and that affect employee success include assimilation, supervisor–subordinate communication, peer relationships, and organizational conflict. In addition, employees can face three types of organizational dilemmas during their careers, including emotion labor, stress and burnout, and work–life conflict.

Three of the most significant societal forces that impact organizational communication are history, globalization, and power. Although each influences beliefs about organizational communication and its performance, power differences in organizations can result in three specific communication problems for workers—bullying, sexual harassment, and employee monitoring.

Ethical issues in organizational communication are key for twenty-first century workers, as is becoming a more effective communicator. When assessing the ethical choices and decisions organizations should make, people usually approach the process from the individual perspective or the communal perspective. Each approach has consequences for the organization, and the most ethical approach combines the two perspectives. Finally, negotiation skills are among the most important organizational communication skills one can develop, and numerous techniques exist for becoming a better negotiator.

KEY TERMS

organizations 257
function 258
production 258
maintenance 258
innovation 258
structure 258
downward communication 258
upward communication 258
horizontal communication 258

hierarchy 258
formal structure 258
informal structure 258
societal role 259
integration role 259
political role 259
pattern maintenance role 259
economic production role 259
organizational culture 260

assimilation 261
organizational identification 261
anticipatory socialization 262
encounter stage 265
metamorphosis 266
semantic-information distance 267
upward distortion 267
perceptual co-orientation 267
openness 268

TEST YOUR KNOWLEDGE

1. What are the benefits of studying organizational communication?

2. What typical communication structures occur in organizations that focus on economic production?

3. What is organizational identification? How is it related to the process of assimilation?

4. What are the three types of uncertainty-reducing strategies that newcomers to an organization use during the assimilation process?

5. How are (1) emotion labor, (2) stress and burnout, and (3) work–life conflict related to one another? How do they differ?

6. What is globalization? What are the communication implications of globalization?

APPLY WHAT YOU KNOW

1. **Understanding Emotion Labor**
   Think of five jobs that require employees to engage in emotion labor and delineate the emotions that these employees are "expected" to display. What emotions are they expected to suppress? What contradictory emotions and behaviors are they expected to perform? Which of the five jobs that you listed appears to have the heaviest emotion labor load?

2. **Understanding Relationships at Work**
   Form a group with one or more of your classmates. Assume that you are a work group that has been charged with developing a fraternization policy for your job. Develop a policy about the types of relationships that are appropriate in your workplace and how people who have these relationships should communicate and behave while at work.

3. **Improving Your Job Interview Skills**
   Go to Job.Interview.net's "Mock Interviews" site at www.job-interview.net/sample/Demosamp.htm and review the information about communicating effectively during job interviews. Engage in one of the mock interviews provided, and then write a brief analysis of your performance. Explain what you did well and what you could have done better.

EXPLORE

1. Go to the *Psychology Today* workplace Web site at www.psychologytoday.com/pto/self_tests.php. Select one of the "Self Tests" listed on that page (e.g., the Sensitivity to Criticism Test or one of the other tests listed there). After completing the test, analyze your score. Does the score you received reflect your understanding of yourself and your work life? Which of your answers concern you? What could you do to improve your score (and your life or career)?

2. Go to the Job Interview Web site at www.job-interview.net/; select one of the topics listed on the page and click it to read the material available on that topic. Select a topic that can help you prepare for future interviews. After reading the material provided, develop a short checklist of helpful hints for interviewing that you can keep on hand for future interviews.

3. Go to the Center for Work-Life Policy Web site's newsroom at www.worklifepolicy.org/inded.hpp/section/press_releases. Click on one of the links to a recent press release related to work–life issues and policy. After reading the press release, write a brief summary of the press release that you could share with your classmates.

Communicating in Public:
Rhetoric

11

I was asked to give the eulogy at my best friend's funeral. I had never given a speech like that, and at first, I wasn't sure what I would say. I decided that I should talk about what a special person he was and tell some stories about the thoughtful things he did and the crazy stunts he pulled. I figured we needed to remember his life as much as we needed to mourn his death.

—Dan

Dan recognized the power of rhetorical communication as a means of honoring and remembering his friend. Rhetoric describes communication that is used to influence the attitudes or behaviors of others. Dan's eulogy was rhetorical in that it was designed to influence how his listeners viewed his deceased friend; through his speech, he encouraged them to see his friend as unique, fun, and thoughtful. On other occasions, communicators might use rhetoric to influence people to vote a particular way, to recognize Pope John Paul II as a saint, or to participate in a Walk for the Cure for breast cancer.

Dan's speech served important cultural and personal functions, and gaining insight into such functions is, by itself, an important reason to study the art of rhetoric. But people study rhetoric, which comes from the ancient Greek word for oratory, for a variety of other important reasons as well, which we will explore throughout this chapter. In the final chapter of this book, we will focus on improving communication by providing instruction on writing and delivering a public speech. However, most of us spend less time as speakers than as receivers of rhetorical communication. Therefore, this chapter focuses on the listening end of rhetoric.

In Chapter 2 we examined the history of communication research and its roots in the study of rhetoric. Here we explore the place of rhetoric in the overall study of communication today. We will first consider the functions and definition of rhetoric. We then examine how characteristics of individual public speakers, or *rhetors*, make them credible and influence what they say and how they relate to their audiences. We then turn our focus to a broader topic—the intersection of society and rhetoric—by examining major rhetorical events, discussing important democratic functions of rhetoric, revealing how justice can be served by rhetoric, and finally, by exploring ways in which rhetoric can bring about social change. But, first, we explain what we mean by *rhetoric*.

Once you have read this chapter, you will be able to:

■ Describe some of the key issues in the history of rhetoric.
■ Identify cultural and social influences on the development of rhetoric.
■ Identify and define the three artistic proofs (ethos, pathos, logos).
■ Explain four functions of rhetoric: reaffirming cultural values, increasing democratic participation, securing justice, and promoting social change.

THE IMPORTANCE OF RHETORIC

Rhetorical communication serves at least three important functions in our society. First, as you may have surmised, rhetoric is essential to a vital democracy. For people to make informed decisions (and vote) about a range of issues, they must listen critically, and sometimes speak carefully, about these topics. By advocating for one's perspective and engaging with the perspectives of others, people can make decisions together regarding the common good. Hence, rhetoric can strengthen democratic society, and speeches or other types of communication to the public can serve important political and social functions. For example, the debates about legalizing gay marriage reflect a vibrant democratic system in which people and institutions explain their views and use rhetoric to help shape how others under this issue. In some cases, decisions about gay marriage are made in the voting booth, as in Arizona and California (see *Communication in Society: Gay Marriage Debate and the Framing of "Marriage"*), sometimes courts make these decisions as in Iowa and Massachusetts, and recently the Vermont legislature voted to approve same-sex marriage.

Rhetoric is used to move people to view issues in a particular way and in different contexts.

Second, rhetoric helps people seek justice. Probably one of the most obvious examples of this is how lawyers use rhetoric in the courtroom to persuade a jury that someone is guilty or not guilty of a crime. Similarly, attorneys argue before the Supreme Court that certain laws or practices are just or unjust. The use of rhetoric in these situations helps society pursue a just course of action. Jurors need rhetorical skills as well; they need to listen carefully and critically not only to what is said, but how it is said, and they must be able to persuade other jurors of the proper verdict. Speakers also use rhetoric to persuade others to pursue social justice—for example, to bring about a better environment or to treat animals more ethically—or to take a position on the many other social issues confronting the world today.

Third, rhetoric helps people clarify their own beliefs and actions. For example, after the attacks on September 11, 2001, many people, like our student in *It Happened to Me: Denise*, p. 294, were not sure what to believe about why the United States was attacked, nor were they sure how they should respond or behave. Therefore, they turned to experts and national leaders, such as the president, to gather information that could help them clarify their beliefs and understanding. In his speech after 9/11, President Bush told the nation and the world that "America was targeted for attack because we're the brightest beacon for freedom and opportunity in the world. And no one will keep that light from shining." Many people who heard his message felt that it spoke to their own views and helped them articulate how they were feeling. On the other hand, at least a few people who heard the message realized that it did not reflect their feelings, but in thinking and talking about their reaction to the speech, they were better able to explain to themselves and others what they *did* believe.

In addition to serving important functions in society, rhetoric is also an important area of academic inquiry. Studying rhetoric as a field of scholarship is useful for four reasons. First, the study of public communication generates findings that help people understand the range of viewpoints around large social issues. For example, if you wanted to understand the reasoning behind the U.S.

Supporters of same-sex marriage protested against the passage of California's Proposition 8.

Proposition 8 in California and 102 in Arizona were passed in November 2008, both defining marriage as a union between a man and a woman.

As the debate over gay marriage continues, what it means to be married is the crux of the arguments made by both sides of the issue. So what does it mean to be married? Interpretations of the Bible's definition (or lack of) by proponents and opponents of gay marriage have been prevalent in the media.

According to The Church of Jesus Christ of Latter-day Saints (2008), a major opponent of gay marriage, "Marriage is sacred, ordained of God from before the foundation of the world. After creating Adam and Eve, the Lord God pronounced them husband and wife, of which Adam said, 'Therefore shall a man leave his father and his mother, and shall cleave unto his wife: and they shall be one flesh' (Genesis 2:24). Jesus Christ cited Adam's declaration when he affirmed the divine origins of the marriage covenant: 'Have ye not read, that he which made them at the beginning made them male and female, and said, For this cause shall a man leave father and mother, and shall cleave to his wife: and they twain shall be one flesh? Wherefore they are no more twain, but one flesh' (Matthew 19:4–6)."

Further, "Marriage between a man and a woman is central to the plan of salvation. The sacred nature of marriage is closely linked to the power of procreation. Only a man and a woman together have the natural biological capacity to conceive children. This power of procreation—to create life and bring God's spirit children into the world—is sacred and precious. Misuse of this power undermines the institution of the family and thereby weakens the social fabric. Strong families serve as the fundamental institution for transmitting to future generations the moral strengths, traditions, and values that sustain civilization" (Church, 2008).

According to proponents of gay marriage, "'marriage' in America refers to two separate things, a religious institution and a civil one, though it is most often enacted as a messy conflation of the two. As a civil institution, marriage offers practical benefits to both partners: contractual rights having to do with taxes; insurance; the care and custody of children; visitation rights; and inheritance. As a religious institution, marriage offers something else: a commitment of both partners before God to love, honor and cherish each other—in sickness and in health, for richer and poorer—in accordance with God's will. In a religious marriage, two people promise to take care of each other, profoundly, the way they believe God cares for them. Biblical literalists will disagree, but the Bible is a living document, powerful for more than 2,000 years because its truths speak to us even as we change through history. In that light, Scripture gives us no good reason why gays and lesbians should not be (civilly and religiously) married—and a number of excellent reasons why they should" (Miller, 2008).

Proponents argue that gay-marriage opponents are really exercised about homosexuality, specifically sex between men, and not the definition of marriage. To that, Lisa Miller (2008) of *Newsweek* argues, "Paul was tough on homosexuality, though recently progressive scholars have argued that his condemnation of men who "were inflamed with lust for one another" (which he calls "a perversion") is really a critique of the worst kind of wickedness: self-delusion, violence, promiscuity and debauchery. In his book "The Arrogance of Nations," the scholar Neil Elliott argues that Paul is referring in this famous passage to the depravity of the Roman emperors, the craven habits of Nero and Caligula, a reference his audience would have grasped instantly. "Paul is not talking about what we call homosexuality at all," Elliott says. "He's talking about a certain group of people who have done everything in this list. We're not dealing with anything like gay love or gay marriage. We're talking about really, really violent people who meet their end and are judged by God." In any case, one might add, Paul argued more strenuously against divorce—and at least half of the Christians in America disregard that teaching.

As the debate over gay marriage continues—and even as new issues emerge in the media—try to pay particular attention to how issues are framed and how emphasis is placed on different aspects (such as definitions) in order to make arguments more compelling and credible.

immigration policy, you could examine the rhetoric of people who are attempting to influence that policy. You could read the interviews, speeches, and press releases of people who support the Minute Man project along the Arizona–Mexico border; you might listen to the president's speeches on immigration; you could examine the Catholic Church's views on pending immigration legislation; and you could review the public comments of various members of Congress, some of whom are themselves the children or grandchildren of immigrants. After considering this information, you should better understand how U.S. immigration policies respond to these varied perspectives.

It Happened to Me: Denise

When the president was going to speak about 9/11 for the first time, I was right there listening. Most of the people I knew, including me, were frightened and not sure what to believe or how to understand the attacks. We wanted to know what was really happening and what he was doing to protect the United States.

Second, the study of rhetoric helps people better understand their own and others' cultures. Both consciously and unconsciously, through listening to and analyzing public communication, people learn the expectations of their own cultures—what it means to be a good parent, how to present oneself, how to decorate one's home, and much more. In addition, through rhetoric, individuals can study others' cultures to understand them better. For example, right now many people wish to increase their understanding of Islamic cultures; one way they are attempting to do so is by analyzing the public communication of people in those cultures.

Third, studying rhetoric and public communication can help people critically evaluate messages designed to influence them. For example, some public communication is designed to convince consumers to purchase products. Other rhetoric tries to persuade people to support particular policies or to vote for or against certain politicians or propositions. As targets for these persuasive messages, people can learn to listen critically and analyze these messages so they can respond appropriately.

Finally, some people study public communication in order to become better public communicators or to understand what makes specific public communicators effective or ineffective. By watching others, they may learn what to do and what not to do in public speaking situations. We examine the skills involved in creating and delivering public speeches in Chapter 14, but you can also learn about public speaking by analyzing the rhetoric of those who speak in public. In addition, you can determine why some speakers are more successful or persuasive than others by analyzing their public communication. For example, some observers have tried to understand how Bill Clinton has become a more popular and respected figure today than he was at the end of his presidential term. To do so, they have analyzed his speeches, interviews, and public conversations to evaluate the rhetorical skills he has used in shaping his image.

Truth and Rhetoric

From the fifth century B.C., teachers and scholars of rhetoric have argued over the fundamental purpose of rhetoric. Is it intended to help speakers and listeners discern truth, or is its purpose to persuade others? If persuasion is the goal, then truth plays a smaller, perhaps even nonexistent, role.

The people who taught persuasive speaking skills in the Greek city-states were called **sophists**. In fact, they were the first to call their subject matter "rhetoric." Their approach to rhetoric was practical; they believed that rhetoric's purpose was to persuade. Therefore, they taught speakers to adjust their notions of right or wrong, true or untrue, depending on the particular speaking situation and their goals. Essentially, they believed that the ends justified the means. Even the most famous sophist, Gorgias, was not concerned about right/wrong, true/false or other

sophists
the people who taught persuasive speaking skills in the Greek city-states

ethical values. He and other sophists felt free to espouse any view or belief depending on whom they were attempting to persuade.

However, others disagreed with this approach. One of the more prominent of these was Plato (429–347 B.C.), who strongly opposed this relativistic view of rhetoric. In his well-known dialogue, *Gorgias,* he disparagingly compared this view of rhetoric to "cookery," in which a set of elements (or ingredients) were "mixed together" to create the final speech (or dish). Plato thought speakers should use rhetoric to search for universal principles of truth and that these truths should then influence people's behavior. In fact, he thought the best way to search for truth was through oral dialogue, and in the *Phaedrus* he argued for a philosophical rhetoric based on truth (Conley, 1994; Infante, Ranceer, & Womack, 1990).

Not unlike students today, Plato's student Aristotle (384–322 B.C.) challenged his teacher's arguments. He did not agree with Plato's emphasis on the relationship of absolute truth to rhetoric; instead he believed speakers needed to focus on skillful persuasion so they could defend truth and justice. As you might guess, he took a more relativistic position on truth and rhetoric than did Plato, but a less relativistic one than did the sophists.

Aristotle defined rhetoric as "the art of discovering all the available means of persuasion in a given situation" (Aristotle, 350 B.C./ 1991, p. 42). Thus, he focused more on persuasion than on truth. With this perspective in mind, he sought to create general rules of rhetoric that would work in any situation and could be passed down to future generations. He was so successful that his text *The Rhetoric* has been read as a theory of rhetoric and used as a handbook for public speaking for more than 2,000 years.

When the Romans conquered the Greeks in 146 B.C., they incorporated the writings of the Greek philosophers into Roman education. Cicero (106–43 B.C.), a prominent lawyer and politician, is often considered the greatest Roman **orator**, or public speaker, and the most influential theorist of ancient rhetoric (see *Did You Know? The Power of Communication*, on p. 296). Cicero based many of his ideas on Aristotle's writing. Because he believed that speakers should use rhetoric for the benefit of Roman society, he viewed truth as whatever was best for Romans as a whole. Unlike the sophists, he did not believe that people should use rhetoric to benefit themselves or to become rich. Thus he held a moderately relativistic position on the role of truth in rhetoric.

Cicero offered guidelines for organizing speeches and was a master of style; in fact, his speeches are still read today because they are so effective and eloquent. He is known best for identifying the three purposes or goals of public speaking: to instruct, to please, and to win over. Modern public speaking courses require mastery of these three types of speeches, which we now refer to as speeches to inform, to entertain, and to persuade.

After the Roman Empire collapsed, the Catholic Church replaced secular educational institutions as the leading disseminator of knowledge in the West. Once again the issue of truth's relationship to rhetoric became important. First, since rhetoric had developed from a non-Christian tradition, concerns arose about its relevance and appropriateness to Christianity. The most prominent thinker and writer of this era was Augustine of Hippo (354–430 A.D.), whom you may know as St. Augustine. He was educated as a rhetorician before converting to Christianity, and he struggled to reconcile his rhetorical training with his religious beliefs.

Augustine's view of truth was close to Plato's—that truth exists in an absolute way—and he promoted the idea that rhetoric could impart the divine truth (Conley, 1994). From this perspective, ethical decisions were not situation specific; choices were always right or wrong, good or evil, as explained by the church. St. Augustine argued that rhetoric could help propagate Christian beliefs; consequently, his views were widely accepted, and debates about the relevance of rhetoric for Christianity largely ended.

orator
a public speaker

How do you view the sophists' relativistic approach to rhetoric? Have you ever been in a situation in a class or debate where you were required to argue for a position that clashed with your personal values? How did it feel to make the argument?

Did You Know?
The Power of Communication

Talk about the power of communication! Cicero was a persuasive orator. He was active in politics and promoted a democratic view that often pitted him against the powerful military generals who wanted to turn Rome into an empire. In hindsight, it was inevitable that he would run afoul of some powerful, aspiring politician—as he did when his assassination was successfully carried out by orders from Marc Antony, Caesar's second in command. It is said that after he was killed, his hands were cut off, because he used them to write his powerful speeches. Others say that his head was displayed in the forum with a golden pin stuck through the tongue.

PARAPHRASED FROM: Crowley & Hawhee, 1999, p. 27

The Dissemination of Rhetoric

While much of Europe declined during the early Middle Ages (500–1050 C.E.), Islam became a major intellectual, artistic, and military force in the world. North African Muslims invaded Spain in 711 C.E. and eventually established a library of approximately 500,000 books at Toledo, one of Moorish Spain's most important cultural seats. This library included works by Aristotle and Plato as well as other Greek and Roman philosophers, and the Moors preserved and translated these texts. Ultimately scholars from all over Europe read and translated these works (Dues & Brown, 2004), and knowledge of rhetorical principles became more widespread.

In addition, during the Middle Ages, the seven liberal arts of the Romans became the curriculum in schools across Europe.

WHAT IS RHETORIC? A BROADER VIEW

When you think of rhetoric, you may think about overblown statements, exaggerations, or even outright lies and misstatements. Unfortunately, this kind of rhetoric is all too common today. However, as we saw in this chapter, rhetoric has a rich history, and it serves important functions in a democratic society. As you saw in the example at the beginning of the chapter, in its truest sense, rhetoric refers to communication that is used to influence others. Thus, rhetoricians would not view the president's communication following 9/11 as simply an attempt to provide information, but rather as an attempt to guide us to view this topic in a particular way for his particular goals. A person may use rhetoric to attempt to influence a friend, family member, or colleague. But in both the historical and the contemporary sense, rhetoric focuses primarily on public communication or messages designed for large audiences.

The earliest study of communication focused on public communication. The field did not yet consider interpersonal, organizational, small group, or any of the other communication contexts that we cover in this book. Why did this keen interest in public communication exist? Early on, people saw rhetoric as vital to their participation in society, and they wanted to know how to use it effectively (Dues & Brown, 2004). Because democracy depends on citizen participation, many universities continue to offer courses in public speaking and argumentation. The use of communication in the public arena is still seen as far more important in society than in other communication contexts, as it is in the public arena that decisions about going to war, justice, and other social issues are negotiated.

Nearly forty years ago, Douglas Ehninger, a communication professor, suggested that throughout history people have had different ideas of what rhetoric is and the purpose it serves (1967). Consequently, he delineated four periods in the history of rhetoric based on how the term was defined and used. Ehninger's findings suggest that if you are asked "What is rhetoric?" you must respond "It depends on the society it functions in." Ehninger's thinking sparked interest in connecting rhetoric to the cultural, social, and historical forces that exist in any particular time and in exploring how these forces shape public communication. Therefore, scholars began to research the ways that public communication serves social needs in societies around the world. For example, they looked at how the uses of rhetoric in a religious state, or theocracy, may differ from those in a secular, democratic one. In addition, their research showed that the methods and reasons that people speak out in public depend on how such communication is received. While Ehninger focused on the European tradition, his argument stirred interest in understanding how non-Western cultures developed their own rhetorical traditions (Lucaites, Condit, & Caudill, 1999). See *Did You Know? Scholarly Definitions of Rhetoric*.

Did You Know?
Scholarly Definitions of Rhetoric

As you can see from the following list, the term rhetoric *has been defined again and again, with many variations. Which definitions are most helpful in thinking about using communication strategically and which ones are least useful? Which ones are most helpful in contemporary society? Why?*

Plato: Rhetoric is "the art of winning the soul by discourse."

Aristotle: Rhetoric is "the faculty of discovering in any particular case all of the available means of persuasion."

Quintillian: "Rhetoric is the art of speaking well."

George Campbell: "[Rhetoric] is that art or talent by which discourse is adapted to its end. The four ends of discourse are to enlighten the understanding, please the imagination, move the passion, and influence the will."

I. A. Richards: "Rhetoric is the study of misunderstandings and their remedies."

Kenneth Burke: "The most characteristic concern of rhetoric [is] the manipulation of men's beliefs for political ends . . . the basic function of rhetoric [is] the use of words by human agents to form attitudes or to induce actions in other human agents."

Lloyd Bitzer: ". . . rhetoric is a mode of altering reality, not by the direct application of energy to objects, but by the creation of discourse which changes reality through the mediation of thought and action."

Douglas Ehninger: "[Rhetoric is] that discipline which studies all of the ways in which men may influence each other's thinking and behavior through the strategic use of symbols."

Gerard A. Hauser: "Rhetoric is an instrumental use of language. One person engages another person in an exchange of symbols to accomplish some goal. It is not communication for communication's sake. Rhetoric is communication that attempts to coordinate social action. For this reason, rhetorical communication is explicitly pragmatic. Its goal is to influence human choices on specific matters that require immediate attention."

John Locke: "[Rhetoric,] that powerful instrument of error and deceit."

Alfred North Whitehead: "The creation of the world—said Plato—is the victory of persuasion over force. The worth of men consists in their liability to persuasion."

SOURCE: Excerpts taken from: Eidenmuller, M. E. (n.d.) Scholarly definitions of rhetoric. Retrieved June 26, 2006, from www.americanrhetoric.com/rhetoricdefinitions.htm

FROM: www.americanrhetoric.com. Reprinted by permission.

rhetor
a person or institution that addresses
a large audience; the originator of a
communication message but not
necessarily the one delivering it

The European rhetorical tradition is only one of many in the world, and public communication functions in different ways in other parts of the world. Rhetorical scholars are increasingly interested in understanding these differences (Kennedy, 1998). The tradition in the United States emerged from the European tradition, brought by European immigrants to North America. Along with rhetorical traditions, the new Americans also imported European cultural traditions, social expectations, political assumptions, and religious beliefs—all of which inform how public communication functions. This view of rhetoric—as a way of using communication that grows out of particular times, places, and political and social institutions—has become the dominant way of thinking about public communication. The historical study of public communication has not been limited to the European tradition; cultures worldwide have used it as a tool to persuade people toward any number of goals. Some speakers used communication skills to motivate soldiers prior to battle, others to change something in their society or to draw listeners to their religion.

It can be difficult to research and study rhetoric use historically and/or globally because the word *rhetoric* is not used in all cultures to describe that which is called "rhetoric" in the European tradition. The term comes to the English language from the Greek *rhetor*. A **rhetor** is a person or institution that addresses to the public. George Kennedy, a scholar of the ancient world, focuses less on the word, and more on the concept itself. "Rhetoric is apparently a form of energy that drives and is imparted to communication. . . . All communication carries some rhetorical energy" (1998, p. 215). In this sense, rhetoric is not a Western cultural phenomenon, but a facet of communication across cultures—it is the motive for communicating.

In some cultures, the social position of the rhetor is key to the ability of the rhetor to speak. In some cultures, it is important that the rhetor is an elder. In others, it was and sometimes still is important that the rhetor be male. In some cultures, it was and is key that the rhetor be from a high status family. In others, everyone is able to speak. These cultural differences influence who had the ability to speak and who needed to study rhetoric to be the most capable communicators.

To understand how these social positions differ across cultures, it is important to know how different cultures and societies are structured. In some cultures, there were and are monarchies; while in other cultures, religious leaders are in the most powerful positions. Some cultures are led by a group, instead of a single leader. Relationships to certain families, or religious leaders, or other characteristics can lead to empowerment (or disempowerment). Yet, how one's rhetoric is received is very much dependent on where one is in society.

In his broad survey of rhetoric around the world, George Kennedy was impressed by "the many forms of formal language used all over the world, including varieties of indirect speech, the large corpus of distinguished oratory preserved in Chinese historical works (see *Did You Know? Ancient Chinese Rhetoric*) the emergence of forms of sophistry in India and China, and the remarkable apodeictic oratory of the Aztec *huehuetlatolli*" (1998, p. 220). While we can look upon these cultural differences in the past, these differences are still important today. As you think about the role of rhetoric around the world, consider how decisions are made in different societies. You might also contemplate how our own culture is changing as we take part in public debates over such far-reaching topics as gay marriage, immigration and employer sanctions, retirement and pension plans, and more.

RHETORIC AND THE INDIVIDUAL

It may be easiest to think about a rhetor as a specific public speaker, and this is the traditional view. For example, when the president speaks to the nation, the president is a rhetor. However, as notions of rhetoric have expanded over time, corporations, organizations, and governments also have come to be thought of as rhetors. Thus, a rhetor is the originator of a communication message, not necessarily the person delivering it.

Did You Know?
Ancient Chinese Rhetoric

It is important to remember that the concept of rhetoric was not unique to the Greeks. For example, the ancient Chinese had a well-developed sense of the power and impact of language on their social, political, and individual lives. The Western study of rhetoric is comparable to the Chinese Ming Bian Xue: the study of naming (Ming) and argumentation (Bian). From the fifth to the third century B.C. China had five schools of thought in rhetorical philosophy:

School of *Ming*: These philosophers were interested in the function of language in political settings as well as in rational thinking. They lived in the same time period and shared some similarity in worldview and theoretical perspectives with the Greek sophists. Both recognized the power of language, and were intelligent, professional, eloquent speakers who traveled around selling their expertise. But unlike the Greek sophists, the Chinese *Mingjia* used their psychological and rational appeals in mostly private settings.

***Confucianism*:** This philosophy is concerned with morality and three principles—*ren* (benevolence), *li* (rites), and *zhong* (the middle way). Each directly affects rhetorical perspectives. Confucians were primarily interested in speech as an ethical issue, believing that proper use of language keeps society orderly and moral. A person with high moral standards is ethical in speech and action, knows his audience, and can use language appropriately. You can see that ancient Chinese and Greek thinkers have much in common.

School of *Mohism*: This philosophy closely resembles Western logical, religious, and ethical systems. It is deeply concerned with questions about sources of knowledge, uses of names, and methods of inference, but always with a preference for a commonsense attitude. This very practical, utilitarian approach threatened the then-ruling class in China and was considered unethical by the standards of Confucianism. Those associated with *Mohism* became unfairly equated with the *Mingjia* and rejected for their lack of concern for the morals of society.

School of *Daoism*: The three schools of thought we have described thus far all assumed that reality could be represented by language, and language could affect social, political, and moral conditions. In contrast, Daoism is a mystical philosophy that points out the limitation of speech. Instead, it advocates the boundlessness of the mind, the wealth of rhetorical possibilities, and the artfulness of living wisely and freely.

School of *Han Feizi*: Han Feizi was a legalist who viewed language through the lens of political power, specifically the power struggle between a ruler and his ministers. He believed in "government of the ruler, by the ruler, and for the ruler." He described deceptive and cunning rhetorical strategies using audience psychology and practicality. This created an ideology of despotism in which the sole authority was a living god who exerted total political control over his people and was thus capable of great cultural, intellectual, and economic devastation.

ADAPTED FROM: Lu, X. (1998). *Rhetoric in ancient China fifth to third century B.C.E: A comparison with classical Greek rhetoric*. Columbia, SC: University of South Carolina Press, p. 72.

artistic proofs
artistic skills of a rhetor that influence effectiveness

ethos
credibility

Like other areas of communication studies, the study of rhetoric acknowledges the tension between individual forces and societal forces. In this segment of the chapter, we look at the individual forces that make for more or less effective public communicators or rhetors. These forces include the rhetor's **artistic proofs**, or artistic skills of the rhetor that influence effectiveness; position in society; and relationship to the audience.

In the *Art of Rhetoric*, Aristotle argued that there are three artistic proofs: ethos, pathos, and logos. Of these three, **ethos**, or credibility, was the most important.

What characteristics do you think are important to a speaker's credibility, or ethos? Which of Aristotle's list apply today? Which characteristics are most important to you?

Ethos

If ethos is the most important artistic proof, where does it come from and how does the rhetor achieve it? Aristotle suggested that rhetors gain credibility from a number of individual characteristics, but he focused his attention on three: good sense, moral character, and goodwill. He also included family background, attractiveness, and athletic ability among the characteristics of a good rhetor. (Advertising commonly uses this aspect of ethos in using attractive models, celebrated athletes, and others to promote products).

Some of the individual characteristics of good speakers may seem to be out of their control. Consider former Pittsburgh Steelers football player Lynn Swann's candidacy for governor of Pennsylvania in 2006. If you are running against him, you cannot suddenly change your communication style to show you are similarly athletic, if you are not. Likewise, you might not be able to make yourself look like a magazine model for a job interview or presentation, but you can dress sharply and fix your hair to increase your attractiveness. You can also emphasize your good sense, character, and goodwill.

Other aspects of credibility are more in the control of the rhetor. For example, the 2009 allegations over corruption by the governor of Illinois, Rod Blagojevich, have tainted his credibility. Similarly, the seeming inability of Sarah Palin to answer foreign-policy questions during the 2008 campaign, as well as charges that she inappropriately put pressure on the Alaska public safety commissioner to fire her ex-brother-in-law who was a state trooper, also hurt her credibility. In both of these cases, not all audiences came to the same conclusions based upon the media coverage. Since then, Governor Palin has remained popular among many U.S. Americans and she likely has a brighter political future than does Blagojevich, who was impeached and banned from holding future office in the state of Illinois.

Thus, rhetors can create and project *personas* that help them communicate messages effectively. **Persona** describes the identity one creates through one's public communication efforts. Persona is related to the notion of identity that we discussed in Chapter 3. However, while individual identities are constructed through larger social categories, one's persona typically is constructed rhetorically. For example, if you listen to a famous speaker, such as Martin Luther King, Jr. or Malcolm X, you obtain a sense of the persona they created for their audiences. However, both of these men likely sounded quite different at the dinner table or while socializing with friends. Thus, a speaker's public persona may be quite different from his or her private one. In contrast, a speaker's social identities, such as race, ethnicity, age, and nationality, remain virtually the same from situation to situation and are not under the speaker's control. The public persona a speaker projects can enhance her ethos if audiences find the persona credible, informed, or intelligent; it can diminish her ethos if audiences perceive the persona to be untrustworthy, deceitful, unintelligent, or misinformed.

Interpretations of ethos are influenced not only by how a speaker presents herself or himself but also by social factors such as stereotypes, assumptions, and other biases. For example, sometimes people hear accents that increase or decrease their perceptions of the speaker's intelligence. British accents tend to increase credibility in the United States, while southern accents may have the opposite effect, especially in the northern United States.

Malcolm X created a very powerful persona that drew many to his view on the path to equality, justice and freedom.

persona
the identity one creates through one's public communication efforts

pathos
the rhetorical use of emotions to affect audience decision making

Pathos

Pathos refers to the rhetorical use of emotions to affect audience decision making. Speakers often use emotion to influence the audience to identify with a particular perspective. In a court case, the prosecuting lawyer may reenact the crime to help the jury see the case from the point of view of the victim. An effective reenactment may influence the jury to emotionally identify and thus side with the prosecution rather than the defense. In late 2004, a jury convicted Scott Peterson of murdering his wife, Laci, and their unborn son. While the jury deliberated about the penalty for this crime, the prosecuting attorney, Dave Harris, projected large photographs of the badly decomposed bodies of Laci Peterson and her fetus. He argued that "Leaving his wife's body to rot in the bottom of the ocean, leaving his son's body to be found as trash in debris, that's not something that should be rewarded by sparing his life" (Ryan, 2004). The attorney used these troubling photographs and descriptions to provoke strong emotional responses, hoping to sway the jury toward his view. In this case, the attorney's rhetorical strategy proved effective, as Scott Peterson did receive the death penalty.

Emotional appeals do not have to be so extreme and often are more subtle. For example, the athletic and alumni Web sites for many universities incorporate pathos to invite participation in their events and support for their organizations. Some of these emotional appeals may involve feelings of pride by associating with the university, as well as positive memories that alumni may have about their student days. You may have similar feelings some day.

Logos

The term **logos**, or rational appeals, refers to the use of rhetoric to help the audience see the rationale for a particular conclusion. While the word *logos* looks like logic, it is not as narrowly defined. Rather, logos refers to reasoning or rationality more generally. For example, a lawyer may use evidence such as fingerprints to build a case and explain how a crime occurred, or a politician may point to her voting record to establish her credibility as a conservative.

One of the most pressing health and social issues in the United States today is obesity, as "more than 60% of us are overweight, and the percentage of us who are considered obese has nearly doubled since 1980" (Tumulty, 2006, p. 41). In addition, "nearly 400 obesity-related bills were introduced in state legislatures across the country last year—more than double the number in 2003" (p. 41). The federal government is also concerned about the costs associated with obesity. Yet, persuading U.S. Americans to lose weight is not easy. A logos-centered approach would focus on the health risks of obesity, including diabetes and shortened life spans. Another logos-centered approach might emphasize nutrition and the health-related rationale behind eating some foods while avoiding others. Information about the benefits of exercise would offer further rational appeals for changing sedentary lifestyles.

Aristotle felt that combining ethos, pathos, and logos was more effective than relying on only one kind of proof. In this case, logos could offer the rationale for losing weight as well as suggestions for how one might do so. Combining these appeals with the pathos-based approach of television shows like *The Biggest Loser* might enhance the impact on waistlines. And by using logos as well as pathos, a rhetor might appear well-formed on the topic of obesity, and this could enhance his or her ethos.

Social Position

Related to the concept of ethos is the social position from which a rhetor speaks. Aristotle noted that those who came from noble families were better positioned as rhetors. Yet **social position** refers to more than the notoriety of one's family. One's social position comes from the way society is structured. Everyone is located in more than one position in the social structure as she or he speaks—as a student, a customer, a friend, a voter, and so on. As a receiver of public communication, you should always consider the position or positions from which the rhetor is speaking.

logos
rational appeals; the use of rhetoric to help the audience see the rationale for a particular conclusion

social position
place in the social hierarchy, which comes from the way society is structured

If this officer were to testify against you in court, how might your different social positions influence how the officer's testimony and your testimony are heard?
Phil Sears/The *New York Times*

What aspects of social position might help or hinder a speaker's ability to advocate a point of view? The answer is that it depends on the society and the situation. We expect certain people to speak in certain situations, such as family members at a funeral, or the governor after a natural disaster. In these cases, the rhetor's authority comes from a combination of her or his position and the audience members' expectations. Yet these social positions are also hierarchical, meaning that some positions have more power than others. For example, if you, as a student, were to speak out about U.S. immigration policies, you would be less influential than the president is when he speaks about the same topic. Even if you spoke well, you could not make up for the difference in social positions between a student and a president. Social positions and positions of power are deeply intertwined, as social positions gain their power from the society that supports the structure. This power structure allows certain rhetors to be more effective than others in promoting a message.

As noted in the extreme example of the student and the president, people's rhetorical positions can vary widely. Barbara Biesecker (1992), a communication scholar, has examined these variations with regard to women and the ways that they have been allowed or not allowed to speak in society. She argues that before women gained the right to vote and participate in political debates, they were allowed to speak only on issues of the home. The home was seen as a traditional domain of women, whereas the world outside the home, and issues like war, taxes, and crime, were seen as more properly the domains of men.

Think about how other social groups have attempted unsuccessfully to speak publicly about various issues. In societies such as India that have strong caste systems, lower castes have few rhetorical mechanisms for changing the rules that guide their lives: Compared with higher castes, fewer of them have access to the Internet; they are less able to garner media coverage of their issues; and thus they have fewer opportunities to be heard by those in power. In her study of the use of Native Americans as sports mascots, Janis King (2002) focused on the rhetoric of a columnist in *Indian Country Today*. In her analysis, she concluded that Native Americans have few opportunities to change the use of these mascots, as "team owners and the majority of the fans are White. And it is these individuals who have the power to eliminate the mascots, clothing and actions" (p. 211).

Social institutions, also considered rhetors according to our definition, have distinct social positions that contribute to the effectiveness or persuasiveness of their public messages. For example, when the U.S. Supreme Court issues a ruling, it sends a public message that—coming from its position of power within our social structure—has tremendous implications for the ways we live. When the court ruled in *Loving v. Virginia* (1967) that laws forbidding interracial marriage were unconstitutional, this public message had important implications for the sixteen states with antimiscegenation laws. The Court opinion stated that "Under our Constitution, the freedom to marry, or not marry, a person of another race resides with the individual and cannot be infringed by the State" (*Loving v. Virginia*, 388 U.S. 1 (1967)). By emphasizing the individual's right to choose whom to marry, the Court underscored the importance of individualism as a value in our society and demonstrated its power to shape the way race functions in the United States. Other social institutions, including those involved in medicine, religion, the military, and education, also exercise their power through rhetoric.

Audiences, too, have social positions, and these affect the way they listen. For example, many high school administrators have entertained heated discussions regarding students' right to eat lunch off-campus. Parents, who don't have to eat on campus and are concerned about their children's safety, tend to favor closing the campuses. In contrast, students, who do have to eat on campus and tend to see fewer risks associated with leaving campus, typically support policies that allow them to leave during the lunch hour. In this instance, the social positions of the participants affect their perspectives on this issue. In general, audiences respond to arguments based on what they perceive to be in their own best interests.

Relationship to Audiences

Rhetorical discourse must always be adapted to its audiences in order to influence them. While a rhetor may assume that all audiences are the same and much like him or her, this would be a mistake. The cultural, social, and political assumptions and perspectives of different audiences can vary considerably. For example, in the aftermath of Hurricane Katrina, polls showed that Whites and African Americans had very different views on the role of race in the response to this disaster. A Pew Research Center Survey (2005) found that 66 percent of African Americans felt that the response would have been faster if the victims were White, whereas only 17 percent of Whites felt that way (http://people-press.org/reports/display.php3?ReportID=255). One common mistake of speakers is to think only of the dominant culture, overlooking minorities who may also be part of the audience. The wide disparity in the ways racial groups viewed the government's response to Katrina serves as an important reminder of the range of opinions that may be represented in any audience.

Who, then, is the rhetorical audience for any particular message? Rhetorical scholar Lloyd Bitzer (1968) argued that only those people who could take the appropriate action are part of the **rhetorical audience**. In other words, if a candidate for president of the United States wanted to persuade a group of people to vote for her, only those people in the audience who are U.S. citizens and registered voters are part of the rhetorical audience. While citizens of other nations or minors may be physically present for the campaign pitch, because they cannot vote for this candidate, they would not be part of the rhetorical audience. Thinking about the audience in this way may help the speaker design an appropriate, appealing, and persuasive message.

Yet, this perspective on audience is quite narrow. As you may have noticed from following presidential elections, U.S. citizens are not the only people who pay attention to campaign rhetoric. People around the world are also quite interested in who is elected and which policies—economic, military, cultural—this president will pursue. We live in a global environment in which the actions of the United States impact others around the world. Thus, the presidential candidate can use rhetoric to construct the desired rhetorical audience, perhaps including non-U.S. citizens. For example, a candidate might refer to "our friends" in a particular nation and assure them of continued U.S. support. Although the citizens of that nation cannot vote in the United States, they might play an important part in the success of the president's term and the international vision of the United States. The recent election of Joseph Cao to Congress from Louisiana underscores the rhetorical message sent. While many people do not live in his congressional district, the election of the first Vietnamese American to Congress sends a powerful message about the "American Dream" worldwide (see *Alternative View: The First Vietnamese American in Congress*, on p. 304).

In addition to being broader than a speaker might initially think, audiences, like society, also are fragmented. French theorist Michel Maffesoli (1996) has suggested that society is constituted of multiple "tribes," or identity groups, with their own ways of seeing the world. These groups often are marked by how they consume products, wear clothing, or participate in certain activities. These tribes might include NASCAR dads, soccer moms, or goths. Maffesoli's view of society can help illuminate the complexity of audiences and how rhetoric works in differing contexts with various groups. For example, at his sister's wedding, Tom

rhetorical audience
those people who can take the appropriate action in response to a message

Alternative VIEW
The First Vietnamese American in Congress

2008 was a year of many political "firsts," not the least of which included the election of Barack Obama as the first African American president of the United States. Making waves in New Orleans, however, is Joseph Cao, the first Vietnamese American elected to Congress. This is a brief look into his life.

Joseph Cao is the first Vietnamese American elected to Congress. He is a Republican from Louisiana's 2nd District.

Anh "Joseph" Cao—the hot new property in Congress, Mr. Upset, the first Vietnamese American elected to the U.S. House or Senate, the first Republican to win Louisiana's 2nd Congressional District since before Louis Armstrong was born—is driving across this Gothic American bayou. He's relating how, as a Jesuit seminarian in the slums of Mexico nearly 20 years ago, he experienced a crisis of faith. He was dispirited by how God could let such human misery exist, he says and then stops himself. "Do you ever read Kierkegaard?" he asks.

Um, the 19th-century Danish philosopher is in our memory bank, but "Fear and Trembling" has not been on our coffee table for quite some time.

"Kierkegaard had this story about a man going through life. The man reached an abyss. He had to make what Kierkegaard called the leap of faith. In life's journey, you sometimes reach a level of uncertainty that you have to make such a leap.

"That's what happened to me in Mexico. I was working in extremely poor conditions, and I wanted to promote social change. I came to believe, over the course of two or three years, that the best way to do that would be to enter public office. It would also allow me to have a family—the celibate life can be quite lonely. So I drafted a course of action for myself to enter politics. But it was a quite painful discernment. It implied I would have to leave the seminary. I would have to start life over again. I would have to make that leap of faith."

Cao (pronounced "gow") is 41. He is soft-spoken, with neatly combed, thick black hair. His trade, until recently, was immigration and personal-injury lawyer. He stands just under 5-2. Soaking wet, he might weigh 125 pounds. He is a very good listener. He smiles, but not all the time. He runs five miles every day before dawn.

He is telling this story in his lightly accented English, a reminder that he was airlifted as a child out of Saigon "two or three days" before that city fell to communist forces. He makes scant mention of other hardships: arriving in Indiana without his parents, a terrified 8-year-old who spoke no English; leaving the seminary in 1996 in a weathered Honda Accord bound for his sister's house in Falls Church; arriving there with $20 to his name and no prospects save for his faith, determination and intellect. (In this tableau, Hurricane Katrina washing out his New Orleans home with eight feet of water in 2005 is not anything much to discuss.)

So—he's back to his story now—his stunning victory earlier this month over veteran congressman William "Cold Cash" Jefferson, he of the beaucoup federal indictments and $90,000 in marked bills in his freezer. It didn't surprise Cao at all.

He's been running for office for 10 years. It's just in the past few weeks that anyone noticed. "Nobody gave him a chance, and all of a sudden—boom!—he was right there," gushes Eddie White, a retired electrician who has a fishing shack just down the canal from Cao's home way out in the bayous of east New Orleans. "It's like the American dream."

noticed that the groom's Jewish American family stood up to praise the groom and tell the bride's family about their newest family member in glowing terms. Yet, because praising a family member in public is viewed negatively among Japanese Americans, some audience members felt uncomfortable with this rhetorical practice. Neither approach is "correct." The story serves to illustrate that cultures differ in their rules for how public communication functions or how it is used or interpreted.

Scholars have studied the ways that rhetoric functions among various audiences. For example, Eric King Watts and Mark Orbe (2002) examined Budweiser beer's advertising campaign that used "Whassup?!" and other aspects of African American culture with White audiences. They explored the meanings and functions of this type of public communication and how it influenced interracial relations. They concluded that this advertising works because of White ambivalence about Black culture. That is, the ads allow Whites to embrace Black culture through consumption, but without participating in it. For example, rhetorical scholar Meagan Parker (2008) analyzed James Forman's "Black Manifesto," which many people see as a rhetorical failure. James Forman's "Black Manifesto" called for reparations from White Christian churches and Jewish synagogues to be paid to African Americans. It was adopted in 1969 by the Black Economic Development Conference in Detroit. It criticized these religious organizations for their role in slavery and creating a racist society. Parker's analysis, however, shows that a number of Black audience members did embrace the work and the leadership role assigned to them, while many White audience members did not like the place they were assigned by the "Black Manifesto." The rhetorical function of the "Black Manifesto," then, depends on the interplay among its audiences, the rhetor, and the rhetorical text.

Much more work needs to be done on the use of specific rhetorical devices among diverse cultural audiences so that we can better understand their complex functions. Nevertheless, as you interact in settings that are culturally different from your own, be aware that certain aspects of communication may serve unique purposes and have distinct meanings.

In summary, a rhetor's effectiveness depends on a configuration of characteristics such as artistic proofs—ethos, pathos, and logos—as well as social position and relationship to audiences. (See *Visual Summary 11.1: Elements of Rhetorical Effectiveness*, on p. 306). Many factors contribute to our impression that one speaker is more charismatic and powerful than another. Audience members may not always agree on which speaker is the best, but most can say which one moves them and which leaves them cold—or drowsy! Considering individual rhetor characteristics gives us only a partial view of rhetoric. Let's broaden our focus to examine the relationship between rhetoric and society and the roles rhetoric plays in giving meaning to major events, fulfilling democratic functions, and bringing about justice and social change.

"NASCAR dads" have been identified as a potential audience that might be considered a contemporary U.S. "tribe."

Fred Conrad/The *New York Times*

THE INDIVIDUAL, RHETORIC, AND SOCIETY

Rhetoric always arises within a specific social context. Since each society is structured in its own way, each one has unique functions for rhetoric. Thus the distinct cultural forces that influence individual societies should be considered when studying their rhetoric.

Research has shown that the technological means of communication available to a society influence its rhetorical tradition. For example, rhetorical scholar Xing Lu (1998) examined the way that Chinese rhetoric responded to historical shifts. She notes that once the Zhou dynasty declined (approximately eleventh to eighth centuries, B.C.) and China instituted a more decentralized political system with many

Elements of Rhetorical Effectiveness

Aristotle's Artistic Proofs

Ethos
- Credibility
  - Good sense
  - Moral character
  - Good will

Pathos
- Emotional appeals

Logos
- Rational appeals

Social Position

Ethos
- Family status
- Social structure

Relationship to the Audience
- Rhetorical audience
- Multiple audiences

kings, advisers to the kings developed a rhetoric "to persuade them to adopt certain policies either for governing their own people or for conquering the neighboring states" (p. 65). Many philosophers in this period became political consultants; Mencius, for example, used this type of persuasive rhetoric to advise the kings of Qi and Liang based on his philosophy of benevolence (p. 65). Of course, the culture of ancient China differs dramatically from our contemporary culture, and rhetoric serves different needs from era to era and society to society. In the United States today, rhetoric serves four important democratic functions that comprise the basis of how we come to decisions and work together on the societal level. We will look at these four functions next.

Reaffirming Cultural Values

The term **rhetorical event** refers to any event that generates a significant amount of public discourse. Such "explosions" of rhetoric give insight into the ways meaning is constructed and rhetoric and cultural values are affirmed. For example, unusual weather or natural disasters incite a great deal of rhetorical discourse that attempts to explain what has occurred. Some of the discourse usually comes from scientists, who provide scientific explanations about the event (say, the tsunami of 2004). Other discourse may come from religious leaders, who try to connect such natural disasters to a religious meaning. After the attacks on September 11, 2001, for instance, Reverend Jerry Falwell "sparked an uproar by saying that liberal civil-rights groups, homosexuals and abortion-rights supporters were partly responsible for last week's terrorist attacks" (Harris, 2001, p. C4). He later apologized for his remarks, but his voice was a powerful one, growing from individuals' need to understand what had happened and why.

Part of the function of rhetorical events, then, is to reaffirm cultural values. Every four years, for example, the United States inaugurates a president, and the speeches given, particularly the president's inaugural speech, highlight important U.S. American values along with that president's goals. However, holidays, sports events, weddings, funerals, retirement parties, campaign speeches, declarations of war, and protest marches also are rhetorical events. This is because these occasions often include speakers who celebrate cultural values at the same time that they deliver relevant content to their audience.

Increasing Democratic Participation

As noted, among the ancient Greeks, rhetoric was valued for its use in civic life. The belief that advocating for one's ideas is in the best interests of society is a cornerstone of democracy. Not all societies are democracies, of course, and in those nondemocratic societies rhetoric has served very different purposes. For our discussion we will examine aspects of rhetorical communication that influence citizen participation, a key part of the democratic process.

Deliberative rhetoric, the type of rhetoric used to argue what a society should do in the future, is deeply embedded in the democratic process. When legislators argue about raising taxes to pay for new roads or increasing funding for education, they are engaged in deliberative rhetoric. A speaker's ability to advocate effectively drives the open discussion and debate about what society should or should not do.

Also essential to a democracy is citizens' ability to evaluate the many important arguments they hear. In 2003, the United States argued in front of the United Nations Security Council that Saddam Hussein had weapons

rhetorical event
any event that generates a significant amount of public discourse

deliberative rhetoric
the type of rhetoric used to argue what a society should do in the future

Congress engages in deliberative rhetoric to decide what future actions the United States should take.

public sphere
the arena in which deliberative decision making occurs through the exchange of ideas and arguments

forensic rhetoric
rhetoric that addresses events that happened in the past with the goal of setting things right after an injustice has occurred

of mass destruction and that, therefore, military intervention was needed. In hindsight, both government officials and citizens can see the errors made in arguments for the invasion. However, at the time, social position (as discussed on p. 301) played an important role in the persuasiveness of the argument to go to war. Because Colin Powell was secretary of state and was well respected nationally and internationally, he spoke from a position of power and credibility. Donald Rumsfeld, as secretary of defense, also spoke in favor of invading Iraq, as did President George W. Bush on a number of occasions. In this instance, however, as well as in many others, citizens in a democracy benefit from listening to a variety of arguments and evaluating them based on the evidence available—without the undue influence of social position.

Another important area of inquiry within rhetorical studies as it relates to democracy focuses on the public sphere. The **public sphere** is the arena in which deliberative decision making occurs through the exchange of ideas and arguments. For example, legislative bodies such as Congress are places where decisions are made about a range of issues, including social security, taxes, and education. Also, protests against the World Trade Association, underground and alternative magazines and newspapers, and performance art that critiques social issues all constitute types of public sphere rhetoric, but are sometimes referred to as *counter-publics*, as they occur outside the mainstream media and institutions. This type of rhetoric is also central to the functioning of a democratic society, because it typically includes the voices of less powerful or marginalized individuals and groups.

Bringing About Justice

As we noted earlier in this chapter, a specific type of rhetoric is used in courts of law to bring about justice. Called **forensic rhetoric**, this form addresses events that happened in the past, as in "Where were you on the night of April 24?" The goal of forensic rhetoric is to set things right after an injustice has occurred. Forensic rhetoric is similar to forensic medicine, which focuses on medical insights that support judicial concerns, in that both contribute to efforts to achieve justice. You are probably familiar with the use of forensic inquiry in the television show *CSI*, where forensic evidence is collected to solve crimes.

TWO PARKING TICKETS AND FOUR OUTSTANDING LIBRARY FINES ...I THINK WE CAN TRUST THE JURY TO MAKE THE LINK WITH THESE RECENT GANGLAND KILLINGS!

Courtroom speeches are part of the rhetorical tradition, and they certainly should be persuasive. In ancient Greece, citizens who were charged with a crime or who wanted to charge someone else for illegal behavior had to speak for themselves in court. Consequently, studying rhetoric was extremely important. Today, however, parties in court usually hire attorneys to speak for them, or one is appointed. This is one reason that the motivation to become an effective speaker has declined over the centuries.

Another function of rhetoric in the context of justice is to allow citizens to exchange and negotiate ideas about what constitutes "just" and "unjust." As we look back over United States history, we can see how notions of justice have changed. In 1692, people in Salem, Massachusetts, felt that justice was served when they hanged nineteen people and jailed hundreds more for practicing witchcraft. Today, we see these trials as examples of injustice. In 1872, Susan B. Anthony, along with a number of other women, voted in Rochester, New York. She was arrested and convicted of violating laws that prevented women from voting. Today, most people view Susan B. Anthony's actions as not only just but courageous. For another example that highlights the changing nature of rhetoric and justice, see *Alternative View: Rhetoric and Justice*, where you can read the rhetoric of Judge Jackie Glass who sentenced O. J. Simpson in 2008.

Alternative VIEW
Rhetoric and Justice

Following are portions of the sentencing speech handed down by Judge Jackie Glass of Las Vegas to O. J. Simpson, who was convicted on twelve charges including conspiracy to commit a crime, robbery, assault and kidnapping with a deadly weapon stemming from a September 13, 2007, incident at Las Vegas' Palace Station hotel and casino.

Earlier in this case, at a bail hearing, I asked—said—to Mr. Simpson I didn't know if he was arrogant or ignorant or both. And during the trial and through this proceeding, I got this answer, and it was both.

At the time—not after you've been locked up for 64 days at the time of this event—and at the time I saw you at the bail hearing, it was clear to the court that you believed you could do in Las Vegas what you couldn't do elsewhere. You could get your stuff back.

. . . And that was a violent event. Guns were brought. Gun—at least one gun was drawn. The potential for harm to occur in that room was tremendous. And I don't know—I don't know how fortunate you consider yourself to be at this moment—but really, truly, if the gun had gone off and bullets started flying, not only could one in the room have been hurt, but some poor tourists walking down the hallway or worker at that hotel could have been hurt. That is why we have rules in the state of Nevada that say you can't take back your own property by force, anybody else's property by force. You can't do it. There's no self-help. You cannot do it. But you did.

I actually am surprised that I heard from you, Mr. Simpson. I believed there wasn't going to be a statement from you, and I was going to be concerned about your lack of responsibility for this action. And it's kind of a fine line in what you said to me. I hear what you said and what Mr. Galanter said, which is I didn't intend to do anything wrong, so I must not have done something wrong, so there was no criminal intent, it was just all stupidity. I have to tell you now, it was much more than stupidity. And it's rare that I have somebody talking to me at a sentencing about mens rea (legal term for "guilty mind") and criminal intent. It doesn't matter. You went to the room, and you took guns—meaning you and the group. You used force. You took property, whether it was yours or somebody else's. And in this state, that amounts to robbery, with use of a deadly weapon.

OK. The problem is that I can't ignore that the behavior at the time on September 13th was reckless. It disregarded the law, the law was broken, force was used, guns were used—or at least a gun was used—there was another gun there. The potential for harm was great. You're fortunate nothing happened. Property was stolen. The jury convicted you, and now I'll sentence you.

As you can see, laws and court judgments can only determine what is just and unjust within specific situations at particular moments in history. For example, Dred Scott was a nineteenth-century slave who tried to buy freedom for himself and his wife, but when the owner refused, he sought freedom through the court system. The U.S. Supreme Court ultimately ruled that he was neither a citizen—and therefore could not bring a case in federal court—nor entitled to his freedom, as he was someone's personal property. Today, we would be shocked at this kind of Supreme Court ruling. As a nation, we have decided that slavery is an injustice, but coming to this decision involved considerable public communication or rhetoric about slavery. It also involved a bloody war. Nevertheless, debates about citizenship and racial restrictions on who was eligible to be a U.S. citizen continued well into the twentieth century.

Hindsight makes it easy to see that slavery or the denial of rights to women or Blacks is unjust. In many cases, however, considerable disagreement exists about what is just. For example, the U.S. military has been grappling with cases of torture at Abu Ghraib prison in Iraq in 2003, and in secret prisons around the world. Some of the photographs of naked prisoners at Abu Ghraib were broadcast on television. What is the just response to this set of events? As the discussion about justice ensues, some will argue that these soldiers were under orders

social movement
a large, organized body of people who are attempting to create social change

from their superiors, and thus not responsible, while others will argue that each person is responsible for her or his own acts. Lawyers are generally at the forefront of these discussions, at least in the courtroom, but the public, the press, and politicians also weigh in.

In the effort to find justice, Ameneh Bahrami, an Iranian woman, has asked that Islamic law be imposed on the man who threw acid on her face, which resulted in disfiguring and blinding her. This man, Majid Movahedi, wanted to marry Bahrami, but she declined his marriage proposal. Recently, "an Iranian court ordered that five drops of the same chemical be placed in each of her attacker's eyes, acceding to Bahrami's demand that he be punished according to a principle in Islamic jurisprudence that allows a victim to seek retribution for a crime" (Erdbrink, 2008, p. A1). While recognizing cultural and religious differences, is this justice? How do we determine what is just and what is unjust, except through public discussion and deliberation? As you contemplate these types of questions you will undoubtedly realize that many different kinds of punishments were (and are) acceptable in different periods and places. Justice is not something that is easily settled nor universally agreed upon. Through our public discussions about what is right and what is wrong, what is just and what is unjust, we try to move our fellow citizens toward building a more just society. Rhetoric plays a key role in these discussions and the attempts to persuade others about justice, whether inside or outside the courtroom.

Prompting Social Change

As you can see from the Dred Scott case and others, laws do not always ensure justice for all. Thus, people who want to bring about social change and promote their views of justice often use rhetoric to mobilize large numbers of people. If a mobilization succeeds, it can lead to a **social movement**—a mass movement of people who are attempting to create social change. Scholars have studied the public messages of social movements, such as the movement to abolish slavery, the women's suffrage movement, and the anti–Vietnam War movement. Social-movement scholars also have tried to understand opposition to such messages and movements and to evaluate how persuasive the opposition is.

Other social movements that have received attention from rhetoricians include the Chicano movement (Delgado, 1995), the environmental movement (DeLuca, 1999), and the gay/lesbian movement (Darsey, 1991). In this latter study, Darsey tracked the changing arguments of gay rights activists over time in relation to the changing contexts of sexual liberation, antigay legislation, and AIDS. For example, during the 1969 Stonewall Riots, an event that occurred in New York's Greenwich Village, gays and lesbians challenged negative cultural stereotypes by expressing the message that "gay is good" (Darsey, 1981, p. 241). However, as the American Psychiatric Association deleted homosexuality from their list of mental disorders in 1973, the rhetoric shifted to gay rights, and then, as AIDS became a health crisis in the gay community, the rhetoric again shifted to focus on public policies related to health care (Darsey, 1991). The goals of this study and other similar ones are to understand the arguments that activists in social movements make, the social and historical context in which they put forth these arguments, the events that spark the emergence of social movement discourse, the resistance to the arguments, and why arguments on both sides are or are not persuasive.

Janice Dickinson, owner of a modeling agency, and some models protest against the use of fur. They are using rhetoric to try to change how we view and use animals.

As you can see, public messages are deeply embedded in the culture of their times. In past eras, debates and speeches about slavery, women's suffrage, and U.S. involvement in the Vietnam War permeated the daily life of U.S. Americans. Today, far more rhetoric focuses on terrorism, Iraq, and gay marriage. As people perceive wrongs that need to be corrected, social movements emerge, and people utilize rhetoric to argue for the desired changes. Because social movements typically are controversial, others who prefer to maintain the status quo will oppose the movement, and they will also use rhetoric to argue against change. This has been the case in every social movement mentioned.

Today, the uses of rhetoric extend far beyond the traditional medium of public speaking. People who desire to change our society turn to using every available means of communicating. This means that rhetoric is a part of our everyday lives and it is relayed via advertising, the Internet, and in email messages, text messages, television programming, and newspapers. In the next chapter, we turn to an examination of media, but rhetoric is embedded in media messages as well. While these may seem to be discrete chapters, the connections between various aspects of communication cannot be so easily segmented.

In sum, rhetoric plays an important role in a society. It can provide meaning and shape our thoughts about major events. It can also serve democratic functions in the political life of a society. Furthermore, rhetoric can bring about justice and provide momentum for major social changes, as it has in historical movements, and as it continues to do today. (For a summary of these functions, see *Visual Summary 11.2: Functions of Rhetoric*, on p. 313.) But how can you use these ideas about rhetoric to become more ethical and effective consumers of rhetorical messages? These are the topics of the next two sections.

ETHICS AND RHETORIC

When we examine ethics and rhetoric we must consider the ethics of both the rhetor and the audience because they are interrelated. As in other aspects of communication, deception and deliberate misrepresentation of information are important ethical issues. While rhetors may in limited and specific instances feel the need to deceive audiences—such as in cases of immediate national security—outright lying rarely can be justified. In the context of rhetoric, outright lying is not usually the ethical concern. More commonly, rhetors push against the boundaries of ethical communication by omitting facts or taking information out of context. In addition, some rhetors may demean or disparage a particular social group—either overtly or in a subtle way. And, of course, each rhetor is generally promoting only one among many possible points of view—an aspect of rhetoric that is not unethical but needs to be considered by those in the audience.

Using what you know about rhetoric, then, what can you do to become an ethical receiver of rhetorical communication? Here are some guidelines:

- Be willing to listen to a range of perspectives on a particular topic. While you may not initially agree with a particular rhetor, you should consider her or his perspective (Makau, 1997), including why you do or do not agree.
- Be willing to speak out if you know that a rhetor is giving misinformation or deceiving an audience.
- Don't be silenced by information overload. If a speaker gives too much information, focus on the main points and be critical of this kind of presentation.
- Listen critically to the rhetor; don't accept the arguments presented at face value.
- Be willing to speak out publicly if a rhetor communicates in a way that dehumanizes or demeans others (Johannesen, 1997).

- Listen to and fairly assess what you hear, which may require that you postpone judgment until you hear the entire message.
- Be willing to change your mind as more evidence becomes available.

BECOMING A MORE EFFECTIVE RECEIVER OF RHETORIC

Rhetorical communication invites you to view the world in a particular way. At one time, rhetors attempted to persuade people that slavery was wrong, while other rhetors argued that slavery was morally just. While you are not confronted with this debate today, you are faced with equally important issues that spark rhetoric from a range of perspectives. For example, some politicians argue that the United States should continue to expand the walls along its border with Mexico to keep out illegal immigrants, while others advocate for a guest-worker program that would ease access for Mexican immigrant workers. How can you become a better listener and, in the process, learn to evaluate conflicting rhetorical messages such as these? The following strategies can help.

The term **rhetorical critic** refers to an informed consumer of rhetorical discourse who is prepared to analyze rhetorical texts. You may think that a critic's job is simply to be negative about whatever is under analysis. However, everyone is a critic in everyday life. When you react to a movie, you are a movie critic; when you say what you think about your dinner, you are a food critic. Of course, you don't dislike every movie and every meal. In both cases you think about why you liked or disliked parts of the movie or the meal. You have reasons for coming to your conclusions. Although some people reserve the term *rhetorical critic* for those who work in academia, we see it differently. We consider anyone who pursues sustained and detailed analyses of rhetorical discourse to be a rhetorical critic.

We hope that you and your fellow citizens all become more attuned to the sensitivities of rhetorical discourse and that you become strong analysts of it, as it has tremendous influence on the ways you conduct your everyday life and the way society functions. For example, rhetorical discourse likely shapes your understanding of what it means to be a good parent. Do you think that good parents have to sacrifice everything for their children? Pay for their college educations? Do good parents expect their children to take care of them in their old age? Or should good parents do everything possible to avoid being a burden? Of course, no "right" answer exists for any of these questions. But it's important to be aware that you do have some ideas about what good parenting is. It's also important to be aware that these ideas came from a barrage of rhetorical messages from newspaper reporters, magazine writers, psychologists, religious organizations, and others. Becoming more aware of your opinions and where they come from can make you a more effective rhetorical critic.

Some rhetoricians also believe that being an informed rhetorical critic can help people better appreciate the artistic aspects of discourse (Darsey, 1994), as well as what makes a particular rhetorical message effective or persuasive. When you read the excerpt from a famous antislavery speech in *Did You Know? Frederick Douglass*, on p. 314, consider what makes it effective. What are the artistic aspects of this speech? Why didn't Douglass simply say, "Slavery is wrong"?

Rhetorical criticism is a method for generating knowledge about rhetoric. Through attentiveness to how rhetoric has functioned and continues to function in various contexts, you can build an understanding of your culture, society, and the ideas that predominated during a given period. Hence, an analysis of any one rhetorical message should be seen as part of a much larger and ongoing dialogue.

rhetorical critic
an informed consumer of rhetorical discourse who is prepared to analyze rhetorical texts

Functions of Rhetoric

REAFFIRMING CULTURAL VALUES

Pope Benedict XVI speaking at the Vatican, April 23, 2005.

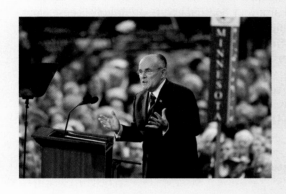

INCREASING DEMOCRATIC PARTICIPATION

Former governor Rudy Giuliani delivers the keynote address at the 2008 Republican National Convention in Minneapolis, Minnesota.

PROMPTING SOCIAL CHANGE

Feminist and activist Gloria Steinem speaking at a rally.

BRINGING ABOUT JUSTICE

Attorney Johnnie Cochran holding a press conference for client Abner Louima, July 12, 2001.

Did You Know?
Frederick Douglass

When Frederick Douglass began to speak out against slavery, many White Americans did not believe he had really been a slave, nor that he was African American. In her biography of Douglass, Sandra Thomas explains: "People gradually began to doubt that Douglass was telling the truth about himself. Reporting on a lecture that he gave in 1844, the Liberator *wrote that many people in the audience refused to believe his stories: 'How a man, only six years out of bondage, and who had never gone to school could speak with such eloquence—with such precision of language and power of thought—they were utterly at a loss to devise.'" Unfortunately, this response to minority speakers may not be unusual.*

Here is a famous excerpt from a speech Douglass gave about the Fourth of July. How do the aesthetic aspects of this speech help move an audience?

What, to the American slave, is your 4th of July? I answer; a day that reveals to him, more than all other days in the year, the gross injustice and cruelty to which he is the constant victim. To him, your celebration is a sham; your boasted liberty, an unholy license; your national greatness, swelling vanity; your sounds of rejoicing are empty and heartless; your denunciation of tyrants, brass-fronted impudence; your shouts of liberty and equality, hollow mockery; your prayers and hymns, your sermons and thanksgivings, with all your religious parade and solemnity, are, to Him, mere bombast, fraud, deception, impiety, and hypocrisy—a thin veil to cover up crimes which would disgrace a nation of savages. There is not a nation on the earth guilty of practices more shocking and bloody than are the people of the United States, at this very hour.

SOURCES: Douglass, F. (1852, July 5). The meaning of July Fourth for the Negro. Retrieved June 26, 2006, from www.pbs.org/wgbh/aia/part4/4h2927t.html

Thomas, S. (n.d.). From slave to abolitionist/editor. Retrieved June 26, 2006, from www.history.rochester.edu/class/douglass/part2.html

Frederick Douglass was a powerful rhetor who spoke out against slavery in the United States.

A variety of approaches to rhetorical criticism exist. We cannot cover all the major approaches to rhetorical criticism in this introductory course. There are many courses and textbooks that focus on rhetorical criticism. Instead we hope to teach you to listen carefully to how rhetoric functions every day and to analyze what purposes it serves. As you listen to rhetoric from presidents, governors, mayors, church leaders, or others, ask yourself, how does this message reinforce the status quo? How does it argue for change? What ideas are mentioned and what ideas are absent? How and why is it persuasive, and how might it influence the public in making public policy decisions?

Rhetorical scholar Michael McGee (1990) argues that people understand the world through rhetorical fragments. In other words, they piece together their understanding of the world through sound bites, pieces of speeches, partial readings of events, news coverage, and so on. For example, with all the potential information available, including Web logs, consider how much discourse you may miss about any particular issue, such as the response to Hurricane Katrina. Because you can only consume a limited amount of the rhetoric generated, and because the rhetorical environment is always changing, the ways in which you understand and think about the world will always be changing as well.

As a participant in a democratic society you are inevitably going to be swimming in rhetorical communication. By studying the use of rhetoric in these messages, you can empower yourself to better understand the messages and the issues, and even become a better rhetor yourself.

SUMMARY

Rhetoric is important in our society for at least three reasons.

- It is vital to the functioning of a democracy.
- It plays an important role in finding justice.
- It helps us understand our world.

The study of rhetoric is important for four reasons. It allows us:

- to understand the many issues we are facing,
- to reinforce or resist dominant cultural values,
- to critically analyze the many rhetorical messages we encounter, and
- to improve our own rhetorical communication.

Rhetoric is tied intimately to the social, cultural, and historical environment in which it functions. It is persuasive communication that is typically directed toward a large audience, and its purpose is to influence how the audience sees or understands the world and actions each person in it might take to change that world.

Characteristics of individual public speakers, or rhetors, play an important role in effective public communication. Such characteristics include the ethos, pathos, and logos of the speaker; the position in society of the speaker; and the speaker's relationship to the audience. Rhetors do not have to be individuals; they also can be organizations, institutions, and corporations.

Rhetoric plays an important role in society. It can provide meaning and shape public thinking about major events, and it can serve democratic functions in the political life of a society. Rhetoric also can bring about justice and provide momentum for major social changes.

Finally, all citizens can become rhetorical critics by improving their skill at evaluating the many rhetorical messages they receive every day. An effective rhetorical critic knows that any rhetoric must be viewed in the social, historical, and political context in which it is produced. Second, the rhetorical critic learns to listen carefully to how rhetoric functions in everyday situations and what functions it serves—for example, as a means to reinforce the status quo, or to argue for change. Third, by becoming more effective rhetorical critics, citizens also become more effective rhetors.

KEY TERMS

sophists 294
orator 295
rhetor 298
artistic proofs 299
ethos 299
persona 300

pathos 300
logos 301
social position 301
rhetorical audience 303
rhetorical event 307
deliberative rhetoric 307

public sphere 308
forensic rhetoric 308
social movement 310
rhetorical critic 312

TEST YOUR KNOWLEDGE

1. What are the four periods in the history of rhetoric? How was rhetoric seen in each period?

2. What are the most important individual characteristics of rhetors?

3. What is a rhetorical event? Give a contemporary or historical example and explain why you think it is a rhetorical event.

4. Why is rhetoric important in a democratic society?

5. How can rhetoric bring about justice and social change?

APPLY WHAT YOU KNOW

1. **Create a List of Ten Speakers You Have Heard** This list might include politicians such as Hillary Clinton, John Edwards, Arnold Schwarzenegger, Barack Obama, or entertainers such as Margaret Cho, Jon Stewart, Oprah Winfrey, and so on. Put these speakers in order of most to least effective and powerful, and be clear about your reasons for ranking them in this way. Then without revealing your order, exchange lists with a classmate. Rank each other's speakers and see how your rankings compare. If they differ, discuss your reasons. Think about the criteria that you are using.

EXPLORE

1. Go to the American Rhetoric site at www.americanrhetoric.com/top100speechesall.html and examine the list of the top 100 speeches. You can listen to many of them. Which of these speeches seem to you to be the most effective? Why? Think about your criteria for the best speeches.

2. Rhetoric is used to persuade people to various perspectives on many topics. Go to etalkinghead.com at http://directory.etalkinghead.com and you will see a list of blogs. Read some of these blogs representing different political perspectives. What rhetorical strategies do they use to persuade readers? What rhetorical strategies are they not using that they should? What strategies did you find more effective, and which strategies are less effective?

3. Rhetoric is very important in courtroom trials. Go to the companion Web site of *Court TV* at www.courttv.com/trials/index.html and read about some contemporary trials. Notice the rhetorical strategies that are used by prosecuting attorneys as well as those used by defense attorneys. How do they work to establish the credibility of witnesses? Those on trial? How do you know if justice was done?

4. Go to the Web site for those opposed to the Wall Street bailout at www.nowallstreetbailout.com/ Compare this Web site to the Web site for those opposed to California's proposition 8 at: www.noonprop8.com/ Note that both of these Web sites function as rhetors. How do they attempt to build arguments for their positions? How can Web sites function as sites for public deliberation over various issues? Can you find Web sites that take positions opposite to those presented on the above mentioned sites?

12
Communication and Media

chapter outline

The economics of media production shapes mass communication and gives it a unique and powerful role in our society."

I always videotape my favorite soap opera so I can watch it when I have time. Sometimes I can watch it later that day, but sometimes I have to wait until the end of the week and I "veg out" on hours of it. My best friend in college got me hooked on this soap opera, and now it's a part of my everyday life.

This student's experience with television is not unique; many television viewers are devoted to a particular show or two and don't want to miss a single episode. When you think about this behavior on the individual level, you probably view it as an issue of choice or of personal taste. When experts analyze television viewing on the social level, however, they examine the impact media have on individuals and how media messages exert their influence. For example, when the soap opera *The Bold and the Beautiful* ran a segment on HIV in August 2001, experts noted that telephone calls to the National STD and AIDS Hotline rose dramatically (Kennedy, O'Leary, Beck, Pollard, & Simpson, 2004). Thus, soap operas and television programs, like other types of media—including radio, newspapers, magazines, and films—can influence people's lives in important ways.

In this chapter we first look at the importance of media in everyday life. We then briefly examine the major forms of media. Next we investigate how individuals use media and the impact that media messages have on individuals. Then we consider media usage within the context of the societal framework and explore the influence media have on society overall. Finally, we discuss media activism as a means for individuals to express media ethics, and we introduce guidelines for becoming more effective consumers of media. Although the Internet is also a type of media, we address that topic in Chapter 13, where we will focus on the role of computers in communication.

 Once you have read this chapter, you will be able to:

- Understand the history of media.
- Describe various models of media.
- Understand five issues in media studies: social identities, understanding the world, media events, media violence, and media economics.

THE IMPORTANCE OF MEDIA

Media hold a very important place in our society. As an indication of their importance to you, consider these questions. If you met someone who did not own a television or radio, would you be surprised? What if the same person never watched movies or read magazines? Would knowing this change your interaction with the person? What topics could you and couldn't you discuss? If you concluded that many topics would be

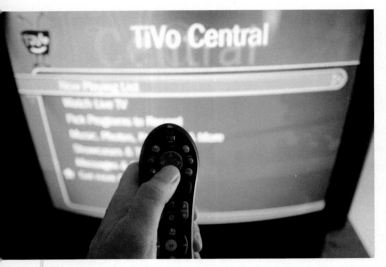

Viewers often record television shows for viewing at their convenience.

When you learned about the devastation of Hurricane Katrina in the Gulf Coast, which communication medium was most important to you? Did you watch television? Use the Internet? Listen to the radio? Read the newspaper? What influenced your communication choices?

off limits, you can see that media messages serve important social functions. For example, they help people bond with others who like or dislike the same shows, movies, advertisements, singers, or actors. Media messages and images also help shape how people view the world and what they understand, and perhaps misunderstand, about events around the globe. Because people are so deeply immersed in this media environment, however, they rarely think about their participation in it. Nevertheless, it is indeed an interaction, as individuals participate in the communication process by selecting certain programs and agreeing or disagreeing with what they hear or see.

Why is media studies important? To begin with, U.S. Americans watch an enormous amount of television, although the exact number of hours is difficult to pin down. Nielsen Media Research (2005) reported that the average U.S. household watched 8 hours and 11 minutes of television per day, which is the highest level recorded since Nielsen began measuring television viewing in the 1950s. The Washington State Department of Health (n.d.) notes that, on average, African Americans watch about two hours per day more than other U.S. Americans. Of all U.S. Americans, children watch the most television and are the center of most concern about television viewing.

People turn to communication media both for information and entertainment. For example, in the first week after September 11, 2001, 81 percent of Americans said they got their news about the attacks primarily from television (Rainie, 2001). They sat glued to their sets, trying to absorb what had happened and to learn as much about it as possible. Many people chose television because they wanted to see the images of the attacks and hear the commentary from news reporters. Of course, not all people turned to television. Why might others have chosen a different communication medium? For one, people at work may have had limited choices for following the events and seeking information and therefore relied on the Internet. Other people may have been traveling and had to rely on the radio for their information.

Media scholars today recognize that they work during an era of rapid media change and development. For example, communication scholars Jennings Bryant and Dorina Miron (2004) identified six kinds of changes that are currently affecting and being affected by mass communication. They include (1) new form, content, and substance in mass communication; (2) new kinds of interactive media, such as the Internet; (3) new media ownership patterns in a global economy; (4) new viewing patterns and habits of audiences; (5) new patterns in family life; and (6) new patterns of interactive media use by youth. Because of the rapid pace of these changes, measuring and studying their impact can be a challenge.

While it is difficult to measure the precise power of media messages, scholars and observers agree that these messages surround and influence people every day. In fact, media reporting has been blamed for influencing both public policy and increased international tensions. For example, in May 2005, *Newsweek* reported that U.S. interrogators had flushed a copy of the Koran down a toilet in Guantánamo Bay prison in Cuba. In response, large riots broke out in the Middle East, protesting the U.S. desecration of a holy book (Thomas, 2005). Although *Newsweek* later retracted its story, a number of politicians held the magazine responsible for these riots and the death and destruction that occurred. Calls for restrictions on media, as, for example, in their ability to cover military actions overseas, are one sign of the power of their messages.

The importance of media in our everyday lives and in our society has been rapidly increasing. We send and receive media messages all day long on email and the

Internet; we watch television, listen to the radio, and engage in other media whether we are at work or home. To help you understand more clearly what is meant by the term *media*, we discuss this topic next.

WHAT ARE MEDIA?

Mediated communication refers to communication that is transmitted through a channel, such as television, film, radio, and print. We often refer to these channels of communication more simply as media.

The word **media** is the plural form of *medium*. While television is one communication medium, many other communication media exist, including film, radio, magazines, advertising, and newspapers. When you pick up the telephone to speak to someone, you are using yet another communication medium. When you write a letter, your communication is mediated by the form of letter writing. In fact, perhaps the only kind of communication that is not mediated is that which takes place face-to-face.

When you think about all the ways that communication is mediated, you can see how complex and varied the field of media studies is. However, media studies typically focus on mass media, or mediated communication intended for a large audience. These mass-mediated messages most often are produced and distributed by large organizations or industries in the business of mass communication. Mass media businesses also are described as **culture industries**, because they produce television shows, made-for-television movies, video games, and other cultural products as an industry. The creation of these cultural products is not driven by individual artists, but by large groups working in corporate contexts. If we think about television shows, magazines, and advertisements as corporate products produced for mass consumption, we tend to look at them differently than we would if we viewed them as artistic works. We will discuss this concept at greater length later.

The study of media is often a moving target, as changes in media are continually occurring. Part of understanding the impact of media on our everyday lives entails understanding the changes that have occurred and what media were available in other time periods. Historically, communication has been framed by what media were available during a given time. Let's now look at some of these industries and the media texts they produce.

When the printing press was invented by Johannes Gutenberg about 1439, it gave rise to mass production of printed books and pamphlets. The use of pamphlets as a communication medium became very important in the American Revolution during the eighteenth century (Bailyn & Garrett, 1965). Many of the ideas that led to the Revolution were reflected in pamphlets that were printed and sold in the colonies. One famous example of such a pamphlet is Thomas Paine's *Common Sense*.

One of the first media addressing a large public was the newspaper. During the nineteenth century, many newspapers grew in distribution and readership as the cost of mass printing declined. As expansion westward continued in the United States, the newspaper played a critical role in community building. Newspapers flourished during this period in staggering numbers. For example, "Before the end of 1867, at least four newspapers had been published in Cheyenne, a town that still had a population well under 800, in the Wyoming Territory" (Boorstin, 1965, p. 131). Looking back upon that period, it is astonishing just how many newspapers some of these small towns were able to support. These numbers are all the more staggering given the current decline in newspaper readership. As you can see, different eras embraced different communication media.

The United States was a major player in the development of the newspaper medium. It is estimated that "Of about 7200 daily newspapers published in the world in the mid-20th century, about one-quarter were published in the United States" (Boorstin, 1965, p. 133). The unique community relationship established by the early newspapers, along with freedom of the press, may help to explain this explosion of newspaper readership in the United States.

media
the plural form of *medium*, a channel of communication

culture industries
large organizations in the business of mass communication that produce, distribute, or show various media texts (cultural products) as an industry

mass-market paperbacks
popular books addressed to a large audience and widely distributed

e-books
electronic books read on a computer screen instead of a printed page

Today, when most people think of newspapers, they first think of large-circulation papers in large metropolitan areas, such as the *New York Times*, *Washington Post*, and *Los Angeles Times*. They might also think about smaller, local papers, including the *Santa Fe New Mexican*, the *Wichita Eagle*, and the *Knoxville News Sentinel*. Large-circulation newspapers serve different needs from local papers, so some people subscribe to both. Other newspapers target specific demographic groups, such as immigrant communities, ethnic and racial communities, gay and lesbian communities, or retirees. Some are bilingual. Others are referred to as the "alternative" press. These alternative-press newspapers attempt to present perspectives and voices that may not be heard in the mainstream press. Examples of alternative papers include the *Seattle Stranger*, the *San Francisco Bay Guardian*, and the *Village Voice*, published in New York City.

Another development that followed the lowered cost of mass printing was the development of the magazine. Magazines are produced weekly, monthly, bimonthly, or quarterly. Some, such as the newsmagazines *Newsweek* and *Time*, target a general audience. Some magazines focus on very specific topics, as shown by the titles *Geck Monthly*, *Philadelphia*, and *Successful Farming*. Like newspapers, magazines offer important forums for political discussions, but they also address distinct interests, such as crafts, hobbies, or travel.

Newspapers are a very important communication medium and are one of the oldest.
Michael Kamber/The *New York Times*

Popular books are another medium addressed to a large audience. Sometimes called **mass-market paperbacks**, these books include romance novels, self-help books, and comic books, as well as other genres that are produced in very large numbers and distributed through supermarkets, airport stores, drugstores, as well as bookstores. **E-books** (electronic books) constitute a recent development in mass media. E-books are books read on a computer screen instead of a printed page. Currently, it is not clear how important a form of media this will become, as many readers still prefer to read the printed page.

Movies developed in the late nineteenth century but flourished in the twentieth century. Although today people can make movies relatively cheaply with digital video, high-quality productions that draw large audiences are typically expensive to produce, distribute, and advertise. Therefore, movie studios with adequate resources dominate the motion picture industry. While some documentary movies do become popular, such as *March of the Penguins*, *Fahrenheit 9/11*, and *Supersize Me*, most best-selling movies are purely entertainment-oriented, such as *The Dark Knight*, *WALL-E*, and *Iron Man*. Typically, large-budget films receive the widest distribution and the most publicity, but small-budget films can also reach audiences and sometimes offer alternative views.

Like movies, radio technology emerged in the late nineteenth century. At first, it had important applications at sea, and radio was not used for commercial purposes until the twentieth century. The first commercial broadcasting station is generally considered to be KDKA in Pittsburgh, Pennsylvania, which was established in 1920. (You can read about this history on their Web page at www.kdkaradio.com/) With the continuing development of communication technology, radio quickly became widely available to the public. As journalism professor Jane Chapman notes, "Radio's take-off was swift, and public enthusiasm for it peaked during the 'golden age' of the 1930s and 1940s" (2005, p. 147). During that time, radio stations broadcast a wide range of programs, including news commentary, quiz shows, soap operas, and comedies. With the rise of television, the Internet, and other competing media, radio broadcasting has become much more specialized. Thus, radio stations target the tastes of specific audiences by broadcasting classical music, jazz, country music, news, sports, or other focused content. Audiences for these specialized programs are often targeted based on identities, such as age, socioeconomic class, race and ethnicity, or language. Today, radio is also broadcast over the Internet, via satellite, and through podcasts. And while commercial enterprises dominate radio in the United States, nonprofit radio, such as National Public Radio and Pacifica, also exists.

Popular music, another form of mass media, existed long before radio, and people listened to it live in public and private venues and, later, on gramophones and record players. Popular music now also plays on television and via other communication media, such as CDs, DVDs, and MP3 players. As different trends grew in popularity, a large number of commercial enterprises arose to glean the profits. In turn, many smaller companies have gone out of business or been bought out, so that fewer, but larger, music corporations select, produce, and distribute the music we hear today.

Television is among the most familiar forms of communication media. Early in its development, in the mid-twentieth century, networks such as ABC, CBS, and NBC dominated, since they were the only providers of content. The rise of cable television, with its multiple specialized channels, has somewhat displaced the networks, yet they remain important and continue to draw large audiences. Since its inception, cable television has expanded to include pay channels, such as HBO, Showtime, and Cinemax. In addition, satellite television is challenging cable television, but it is still developing its audience. The United States has some nonprofit television stations, with the most notable being public television and Deep Dish TV, which is a satellite network with alternative programming. However, because television programming is expensive, commercial enterprises continue to dominate the medium.

The recent rapid rise of digital technology has provided openings for new forms of communication media. Not only has television gone digital as of June 12, 2009, enhancing picture quality, but this digital technology has made multicasting and interactive television possible. Digital technology has also made a number of other communication media possible today. Some of these new communication media are the result of innovative media technologies, such as the iPhone, BlackBerry Storm, Skype Internet phone system, and YouTube. These recent technologies are sometimes grouped under the name **new media**. New media are rapidly developing and many more communication media will become available in the coming years. The speed of these changes has led some scholars, such as Paul Virilio (2006), to speculate on the relationships between technological change and the speed of these new technological developments. The ways that these increasingly rapid changes sweep over our culture and ourselves make them a driving force in shaping our world. All told, these many forms of mass media saturate our world and penetrate deeply into our individual consciousness, yet we still have some choices regarding which messages to accept. Let's see how this works.

new media
refers to the new communication technologies of the late twentieth century and early twenty-first century

Skype allows people to see and talk to people around the world. It changes how we might stay connected as people move around the globe.

THE INDIVIDUAL AND MEDIA

Media scholars are interested in the impact media messages have on individuals, but they are also interested in how individuals decide which media messages to consume or avoid. Marketers and media producers especially want to know how they might predict and characterize individuals' choices so that they can more effectively influence consumer choice. In this section of the chapter we'll explore

Figure 12.1: The Linear Model
The linear model emphasizes the effect of media messages on the individual. Communication in this model is largely (although not entirely) one-way.

both aspects of individual media consumption—how media messages influence us and how we become **active agents**, or active seekers, of various media messages and resisters of others. With the term *active agent*, we stress that even though people inhabit a densely media-rich environment, they need not be passively bombarded by media messages.

How Media Messages Impact the Individual

One approach to studying the impact of media messages on individuals relies on the **linear model**. As suggested by its name, this model portrays communication as a process that occurs in a linear fashion—for example, on a path from the television to the viewer (see Figure 12.1). In this traditional approach, scholars focus on the sender, the medium, the audience, and the effect of the message. This model views communication as a process that moves from one source to many receivers. While researchers who utilize this approach recognize that people are not passive viewers or consumers of media messages, they are interested only in measuring the influence of media messages on the individual, not vice versa.

By understanding the effects of media messages, communication scholars in this tradition hope to assist public policy debates about media regulation. For example, their research might inform debates about how violence or sexuality on television and in movies affects viewers. So, on a societal level, research based on the linear model often impacts public policy decision making. On an individual level, this kind of research may help you select the types of television shows you watch or the movies you allow your children to see.

As an analytic tool the linear model of media analysis has its limits. For example, critics argue that its simplicity cannot account for the multiple ways that people respond to media messages (Sproule, 1989). Viewers are not merely passive receivers of messages, these critics say, nor do they necessarily believe or imitate everything they watch on television or read in magazines. Those who watched *The Osbournes*, for example, did not necessarily model their family behaviors on the show's characters. Nor did everyone believe that O. J. Simpson was innocent after watching his murder trial.

On the other hand, the linear model does highlight the power and influence of media messages. Some people did try to imitate the antics of Johnny Knoxville on the MTV television show *Jackass*, resulting in very serious injuries despite televised warnings against trying to imitate the stunts. And in a classic example, many listeners of Orson Welles' radio broadcast *War of the Worlds*, did believe that Martians were landing in New Jersey in 1938, setting off mass panic.

Scholars who study media influence work in an area called **mass media effects**. Their studies try to measure the influence that media have on people's everyday lives. The study of mass media effects has undergone significant changes over the years, as researchers have disagreed about how much effect a particular media message has (McQuail, 1987). In the 1930s, Paul Lazarsfeld and his colleagues studied radio's effect on listeners, and in particular, its effect on voting behavior. This study, titled *The People's Choice* (Lazarsfeld, Berelson, & Gaudet, 1948), argued that media had limited effects, as they found that radio tended to reinforce preexisting beliefs rather than shape new ones.

active agents
seekers of various media messages and resisters of others

linear model
portrayal of communication as a process occurring largely in one direction

mass media effects
the influence that media have on people's everyday lives

Today, the focus on effects remains important in media research. For example, contemporary researchers have examined media images of beautiful bodies and how those images influence people's perceptions of their own bodies and their resultant behavior in response to those images—including dieting, working out, taking diet pills, and having plastic surgery. In their study of the effects of entertainment television and sports media, Kimberly Bissell and Peiqin Zhou (2004) found a high correlation between the thin images of women's bodies that appear repeatedly in entertainment television and eating disorders among college-age women who watched those shows.

Another area of inquiry among media-effects scholars involves media images of violence. In their study of media usage among middle-school children in ten regions in the United States, Michael Slater and his colleagues found that aggressive young people seek out violent media and that exposure to media violence can predict aggression (Slater, Henry, Swaim, & Anderson, 2003). Thus, they see media violence and aggression as mutually reinforcing and call their model a *downward spiral model* to describe the powerful, negative influence the interaction has on youth. Those youth who are prone to violent behaviors seek out violent media that reinforce more violent behavior.

Promoting health through media messages is another significant area of inquiry among those scholars seeking to understand media effects. In a recent study on antidrug advertisements for adolescents, Hunyi Cho and Franklin J. Boster (2008) found that framing loss rather than gain in these advertisements was more effective among those who had friends who did use drugs. There was no difference among those adolescents whose friends did not use drugs. In order to engage the most effective communication messages to promote public health, media effects scholars are also trying to better understand how media messages can be more effective.

How Individuals Choose Media Messages

As noted, advertisers, political campaign strategists, and communication scholars all want to understand which groups of people consume which media texts. They want to know who watches *Grey's Anatomy*, who reads the *New York Times*, and who reads *People* magazine. You can probably imagine why advertisers and campaign strategists would like to know these things. With this type of information, advertisers can target their messages more accurately to influence consumers, and campaign strategists can focus their message to attract more votes. But, why would media scholars be interested in this information?

Media scholars need this information so that they can correctly target their research. For example, if scholars want to study the effect of a particular **media text**, say, a television show, advertisement, or movie, they need to know which audience group to study. If they want to know how people interpret a particular media text, they need to know who the audience for that text is. Or if scholars want to know about the economic influence of particular media texts, they need to know which audience groups advertisers target with these messages.

On an individual level, you are constantly faced with media choices. And your choices have increased considerably in the past decade, with the rise of cable and satellite television, the Internet, DVDs, and blogging. Researchers are interested in not only *what* we choose but *how* we choose. See how one of our students considers this in *It Happened to Me: Josh*.

media text
a television show, advertisement, movie, or other media event

It Happened to Me: Josh

I love comedies, but I seem to be the only person who doesn't like Will Ferrell movies. We saw *Stepbrothers* with some friends and I just wasn't impressed. Some of the scenes were verbally and physically exaggerated and every time I looked around and saw others laughing, I wondered why I didn't find it funny. I'd say Ferrell's last funny movie was *Old School*, and I think I like it because Vince Vaughn is more my style of humor. To me, Will Ferrell's type of humor is more slapstick, and I like a more "dry" humor. I always give every movie a chance, but I know that I have my favorite actors.

selective exposure
the idea that people seek media messages and/or interpret media texts in ways that confirm their beliefs and, conversely, resist or avoid messages that challenge their beliefs

uses and gratifications
the idea that people use media messages and find various types of gratifications in some media texts rather than in others

In what ways do you selectively expose yourself to media messages? Do you generally listen to the same news commentators rather than seeking alternative voices? Do you watch the same shows your friends watch, or do you look for something different?

Many romance novel readers find affirmation in their personal identities and connection with other romance novel readers.

Although Josh doesn't mention it directly, both what people choose and how they choose are related to individual identity. And, as we noted in Chapter 3, identities are not fixed; they are dynamic, meaning that they change over time and from situation to situation, and with them, media choices change as well. For example, as a child, Josh may have been a fan of Saturday morning cartoons or *Sesame Street*, while as a young adult, he preferred MTV's *Real World*, or *Monday Night Football*. Thus, Josh's age and the ages of his friends likely influence the movies he selects. But age is only one aspect of identity—and perhaps one of the simplest factors that influence media choices. Other aspects, such as regional identity, might also have an impact but be more difficult to correlate with media tastes.

Selective exposure theories help us understand how identity plays a role in media tastes and preferences. These theories are based on the idea that people seek media messages and/or interpret media texts in ways that confirm their beliefs and, conversely, that they resist or avoid messages that challenge their beliefs. Depending upon their political beliefs, some people enjoyed watching Tina Fey as Governor Sarah Palin on *Saturday Night Live*. (See *Communication in Society: Saturday Night Live's Tina Fey Wins Associated Press' Entertainer of the Year, Makes Huge Impact on the 2008 Presidential Election*). Thus, if you believe that wearing fur is wrong, you are likely to seek media messages that confirm this belief or see any portrayal of fur-wearing in media in a negative way. If you believe that racism no longer exists, then you are likely to interpret messages you receive as confirming or reinforcing this perception. In their study of *The Cosby Show*, Sut Jhally and Justin Lewis (1992) set up focus groups. Twenty-six of these focus groups were composed of White viewers of the show, and twenty-three were composed of African American viewers. In analyzing the White focus group responses, Jhally and Lewis found that Whites were more likely to think that *The Cosby Show* proved Black people can succeed; therefore, they said, African Americans who did not succeed were to blame for their own failure. In other words, as the White focus groups saw it, personal failings rather than discrimination or racism were what blocked success. In contrast, Black respondents saw *The Cosby Show* as a "cultural breakthrough" in terms of positive portrayals of Black culture (p. 121). Thus, they expressed far more concern about the pervasive negative images of African Americans in media and the influences of those images on viewers. As you can see, while both racial groups were watching the same television show, their interpretations were very different. Selective exposure theories point to the ways that both groups interpret the show to confirm their own beliefs and views. For another look at the way audiences perceive media messages, see *Alternative View: Hostile Media Effect*, on p. 328.

One media phenomenon that highlighted the practice of selective exposure was the release of the movies *The Passion of the Christ* and *Fahrenheit 9/11*. Both films were popular, but they played to audiences with divergent political views. As one commentator concluded, "Ultimately, *Fahrenheit 9/11* is propaganda for the converted. Just as Christians voted for their faith at the box office with *Passion of the Christ*, so liberals now have an opportunity to have their ballots counted too. But few minds will be changed" (Saulsbury, 2004). Selective exposure theory would explain why each of the two audiences sought the movie that confirmed their belief. Those who subscribe to selective exposure theory argue that people rarely inhabit a media environment that challenges their social identities, including their religious and political beliefs, notions about gender, or ideas about race.

Another line of media research, called **uses and gratifications** studies, explores how people use media messages and what types of gratifications they find in some media texts rather than others. Working within this approach, researchers might

COMMUNICATION IN SOCIETY

Saturday Night Live's Tina Fey Wins Associated Press' Entertainer of the Year, Makes Huge Impact on the 2008 Presidential Election

Fey was voted The Associated Press' Entertainer of the Year, an annual honor chosen by newspaper editors and broadcast producers across the country. Fey was selected by AP members as the performer who had the greatest impact on culture and entertainment in 2008.

[It] was Fey who most impressed voters largely with her indelible impression of Gov. Sarah Palin on "Saturday Night Live." Her cameos on her old show (where she had been a head writer until 2006) helped drive the show to record ratings and eventually drew an appearance from Palin herself. "Tina Fey is such an obvious choice," said Sharon Eberson, entertainment editor of the Pittsburgh Post-Gazette. "She gave us funny when we really needed it and, in a year when women in politics were making huge strides, Fey stood out in the world of entertainment."

As soon as Palin was chosen as Sen. John McCain's running mate, conjecture mounted that the similar-looking Fey would have to return to "SNL" to play her.

In an interview earlier this fall, Fey recalled watching early TV coverage of Palin: "That was the first time I thought, 'Well, I kinda do look like her. I'd better really listen to how this lady talks.'"

Fey debuted the impression on the "SNL" season premiere and a sensation quickly followed. She made four more pre-election appearances as Palin on the late-night satire.

"From the winks to the nods to the accent, she nailed it," said Marc Bona, assistant entertainment editor of the Plain Dealer in Cleveland. "And she did so at a time when it seemed the whole country was tuned in—both to the presidential race as well as 'Saturday Night Live.'"

[So how did Fey impact the 2008 election? It depends on a person's party affiliation.] A recent Washington

Tina Fey as Sarah Palin and Amy Poehler as Hillary Clinton may have influenced the 2008 presidential election.

Times poll found that independent voters [credited] the "Tina Fey effect" with turning them off to the McCain ticket. But some experts argue that comedy sketches [did] not change voters' minds.

"Jokes and impersonations only leave lasting damage if they resonate with existing narratives the voter internalized," said Dorothy James, a professor of government at Connecticut College. "Most people who strongly identify as Republicans have internalized the narrative that Gov. Palin is a breath of fresh air, a maverick. Tina Fey's impersonation only angers them, and may increase their support for Palin, "James said.

"Those who strongly identify as Democrats have an alternative narrative—that she is grammatically chaotic, tied to party talking points, ignorant and unprepared. Fey's impersonation only reinforces existing attitudes there."

FROM: "Tina Fey voted AP Entertainer of the Year," The Associated Press, December 23, 2008. Used with permission of The Associated Press. Copyright © 2009. All rights reserved.

want to know why viewers watch the soap opera *All My Children* instead of *General Hospital, The Amazing Race* instead of *Law and Order,* or *Wife Swap* instead of *Survivor.* For example, a researcher might note that a certain type of entertainment is popular—say, violent movies, romance novels, or wrestling—and wish to explore why so many people seek out those kinds of texts and what needs they satisfy. Denis McQuail and his colleagues suggested four general uses and gratifications that audiences have for media texts: (1) information, (2) personal identity, (3) integration and social interaction, and (4) entertainment (1987,

Alternative VIEW
Hostile Media Effect

Selective exposure theories tell us that people tend to consume media that reinforce or support their own views. Yet, some media researchers counter this idea. Why? Researchers have found that people on both sides of an issue can be exposed to the same media coverage, and when asked what they thought of the coverage, both groups say that it was biased against their views. If both sides find the same coverage biased, it may undermine the idea that people only seek messages that confirm their views. Thus, the researchers concluded that while bias in media news stories surely does occur, another kind of bias rests with the viewer—a phenomenon called the "hostile media effect" because it reflects a general hostility toward media. In their study, Albert C. Gunther and Kathleen Schmitt (2004) used the controversy over genetically modified foods to understand the hostile media effect. To summarize part of the study's findings,

regardless of respondents' position on genetically modified foods, they viewed news media stories as biased against them. However, when respondents saw the same information in a student essay format, the hostility tended to be absent or at least minimal. The researchers conclude, then, that the hostile media effect is created by the perception that a media message has the potential to influence large numbers of people for or against a particular viewpoint.

If the selective exposure theory (page 326 in this chapter) is correct, and people tend to select media messages that support their own views, why would they then interpret these messages to be biased against them? There is no easy answer, but perhaps questions of bias and media selection need to be thought about in more complicated ways. When charges of bias arise against a media source, how often do we consider that the bias may be our own?

SOURCE: Gunther, A. C. & Schmitt, K. (2004). Mapping boundaries of the hostile media effect. *Journal of Communication, 54*, 55–70.

p. 73). The first motivation, information seeking, is straightforward: Audiences want to learn from some media presentations, as in the case of a news event. The second motivation, personal identity, refers to the idea that viewers may use media messages to affirm some aspect of their personal identity—for example, as mothers, consumers, or political conservatives. The third motivation, integration and social interaction, underscores the role that media can play in helping people connect with others, as they do when discussing sports or the events on a soap opera. Finally, the entertainment motivation refers to the use of media for pleasure, or the desire simply to be entertained. Of course, these motivations can overlap, so that we can watch a program for information, while at the same time using it as a topic for conversation with others, which would fit within McQuail's third motivation.

Understanding why some groups choose one program over another highlights the cultural values at work in the consumption of media. In his study of television preferences among Israeli adults, Jonathan Cohen (2002) examined viewing habits and choice. He found that factors influencing media selection included loyalty to particular channels, preferences for certain types of shows, and even the language of the programs, as most preferred to watch shows in Hebrew. His conclusion was that "Most Israeli viewers seem to prefer native programming, whether due to language problems or to cultural resonance" (p. 218). Cohen suggests that Israeli audiences use television to affirm their Israeli identities, entertain themselves, and sometimes as a context to interact socially with other Israelis.

Determining why people seek specific media texts and not other texts is very important from an economic perspective. After all, a media corporation does not want to spend a lot of money on a television show or magazine if it is going to fail. However, it is notoriously difficult to predict which media texts will become popular and which will not. *Desperate Housewives*, for example, was described as

"the surprise hit of the television season" (Glaister, 2005). So, to the dismay of media honchos, despite the research, there is no completely foolproof way to predict audience response.

Of course, the inability to accurately predict audience response does not mean that media producers have no information on trends. In certain eras, viewers are more interested in Westerns or police dramas, reality shows or evening soap operas than they are during other periods. Today, reality shows are quite popular. Furthermore, advertisers know that some groups prefer to consume certain kinds of media. For example, the advertising that appears during televised football games reveals what advertisers have learned about that audience through careful market research and analysis.

How Individuals Resist Media Messages

While media messages bombard people every day, individuals do not necessarily, or even easily, accept all that they receive. In addition, people actively resist certain media texts. For example, some people sought out and watched *Kill Bill* films, *Pulp Fiction*, and similarly violent movies. Others actively avoided them. Why? We resist media texts every day for many reasons, including something as hard to quantify as individual taste and something as personal as what we see as negative portrayals of our political, moral, or religious views; our interests, age, or level of education; or our gender, sexuality, and racial and ethnic identities. In their study of Madonna's video, "Open Your Heart," Jane Brown and Laurie Schulze (1995) found that females resisted the performance, which they saw as playing to male pleasure. Other far-less-political reasons can create consumer resistance as well, as our student reveals in *It Happened to Me: LeAnn*.

It Happened to Me: LeAnn

My mother wanted me to go see *Crash* because she thought it had important things to say about race and class conflicts. She may be right, but I said no anyway, even though she mentioned it four or five times. I rarely go to the movies because I don't like being in crowds, and I really don't like the high prices of the tickets. I have to be extremely excited about a movie to see it in a theater, and I just didn't feel the excitement for that one.

Resisting media messages entails much more than simply whether we go to a particular movie or watch a particular video. It is also about how we resist the power of media to shape our identities. For example, in one study, Meenakshi Gigi Durham (2004) interviewed South Asian immigrant girls living in America. She explored the question of how these girls dealt with traditional Indian notions of female gender expectations in the context of available media. She found that the only mainstream U.S. show they liked to watch was *Friends,* which they found to be funny, while they disliked *Dawson's Creek*, which they thought was unrealistic. In general, they distanced themselves from mainstream U.S. media. In contrast, they consumed large amounts of media (films, popular music) from India, which they rented from Indian grocery stores and restaurants, borrowed from others, and watched or downloaded from the Internet. They particularly identified with the narratives in *Mississippi Masala, Bend It Like Beckham,* and *American Desi*—three Indian films with narratives involving "the taboo relationships between Indian girls and men of different racial/cultural backgrounds" (p. 154). Durham concludes that these adolescent girls use media to create new identities, and that these identities do not conform to stereotypes of either Asian Indian women or U.S. American women.

Of course, as noted earlier, we resist and avoid media texts not only for identity reasons, but also as a matter of taste. When an individual chooses not to watch a particular television show, she or he is resisting it. However, when someone dislikes a particular television show, the reasons may go beyond individual taste.

A television show produced by Radio Canada from 2004 to 2006, *Les Bougon*, highlighted the interrelatedness of social identities and media consumption—and the complexities of consumption and resistance. *Les Bougon* was described in the *New York Times* as "a politically incorrect version of *Father Knows Best*, with twists so wicked and crude that even fans of *The Simpsons* might blush" (Krauss, 2004). *Macleans*, a Canadian newsmagazine, described the Bougon family as "rough, truculent, beer-soaked urban trash. In their commitment to not working, though, they come out as likeable, funny anarchists" (Aubin, 2004). This representation of a poor family created a controversy in Canada, as well as high ratings. This television show was popular across social class identities in Québec, even if the classes interpret it differently. For example, poor people may have liked the show because they interpreted it as empowering to their identities, and they saw this family as heroes for using the system to their advantage. In contrast, well-to-do viewers may have appreciated the program as a satire. Others, in any social class, may simply have seen a tight-knit family loving and protecting each other to survive (Cernetig, 2004).

Thus, you can see that how one interpreted the show could determine why one embraces or resists it. The president of the Canadian National Anti-Poverty Organization, for example, objected to it for what he saw as the stereotyping of poor people. Others might have resisted it because they found it crude. As this French-language show is dubbed into English and reaches a wider audience, new social and individual forces may lead to new interpretations and new reasons for acceptance or resistance.

As you have seen through our discussion, communication researchers are interested in all aspects of the relationship between individuals and the media messages that surround them. First, they wonder what effect media messages have on individuals, and second, they explore how individuals choose, resist, and interpret these messages. Research has revealed that the answers to both questions involve complex processes related to individual identity, individual needs, and individual taste. Audiences respond to and interpret texts based on both their individual and social identities, and therefore, different social groups can consume the same text while being affected by it differently and interpreting it differently. However, all individual responses and choices occur in a larger social context. Thus, to provide a more complete picture, we now shift our attention to the role of media at the societal level.

Les Bougon was a popular television show in Québec, although it does not focus on an idealized family.

THE INDIVIDUAL, MEDIA, AND SOCIETY

Why do media play such an important role in society? One reason is that they often serve as the voice of the community. In this way, media offer people a means of thinking about themselves and their place in the world, and they represent the societal forces around them. As individuals, we can only choose from among the media choices available. Societal forces, including the government, economics, media organizations, and advertisers, largely determine which media options are available. In the following section we'll look at three important roles that media play in society: confirming social identities, helping people understand the world, and helping individuals understand important public events. And finally, because no discussion of media and society would be complete without a discussion of media violence and media economics, we will conclude with these topics.

Confirming Social Identities

As we've noted, media influence our understanding of social identities, such as our own gender or age identity, as well as the identities of others. This is one of the functions of media usage that we examined as we discussed uses and gratifications. For example, images we see on television, in films, magazines, and newspapers shape our sense of what a man or woman is. These views often create or enforce a hierarchy of identities, often portraying men as more powerful than women. Thus, media messages not only shape the way we understand social identities; they also show us which social identities are valued. For example, as Associated Press reviewer Christy Lemire (2005) noted in her review of the film *Deuce Bigalow: European Gigolo*, "Making fun of homosexuality seems to be the one area of humor that has yet to be ruled off-limits by political correctness; such jokes also appeared in the far superior *Wedding Crashers* earlier this summer." If Lemire's analysis is correct, this "permission" to joke about one particular social identity can reinforce a hierarchy in which heterosexuality is valued over homosexuality.

One approach to understanding how and what media communicate about various social identities is content analysis. **Content analysis** focuses on some specific aspect of a text's content. Bernard Berelson (1952/1971), a behavioral scientist, explains that content analysis took off during the late 1930s, with the work of Harold Laswell and his colleagues (see Chapter 2), who were concerned with "propaganda and public opinion and the emergence of radio as a great mass medium of communication" (pp. 22–23).

How does content analysis work? To begin, a researcher might want to know how many non-White characters appear on the television show the *Monk*, which is set in San Francisco, a very multiethnic and multicultural city, or on *Southland*, a show set in a city (Los Angeles) where Whites are a minority population. The researcher would thus watch a number of episodes, count the number of non-White characters, note the kinds of roles they play and which characters are central, and finally, draw conclusions based on these data. Researcher Caroline Aoyagi (2004) conducted such a study on shows set in the State of Hawai'i and concluded the following:

> No one can blame the big television networks for their love affair with the beautiful islands of Hawaii, but as several new shows are set to launch or are already on air, the lack of Asian Pacific Americans in the shows' casts have many wondering: what Hawaii is this?

content analysis
approach to understanding media that focuses on specific aspect of the content of a text or group of texts

Content analysis can provide data on representation of various groups, as well as topics, violence, and other items.

In a state where Asian Pacific Islander Americans [APIA] make up more than 80 percent of the population and whites are considered the minority, a look at the new line-up of shows for FOX, the WB network, and NBC show no APIA lead actors and only one or two APIAs in supporting roles (p. 1).

A content analysis of television shows, thus, can provide data on racial representation in media. Content analysis also can reveal the kinds of topics that arise most often, the way episodes and conflicts are resolved most frequently, the number and types of conflicts that occur, and many other issues. For example, in their study of television news in Los Angeles and Orange County, California, Travis Dixon and Daniel Linz (2002) employed content analysis to determine whether correlations existed between pretrial publicity and race. Using the American Bar Association's definition of potentially prejudicial information, they found that "Blacks and Latinos are twice as likely as Whites to have prejudicial information aired about them, and Latinos are three times more likely than Whites to have prejudicial information aired when they victimize Whites" (p. 133). Through content analysis, then, these two scholars were able to show a strong correlation between the race of the accused and the reporting of prejudicial information in the news. Moreover, they found that reporting of prejudicial information dramatically increased when the crime victim was White. Here you can see how media confirm social identities.

Similarly, Cheryl Law and Magdala Peixoto Labre (2002) conducted a content analysis of images of male bodies in thirty years of popular magazines, specifically, *GQ, Rolling Stone*, and *Sports Illustrated*. They found that "the images of men in popular magazines became more lean and muscular from 1967 to 1997, and that the V-shaped male figure also became more prevalent over time" (p. 705). As the researchers report, "this content analysis suggests that the new ideal seen in the mass media does not represent the body type most men have" (p. 706), and they speculate on the effect these images have on men's behavior, for example, their use of steroids, diets, and workouts. Yet, as this was not a media-effects study (see page 324), the researchers did not survey male readers of these magazines to find out whether they actually went on diets, used steroids, and so on. Clearly, the point of the study is to highlight what media messages communicate to men (and women) about the ideal male image and male social identity.

Images of male beauty are socially constructed.

As noted, content analysis by itself does not reveal why viewers choose to watch particular television shows or consume other kinds of media messages. Collecting demographic information about an audience's racial, ethnic, or age composition may give some insight as to which groups are drawn to what kind of content, but, again, this is not the primary purpose of content analysis. In their study, for example, Dixon and Linz did not try to explain whether or why southern Californians preferred pretrial television news coverage with prejudicial information about minorities, or why the television news industry produces this kind of news. What their data do confirm, however, is that Blacks and Latinos are represented more negatively in news programs.

Some studies use a more detailed analysis of media messages than content analysis does, and this approach can help us better understand which social identities are being confirmed and elevated. Such studies, which rely on textual analysis, typically focus on fewer media texts than content analyses do. Researchers who conduct textual analyses of media messages take an approach similar to literary critics when they explore meanings in a literary work. However, in textual analysis, any kind of media image can be considered a text. For example, in her study of the news coverage of Freaknik, a spring break event that used to draw African American college students to Atlanta, Marian Meyers (2004) looked closely at the news reports of sexual violence against African American women perpetrated by African American men. "In essence," she wrote, "the news criminalized Black men primarily with respect to property damage while decriminalizing them concerning their abuse of women. The safety of Black women appears of less consequence than that of property" (p. 113). Thus, these news reports confirmed an identity of Black men as criminals while undermining the identity of Black women as crime victims.

In her study of masculinity, Helene Shugart (2008) focused on the media construction of the "metrosexual" in the context of commercialism. Metrosexuals are men who are very attentive to their appearance, not only their physiques, but also their clothing, hair styles, and so forth. In her textual analysis of the metrosexual, Shugart found that metrosexuality "bore all the hallmarks of a fad or a trend" (p. 295), but metrosexuality also "served a vital and strategic rhetoric function as part of a much larger and ongoing cultural discourse about masculinity(ies)" (p. 295). Because commercialism has threatened traditional masculinity by insisting on enhancing masculinity through the purchase of various products, metrosexuality helped to reconcile the contradiction between the commercial masculinity and a more traditional or normative masculinity.

Thus, what people see, hear, and read in the media can confirm identities, but so can their media choices. Although our social identities are not absolute predictors of media choices, trends do emerge if we look at the correlations between media consumption and various social identities. Nielsen Media Research has studied the most popular television shows among all U.S. Americans and among African Americans as a subgroup, revealing that their choices are similar in some respects and different in others, and thus, that racial identities do somewhat correlate with media consumption, as noted in *Did You Know? Nielsen Media Research*, on p. 334.

In addition, people often choose media images that not only confirm their identities but also that help them deal with the various issues involved in any identity. For example, some women are drawn to the TBS show *The Closer*, which features a strong woman police detective (played by Kyra Sedgwick) who is tough, very smart, very southern, and feminine and who works in a male-dominated environment. Thus, she provides a role model to help women envision how they can operate successfully in a masculine environment and retain their gender identity.

How does media coverage favor some identities over others? The amount of coverage, as revealed by content analysis, sometimes is the controlling factor. For example, in their study of the Salt Lake City Olympics in 2002, Billings and Eastman (2003) found that NBC devoted more time to reporting on male athletes and White athletes than on other groups. Moreover, U.S. American athletes "were depicted as being more composed and courageous, [and were] the most mentioned, most profiled, and most promoted of all athletes" (p. 584). The potential effect of this imbalance is that the national identity of the White U.S. American audience are reinforced and confirmed, while the national identities of other viewers are disconfirmed or undermined. Remember, however, that more extensive coverage can also have the opposite effect. For example, if an identity is portrayed with great frequency in a negative way, that identity can be undermined, as Dixon and Linz found in their analysis of pretrial coverage in southern California (2002).

What kinds of shows or movies do you like to watch, and which aspects of your social identities might guide these media choices? How might these choices sustain or challenge your social identities?

Did You Know?

Nielsen Media Research

Nielsen ratings are widely used in the television industry to determine audience viewing; and they are used to set advertising rates. Note their findings on the top rated television shows for African Americans and for the U.S. population at large, shown in the tables included here. How might social identities play a role in the popularity of some television shows?

The following were the highest rated prime time television programs in African American households for one week in December 2008:

Rank	Program	Network	Household Rating %
1	*60 Minutes*	CBS	12.5
2	*NBC Sunday Night Football*	NBC	11.1
3	*The OC*	FOX	8.8
4	*Cold Case*	CBS	7.7
5	*Law and Order*	NBC	7.6
6	*Million Dollar Password*	CBS	7.3
6	*CSI: Miami*	CBS	7.3
8	*CSI: New York*	CBS	7.1
9	*The Unit*	CBS	6.9
10	*Sunday Night Football in America* (Pre-Kickoff Show)	NBC	6.6

The following were the highest rated prime time television programs in all U.S. households (including African American homes) for one week in December 2008.

Rank	Program	Network	Household Rating %
1	*NBC Sunday Night Football*	NBC	9.0
2	*60 Minutes*	CBS	8.7
3	*Two and a Half Men*	CBS	7.4
4	*The Mentalist*	CBS	6.6
4	*NCIS*	CBS	6.6
6	*Million Dollar Password*	CBS	6.3
7	*Cold Case*	CBS	6.1
7	*Football in America* (Pre-Kickoff Show)	NBC	6.1
9	*CSI: Miami*	CBS	5.8
10	*CSI*	CBS	5.0
10	*The Ghost Whisperer*	CBS	5.0

SOURCE: Nielsen Media Research. (n.d.). Top primetime programs—African American homes. Retrieved January 6, 2009, from www.nielsenmedia.com/nc/portal/site/Public/menuitem.43afce2fac27e890311ba0 a347a062a0/?show=%2FFilters%2FPublic%2Ftop_tv_ratings%2Famong_african_americans&selOne Index=3&vgnextoid=9e4df9669fa14010VgnVCM100000880a260aRCRD
Nielsen Media Research. (n.d.). Highest-rated primetime programs—total U.S. homes. Retrieved January 6, 2009, from www.nielsenmeida.com/nc/portal/site/Public/menuitem.43afce2fac27e890311ba0a347a062a0/ ?show=%FFilters%2FPublic%2Ftop_tv_ratings%2Fbroadcast_tv&selOneIndex=0&vgnextoid=9e4df966 9fa14010VgnVCM100000880a260aRCRD

As you learned in Chapter 3, social identities help shape individuals' outlook on the world; at the same time, individuals interpret media texts from their identity positions. Media critics have been instrumental in bringing to the public's attention these issues of identity confirmation and media bias in portraying identities. As a result, many with identities that media portray less positively have come to recognize their exclusion. The effect can be anger or disengagement when few, if any, images exist of one's own social group acting in positive ways.

Understanding the World

Media play a key role in helping people understand the world. Most people will never travel to the Ukraine, North Korea, Iraq, Palestine, Rwanda, Indonesia, Somalia, or Brazil, but they can learn something about these places through media. They may see these distant regions on the Travel Channel or in *National Geographic* magazine, or they may see news about them on CNN, MSNBC, or other news channels.

However, the texts produced by media organizations concerning such places can distort their image as well as enhance it, especially if viewers have never been to the parts of the world represented. In her study of AP wire photographs of Afghan women—both during and after the Taliban regime—Shahira Fahmy (2004) found that "1 percent of [published] AP photographs portrayed women revealing their face and hair." Thus, even after the fall of the Taliban, Afghan women are depicted wearing their burqas. And this despite that fact that many photos exist that portray "images of Afghan women removing their burqas as a sign of liberation" (p. 110). In this study, Fahmy brings to light the discrepancy between the pool of available AP photographs and the ones selected for publication in the United States, noting that the ones that editors select shape and sometimes distort our impressions of the subject.

As another example of the media's power to shape knowledge and understanding, prior to the disappearance of Natalee Holloway in Aruba in spring of 2005, there had been little U.S. news coverage of this Caribbean island. Many U.S. Americans did not know that Aruba was Dutch or that it operated under the Dutch legal system—much less what the technicalities of that system were. In contrast, media provide U.S. audiences with extensive detail on the British royal family. As you can see, by choosing what to cover and how extensively, media shape audience understanding of what is and isn't important in the world.

This power of media coverage to influence individuals' view of the world is referred to as its **agenda-setting capacity**. Thus, in agenda-setting research, scholars focus on audience perceptions of reality and attempt to discover how or whether media coverage correlates with these audience perceptions. For example, Lowry, Nio, and Leitner (2003) studied correlations between crime rates, news coverage on crime, and public attitudes about crime from 1978 to 1998. Existing data indicated that in March 1992, only 5 percent of the public thought that crime was the most important problem. By August 1994, however, 52 percent felt that way. What accounted for this jump? By correlating the amount of television news coverage with the crime rates, the researchers found that the amount of news coverage was far more influential than actual crime rates in this change in public perception. By focusing so much attention on crime reporting, the theory goes, media set the public agenda for what was important. Agenda-setting studies often look at long time periods, as the crime-coverage study did, in order to correlate media coverage to changes in audience perceptions.

In another study using an agenda-setting perspective, Jochen Peter (2003) focused on the issue of fourteen European nations and their integration into the European Union (EU). Here, however, he did not find a simple correlation between more news coverage of EU integration and public attitudes about the importance of this issue. Instead he found that when political elites agreed about integration, public involvement or interest in the issue declined. However, coverage of disagreement

agenda-setting capacity
the power of media coverage to influence individuals' view of the world

Cultivation theory has been used to emphasize the role of news coverage of crime in the perceptions of crime rates.

among political elites over EU integration did correlate with public involvement in the issue. Thus, content and the degree of exposure play parts in setting the public's agenda.

Media messages also play a critical role in acculturating individuals. **Cultivation theory** proposes that long-term immersion in a media environment leads to "cultivation," or enculturation, into shared beliefs about the world. Unlike other approaches that focus on specific media messages, television programs, movies, or other kinds of text, "Cultivation analysis is concerned with the more general and pervasive consequences of cumulative exposure to cultural media" (Morgan & Signorielli, 1990, p. 16). Initiated by George Gerbner and his colleagues, cultivation analysis seeks to uncover how television, in particular, influences those who are heavy viewers. Those who watch television news, the theory goes, will share certain beliefs or distortions about the world. Moreover, this theory argues that media coverage shapes attitudes about one's own society and the issues it faces. For example, although crime rates have gone down overall in recent years, many U.S. Americans feel more insecure than ever. In their study on fear of crime, Daniel Romer, Kathleen Hall Jamieson, and Sean Aday (2003) surveyed 2,300 Philadelphia residents. Within that population group, they found a relationship between the widespread belief that crime is a significant problem and the amount of local television news coverage of crimes. The point of the study is that Philadelphia media coverage cultivates attitudes and beliefs that shape everyday life in Philadelphia, with a key element of daily life being an exaggerated fear of crime.

In another cultivation study, Woo and Dominick (2003) focused on international students in the United States who watch daytime television talk shows. Because these programs emphasize "interpersonal conflict, betrayal, disloyalty, cheating and lying" (p. 112), Woo and Dominick theorized that watching them might affect the students' acculturation and perceptions of human relations in the United States. They found that those international students who scored low on acculturation, meaning that they were not highly integrated into U.S. society, and who watched a lot of these talk shows tended to think more negatively about relationships in the United States— much as these talk shows portray them. In both these studies, then, immersion in the television environment shaped, or cultivated, a particular view of the world.

A different way of explaining how media influence how we understand the world is through **hegemony**. Hegemony refers to the process by which people consent to particular understandings as reflected in media representations. In other words, we come to understand what a "mother" means through often idealized images of mothers on television programs, films, and other media. While there are no laws that regulate what a "mother" must do, we consent to these images of motherhood and we expect mothers to engage in certain behaviors, such as throwing birthday parties for their children. In contrast, our hegemonic understanding of "fathers" does not include that kind of activity. Fathers can, of course, throw birthday parties for their children, but it is not part of the hegemonic construction of fatherhood.

Masculinity, as represented in media content, has been a rich site for investigating how hegemony functions. For example, in his work on hegemony, communication scholar Nick Trujillo (1991) studied the media representations of Nolan Ryan, a baseball pitcher, to show how masculinity is constructed. He found five features of how Ryan was portrayed: (1) male athletic power, (2) ideal image of the capitalist worker, (3) family patriarch, (4) White rural cowboy, and (5) a symbol of male

cultivation theory
idea that long-term immersion in a media environment leads to "cultivation," or enculturation, into shared beliefs about the world

hegemony
the process by which we consent to social constructions, rather than having them imposed on us

(hetero)sexuality. Trujillo asks that we consider the negative consequences of this construction of masculinity. Similarly, in his studies of the television programs, *Coach* and *Home Improvement*, communication scholar Robert Hanke (1998) analyzes how hegemonic notions of masculinity are used to create the humor in these situation comedies. In his study of the television show, *thirtysomething*, Hanke (1990) also analyzes the way that hegemonic masculinity shifts slightly to focus on men "who are more open to domestic concerns and interpersonal relationships" (p. 245). His analysis focuses on hegemony as a process in which masculinity shifts to respond to changing social needs. Hegemony is a process by which we all participate in the social construction of ourselves and others. If we violate these hegemonic notions, we risk alienation. This approach to the study of media content helps us better understand the contours and limits of how we might present ourselves and interpret others, as hegemony outlines what is acceptable and, even, ideal.

Interpreting Media Events

The term **media event** applies to those occasions or catastrophes that interrupt regular programming. Like rhetorical events, which we discussed in the last chapter, media events create vast numbers of media messages. Examples include the funeral of John F. Kennedy, the Olympics, or the attacks of September 11, 2001. Media scholars are interested in the coverage of such events because such coverage can shape viewers' understanding of what has occurred and create powerful responses. For example, Daniel Dayan and Elihu Katz (1992) found that media events bring society closer together. As a new form of "high holidays of mass communication" (p. 1), these events both reinforce and celebrate national identity.

Some media events are staged by public relations officers to garner media attention on a particular issue. When the president of the United States calls a press conference, for example, he is creating a media event. Then, of course, the representatives of various news media are present to report what he says. In these cases, the president and his public relations staff carefully control many aspects of the conference—where it will be staged, what kinds of issues will be raised, who will be present, what video images will be shown, and so on. Other politicians, movie stars, and lawyers in high-profile cases also commonly create media events to bring attention to themselves and/or their causes.

Not everyone, however, can attract this kind of media attention. People seeking media attention who lack notoriety or celebrity must use other measures. For example, when President Bush visited Canada in 2004, Canadian protestors created a media event by planning large public protests in various cities. Antilogging protestors have created media events by taking up residence in trees, chaining themselves to trees, or dangling from ropes tied to trees. During the World Trade Organization meetings in Seattle in 1999, protestors used the Internet and alternative newspapers to plan a large march in downtown Seattle. The violence that erupted between police and some protesters drew considerable media attention and was broadcast widely (DeLuca & Peeples, 2002).

Media events often focus on important rituals while promoting a variety of less obvious messages, or subtexts. Examples of rituals include royal marriages, royal funerals, and presidential inaugurations. These events, media observers say, go well beyond the occasion to promote important cultural values through media coverage. For example, in their analysis of the British queen's Golden Jubilee, Claire Wardle and Emily West (2004) concluded that the British press framed the event not simply as an anniversary celebration for the queen, but as a sign of British national strength, thus converting it to a nationalistic celebration.

Media events are filled with messages that shape one's view of the world and invite one to view the world in a particular way. The funerals of Yasser Arafat and Ronald Reagan in 2004, both inaugurations of George W. Bush and Barack Obama and many other media events are worthy of examination for the underlying assumptions and meanings they communicate beyond reporting the facts. For example, in

media event
occasions or catastrophes that interrupt regular programming

As you think about Hurricane Katrina and the devastation left behind, what do you think are some of the messages that were sent in media coverage and in the speeches by President Bush and other elected leaders? What did the coverage reveal about our national identity and who we are? How was your own identity shaped by these media messages?

addition to explaining what occurred, such events can stimulate nationalistic feelings or reinforce specific political beliefs and positions. They also may serve as celebrations of a particular nation's history or values. Another example of a powerful media event was the earthquake and tsunami of 2004. Media played a key role in bringing attention to this human tragedy, which in turn prompted huge numbers of people to make donations to relief organizations. Early concerns about the U.S. government's stinginess were also reported. The *New York Times* (Are We Stingy, 2004), for example, ran an editorial which noted that "America, the world's richest nation, would contribute $15 million. That's less than half of what Republicans plan to spend on the Bush inaugural festivities." In response to media attention, the U.S. government substantially raised its financial commitment.

Monitoring Media Violence

Representations of violent acts in media are common and are an increasingly important area of research, as well as a concern among parents and others. As you might surmise, our society is ambivalent about **media violence**, as indicated by the range of responses to it. On the one hand, a large number of people must be entertained by it, or why would there be so many books, movies, video games, and so on that include it? On the other hand, media producers and editors make intentional decisions to keep certain violent images out of the public view (beheadings, coffins, bodies). In addition, we are inventing tools such as parental control devices for television to protect certain members of society from witnessing violence. These conflicting trends reveal tensions between the principles of censorship, freedom of the press, and protection of children.

While no clear-cut definition of violence exists, most people generally consider shootings, stabbings, and other kinds of killings to be violent. Slapping, hitting, and fighting of all types also can constitute violence. Most of the concern about media violence focuses on the impact such violence may have on children. The American Academy of Pediatrics, for example, is particularly concerned about the impact of media violence on children under 8 years old. Based on current research (2002), they have concluded that media violence has the following effects on children:

- increased aggressiveness and antisocial behavior,
- increased fear of becoming victims,
- less sensitivity to violence and to victims of violence,
- increased appetite for more violence in entertainment and in real life.

Parents play an important role in their children's media viewing, as well as the way in which their children interpret programs.

These concerns are not new. People, especially parents, began to worry about media violence in television almost as soon as broadcasting began in 1946 (Anderson & Bushman, 2002). Also, as we noted earlier, numerous studies have shown that "media violence contributes to a more violent society" (p. 2377). Research has also demonstrated that while cartoons are far more violent than prime time television, an intervention by parents and adults can influence how children respond to those violent images. For example, in her study of five- to seven- and ten- to twelve-year-old children, Amy Nathanson (2004) found that when parents and other adults simply discussed the production techniques of a program, this either had no effect on children, or it increased the impact of the violent images. In contrast, when parents underscored the fictional nature of a program's characters, the children were better able to deal with the violence and were less afraid.

In response to concerns about children and television content, in 1998 the Federal Communications Commission (FCC, 2003) mandated that half of all new televisions 13 inches or larger manufactured after July 1, 1999, and *all* sets 13 inches or larger manufactured after January 1, 2000 must have a **V-chip** installed. A V-chip identifies program ratings by content and can block programming that is designated by the owner, typically the parent(s). For example, a parent who does not want a child to watch programs with TV-14 ratings can block such programs from being shown. Similar systems have been developed to block access to certain kinds of Web sites on the Internet and other media.

Of course, not all violent images presented in media are fictional. Television news journalists must decide what is and is not too horrifying to broadcast. For example, recent Internet broadcasts of hostages in Iraq being beheaded have not been shown on U.S. network television. Images of people leaping to their deaths from the World Trade Center towers on September 11, 2001, also were considered too troubling to broadcast.

The Federal Communications Commission has oversight of the appropriateness of television programming, but it focuses more on the major network channels than on cable channels. Moreover, the commission can fine broadcasters for presenting inappropriate materials, but these fines are typically for indecency rather than violence. Fear of audience reaction has kept some media from broadcasting more graphic, but accurate, images of violence in Iraq, as shown in a recent study conducted at American University. Sometimes broadcasters warn audiences that an upcoming image may not be suitable for all audiences—one approach to dealing with extremely violent images. For example, some television newscasters provided such warnings before showing the numerous bodies of victims of the 2004 tsunami. Cable broadcasts, particularly pay-per-view, have more leeway in their programming, since the assumption is that viewers have actively sought out and paid for a particular type of programming.

Analyzing Media Economics

Mass communication today is dominated by the large corporations that produce and distribute media messages. Thus, the economics of media production shapes mass communication and gives it a unique and powerful role in our society. No individual can easily compete with a multinational corporation in producing and distributing media messages. Therefore, these huge media corporations determine which messages are available, and which impact our society in important ways. For example, Rupert Murdoch's News Corporation, and Disney own many television and radio stations, as well as production and distribution companies, so these corporations have enormous influence on the messages that fill the media environment.

In the area of media studies concerned with economic issues, scholars focus on **political economy**, or the ways in which media institutions produce texts in a capitalist system and the legal and regulatory frameworks that shape their options for doing so. Political economists also examine how these media products are marketed in order to understand what they reveal about our society. This approach is an extension of the work of Karl Marx, the influential nineteenth-century socialist thinker, and it emphasizes the economics of media, rather than its messages or audiences—although all these components are interrelated. An example of this theory's application can be seen in one researcher's analysis of the recent decision by ABC to no longer to broadcast the Miss America pageant. After all, the researcher noted, "a little more than a decade ago" this pageant "had copped about 27 million viewers; last month it drew a record-low 9.8 million" (de Moraes, 2004). With a small viewing audience, the demand for and price of advertising during the pageant also dropped. Thus, the theory goes, economic factors largely determine what media content people are exposed to.

V-chip
device that identifies television program ratings by content and can block programming designated by the owner

political economy
the ways in which media institutions produce texts in a capitalist system and the legal and regulatory frameworks that shape their options for doing so

Earlier in this chapter we introduced the term *culture industries* to refer to organizations that produce, distribute, or show various media texts. In the United States, these culture industries most often are media corporations or media industries that operate as for-profit organizations. In some other countries, however, culture industries are more like U.S. public television—meaning that they are nonprofit media organizations—and this economic structure affects content and programming. Consider for a moment how a nonprofit media organization might develop programming as compared with a for-profit organization. What factors might guide their decision making? PBS, for example, needs to please the public and the government, both of which fund it. In contrast, for-profit networks need to please shareholders and advertisers as well as the public.

While television networks have historically been identified with specific nations—for example, CBC with Canada, BBC with Britain—globalization is leading to transnational television networks. Thus, many media corporations with significant financial backing are moving in this direction. Initial attempts at transnational broadcasting in the early 1980s to mid-1990s faced many difficulties, and most did not survive (Chalaby, 2003). Today, however, transnational television networks are growing, and some of these include U.S.-based networks such as CNN International and MTV. Some are European-based, such as BBC World, Euronews, and Skynews. More studies need to be done to determine what impact this global flow of information and entertainment is having on societies.

In China, another kind of change is occurring in the mass media system, related in part to globalization. Extensive reforms have been taking place across the economy, and the state-owned mass media system has experienced changes as a result. These changes include the "rise of semi-independent newspapers and broadcasting stations, the proliferation of private Internet content providers and unlicensed cable networks, and increasing cross-investment by the media into other commercial enterprises, including joint ventures with international media giants" (Akhavan-Majid, 2004, p. 553). In her study of these new Chinese media, Akhavan-Majid argues that "non-state actors (e.g., citizens, journalists, entrepreneurs)" (2004, p. 554) have used loopholes in official Chinese policies to creatively open new media opportunities. As you can see, changes in political and economic structures can be intimately intertwined with changes in mass media.

Political economists also analyze the mergers and acquisitions that occur in the media industry as a way of understanding changes in programming. For example, when NBC acquired the Bravo channel (2001), it added performing arts and arts films to its roster as well as some riskier programs, including *Boy Meets Boy* (2003), *Queer Eye for the Straight Guy* (2003–2007) (and now *Girl* (2008)), and *Celebrity Poker Showdown* (2004–2006). In a news release related to this sale, Bob Wright, Vice Chairman of General Electric and Chairman and CEO of NBC said, "Bravo, with its desirable demographic, is a perfect strategic addition to our portfolio, providing a particularly good fit with NBC's network and cable viewers" (Cablevision, 2000). In analyzing these developments, a political economist might focus on the economic reasons behind this acquisition and the potential future revenues to be generated by appealing to this desirable demographic group. (*Desirable* typically refers to an audience with the size and demographic profile to bring in high advertising revenues.) As they continue to search for desirable audiences, Bravo now has moved to new television programming, including *Top Chef, Project Runway, Kathy Griffin: My Life on the D-List,* and *Tabatha's Salon Takeover.*

Of course, political economists cannot predict the kinds of media texts that will emerge from any specific merger. They know that television stations seek viewers who are more affluent so they can attract more advertisers, but political economists do not know (nor does anyone) what kinds of shows will attract affluent viewers. While television production companies try to create—and television networks try to buy—television programs that will draw large audiences, they do not always succeed. Political economists cannot and do not predict such successes either. Instead, they focus on the ways that corporate media influence the information we get, the impact that capitalist media corporations have on society, and the demands that this political and economic structure places on journalists, broadcasters, and other media workers.

In their study of commitment to local television news coverage, David Scott, Robert Gobetz, and Mike Chanslor (2008) compared television stations owned by chains with television stations that were independently owned. They found that "the news department operated by a small media group produced more local news, more locally produced video, more use of on-air reporters, and fewer news promotions than the larger chain-based broadcast group investigated" (p. 84). In the context of the 2003 Federal Communications Commission decision to relax restrictions on ownership of media, these findings point to the importance of understanding the complex relationships between media economics, media ownership, and media content.

In other words, because news is sold for profit, the profit motive shapes what readers consider "news." This commercial pressure impacts the work of journalists, as well as the way media organizations are run. One leading scholar in this area, Robert McChesney (1998), explains these concerns:

> The American media system is spinning out of control in a hyper-commercialized frenzy. Fewer than ten transnational media conglomerates dominate much of our media; fewer than two dozen account for the overwhelming majority of our newspapers, magazines, films, television, radio, and books. With every aspect of our media culture now fair game for commercial exploitation, we can look forward to the full-scale commercialization of sports, arts, and education, the disappearance of notions of public service from public discourse, and the degeneration of journalism, political coverage, and children's programming under commercial pressure. (p. 4)

By focusing on the political and economic structures in which media industries operate, political economists offer a unique perspective on the impact of media in our lives. Their analysis of areas that many people ignore reveals the potential impact that the business of media has on all of us.

Societal issues very much influence individuals' interactions with media. More-over, both personal and social identities are key to one's interactions with media and how one interprets media violence. Given the profits to be made, media economics ensures that media violence will remain pervasive as long as people continue to purchase products with violent content.

ETHICS AND MEDIA

Because media messages are so powerful, they can generate powerful responses. One potential response is **media activism**, or the practice of organizing to communicate displeasure with certain media images and messages, as well as to force change in future media texts. The issues that media activists address are important because they highlight many significant ethical questions surrounding mediated communication. Media activism, of course, is not limited to the United States. Media activist groups have mobilized around the world—for example, in Canada, Belgium, Australia, and Brazil—to express ethical concerns about media coverage on a range of issues.

Voicing ethical concerns through media activism is not a recent phenomenon. People have been concerned about media content and images for centuries. The notions of freedom of speech and freedom of the press articulated in the U.S. Constitution reflect one response to media control. In the early twentieth century, as silent

media activism
the practice of organizing to communicate displeasure with certain media images and messages, as well as to force change in future media texts

Did You Know?
The Hays Code

All the following regulations are taken from the Hays Code. Which, if any, still appear relevant to you? Why?

- Dances which emphasize indecent movements are to be regarded as obscene.
- Complete nudity is never permitted. This includes nudity in fact or in silhouette, or any lecherous or licentious notice thereof by other characters in the picture.
- The use of the Flag shall be consistently respectful.
- No film or episode may throw ridicule on any religious faith.
- The use of liquor in American life, when not required by the plot or for proper characterization, will not be shown.
- Adultery, sometimes necessary plot material, must not be explicitly treated, or justified, or presented attractively.
- Illegal drug traffic must never be presented.
- White slavery shall not be treated.

EXCERPTED FROM: The Motion Picture Production Code of 1930 (Hays Code). Retrieved June 26, 2006, from www.artsreformation.com/a001/hays-code.html

movies became popular entertainment, concerns about their racy content and the transition to talking movies led to calls for government regulation of media. In an attempt to avoid government regulation, Hollywood established the Hays Office, to create its own system of regulation. The **Hays Code**, which was published in 1930, established strict rules for media content with the goal of wholesome entertainment (see *Did You Know? The Hays Code*). Some of the Hays regulations still apply today, such as the ban on exposing children's sex organs. Other regulations, however, have become outdated, such as the ban against portraying sexual relationships between interracial couples or using vulgar expressions or profanity, which the code specified as including the words "God, Lord, Jesus, Christ—unless used reverently—Hell, S.O.B., damn, Gawd."

While the Hays code came about because of media activism in the 1920s, it set industry standards until the late 1960s, when the **MPAA** (Motion Picture Association of America) devised its rating codes. These codes have changed slightly since then, but most people are familiar with the G, PG, PG-13, R, and NC-17 ratings. Today, media activism has concentrated largely on the ethics of four areas: children's programming, representations of cultural groups, news reporting, and alternative programming. Let's look at each of these in turn.

Complaints about content in television shows and its impact on children led to the creation of the **TV Parental Guidelines** (by the TV Parental Guidelines Monitoring Board), which are a self-regulating system of the television industry. These guidelines rate programs in terms of appropriateness for particular age groups. You have probably noticed the rating codes in the upper-left corner of the television screen. (An explanation of the ratings is available at **www.tvguidelines.org/ratings.htm**.) This kind of rating system is voluntary, so unless an adult activates the V-chip, or an adult is present to change the channel or turn off the television, the rating system may have no impact.

The second ethical focus of media activists has been distortions perpetrated or reinforced by media. The concern here is that such portrayals create stereotypes and misunderstandings. Minority groups, in particular, have had such concerns, as we can see in the number of media activist groups focused on media representations of racial and sexual minorities.

Hays Code
self-imposed rules for Hollywood media content instituted in 1930 with the goal of creating "wholesome entertainment"

MPAA
Motion Picture Association of America

TV Parental Guidelines
a self-regulating system of the television industry that rates programs in terms of appropriateness for particular age groups

These activists argue that when people have limited contact with minority groups, they are likely to gain false impressions from media misrepresentations. In turn, these distorted images may lead to hate crimes or discriminatory government policies, such as racial profiling. Media activist groups that monitor media producers and challenge them to create responsible and accurate images include MANAA (Media Action Network for Asian Americans) and GLAAD (Gay and Lesbian Alliance Against Defamation) as well as organizations that have broader goals but that include a media activist focus, such as the National Organization for Women (NOW) and the League of United Latin American Citizens (LULAC).

A third category of activist groups has focused on structural issues in media industries and their impact on consumers. For example, organizations like FAIR (Fairness and Accuracy in Reporting) focus on the news media and their misrepresentation of certain issues, their lack of independence, and the resulting lack of diverse viewpoints. FAIR recently criticized the Corporation for Public Broadcasting's chair for attempting to pressure public television into producing more politically conservative television programs. Go to **www.fair.org** for more information on their many activities.

The fourth ethical focus of media activists has been to find and provide media texts that offer alternatives to mainstream sources. For example, Clean Flicks was created for those who are concerned that movies have too much violence and sex, so it offers alternatives that are free of profanity, graphic violence, nudity, and sexual content. And many newspapers, radio programs, and Internet sites have now been developed for those who want alternatives to mainstream news media coverage so that they can hear a diversity of voices and opinions. Earlier we discussed the alternative press, but there is also alternative radio programming, such as Air America, and other alternative media outlets, such as Amy Goodman's daily television program called *Democracy Now!* Other alternative views are expressed as humor in print and online in *The Onion* and on television on *The Daily Show* and *The Colbert Report*.

Finally, some activists use media to communicate specific ethical concerns and messages to a wide audience. Thus, despite the fact that they lack the backing of huge media corporations, activists have used media to educate or influence audiences regarding cruelty to animals, the situation in Palestine and the Middle East, violence against women, anti-Semitism, anti-Catholicism, genocide, racism, and more. To get their messages out, these groups set up Web sites, Web casts, and sometimes even advertisements on television or in mainstream newspapers or magazines.

As new media outlets develop (for example via the Internet, cable TV, and satellite radio) and the world continues to confront new challenges, new ethical issues and new ways of communicating will continue to emerge. We cannot forecast the future, but we do know that the changes occurring in the media environment show no signs of abating. Media activists will continue to try to shape the media messages we receive, while at the same time, media producers will continue to try to sell what people are interested in purchasing. And so, bombarded as you are by media and the messages of a range of media activists, how can you become a responsible media consumer? Let's explore this topic next.

The GLAAD Media Awards is an annual event that honors responsible and accurate media images of lesbians, gays, transgendered individuals, and bisexuals.

Funny, whenever I listen to this station I get a craving for a caramel frappuccino.

STARBUCKS GETS A RADIO STATION

©David Brown/www.CartoonStock.com

✕ BECOMING A MORE EFFECTIVE CONSUMER OF MEDIA

As a consumer of practically nonstop messages coming from radio, television, newspapers, magazines, advertisements, movies, and so on, you need strategies for dealing with this complex media environment. The solution cannot be boiled down to a set of simple guidelines, of course, but here are some ideas to consider when interacting with media. The guidelines for becoming a better consumer of media reflect the overall ethical guidelines we laid out in Chapter 1 for receivers of communication. That is, to become more effective in your media consumption, become active in your media choices, be mindful of the media choices you make, and speak out if you find media content offensive.

Be an Active Agent

How can you become an active consumer of media? First, don't just watch or read whatever is available. Make deliberate choices about media you expose yourself to so that you can control the effect that media messages have on you. As you become more selective, you express a set of media-related values, which in turn, indicates to media providers what type of media programming they should be providing.

As an active agent, then, seek out those media that meet your needs and avoid or resist others. In order to be a truly active agent, however, you have to think about the basis for your media choices. Are you avoiding some media messages simply because they challenge your beliefs? If so, this probably is not the best way to navigate through the media environment. Sometimes, you can benefit from being open-minded about the views and perspectives of others.

Broaden Your Media Horizons

People often live within the confines of a particular media environment, and like a fish in water, can't see the limits. With the vast possibilities now available via the Internet, in libraries, and other media outlets, you have access to practically the whole world. Even if your only language is English, you have many media options available to you.

As you work to broaden your horizons, obtain a range of views on world events. Try to understand why other people view the world the way they do—no matter how different their views are from your own. Try to understand the rising anti-Americanism coming from around the world. While you may not agree with what you hear, seeing the complexity of issues can help you better understand your world.

Overall, being a responsible and effective consumer of media is not easy. It certainly does not involve lounging around watching whatever is on television. Becoming an active partner in this complex communication process is a challenge—one we hope you will take up.

Talk Back

You can benefit from talking back or challenging the messages you receive via news commentators, politicians, reporters, or even characters in television programs. In other words, if you hear something you disagree with or that sounds wrong, point this out, even if it is only to yourself. For example, suppose you hear a reporter covering a natural disaster refer to "innocent victims." What, you might ask yourself, is a "guilty victim" in the context of an earthquake, or in any context for that matter? Questioning and noticing these kinds of empty phrases makes you a more active consumer of media. As you watch or listen, you might also consider why one news story is given more time than another one, or why a particular story is reported at all, and what that prioritizing and selection communicates about what is and isn't valued.

Talking back also includes being attentive to the ethical implications of media to which you are exposed, particularly if it benefits some social identities at the expense of others. More specifically, be aware of the ways that, for example, women and racial minorities, sexual minorities, and religious minorities are portrayed and what impact these images may have on the group depicted. If you do attend movies that mock particular cultural or religious groups, that denigrate women, or that misrepresent the experiences of certain individuals, consider the implications. You not only ratify this depiction by your attendance, but also you encourage the production of more of this type of media with your dollars.

Talking back, however, can involve much more than talking to the images that come to you in media or making choices about which images to support or resist. If you find something particularly objectionable, you can contact the television station, magazine, or newspaper that has offended you. For example, if you believe that specific programs manipulate or attempt to unfairly influence children, let the producers of those programs, and the companies that advertise in that medium, know exactly how you feel. Or you can complain to the Federal Communications Commission—the federal agency that regulates radio, television, wire, cable, and satellite. On the other hand, if you believe specific media have a positive influence and should be more widely produced or distributed, let advertisers and media companies know that as well. Certainly, praising a job well done is as important a form of talking back as is raising objections.

In general, few consumers are sufficiently deliberate about the media messages they select. But because media messages have such a powerful impact on consumers, and because you can have some influence on the availability of specific types of media, you benefit society when you become an active and critical media consumer.

You can talk back to your television, as well as discuss the media messages with your family and friends.

SUMMARY

Media, in all their variety, play a powerful role in our lives. They influence how we see ourselves and the world around us through both entertainment and information. We refer to the messages that come to us via media as *mediated communication* because they are mediated, or transmitted, through a channel, such as television, film, radio, and print. Mass media communication refers to communication that is directed at a mass audience. Each individuals chooses which types of media texts to watch, read, listen to, purchase, or avoid.

Media scholars are interested in how we make these decisions, and marketers and media producers also want to know how they might predict and characterize our choices: how we choose what to consume and how we resist the rest. Complicating our individual choices, however, are social forces that shape the media options that are available.

Media play a number of important roles in our lives as individuals as well as in our society: confirming our social identities, helping us understand the world, and helping us understand important public events. In addition, media shape the images of real and imagined violence and wield enormous economic influence.

Media activism—the practice of organizing to communicate displeasure with certain media images and messages—is one way that people express their ethical views and respond to objectionable media messages and powerful media corporations. Today, media activism has concentrated largely in four areas: children's programming, representations of cultural groups, news reporting, and alternative programming.

Finally, consumers of media can and should become more aware of their own media consumption habits. Guidelines for improving media consumption skills include being active in making media choices, broadening media horizons, and speaking out when media content is offensive.

KEY TERMS

media 321	media text 325	media violence 338
culture industries 321	selective exposure 326	V-chip 339
mass-market paperbacks 322	uses and gratifications 326	political economy 339
e-books 322	content analysis 331	media activism 341
new media 323	agenda-setting capacity 335	Hays Code 342
active agents 324	cultivation theory 336	MPAA 342
linear model 324	hegemony 336	TV Parental Guidelines 342
mass media effects 324	media event 337	

TEST YOUR KNOWLEDGE

1. What are some of the most common communication media?

2. What are strategies that media consumers use to select and reject media texts?

3. How do media events reaffirm values and social identities?

4. What are common concerns about media violence, and how are these concerns being addressed?

5. How do media activists respond to media messages they find objectionable? What are some concerns that contemporary media activists have raised?

APPLY WHAT YOU KNOW

1. Research a popular media text—for example, a magazine, television show, or newspaper—that targets an identity group different from your own. What elements do you find in this text that differ from a text targeted at one of your identity groups?

2. Select and study a media event such as the Super Bowl, Miss America Pageant, or a famous murder trial, and identify the rituals that surround this event.

How does the media event affirm U.S. cultural values?

3. Select a media activist group to study. Go to their Web page and identify their concerns about media. What strategies do they use to promote their messages? Who is their audience? How do they plan to change media in the ways that concern them?

EXPLORE

1. Go to the Nielsen Web page at www.nielsenmedia. com and read about the company and how it researches media audiences. Who are the main audiences for the products of this company? How does Nielsen do its research? What are the nineteen markets where they do research on Hispanic household audiences?

2. Go to the home page of the Public Broadcasting System at www.pbs.org and read about public television. When was it founded? What is its relationship, if any, to local, state, or federal governments? How do the mission and philosophy of public television differ from those of other culture industries?

3. For an advertising campaign, Molson Brewing Company, a Canadian company, created a character named Joe Canadian. Watch this advertisement for Molson at: www.coolcanuckaward.ca/ joe_canadian.htm

   Do you think Joe Canadian appeals to Canadians? Why? Given this advertising campaign, how do you think Canadians would feel if felt when Molson announced a merger with a U.S. brewing company?

13

Computer-Mediated Communication

chapter outline

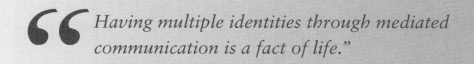

Having multiple identities through mediated communication is a fact of life."

Every day I check my Facebook page to see if anything new has happened with my friends. First, I like to look at people's statuses to see what they are doing in that moment—maybe they are studying for an exam or maybe they are out at work. I also look to see if my friends have added any new photos, especially from this weekend's camping trip and Matt's birthday party. I hope no one posts any embarrassing pictures of me, especially since I have family members new to Facebook! Today, I also changed my profile picture since I got a new haircut yesterday, and I updated my favorite music to include Kanye West. His concert was the best I've ever been to!

This experience of our student Danielle illustrates a number of issues addressed in this chapter. For example, how do people present themselves online and how do they communicate as a result of their choices? Also, how has the prevalence of social networking sites such as Facebook changed how people communicate? How does computer-mediated communication affect individuals' identities and their relationships with others?

In this chapter we will move away from our discussion about mediated communication that is directed at a larger audience. We will focus instead on media that facilitate *interpersonal communication*. More specifically, we focus on *computer-mediated* communication (CMC), which is playing an increasingly important role in most of our lives. In exploring this topic, we first describe the importance of CMC and then compare it with other forms of mediated communication, as well as with face-to-face *communication*. We will examine individuals' use of CMC, including the identity issues it raises and the effect it has on interpersonal relationships. We then examine the impact of societal forces on CMC—including how gender, race, and ethnicity impact CMC and who does and does not have access to it. Finally, we discuss the future of CMC and ethical issues related to it. We conclude with suggestions for improving your computer-mediated communication.

 Once you have read this chapter you will be able to:

- Identify reasons for learning about computer-mediated communication.
- Define *computer-mediated communication* (CMC).
- Describe differences between face-to-face communication and CMC.
- Describe issues that arise in identity and relationship development.
- Understand the role of power and privilege in computer-mediated communication.
- Describe the digital divide and possible solutions.
- Describe ethical challenges in CMC.
- Discuss three ways to improve your own mediated-communication skills.

THE IMPORTANCE OF COMPUTER-MEDIATED COMMUNICATION

Text messages and instant messages are increasingly popular ways to communicate in the United States, particularly for adolescents and college students.

Most of us now engage in mediated communication almost constantly. In any one day, you may contact your professor by email, communicate with other students via an online discussion board, connect with friends on Facebook like our student Danielle, text message your friends to let them know what you're doing, and call your parents on your cell phone to say hi. Not everyone is enthralled with new communication technology. See *Alternative View: "With Friends Like These . . ."*

As of December 2008, about 75 percent of adults and 93 percent of young people in the United States use the Internet (Jones & Fox, 2009); a recent study at Rutgers University found that about 20 percent of people on campus were using mobile devices at any one time (Katz, 2007). In addition to their pervasiveness, recent communication technologies are important because they have been adopted at such a fast rate. In fifteen short years, the Internet has changed the way we inform ourselves, educate ourselves, work, shop, bank, and stay in touch with others

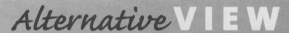

Alternative VIEW

"With Friends Like These . . ."

Facebook has 59 million users—and 2 million new ones join each week. But you won't catch Tom Hodgkinson volunteering his personal information— not now that he knows the politics of the people behind the social networking site.

I despise Facebook. This enormously successful American business describes itself as "a social utility that connects you with the people around you." But hang on. Why on God's earth would I need a computer to connect with the people around me? Why should my relationships be mediated through the imagination of a bunch of supergeeks in California? What was wrong with the pub?

And does Facebook really connect people? Doesn't it rather disconnect us, since instead of doing something enjoyable such as talking and eating and dancing and drinking with my friends. I am merely sending them little ungrammatical notes and amusing photos in cyberspace, while chained to my desk? A friend of mine recently told me that he had spent a Saturday night at home alone on Facebook, drinking at his desk. What a gloomy image. Far from connecting us, Facebook actually isolates us at our workstations.

Facebook appeals to a kind of vanity and self-importance in us, too. If I put up a flattering picture of myself with a list of my favourite things, I can construct an artificial representation of who I am in order to get sex or approval. ("I like Facebook," said another friend. "I got a shag out of it.") It also encourages a disturbing competitivness around friendship: it seems that with friends today, quality counts for nothing and quantity is king. The more friends you have, the better you are. You are "popular," in the sense much loved in American high schools. . . .

Most of us engage in mediated communication almost constantly. About 75 percent of adults and 93 percent of young people in the United States use the Internet.

All of the above would have been enough to make me reject Facebook for ever. But there are more reasons to hate it. Many more.

Facebook is a well-funded project, and the people behind the funding, a group of Silicon Valley venture capitalists, have a clearly thought out ideology that they are hoping to spread around the world. Facebook is one manifestation of this ideology. Like PayPal before it, it is a social experiment, an expression of a particular kind of neoconservative libertarianism. On Facebook, you can be free to be who you want to be, as long as you don't mind being bombarded by adverts for the world's biggest brands. As with PayPal, national boundaries are a thing of the past. . . . PayPal was a way of moving money around the world with no restriction. . . .

Clearly, Facebook is another uber-capitalist experiment: can you make money out of friendship? Can you create communities free of national boundaries—and then sell Coca-Cola to them? Facebook is profoundly uncreative. It makes nothing at all. It simply mediates in relationships that were happening anyway. . . .

Now even if you don't buy the idea that Facebook is some kind of extension of the American imperialist programme crossed with a massive information-gathering tool, there is no way to denying that as a business, it is pure mega-genius. Some net nerds have suggested that its $15bn valuation is excessive, but I would argue that if anything that is too modest. Its scale really is dizzying, and the potential for growth is virtually limitless. "We want everyone to be able to use Facebook," says the impersonal voice of Big Brother on the website. I'll bet they do. It is Facebook's enormous potential that led Microsoft to buy 1.6% for $240m. . . .

The creators of the site need do very little bar fiddle with the programme. In the main, they simply sit back and watch as millions of Facebook addicts voluntarily upload their ID details, photographs and lists of their favorite consumer objects. Once in receipt of this vast database of human beings, Facebook then simply has to sell the information back to advertisers, or, as Zuckerberg puts it in a recent blog post, "to try to help people share information with their friends about things they do on the web." And indeed, this is precisely what's happening. On November 6 last year, Facebook announced that 12 global brands had climbed on board. They included Coca-Cola, Blockbuster, Verizon, Sony Pictures and Condé Nast. . . .

Futhermore, have you Facebook users ever actually read the privacy policy? It tells you that you don't have much privacy. Facebook pretends to be about freedom, but isn't it really more like an ideologically motivated virtual totalitarian regime with a population that will very soon exceed the UK's? Thiel and the rest have created their own country, a country of consumers. . . .

Or you might reflect that you don't really want to be part of this heavily-funded programme to create an arid global virtual republic, where your own self and your relationships with your friends are converted into commodities on sale to giant global brands. You may decide that you don't want to be part of this takeover bid for the world.

For my own part, I am going to retreat from the whole thing, remain as unplugged as possible, and spend the time I save by not going on Facebook doing something useful, such as reading books. . . . And if I want to connect with the people around me, I will revert to an old piece of technology. It's free, it's easy and it delivers a uniquely individual experience in sharing information: it's called talking.

FROM: "With Friends Like These...," by Tom Hodgkinson, *The Guardian*, January 14, 2008, www.guardian.co.uk. Copyright Guardian News & Media Ltd 2008. Reprinted by permission.

(Rainie et al. 2005, p. 57). Wireless and cell phone technology have spread even faster. Since the first handheld cellular telephone call was made in Manhattan in April 1983, about 2.8 billion (out of 6.6 billion) people worldwide now use mobile phones (Castells, Qiu, & Fernandez-Ardevol, 2006). The ability to access and use these communication technologies depends on, among other things, one's age, income, geographical location, race, and ethnicity. The issue of access is an important one, which we discuss later in this chapter.

Most people use CMC for four basic activities: (1) exchanging email and instant messages, (2) seeking and exchanging information, (3) entertainment, and (4) financial transactions (Daily Internet Activities, 2008). Let's look at each in turn.

Exchanging messages is still the most common use of CMC—about 60 percent of Internet users send/receive email messages on a typical day—but using the Internet to search for information is rapidly catching up (Fallows, 2008). Email is mostly used by older folks as young people prefer sending text messages on their phones or

social networking site (SNS)
a Web site where one user can publish information about himself or herself for the purpose of connecting with others and sharing personal or professional interests

blogs
short for Web logs; a Web site, like a journal, maintained by an individual with regular entries of commentary, descriptions of events, or other material such as graphics or video

keeping touch through **social networking sites** (**SNS**), as our student Danielle does (Lenhart, Madden, Macgill, & Smith, 2007).

Gathering and exchanging information is the second most common use of the Internet, as illustrated below by Nicole in *It Happened to Me*. According to a recent study, the percentage of Internet users who use search engines on a typical day has been steadily rising from about one-third in 2002 to just under 50 percent in 2008 (Fallows, 2008); popular searches are for news and weather, but the amount of information that we have at our fingertips is indeed staggering. You have probably gone online to search for answers to specific questions, like finding the best margarita recipe; locating phone numbers, addresses, and directions; or seeking information about unfamiliar illnesses. Others access the Internet to follow news on commercial Web sites or **blogs** (short for Web logs). According to a recent study conducted by Technocrati.com—a blog search engine that tracks in eighty-one languages around the world—there are now about 70 million blogs worldwide, and bloggers collectively create almost 1 million posts every day (State of the Blogosphere, 2008). In the beginning, blogs were created for political and technical users, but today's blogs are increasingly created by nonprofessionals for much smaller audiences (Nardi, Schiano, Gumbrecht, & Swartz, 2004).

Blogging activity has increased exponentially since 1999, partly because mainstream media have highlighted the "grassroots power of blogs as alternative news sources," and because blogging software allows users the ability to update rapidly and easily (Herring, Scheidt, Wright, & Bonus, 2005, p. 142). People blog for many reasons: to document their life, to express opinions or commentary, for catharsis or as an outlet for thoughts and feelings, to test ideas or "muse," and as community forum (Nardi, Schiano, Gumbrecht, & Swartz, 2004). For example, religious blogs are increasingly popular—a place where individuals can express their thoughts and feelings about their own personal faith, connect with others with similar beliefs, as well as to a wider public audience (Cheong, Halavais, & Kwon, 2008).

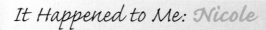

It Happened to Me: Nicole

While I was working on a paper for my communication class, I was thinking about how difficult and more time-consuming research must have been for students in the past. I can't imagine not having the Internet to gain access to information quickly. When I have to go to the library to do research, it takes me so much longer than when I go online.

Not surprisingly, teens are much more likely than adults to blog and read blogs. A recent report showed that about 30 percent of teens surveyed had created their own journal or blog—compared to only 11 percent of adults (Lenhart, Madden, Macgill, & Smith, 2007). The most common information-gathering use of the Internet for college students, however, is for doing course research online (Jones & Madden, 2002).

Some of your online research may involve podcasts, as colleges and universities now provide podcasts of various lecture series and important speakers on campus. People are increasingly using the Internet to download podcasts. Currently, 19 percent of all Internet users say they have downloaded a podcast so they could listen to it or view it later. Popular podcast topics are technology, comedy, religion and spirituality, and business—and you can receive your daily news-fix through podcasts of newspapers and magazines like the *Wall Street Journal* and the *Economist* (Madden & Jones, 2008). Some experts worry about our overreliance on the Internet for information. They speculate that because we have learned to "skim" information on the Internet; we no longer need to remember information since it is always at our fingertips—making us less able to concentrate and recall information (Carr, 2008). The importance of Internet search activities in our lives may be seen in the fact that "Google" is now a verb. If we need information, we google it!

Often the Internet is used for hobbies and entertainment. As one might expect, these activities are more prevalent among adolescents, college students, and those with high-speed connections at home (Griffith & Fox, 2007). Two popular online activities are video games and downloading music. For example, 53 percent of American adults age eighteen and older play video games—often on the Internet; and about 20 percent play every day or almost every day (Lenhart, Jones, & Macgill, 2008). While the number of video gamers among adults is substantial, it is still well under the number of teens who play. Fully 97 percent of teens play computer, Web, portable, or console games. Almost 50 percent play daily, typically for an hour or more (Lenhart, Kahne, Middaught, Macgill, Evans, & Vitak, 2008). Eighty-three percent of teens say they download music from the Internet (Leggatt, 2007). Of course, many people go online for no reason other than to surf the Net for fun.

Financial applications are another increasingly common use of the Internet—which includes shopping, paying bills, banking, and managing stock portfolios. Most of us have had some experience with this aspect of CMC. In fact, transaction-based activities have grown faster than any other type of online activity (Fallows, 2005). We should note, however, that information-seeking and financial activities are most popular among users with higher income and education levels, those with more experience online, and those with broadband access at home (Madden & Rainie, 2003).

While the Internet and other communication technologies seem pervasive and ordinary to us now, the pace at which these technologies entered and influenced our lives is unprecedented. One way to understand how rapidly communication technologies have developed is to think of all human history compressed to a single twenty-four-hour period. Using this measure, the alphabet came into existence roughly twenty hours into the day, and printing was invented after about twenty-three hours and thirty-eight minutes (A.D. 1451)! Recent advances in communication technology, like the computer, have all occurred during the last five minutes, or one-tenth of 1 percent of human history (Chesebro & Bonsall, 1989).

So, it's easy to see that many everyday activities and transactions that used to be conducted face to face are now being carried out in cyberspace using computer-mediated communication. How do these changing patterns affect our everyday communication, our identity, and our relationships? We begin answering these questions in the next section as we define CMC and describe how it differs from face-to-face communication.

WHAT IS COMPUTER-MEDIATED COMMUNICATION?

Before the computer, electronic communication technology was **analog** based, meaning that information was transmitted in a continuous numerical format. Analog technologies included inventions like the telegraph, telephone, radio, and phonograph (see Table 13.1). The invention of the first commercial computer in 1951 led to the **digital** communication revolution. Digital technology was revolutionary because digital information (based on only two values—0 and 1) is easier to store and manipulate, and this technology eventually led to the development of cable television, digital TV and radio, satellites, videogames, and the Internet.

Computer-mediated communication (CMC), which developed alongside computer technology, is the exchange of messages carried through an *intervening* system of digital electronic storage and transmitted between two or more people. CMC differs from face-to-face (FtF) communication because with FtF, messages are transmitted more or less directly, without the aid of exterior technology (Wood & Smith, 2005, p. 6)—a difference with significant implications, as you will soon see. In contrast, most CMC involves communicating online, using the Internet and the Web. As you probably know, the **Internet** is a system of networks that connects millions of computers around the world, and the **World Wide Web (WWW)** is one of a number of services that moves over the Internet. Other services deployed over the Internet

analog
information that is transmitted in a continuous numerical format

digital
information that is transmitted in a numerical format based on only two values (0 and 1)

computer-mediated communication (CMC)
the exchange of messages carried through an intervening system of digital electronic storage and transmitted between two or more people

Internet
a system of networks that connects millions of computers around the world

World Wide Web (WWW)
one of a number of services that moves over the Internet; it uses HTML (hypertext markup language) as its document format

cyberspace
synonymous with the Internet or
online world

TABLE 13.1   Communication Technologies Timeline

Analog	
1844	**Telegraph**
1876	**Telephone**
1921	**Wirephoto**
1927	**Television**

Digital	
1951	**First commercial computer available (though invented in 1931)**
1969	**AARPNET (Advance Research Project Agency-Network) predecessor of Internet**
1977–78	**Bulletin Board Systems (BBS)**
1978–80	**Multiuser Domains (MUDs)**
1983	**Personal Computer**
1988	**Internet Relay Chat (IRC)**
1990	**Internet**
1989–91	**World Wide Web (WWW)**
1989	**First commercial email (though email invented in 1971)**
1992	**First Short Messaging Service (SMS) message sent (in Finland)**
1997	**Instant messaging**
2004	**Social Networking Sites (SNS)**

Adapted: Retrieved June 23, 2006, from; www.pbs.org/wgbh/amex/telephone/timeline/timeline_text.html
www.zakon.org/robert/internet/timeline/; http://computer.howstuffworks.com/instant-messaging1.htm

include email, instant messaging, and newsgroups; each service uses a particular document format, which for the WWW is HTML. This chapter focuses on CMC that is interactive and mostly text-based.

Online CMC encompasses a wide range of communication possibilities, from personal and commercial Web pages to the more interactive email, chats, bulletin board systems (BBS), and MMOGS (massively text-based mulltiplayer online games) (see Table 13.2). Most CMC scholars, including the authors of this book, are interested in these interactive pursuits, where the "real give and take of social life" in **cyberspace** occurs (Walther & Parks, 2002, p. 3).

Portable devices, like phones and laptops, now use wireless technology, allowing us to be connected to the Internet practically wherever we go.

The invention of wireless technology has had a tremendous impact on our lives. It affords us convenience, allows us to be connected to the Internet practically wherever we go. Portable devices, like phones and laptops, now use wireless technology and do not need to be physically connected to a computer or any other device. You can talk on the phone while walking the dog, take notes on your computer during class, access MapQuest or phone directories while traveling, or answer work email while sitting in a doctor's office (Goggin, 2006; History of Wireless Technology, n.d.).

While cell phones are not, technically speaking, *computer*-mediated communication, they allow us access to the Internet (CMC), and are now an important form of mediated communication around the world (Goggin, 2006). According to a recent report, 62 percent of all Americans have either used a cell phone or PDA for a

TABLE 13.2   Common Computer-Mediated Communication Technologies

Email	Exchange of textual (word-based) messages between two or more parties.
Blog ("Web log")	Web site, like a journal, maintained by an individual with regular entries of commentary, descriptions of events, or other material such as graphics or video. Entries are commonly displayed in reverse-chronological order.
Bulletin Board Systems	A form of email that communicates to a larger audience. Messages are sent to a single computer address, where they are "posted" for others to read and respond to.
Chats	A type of real-time discussion. Text-based messages sent to and simultaneously read by a group of people.
MMOGs (Massively Multiplayer Online Games)	Text-based "virtual reality" game. Real-time interaction. Participants interact with environment, objects, and other participants.
Instant Messages	Text-based message system allows two people to exchange real-time messages—like a private chat.
Short Messaging service (SMS) or text messages	Very brief text messages exchanged on mobile phones.
SNS (Social Networking Sites)	Web-based service where people construct their profiles, identify others with whom they share a connection, and interact with their lists of connections and others within the system.
Twitter	Social networking and microblogging service, that allows its users to send and read other users' updates (otherwise known as **tweets**), which are text-based posts of up to 140 characters in length.

Adapted from: Thurlow, Lengel, & Tomic, 2004, pp. 28–29, Wood & Smith, 2005, pp. 10–15; "Twitter," from Wikipedia, the free encyclopedia. Retrieved March 30, 2009, from http://en.wikipedia.org/wiki/Twitter

nonvoice data application or logged on to the Internet while away from home or work by using a wireless laptop or a handheld connection. In fact, when asked how hard it would be to give up a specific technology, those surveyed said that the cell phone would be the most difficult to do without, followed by the Internet, TV, and landline telephone (Horrigan, 2008a).

Most CMC on the Internet is text-based (word-based), although possibilities for incorporating audio and video exist—reflecting a general trend in technology toward the integration of communication modes. For example, telephone technology can be integrated with video technology so you can use your cell phone as a video recorder or your computer as a telephone, and if you add a Webcam, you can have video with your telephone. However, predictions that multimedia uses of CMC would eclipse text-based messages have not yet been realized. As one communication scholar (Herring, 2004) points out, the most recent innovations are all text-based. Text messaging, for example, is email sent over mobile phones, IM is a form of text chat, and blogs are Web pages.

The fact that CMC is a relatively recent form of communication and is rapidly changing makes it difficult to arrive at definitive conclusions about its exact role in everyday life. Researching this aspect of communication can be like trying to hit a moving target. However, with a basic understanding of what CMC is, and the significant ways in which it differs from FtF communication, we can begin to assess its increasingly important role.

To begin, consider this question. Have you ever debated whether to communicate a message by email, text message, or in person? Perhaps you had a difficult issue to discuss and were unsure what the most effective mode of communication would be. If so, you had good reason to feel unsure. CMC and face-to-face communication differ in several ways, and these differences can impact the outcome of your conversation. There are many different ways to understand the relationship between face to face and CMC, and scholars do not agree on which is the most useful. However,

tweets
text-based updates, 140 characters or less sent through social networking and microblogging services

media deficit approach
a theoretical perspective that sees mediated communication as deficient, in comparison to face-to-face communication

media augmentation approach
a theoretical perspective that views mediated communication as complementing or augmenting face-to-face communication

social presence
degree of psychological closeness or immediacy engendered by various media

media richness
the potential information-carrying capacity of a communication medium

most experts fall into one of two research camps: One is the **media deficit approach**, which basically sees mediated communication as deficient when compared to face-to-face communication; the other is the **media augmentation approach**, which views mediated communication as complementing or augmenting face-to-face communication. Those who hold the deficit approach focus on two unique characteristics of mediated communication: (1) It filters out nonverbal cues, and (2) It occurs asynchronously, meaning there may be a delay between the time the message is sent and when it is responded to. Let's look at these two important properties.

Filtered Communication

As we learned in Chapter 6, nonverbal cues are extremely important in understanding the totality of another person's communication. And the Internet is a "cues-filtered-out" form of communication. In comparison, the telephone filters out some cues but does allow others, like the speed, tone, and quality of voice.

There are two "deficit" theories that help us understand the impact filtering has on CMC: **social presence** theory and **media richness** theory. See Table 13.3. Social presence refers to the feelings of psychological closeness or immediacy that people experience when interacting with each other (Short, Williams, & Christie, 1976). This closeness or intimacy generally is communicated through nonverbal cues, like smiling, leaning forward, and having a relaxed body posture. Social presence theory suggests that face-to-face communication is generally high in social presence, and media vary in the amount of social presence they convey. For example, telephone communication conveys less social presence than face-to-face interaction, but more than email communication—where all nonverbal cues are filtered out. The implication is that media low in social presence seem more impersonal, less sensitive, and less relationship focused.

Media richness theory views CMC similarly. Media richness describes the potential information-carrying capacity of a communication media (Daft & Lengel, 1984, 1986): *Visual Summary 13.1: Media Richness Theory*, on p. 358. According to this theory, face-to-face communication is the richest medium for communicating, because you can see facial expressions and body gestures as well as hear the tone, speed, and quality of the voice. All these factors relay a tremendous amount of information and allow you to interpret messages more accurately. You not only hear the words, or the content of the message, but you also receive the relational messages that are being sent nonverbally and that reveal how that person feels about you. If the other person is smiling, leaning toward you, and maintaining eye contact, you probably infer that the person is happy or glad to talk with you. If the person is scowling and avoiding eye contact, you might infer that she is angry or unhappy with you.

Another relatively rich medium is video/audio communication, which some people conduct through personal Webcams on their home computers. In using a

TABLE 13.3	Characteristics of Common Communication Technologies		
	Social Presence	**Media Richness**	**Synchronicity**
Telephone	Some	Rich	Synchronous
Video (live)	High	Rich	Synchronous
Video (recording)	High	Rich	Asynchronous
Chats	Low	Less rich	Synchronous
Email	Low	Lean	Asynchronous
Bulletin board	Low	Lean	Asynchronous
Instant messaging	Low	Lean	Synchronous

emoticons
pictographs used in email to convey relational information

Webcam, you might miss some immediate context cues, such as body posture or gestures, but you would have the benefit of seeing some nonverbal behaviors. Less rich is the telephone. On the phone, conversation partners can process the audio information and discern some paralinguistic cues, but they don't see facial expression, eye gaze, or gestures.

The very leanest of media, according to media richness theory, is email. Here, nonverbal cues appear to be completely absent. On the other hand, some relational and nonverbal information can be communicated in CMC. For example, some people convey relational information by **emoticons**, or pictographs, such as the smiley face—:)—or they use abbreviations like LOL (laughing out loud) or H&K (hugs and kisses). See *Did You Know? Emoticons*, to see the full array of pictographs.

Of course, writing (including writing emails and text messages) is a form of communication that includes many techniques for expressing mood and feelings.

Did You Know?
Emoticons

Have you ever had an email conversation where you wondered whether a person meant what he or she "said"? The solution is "pictographs" conveying an emotion and made of letters or symbols. The only weird thing is you have to get used to "reading" them sideways.

:-)	Smile
;-)	Smile with a wink
:<})	User with mustache, smiling
:-||	Mad
:-(	Sad
:'-(	Crying
:~	Also crying
:-))	Really happy
:-D	Big grin
:-*	A kiss
:-P~	A lick
:-o	Wow! Or I'm surprised
:-|	Grim
:-P	Sticking out your tongue
:-	User happens to be Popeye
:-/	Perplexed
=:O	Frightened (hair standing on end)
=8O	Bug-eyed with fright
:-}	Embarassed smile
:-)<>>>>>	Basic smiley with a necktie
;-^)	Tongue in cheek
%*@:-(	Hung over
:-~~~	Drooling
>:)	Perplexed look

SOURCE: Mobile Computing Definitions: Emoticons. Retrieved March 29, 2009, from http://searchmobilecomputing.techtarget.com/sDefinition/0,,sid40_gci212057,00.html

Media Richness Theory
(potential information-carrying capacity)

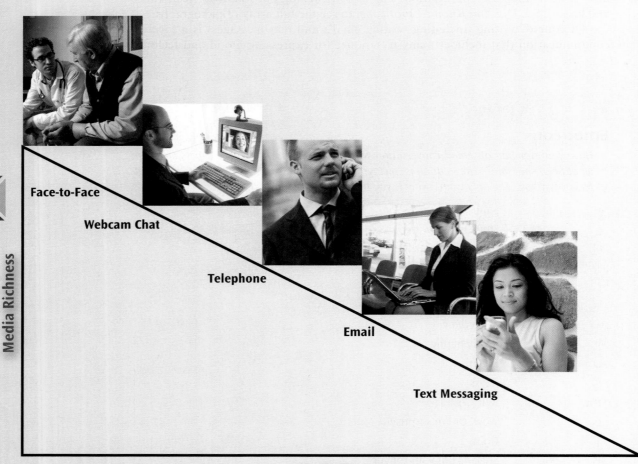

Media Richness

Face-to-Face

Webcam Chat

Telephone

Email

Text Messaging

Media Type

For example, moods can be expressed by punctuation, by the length of sentences, and by numbers of adjectives or adverbs. One can also communicate intonation by emphasizing particular words in a sentence, or by repetition. Using capital letters counts as shouting, as you can see in the following message; many people avoid this to keep from offending others. Is there any question about the tone of this message?

> I just DON'T understand you; it just doesn't MAKE ANY SENSE. Why would you not want to spend the weekend here? WHY? I worked overtime for three weeks in a row so I could have the weekend off, told all my friends that you were coming to visit, and NOW you tell me you can't make it. I JUST DON'T BELIEVE IT!!!!!

Asynchronous Interaction

Another difference between face-to-face and CMC is the degree to which the exchange of messages is synchronous or asynchronous. Face-to-face communication and media such as the telephone and CMC chats are synchronous; that is, messages are sent and received at the same time. However, email, bulletin board messages, and text messages are asynchronous, since with these media you can send a message that may be received at a later time. Text messaging may be synchronous—or not—depending on whether or not the other person acknowledges and responds.

While **asynchronicity** affords convenience, deficit theorists point to the fact that the interaction is not being shared in the moment, leading to an "absent presence," or a lack of shared reality (Gergen, 2002). In some work contexts, this lack of presence may not matter much. In other work contexts, such as carrying out negotiations, asynchronicity (and filtering of cues) may have serious impacts, such as colleagues misinterpreting written messages.

Asynchronicity in CMC may also impact personal relationships, because the notion of friendship includes shared experiences, feelings, and activities. So, when you receive terrific news that you want to share with your best friend, telling him or her through an email message or delayed text message (if your friend does not respond immediately) does not have the same impact.

Another problem of asynchronicity is that one doesn't know if the other person has received a sent message because the sender does not receive any "in the moment" response. In addition, silences or nonresponses in CMC interaction can be problematic. In face-to-face interaction, silences can be very meaningful and usually are interpreted by nonverbal cues—to mean hesitation, reflection, or perhaps anger. But silence over email is just a gap in the exchange of written words and might mean anything. A lack of response to an email or to a bulletin board discussion may be taken as lack of interest. However, the silence may simply mean that the person was called away or was having email problems. Yet, the implications for relationships can be severe, as the following quote indicates: "Disappearance of an email may impair a relationship conducted entirely in text if the unreliability of the medium of communication is instead attributed to neglect by the writer. Either may be taken, by a fearful, suspicious, or attentive correspondent, as breach of tacit commitment to reply, even if the silence is quite unintended" (Rooksby, 2002, p. 112).

How do these characteristics of filtering and asynchronicity in CMC affect communication in everyday life? Deficit theorists recognize that the answer partly depends on the purpose of the conversation and the context. In contexts where messages communicate basic information—such as getting an e-vite or driving directions from a friend—the filtering of nonverbal cues and the leanness of the medium may not be a problem. However, communicating personal feelings may be a different story, such as using text messaging to break up with someone. Personal

asynchronicity
occurs when a message is sent and received at different times

Telephone communication conveys more nonverbal cues than email does, but less than face-to-face communication.

preferences may also come into play. Some shy people prefer mediated communication over face-to-face meetings (Auter, 2007). Also, age makes a difference; your grandmother probably prefers to talk with you in person or on the telephone, rather than by text messages. In the end, deficit theorists emphasize CMC's deficiencies by comparing CMC and face-to-face communication—noting its lack of both social presence and information-carrying richness.

These theorists also believe that using communication technology weakens relationships by replacing direct, personal contact with less rich contact, increasing the prevalence of social isolation throughout society (e.g., McPherson et al., 2006, cited in Boase, 2008). They note, that people can "hide" behind cellphone conversations, for example, so as to not communicate with those around them (Gergen, 2002). Some also fear that mobile communication may result in a psychological "emptying out" of public space, where people's bodies are present, but personalities are engaged elsewhere, resulting in the stress of always being somewhere else no matter where one might be (Katz, 2007, p. 390). Evidence to support these claims is a 2000 national survey where 1 to 7 people surveyed reported that the cell phone reduced their social relationship quality (Katz & Rice, 2002).

A more recent approach views CMC as complementing or augmenting face-to-face encounters. These scholars point to evidence that contradicts a strict deficit view. For example, they note that having prior information about a writer helps one interpret CMC relational messages, which render email communication less lean. For example, interpreting the phrase "that's just great for you" would be easier if one knew something about the writer and the context. Is the writer often sarcastic? Is her current mood supportive or hostile? Also, having experience with CMC often makes it easier to interpret filtered communication (Rooksby, 2002). In addition, the asynchrony of message can have positive effects: It can give people time to formulate their messages when more time is needed such as in a conflict situation or when there is a language deficiency (Osman & Herring, 2007; Thompson & Ku, 2005). The lack of physical data that may trigger stereotypes, which is also a benefit (Merryfield, 2003).

Further, many of these experts do not view mediated and face-to-face communication as two different realities, rather they emphasize that people simply use multiple media, in addition to face-to-face interaction to fit their social needs and lifestyles (Boase, 2008; Sawhney, 2007). For example, a series of research studies compared college students' interpersonal interaction online, face to face, and on the telephone. The results showed that students did not rate the quality of their FtF conversation any higher than their telephone or online conversations, and the authors of the study concluded that people do not perceive face-to-face communication as vastly superior to online communication and that "instead of a trade-off between high quality FtF conversations and lower quality Internet interaction, students are supplementing high quality FtF conversations and telephone calls with really good Internet interactions" (Baym, Zhang, & Lin, 2004, p. 316). Another study, using **social network theory**, found similar results. Social network theory proposes that the patterns of ties among people affect social behavior and communication. Specifically, the theory predicts that the more people are socially connected, the more intensely they are likely to communicate using various media available to them. Indeed, the study found that people who had more frequent FtF social contacts also had more frequent online contacts and even had more intimate Internet social contacts. These findings suggest that, as with previous advances in communication technology (for example, the telephone), CMC enhances the process of connecting people rather than isolating them (Bimie & Horvath, 2002).

More recent research results, now including cell phone use, come to similar conclusions, that cell phones and the Internet have not weakened relationships by acting as insufficient substitutes for in-person contact, rather individuals use various media to connect with their different social networks. It appears that people use mobile phones to stay in contact with people they already know well and use the Internet to expand their social network—getting to know people, or staying in touch with people who are geographically distant. They may get to know someone on the Internet, and as these ties become close they are often contacted through other means, either in person or by phone (Boase, 2008; Katz, 2007; Kim, Kim, Park, & Rice, 2007; Ling, 2004). At least one expert suggests that mobile phones can even restore the comfort and intimacy that was degraded by twentieth-century technologies, especially the television (Gergen, 2002).

One scholar suggests that we use the term *personal communication system* to convey the idea that individuals draw on multiple kinds of communication technologies together with in-person contact. The word *personal* notes that the use of communication media is centered on the individual and that individuals can combine various media differently, to suit their needs and personal preferences. "The word 'system' implies that individuals combine various communication media together to connect with their own personal networks, rather than using them separately to connect with separate social worlds" (Boase, 2008, p. 492).

Media augmentation experts acknowledge that some skepticism about the impact of new communication technologies is understandable, but they caution that we should not assume that online communication is inferior to FtF communication:

> When a technology grabs hold and diffuses as rapidly as the Internet, it is reasonable to be concerned about its impact. However, understanding these impacts requires demystifying the Internet. Rather than studying "the Internet" we need to differentiate between the multiple aspects of this complex and pervasive technology and to distinguish the Internet clearly from other strategies for accomplishing the same cultural goals. We need to understand that users may be influenced by the technologies' affordances, but they also appropriate technologies to serve their needs. . . . Before we have built a strong foundation for such studies, any pronouncements about the Internet's dangers or salvations should be treated with skepticism (Baym, Zhang, & Lin, 2004, p. 316).

Think of a recent conflict you've had and describe how it might have been different if the communication medium had been different. How might it have gone over the telephone? Face-to-face? Text messaging?

Now that we have defined CMC and described various ways of understanding it, let's look more closely at how personal identity is performed and managed in CMC.

COMPUTER-MEDIATED COMMUNICATION AND THE INDIVIDUAL

As you can now see, CMC's unique properties can powerfully impact communication between individuals. The combined effects of filtering and asynchronicity have important implications for identity performance and, in turn, for personal relationships. Let's examine the way this works.

Managing Identity

How does CMC affect one's identity? And how do people communicate and manage their identities when using CMC? The same characteristics that filter out nonverbal cues and make CMC a leaner form of communication add an interesting dimension to how communicators present themselves online. The primary effect of this is that we can control the amount of information we disclose about ourselves, which provides a certain fluidity to our identities that we don't have in face-to-face communication. Think back to Danielle's dilemma in the opening vignette. She made several decisions about how she wanted to present herself on Facebook. As we noted in Chapter 3, one's identity, or self-concept, is developed and expressed through communication with others. Early CMC researchers thought that people maintained separate identities online and offline. As CMC becomes the norm in our lives, researchers no longer hold this view (Zywica & Danowski, 2008, p. 7), but do suggest that CMC communication provides the opportunity to express our identities in various ways, not possible in face-to-face communication. Three identity management issues are discussed next. At one extreme is the possibility of being anonymous or presenting yourself as someone you are not in real life (*psuedoidentity*). A more common issue in CMC is making decisions about what type of information about yourself you want to present to others online—a topic related to impression management that we discussed in Chapter 9.

Anonymity and Psuedoanonymity

When you communicate with someone over email or in an online course discussion forum, unless they infer information from your name, they would not know your age, gender, race, nationality, or many of the other cues that lead others to perceive you in a particular way. So CMC offers the possibility of controlling more aspects of your identity for public consideration than has ever before been possible. It also

In virtual worlds, as many as 10,000 people at one time, through their avatars, can be involved in a gamut of activities, from just hanging out, to playing games, or participating in educational activities.

gives the opportunity for deception. If you have represented yourself as something you are not on a discussion board or on your Facebook or MySpace profile, you aren't alone. Forty-nine percent of young people say they put false information on their SNS (Social Network Site) and they give many reasons for doing so. Fabricating data on SNSs may protect you from unwanted advances from strangers but some young people say they put false information on their SNS profile to protect themselves from the watchful eye of their parents (boyd, 2007b). There is one account of three girls whose parents were offended by the information the teens had revealed on their MySpace profiles. So the friends created a second account using fake names and details, which they then linked to each other's second profile; they then uploaded the offending material, inviting their friends to do the same. In doing so, they created a network that completely mirrored the network that their parent had seen (boyd, 2007b).

This anonymity may be beneficial or detrimental, depending on your viewpoint. Communication researchers Andrew F. Wood and Matthew J. Smith (2005) identify three issues in the complex relationship between anonymity and identity in CMC. The first has to do with the informative aspect of the identity. On the one hand, knowing something about the persons sending information gives a context for judging their messages. If you know, for example, that the person answering your medical question online is a doctor, that person seems more credible than a person without a medical degree. On the other hand, information on age, gender, and race can form the basis for stereotyping and prejudice.

A second issue related to CMC and anonymity is that the combination has generated a new set of group norms. One might say that the freedom granted by anonymity has led people to be less responsible in their communication. People sometimes treat others more carelessly over email than in person. One professor noted that in online courses, "students are sometimes aggressive . . . something that never happened in face-to-face classes" (Smith, Ferguson, & Caris, 2001, p. 25). In addition, anonymity permits the generation of email rumors and hoaxes, such as warnings that canola oil can cause cancer or that companies like Microsoft will give away free money to people who forward the email message to five additional people. (For information about evaluating these types of messages, go to David Emery's Web site at http://urbanlegends.about.com/od/Internet/a/current_netlore.htm).

Anonymity can also lead to bad behavior in virtual worlds. Recently two players were banned from "Second Life" for depicting sexual activity between an adult and a child (Serious Trouble, 2007).

Even more annoying are the millions of **spam** messages (unwanted commercial messages and advertisements sent through email), which might be greatly reduced if addresses or spammers' identities were easier to trace (see Figure 13.1). **Phishing** (fraudulently attempting to get consumer banking and credit card information) is another problem for Internet users. Increasing numbers of fake emails are showing up in people's email inboxes, "warning" them that their account information needs to be checked then pointing them to Web sites where they are asked to enter their financial information. Technology companies and banks are aggressively pursuing those who send spam and phishing messages (Fox, 2005; Seagraves, 2004).

Figure 13.1: Model of Spam messages

Spam, an ongoing problem, rapidly changes how it infects and sends messages, as other people work to block it.

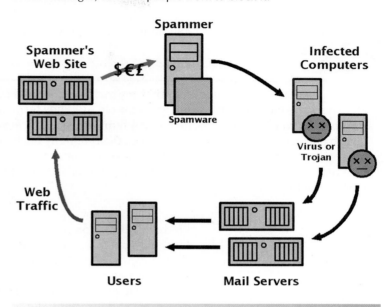

A third issue regarding anonymity has to do with its capacity to liberate speech, which has both positive and negative aspects. For example, without knowing who has issued a statement, the legal restrictions on speech are difficult to enforce. So if someone, while **spoofing** (misrepresenting oneself online), makes racist or libelous statements, it is almost impossible to implement legal sanctions. On the other hand, anonymity may have benefits. For example, it can give some people courage to express unpopular opinions or question conventional wisdom, which they might be afraid to do in face-to-face interaction.

Beyond anonymity is a phenomenon made possible by CMC—**pseudoanonymity**, or projecting a false identity. For example, people can invent identities through very acceptable means as in MMOGs (massively multiplayer online games), like "World of Warcraft," "EverQuest II," "Karaoke Revolution," or virtual worlds like "Second Life" and "Entropia Universe." The original multiplayer game was "Dungeons & Dragons" but hundreds of MMOGs now exist on the Internet—some for gaming, others, like Second Life have been used for socializing or pedagogical purposes, or for commercial ventures. In these virtual worlds, as many as 10,000 people (or their **avatars**—digital alter egos/versions of themselves) can be involved at the same time, engaged in a gamut of activities, everything from just hanging out, to holding charity fund-raisers, to operating sex clubs (Siklos, 2006). Some universities have developed sites on "Second Life" where professors and students can interact virtually, and a big American bank is using PIXELearning's simulator for "diversity and inclusion training" (Serious Trouble, 2007, p. 4).

Deception also can occur in MMOGs, even though the community is based on false identities. For example, in one MMOG called Bluesky, a player and her boyfriend decided to see if other players would notice if they took turns playing a character. They found it was very easy to do. And then they decided to "confess" to the other players. The reactions were mixed (Kendall, 2002).

In this example, the feeling of betrayal is complex and perhaps surprising. Some players saw this experiment as a dishonest representation of identity—even though identities in this game were understood by all to be assumed, or false. In this case,

spam
unwanted commercial messages and advertisements sent through email

phishing
email messages that try (fraudulently) to get consumer banking and credit card information

spoofing
misrepresenting oneself online

pseudoanonymity
projecting a false identity

avatar
a computer user's representation of himself/herself or alter ego

the outcome was comparatively benign. In other cases, however, people have misrepresented themselves with results that were far more significant. See *It Happened to Me: Vivian* to read an account by one of our students of a troubling Internet-related incident involving one of her teachers. You may remember a few years ago that sites like MySpace were implicated in a series of sexual interactions between adults and minors, although some researchers say that concerns about sexual predators on SNS were greatly exaggerated (boyd & Ellison, 2007).

It Happened to Me: Vivian

At my high school, it was discovered that my math teacher had been communicating over the Internet with a thirteen-year-old girl. They formed a relationship, and when he went to meet her, he found a female police officer waiting for him. So both participants were lying. The police officer told my teacher she was a young girl, and my math teacher told her he was a sixteen-year-old boy. My math teacher was arrested for pursuing a sexual relationship with a minor, and he was fired from his job.

Impression Management Online

You may have never taken advantage of online anonymity, and with the rise of SNSs the whole point is to be seen and known; but like our student Danielle, you probably have made decisions about what kind of information to reveal about yourself on SNSs like Facebook and MySpace. How do you decide what type of information to present to others? A MySpace profile can be seen as a sort of *digital body* where individuals must "write themselves into being" (boyd, 2007, p. 13). There seems to be three different types of SNS profile presentations: *authentic* (presenting true information about the self—real name and location); *authentic ironic* (presenting true information but modifying it using sarcasm, irony or satire); or *Fakesters*, whose profiles claim that they are celebrities, objects, places, activities or obscure in-jokes (Marwick, 2005).

Researchers have discovered that some decisions concerning what to reveal on SNSs are related to a person's age, their self-esteem, and their popularity. As it turns out, younger adolescents experiment more with online identities than do young adults (Valkenburg & Peter, 2007a, 2007b). Perhaps not surprisingly, people with low self-esteem tend to reveal more information about themselves online, and present exaggerated information—rather than making strategic moves to enhance their popularity. This may be that they feel more comfortable expressing their true selves online than they do offline (Zywica & Danowski, 2008). Popular users say they would most often change their profile picture in order to appear popular on Facebook and also change their Facebook profiles, like noting new activities or interests and add friends (Zywica & Danowski, 2008).

Another aspect of self-presentation is listing friendship links, which serve as another expression of one's online identity, since "You are who you know." Sometimes "friends" on SNSs are not the same as friends in the everyday sense, but rather provide context by offering users a kind of imagined audience to interact with (boyd & Ellison, 2007). But adding too many friends can have the opposite effect—raising doubts about one's popularity and desirability (Tong, Van Der Heide, Langwell, & Walther, 2008).

How much personal information to include in an SNS profile may also be determined by privacy and security concerns. One researcher says there is a *privacy paradox* that occurs when young people are not aware of the public nature of the Internet and that disclosing too much information on SNSs can have detrimental effects. For example, spammers used freely accessible profile data from SNSs to craft a *phishing* scheme that appeared to originate from a friend on the network. Their targets were much more likely to give away information to this "friend" than they were to a perceived "stranger" (boyd & Ellison, 2007). Potential employees can also access profile information and according to one study, 34 percent of employers surveyed admit to dismissing a candidate from consideration because of what they found on social networking sites (see *Communication in Society: Putting Your Best Cyberface Forward* and *Did You Know? Employers Admit to Disqualifying Candidates Due to Facebook Content*, on p. 366).

COMMUNICATION IN SOCIETY
Putting Your Best Cyberface Forward

This article from the Toronto Sun *describes survey findings that can help Canadians (and others) to put their best image online.*

Chances are you have more than one email address and at least one of your online identities contains a fun or cute word. But if you're gunning for a promotion or applying for a new job, it may be time to switch from "bon bon girl" to something more reflective of your career aspirations. "Everyone is an individual brand—the 'you' brand," says Mitch Joel, president of Twist Image, a Montreal-based digital marketing agency. "If managed incorrectly, this can have negative consequences when it comes to getting a job, advancing your career or maintaining a positive reputation."

He's responding to the results of an MSN Canada/Ipsos-Reid survey that found four of 10 Canadians don't know how to use the Internet to promote themselves or their careers. The survey raised several red flags, says Joel, who adds that the lines between your online persona and real life brand are blurring. Creating a carefully-polished online image begins with your email address. According to the survey, 80 percent of Canadians describe one of their online identities as "personal"—a variation of their name, a nickname or personality trait. One quarter use a fun word that reflects an image or hobby. But what happens when "bon bon girl" grows up? "I push everyone to use their own name in their address," Joel says.

The survey found 67 percent of email users have more than one email address. To protect your privacy but still be visible, Joel recommends using consistent personal information in all online activities, such as the same photo and same email alias for all your accounts. The idea: To become recognizable across many channels.

But don't stop there. You should also regularly Google your name. If you find an unprofessional or unflattering YouTube clip of yourself, chances are the human resources professional checking out potential job candidates will find it, too. Polish your image or delete inappropriate information. "People search you just like you search them," Joel says. . . . Security must always be top of mind, but it shouldn't overshadow your digital image.

Take your online brand one step further by actively searching for environments where you can thrive. "Even within Facebook, there are segments and niches that reflect interests like geography and marketing," Joel says. "Make sure you're well connected." . . . Develop a strong online brand with the following additional strategies:

The majority of Canadians (85 percent) avoid putting personal information about themselves on the Internet to protect their privacy and reputation. But if you're not online, you're not proactively promoting your personal brand. Fewer than 5 percent of Canadians would change their email alias if they could get their first request. Reconsider this. Own an email alias featuring your name, rather than a vague variation, and use that ID in all your email accounts.

To summarize, the anonymity of CMC affords many possibilities for performing and managing identities, but it also brings with it ethical challenges, which we discuss later in the chapter. Let's now turn our attention to how relationships develop and are maintained through CMC.

Relationship Development

Today, most of us carry on relationships through CMC. In fact, you probably have some relationships that exist only online, like acquaintances you met in an online course or on a bulletin board. You may have other friends with whom you interact both on- and offline. Before we go any further in this discussion, let's disprove two misconceptions about people in online relationships. First we'll consider the notion that people who spend a lot of time online are introverted and prefer the filtered CMC because they can't establish "real" relationships.

Research indicates that when *some* people increase online interaction, they do decrease contact with their real friends and acquaintances (Kraut, Kiesler,

Did You Know?

Employers Admit to Disqualifying Candidates Due to Facebook Content

My conversations with dozens and perhaps even hundreds of employers who hire college students for internships and recent graduates for entry level jobs have led me to believe that about 75 percent are searching social networking sites such as Facebook and MySpace as part of their background checking process. But one question that was harder to answer was how many of those employers have declined to hire a candidate because of content on those sites.

Careerbuilder recently surveyed hiring managers and found that of those admit to screening job candidates using Facebook, MySpace, and other social networking sites, 34 percent admit to dismissing a candidate from consideration because of what they found on the social networking sites. The top areas for concern among these hiring managers were:

- 41%—candidate posted information about them drinking or using drugs
- 40%—candidate posted provocative or inappropriate photographs or information
- 29%—candidate had poor communication skills
- 28%—candidate bad-mouthed their previous company or fellow employee
- 27%—candidate lied about qualifications
- 22%—candidate used discriminatory remarks related to race, gender, religion, etc.
- 22%—candidate's screen name was unprofessional
- 21%—candidate was linked to criminal behavior
- 19%—candidate shared confidential information from previous employers

I've said it before and I'll say it again: don't put anything online on any site unless you would feel comfortable sharing that information with your favorite grandmother. Posting information online is like getting a tattoo in that there's nothing inherently wrong with it but you have to understand that it is permanent and that people who you may not want to see it will at times see it.

Excerpt posted by Steven Rothberg, CollegeRecruiter.com on September 26, 2008. Courtesy of CollegeRecruiter.com job board.

Mukhopadhya, & Scherlis, 1998; Nie & Erbring, 2000). For example, young people who suffered from depression were more likely to use the Internet to make friends (Hwang, Cheong, & Feeley, 2008). However, most researchers have argued that Internet socializing complements rather than replaces traditional socializing and that frequent Internet users might have more active social lives than nonusers (Finn & Korukonda, 2004).

Another related myth was that offline relationships were more real than Internet relationships and that people viewed their online and offline relationships differently. As we noted earlier, many relationships are maintained through multiple media, Internet, telephone, and face-to-face encounters. While the Internet is especially useful for maintaining long-distance relationships, you probably have many local relationships that exist both online and offline (Baym, Zhang, & Lin, 2004; Beer, 2008).

Having considered this alternative view of cyber-socializing, let's consider the impact of CMC on three types of relationships: friendships, romantic relationships, and relationships in the workplace.

Friendships

While online and offline relationships have much in common, there are several ways in which CMC impacts our relational development: Online relationships offer a larger **field of availables**, and they overcome limits of time and space.

What do we mean by *field of availables*? This term describes the fact that the field of potential partners and friends accessible through CMC is much larger than in face-to-face relationships. This is true for two reasons. First, you can come into contact with many more people online than you ever would in person. Moreover, when online, you have fewer reasons to dismiss someone as a potential friend or partner, because initial physical cues are not present. The fact that you engage with someone in a chat room, over email, or on a discussion board means that you already have something in common, which is a powerful means of attraction.

How do CMC interactions overcome limits in time or space? Before the prevalence of CMC, interactions were limited to the people one met during the day or talked to on the telephone. Through CMC, however, people can communicate with others who have completely different schedules, who live in any time zone, anywhere in the world. In addition, through the asynchronicity of email, people can develop relationships without ever meeting face-to-face or even in real time.

This lack of constraint in time and space has both positive and negative implications for friendships. On the positive side, online relationships may be more durable. For example, if you have a relationship that is strictly online and you relocate to another region of the country (or even overseas), the relationship may not be affected. As people are increasingly mobile, CMC affords more continuity than was possible before (Kendall, 2002).

On the other hand, online relationships are in some ways more fragile and so require more trust (boyd, 2003; Carter, 2004; Rooksby, 2002). As one MMOGer said:

> You have these friends, but maybe the worst thing is knowing that the last time you "see" somebody may be the last time you ever see them. There's no guarantee that they're ever coming back. This happened last year. [One of our players] just disappeared. (Kendall, 2002, p. 149).

For this reason, many people who develop friendships on discussion boards or in chat rooms also exchange email addresses or phone numbers, or even meet offline, in order to establish more trust in the relationship (Kendall, 2002). As noted earlier, many of our friendships are maintained through both online and offline interaction. Most SNSs primarily support preexisting social relations. Facebook is used to maintain existing offline relationships or to solidify offline connections, as opposed to being a vehicle for meeting new people—some common element, such as a shared class at school exists (boyd & Ellison, 2007; Ellison, Steinfeld, & Lampe, 2007). Communication researcher Joseph Walther (1996) suggested that sometimes those in Internet relationships develop intimacy quickly. Walther termed this phenomenon **hyperpersonal relationships**. He based his conclusions on social information processing theory (SIPT), which predicts that the speed at which a relationship develops is related to the amount of time available for message exchange (Walther, 1996). So when time is limited, the theory predicts that communication will appear impersonal, more task focused, and less social in nature. Accordingly, communicators would focus on completing the task at hand and social concerns would become secondary. Consequently, when time is limited, messages do not accumulate as quickly as in FtF, resulting in a slower rate of relationship development.

Walther suggests that early research on CMC may have viewed it as impersonal because the researchers focused on instances in which people met one time only, especially in task/work situations. In contrast, in hyperpersonal communication carried out via

field of availables
potential partners and friends, typically much larger via CMC than via face-to-face relationships

hyperpersonal relationships
Internet relationships that develop intimacy more quickly than face-to-face relationships

Through CMC, people can communicate with others who live in any time zone anywhere in the world.

email, participants place great importance on the few cues that aren't filtered out. In fact, people seem to "fill in the blanks" about the personality of the sender from online email messages (Rosen, Cheever, Cummings, & Felt, 2008). They also can take time to craft their messages.

A recent study tested whether people's anticipation of future interactions influence how they view an online relationship. It turns out that individuals who expected future contact with their conversational partners in the study were more positive about the initial interaction and reported the most positive relational tone. Likewise, those who did not expect future contact and attained an initial negative impression reported the lowest levels of relational positivity (Ramirez, 2007). For example, when people sit at the computer late at night, replying to a newfound friend, they tend to give the written words great meaning and to disclose more rapidly than they might in face-to-face interaction (McKenna, Green, & Gleason, 2002).

There is some suggestion that the timing of moving a CMC-only relationship from online to offline may be important; some researchers suggest that it is better to move a relationship offline fairly soon after an initial meeting, before people develop an idealized notion of their online partner and have unrealistic expectations (Ramirez & Zhang, 2007, p. 306).

Romantic Relationships

Who becomes involved in online romantic relationships, and how does online romance differ from in-person romance? We've already discussed the qualities that allow friendships to develop more easily online: anonymity, increased field of availables, and no time or space limits, all of which also impact the development of online romantic relationships. Dating Web sites continue to flourish. According to one survey, 37 percent of single American Internet users who are looking for a romantic partner have gone to a dating Web site (Madden & Lenhart, 2006). These Web sites have refined their methods, and now emphasize a more scientific approach, which often includes compatibility and personality testing. Others focus on niche marketing, including Spark Networks, whose online dating sites include JDate for Jewish singles, as well as CatholicMingle.com, InterracialSingles.net, BlackSingles.com, LatinSinglesConnection.com, and Chemistry.com that promotes itself as more inclusive than other sites such as Eharmony.com (Facenda, 2008). These sites seem to be used by people across all income and educational levels and by both males and females. Sites like lavalifePRIME, BOOMj.com, and PrimeSingles.net are among those offering social networking for older singles (Jayson, 2008). In one study, people around forty years of age were the most active online daters, probably because it is relatively difficult for people of this age group to find a romantic partner using more traditional strategies. Singles in this age group are often divorced and have to combine taking care of children with a busy career (Valkenburg & Peter, 2007b). Also, younger people are increasingly using Facebook and Facebook's new online dating sites—are you Interested and Meet New People—to find romantic partners (Krauss, 2008).

Psychologists have identified three qualities of Internet communication that are particularly relevant to romantic relationships: The ease of finding similar others, of "getting past the gates," and of achieving intimate exchanges (McKenna et al., 2002, p. 2). These three qualities are particularly relevant to online romantic relationships.

To begin, it's easy to see how one can meet people with similar interests via online bulletin boards, discussion boards, or singles chat rooms, where people gather precisely because they share an interest. In contrast, finding people with similar interests offline may be more difficult.

Second, and perhaps even more important, when meeting online, it's easier to get past the barriers that people sometimes close to each other because of features such as physical appearance, visible shyness, or lack of strong social skills. Getting beyond these obstacles can increase self-esteem and confidence, which, in turn, can lead to more ease in initiating relationships.

Third, CMC may give rise to easier, quicker self-disclosure and intimacy as noted earlier. For example, on Internet dating sites, profiles are set up to reveal extensive information about potential partners. In addition to surface-level information like eye color, drinking and smoking habits, relationship status, number and types of

"If you really want to know why I'm dumping you, you may want to check out my website where there's a long, detailed explanation posted."

pets, and occupation, individuals are asked to reveal more in-depth information about themselves—to describe their personality, interests (what they read, the music they listen to, and so forth), their ideal date, their political persuasion—and are encouraged to open up about all aspects of themselves. It is easy to see how these CMC in this context may lead to more hyperpersonal relationships (where people develop intimacy more quickly) and that romantic relationships may develop more quickly online than offline (Henderson & Gilding, 2004; Whitty, 2007).

However, developing online relationships poses dangers, as the characteristics of the medium (anonymity, fewer nonverbal or body-language cues) provide opportunities for deception and fraud, as described earlier by Vivian, and experienced and described by one of our students: She met a man online and thought they had a lot in common, but when she met him in person, he was very different (physically, emotionally, and professionally) from the way he had presented himself online. In fact, he was "a bit scary," and she never saw or talked to him again. In one study of online dating practices, researchers found that 50 percent of the participants admitted to misrepresenting themselves on the dating site, lying about their looks, their current relationships, age, weight, socioeconomic status, and interests (Whitty, 2007). Increasing numbers of people have been swindled out of thousands of dollars by professional criminals posing as potential suitors who ask for money after gaining the trust and interest of dating partners (Mangla, 2008). So, one has to be very careful (Madden & Lenhart, 2006). Some suggestions for safe dating online appear in *Did You Know? Safety Tips for Dating Online*, on p. 370.

Nonetheless, people can and do form close, lasting relationships on the Internet, and in some cases they gain intimacy rapidly. Many of the same things that make offline romantic relationships work are important in online relationships, such as intimacy, trust, and communication satisfaction (Anderson & Emmers-Sommer, 2006). But can these relationships survive face-to-face meetings? The answer depends on whether one has engaged in honest self-disclosure, communicated one's true self, and established solid commonality. Thus, an online relationship that is based on

Did You Know?
Safety Tips for Dating Online

1. Avoid giving out personal information such as your home address or telephone number to people you meet on the net; not everyone is what they seem. There are predators out there, but they won't look like wolves; they'll be disguised as sheep.
2. Exercise caution when agreeing to meet anyone in person whom you've met on the net. Before you arrange any such meeting, at least try to address the following:
   a. Can you verify, through a third party whom you know and trust, the true identity of this person?
   b. Is there a way to verify the information provided by this person?
3. If you choose to arrange a meeting, make it on YOUR terms:
   a. Meet in as public a place as possible.
   b. Arrange your own transportation to and from the meeting.
   c. Bring a friend along for security; consider a "double-date" the first time.
   d. Set your conditions for the encounter, and don't let your new friend change them.
   e. Stay near other people and in lighted areas throughout the meeting.
   f. If things go awry, can you positively identify the person to the police?
4. Limit meetings to public places until you are comfortable with the other person and certain of who they are and what they want from the relationship.

FROM: "Romance on the Internet," *The Police Notebook*, University of Oklahoma Department of Public Safety, www.ou.edu. Reprinted by permission.

It Happened to Me: Jenna

A friend of mine met someone from another state over the Internet, and they currently have a successful relationship. They spent a lot time (several years) getting to know each other until he moved to her area because of his job. I've seen them together, and I think their relationship is successful because they were both totally honest during the online phase, so there were no surprises when they finally met. Plus, they established a pattern of honesty as a foundation for the relationship.

"mutual self-disclosure and common interests rather than superficial features such as physical attraction, provide[s] a more stable and durable basis for the relationship . . . [which] enables it to survive and flourish once those 'gates' do come into operation when partners meet in person" (McKenna et al., 2002, p. 24).

The characteristics of such a successful online romantic relationship are shown in the experience recounted by one of our students in *It Happened to Me: Jenna*.

The Downside to Being on the Internet

While the Internet enables people to express themselves and find a space to talk about their difficult or personal issues, some people are concerned that the Internet can become addictive and harmful. Since 1996, some doctors believed that increasing amounts of Internet users are suffering from Internet Addiction Disorder (IAD) (Juan, 2006). According to Dr. Jerald Block, of the Oregon Health and Science University in Portland, the four symptoms of addiction are: "victims 'forget to eat and sleep'; they crave more advanced tech and more time online as they're numbed by 'resistance' to the kicks they get from their current system; prying them away from their computer results in 'genuine withdrawal symptoms'; and they begin to become more argumentative, more fatigued, more isolated from society, and perform worse in tests" (as cited in Haines, 2008, 2).

At the extreme, some video game players who have been labeled addicts have died from excessive video game playing. In 2002, a twenty-seven-year-old Taiwanese man collapsed and died after playing computer games for thirty-two hours nonstop (Farrell, 2002); in 2005, a twenty-eight-year-old South Korean man collapsed after playing the game Starcraft for fifty hours straight (BBC News, 2005).

If online addiction can have severe consequences to one's well-being and relationships, why do people become addicted? The Center for On-Line Addiction (2000) argues that people become addicted to online gambling for three reasons: accessibility, control, and excitement (ACE model). While this model applies to online gambling, the influences on addiction can be applied to other addictions, such as video games and pornography. Accessibility refers to fact that the Internet provides convenience, that "the hassles and limitations of real-life are removed, [and] we now live in a culture where we can indulge in these activities to seek out immediate gratification and satisfy our impulsive whims" (Center for On-Line Addiction, 2000). Control literally refers to the control that people can exercise over their own online activity—people can do what they want when they want. Last, Excitement refers to the emotional "rush" or "high" that people get when they win a game or do anything else that causes arousal or excitement. Thus, while the Internet affords us the opportunities to meet new people, maintain relationships, find information, and express ourselves, we must also be aware of our Internet use and how it may be affecting our identities in negative ways.

Work Relationships

CMC has had a huge impact on work relationships. The impact varies, however, depending on the type of relationship—whether it is a superior–subordinate relationship, a peer relationship, or a team relationship. CMC plays a unique role in each type.

Superior–Subordinate Communication.   A major impact of online communication in the workplace is its status-leveling effect, giving subordinates far more access to high-level administrators than ever before. Before CMC, receptionists and secretaries were the gatekeepers and controlled access to the boss. However, with email, anyone can have instant access to superiors. In addition, communicating by email gives subordinates the opportunity to think carefully about their communication before sending it.

CMC also gives superiors a way of checking up on subordinates. For example, the messages sent through email may be stored forever on company servers, so management can monitor employees' correspondence (Thurlow, Lengel, & Tomic, 2004). Many companies now monitor employee email and Internet usage, and Web-based security cameras are increasingly common. Also, very new technologies such as GPS and employee badges with radio frequency identification (RFID) tags provide an even higher level of employee monitoring. These tracking systems can record, display, and archive the exact location of any employee, both inside and outside the office, at any time—an extension of in-house security measures that include the monitoring of email and the control of access to corporate computing resources (James, 2003).

While most workers think that communication technologies have improved their ability to do their job, their ability to share ideas with co-workers, and have provided more job flexibility, there are some concerns. According to a recent report, almost half the workers surveyed said that these technologies result in longer hours, increased stress level, and difficulty disconnecting from work when they are at home. Many continue their work after they get home, and are expected to read email and be available for cell phone calls after work (Madden & Jones, 2008).

Another issue raised by CMC between superiors and subordinates concerns decisions about what should be handled over email versus face-to-face. Misunderstandings can occur with email, as indicated by our student in *It Happened to Me: Cruzita*.

It Happened to Me: Cruzita

I sent my manager an email requesting some time off, but she didn't receive it. When I found out that I did not get the weekend off, I was mad at her, but she had no idea I had sent her an email. If my manager and I had communicated face to face, we would not have had a mix-up of this kind.

Peer Communication. While the field of availables may increase through CMC in work contexts, access to certain kinds of information often decreases when one relies on CMC. For example, in face-to-face work contexts, you can observe the person in the next office during meetings and talk with them in the halls or mailroom. However, if you are communicating with coworkers at another location only through CMC, you have little information about them. This lack of information increases uncertainty as well as the potential for disagreements and misunderstanding, as revealed in this story reported in *It Happened to Me: Mei-Lin.*

It Happened to Me: Mei-Lin

I sent an urgent email to a colleague requesting information for a report I was writing. He didn't respond, and I became very irritated at his lack of response. A few days later I found out that his child had been in a serious accident, and he had missed work for several days. If we had been located in the same office, I would have known immediately what was wrong, would have responded more appropriately to his absence, and could have gotten the information I needed in some other way.

To summarize, online relationships have unique characteristics that distinguish them from in-person relationships. While these characteristics expand opportunities for relationship development, they also present challenges, and each type of relationship, whether a friendship, a romance, or a work relationship, has unique challenges. When we expand the frame of reference beyond individuals, as we do in the next section, you will encounter a new set of CMC-related issues and challenges—those posed by societal forces.

◪ THE INDIVIDUAL, COMMUNICATION TECHNOLOGY, AND SOCIETY

It's important to remember that all online activities—whether for fun, socializing, information-seeking, or whatever—are all enacted by humans within a social context and the larger society. These activities both reflect and influence larger societal norms. For example, do our various identities (gender, age, ethnicity, race, etc.) influence how we use communication technologies? Let's consider gender. In one study, college students were asked to identify various computer activities as *masculine* or *feminine* or *neutral.* Not surprisingly, they identified arcade-style computer games as the most masculine activity, as well as high-tech peripherals (PDA, digital camera), banking, and downloading music. In contrast, they identified emailing, Internet chat rooms, studying online, and shopping as feminine activities (Selwyn, 2007). These perceptions seem to represent traditional gender roles—men being more oriented toward action and females more interpersonally oriented (Jackson, Ervin, Gardner, & Schmitt, 2001). The authors conclude that the results suggest "that it is erroneous to presume that gender stereotyping of new technologies—and in particular the computer—has ceased to exist" (Selwyn, 2007, p. 534). How accurate are these stereotypes? It seems likely that males and females are socialized to use communication technologies in very different ways and that these uses reflect societal attitudes about gender.

As it turns out, some of the perceptions are accurate. Males tend to use the Internet to search more than females do (Fallows, 2008), they are more likely to play online games and to play a larger variety of games (Lenhart et al., 2007), are more likely to download podcasts (Madden & Jones, 2008). Women tend to email more than men and visit SNSs more frequently (boyd, 2007b), they tend to communicate more in online discussions than men do (Caspi, Chajut, & Saporta, 2008). [There is some evidence that women are a bit more anxious about the relatively advanced and complex computer technology and so are less likely to play complicated online games than men are (Wang & Wang, 2008),

The military forces rely on computer-mediated communication to accomplish work goals.

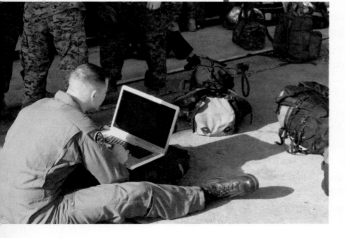

although other evidence points to males and females having equal levels of computer skills (Cheong, 2008).] However, some of the students' perceptions are unfounded stereotypes. For example, women are not more likely to shop online, male and females participate in online shopping equally (Horrigan, 2008b). Taken together, all this evidence suggests that communication technologies use probably does reflect the gendered activities in larger society and probably reinforces those patterns.

Age is another important factor in CMC. As one might expect, young Americans are much more comfortable with new technologies than are older folks, and they tend to use communication technologies in different ways. Young people are more likely to search for information online (Fallows, 2008; Griffin, 2007), more likely than older adults to play games (Lenhart & Macgill, 2008), more likely to download music and podcasts (Madden & Jones, 2008) and less likely to use email. They are more likely than older folks to create their own blog or personal Web page and share their own artistic creations online (Lenhart, Madden, Macgill, & Smith, 2008). The same patterns extends to cell phones, young people are more likely to use SMS than older people (Horrigan, 2008a).

Ethnicity plays less of a role online but does play a part in cell phone use. More Latinos have cell phones than people of other ethnicity/races. For English-speaking Hispanics, the cell phone is an oft-used and multifaceted device—more so than is the case for White or Black Americans (Horrigan, 2008a). We'll discuss more about other identities (race, social class, and education) a little later.

Another way that individual use of communication technologies intersects with societal forces is in various online community-building and political activities. A growing body of research suggests that individual blogs can create space for community growth, bringing otherwise strangers together around very personal and emotional topics, such as religion, breast cancer, suicide, and depression. For example, Rodgers and Chen (2005) analyzed more than 33,200 postings from an online breast cancer bulletin board and found that there were many benefits to participating on the discussion board, including receiving/giving information, receiving/giving social support, affect toward the discussion board, optimism toward breast cancer, increased skill of ability to cope with the disease, improved mood, decreased psychological distress, and strategies to manage stress. Thus, blogging serves as not only a mode of personal expression, but also as a community-building medium. As Nardi, Schiano, and Gumbrecht (2004) state, "Bloggers aren't letting 900 million people read their diary, but they are standing before 900 million, sometimes in an attitude of indifference, sometimes with the hope of reaching out to new people in the ever-expanding blogosphere" (p. 231).

Online space serves increasingly for political action, as shown in the 2008 U.S. presidential campaign. Three online activities have become especially prominent as the presidential primary campaigns have progressed: watching online political videos, using social networking sites such as Facebook or MySpace to gather information or to become involved (especially for younger voters), and making political contributions online (Rainie & Smith, 2008).

Research has shown that not everyone participates equally in the communication technology revolution, nor does everyone have access to digital life and cyberspace. This issue of access is perhaps the most important way that societal forces affect computer-mediated communication.

Power, Access, and the Digital Divide

According to a recent Pew report on the Internet and American life, about 25 percent of Americans are not online (Horrigan, 2008c), and in many countries, only a fraction of the population has access to computers and the Internet. (See Table 13.4.) While there is high Internet usage in Asia, Western Europe, North American, and in high-tech economies such as South Korea, China, and Japan, usage in developing countries, and especially in Africa is pitiful. Many of these emerging economies lack telephone services (Wray, (2007); www.internetworldstats.com/stats.htm.) In Africa, Internet penetration is 5 percent compared to 15 percent in Asia, 21 percent the Middle East, almost 25 percent

TABLE 13.4 The Global Digital Divide

(Percentage of Internet Users as of 2008)

Country	% of Population
Netherlands	90
Norway	88
Iceland	84
Canada	84
Japan	74
U.S.A	72
S. Korea	70
Germany	64
Spain	63
Chile	45
Mexico	21
China	19
Tunisia	17
Nigeria	17
Egypt	10
Bolivia	6
India	5
Laos	1.5
Somalia	1

in Latin and South America, almost 50 percent in Europe, and 75 percent in North America. As you can see in Table 13.4, there are pockets of low Internet use all over the world (Albania, 13 percent; Bolivia, 6 percent; India, 5 percent; Laos, 1.5 percent; and Somalia, 1 percent).

This inequity of access between the haves and the have-nots has been called the *digital divide*, and it exists domestically, within the United States, and also on a global scale. Why do differences in access matter? In a global society, information is an important commodity. Everybody needs it to function. In addition, to function effectively in society, people need **cultural capital** (Bourdieu, 1986), or certain bodies of cultural knowledge and cultural competencies. Those with the most power in a society decide what constitutes cultural capital, and they pass it down to children, just as they bestow economic capital.

In the United States and much of the world, cultural capital includes the ability to access and use CMC in appropriate ways. This ability is especially important in an increasingly computer-based and "networked" society. (Go to www.computeruser.com/resources/dictionary/index.html for an overview of the latest computer terminology and acronyms, meanings for emoticons, domain names, and more.) It is easy to see that without these skills and knowledge, one might feel disconnected from the center of society (van Dijk, 2004, Rojas, Straubhaar, Roychowdhury, & Okur, 2004;). For example, a researcher told of a man who had no experience with computers: "When the man went for a haircut, he was told to check in at the computer terminal at the counter. He was too embarrassed to admit not knowing how to use the keyboard or cursor, so he left the shop without getting a haircut." Why is this man on the far side of the digital divide? What factors keep him, and so many others, from having access to the Internet?

Who Is Online?

Many studies show that in the United States, the people most likely to have access to and use the Internet

- are young or middle-aged,
- have a college degree or are currently students, or
- have a comfortable income.

Gender differences, once a feature underlying the digital divide in the United States, have all but disappeared, and researchers find little difference in how often men versus women access the Internet (Fallows, 2005).

Racial and ethnic disparities are shrinking rapidly, especially among adolescents—the fastest-growing group of Internet users—but socioeconomic status and education level make a tremendous difference in Internet access (see Table 13.5). People who make more than $50,000 a year are almost twice as likely to be online as those making less than $30,000 (92 percent vs. 56 percent). Those with some college training are more than twice as likely to be online (87 percent) as those without a high school diploma (38 percent). A recent study showed how low levels of education and limited English ability largely explain the gap in Internet use between Hispanics and non-Hispanics. Overall 71 percent of Whites, 70 percent African Americans, and 54 percent of Latinos are online. However, for those Latinos without a high school education, only about 30 percent use the Internet compared to 95 percent

cultural capital
cultural knowledge and cultural competencies that people need to function effectively in society

of those who have a college education. For those making less than $30,000 a year only 56 percent use the Internet, those making $50,000 to $75,000—92 percent use the Internet. Forty-one percent of Latino adults have not finished high school, compared with about one in ten non-Hispanic Whites and one in five African Americans. Language is also a powerful factor, as Internet use is much higher among Latinos (79 percent) who speak and read English fluently than among those who have limited English abilities or who only speak Spanish (30 percent). When the different levels of language or education are controlled statistically, Hispanics and non-Hispanics show similar levels of Internet use (Fox & Livingston, 2007).

Age also makes a difference. Ninety-one percent of young people (ages 18–29) are online, compared to 86 percent of people in their thirties and forties, 74 percent of people ages fifty to sixty-four, and only 38 percent of those sixty-five and older. What accounts for these discrepancies?

What Keeps People Offline?

While the digital divide is shrinking, certain groups continue to lag: Americans sixty-five and older, African Americans, those with low incomes and less education, and people with physical disabilities. Twenty-two percent of Americans have never been online and are categorized as the "truly disconnected"; this number has remained constant for the past three years (Fox, 2005). About 30 percent of these nonusers simply have no access, and about 30 percent said they have no desire to go online—even if they live in a home with Internet access. Some say that going online is not a good use of their time. Others are reluctant because of frustrating previous online experiences; others say they don't go online because getting access is too expensive (Fox, 2005).

TABLE 13.5   Demographics of Internet Users

Below is the percentage of each group who use the Internet, according to our December 2008 survey. As an example, 75% of adult women use the Internet.

	Use the Internet
Total adults	74%
Women	75
Men	73
Age	
18–29	87%
30–49	82
50–64	72
65+	41
Race/ethnicity	
White, non-Hispanic	77%
Black, non-Hispanic	64
Hispanic	58
Geography	
Urban	71%
Suburban	74
Rural	63
Household income	
Less than $30,000/yr	57%
$30,000–$49,999	77
$50,000–$74,999	90
$75,000+	94
Educational attainment	
Less than high school	35%
High School	67
Some College	85
College+	95

From: Pew Internet and American Life Project, www.pewinternet.org. Used by permission.

Some of these reasons may flow from the lack of a specific type of cultural capital—**technocapital**, or access to technological skills and resources. What hinders people from acquiring technocapital? One reason might be competing social and cultural influences that go beyond the lack of funds to buy computers or access to the Internet. For example, one study found that family attitudes and resources, the educational system, peer pressure, and institutional structures and deficiencies were among the factors that turned people away from computer use (Jackson, Barbatsis, Biocca, von Eye, Zhao, & Fitzgerald, 2004).

This particular study investigated computer use in a poor neighborhood in Austin, Texas—a technologically progressive city with a number of programs to ensure public access to CMC. Via interviews and surveys, researchers discovered that many of the poorest families in Austin, even though they had radios, cell phones, and televisions, did not own computers or have access to the Internet. Further, while some

technocapital
access to technological skills and resources

parents understood the importance of computer skills, they did not feel they had the time or energy to communicate this to their children. Moreover, although they owned other electronic devices, they did not feel they had the funds needed for computers. In addition, the neighborhood school, like most schools in poor neighborhoods, lacked sufficient computer facilities and adequate computer training (Jackson et al., 2004).

These inequities in educational resources, combined with parental attitudes, reinforce students' notion that computers and computer skills are not for them, and so they acquire a negative attitude toward computer technology. A more recent study found similar results. This study tried to identify what determined people's "Internet connectedness" and found that, even more important than SES status, ethnicity, or access to a home computer were the social environment or whether people have family and friends who also use the Internet and who can help them resolve Internet-related problems, and whether they view the Internet as central to important activities. These activities included getting in touch with people when looking for a job, gaining skills for career development, getting work done, amusement, staying on top of what is happening in the community, socializing, getting advice on how to deal with other people such as doctors and health professionals (Jung, 2008). Like the earlier study, this research shows that the social environment greatly influences whether or not people are digitally connected. These same people may be avid videogame players, but they see computer skills as being for others, not for them, and as irrelevant to their lives. So, for this group, inadequacies in the educational system reinforce the cultural capital inequities (Bourdieu, 1986).

Institutional structures also reinforce the social divide. Many low income people say that TV and billboard Internet ads are irrelevant to them. Indeed, most of these ads, often showing White, middle-class people (professionals or college students) touting the advantages of getting "connected," probably are not directed at them. They also don't use the free computers in the public libraries because they regard libraries as unfriendly places (Rojas, Straubhaar, Rochowdhury, & Okur, 2004). Thus, the digital divide has deep societal and cultural roots, and arises from far more than a lack of access to computers.

One specific example of this claim has been explored by communication researcher Cheris Kramarae (1998), who points out that the primary users in the early days of the Internet determined, without much discussion, the basic linguistic conventions that all the rest of us are expected to use (including emoticons and commonly used abbreviations). Most of these early users were English-speaking, technically skilled White elites, and CMC conventions reflect their styles of thought and social interaction. One implication is that people who have not yet learned the language of emoticons or the shorthand of email text (shown in *Did You Know? Cyberspace Shorthand*) can have a powerful sense of being excluded (Rooksby, 2002, p. 121). Perhaps future technology will allow for more and different types of cues to be included in CMC, making it richer and more familiar to a variety of users.

Globalization and the Digital Divide

Even compared with the domestic divide we have just been describing, still larger digital inequities exist on a global scale. The issues of who does and does not have technocapital, and whose culture dominates it, are relevant in our current global economy. Why? Some activists and policymakers hope that, facilitated by CMC, economic globalization—meaning increased mobility of goods, services, labor, and capital—can lead to a more democratic and equitable world; and some evidence supports this hope. For example, outsourcing American jobs to overseas locations has provided income opportunities for many in English-speaking countries such as Ireland and India. And, in spite of some governments' attempts to limit their citizens' access to CMC, the Internet provides information, world news, and possibilities for interpersonal communication that were not available previously (Scanlon, 2003; Wheeler, 2001).

However, other evidence suggests that globalization primarily benefits wealthy Western nations, promoting their cultural values and technology and enriching their

Did You Know?

Cyberspace Shorthand

Those who use email and IM a great deal know the "shorthand" cyber language conventions, shown in an online course chat room conversation below. Does it matter if you don't know or use these conventions?

Sandra: wait lemme ask u a quick question b/c u seem to grasp this stuff well. can u try to explain the MUDs to me? do u know what they are? I was confused a lil by that

Paul: I think it means you can be "Skater Girl1" or "Tiny Princess." I am not sure. I got a little confused too b/c names for all this stuff keep changing.

Sandra: yeah, i hear u there

Paul: Well, I'm sure you will run into other people on times that are listed.

Sandra: thanks for staying

Paul: Good luck with your chatting. I will not be entering the chat room again.

Sandra: i'll talk to u later

Paul: No Problem.

Sandra: c u Paul

Paul: Good luck with the rest of the class.

Sandra: thanks

Sandra: u too!

countries. Evidence here includes the fact that Western countries control and profit from the majority of CMC hardware and software. Furthermore, English has become the dominant language of the Internet, and most software is developed in English, even though only a small percentage of the world's population speaks English (Herring, 2004; Keniston, 2001). What is the impact of these facts?

Concerned with this question, researcher Fernando Delgado (2002) examined this Western domination of communication technology and media products (music, film, television). He makes the case that this domination widens the digital divide and impacts interpersonal communication across cultures. Specifically, he argues that people in poorer countries are left behind by the CMC revolution, and they resent the control wielded by Western technology.

Some richer countries have simply modified Western software to meet their cultural norms. For example, the Japanese supplement U.S. computer-supported cooperative work (CSCW) software with video images and large display monitors to reflect their cultural preference for close attention to nonverbal cues in interpersonal communication. In addition, for some very delicate communication contexts, like business negotiation, the Japanese do not believe that CMC can ever substitute for face-to-face communication (Heaton, 2001). South Korea, with its booming online gaming industry, is the world leader in high-speed Internet connection (Lacy, 2005), and South Korean youth have the most sophisticated media habits in the world (Fine, 2006). However, poorer countries often do not have the resources to develop their own software or modify existing programs and are faced with communication technology that their citizens might not easily use.

Closing the Digital Divide

Two theories address strategies for lessening the digital divide. The first is called **diffusion of innovations**, developed by communication scholar Everett Rogers (2003). This theory explains why some innovations, like computer and Internet technology, are accepted by some people and rejected by others. For example, the theory posits that in order for people to accept a new technology, they have to see its

diffusion of innovations theory that explains why some innovations, like computers and Internet technology, are accepted by some people and rejected by others

usefulness, and they have to find it compatible with their values and lifestyle. Communication also plays a key role; if people important to the individual, such as peers for adolescents, adopt the innovation first, then the next individual is more likely to adopt it. According to this theory, giving people access to computers and the Internet is an important first step in getting more people online, as this exposure tends to diffuse, or spread, but exposure is not enough to close the digital divide.

The second theory, proposed by Dutch sociologist Jan van Dijk (2004), also emphasizes that lack of access to computer hardware is only one part of exclusion from the digital world. To cross the digital divide, this theory goes, people must have access to technocapital on four levels: mental, material, skills, and usage. Furthermore, each level builds on the previous one.

Mental access, the first and perhaps most important level, relates to motivation and to acceptance of CMC as meaningful. In other words, to cross the digital divide, people must be convinced that computer and Internet skills are important. As we noted earlier, however, they often face competing influences. For example, many older people and some poorer people do not see the benefit for themselves. Those concerned with minimizing the digital divide recommend that more attention and effort be directed to overcoming these mental-access barriers (Lenhart et al., 2003).

The second level—*material access* to computer hardware—is where most public policy currently focuses. For example, one U.S. program uses telephone taxes to pay for Internet connections in elementary schools; state and local funds are used to pay for Internet connections at public libraries; and companies donating computer and technical training are given tax incentives (Lenhart et al., 2003; Marriot, 2006). With a global market in mind, engineers have developed a $100 laptop with a seven-inch color screen, the capacity for wireless Internet connection, and a hand crank that supplies ten minutes of power for every minute of cranking (Hutchinson, 2006). Clearly, without access to hardware and low-cost Internet connections, one cannot acquire technocapital.

The third level—*skills access*—is also critical. Many nonusers view lack of training and lack of user-friendly technology as barriers, and frustration levels can be significant. Thus, to facilitate skills access, hardware and software developers must better understand the minds of users, taking into consideration their diverse cultural communication norms and practices. In other words, we need "technology that can think like the user" and that can think like users from many cultural backgrounds (Jackson et al., 2004, p. 180).

Finally, *usage access* means knowing how to use a variety of computer applications. For example, learning to use the Internet or build a Web site takes more know-how than using the computer to play games or send email. Even if people have computers, the lack of technological proficiency and social resources may frustrate Internet use, leading to what some experts call a *secondary digital divide* (inequalities in Internet skills, problem-solving behaviors, and Internet usage patterns) in high-tech societies (Cheong, 2008). People's computer usage knowledge is often related to their educational level. One study showed that even when people have the same access to computers, those with more education tend to have more usage knowledge and use the Internet for more varied applications. More importantly, they use the computer in ways that ultimately enhance them professionally and personally; for example, they visit sites that provide useful information about national and international news, health and financial information, government services, and product information (Hargittai & Hinnant, 2008). Knowing how to use a broad range of applications would provide less-educated and lower income people with more technocapital and the social and economic opportunities that come with participation in the "connected" life (Jackson et al., 2004).

The digital divide makes computer-mediated communication much less likely in many areas of the world, such as this United Nations–funded classroom in Ethiopia.

Vanessa Vick/The *New York Times*

ETHICS AND COMPUTER-MEDIATED COMMUNICATION

One message we hope you take from this chapter is that CMC, in itself, is neither better nor worse than face-to-face communication. It is simply different. However, these differences allow for irresponsible, thoughtless, or even unethical communication online. How can you become an ethical user of CMC? There are at least two areas of ethical consideration. The first concerns presentation of identity online, and the second involves building online relationships.

Ethics and Online Identity

As we discussed earlier, the issue of identity and ethics online is complex, and one can take various positions on these issues. An extreme position would be that one should never misrepresent oneself. On the other hand, CMC clearly offers legitimate opportunities (like MMOGs), where one can take on an entirely new identity. A guiding principle, however, as noted in *Did You Know? The Ten Commandments of Computer Ethics* is that one should "do no harm" to others.

An increasing problem is the incivility of messages on bulletin boards and blogs. When bloggers disclose their feelings and opinions, they become vulnerable to personal attacks via comments left by readers. Women, who host more personal blogs, are often targets of vulgar or insulting comments—comments that can range from death threats to manipulated photos (Stone, 2007). Some Web site and software developers have suggested that a set of guidelines for conduct be created and implemented to bring civility to the Web (Stone, 2007). They suggest that bloggers control if and when they will allow anonymous comments by strangers, and they also recommend that bloggers make it known on their page which behaviors they will tolerate. Incorporating these standards is a difficult project considering the size of the community and how some consider standards of Web conduct a violation of free speech.

Communication, of course, is interactive and reciprocal; it takes two people to engage in any interaction, and both have responsibility. As we discussed in Chapter 1, the receiver is responsible for being somewhat skeptical of others' communication. In this case of CMC, skepticism should focus on how people present their identity—particularly in certain contexts (for example, chat rooms or other online venues).

Did You Know?

The Ten Commandments of Computer Ethics

1. Thou shalt not use a computer to harm other people.
2. Thou shalt not interfere with other people's computer work.
3. Thou shalt not snoop around in other people's computer files.
4. Thou shalt not use a computer to steal.
5. Thou shalt not use a computer to bear false witness.
6. Thou shalt not copy or use proprietary software for which you have not paid.
7. Thou shalt not use other people's computer resources without authorization or proper compensation.
8. Thou shalt not appropriate other people's intellectual output.
9. Thou shalt think about the social consequences of the program you are writing or the system you are designing.
10. Thou shalt always use a computer in ways that ensure consideration and respect for your fellow humans.

As we noted earlier, as a reflection of their identities, people often express their deeply held feelings online, in a blog, in a course discussion forum, or on a listserve or bulletin board. It is important to be aware of how your comments may affect another's identity and how your comments do, or do not, contribute to civil dialogue on the Web.

One idea under discussion for addressing identity problems is a mandatory Internet ID. This fixed identity would "travel" with a user from site to site. While the benefits include decreasing some crime (particularly the exploitation of children) and some unethical behavior, it raises the issue of basic privacy rights. Moreover, for some people, anonymity is part of the "fun" of the Internet. In addition, finding a way to implement an effective ID that would protect everyone and *not* be susceptible to fraud or identity theft would be challenging.

One possible solution would be to tailor the ID requirements to the context. For example, some sites could require ID, while others would not, and the users at those sites would follow a "buyer beware" guideline. Internet users could then choose their sites based on their own comfort levels.

What do you think about a mandatory identity that would be required for Internet users? What would be the advantages? Disadvantages?

Building Relationships Online

The first step in building ethical relationships online is to remember how CMC differs from face-to-face communication. Because nonverbal cues are filtered in CMC, you need to provide as much information as you can to help the receiver discern the tone of your message. For example, you may have to explain in words (or emoticons) that humorous tone that would be communicated by facial expressions or gestures in face-to-face conversation.

A second step is to consider whether an online communication is appropriate for your message, and here, relevant factors are your relationship with the receiver and the purpose of the message. For example, in a work context, a lean email message can convey essential information. However, personal messages may be better delivered in person, especially if miscommunication is likely and you need immediate feedback to make sure you are understood.

◩ IMPROVING YOUR MEDIATED COMMUNICATION SKILLS

What should you take from this chapter that can help you be a better CMC communicator? First, you can strive to communicate more politely, especially via email cell phone; and second, you can learn to evaluate CMC information more carefully.

Email Etiquette

Because email is still prevalent in some work and social contexts, it is worth considering how to increase its effectiveness. The most important guideline is to think before writing a message and clicking the send button. Remember that what you put in writing can never be unwritten and that others besides the intended recipient may see it. Here are a few specific suggestions:

- Send email only to those who will want or need to use it. Don't forward the joke about the pope, the rabbi, and the e-business consultant to everyone. Those who don't share your sense of humor—or are too busy to laugh—might lose respect for you.

- Give your email a context. That is, don't just say "FYI" or "Hi" in the subject area of the email; let the recipient know specifically what you're writing about. This is especially important in work contexts. Because of the status-leveling effects of email, busy, important people get many more messages now than they ever did by telephone, so they want to know the subject of those messages.

- Check your spelling carefully. While the standards for spelling and grammar have been lowered a little for email, sending emails full of typos and grammar mistakes communicates a lack of respect for yourself and the recipient.

As a society, we are in the process of inventing rules for polite ways to use new communication technologies. Email messaging has been around for a while, but cell phones are a new technology and we're still figuring out how to use them in ways that promote smooth and effective relational communication. Indianchild.com, "India's Web site dedicated to Internet safety" offers the following suggestions for cell phone etiquette in most public places.

- **Know when to turn off your phone or set it to vibrate it.** Meetings, movies, worship, and seminars are culturally agreed-upon no-cell zones. Put it in vibrate mode when in places where you can take a call, but don't want to disturb others.

- **Be brief.** When you get a call and you're with friends, keep the call short.

- **Ask permission to use the phone when appropriate.** For example, if you are expecting a call during a meeting, inform others at the beginning of the meeting that you are expecting an important call and get their permission to take the call.

- **Be polite.** Don't scream; speak in a lower-than-normal voice. You will be heard by the caller, and not by others in the room According to a new survey, speaking too loudly on mobile phones is the most irritating thing about people using cell phones in public. More than half of those questioned said that loud talking was even more annoying than ringtones or even taking calls while at the dinner table. Go to www.textually.org/textually/archives/cat_cell_phone_etiquette.htm for an overview of cell phone etiquette.

- **Don't distract.** Avoid talking where you may be distracting to others. For example in places of business (waiting rooms, banks) where people may be concentrating or reading.

- **Be careful when using phones while driving.** It is not only very dangerous, but also unlawful in many states in the United States and in most countries to drive and talk on your cell phone, unless using a hands-free device.

Evaluating Internet Information

While the Internet provides a wealth of information, it is not all equally credible. Thus, perhaps the most important questions to ask when reviewing information are *What is its source?* and *Is it credible?* Is the information one person's opinion, or is it based on solid research? For example, when you are gathering information for a course research project, academic journal articles accessed through EBSCO, LexisNexis®, or another online database are preferable to student papers posted on the Internet or Web sites that do not identify the source of the information.

A second question to ask yourself concerns the motivation of the information source. *Is the Web site sponsored by an organization that has a particular political viewpoint, or is it a more balanced source?* For example, if you are searching for information about the abortion debate or globalization, most Web sites you access are likely to have a particular viewpoint. This does not mean they don't provide useful information, just that you need to recognize the biases and use the information accordingly.

It is also important to recognize that many search engines, like Yahoo and Google, are commercialized. Businesses pay these search engines to post their Web sites first. Therefore, if you are trying to find information on the top ten computer companies in the United States, you will most likely get Web addresses of companies trying to sell you computer hardware and software rather than an objective rating.

As we move forward, CMC will inevitably be a part of our lives. It is deeply imbedded in the way we do business and research and in the ways we socialize and connect with others. Clearly, we have much to think about as we use this tool. In every context, we should strive to communicate responsibly, ethically, equitably, and with social awareness.

SUMMARY

Computer-mediated communication (CMC) is worthy of study because of its pervasiveness and the rapidity with which this technology has been adopted. Many common daily activities—casual comunication, information-seeking, entertainment, and financial transactions—now are frequently carried out through CMC. The most frequently used CMC, and the focus of this chapter, is *interactive, mostly text-based* communication technologies, such as email, IM, text messages, and bulletin boards. There are two views of the relationship between CMC and face-to-face communication: the media deficit approach and the media augmentation complementarity approach. The pervasiveness of this interactive technology has a huge impact on relationships given the differences between CMC and face-to-face interaction. Specifically, CMC filters out most of the nonverbal cues we use in face-to-face communication, and it can be conducted asynchronously.

Compared with face-to-face communication, CMC affords more control over how people present themselves. Specifically, CMC affords one the possibility of performing multiple identities, being anonymous, or even assuming a false identity (pseudoanonymity). In addition, CMC relationships differ from in-person relationships in that CMC affords one access to many more potential relationships, and these relationships are not bound by time or space. These characteristics have implications: They make CMC relationships somewhat more durable but in some respects more fragile.

CMC is also affected by societal forces, especially in terms of who has access to it. The digital divide—the differential access to CMC by various income, racial, and national groups—separates those who have access from those who do not. Power also comes into play in the digital divide, as it does in other parts of society, as the most powerful are the ones who develop and define computer literacy and expertise—sometimes excluding those from less powerful groups.

Communicating ethically using CMC is especially important in the presentation of identity online and in building online relationships. Suggestions for communicating effectively using CMC include following email etiquette and carefully evaluating Internet information.

KEY TERMS

social networking site (SNS) 352
blogs 352
analog 353
digital 353
computer-mediated communication (CMC) 353
Internet 353
World Wide Web (WWW) 353
cyberspace 354

tweets 355
media deficit approach 356
media augmentation approach 356
social presence 356
media richness 356
emoticons 357
asynchronicity 359
spam 363
phishing 363

spoofing 363
pseudoanonymity 363
avatar 363
field of availables 367
hyperpersonal relationships 367
cultural capital 374
technocapital 375
diffusion of innovations 377

TEST YOUR KNOWLEDGE

1. What are the key differences between CMC and face-to-face communication?

2. Why is it so easy to misrepresent one's identity online? What ethical guidelines should people follow when constructing identities online?

3. What are some differences in how Internet relationships develop compared to in-person relationships?

4. Why is trust much more important when working together online than it is when working face to face? What can we do to build trust in online working relationships?

5. What is the digital divide? What are the most important factors that determine whether one has access to computers and the Internet? What might be done to decrease or eliminate this divide?

APPLY WHAT YOU KNOW

1. Don't use any CMC for two days and then answer the following questions. To what extent did you miss this form of communication? What did you miss most? Least? What might you conclude about the role CMC plays in your everyday life and relationships? How do you view those who have limited access to CMC?

2. Select any personal Web page from the Internet and describe the identity you think the person is trying to project. Describe the elements that contribute to this identity. What kind of information is presented? What information is missing?

3. Visit a MUD (multiuser domain) (go to www.mudconnector.com/ for a list and access to many MUDs). Log in and participate for a while. Then answer the following questions: Did you enjoy the experience? Why or why not? Did you try to project a different identity than you usually do? Describe your interaction with other players. How did your communication with them differ from CMC in other contexts, for example, bulletin boards or email? Why?

EXPLORE

1. Go to ComputerUser.com's online dictionary at www.computeruser.com/resources/dictionary/noframes/index.html This high-tech dictionary offers definitions for the latest computer terminology, including acronyms, emoticons, domain names, and chat lingo. Click on "Random Term" a few times.

   How much of this information are you familiar with? Imagine someone who knows none of this information. In his or her day-to-day CMC activity be limited?

2. Go to The Telephone, a Web site created for PBS's program The American Experience, found at www.pbs.org/wgbh/amex/telephone/index.html This site's "Technology Timeline" provides information about the invention of the telephone, radio, television, Internet, and other technological innovations. If you had to give up one of these inventions, which would it be? How would your day-to-day communication be different without this invention? How would you compensate for the lack?

3. Go to Hobbes' Internet Timeline at www.zakon.org/robert/Internet/timeline/ This is a very interesting, detailed, and up-to-date timeline of the Internet maintained by Robert H. Zakon. It includes all-important dates in the development of the Internet, leading up to the present time. At what point on this timeline did you begin using the Internet? Has the rapidly increasing number of Web sites affected your CMC use? If so, how?

14
Speaking in Public

chapter outline

ANTICIPATING YOUR PRESENTATION
Becoming an Ethical Public Speaker
Overcoming Your Fear of Public Speaking

UNDERSTANDING THE COMMUNICATION EVENT
Identifying Your General Purpose
Selecting Your Topic
Identifying a Specific Purpose

UNDERSTANDING AND RELATING TO AUDIENCES
Determining What Your Audience Knows
Determining Who Your Audience Is
Determining What Your Audience Knows About You
Considering What Your Audience Expects

DEVELOPING YOUR TOPIC
Narrowing Your Topic
Identifying Your Thesis Statement
Finding Supporting Materials

ORGANIZING YOUR PRESENTATION
Selecting Your Organizational Pattern
Creating Your Outline
Developing Your Introduction, Conclusion, and Transitions

DELIVERING YOUR SPEECH
Selecting a Style
Incorporating Visual Aids
Being Aware of the Time
Considering the Means of Delivery
Projecting a Persona
Practicing Your Speech

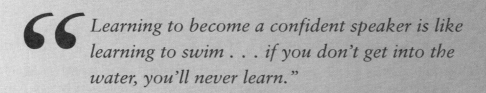

> *Learning to become a confident speaker is like learning to swim . . . if you don't get into the water, you'll never learn."*

You know, it was scary. It was wonderful. But I remember it being a horrifying experience. Really embarrassing to forget the words, forget the words. That's why I didn't sing for a very long time until they invented Teleprompters. It still scares me to this day.

> Barbra Streisand, describing her stage fright in front
> of 135,000 people at Central Park in 1967 (CBS, 2008).

We often think about stage fright or our own fear of standing in front of others when we think about public speaking. As you can see from this opening quote, even someone who performs in front of others as often as Barbra Streisand, can experience this fear when speaking in public. It is something that all public presenters learn to use to help them perform even better. It's a fact—when responding to public opinion polls, people often rate speaking in front of an audience as their number-one fear (Schneier & Welkowitz, 1996). Some nervousness is normal, to be expected, and actually helps motivate speakers to do their best—as we'll see later in the chapter.

Despite the anxieties that surround it, speaking in public is a cornerstone of U.S. society, which is based on the participation of its citizens. As members of a democratic society, citizens need to become adept public speakers so that they can advocate for what they think is best (Gayle, 2004). Also, learning to speak up for your interests can be important, particularly at the local level—for example, in the context of student organizations or city council meetings.

In addition, public speaking skills are a requirement for success in most jobs. Increasingly, businesses want employees who can speak well in public and address meetings (Osterman, 2005). This is true for teachers, social workers, bankers, financial planners, and those who work in public relations, but it also applies to those in technical fields, such as engineers, accountants, nurses, medical examiners, police officers, soldiers, and professional athletes.

In this chapter, we focus on helping you become a more confident and capable speaker. Unlike the previous chapters in this book, which are designed primarily to help you understand communication concepts, this chapter focuses on developing communication skills. As you read this chapter, however, you will see how concepts you encountered in Chapter 5 (Verbal Communication), Chapter 6 (Nonverbal Communication), and Chapter 11 (Communicating in Public: Rhetoric) can help you in public speaking.

One disclaimer: Although this chapter provides you with guidelines for effective public speaking, learning to be an effective speaker is not as simple as following directions on a cake mix box. Following a recipe's instructions typically results in a fairly good cake, but for a really original cake, the baker draws on artistry, practice, and lessons learned from others. In short, public speaking is an *art*. While following a formula may result in a satisfactory speech, when you add your own ingredients, you will become an even better speaker. And, of course, a good speaker also needs to practice, practice, and practice!

In the following sections, we introduce the basic elements of speech preparation. We'll look at the range of communication events at which people may be called to speak, the importance of understanding audiences, and the basics of constructing, organizing, and delivering a speech. Taken together, these elements supply the foundations for effective public speaking.

Once you have read this chapter, you will be able to:

- Analyze a speech event and analyze the analyze.
- Develop a speech topic.
- Understand various ways to organize a speech presentation.
- Understand how to deliver a speech presentation.

ANTICIPATING YOUR PRESENTATION

Before getting into the mechanics of public speaking, we want to discuss two important concerns: the ethics of public speaking and the fear that most people feel as they anticipate stepping in front of an audience. Let's look first at the place of ethics in public speech.

Becoming an Ethical Public Speaker

We have stressed the importance of ethical communication in all contexts in this book, and public speaking will be no exception. According to authors of *The Speaker's Handbook* (Sprague & Stuart, 2005), effective public speaking involves a commitment to ethical communication principles and at least two specific guidelines: respect for the integrity of your audience and respect for the integrity of ideas. Respecting your audience's integrity means that you recognize that you have a special kind of power in the public speaking situation. "When audience members entrust you with their time and attention, you take on an obligation to treat them with fairness and concern" (Sprague & Stuart, 2005, p. 33). This means that you do not try to manipulate them into making decisions that might endanger their health or safety and that you do not say anything that might deceive them. Your listeners don't have to agree with what you say, but they should be better off, perhaps having more valid options to consider, for having listened to you.

A second and related ethical principle involves respect for the integrity of ideas. An ethical public speaker gives credit for information taken from other sources. If you are using others' ideas or quoting others' words, give them credit. The careers of even prominent scholars and politicians have suffered when they quoted another's speech as their own. Respecting the integrity of ideas also means that you have an ethical responsibility to be honest with your audience. For example, if you cite statistics, you have a responsibility to be certain that they are accurate, well-researched numbers. You also have a responsibility to tell the whole truth. For example, you leave a false impression if you say, "During my time at Harvard," when you only spent a week there visiting your cousin.

Oversimplifying complex ideas and concepts is another way that speakers may undermine the integrity of ideas and hurt their image with audiences. For example, if you were to claim that "Philadelphia is the best place to live," you may put off some people who believe some other city is a better place to live. There is no single set of criteria that all people use to judge this type of thing. In its annual rankings of the best places to live, *Money* magazine uses a number of criteria. On the Web site, you can use these criteria to determine how important some of these factors are to you, and perhaps see where the "best place" might be for you to live (but not everyone else) at **http://money.cnn.com/magazines/moneymag/bplive/2008/index.html.**

Well-known public performers, such as Barbra Streisand, can also experience fear in front of audiences.

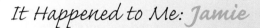

Overcoming Your Fear of Public Speaking

You should know that it is normal to experience some fear of public speaking, or stage fright, when you deliver a speech. Even people you wouldn't expect to experience stage fright, do—as you saw in the opening vignette about Barbra Streisand, and as you can see in *Communication in Society: The Political Power of Public Speaking.* The well-known actor Mel Gibson is reputed to have been so overcome with nervousness in front of other people during his first performance that he had to sit down. His legs were too weak to support him. Extreme fear of public speaking is the number-one social phobia in the United States (Bruce & Saeed, 1999).

Speakers may express their anxiety in a variety of ways, but some of the most common symptoms include shaking in the hands and legs, voice fluctuations, and rapid speech. Moreover, most speakers worry that their nervousness is going to be obvious to the audience. Fortunately, many signs of anxiety are not visible. For example, if your hands sweat or your heart pounds when you speak, the audience will probably not notice. You, may be the only person who knows you're nervous as you can see in *It Happened to Me: Jamie.*

It Happened to Me: Jamie

When you called on me, my stomach sank. I was ready to run out of the building. When I started my speech, I felt as though sweat was pouring down my forehead. Then, I thought about all the tools you gave us. In an instant, it seemed, I was done. I stood there, ready for criticism on how bad my speech was. But the class applauded. They had not seen that I was at all nervous. You even commented that I seemed like a natural speaker.

As a speaker, your goal is not to eliminate these feelings but to use them to invigorate your presentation. Having some stage fright can motivate you to prepare carefully: It can give you the energy and alertness that make your presentation lively and interesting. Public speaking instructors usually say that they worry more about students who are not nervous, as it may reflect lack of concern and motivation, than about those who are.

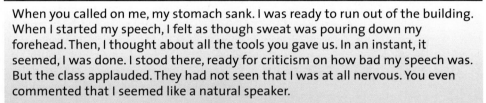

COMMUNICATION IN SOCIETY
The Political Power of Public Speaking

Many people do not pay enough attention to the public speaking of political candidates. However, we can learn the most about these candidates from their public oration.

The time has come to finally confront a question we have too long avoided: What value should voters actually place on a politician's oratorical skill?

Regrettably, most voters are woefully ill-equipped to judge candidates on the basis of their presentation skills. We rarely attend speeches or lectures except in mandatory classroom or business settings, and we have about as much framework for forming critical opinions concerning whether an orator is sharp or lame, sincere or deceptive, as we would about the finer points of formal ballet.

We do ourselves damage with such ignorance and inattention. Lacking the capacity to formulate opinions that go much beyond blind hunches, we resort to a range of sloppy, superficial proxy considerations like the one that seems to have delivered us President George W. Bush: namely, a good ol' boy who appears like the type we'd like to plunk down and have a beer with.

The joke, of course, is one us. We'll never get a chance to hoist a pint with the prez. But we certainly are going to be compelled to listen to him or her, again and again, give speeches, address the news media, report to Congress and explain—in words alone—what lies ahead. For better or worse, it is the "president of the spoken word" we are electing.

To dismiss verbal capability as incidental or unimportant leaves a mighty large gap in the checklist of virtues we hunger to assess in our would-be political leaders. Spoken words, slight as they are, still represent the single best opportunity we have to really "know" these candidates (yes, better than slick TV ads, spit-polished resumes and perpetually rejiggered position papers).

FROM: "Public speaking matters—listen to our president," by Bob Katz, *Los Angeles Times*, March 24, 2008, www.latimes.com.
Copyright © 2008, Los Angeles Times. Reprinted by permission.

Toastmasters International is an organization focused on promoting public speaking.

Although you may feel that your nervousness is too much to overcome, statistics are on your side. Researchers have found that only "one out of 20 people suffers such serious fear of speaking that he or she is essentially unable to get through a public speech" (Sprague & Stuart, 2005, p. 73). Your own anxiety likely will not be so severe as to prevent you from delivering your speech. Still, several strategies can help you manage it.

First, prepare carefully. What does this mean? In short, experts have discovered that it is not the amount of time you spend preparing, but *how* you prepare. People who are extremely anxious about giving a speech tend to spend most of their time preparing notes. On the other hand, speakers who are less anxious, and more effective, prepare careful notes, but they also spend considerable time analyzing their anticipated audience (Ayres, 1996), a subject we will turn to later.

Second, practice your speech before you give it—another subject we address later in the chapter. There is no substitute for practice. However, going over the points silently in your head does not count as practice. Practice means giving your speech out loud (possibly in front of a mirror) while timing it and later asking a sympathetic friend or friends to listen to it and give you feedback.

Third, once you are in front of your real audience, focus on the faces in the audience who look friendly—who may be smiling or nodding in agreement. The peak anxiety time for most speakers is the first moment of confronting the audience (Behnke & Sawyer, 1999, 2004). Receiving positive reinforcement early on is an excellent way to get over this initial anxiety.

Fourth, try relaxation techniques just before speaking. While the fear may be in your head, it manifests itself in physiological changes in your body: Your muscles tense, your breathing becomes shallow, and adrenaline pumps through your system (Behnke & Sawyer, 2004). Effective relaxation techniques for such situations include taking several deep, even breaths; yawning once or twice to relax your throat; smiling, shaking hands and talking with attendees; taking sips of water (avoid caffeine); and looking at your notes. Visit the Great Speaking Center's "Stage Fright Strategies" at **www.antion.com/articles/stagefright.htm** for many more suggestions. While you may feel very nervous, your inner anxiety is not often easy for your audience members to see. Do not assume that they see how nervous you feel—and it's best not to mention it. Project confidence, and you will feel more confident as you speak.

Finally, the strategy most public speaking instructors and students use to overcome anxiety is to take the opportunity to give lots of speeches (Levasseur, Dean, & Pfaff, 2004). Public speaking becomes easier and easier with each speech. As one seasoned speaker said, "Learning to become a confident speaker is like learning to swim. You can watch people swim, read about it, listen to people talk about it, but if you don't get into the water, you'll never learn" (Sanow, 2005). Take opportunities to hone your public-speaking skills. Volunteer to give speeches or become a member of Toastmasters International or a local group of public speakers. *Visual Summary 14.1* highlights the process of developing your speech.

UNDERSTANDING THE COMMUNICATION EVENT

If you volunteer to speak in public, you likely have an excellent understanding of why you want to speak and what you hope to accomplish. If, for example, you want to advocate for building a light-rail system in your city, you know something about the communication event, your purpose for speaking in front of the city council, and what you want to accomplish.

Developing Your Speech

Phase 1: Understand the Communication Event

Identify your general purpose.

Select your topic.

Identify your specific purpose.

Phase 2: Understand and Relate to the Audience

Determine what your audience knows.

Developing Your Speech

Phase 3: Develop Your Topic

Narrow your topic.

Identify your thesis statement.

Find supporting materials.

Consider the types of supporting materials.

Select an organizational pattern.

Create an outline.

Develop your introduction, conclusion, and transitions.

Phase 4: Organize Your Presentation

Phase 5: Deliver Your Presentation

Determine an appropriate style (type of language and phrasing).

Consider incorporating visual aids.

Be aware of the time.

Consider the means of delivery.

Develop a persona.

US Airways Captain Sullenberger was honored for a safe emergency landing of Flight 1549 in the Hudson River. How might speakers prepare effective, appropriate speeches at events like this one?

In contrast, when you are asked to speak in a public setting, someone else has, for the most part, already determined the purpose of the speech. For example, if you are asked to make a toast at a friend's wedding, you know why you will be speaking and when you will be speaking, but you may want to clarify who your audience will be and what expectations your friend has for your toast. Other purposes for speaking include introducing someone to an audience, making a presentation to clients, or presenting a petition to your homeowner's association on behalf of your neighbors. Whatever the purpose, and whether you've volunteered or been selected to speak, you can refer to *Did You Know? Communication Event Checklist* to make sure you've obtained all the preliminary information you need.

If you do not have complete, accurate information about the communication event, you may not prepare your speech appropriately. This once happened to Jess Alberts, one author of this textbook. She was asked to speak about relational communication at a retirement community on Valentine's Day for couples who had been married for 50 years or more. However, when she showed up to give her speech, she discovered another event had drawn all the married couples, and her entire audience was composed of widows and widowers! Needless to say, the speech she had prepared was not appropriate to the occasion. So she collected her thoughts, took a deep breath, and revised her speech as she went along—focusing on relational communication in general—illustrating the importance of improvisation and flexibility in speech delivery, a topic we take up later in the chapter.

How do speakers begin to prepare an effective, appropriate speech? Based on their understanding of the communication event, they first focus on the general purpose of their speech, which usually will fall into one of several traditional categories. In addition, speakers must carefully select a topic that suits their general purpose. Finally, they must zero in on the specific purpose of their speech. We'll look at each of these steps in turn.

Identifying Your General Purpose

To determine the most appropriate and effective type of speech for any particular event, you can begin by considering other speeches you have heard at similar communication events. At some point you have probably been present for a toast given by the best man at a wedding, so you know that it should offer a light-hearted, but positive, review of the couple's meeting and dating. It may also include stories that shed light on the couple's romantic commitment. The general purpose of this speech is to evoke fond memories and support for the couple.

Did You Know?
Communication Event Checklist

_____ 1. Do you know when you are expected to speak (date as well as time)?

_____ 2. Do you know where you are to speak?

_____ 3. Do you know why you are speaking?

_____ 4. What do you know about the audience?

_____ 5. Have you requested audiovisual equipment in advance, if you want to use it?

_____ 6. Do you have a name and phone number for a contact person in case a question or emergency arises?

You might remember from reading Chapter 11 that the great Roman orator Cicero, identified three objectives for public speaking: to inform, to persuade, and to entertain. These three types of speeches are still taught in most public-speaking courses today (McKerrow, Gronbeck, Ehninger, & Monroe, 2003; O'Hair, Stewart, & Rubenstein, 2004). However, the objective "to entertain" has been broadened to "to evoke feeling," which is a more accurate description of what this type of speech can do. We will refer to this third type as the *evocative speech*.

"I don't like the look of this"

©Robert Thompson/www.CartoonStock.com

The *informative speech* explains, instructs, defines, clarifies, demonstrates, or teaches. As we explained in Chapter 11 on rhetoric, the *persuasive speech* attempts to influence, convince, motivate, sell, preach, or stimulate action. Finally, the purpose of the *evocative speech* is to entertain, inspire, celebrate, commemorate, or build community (Sprague & Stuart, 2005, p. 65). A common type of evocative speech, including the wedding toast, celebrates aspects of a person or topic. Sometimes evocative speeches are also known as **special-occasion speeches**, and they include speeches given at retirement dinners, award ceremonies, weddings, graduations, and funerals.

Obviously, the three general purposes do not function in isolation. Speakers often persuade others by informing them about something, or they inform audiences by entertaining them. Gus Van Sant's film *Milk* may have been made primarily to persuade audiences to adopt a particular political point of view, but many viewers found the film evocative as well as informative. So, given that most speeches have more than just one aim, the one that is dominant is known as its **general purpose**. Once you identify the general purpose of your speech, you are prepared to focus your presentation and achieve your most important communication goals. The next step will be to select a topic that suits your purpose.

Selecting Your Topic

Selecting a topic can be the most interesting and the most difficult part of any speech presentation. Assuming that the topic is not already determined for you, here are some guidelines to help you choose:

- **Consider the communication event.** What are the expectations for your presentation? What types of topics would be appropriate to speak about?

- **Consider your interests.** Take an inventory. What are some unusual experiences you've had? What subjects do you know a lot about? What topics do you feel strongly about? What would you like to learn more about?

- **Consider your relationship to the communication event.** Why are you being asked to speak? Do you have a special relationship to someone, for example, the bride or the deceased? If so, you may have special insight into topics the audience would consider appropriate and effective. Have you been chosen because you are an expert in a particular area? If so, the audience will expect you to demonstrate that expertise and to answer questions effectively.

In selecting your topic, be sure your purpose matches the communication event. For example, because of her expertise in representing business owners, a lawyer is asked to speak at a chamber of commerce meeting for people who want

If you had to give a speech today to the graduating class of the high school you attended, what topics might you consider for your speech?

special-occasion speeches
evocative speeches intended to entertain, inspire, celebrate, commemorate, or build community

general purpose
whichever of three goals—to inform, persuade, or entertain—dominates a speech

to start their own businesses. In keeping with this communication event, she decides to prepare an informative speech on the advantages and disadvantages of various business structures—sole proprietorships, partnerships, limited liability companies, or corporations. However, if in doing the research for her presentation, she decides that she cannot cover all these structures in the time allotted, she may need to narrow her topic. Later in the chapter, we'll discuss speech topics again, when we guide you through the important process of narrowing a broad topic to an appropriately focused one.

Identifying a Specific Purpose

Once you know the general purpose of your speech and have selected your speech topic, you can begin focusing on the specific purpose of your speech. As discussed earlier, your general purpose may be to inform or persuade your audience, or it may be to evoke some feeling from them. Your **specific purpose** focuses on what you would like to inform or persuade your audience about or what type of feelings you want to evoke. Identifying your specific purpose helps you focus your topic and establish your organizational structure. You should be able to state this purpose clearly in writing, as shown in the following examples:

> **General Purpose:** To inform
> **Specific Purpose:** To inform my audience about how to prevent skin cancer
>
> **General Purpose:** To persuade
> **Specific Purpose:** To persuade my audience that gay marriages should be legalized
>
> **General Purpose:** To evoke feelings
> **Specific Purpose:** To evoke positive and warm memories of my Uncle Joe

Typically, you will need to revise your purpose statement several times to make it specific enough. For example, if you have written that the purpose of your speech is to inform your audience about same-sex relationships, you do not yet have a specific enough focus. Like most topics, same-sex relationships is a huge subject that could be approached from a wide range of perspectives, including types of friendships, gay marriage around the world, gay relationships throughout history, and famous same-sex relationships. Thus, you must be more specific. What about same-sex relationships do you want your audience to know? If the audience consists of historians and history students, you might want to focus on the history of same-sex relationships in the United States, since they might be most interested in this historical perspective. If the audience consists of lawyers, you might want to focus on the legal status of same-sex relationships in various states and nations. As you can see from this example, part of identifying your specific purpose involves adapting it to your audience, the topic we take up next. Understanding and relating to your audience are crucial aspects of public speaking because, regardless of purpose or goals, you cannot have a successful presentation unless you adapt your speech to your audience.

UNDERSTANDING AND RELATING TO AUDIENCES

As we pointed out in Chapter 11 (Rhetoric), consideration of your audience should be paramount in any public speaking situation. Thus, you need to do an **audience analysis**, the process of determining what the audience already knows or wants to know about your topic, who they are (demographics), what they know or need to know about you, and what their expectations might be for the presentation.

specific purpose
what a speaker wants to inform or persuade an audience about, or the type of feelings the speaker wants to evoke

audience analysis
the process of determining what an audience already knows or wants to know about a topic, who they are, what they know or need to know about the speaker, and what their expectations might be for the presentation

Determining What Your Audience Knows

How can you gather information about your audience? You can begin through discussion with the person who invited you to speak. The information you gather from this discussion, gained by posing the following types of questions, can help you adapt to your audience (Yook, 2004).

- **Open-ended questions** are useful in exploring issues, as they give the person being questioned free rein. For example, ask, "How much does the audience know about gay marriage?"
- **Closed questions** are answerable in a few words. For example, ask, "Will most people in the audience be males? Females? Under 35? Over 35?"
- **Secondary questions** follow up on a previous question. For example, you might ask, "Are gay marriages a concern for people in this audience?"
- **Neutral questions** give the person being questioned a chance to respond without any influence from the interviewer. For example, "What do you think the audience would like to know about?"

Determining Who Your Audience Is

Another important aspect of the audience analysis involves gathering the information you need about their demographic characteristics. Demographic characteristics are the large identity-related social-categories introduced in Chapter 3. Thus, in doing a **demographic analysis**, you consider the ages, races, sexes, sexual orientations, religions, and social-class backgrounds of your audience. People who share particular demographic characteristics also often share a set of historical or cultural references, and you might use some of these in your speech. For example, if the audience members are all in one age group, they may know the same television shows, popular songs, and fashions, and hearing these references in your speech can help draw them in.

You may already be familiar with the demographics of the group, as would be the case if you were making a presentation to your religious congregation. If you are unsure of the audience composition, you can ask for more information from the person who invited you to speak. Note, however, that not all demographic information is necessary or helpful in preparing your speech. If you are putting together a presentation for your city council about light rail, for example, you don't need to know if the council members are married, divorced, gay, or straight.

Sometimes demographic information about your audience can lead you to make erroneous judgments. For example, if you are speaking about the controversies surrounding Title IX and its effects on men's college sports, knowing that your audience will be composed primarily of males may be helpful. On the other hand, knowing simply that your audience is overwhelmingly White may not help you prepare a speech about politics. Although voter analyses showed that the majority of Whites voted Republican in 2000, whereas the majority of Asians, Hispanics, and Blacks voted Democrat, you may be wrong if you rely solely on these data and assume that your audience is Republican (Von Drehle, 2004, p. 7). The lesson? Use demographic information in preparing a speech, but be careful in doing so, because you can end up playing into stereotypes about social groups.

open-ended questions
questions that give the person being questioned free rein in answering

closed questions
questions that are answerable in a few words

secondary questions
questions that follow up on a previous question

neutral questions
questions that give the person being questioned a chance to respond without any influence from the interviewer

demographic analysis
the portion of an audience analysis that considers the ages, races, sexes, sexual orientations, religions, and social class of the audience

Have you ever been in an audience when a speaker made an inappropriate assumption about you based on demographics? How did you respond? If you haven't had this experience, try to imagine a situation in which this could happen.

Audiences can be complex groups of people who may share some interests, but differ on others. Demographic information can be helpful, but avoid playing into stereotypes.

In addition to having demographic information, you also need to know something of the interests of the audience and their relationship to the topic. If you are presenting a persuasive speech, it is especially important to know as much as you can about the range of audience attitudes and where they stand on the topic. As emphasized in Chapter 11, it would be a mistake to assume that all audience members share your beliefs and attitudes. For example, if you are giving a speech to other students advocating the elimination of race-based scholarships, you need to know where they stand on the issue so that you will be prepared to address their potential objections. For other types of speeches and topics, audience values and attitudes *may* be less important—for example, giving an informative speech to college transfer students on registration procedures.

One caveat: Because technology is playing an increasing role in communication, you may not always be able to tell who is or will be in your audience. For example, if your presentation is Webcast or recorded for future viewing, you may not have physical contact with the multiple audiences who will listen to your presentation. Sometimes this happens with classes that are part of the distance-learning curriculum, where the instructor is in one room and students watch from many locations. One can do little to analyze these more remote potential audiences. Therefore, our discussion here focuses only on the audience that will be sitting in the same room with you as you make your presentation.

Determining What Your Audience Knows About You

As you plan your presentation, in addition to analyzing the characteristics of your audience, also consider how they will perceive you and how you want them to perceive you. For example, will your audience have heard of you? Will they know your qualifications? If they do not know you, what will they see when you stand before them? Will they consider you a member of their group?

If your audience knows you in one context but you are speaking in another, you may have to make a special effort to establish your credibility, or *ethos*. For example, if your audience knows you primarily as a student and you want to speak about stem-cell research, you must establish your expertise by referring to the sources you have consulted or the experts you have interviewed.

Considering What Your Audience Expects

To anticipate audience expectations, you need to consider several factors. First, what is the nature of the event? If you are speaking at a wedding, graduation party, or baby shower, the audience will expect an evocative speech that is brief, upbeat, and optimistic about the honorees. One author of this textbook, Tom Nakayama, was invited to speak at a communication conference in Ireland. In accepting this invitation, he asked the inviter about the audience and what to expect. Since this was an informative speech in an academic setting, he was told about the academic interests, backgrounds, and theoretical orientations of the audience, which helped him focus his speech preparations.

Second, how much will the audience members already know about your topic? Knowing this is especially important if the general purpose of your speech is to inform. If your audience is already very familiar with the topic, you can design your speech with more advanced material, examples, and illustrations.

Third, what cultural factors, if any, may be relevant? For example, Judith Martin, another of the text's authors, was recently asked to speak at a *Quinceañera* party, an event that celebrates the coming of age of Mexican and Mexican American girls. As part of the ceremony, the girl's *padrinos* and *madrinas* (godparents)

A *Quinceañera* party is an important Latina event that shapes audience expectations.

Donna Alberico/The *New York Times*

give a short evocative speech and present a gift. At a *Quinceañera*, the audience expectation is that the speakers will describe their commitment to nurturing and educating their goddaughter, and they give her a Bible, rosary, jewelry, or other gifts to symbolize her transition from girlhood to womanhood. As a *madrina*, Judith had to educate herself about the audience's expectations before she could prepare her speech.

Cultural backgrounds of an audience may also influence expectations about speech organization. For example, in reporting on public speaking practices in their country, Kenyan students and professors observed that Kenyan speeches did not necessarily follow the linear format expected in the United State One described Kenyan speeches as often being circular, resembling a bicycle wheel, with the speaker wandering out repeatedly to the rim to make a point or tell a story and then returning to the center, or thesis (Miller, 2002). As you can see, in today's diverse world, even rigorous audience analysis may not prepare a speaker to meet the expectations of everyone in the audience.

DEVELOPING YOUR TOPIC

At this stage, you have determined the general and specific purposes of your speech, and you have selected a topic. You have also completed your audience analysis. Thus, you have the foundation for developing your topic—first, by narrowing your topic, then by identifying your thesis statement, and finally, by locating supporting materials.

Narrowing Your Topic

The purpose of your speech should be your guide in narrowing your topic. Thus, if your general purpose is to inform your audience, you will be most successful if you focus on aspects of the topic that are most likely to affect your listeners. For example, if your topic is social unrest in Nigeria, you may engage your audience by demonstrating how Nigerian social unrest can affect the cost of gasoline at the pump. Once they see that the topic has relevance to them, they will be more likely to take in the information you plan to present.

If your general purpose is to persuade, you should narrow your topic by selecting and developing strong reasons for a particular viewpoint (logos) and appeals that will have a strong emotional impact on the audience (pathos). Sometimes speakers use personal stories to help the audience identify with the need for change. At their best, persuasive speeches not only move the audience to the speaker's view, but also motivate them to act. Thus, if you want to persuade your audience that outsourcing jobs will negatively impact their wages and future job opportunities, you could also point to actions they can take to stop or protest outsourcing. Finally, if your general purpose is to evoke feeling, such as when you are giving an award to someone, you will narrow your topic by selecting key achievements of the recipient.

Identifying Your Thesis Statement

Your next step is to rephrase your specific purpose (see page 392) as a **thesis statement**, or a statement of your topic and your position on it. For example, if your specific purpose is to argue for lowering the drinking age, you might articulate your thesis statement this way: "The drinking age should be lowered to eighteen years old." This is an effective thesis statement because it clearly sets out the proposition to be considered.

The thesis statement is important because it is the foundation on which you construct your presentation. Thus, each of the main points you want to convey

thesis statement
a statement of the topic of a speech and the speaker's position on it

should clearly connect to your thesis statement. Moreover, each main point should develop your thesis statement. For example, to go back to the drinking-age argument, say that you have three main points: (1) the logic of recognizing eighteen-year-olds as adults, (2) the logic of matching the drinking age in other countries, and (3) the need to teach the responsibilities of adulthood. You can tell that these three points develop your thesis statement because separately and together they advance the argument that the drinking age should be lowered.

Finding Supporting Materials

Some topics require extensive research, particularly those on which you are not considered an expert. However, all speech preparations should include some research to find **supporting materials**—information that supports your ideas.

Library research is often the best way to gather supporting materials.

Where can you find supporting materials? There are at least three sources: electronic, print, and personal. You can start with the electronic card catalog at your school or university, accessing databases and various online journals. You will also want to search the Internet, which is increasingly becoming an excellent and acceptable source for research, even scholarly studies. One caution about Internet sources, however: You must evaluate them carefully, as you should any source. (See Chapter 13 for tips on evaluating Internet sources.) Referring to credible sources is especially important for informative and persuasive speeches.

Print sources include books, magazines, and newspapers. Again, evaluate the source. Newspapers like *The Wall Street Journal* or *The Washington Post* are considered highly reliable. Note that some print materials (for example, *The New American, Ms. Magazine*) have a specific point of view. You may use such sources to support your point, but you should acknowledge their viewpoint or bias in your speech. You can find magazines that address every topic imaginable—from general news (for example, *Newsweek*) to specific hobbies (such as *Model Railroader, Scrapbooking, Sky and Telescope*). Use Internet databases like EBSCO or NexisLexis® to help you locate print magazine articles that address your speech topic. In addition to newspapers and magazines, encyclopedias and other reference works, such as the *Statistical Abstract of the United States*, the *People's Almanac*, and the *Guinness Book of World Records*, offer a wealth of information on a variety of topics.

A final source of supporting materials can be face-to-face interviews. You might want to interview people who can give you facts, opinions, and background information on your topic. In addition, you can use interviews to find leads to other sources, including the faculty at your college or university. Most professors have a wealth of information in several areas of expertise and enjoy sharing that information, including where you might do further research. Before any interview, be sure to prepare well. Know what kind of information you're looking for, contact the potential interviewees in advance to make appointments, and be able to explain why you chose them (this shows you've done some homework).

As you identify and use any of these kinds of sources, take careful notes, since you may need to refer to them. Moreover, some instructors ask that each student submit references with their speaking outline.

supporting materials
information that supports the speaker's ideas

Once you have a collection of relevant sources, what kinds of material do you look for within them? Statistics, examples, personal narratives, and testimony by others can all be useful in bolstering your points. Visual aids also provide effective support, especially when a topic is complex. Let's look at the uses for each of these types of support materials.

Statistics

Statistics can highlight the size of a problem or help when making comparisons. See *It Happened to Me: Lisa* to read how the use of statistics can impact your audience. For example, the Pew Forum on Religion and Public Life reported in a 2008 survey that nearly two-thirds (65 percent) of U.S. Americans with religious affiliations believe that many religions can lead to eternal life (2008 Dec.). In contrast, only 29 percent agreed that their religion "is the one, true faith leading to eternal life." The rest did not know or did not answer.

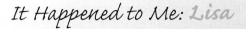
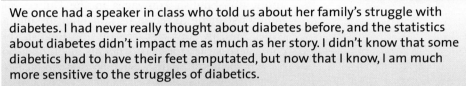

It Happened to Me: Lisa

We once had a speaker in class who told us about her family's struggle with diabetes. I had never really thought about diabetes before, and the statistics about diabetes didn't impact me as much as her story. I didn't know that some diabetics had to have their feet amputated, but now that I know, I am much more sensitive to the struggles of diabetics.

While it may seem that religious U.S. Americans are very tolerant of other religions, the percentages of those who believe that other religions can lead to eternal life are declining. In 2007, about 70 percent felt this way about other religions; in 2002, about 76 percent felt similarly that other religions can lead to eternal life. It is important to note in these statistics that the trend is toward religious exclusivity and that this trend is rapidly changing among White evangelicals and Black Protestants. From 2007 to 2008, White evangelicals moved from 56 percent to 47 percent, while Black Protestants fell from 59 percent to 49 percent, among those who felt that other religions can lead to eternal life. This rapid shift in one year among these two groups is worth noting and can be an important part of the message about religion in our society and its related future trends.

If you are dealing with very large numbers, round them off. For example, according to the U.S. Census Bureau, 178,014 people in the United States spoke the Navajo language in 2000 (U.S. Census Bureau, 2003 Feb.). Your audience is more likely to remember this statistic if you round it off and say that there are almost 200,000 (or just over 175,000) Navajo speakers in the United States.

When citing statistics, however, be careful about attributing meaning to them, as the reasons for statistical differences are not always apparent or reported with the statistical data. For example, the *Statistical Abstract of the United States 2009* tells us that in 2007, 8.1 percent of the workforce in Massachusetts was employed in science and engineering occupations. In the neighboring state of Rhode Island, however, only 4.7 percent held jobs in those same sectors. This data source does not indicate *why* there is such a large difference in these two neighboring states. While you might speculate that Massachusetts has more favorable tax rates for science and engineering businesses, this disparity could be explained in other ways. Perhaps Massachusetts students who score very high in math and science (Vaznis, 2008) drive the economy toward science and engineering. You could come up with other explanations, but the *Statistical Abstract* does not explain this difference in employment and, unless you have support for your explanation, you should make it clear that you are merely speculating.

Examples

A second type of supporting material, examples, can also add power to a presentation. One might give a brief example to illustrate a point in passing or use a more extended example, woven throughout a speech. Examples provide a concrete and realistic way of thinking about a topic and clarifying it. If you were to speak about nonfiction television programming, for example, your audience may better understand your point if you name specific programs, such as *60 Minutes, Nova,* or *Monday Night Football.* Without these examples, some audience members might think you are referring to reality television programs, such as *Survivor, Amazing Race,* and *Big Brother.* Often you can support your points with examples, particularly if you make personal connections to some of the shows that you discuss (Lucas, 2004), such as, "When I watch *60 Minutes* I always . . ." or "My sister, who is a producer on *60 Minutes,* reports that . . . ."

Personal Narratives

A third kind of support for your presentation—personal narratives and testimony of others—can give your speech a human touch. For example, if you are speaking about non-English languages in the United States and you describe your own family's struggle to retain its non-English language, your story adds weight to the issue. And, in your research on non-English speakers in the U.S., you may have come across the stories of students at "Indian boarding schools" who were beaten for not speaking English. Such stories enhance your topic with pathos.

ORGANIZING YOUR PRESENTATION

Like well-written essays, oral presentations need a clear structure as well as a sound foundation in research. If your presentation lacks a clear organizational structure, the audience may not be able to follow your thinking, and you are likely to lose their attention and interest. Sometimes students think that because *they* understand their speech, the audience will as well. The key here is making certain the audience, who has never before heard the presentation, understands.

Organizing an effective presentation means choosing and following a pattern that is compatible with your topic and that will make sense to your audience, whose expectations you will have in mind after doing the kind of research outlined in the previous sections. Organizing a presentation also involves creating an outline that can serve as the framework for your material. To anchor your organizational structure, you will develop an introduction, a conclusion, and transitions. Let's look at the subject of patterns first.

Selecting Your Organizational Pattern

In most cases, a speech should be organized around three to five main points. If you have fewer than three points, you may not yet have sufficiently researched or thought about your topic. For example, if you are making an informational presentation comparing and contrasting the European Union (EU) and the United States, and you have only two points—(1) that the EU and the United States each have a common currency and (2) that neither regulates travel across internal borders—you have not even scratched the surface of the many major differences and similarities between the two. Once you learn more about the topic, you may realize that it is too large for a short presentation and decide to adopt a narrower focus—say, on how the monetary systems of the two bodies differ.

Alternatively, if you have done sufficient research and can only come up with two points, it might be a sign that you have narrowed your topic too much, so that you simply don't have enough to say about it. You may find, for example, that the topic of hepatitis D is too narrow for a speech addressed to a nonmedical audience. If so, you may need to broaden your topic to hepatitis in general. Then your main points could be (1) the five kinds of hepatitis, (2) how transmission occurs, and (3) steps people can take to avoid catching it. This broader discussion offers relevant information to a general audience.

If you have more than five main points, your audience may find your presentation difficult to follow. In this case, determine if you can combine several points into one larger point, or if you can eliminate any main points. Alternatively, if you have too many main points, your topic may just be overly broad.

Once you have identified your main points, divide them into subpoints. These subpoints should all clearly relate to their corresponding main points. Returning to the European Union example, you could divide a main point about the European monetary system into the following subpoints: (1) the introduction of the Euro, which is the primary monetary unit of the EU; (2) the population's acceptance of the Euro; and (3) the rising strength of the Euro against the U.S. dollar. Again, limit yourself to three to five subpoints for each main point, since you can lose your audience if you include too many.

Once you have all your main points and subpoints, you need to consider how to arrange them. Speakers in the United States generally follow one of five organizational patterns: chronological, spatial, topical, problem–solution, or cause–effect. A **chronological pattern** follows a timeline; for example, a speech on the life of a famous person, like Susan B. Anthony, lends itself well to a chronological outline.

Topic: Life of Susan B. Anthony

   I. Her birth and formative years (1820–1840)

  II. Her fight to end slavery (1840–1860)

 III. Her fight for women's rights (1860–her death in 1902)

A **spatial pattern** arranges points by location and can be used to describe something small (for example, parts of a flower—moving from the edge to its center) or something large (for example, Ellis Island, in New York—moving along a central hallway).

Topic: A Tour of Ellis Island

    I. The Baggage Room

   II. The Registry Room

  III. The Hearing Room

  IV. The Bunk Room [www.nps.gov/elis/planyourvisit/maps.htm]

A **topical pattern** of organization, the most common, is used when your main points have no innate pattern except the one you impose on them. This situation requires more thinking because the points have no predetermined relationship, and you will need to find the scheme that is most logical and will work best for your audience.

Topic: Skin Cancer

   I. What is skin cancer?

  II. Who is most at risk?

 III. How can one prevent skin cancer?

The fourth common pattern is the **problem–solution pattern**, in which you describe various aspects of a problem and then propose solutions. This pattern frequently is used in persuasive speeches.

Topic: Why Gay Marriage Should Be Legalized

    I. Lack of health benefits for gay couples

   II. Hospital visitation problems

  III. Inheritance problems

  IV. Benefits and advantages of legalizing gay marriage

chronological pattern
one that follows a timeline

spatial pattern
one that arranges points by location and can be used to describe something small

topical pattern
one that has no innate organization except that imposed by the speaker

problem–solution pattern
one in which the speaker describes various aspects of a problem and then proposes solutions

A final approach to organization, referred to as the **cause–effect pattern**, is often used to create understanding and agreement, and sometimes to argue for a specific action.

Topic: Global Warming

   I. Causes

         Subpoints: technology, energy consumption, and overpopulation

   II. Effects

         Subpoints: higher temperatures, rising sea levels, and melting ice caps

   III. How to slow global warming

Creating Your Outline

Once you have selected your pattern, you will have a good idea of the order in which you want to present your points. Thus, you are ready to create your outline. You are probably already familiar with how to outline. In the past, you may have used outlining chiefly to organize your written compositions. However, outlining also is useful in organizing a public speaking presentation.

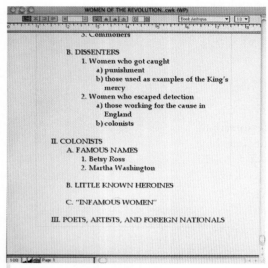

Outlining your speech is a very important part of the public speaking process.

An outline should be considered a working document, and thus, you shouldn't hesitate to change it again and again. For example, as you work on it, you may see points that you wish to reorder, details that you want to emphasize more—or less, and new examples that you want to include.

Let's look at some sample outlines—first, for a speech to inform, which uses a topical pattern as its framework. In the following outline, you will see several items in parentheses and brackets. These are meant to show how you can incorporate *signposts*, or transitions, which help your audience understand your organization. You may choose to include these kinds of signposts in your own outline. Note also that some entries are complete sentences, while others are fragments. This is meant to indicate that an outline is a flexible form, and you can create it in the way that best captures your ideas but keeps them well structured.

General Purpose: To inform the audience

Specific Purpose: To inform the audience about the history of same-sex marriage

Thesis statement: Same-sex marriage is not a recent invention, but it has been controversial throughout its history.

   I. Introduction

      A. Gay marriage is a very prominent topic today.

      B. California Proposition 8, and other state elections, have placed this issue at the forefront of public deliberation.

      C. State thesis: It is important to understand that same-sex marriage is not a recent invention.

      D. Explain that understanding this history can enrich our understanding of the deliberations currently taking place across the country.

   II. What is "marriage"?

      First, let's look at the history of marriage. (signpost)

      A. Marriage as a legal institution.

      B. Marriage as a religious institution.

      Next we'll look at some of the ways that marriage has changed over time. (signpost/transition)

cause–effect pattern
one used to create understanding and agreement, and sometimes to argue for a specific action

III. How has the notion of marriage expanded within the United States?
     Second, let's look at some of the changing notions of marriage in the U.S. (signpost)

   A. Barriers facing slaves and marriage.
   B. Barriers facing interracial marriage.
   C. Barriers facing polygamous marriages.

   Next we will look at some same-sex marriages in history. (transition)

IV. Same-sex relationships were recognized by societies in the past.
     Third, let's look at some of the ways that societies recognized same-sex marriages. (signpost)

   A. Church recognition: Same-sex marriages in Catholic and Eastern Orthodox Churches in Medieval Europe (Boswell, 1995).
   B. State recognition: Same-sex marriages in sixteenth-century France (Tulchin, 2007).
   C. Anti-gay repression is largely a post-WWII phenomenon in the U.S. (Chauncey, 2004).

V. Conclusion
     In conclusion, same-sex relationships were recognized by churches and governments in the past.

   A. In this speech, I've reviewed the changing definitions of marriage.
   B. Same-sex marriage is not a recent invention.
   C. Understanding the rich history of human relationships and the churches and states that recognize the complexities of these relationships can only enhance our discussion about these issues.

REFERENCES

Boswell, J. (1995). *Same-sex unions in pre-modern Europe.* New York: Vintage.

Chauncey, G. (2004). *Why marriage: The history shaping today's debate over gay equality.* Cambridge, MA: Perseus Books.

Cott, N. F. (2002). *Public vows: A history of marriage and the nation.* Cambridge, MA: Harvard University Press.

Tulchin, A. A. (2007). Same-sex couples creating households in Old Regime France: The uses of the *affrèrement. Journal of Modern History, 79,* 613–647.

Note that this informative speech does have some elements of persuasion. In this example, informing the audience about this history can be indirectly persuasive, particularly when the historical information is seen to connect to other barriers to marriage. The primary purpose of the speech, however, is focused on informing the audience about the complex history of marriage and gay marriage. As the speaker practices and refines this speech, he or she can shape the emphasis to be more informative and focus on what understanding this history can do for the audience.

In a persuasive speech, the outline should reflect a slightly different format. In persuasive speeches, the speaker first needs to convince the audience that a problem exists. Then the speaker moves to persuading them that something needs to be done about it. Often, the speaker also presents a particular solution that he or she wants the audience to embrace. Therefore, a persuasive outline might look like this:

General purpose: To persuade the audience

Specific purpose: To persuade the audience that gay marriage should be legalized

Thesis: The United States should legalize gay marriage.

I. Introduction
   A. Tell Keith & Jeff story. Jeff was a flight attendant on American Airlines Flight #11, which crashed into the World Trade Center on 9/11: Because gay and lesbian couples do not have the same rights and protections under the law that straight married couples do, Keith suffered through an expensive and stressful legal battle to get Jeff's death certificate and settle his legal affairs.
   B. Focus on feelings that most people in audience will have about 9/11 and about loss.
   C. State thesis: That the United States should legalize gay marriage.
   D. Explain that the denial of same-sex marriage creates enormous inequalities, the subject we will look at next. (signpost)

II. Problems posed by absence of gay marriage
   A. Problems of children with gay or lesbian parents
   B. Problems for gay/lesbian employees (who aren't eligible for partners' benefits)
   C. Problems of gay/lesbian senior citizens (who can't collect social security benefits of their deceased partners)
   D. Denial of 49 rights that married couples have, including hospital visitation, social security benefits, pensions, family leave, and immigration rights

III. Solution
   There is a solution to this civil rights issue. (signpost/transition)
   A. Recognize the separation of church and state.
   B. Legalize same-sex marriage.

IV. Benefits and advantages
   Legalizing same-sex marriage has several benefits, as we will see next. (signpost/transition)
   A. Will solve civil rights disparities
   B. Will create stronger families for gay parents with children
   C. Will create more equitable situations for gay senior citizens
   D. Will create a more equitable society for all Americans
   E. Encourage audience to sign the "million for marriage" petition. (call to action)

V. Conclusion
   A. Summarize main points.
   B. Restate the solution—legalize gay marriage in the United States
   C. Return to Keith and Jeff story to provide closure.

REFERENCES
Human Rights Campaign. (2003). Keith and Jeff. Retrieved June 25, 2006, from **www.hrc.org/millionformarriage/hrc_adcenter/keith_jeff.html**

The persuasive outline differs from the informative one in that it focuses on convincing the audience that a problem exists and that it needs a solution. Furthermore, it offers a solution that requires taking a stand—signing the "million for marriage" petition, for example. Note that although this is primarily a persuasive speech, it includes both informative elements (problems that gay couples face) and evocative elements (the story of Jeff and Keith; the references to 9/11 and loss). With these two examples you can see that an outline can be spare, as is the one about gay marriage, or more fleshed out, as is the one about gay marriage. The idea is to create a sound organizational structure and a road map from which you can best build your presentation.

Developing Your Introduction, Conclusion, and Transitions

After you have developed your outline, arranging your points and subpoints according to the pattern you have chosen, you will need to develop this skeleton into a full-bodied presentation. In doing so, you will pay special attention to your introduction and conclusion. Writing the introduction and conclusion often requires more attention than beginning speakers expect. Why? Audiences usually remember much more about these opening and closing elements than they do about the body of the speech, and they also may judge the speaker primarily by these elements. Why is this true?

From your **introduction**, audience members gain a first impression of your speech's content and of you as the speaker, so both the content and presentation of the introduction are very important. You'll want to start with a bang, not a whimper. To do this, your introduction should (1) gain audience attention, (2) focus their attention on your topic by relating it to them, (3) give them an overview of your organizational pattern, and (4) help them understand your thesis.

You can gain audience attention with a snappy quotation, a startling fact, a personal example, or a shocking statistic connected to your speech topic. For example, in a presentation about domestic violence, if you start out by saying that most child murders are committed by family members (Bureau of Justice Statistics, 2006) (see **www.ojp.usdoj.gov/bjs/cvict_c.htm**), the audience will want to learn more. As noted earlier, speakers will sometimes tell a story about themselves. This approach both captures attention and establishes the speaker's relationship to the topic—perhaps his own experience with domestic violence.

Once you have gotten the audience's attention, you need to get it focused on your specific topic. For example, why should this statistic about children or a personal story about domestic violence matter to them? You can probably think of a number of reasons, such as concern for problems in their own family, a friend's family, or a neighbor's family. Thus, if the topic of your presentation is warning signs of domestic violence, you have found a dramatic way to focus audience attention on the topic.

Your next task is to present your thesis statement so the audience understands the point of the speech. So, if your topic is domestic violence, you might say, "I plan to show you the four warning signs of domestic violence." In the final part of your introduction, you would preview the overall organization, or pattern, of the presentation. Previewing the organization will make it easier for your audience to follow your speech. When you preview, you name the four warning signs: "negative inner feelings, partner's lack of control, partner's controlling behavior, and partner's diminishment of spouse." Then, of course, you need to be sure to follow through on each of these points in the body of the speech and in the order you named them. You may want to point your audience to more information such as this Web site **www.helpguide.org/mental/domestic_violence_abuse_types_signs_causes_effects.htm** as an additional resource.

As you move from main point to main point, and from subpoint to subpoint, insert transitions to help your audience understand your organization. These transitions are called **signposts**, and you saw them inserted in the outlines we worked through earlier. Signposts tell the audience where you are in the overall organization, thus making it easier for them to follow along and stay oriented. Common signposts include phrases such as, "my second point is" or "a second stage of the"

An interesting introduction can grab your audience's attention.

introduction
opening material of a speech from which the audience members gain a first impression of the speech's content and of the speaker

signposts
transitions in a speech that help an audience understand the speaker's organization, making it easier for them to follow

FIGURE 14.1: Basic Speech Structure

I. Introduction	III. Second Main Point
A. Attention-getting step	A. Signpost your second point.
B. Connection to audience	B. Make your point (include supporting material).
C. Thesis statement	C. Transition to your next point.
D. Preview of main points	IV. Third Main Point
E. Transition to first point	A. Signpost your third point.
II. First Main Point	B. Make your point (include supporting material).
A. Signpost your first point.	C. Transition to conclusion.
B. Make your point (include supporting material).	V. Conclusion
C. Transition to your next point.	A. Review main points.
	B. Connect back to audience.
	C. Create a memorable conclusion.

conclusion
closing material of a speech where the speaker reviews the main points, may challenge the audience to act, and leaves the audience with a positive view of speaker and topic

or "in addition." These devices are not merely mechanical. You can use them in an artful way to help your words and ideas flow together gracefully.

As you transition into your conclusion, you must be sure to provide a signpost so that the audience knows you are preparing to end your speech. Sometimes speakers are direct, and they say, "In conclusion," or "As I wrap up my discussion." This approach is very clear and tells the audience where you are in the presentation.

The **conclusion** should accomplish several goals. First, it should review the three to five main points in the body of your presentation. Second, if you are giving a persuasive speech, during the conclusion, you will challenge the audience to act. Actions may include finding out more about the topic, or becoming more involved in the issue—for example, by registering to vote, donating blood, or signing a petition. As you formulate this challenge, or call the audience to action, consider how you want your presentation to impact their lives. Do you want them to vote a particular way? Change their eating habits? Use sunscreen?

Finally, the conclusion should leave the audience with a positive view of you and your topic. For example, you might end with a memorable quote or an amusing anecdote. Sometimes speakers return to their opening example to reach closure on the issue. For example, if your topic is skin cancer, you might open with a story about a friend or family member who had this disease. Then, when you close the speech, you might return to your example and tell the audience how your friend (or family member) is currently doing. Whatever closing technique you choose, remember that public speaking is an art that requires artistic judgment. There is no one right or wrong way to do it, only more effective and less effective ones. See Figure 14.1 for an outline of the basic speech structure that has just been described.

Next we discuss issues surrounding speech delivery. Many people think of public speaking as being all about delivery, but delivery is, as we hope you have seen, only one aspect of the entire process.

Can you think of a speaker you've heard who used signposts effectively? If not, pay attention over the next few weeks to all the presentations you hear—in class, on TV, on the radio—and note the effective or ineffective use of signposts.

DELIVERING YOUR SPEECH

In the context of public speaking, delivery refers to the presentation of the speech you have researched, organized, outlined, and practiced. Delivery relies on both verbal communication (Chapter 5) and nonverbal communication (Chapter 6). Delivery *is* important, of course, because it is what is most immediate to the audience. In this section, we focus on six important aspects of delivery:

selecting a style, incorporating your visual aids, being aware of time, speaking extemporaneously, developing a speaking persona, and finally, putting your speech into action.

Selecting a Style

style
the type of language and phrasing a speaker uses and the effect the language and phrasing create

Style refers to the type of language and phrasing a speaker uses and the effect the language and phrasing create. Styles range from very plain and direct, at one end of the spectrum, to very ornate and indirect, at the other end. Ornate styles were common in the nineteenth century, but are less so today. For example, here is a section from Daniel Webster's 1825 "Bunker Hill Monument Oration," which has an extremely ornate style:

> "The great event in the history of the continent, which we are now met here to commemorate, that prodigy of modern times, at once the wonder and the blessing of the world, is the American Revolution. In a day of extraordinary prosperity and happiness, of high national honor, distinction, and power, we are brought together, in this place, by our love of country, by our admiration of exalted character, by our gratitude for signal services and patriotic devotion" (Webster, 1989/1825, p. 127).

A plainer style of this same speech might sound like this: "The American Revolution was a great event in our history, and we are here to commemorate its importance by erecting this monument." The more ornate style attempts to stimulate a more emotional response and, in this case, create great pride in the establishment of the United States. The plainer style gets right to the point and values economy in wording.

The key is to select a style that is appropriate for the speech you are giving. For example, you may use a plain style if you are giving instructions, but you may use a more eloquent style if you are celebrating someone's accomplishments. Being aware of speech style is important, as the style you use can enhance or undermine your message. For example, if you were speaking at a meeting of the local school board and used too informal a style—for example, referring to the members of board as "dudes"—the audience likely would focus more on you than your topic. In this instance, your style would interfere with your ability to convey your message.

Two main elements that contribute to style are clarity and appropriateness of language and phrasing. Your speech style has the element of clarity if listeners are able to grasp the message you intended to communicate. Using precise language increases clarity. In everyday conversation, speakers often use words and phrases without much attention to precision. For example, if someone says, "Bob's totally gross," we learn little about Bob; we only know that the speaker has some objection to him. But if the speaker says, "I don't like Bob because he uses vulgar language and ridicules his friends," then we know more specifically how he perceives Bob.

As another example of the importance of precise word choice, consider the range of words you have to choose from in describing how someone died: *Killed, murdered, terminated, exterminated,* and *assassinated* are only a few of the possibilities, with each conveying a different message. If someone was *killed,* it sounds less intentional than if someone were *murdered.* To say that someone was *terminated* sounds very casual and flippant, like a character in a science fiction or action movie, while *exterminated* communicates a far more sinister death, perhaps involving genocide or mass murders. If someone is *assassinated,* it communicates political reasons. The lesson here is that you need to think carefully about the words you use and what they communicate.

In addition to focusing on the clarity of your language, you also need to consider its appropriateness, which generally refers to how formal or informal it should be. In general, speakers tend to strive for a more formal style when they are speaking to a larger audience and a less formal style with smaller audiences. Speakers also are apt to use a more formal style during more ceremonial occasions, such as a big public wedding or funeral, and a less formal style for more casual events, such as a family holiday dinner. Though we can't offer a strict formula for choosing a level of formality or appropriateness, one guideline is to match your style of presentation to the type of clothing you might wear to a particular event. Just as you wouldn't wear your favorite cut-offs and tank top to make a presentation to an important client, you shouldn't use a very informal style of speech during the presentation. Similarly, as you may have been told, if you don't know what to wear, it is often better to overdress than to underdress, and it is usually best to speak a little more formally than to speak too informally. Becoming too familiar with an audience, especially one that does not know you, may alienate them.

Concerns about appropriateness of style also cover your choice of topics, examples, and visual aids. We cannot offer any easy answers regarding inclusion of controversial subject matter or visual images, but as a public speaker, you should be aware that the choices you make in this regard can enhance or undermine your ability to get your message across. If you are considering a controversial topic, your audience research and analysis become crucial, as some audiences may be more receptive to certain ideas than other ideas.

Incorporating Visual Aids

As a student in elementary school, you may have used visual aids in show-and-tell speeches. In these speeches, the visual aid—perhaps a favorite toy, gift, or souvenir—was at the center. As part of your college coursework, your instructors may also require that you use visual aids in speeches. Even if you are not required to do so, you should consider the possibility. **Visual aids** are any audiovisual materials that help you reach your speech goals. Some of the most common kinds are video clips, photographs, DVD segments, and PowerPoint slides.

Always select and incorporate visual aids carefully, remembering that their purpose is to augment and enhance your presentation, not to detract from your presentation or substitute for content, as Edward Tufte instructs in *Alternative View: PowerPoint Is Evil: Power Corrupts. PowerPoint Corrupts Absolutely.* To determine whether the visual aid is going to augment or detract, ask yourself why you are using it and how it will support your speech goals. Here are some guidelines for handling visual aids effectively:

1. Prepare visual aids in advance. If you use the blackboard as a visual aid, for example, you communicate informality and lack of preparation. The lack of preparation can be insulting to some audiences, who may have made a major effort to come to hear your presentation. If, on the other hand, you incorporate relevant and well-designed PowerPoint slides, you communicate that you have carefully and thoughtfully prepared your presentation.
2. Make sure that your visual aids are easy to see. If your visual aid is too small, it will frustrate your audience. As you speak about something they have difficulty seeing, many audiences will tune you out. Once you have lost your audience, it is very difficult to recapture their attention, and you won't reach your speech goals.
3. Make sure that the equipment you need will be available when you speak. For example, if you want to use a PowerPoint presentation, be sure that the room has the appropriate equipment. Today, many classrooms do, but it is always best to check. Sometimes classrooms only have overhead projectors, and if you know this, you can prepare overhead transparencies to use in your presentation.

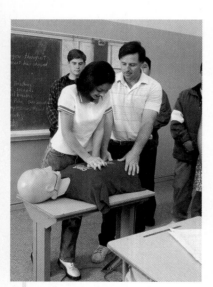

Visual aids can be helpful in explaining ideas and instructions. In this photo, students receive hands-on training in CPR.

visual aids
audiovisual materials that help a speaker reach intended speech goals

Alternative VIEW

PowerPoint Is Evil: Power Corrupts. PowerPoint Corrupts Absolutely.

By Edward Tufte

Imagine a widely used and expensive prescription drug that promised to make us beautiful but didn't. Instead the drug had frequent, serious side effects: It induced stupidity, turned everyone into bores, wasted time, and degraded the quality and credibility of communication. These side effects would rightly lead to a worldwide product recall.

Yet several hundred million copies of Microsoft PowerPoint are churning out trillions of slides each year. . . . The standard PowerPoint presentation elevates format over content, betraying an attitude of commercialism that turns everything into a sales pitch. . . .

In a business setting, a PowerPoint slide typically shows 40 words, which is about eight seconds' worth of silent reading material. With so little information per slide, many, many slides are needed. Audiences consequently endure a relentless sequentiality, one damn slide after another. When information is stacked in time, it is difficult to understand context and evaluate relationships.

Visual reasoning usually works more effectively when relevant information is shown side by side. Often, the more intense the detail, the greater the clarity and understanding. This is especially so for statistical data, where the fundamental analytical act is to make comparisons. . . .

Presentations largely stand or fall on the quality, relevance, and integrity of the content. If your numbers are boring, then you've got the wrong numbers. If your words or images are not on point, making them dance in color won't make them relevant. Audience boredom is usually a content failure, not a decoration failure.

At a minimum, a presentation format should do no harm. Yet the PowerPoint style routinely disrupts, dominates, and trivializes content. Thus PowerPoint presentations too often resemble a school play—very loud, very slow, and very simple.

The practical conclusions are clear. PowerPoint is a competent slide manager and projector. But rather than supplementing a presentation, it has become a substitute for it. Such misuse ignores the most important rule of speaking: Respect your audience.

FROM: "PowerPoint Is Evil," by Edward Tufte as appeared in *Wired Magazine*, September 2003. Reprinted by permission, from Edward R. Tufte, *The Cognitive Style of PowerPoint* (Cheshire, Connecticut, Graphics Press, 2003).

4. Prepare for technology failures. Computers fail, projectors fail, and DVD players are not always correctly connected to LCD projectors. No equipment is foolproof, so you may not be able to show your visual aids. Thus, make sure that your speech can stand on its own and that you are prepared to speak successfully without the visual aids.

5. In using your visual aid, follow these three steps: (a) introduce the visual aid to your audience by explaining what they will see, (b) point to the parts of the visual aid that you want them to focus on, and (c) reaffirm the major point of the visual aid, thus pointing the audience to the conclusion you want them to draw. In a sense, this use of visual aids is a microcosm of your overall speech—that is, it has an introduction, body, and conclusion.

Although visual aids can help you reach your speech goals, they also can distract the audience from your main points. For example, if you distribute a handout during your speech, audiences will tend to focus on the handout, and you will lose their attention. Also, if you finish with a visual aid but leave it up on the screen, the audience will continue to focus on it rather than on you. Finally, when you use your visual aid, be sure to speak to your audience, not to the visual aid. While it may be tempting to avoid eye contact with the audience by focusing on your visual aid, you risk disconnecting with them. To use visual aids in a way that will help you meet your speech goal, refer to *Did You Know? Visual Aid Checklist*, on p. 408.

Did You Know?
Visual Aid Checklist

_____ 1. Do you have the equipment you need for your visual aid at the speech location?

_____ 2. Have you prepared your visual aid in advance of your speech?

_____ 3. If you are using PowerPoint, have you created the appropriate number of slides? Have you included enough but not too much information on each?

_____ 4. Will everyone be able to see the visual aid?

_____ 5. Have you practiced speaking to an audience and maintaining your connection with them?

_____ 6. Will you be able to put up and take down your visual aid so that the audience can focus on you and your topic?

_____ 7. Have you anticipated problems with technology?

As your own classroom experience likely has demonstrated, when used well, visual aids can be very effective in helping an audience understand a topic. Thus, when you use them, be sure that they strengthen your presentation and make your points clearer. For example, in a presentation on gay marriage, you could develop a visual aid, such as a map that shows the status of gay marriage and civil union in different places. As with most things in life, however, the key to success is balance. Focusing too much on the visual aids reduces your contact with the audience, which is most often established through eye contact.

After you have selected your style of presentation and incorporated your visual aids, you are ready to consider the presentation of your speech. In the following sections, we will look at several guidelines for your delivery.

Being Aware of the Time

In the United States, we often think about time as absolute—a phenomenon that can be broken down into clearly measurable units: seconds, minutes, and hours. Yet, communication scholars have repeatedly shown that notions of time are relative, as described in Chapter 6. Many public speakers experience this relative nature of time. Some, for example, feel they have been speaking for a very long time, while their audience may feel that they have heard only a short speech. More often, speakers feel that they have not spoken very long, while their audience is wondering whether the speech will ever end.

Knowing how long to speak is an important aspect of the art of public speaking. The length of any speech should be guided by audience expectations in a particular context as well as by your content. In some instances, the guidelines are rather loose, such as speeches at weddings and retirements. In other cases, the time limits are very strict, and you may be cut off before you finish. For example, a citizen advocating a position in city council meetings often faces strict time limits. In this case, you should adhere to those time guidelines.

If your speech is significantly longer than expected, your audience may become restless, impatient, and finally hostile. On the other hand, if your speech is significantly shorter than the time expected, your audience may leave feeling disappointed or shortchanged. They may have made a significant effort to be at your presentation with expectations that now remain unfulfilled. Also, your speech may be part of a larger program, and the planners are depending on you to fill a particular time slot.

In classroom speech situations, you are often told how long to speak—say, for five minutes. In this situation, your audience expects you to speak for only five minutes. One way to make sure you comply is to time yourself when you practice your speech. Doing this will ensure that you know how long your speech runs and whether you need to adjust it. If you have prepared, practiced, and timed your speech, you should have no problem meeting your time requirement.

Considering the Means of Delivery

Speakers have several means for delivering a message, ranging from spontaneous, off-the-cuff remarks to speeches that are carefully planned, written, revised, and rehearsed. Let's look first at the spontaneous variety.

An **impromptu speech** is one that is delivered with little or no preparation—perhaps because the speaker has been given very little notice or no notice at all. For example, at some celebrations, a person may be asked to speak spontaneously as the surprise recipient of an award. Or a person may be asked to make a few comments at a community or university meeting. Making a comment in class also can be thought of as an impromptu speech.

This man is giving a speech against building a proposed Wal-Mart store in Cazenovia, New York. Community meetings often include many impromptu speeches.

Naturally, this type of speech is often difficult for beginning speakers, but a few guidelines do exist. First, if possible, take a few moments to jot down the major points you wish to make, an interesting way to introduce your topic, and some way of concluding. Organizing your speech in this way will ensure that you cover the important points. Also, be sure to stop after you have made your points. One error beginning speakers often make, especially with impromptu speaking, is to continue long after they have made their point, often repeating what they have already said.

In contrast with the impromptu speech is the **manuscript speech**, one that is written out word-for-word that the speaker reads to the audience. While it may be tempting to take this approach, it is not a good idea. Rarely can a speaker read a speech and manage to make it sound natural. Audiences generally prefer to hear from you directly, as if you are speaking from the heart. Engaging your audience with direct address, including eye contact, is preferable to the more distanced presentation that results from reading. However, reading a speech can be appropriate if the specific word choices are extremely important and your speech is likely to be quoted directly. The president of the United States often reads speeches, as journalists and others are likely to quote him and because lack of attention to word choices can create controversies.

For example, in a question-and-answer session, President George W. Bush once referred to the military response to September 11 as a "crusade." This word choice drew an immediate and strong response. During the Crusades of the medieval period, Christians left their homes to battle Muslims in the Middle East. While President Bush may not have intended to frame the military actions against terrorism as a holy war against non-Christians, his word choice, which was spontaneous rather than scripted, pointed to this interpretation. If he had been speaking from a manuscript speech, he could have avoided this controversy. On the other hand, during a question-and-answer session, some spontaneity is always required.

Lying in the middle ground between spontaneous and manuscript speech is the **extemporaneous speech**—probably the most common type of delivery. Speaking extemporaneously allows you to be a directly engaged but well-prepared speaker. An extemporaneous speech is written ahead of time, but only in outline form. Then, the speaker uses the outline as a guide. Some extemporaneous speakers may include a few extra notes in the outline to help them remember particularly important points or quotations, but the speech is neither written out in its

impromptu speech
speech that is delivered with little or no preparation

manuscript speech
speech that is written out word-for-word and read to the audience

extemporaneous speech
speech that is written ahead of time but only in outline form

entirety nor memorized. By speaking extemporaneously, you will be able to better engage your audience and adapt your speech to their responses. The examples provided earlier (pages 405–407) are typical of the type of outlines extemporaneous speakers use.

Projecting a Persona

Developing a persona, meaning the image a speaker conveys, is one of the most artistic aspects of public speaking. We discussed this in Chapter 11 in our examination of rhetoric. If you have seen Ellen DeGeneres on her talk show, you know that she projects a friendly, down-to-earth, almost naive persona. She dresses informally, she jokes with her audience, and she seems friendly. Her nonverbal communication is very informal and relaxed. For example, she makes direct eye contact with her audience and the television camera; she sometimes slouches in the chair and even does a little "dance" at the beginning of every show. These elements together make up her public persona.

Speakers adopt personas when they deliver speeches. For example, a speaker who appears to be confident, trustworthy, and calm may have had to create this persona and learn how to project that image. Successful national politicians work to develop personas that are attractive to large groups of people. President Clinton, for example, was described by many, even his detractors, as both affable and engaging in public.

As you create your public persona, consider a few factors that shape it. First, the speed at which you speak, or speaking rate, will shape your persona and how people perceive you. Although there is no single, ideal speaking rate, it should vary to fit your message. For example, speaking slowly and deliberately can be very effective if you want to highlight the gravity of a situation. At other times, you may wish to speak more quickly, particularly for a light, humorous presentation. You may also vary your speed as you move from point to point, slowing down, perhaps, to emphasize one item in particular.

If you watch television news, you will have noticed that news broadcasters speak quickly. In comparison, people being interviewed often appear to be speaking too slowly, and sometimes the news journalist cuts them off. Because of the dominance of television and the fast speech used in that medium, audiences generally are receptive to a speaking rate that is faster than the one used in casual conversation. One danger with a rapid rate, especially when the speaker is nervous, is that words often blur together. So when you pick up your pace, be sure to continue to articulate your words carefully.

Eye contact is another important element of creating your persona. Making **eye contact**, or looking directly into the eyes of another, is one of the most direct ways to show your engagement with your audience, and it can lend credibility to your presentation. If you watch *Law and Order* on television, you may have noticed that the lawyers make direct eye contact with the jury in their closing remarks. How might the jury interpret a lawyer's presentation if instead she used a manuscript speech approach? As we saw in Chapter 6, the norm in mainstream U.S. culture is to distrust people who do not look at us directly, and to interpret this as a sign of shyness or dishonesty. Although other cultures—some Native American and some Asian—do not interpret lack of eye contact this way, you should consider your eye contact and adapt it to the context in which you are speaking.

As mentioned, gestures and movement also contribute to one's persona. This part of delivery is known as *kinesics* (Chapter 6). While you may not think that other speakers consider their movements when preparing to speak, the more natural they appear, the more likely it is that they have practiced staging. One of the best ways to ensure that your gestures and movement are effective is to practice them along with your speech—a topic we turn to in the next section.

Think about the persona and public image of a great speaker you've heard. How would you describe her or his persona? Analyze the elements that contribute to that persona: language, body posture, gestures, facial expressions. Describe the speaker's distinctive approach to each of these elements.

eye contact
looking directly into the eyes of another

Finally, although you may think that your delivery begins when you stand up to speak, you begin to present your persona well before that. In some cases, for example, speakers are part of a panel, seated at a table in front of the audience, or a single speaker is introduced by someone else. In both cases, the speakers are constructing their personas while they wait to speak. Fidgeting, rolling the eyes, yawning, chewing gum, being late, and displaying other unflattering nonverbal behaviors may influence how the audience perceives you. Assume that you are "on stage" from the moment you walk into the room until the moment you leave.

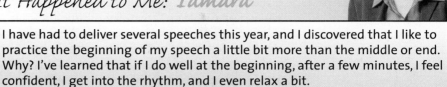

It Happened to Me: Tamara

I have had to deliver several speeches this year, and I discovered that I like to practice the beginning of my speech a little bit more than the middle or end. Why? I've learned that if I do well at the beginning, after a few minutes, I feel confident, I get into the rhythm, and I even relax a bit.

Practicing Your Speech

One of the best ways to become an effective public speaker is to practice. Once your outline is complete, stand up and speak as if you were in front of an audience. Then do this as many times as necessary to ensure that you are familiar with your speech and feel comfortable delivering it.

As we noted earlier, practicing can help you overcome nervousness and meet time requirements. Practice can also help you project natural nonverbal gestures. Typically, the more familiar and comfortable you are with your speech, the more natural will be your gestures, and your goal in extemporaneous speaking is to gesture as you would in conversation. Thus, when you present your speech to friends or family members, ask them to comment on your gestures and movement as well as your content. Often new speakers engage in unconscious, repetitive movements, such as rocking back and forth or fiddling with their hair, and they need someone to make them aware of this fact.

By practicing, you also can focus on your signposting, your speech rate, and your eye contact. In other words, you can work on projecting the type of public persona you desire. Each time you practice your speech, you can focus on a different aspect—one time your gestures; one time the content; and so on—until you feel comfortable with the persona and style you have developed. See *It Happened to Me: Tamara* to learn how one speaker approaches pratice.

Practice, pratice, practice.

Although you may practice your speech many times, your goal is not to memorize it. A memorized speech often sounds memorized, like a recording rather than a real human being. In addition, if you work strictly from memory and you stumble over a word or phrase, you may lose your place and find it difficult to resume your presentation. Instead, during practice, focus on delivering a presentation that is enthusiastic, vibrant, and engaging. Each time you practice, you may come out with different phrasing, different wording, different movements, and so on. When you give your speech, yet another version may appear, but this time, it will likely be a version that you are comfortable presenting. In sum, the public speaking process involves a lot of preparation and practice. We hope that these guidelines will help you become a better speaker.

SUMMARY

The foundations of public speaking include anticipating your presentation, understanding the communication event, understanding audiences, developing your topic, organizing your presentation, and finally, delivering your speech. In anticipating your presentation, you should work on being an ethical public speaker and overcoming unnecessary speech anxiety.

One important lesson of our discussion is that you must understand the larger context for your speech. To do so, understand why you are speaking in public—the general and specific purposes of the event—and identify your audience. You can understand and know your audience by analyzing their demographic characteristics and expectations as well as by examining your relationship to them.

In constructing your speech, you first need to narrow your speech topic, identify a thesis statement, and find your supporting materials. You can then choose an organizational pattern, create an outline for your presentation, and develop an introduction, conclusion, and signposts. After constructing your speech, you are ready to work on delivering it. This involves selecting a style for your presentation, incorporating your visual aids, being aware of time constraints, developing a speaking persona, and practicing (and practicing, and practicing).

KEY TERMS

special-occasion speeches 391
general purpose 391
specific purpose 392
audience analysis 392
open-ended questions 393
closed questions 393
secondary questions 393
neutral questions 393
demographic analysis 393

thesis statement 395
supporting materials 396
chronological pattern 399
spatial pattern 399
topical pattern 399
problem–solution pattern 399
cause–effect pattern 400
introduction 403
signposts 403

conclusion 404
style 405
visual aids 406
impromptu speech 409
manuscript speech 409
extemporaneous speech 409
eye contact 410

TEST YOUR KNOWLEDGE

1. Why is feeling apprehensive about speaking in public a normal reaction?

2. Identify three general purposes in speaking. How is the general purpose different from the specific purpose? Provide some examples.

3. What elements are included in a speech outline?

4. What are some benefits and potential drawbacks of using visual aids?

5. What elements go into a strong introduction and conclusion?

APPLY WHAT YOU KNOW

1. **Research the characteristics of a particular kind of speech.**
Ask your family and friends what they might expect from a speaker who is giving a eulogy, a graduation speech, or a retirement speech. How long would they expect the presentation to be? What level of formality do they expect? Do the people you ask differ in their opinions? What did you learn from this exercise?

Compile your findings in a presentation to your class, following the steps outlined in this chapter.

2. **Learn about techniques for dealing with communication apprehension.**
Talk to some people who frequently speak in public. Ask them for ideas on dealing with nervousness or fears about speaking. Do some library research, to see

what communication researchers have found about communication apprehension. Identify some techniques that will help you deal with communication apprehension. List the techniques that you learned from doing this research.

3. **Watch a videotape of someone you consider to be a good speaker.**
Possibilities include Barack Obama, Oprah Winfrey, Ken Burns, Alec Baldwin, Pat Schroeder, or Helen Thomas. Analyze the speech, the style, and the delivery. How do your favorite speakers organize their speeches? Do they project a particular persona or use a particular style? Take notes as you watch them and compile your notes into a report that identifies some public-speaking skills that you would like to incorporate.

4. **Research some ways that public speaking functions in other cultures.**
How might culture influence how we speak in public?

EXPLORE

1. You must make choices if you decide to use visual aids in a presentation. The government of Canada has put together a discussion on the advantages and disadvantages of using various types of visual aids in *Speaking globally: An exporter's guide to effective presentations* located at: www.canadabusiness.ca/servlet/ BlobServer?blobcol=urldata&blobheader= application/pdf&blobkey=id&blobtable= MungoBlobs&blobwhere=1189794426842. Take a look at Chapter 3. Based on the information provided here, which visual aids would you try in your next presentation? Why?

2. Go to the Americn Rhetoric site at www.americanrhetoric.com/ Listen to the various speaking styles available. Then decide which ones you like and which you dislike. Which qualities attract you? How might knowing what you like and don't like help you in your public speaking?

Glossary

absolute pertaining to the belief that there is a single correct moral standard that holds for everyone, everywhere, every time

active agents seekers of various media messages and resisters of others

adaptors gestures used to manage emotions

affective exchange stage in which people increase the breadth, depth, and frequency of their self-disclosure

age identity a combination of self-perception of age along with what others understand that age to mean

agenda-setting capacity the power of media coverage to influence individuals' view of the world

analog information that is transmitted in a continuous numerical format

analysis paralysis potential pitfall in small group interaction; occurs when excessive analysis prevents a group from moving toward a solution

anticipatory socialization activities and experiences that occur before an individual enters an organization but that later assist in the assimilation process

artifacts clothing and other accessories

artistic proofs artistic skills of a rhetor that influence effectiveness

assertiveness expressing one's opinions forcefully without offending others

assimilation the communicative, behavioral, and cognitive processes that influence individuals to join, identify with, become integrated into, and (occasionally) exit an organization

asynchronicity occurs when a message is sent and received at different times

attractiveness the appeal one person has for another, based on physical appearance, personalities, and/or behavior

attribution theory explanation of the processes we use to judge our own and others' behavior

attributional bias the tendency to attribute one's own negative behavior to external causes and one's positive actions to internal states

audience analysis the process of determining what an audience already knows or wants to know about a topic, who they are, what they know or need to know about the speaker, and what their expectations might be for the presentation

authoritarian leader leader who takes charge, makes all the decisions, and dictates strategies and work tasks

autonomy/connection a dialectical tension in relationships that refers to one's need to connect with others and the simultaneous need to feel independent or autonomous

avatar a computer user's representation of himself/herself or alter ego

avoiding stage of romantic relational dissolution in which couples try not to interact with each other

behaviorism the focus on the study of behavior as a science

blogs short for Web logs; a Web site, like a journal, maintained by an individual with regular entries of commentary, descriptions of events, or other material such as graphics or video

bonding stage of romantic relational development characterized by public commitment

border dwellers people who live between cultures and often experience contradictory cultural patterns

brainstorm to generate as many ideas as possible without critiquing them

bullying repeated hostile behaviors that are or appear to be intended to harm parties unable to defend themselves

burnout a chronic condition that results from the accumulation of daily stress, which manifests itself in a very specific set of characteristics, including exhaustion, cynicism, and ineffectiveness

categorization a cognitive process used to organize information by placing it into larger groupings of information

cause–effect pattern one used to create understanding and agreement, and sometimes to argue for a specific action

change/predictability a dialectical tension in relationships that describes the human desire for events that are new, spontaneous, and unplanned while simultaneously needing some aspects of life to be stable and predictable

channel the means through which a message is transmitted

charismatic leadership a leadership style in which extremely self-confident leaders inspire unusual dedication to themselves by relying upon their strong personalities and charm

chronemics the study of the way people use time as a message

chronological pattern one that follows a timeline

circumscribing stage of romantic relational dissolution in which couples discuss safe topics

closed questions questions that are answerable in a few words

cocultural group a significant minority group within a dominant majority that does not share dominant group values or communication patterns

cocultural theory explores the role of power in daily interactions

cognitive complexity the degree to which a person's constructs are detailed, involved, or numerous

cognitive representation the ability to form mental models of the world

cohort effect the influence of shared characteristics of a group that was born and reared in the same general period

collectivistic orientation a value orientation that stresses the needs of the group

communicating information using nonverbal behaviors to help clarify verbal messages and reveal attitudes and moods

communication ethics the standards of right and wrong that one applies to messages that are sent and received

computer-mediated communication (CMC) the exchange of messages carried through an intervening system of digital electronic storage and transmitted between two or more people

conclusion closing material of a speech where the speaker reviews the main points, may challenge the audience to act, and leaves the audience with a positive view of speaker and topic

confirming communication comments that validate positive self-images of others

congruent verbal and nonverbal messages that express the same meaning

connotative meaning the affective or interpretive meanings attached to a word

constructive marginal people people who thrive in a border-dweller life, while recognizing its tremendous challenges

constructs categories people develop to help them organize information

content analysis approach to understanding media that focuses on specific aspect of the content of a text or group of texts

content meaning the concrete meaning of the message, and the meanings suggested by or associated with the message and the emotions triggered by it

contingent employees individuals who work in temporary positions, part-time or as subcontractors

contradicting verbal and nonverbal messages that send conflicting messages

critical approach an approach used not only to understand human behavior but ultimately to change society

cultivation theory idea that long-term immersion in a media environment leads to "cultivation," or enculturation, into shared beliefs about the world

cultural capital cultural knowledge and cultural competencies that people need to function effectively in society

cultural values beliefs that are so central to a cultural group that they are never questioned

culture learned patterns of perceptions, values, and behaviors shared by a group of people

culture industries large organizations in the business of mass communication that produce, distribute, or show various media texts (cultural products) as an industry

culture shock a feeling of disorientation and discomfort due to the lack of familiar environmental cues

cyberspace synonymous with the Internet or online world

deception concealment, distortion, or lying in communication

decision-making process the four-phase process used by a group to evaluate information and arrive at a decision or solution

decoding receiving a message and interpreting its meaning

deliberative rhetoric the type of rhetoric used to argue what a society should do in the future

demand touching a type of touch used to establish dominance and power

democratic leader leader whose style is characterized by considerable input from group members

demographic analysis the portion of an audience analysis that considers the ages, races, sexes, sexual orientations, religions, and social class of the audience

denotative meaning the dictionary, or literal, meaning of a word

dialect a variation of a language distinguished by its vocabulary, grammar, and pronunciation

dialectic approach recognizes that things need not be perceived as either/or, but may be seen as both/and

dichotomous thinking thinking in which things are perceived as "either/or"—for example, good or bad, big or small, right or wrong

differentiating stage of romantic relational dissolution in which couples increase their interpersonal distance

diffusion of innovations theory that explains why some innovations, like computers and Internet technology, are accepted by some people and rejected by others

digital information that is transmitted in a numerical format based on only two values (0 and 1)

disconfirming communication comments that reject or invalidate a positive or negative self-image of our conversational partners

disqualification communication acts that attempt to deny others the right to speak based on their positions or identities

downward communication in a traditional conduit model of communication, communication with subordinates

Ebonics a version of English that has its roots in West African, Caribbean, and U.S. slave languages

e-books electronic books read on a computer screen instead of a printed page

economic production role organizational role in which the delivery of products or services maximizes profit

ego-defensive function the role prejudice plays in protecting individuals' sense of self-worth

elocution the mechanics of public speaking, including proper pronunciation, posture, and grammar

emblems gestures that stand for a specific verbal meaning

emergence phase the third phase of the decision-making process; occurs when group members express a cooperative attitude

emoticons pictographs used in email to convey relational information

empowerment employees' feelings of self-efficacy

enacting identities performing scripts deemed proper for particular identities

encapsulated marginal people people who feel disintegrated by having to shift cultures

encoding taking ideas and converting them into messages

encounter stage stage in the assimilation process during which individuals learn the norms, expectations, and practices of the organization and begin to accept and adapt to them

Enlightenment eighteenth-century belief that science and reason are the pathways to human knowledge

establishing social control using nonverbal behavior to exercise influence over other people

ethics standards of what is right and wrong, good and bad, moral and immoral

ethnic identity identification with a particular group with which one shares some or all of these characteristics: national or tribal affiliation, religious beliefs, language, and/or cultural and traditional origins and background

ethnocentrism the tendency to view one's own group as the standard against which all other groups are judged

ethnographic relating to studies in which researchers actively engage with participants

ethos credibility

evaluating assessing your reaction to a message

experimenting stage of romantic relational development in which both people seek to learn about each other

exploratory affective exchange stage in which people increase the breadth of their communication

expressing and managing intimacy using nonverbal behaviors to help convey attraction and closeness

expressiveness/privacy a dialectical tension in relationships that describes the need to be open and to self-disclose while also maintaining some sense of privacy

extemporaneous speech speech that is written ahead of time but only in outline form

eye contact looking directly into the eyes of another

feedback the response to a message

field of availables potential partners and friends, typically much larger via CMC than via face-to-face relationships

field of experience the education, life events, and cultural background that a communicator possesses

forensic rhetoric rhetoric that addresses events that happened in the past with the goal of setting things right after an injustice has occurred

formal structure officially designated channels of communication, reflecting explicit or desired patterns of interaction

frame a structure that shapes how people interpret their perceptions

friendship touch touch that is more intimate than social touch and usually conveys warmth, closeness, and caring

function the goals and effects of communication

functional (situational) theory a theory that assumes leadership behaviors can be learned

functional touch the least intimate type of touch; used by certain workers such as dentists, hairstylists, and hospice workers, as part of their livelihood; also known as *professional touch*

fundamental attribution error the tendency to attribute others' negative behavior to internal causes and their positive behaviors to external causes

gender identity how and to what extent one identifies with the social construction of masculinity and femininity

general purpose whichever of three goals—to inform, persuade, or entertain—dominates a speech

general systems theory theory that organizations are a system composed of many subsystems and embedded in larger systems, and that organizations should develop communication strategies that serve both

generalized other the collection of roles, rules, norms, beliefs, and attitudes endorsed by the community in which a person lives

gestures nonverbal communication made with part of the body, including actions such as pointing, waving, or holding up a hand to direct people's attention

globalization the increasing connectedness of the world in economic, political, and cultural realms

group processes the methods, including communication, by which a group accomplishes a task

group roles the shared expectations group members have regarding each individual's communication behavior in the group

grouphate the distaste and aversion that people feel toward working in groups

groupthink a negative, and potentially disastrous, group process characterized by "excessive concurrence thinking"

haptics the study of the communicative function of touch

Hays Code self-imposed rules for Hollywood media content instituted in 1930 with the goal of creating "wholesome entertainment"

healthy feedback the honest and ethical responses receivers provide to the messages of others

hegemony the process by which we consent to social constructions, rather than having them imposed on us

heterogeneous diverse

heuristic use of language to acquire knowledge and understanding

hierarchy a power structure in which some members exercise authority over others

homogeneity a high degree of similarity

horizontal communication in a traditional conduit model of communication, communication with peers

hostile work environment an intimidating, hostile, or offensive workplace atmosphere created by unwelcome and inappropriate sexually based behavior; one of two types of sexual harassment recognized by federal law

human communication a process in which people generate meaning through the exchange of verbal and nonverbal messages

human–nature value orientation the perceived relationship between humans and nature

human relations approach to management that holds that the job of management is actually to educate, interact, and integrate

human resources approach to management that holds that workers are not only economically motivated but that they also bring personal histories and emotional needs to work with them

humanism a system of thought that celebrates human nature and its potential

hyperpersonal relationships Internet relationships that develop intimacy more quickly than face-to-face relationships

iconic signs signs that represent a thing itself and always bear some resemblance to the object to which they refer

identity who a person is; composed of individual and social categories a person identifies with, as well as the categories that others identify with that person

illustrators signals that accompany speech to clarify or emphasize the verbal messages

imaginative use of language to express oneself artistically or creatively

immediacy how close or involved people appear to be with each other

impromptu speech speech that is delivered with little or no preparation

indexical signs signs that reveal something beyond the thing itself

individual roles roles that focus more on individuals' own interests and needs than on those of the group

individualist orientation a value orientation that respects the autonomy and independence of individuals

informal structure unspoken but understood channels of communication, reflecting patterns that develop spontaneously

informative use of language to communicate information or report facts

ingratiation behavior and communication designed to increase liking

initiating stage of romantic relational development in which both people behave so as to appear pleasant and likeable

innovation a function of organizational communication by means of which systems are changed

instrumental use of language to obtain what you need or desire

integrating stage of romantic relational development in which both people portray themselves as a couple

integration role organizational function in which potentially chaotic social conflicts or problems are managed

intensifying stage of romantic relational development in which both people seek to increase intimacy and connectedness

interactional use of language to establish and define social relationships

intercultural communication communication that occurs in interactions between people who are culturally different

Internet a system of networks that connects millions of computers around the world

interpersonal violence physical violence against a partner or child

interpretation the act of assigning meaning to sensory information

interpretive approach contemporary term for humanistic (rhetorical) study

intimate distance (0 to 18 inches) the space used when interacting with those with whom one is very close

introduction opening material of a speech from which the audience members gain a first impression of the speech's content and of the speaker

involuntary long-term travelers people who are border dwellers permanently but not by choice, such as those who relocate to escape war

involuntary short-term travelers people who are border dwellers not by choice and only for a limited time, such as refugees forced to move

jargon the specialized terms that develop in many professions

jealousy a complex and often painful emotion that occurs when a person perceives a threat to an existing relationship

kinesics nonverbal communication sent by the body, including gestures, posture, movement, facial expressions, and eye behavior

Knapp's stage model model of relationship development that views relationships as occurring in "stages" and that focuses on how people communicate as relationships develop and decline

label a name assigned to a category based on one's perception of the category

laissez-faire a leadership style characterized by complete freedom for the group in making decisions

lexical choice vocabulary

linear model portrayal of communication as a process occurring largely in one direction

logos rational appeals; the use of rhetoric to help the audience see the rationale for a particular conclusion

long-term orientation a value orientation in which people stress the importance of virtue

long-term versus short-term orientation the dimension of a society's value orientation that reflects its attitude toward virtue or truth

looking-glass self the idea that self-image results from the images others reflect back to an individual

love-intimate touch the touch most often used with one's romantic partners and family

Machiavellian tactics having a third party convey one's unhappiness about a relationship

maintenance a function of organizational communication in which the stability of existing systems is preserved

manuscript speech speech that is written out word-for-word and read to the audience

mass-market paperbacks popular books addressed to a large audience and widely distributed

mass media effects the influence that media have on people's everyday lives

matching hypothesis the tendency to develop relationships with people who are approximately as attractive as we are

meaning denial the refusal to acknowledge the intended meaning of a message

media the plural form of *medium*, a channel of communication

media activism the practice of organizing to communicate displeasure with certain media images and messages, as well as to force change in future media texts

media augmentation approach a theoretical perspective that views mediated communication as complementing or augmenting face-to-face communication

media deficit approach a theoretical perspective that sees mediated communication as deficient, in comparison to face-to-face communication

media event occasions or catastrophes that interrupt regular programming

media richness the potential information-carrying capacity of a communication medium

media text a television show, advertisement, movie, or other media event

media violence representations of violent acts in media

mediation peaceful third-party intervention

message creation transmitting ideas and emotions via signs and symbols

messages the building blocks of communication events

metamorphosis the final stage of the socialization process during which employees come to see themselves as members of the organization, and colleagues see them this way as well

methodology an accepted set of methods for developing new knowledge about a subject

methods the specific ways that scholars collect and analyze data which they then use to prove or disprove their theories

modernism the belief that through rational thinking, humans can advance and discover universal truth

monochronically engaging in one task or behavior at a time

monotheistic belief in one god

motivation feeling personally invested in accomplishing a specific activity or goal

MPAA Motion Picture Association of America

multiracial identity one who self-identifies as having more than one racial identity

mutable subject to change

national identity a person's citizenship

naturalistic relating to everyday, real-life situations, such as a classroom, café, or shopping mall

neutral questions questions that give the person being questioned a chance to respond without any influence from the interviewer

new media refers to the new communication technologies of the late twentieth century and early twenty-first century

new social contract assumes that loyalty is not expected by workers or organizations and that job security is unlikely

noise any stimulus that can interfere with, or degrade, the quality of a message

nominalists those who argue that any idea can be expressed in any language and that the structure and vocabulary of the language do not influence the speaker's perception of the world

nonverbal behavior all the nonverbal actions people perform

nonverbal codes distinct, organized means of expression that consists of symbols and rules for their use

nonverbal communication nonverbal behavior that has symbolic meaning

open-ended questions questions that give the person being questioned free rein in answering

openness a state in which communicators are willing to share their ideas as well as listen to others in a way that avoids conveying negative or disconfirming feedback

orator a public speaker

organization the process by which one recognizes what sensory input represents

organizational culture a pattern of shared beliefs, values, and behaviors

organizational identification the stage of assimilation that occurs when an employee's values overlap with the organization's values

organizations the set of interactions that members of groups use to accomplish their individual and common goals

orientation the stage in which people first meet and engage in superficial communication

paradigm belief system that represents a particular worldview

paralinguistics all aspects of spoken language except the words themselves; includes rate, volume, pitch, stress

participants the people interacting during communication

particular others the important people in an individual's life whose opinions and behavior influence the various aspects of identity

passing away the process by which relationships decline over time

pathos the rhetorical use of emotions to affect audience decision making

pattern maintenance role organizational role in which learning and expressive functions are performed, while also establishing and perpetuating social and cultural norms

perceptual co-orientation a state in which two people share similar perceptions and recognize that their perceptions agree

performance of identity the process or means by which we show the world who we think we are

persona the identity one creates through one's public communication efforts

personal distance (18 inches to 4 feet) the space used when interacting with friends and acquaintances

personal language use of language to express individuality and personality

phishing email messages that try (fraudulently) to get consumer banking and credit card information

phonology the study of the sounds that compose individual languages and how those sounds communicate meaning

planning the sequence of actions one develops to attain particular goals

political economy the ways in which media institutions produce texts in a capitalist system and the legal and regulatory frameworks that shape their options for doing so

political role organizational function in which valued resources and, thus, power are generated and distributed

polychronically engaging in multiple activities simultaneously

polytheistic belief in more than one god

postmodern approach an approach in which reality is subjective, and power is an important issue

postmodernism a broad intellectual and social movement of the late twentieth century

power distance a value orientation that refers to the extent to which less powerful members of institutions and organizations within a culture expect and accept an unequal distribution of power

pragmatics field of study that emphasizes how language is used in specific situations to accomplish goals

preferred personality a value orientation that expresses whether it is more important for a person to "do" or to "be"

prejudice experiencing aversive or negative feelings toward a group as a whole or toward an individual because she or he belongs to a group

primary groups groups that provide members with a sense of belonging and affection

primary tension the uncertainty commonly felt in the beginning phase of decision making

problem–solution pattern one in which the speaker describes various aspects of a problem and then proposes solutions

production a function of organizational communication in which activity is coordinated toward accomplishing tasks

professional touch type of touch used by certain workers, such as dentists, hairstylists, and hospice workers, as part of their livelihood; also known as *functional touch*

prototype an idealized schema

proxemics the study of how people use spatial cues, including interpersonal distance, territoriality, and other space relationships, to communicate

proximity how close one is to others

pseudoanonymity projecting a false identity

public distance (12 to 25 feet) the distance used for public ceremonies such as lectures and performances

public sphere the arena in which deliberative decision making occurs through the exchange of ideas and arguments

qualitative methods methods in which researchers study naturally occurring communication rather than assembling data and converting it to numbers

quantitative methods methods that convert data to numerical indicators, and then analyze these numbers using statistics to establish relationships among the concepts

quid pro quo requests for sexual favors as a condition of getting or keeping a job or benefit; one of two types of sexual harassment recognized by federal law

racial identity identification with a particular racial group

rationality the ability to communicate through reasoning, bargaining, coalition building, and assertiveness

reasoned skepticism the balance of open-mindedness and critical attitude needed when evaluating others' messages

reflected appraisals the idea that people's self-images arise primarily from the ways that others view them and from the many messages they have received from others about who they are

regulating interaction using nonverbal behaviors to help manage turn-taking during conversation

regulators gestures used to control conversation

regulatory use of language to control or regulate the behaviors of others

reinforcement phase the final phase of the decision-making process when group members reach consensus, and members feel a sense of accomplishment

relational maintenance behaviors that couples perform that help maintain their relationships

relational roles roles that help establish a group's social atmosphere

relational trajectory models relationship development models that view relationship development as more variable than do stage models

relationship meaning what a message conveys about the relationship between the parties

relative pertaining to the belief that moral behavior varies among individuals, groups, and cultures, and across situations

relativists those who argue that language serves not only as a way for us to voice our ideas but "is itself the shaper of ideas, the guide for the individual's mental activity"

relaxation the degree of tension displayed by one's body

religious identity aspect of identity defined by one's spiritual beliefs

Renaissance an era of tremendous intellectual, artistic, and scientific achievements in Europe spanning the fourteenth to the seventeenth centuries

responding showing others how you regard their message

reverse culture shock/reentry shock culture shock experienced by travelers upon returning to their home country

rhetor a person or institution that addresses a large audience; the originator of a communication message but not necessarily the one delivering it

rhetoric communication that is used to influence the attitudes or behaviors of others; the art of persuasion

rhetorical analysis used by researchers to examine texts or public speeches as they occur in society with the aim of interpreting textual meaning

rhetorical audience those people who can take the appropriate action in response to a message

rhetorical critic an informed consumer of rhetorical discourse who is prepared to analyze rhetorical texts

rhetorical event any event that generates a significant amount of public discourse

role expectations the expectation that one will perform in a particular way because of the social role occupied

Sapir-Whorf hypothesis idea that the language people speak determines the way they see the world (a relativist perspective)

schema cognitive structure that represents an individual's understanding of a concept or person

scientific management approach to management advocated by Frederick Taylor, who believed there was a best way to complete any task and that rigorous study would help him find it

script a relatively fixed sequence of events that functions as a guide or template for communication or behavior

secondary groups groups that meet principally to solve problems

secondary questions questions that follow up on a previous question

secondary (recurring) tension conflict or tension found in the second or conflict phase of the decision-making process

selection the process of choosing which sensory information to focus on

selective attention consciously or unconsciously attending to just a narrow range of the full array of sensory information available

selective exposure the idea that people seek media messages and/or interpret media texts in ways that confirm their beliefs and, conversely, resist or avoid messages that challenge their beliefs

self-concept the understanding of one's unique characteristics as well as the similarities to, and differences from, others

self-esteem part of one's self-concept; arises out of how one perceives and interprets reflected appraisals and social comparisons

self-fulfilling prophecy when an individual expects something to occur, the expectation increases the likelihood that it will

self-respect treating others, and expecting to be treated, with respect and dignity

self-serving bias the tendency to give one's self more credit than is due when good things happen and to accept too little responsibility for those things that go wrong

semantic-information distance describes the gap in information and understanding between supervisors and subordinates on specific issues

semantics the study of meaning

sensing the stage of listening most people refer to as "hearing"; when listeners pick up the sound waves directed toward them

servant leadership a leadership style that seeks to ensure that other people's highest priority needs are being served in order to increase teamwork and personal involvement

service-task functions using nonverbal behavior to signal close involvement between people in impersonal relationships and contexts

setting the physical surroundings of a communication event

sexual coercion physically nonviolent pressure to engage in unwanted sex

sexual identity which of the various categories of sexuality one identifies with

shared (collaborative or distributed) leadership a type of leadership style where functional leadership is extended to an organizational level; all members are equal partners and share responsibility for the work of the group

short-term orientation a value orientation that stresses the importance of possessing one fundamental truth

signposts transitions in a speech that help an audience understand the speaker's organization, making it easier for them to follow

similarity degree to which people share the same values, interests, and background

small group communication communication among a small number of people who share a common purpose or goal, who feel connected to each other, and who coordinate their behavior

social class identity an informal ranking of people in a culture based on their income, occupation, education, dwelling, child-rearing habits, and other factors

social distance (4 to 12 feet) the distance most U.S. Americans use when they interact with unfamiliar others

social facilitation the tendency for people to work harder and do better when others are around

social movement a large, organized body of people who are attempting to create social change

social networking site (SNS) a Web site where one user can publish information about himself or herself for the purpose of connecting with others and sharing personal or professional interests

social penetration theory a theory that proposes relationships develop through increases in self-disclosure

social-polite touch touch that is part of daily interaction in the United States; it is more intimate than professional touch but is still impersonal

social position place in the social hierarchy, which comes from the way society is structured

social presence degree of psychological closeness or immediacy engendered by various media

social role the specific position or positions one holds in a society

social science approach contemporary term for the behaviorist approach

societal role social function

sophists the people who taught persuasive speaking skills in the Greek city-states

spam unwanted commercial messages and advertisements sent through email

spatial pattern one that arranges points by location and can be used to describe something small

special-occasion speeches evocative speeches intended to entertain, inspire, celebrate, commemorate, or build community

specific purpose what a speaker wants to inform or persuade an audience about, or the type of feelings the speaker wants to evoke

speech act theory branch of pragmatics that suggests that when people communicate, they do not just say things, they also do things with their words

spoofing misrepresenting oneself online

stable exchange stage in which relational partners engage in the greatest breadth and depth of self-disclosure

stagnating stage of romantic relational dissolution in which couples try to prevent change

stereotype threat process in which reminding individuals of stereotypical expectations regarding important identities can impact their performance

stereotyping creating schemas that overgeneralize attributes of a specific group

structure lines of communication, or a system of pathways, through which messages flow

style the type of language and phrasing a speaker uses and the effect the language and phrasing create

style theory theory that asserts that a leader's manner or style determines his or her success

sudden death the process by which relationships end without prior warning for at least one participant

supporting materials information that supports the speaker's ideas

supportiveness refers to supervisors who provide their subordinates with access to information and resources

symbol something that represents something else and conveys meaning

syntax the rules that govern word order

task roles roles that are directly related to the accomplishment of group goals

technocapital access to technological skills and resources

terminating stage of romantic relational dissolution in which couples end the relationship

textual analysis similar to rhetorical analysis; used to analyze cultural "products," such as media and public speeches

theory a set of statements that explains a particular phenomenon

thesis statement a statement of the topic of a speech and the speaker's position on it

time and motion studies repeated measurements of detailed task variables to determine their most efficient combination

topical pattern one that has no innate organization except that imposed by the speaker

trait theory leadership theory that suggests that leaders are born

transformational leadership a leadership style that empowers group members to work independently from the leader by encouraging group cohesion

truth bias the tendency to not suspect one's intimates of deception

turning point model a model of relationship development in which couples move both toward and away from commitment over the course of their relationship

TV Parental Guidelines a self-regulating system of the television industry that rates programs in terms of appropriateness for particular age groups

tweets text-based updates, 140 characters or less sent through social networking and microblogging services

uncertainty reduction theory theory that argues that much early interaction is dedicated to reducing uncertainty about others and determining if one wishes to interact with them again

understanding interpreting the messages associated with sounds or what the sounds mean

upward communication in a traditional conduit model of communication, communication with superiors

upward distortion occurs when subordinates are hesitant to communicate negative news and present information to superiors in a more positive light than is warranted

urgent organizations companies that try to shorten the time it takes to develop new products and respond to customer demands

uses and gratifications the idea that people use media messages and find various types of gratifications in some media texts rather than in others

value-expressive function the role played by prejudice in allowing people to view their own values, norms, and cultural practices as appropriate and correct

V-chip device that identifies television program ratings by content and can block programming designated by the owner

view of human nature a value orientation that expresses whether humans are fundamentally good, evil, or a mixture

visual aids audiovisual materials that help a speaker reach intended speech goals

vocalizations uttered sounds that do not have the structure of language

voice qualities qualities such as speed, pitch, rhythm, vocal range, and articulation that make up the "music" of the human voice

voluntary long-term travelers people who are border dwellers by choice and for an extended time, such as immigrants

voluntary short-term travelers people who are border dwellers by choice and for a limited time, such as study-abroad students or corporate personnel

withdrawal/avoidance a friendship termination strategy in which friends spend less time together, don't return phone calls, and avoid places where they are likely to see each other

World Wide Web (WWW) one of a number of services that moves over the Internet; it uses HTML (hypertext markup language) as its document format

References

Chapter 1

Alberts, J. K., Yoshimura, C. G., Rabby, M. K., & Loschiavo, R. (2005). Mapping the topography of couples' daily interaction. *Journal of Social and Personal Relationships, 22,* 299–323.

Andersen, P. A., Lustig, M. W., & Andersen, J. F. (1990). Changes in latitude, changes in attitude: The relationship between climate and interpersonal communication predispositions. *Communication Quarterly, 38,* 291–311.

Barnlund, D. C. (1962). Consistency of emergent leadership in groups with changing tasks and members. *Speech Monographs, 29,* 45–52.

Bavelas, J. B., & Smith, B. J. (1982). A method for scaling verbal disqualification. *Human Communication Research, 8,* 214–227.

BBC News. (1998, December 22). Sex, lies and impeachment. BBC Online. Retrieved March 11, 2009, from http://news.bbc.co.uk/2/hi/special_report/1998/12/98/review_of_98/themes/208715.stm

Berlo, D. K. (1960). *The process of communication.* New York: Holt, Rinehart and Winston.

Brewer, M., & Miller, N. (1996). *Intergroup relations.* Pacific Grove, CA: Brooks/Cole.

Buck, R., & VanLear, C. A. (2002). Verbal and nonverbal communication: Distinguishing symbolic, spontaneous and pseudo-spontaneous nonverbal behavior. *Journal of Communication, 52,* 522–541.

Buller, D. B., & Burgoon, J. K. (1996). Interpersonal deception theory. *Communication Theory, 6,* 203–242.

Bush, G. W. (2002, October 7). President Bush outlines Iraqi threat. Office of the Press Secretary. Retrieved April 1, 2006, from www.informationclearinghouse.info/articles3711.htm

Christians, C., & Traber, M. (Eds.). (1997). *Communication ethics and universal values.* Thousand Oaks, CA: Sage.

Deacon, T. (1997). *The symbolic species: The co-evolution of language and the human brain.* New York: Penguin.

Deetz, S. (1990). Reclaiming the subject matter as a guide to mutual understanding: Effectiveness and ethics in interpersonal interaction. *Communication Quarterly, 38,* 226–243.

Dickens, T. E. (2003). General symbol machines: The first stage in the evolution of symbolic communication. *Evolutionary Psychology, 1,* 192–209.

Diener, M. (2002, January). Fair enough: To be a better negotiator, learn to tell the difference between a lie and a *lie. Entrepreneur Magazine.* Retrieved March 16, 2006, from www.Entrepreneurmagazine.com

Dixon, M., & Duck, S. W. (1993). Understanding relationship processes: Uncovering the human search for meaning. In S. W. Duck (Ed.), *Understanding relationship processes, Vol 1: Individuals in relationships* (pp. 175–206). Newbury Park, CA: Sage.

Drzewiecka, J. A., & Alberts, J. K. (1996, November). Ethnic jokes and intercultural interactions. Paper presented at the Speech Communication Association Convention, San Diego, CA.

Duck, S. (1988). *Relating to others.* Chicago: Dorsey.

Duck, S. (1994). *Meaningful relationships: Talking, sense and relating.* Newbury Park, CA: Sage.

Eisenberg, E. M., & Goodall, H. L., Jr. (1997). *Organizational communication: Balancing creativity and constraints.* New York: St. Martin's.

Emanuel, R. (2007). Humanities: Communication's core discipline. *American Communication Journal, 9*(2). Retrieved March 11, 2009, from www.acjournal.org/holdings/vol9/summer/articles/discipline.html

Gergen, K. J. (1982). *Toward transformation in social knowledge.* New York: Springer.

Heinich, R., Molenda, M., Russell, J., & Smaldino, S. (1996). *Instructional media and technologies for learning.* Columbus: Prentice Hall.

Jaksa, J. A., & Pritchard, M. S. (1994). *Communication ethics: Methods of analysis* (2nd ed.). Belmont, CA: Wadsworth.

Johannesen, R. (1990). *Ethics in human communication.* Prospect Heights, IL: Waveland.

Kant, I. (1949). *Fundamental principles of the metaphysic of morals* (T. K. Abbott, Trans.). Indianapolis: Bobbs-Merrill. (Original work published 1785)

Koreans die saving Kim portraits (2004, April 29). *The Guardian.* Retrieved March 10, 2006, from www.guardian.co.uk/korea/article/0,,1205710,00.html

Kruger, P. (1999, June). A leader's journey. *Fast Company,* 116–138.

Laswell, H. D. (1948). The structure and function of communication in society. In L. Bryson (Ed.), *The Communication of Ideas.* New York: Harper.

Long, R., & Pearson, R. (2009, January 30). Impeached Illinois Govenor Rod Blagojevich has been removed from office. *Chicago Tribune Online.* Retrieved March 11, 2009, from www.chicagotribune.com/news/local/chi-blagojevich-impeachment-removal,0,5791846.story

Mabry, E. A. (2001). Ambiguous self-identification and sincere communication in CMC. In L. Anolli, R. Ciceri, & G. Riva (Eds.), *Say not to say: New perspective on miscommunication* (pp. 254–270). Burke, VA: IOS Press.

Martin, J. N., & Nakayama, T. K. (2005). *Experiencing intercultural communication* (2nd ed.). Boston: McGraw-Hill.

McCabe, D. L., & Trevino, L. K. (1996). What we know about cheating in college: Longitudinal trends and recent developments. *Change, 28,* 28–33.

McCornack, S. A., & Parks, M. R. (1986). Deception detection and relationship development: The other side of trust. In M. L. McLaughlin (Ed.), *Communication Yearbook 9* (pp. 377–389). Newbury Park, CA: Sage. Retrieved March 16, 2006, from www.natcom.org/policies/External/Ethicalcomm

Mead, G. H. (1934). *Mind, self, and society.* Chicago: University of Chicago Press.

National Communication Association (2003). What is communication? *Pathways* [excerpt]. Retrieved October 24, 2008, from www.natcom.org/nca/Template2.asp?bid=339

NCA Credo for Ethical Communication. (2005). National Communication Association. Retrieved March 10, 2006, from www.natcom.org/nca/Template2.asp?bid=514

New World Encyclopedia. (2008). Aaron. Retrieved October 24, 2008, from www.newworldencyclopedia.org/entry/Aaron

Nussbaum, J. F. (1989). *Life-span communication: Normative processes.* Hillsdale, NJ: Erlbaum.

Poole, M. S., & Walther, J. B. (2001). *Report of National Communication Association/National Science Foundation funded symposium.* Retrieved March 11, 2009, from www.natcom.org/nca/Template2.asp?bid=394

Roloff, M. E., & Cloven, D. H. (1990). The chilling effect in interpersonal relationships. In D. D. Cahn (Ed.), *Intimates in conflict* (pp. 49–76). Hillsdale, NJ: Erlbaum.

Sartre, J. P. (1973). *Existentialism and humanism* (P. Mairet, Trans.). London: Methuen Ltd. (Original work published 1946)

Schirato, T., & Yell, S. (1996). *Communication & cultural literacy: An introduction.* St. Leonards, Australia: Allen & Unwin.

Schramm, W. (1954). How communication works. In W. Schramm (Ed.), *The process and effects of mass communication.* Urbana, IL: University of Illinois Press.

Schramm, W. (1971). The nature of communication between humans. In W. Schramm & D. F. Roberts (Eds.), *The process and effects of mass communication* (Rev. ed.). Urbana, IL: University of Illinois Press.

Shannon, C. E., & Weaver, W. (1949). *A mathematical model of communication.* Urbana, IL: University of Illinois Press.

Tolhuizen, J. H. (1990, November). *Deception in developing dating relationships.* Paper presented at the Speech Communication Association Convention, Chicago, IL.

Trumble, W., & Brown, L. (Eds.). (2002). *Shorter Oxford English dictionary.* Oxford, England: Oxford University Press.

Verschoor, C. C. (2005, September). AIG remediation emphasizes compliance but not ethics. *Strategic Finance.* Retrieved March 11, 2009, from www.imanet.org/pdf/3291.pdf

Warren, S. F., & Yoder, P. J. (1998). Facilitating the transition from preintentional to intentional communication. In A. M. Wetherby, S. F. Warren, & J. Reichle (Eds.), *Transitions in prelinguistic communication* (pp. 365–385). Baltimore, MD: Paul H. Brookes.

Watzlawick, P., Beavin, J., & Jackson, D. D. (1967). *Pragmatics of human communication.* New York: W. W. Norton.

Westen, D. (2007). *The political brain: The role of emotion in deciding the fate of the nation.* NY: PublicAffairs.

Wokutch, R. E., & Carson, T. L. (1981). The ethics and profitability of bluffing in business. In R. J. Lewick, D. M. Saunders, & J. M. Minton (Eds.), *Negotiation: Readings, exercises, and cases* (pp. 341–353). Boston: Irwin/McGraw-Hill.

Chapter 2

Alberts, J. K. (1988). An analysis of couples' conversational complaint interactions. *Communication Monographs, 5,* 184–197.

Alcoff, L. (Winter 1991–1992). The problem of speaking for others. *Cultural Critique, 20,* 5–32.

Argyle, M. (1969). *Social interaction.* New York: Lieber-Atherton.

Barnlund, D. (1968). *Interpersonal communication: Surveys and studies.* Boston: Houghton Mifflin.

Berger, C. R., & Calabrese, R. J. (1975). Some explorations in initial interaction and beyond: Toward a developmental theory of interpersonal communication. *Human Communication Theory, 1,* 99–112.

Berger, C. R., & Gudykunst, W. B. (1991). Uncertainty and communication. In B. Dervin & M. Voight (Eds.), *Progress in communication sciences* (pp. 21–67). Norwood, NJ: Ablex.

Bernal, M. (1987). *Black Athena denied: The Afroasiatic roots of classical civilization.* Vols. 1–2. New Brunswick, NJ: Rutgers University Press.

Borda, J. L. (2002). The woman suffrage parades of 1910–1913: Possibilities and limitations of an early feminist rhetorical strategy. *Western Journal of Communication 66,* 25–52.

Bormann, E. G. (1980). *Communication theory.* New York: Holt, Rinehart and Winston.

Brookey, R. A. (2001). Bio-rhetoric, background beliefs and the biology of homosexuality. *Argumentation and Advocacy, 37,* 171–183.

Burrell, G., & Morgan, G. (1988). *Sociological paradigms and organizational analysis.* Portsmouth, NH: Heinemann.

Calafell, B. M., & Delgado, F. P. (2004). Reading Latina/o images: Interrogating Americanos. *Critical Studies in Media Communication, 21,* 1–21.

Campbell, K. K. (1994). *Women public speakers in the United States, 1925–1993: A bio-critical sourcebook.* Westport, CT: Greenwood.

Carbaugh, D. (1990). Communication rules in Donahue discourse. In D. Carbaugh (Ed.), Cultural communication and intercultural contact (pp. 119–149). Hillsdale, NJ: Lawrence Erlbaum.

Carbaugh, D. (1999). "Just listen": "Listening" and landscape among the Blackfeet. *Western Journal of Communication, 63,* 250–270.

Carbaugh, D., & Berry, M. (2001). Communicating history, Finnish and American discourses: An ethnographic contribution to intercultural communication inquiry. *Communication Theory, 11,* 352–366.

Cloud, D. L. (1998). The rhetoric of family values: Scapegoating, utopia, and the privatization of social responsibility. *Western Journal of Communication, 62,* 387–419.

Cloud, D. L. (2003). Beyond evil: Understanding power materially and rhetorically. *Rhetoric and Public Affairs. 6,* 531–538.

Cody, M., Murphy, S., & Glik, D. (2007, May). *Affective and behavioral reactions of "accident" vs. "terrorist" framing of disaster.* Paper presented to the annual meeting of the International Communication Association, Montreal, Canada.

Cohen, H. (1994). *The history of speech communication: The emergence of a discipline, 1914–1945.* Annandale, VA: Speech Communication Association.

Cragan, J. F., & Shields, D. C. (1998). *Understanding communication theory: The communicative forces for human action.* Boston, MA: Allyn & Bacon.

Craig, R. T. (1999). Communication theory as a field. *Communication Theory, 9,* 119–161.

Crowley, S., & Hawhee, D. (1999). *Ancient rhetorics for contemporary students* (2nd ed.). Boston, MA: Allyn & Bacon.

Dow, B. J. (2004). Fixing feminism: Women's liberation and the rhetoric of television documentary. *Quarterly Journal of Speech, 90,* 53–80.

Downing, J. R. (2004). American Airlines use of mediated employee channels after the 9/11 attacks. *Public Relations Review, 30,* 37–48.

Dues, M., & Brown, M. (2004). *Boxing Plato's shadow: An introduction to the study of human communication.* Boston: McGraw Hill.

Gergen, K. (1991). *The saturated self: Dilemmas of identity in contemporary life.* New York: HarperCollins Basic Books.

González, M. C. (2000). The four seasons of ethnography: A creation centered ontology for ethnography. *International Journal of Intercultural Relations, 24,* 525–539.

Graham, P., Keenan, T., & Dowd, A. M. (2004). A call to arms at the end of history: A discourse-historical analysis of George W. Bush's declaration of war on terror. *Discourse and Society. 15* (2/3, March/May), 199–221.

Gunn, J. (2004). The rhetoric of exorcism: George W. Bush and the return of political demonology. *Western Journal of Communication, 68,* 1–23.

Hasian, M. A., Jr., & Parry-Giles, T. (1997). "A Stranger to Its Laws": Freedom, civil rights, and the legal ambiguity of Romer v. Evans (1996). *Argumentation & Advocacy, 34,* 27–42.

Herrick, J. A. (2001). *The history and theory of rhetoric: An introduction.* Boston: Allyn & Bacon.

Hovland, C., Janis, I., & Kelly, H. (1953). *Communication and persuasion.* New Haven, CT: Yale University Press.

Hovland, C., & Weiss, W. (1951). The influence of source credibility on communication effectiveness. *Public Opinion Quarterly, 15,* 635–650.

Infante, D. A., Rancer, A. S., & Womack, D. E. (1990). *Building communication theory.* Prospect Heights, IL: Waveland.

Ivie, R. L. (1987). Metaphor and the rhetorical invention of cold war "idealists." *Communication Monographs, 54,* 165–182.

Kerber, L. K. (1997). *Toward an intellectual history of women: Essays by Linda K. Kerber.* Chapel Hill, NC: University of North Carolina Press.

Khan, M. Y. (2007). "Shaking up" vision: The video diary as personal and pedagogical intervention in Mona Hatoum's measures of distance. *Intercultural Education. 18*(4), 317–334.

Knapp, M. L., Daly, J. A., Albada, K. F., & Miller, G. R. (2002). Background and current trends in the study of interpersonal communication. In M. L. Knapp & J. A. Daly (Eds.), *Handbook of interpersonal communication* (pp. 1–20). Thousand Oaks, CA: Sage Publications.

Kraybill, D. B. (1989). *The riddle of Amish culture.* Baltimore: Johns Hopkins University Press.

Laswell, H. D. (1948). The structure and function of communication in society. In L. Bryson (Ed.), *The communication of ideas.* New York: Harper & Row.

Lazarsfeld, P. F. (1944). *The people's choice: How the voter makes up his mind in a presidential campaign.* New York: Columbia University Press.

Lewis, W. F. (1987). Telling America's story: Narrative form and the Reagan presidency. *Quarterly Journal of Speech, 73,* 280–302.

Martin, J. N., & Butler, R. L. W. (2001). Towards an ethic of intercultural communication research. In V. H. Milhouse, M. K. Asante, & P. O. Nwosu (Eds.), *Transcultural realities: Interdisciplinary perspectives on cross-cultural relations* (pp. 283–298). Thousand Oaks, CA: Sage.

Moore, W. E. (1945). James Madison: The speaker. *Quarterly Journal of Speech, 31,* 155–162.

Mumby, D. (1997). Modernism, postmodernism, and communication studies: A rereading of ongoing debates. *Communication Theory, 7,* 1–28.

Nabi, R. L. (2002). Anger, fear, uncertainty and attitudes: A test of the cognitive function model. *Communication Monographs, 69,* 204–216.

Ono, K. A., & Sloop, J. M. (2002). *Shifting borders: Rhetoric, immigration and California's Proposition 187.* Philadelphia: Temple University Press.

Packer, G. (2002, December 8). The liberal quandary over Iraq. *New York Times Magazine,* 104.

Schramm, W. (1955). *The process and effects of mass communication.* Urbana: University of Illinois Press.

Shannon, C., & Weaver, W. (1949). *The mathematical theory of communication.* Urbana: University of Illinois Press.

Strate, L. (1998). An overview of communication analysis, *Antenna, Newsletter of the Mecurians in the Society for the History of Technology, 10.* Retrieved January 10, 2005, from www.mercurians.org/may98/comm.analysis.html

Suter, E. A. (2004). Tradition never goes out of style: The role of tradition in women's naming practices. *Communication Review, 7,* 57–87.

Tanno, D. (1997). *Communication and identity across cultures.* Thousand Oaks, CA: Sage.

Terrill, R. E. (2003). Irony, silence and time: Frederick Douglass on the fifth of July. *Quarterly Journal of Speech, 89,* 216–234.

Vankevich, N. (2003). Confronting the uncomfortable: Postmodernity and the quandary of evil. *Rhetoric and Public Affairs. 6,* 554–566.

Walzer, M. (2002). Can there be a decent left? *Dessent, 49,* 19–24.

Watts, E. K. (2001). Cultivating a Black public voice: W. E. B. Dubois and the "Criteria of Negro Art." *Rhetoric and Public Affairs, 4,* 181–201.

Watzlawick, P., Beavin, J., & Jackson, D. D. (1967). *Pragmatics of human communication.* New York: W. W. Norton.

Wichelns, H. A. (1925; rpt. 1993). The literary criticism of oratory. In M. J. Medhurst (Ed.) *Landmark essays on American public address.* (pp. 1–32). Davis, CA: Hermagoras Press.

Wilson, K. H. (2003). The racial politics of imitation in the nineteenth century. *Quarterly Journal of Speech, 89,* 89–108.

Wrage, E. J. (1947). Public address: A study in social and intellectual history, *Quarterly Journal of Speech, 33* (1947), 451–457.

Zaeske, S. (2002). Signature of citizenship: The rhetoric of women's antislavery petitions. *Quarterly Journal of Speech, 88,* 147–168.

Chapter 3

Abrams, J., O'Connor, J., & Giles, H. (2002). Identity and intergroup communication. In W. B. Gudykunst & B. Mody (Eds.), *Handbook of international and intercultural communication* (2nd ed., pp. 225–240). Thousand Oaks, CA: Sage.

Allen, B. (2004). *Difference matters: Communicating social identity.* Long Grove, IL: Waveland.

Arana, M. (2008, November 30). He's not black. *Washington Post,* p. B1. Retrieved December 31, 2008, from www.washingtonpost.com/wp-dyn/content/article/2008/11/28/AR2008112802219.html

Arnold, T. K. (2004, April 28). Just call them the Olsen "individuals." *USA Today.*

Azuri, L. (2006, November 17). Public debate in Saudi Arabia on employment opportunities for women. *Inquiry and Analysis 300.* Retrieved March 16, 2009, from www.memri.org/bin/articles.cgi?Area=ia&ID=IA30006&Page=archives

Baker, C. (2003, November 30). What is middle class? *The Washington Times.* Retrieved January 16, 2005, from www.washtimes.com/specialreport/20031129105857412r.htm

Bennett-Haigney, B. (1995, August). Faulkner makes history at the Citadel. *NOW Newsletter.* Retrieved March 1, 2006, from www.now.org/nnt/08-95/citadel.html

Berstein, A. (2004, June 14). Commentry. Women's pay: Why the gap remains a chasm. *Business Week.* Retrieved June 17, 2008, from www.businessweek.com/magazine/content/04_24/b3887065.htm

Blumer, H. (1969). *Symbolic interactionism: Perspective and method.* Englewood Cliffs, NJ: Prentice Hall.

Bourdieu, P. (1984). *Distinction: A social critique of the judgment of taste.* (R. Nice, Trans.). London: Routledge & Kegan Paul.

Butler, J. (1990). *Gender trouble: Feminism and the subversion of identity.* New York: Routledge.

Butler, J. (1993). *Bodies that matter: On the discursive limits of "sex."* New York: Routledge.

Candiotti, S., Koppel, A., Zarrella, J., & Bash, D. (2006, October 3). Attorney: Clergyman molested Foley as teen. *CNN.* Retrieved December 31, 2008, from www.cnn.com/2006/POLITICS/10/03/foley.scandal/index.htm

Carbaugh, D. (2007). Cultural discourse analysis: Communication practices and intercultural encounters. *Journal of Intercultural Communication Research, 36,* 167–182.

Condon, J. C. (1984). *With respect to the Japanese.* Yarmouth, ME: Intercultural Press.

Cooley, C. H. (1902). *Human nature and the social order.* New York: Scribner's.

Corey, F. C. (2004). A letter to Paul. *Text and Performance Quarterly, 24,* 185–190.

Corey, F. C., & Nakayama, T. K. (2004). Introduction. Special issue "Religion and Performance." *Text and Performance Quarterly, 24,* 209–211.

Cornell University. (2004). Fear factor: 44 percent of Americans queried in Cornell national poll favor curtailing some liberties for Muslim Americans. *Cornell News.* Retrieved December 6, 2006, from www.news.cornell.edu/releases/Dec04/Muslim.Poll.bpf.html

Crane, R. (2004, April 30). Interview: Mary-Kate and Ashley from 'New York Minute.' *Cinema Confidential.* Retrieved June 22, 2009, from www.cinecon.com/news.php?id=0404301

Croizet, J., & Claire, T. (1998). Extending the concept of stereotype threat to social class: The intellectual underperformance of students from low socioeconomic backgrounds. *Personality and Social Psychology, 24*(5), 588–594.

Davies, R., & Ikeno, O. (Eds.). (2002). *The Japanese mind: Understanding contemporary culture.* Boston: Tuttleman.

Drum Major Institute for Public Policy. (2005). Middle class 2004: How Congress voted. Retrieved June 12, 2006, from www.drummajorinstitute.org/library/report.php?ID=4

Eby, D. (2009, April 6). Actors and self-esteem-boosting self confidence. http://ezinearticles.com/?id=2199637

Edwards, R. (1990). Sensitivity to feedback and the development of the self. *Communication Quarterly, 38,* 101–111.

Erickson, A. L. (1993). *Women and property in early modern England.* London: Routlege.

Foucault, M. (1988). *History of sexuality* (R. Hurley, Trans.). New York: Vintage Books.

Fussell, P. (1992). *Class: A guide through the American status system.* New York: Touchstone.

Guzman, I. M., & Valdivia, A. N. (2004). Brain, brow, and booty: Latina iconicity in U.S. popular culture. *Communication Review, 7,* 205–221.

Hacker, A. (2003). Two nations: Black and White, separate, hostile, unequal. New York: Scribner.

Harwood, J. (2006). Communication as social identity. In G. J. Shepherd, J. St. John, & T. Striphas (Eds.), *Communication as . . . : Perspectives on theory* (pp. 84–90). Thousand Oaks, CA: Sage.

Hecht, M. L. (1993). 2002—A research odyssey. *Communication Monographs, 60,* 76–82.

Hecht, M. L., Jackson R. L., III, & Ribeau, S. A. (2003). *African American communication: Exploring identity and culture.* (2nd ed). Mahwah, NJ: Lawrence Erlbaum Associates.

Heffernan, V. (2006, February 1). Taking Black family trees out of slavery's shadow. *New York Times.* Retrieved June 12, 2006, from www.nytimes.com/2006/02/01/arts/television/01heff.html

Hirschman, C. (2003, May). The rise and fall of the concept of race. Paper presented at the Annual Meeting of the Population Association of America, Minneapolis, MN.

Hutcheson, J., Domke, D., Billeaudeaux, A., and Garland, P. (2004). U.S. national identity, political elites, and a patriotic press following September 11. *Political Communication, 21,* 27–50.

Imbornoni, A. M. (2008). Women's rights movement in the U.S.: Timeline of key events in the American women's rights movement. Retrieved June 18, 2008, from www.infoplease.com/spot/womenstimeline1.html

Johnson, A. G. (2001). *Privilege, power and difference.* Boston: McGraw-Hill.

Jones, N. A., & Smith, A. S. (2001). The two or more races population. *Census 2000 Brief (U.S. Census Bureau Publication No. C2KBR/01-6).* Washington, DC: U.S. Government Printing Office.

Kimmel, M. S. (2005). *The history of men: Essays in the history of American and British masculinities.* Albany: State University of New York Press.

Koshy, S. (2004). *Sexual naturalization: Asian Americans and miscegenation.* Stanford, CA: Stanford University Press.

Kraybill, D. B. (1989). *The riddle of Amish culture.* Baltimore: Johns Hopkins University Press.

Lagarde, D. (2005, September 22–28). Afghanistan: La loi des tribus. *L'Express International,* pp. 30–37.

Lengel, L., & Warren, J. T. (2005). Introduction: Casting gender. In L. Lengel & J. T. Warren (Eds.), *Casting gender: Women and performance in intercultural contexts* (pp. 1–18). New York: Peter Lang.

Loden, M., & Rosener, J. B. (1991). *Workforce America: Managing workforce diversity as a vital resource.* Homewood, IL: Business One Irwin.

Manczak, D. W. (1999, July 1). Raising your child's self-esteem. *Clinical Reference Systems,* 1242.

Martin, J. N., & Harrell, T. (1996). Reentry training for intercultural sojourners. In D. Landis & R. S. Bhagat (Eds.), *Handbook of intercultural training* (2nd ed., pp. 307–326). Thousand Oaks, CA: Sage.

McGlone, M. S., & Aronson, J. (2006). Stereotype threat, identity salience, and spatial reasoning. *Journal of Applied Development Psychology, 27*(5), 486–493.

Mead, G. H. (1934). *Mind, self, and society.* Chicago: University of Chicago Press.

Mikkelsen, E. G., & Einarsen, S. (2001). Bullying in Danish work-life: Prevalence and health correlates. *European Journal of Work and Organizational Psychology, 10,* 393–413.

Milbank, D. (2007, August 29). A senator's wide stance. "I am not gay." *Washington Post,* p. A2. Retrieved December 31, 2008, from http://www.washingtonpost.com/wp-dyn/content/article/2007/08/28/AR2007082801664.html

Office for National Statistics. Retrieved July 8, 2009, from www.ons.gov.uk/about-statistics/classifications/archived/ethnic-interim/presenting-data/index.html

Online Glossary. (2005, January). Prentice Hall. Retrieved January 16, 2005, from www.prenhall.com/rm_student/html/glossary/a_gloss.html

Palladino, G. (1996). *Teenagers: An American history.* New York: Basic Books.

Papalia, D. E., Olds, S. W., & Feldman, R. D. (2002). *A child's world: Infancy through adolescence.* New York: McGraw-Hill.

Pew Forum on Religion and Public Life. (2008, November 20). *How the News Media Covered Religion in the General Election.* Retrieved December 31, 2008, from http://pewforum.org/docs/?DocID=372

Phelps, J. L., Belsky, J., & Crnic, K. (1998). Earned security, daily stress, and parenting: A comparison of five alternative models. *Development and Psychology, 10,* 21–38.

Philipsen, G. (1992). *Speaking culturally: Explorations in social communication.* Albany, NY: SUNY Press.

Rawls, J. (1995). Self-respect, excellence, and shame. In R. S. Dillon (Ed.), *Dignity, character, and self-respect* (pp. 125–131). New York: Routledge.

Robinson, E. (2008, October 21). The Power of Powell's Rebuke. *Washington Post,* p. A17. Retrieved December 31, 2008, from http://www.washingtonpost.com/wp-dyn/content/article/2008/10/20/AR200S1020022393.html.

Roland, C. E., & Foxx, R. M. (2003). Self-respect: A neglected concept. *Philosophical Psychology.* 16(2) 247–288.

Rosenblith, J. F. (1992). *In the beginning: Development from conception to age two.* Newbury Park, CA: Sage.

Rottenberg (2008, June 20). Karma chameleon. *Entertainment Weekly, 998,* 38–43.

Sanders, W. B. (1994). *Gangbangs and drive-bys: Grounded culture and juvenile gang violence.* New York: Aldine de Gruyter.

Sen. Craig restroom tanking as tourist destination. (2008, December 28). *Washington Post.* Retrieved December 31, 2008, from www.cbsnews.com/stories/2008/12/28/ap/strange/main4688671.shtml

Sheridan, V. (2004, November). *From Vietnamese refugee to Irish citizen: Politics, language, culture and identity.* Paper presented at the International Association of Languages and Intercultural Communication, Dublin City University, Dublin, Ireland.

Shih, M., Pittinsky, T. L., & Ambady, N. (1999). Stereotype susceptibility: Identity salience and shifts in quantitative performance. *Psychological Science.* 10(1), 80–83.

Sloop, J. M. (2004). *Disciplining gender: Rhetoric of sex identity in contemporary U.S. culture.* Amherst: University of Massachusetts Press.

Smith, J. L., & White, P. H. (2002). An examination of implicitly activated, explicitly activated, and nullified stereotypes on mathematical performance: It's not just a women's issue. *Sex Roles, 47*(3–4), 179–191.

Steele, C. M., & Aronson, J. (1995). Stereotype threat and intellectual test performance of African Americans. *Journal of Personality and Social Psychology, 69*(5), 797–811.

Sullivan, H. S. (1953). *The interpersonal theory of psychology.* New York: Norton.

Sullivan, T. A., Warren, E., & Westbrook, J. (2001). *The fragile middle class: Americans in debt.* New Haven: Yale University Press.

Taylor, J. (2005, June 6). *Between two worlds.* How many Americans really attend church each week? Retrieved January 30, 2006, from http://theologica.blogspot.com/2005/06/how-many-americans-really-attend.html

Thomas, C. (2000). Straight with a twist: Queer theory and the subject of heterosexuality. In C. Thomas (Ed.), *Straight with a twist: Queer theory and the subject of heterosexuality* (pp. 11–44). Urbana: University of Illinois Press.

Ting-Toomey, S. (1999). *Communicating across cultures.* New York: Guilford.

Waters, M. C. (1990). *Ethnic options: Choosing identities in America.* Berkeley: University of California Press.

Wax, E. (2005, September 26–October 2). Beyond the pull of the tribe: In Kenya, some teens find unity in contemporary culture. *Washington Post,* National Weekly Edition, Vol. 22, No. 49, p. 18.

Chapter 4

Applegate, J. (1982). The impact of construct system development on communication and impression formation in persuasive contexts. *Communication Monographs, 49,* 277–289.

Berger, C., & Bell, R. (1988). Plans and the initiation of social relationships. *Human Communication Research, 15,* 217–235.

Berger, C., Karol, S., & Jordan, J. (1989). When a lot of knowledge is a dangerous thing: The debilitating effects of plan complexity on verbal fluency. *Human Communication Research, 16*(1), 91–119.

Bradbury, T. N., & Fincham, F. D. (1988). Individual difference variables in close relationships: A contextual model of marriage as an integrative framework. *Journal of Personality and Social Psychology, 54,* 713–721.

Braithwaite, C. (1990). Communicative silence: A cross-cultural study of Basso's hypothesis. In D. Carbaugh (Ed.), *Cultural communication and intercultural contact* (pp. 321–327). Hillsdale NJ: Lawrence Erlbaum Associates.

Braithwaite, D. O., & Japp, P. (2005). "They make us miserable in the name of helping us": Communication between people with disabilities and nondisabled others. In E. B. Ray (Ed.), *Case studies in health communication* (2nd ed.). Mahwah, NJ: Erlbaum.

Brislin, R. (2000). *Understanding culture's influence on behavior* (2nd ed.). Bel mont, CA: Wadsworth.

Bruner, J. (1991). *Acts of meaning,* Cambridge: Harvard University Press.

Bruner, J. S. (1958). Neural mechanisms in perception. Research Publication of the Association for Research in Nervous and Mental Disease, 36, 118–143.

Burgoon, J. K., Berger, C. R., & Waldron, V. R. (2000). Mindfulness and interpersonal communication. *Journal of Social Issues, 56,* 105–127.

Burleson, B. R., & Caplan, S. E. (1998). Cognitive complexity. In J. C. McCroskey, J. Daly, & M. M. Martin (Eds.), *Communication and personality: Trait perspectives.* Cresskill, NJ: Hampton.

Chaiken, S. (1986). Physical appearance and social influence. In C. P. Herman, M. P. Zanna, & E. T. Higgins (Eds.), *Physical appearance, stigma, and social behavior: The Ontario Symposium* (Vol. 3, pp. 143–144). Hillsdale, NJ: Erlbaum.

Chapin, J. (2001). It won't happen to me: The role of optimistic bias in African American teens' risky sexual practices. *Howard Journal of Communications, 12,* 49–59.

Classen, C. (1990). Sweet colors, fragrant songs: Sensory models of the Andes and the Amazon. *American Ethnologist, 14,* 722–735.

Classen, C., Howes, D., & Synott, A. (1994). *Aroma: The cultural history of smell.* Florence, KY: Taylor & Frances/Routledge.

Danghel, E. (1996). The symbolism of smell. *Psychiatria Hungarica, 11,* 683–692.

Deutsch, F. M., Sullivan, L., Sage, C., & Basile, N. (1991). The relations among talking, liking, and similarity between friends. *Personality and Social Psychology Bulletin, 17,* 406–411.

Dijk, T. A., van (1977). *Text and context: Explorations in the semantics and pragmatics of discourse.* London: Longman.

Douglas, W. (1990). Uncertainty, information-seeking, and liking during initial interaction. *Western Journal of Speech Communication, 54,* 66–81.

Douthat, R. (2005, November). Does meritocracy work? *Atlantic*, 120–126.

Ehrenreich, B. (2001). *Nickel and dimed: On (not) getting by in America*. New York: Metropolitan Books.

Estroff, H. (2004, September/October). Cupid's comeuppance. *Psychology Today*. Retrieved March 15, 2006, from www.psychologytoday.com/articles/pto-20040921-000001.html

Fehr, B. (1993). How do I love thee: Let me consult my prototype. In S. W. Duck (Ed.), *Understanding relationship processes 1, individuals in relationships* (pp. 87–122). Newbury Park, CA: Sage.

Fisher, K. (1997). Locating frames in the discursive universe. *Sociological Research Online*, 2(3). Retrieved October 25, 2008, from www.socresonline.org.uk/2/3/4.html

Fisk, S. T., & Taylor, S. E. (1991). *Social cognition* (2nd ed.). New York: McGraw-Hill.

Greenough, W. T., Black, J. E., & Wallace, C. S. (1987). Experience and brain development. *Child Development*, 58, 539–559.

Griffin, E. (1994). *A first look at communication theory*. New York: McGraw-Hill.

Gueguen, N., & De Gail, M. (2003). The effect of smiling on helping behavior: Smiling and good Samaritan behavior. *Communication Reports*, 16(2), 133–140.

Hacker, A. (2003). *Two nations: Black and White, separate, hostile, unequal*. New York: Scribner.

Heider, F. (1958). *The psychology of interpersonal relations*, New York: Wiley.

Heine, S. J., & Lehman, D. R. (2004). Move the body, change the self: Acculturative effects on self-concept. In A. Schaller & C. Crandall (Eds.), *The psychological foundations of culture* (pp. 305–31). Hillsdale, NJ: Erlbaum.

Herz, R. S., & Inzlicht, M. (2002). Sex differences in response to physical and social factors involved in human mate selection: The importance of smell for women. *Evolution and Human Behavior*, 23, 359–364.

Jong, P. F. de, Koomen, W., & Mellenbergh, G. J. (1988). Structure of causes for success and failure: A multidimensional scaling analysis of preference judgments. *Journal of Personality and Social Psychology*, 55, 718–725.

Kanizsa, G. (1979). *Organization in vision*. New York: Praeger.

Kellerman, K. (2004). A goal-direct approach to compliance-gaining: Relating differences among goals to differences in behavior. *Communication Research*, 31, 345–347.

Kelley, H. H. (1973). The processes of causal attribution. *American Psychologist*, 28, 107–128.

Kim, M. S. (2002). *Non-Western perspectives on human communication*. Thousand Oaks, CA: Sage.

Kirouac, G., & Hess, U. (1999). Group membership and the decoding of nonverbal behavior. In R. S. Feldman & P. Philippot (Eds.), *The social context of nonverbal behavior* (pp.182–210). New York: Cambridge University Press.

Krivonos, P. D., & Knapp, M. L. (1975). Initiating communication: What do you say when you say hello? *Central States Speech Journal*, 26, 115–125.

Lakoff, G. (1987). *Women, fire, and dangerous things: What categories reveal about the mind*. Chicago: University of Chicago Press.

Langer, E. J. (1978). Rethinking the role of thought in social interaction. In J. H. Harvey, W. Ickes, & R. F. Kidd (Eds.), *New directions in attribution research* (Vol. 2, pp. 3–58). New York: Wiley.

Levinthal, D., & Gavetti, G. (2000, March). Looking forward and looking backward: Cognition and experiential search. *Administrative Science Quarterly*, 1–9.

Lin, M., Harwood, J., & Hummert, M. L. (2008). Young adults' intergenerational communication schemas in Taiwan and the USA. *Journal of Language and Social Psychology*, 27(1), 28–50.

Link, B. G., & Phelan, J. C. (August, 2001). Conceptualizing stigma. *Annual Review of Sociology*, 27, 363–385.

Lupfer, M. B., Weeks, M., & Dupuis, S. (2000). How pervasive is the negativity bias in judgments based on character appraisal? *Personality and Social Psychology Bulletin*, 26, 1353–1366.

Markus, H. R., Mullally, P. R., & Kitayama, S. (1997). Selfways: Diversity in modes of cultural participation. In U. Neisser & D. A. Jopling (Eds.), *The conceptual self in context* (pp. 13–59). Cambridge, UK: Cambridge University Press.

McCoy, N. L., & Pitino, L. (2002). Pheromonal influences on sociosexual behavior in young women. *Physiology and Behavior*, 75, 367–375.

Middle of the Class (2005, July 14). Survey: America. *Economist*. Retrieved March 10, 2006, from www.economist.com/displayStory.cfm?Story_id=4148885

Morgan, M. J. (1977). *Molyneux's question : Vision, touch and the philosophy of perception*. Cambridge, NY: Cambridge University Press.

Neale, M. A., & Bazerman, M. H. (1991). *Cognition and rationality in negotiation*. New York: Free Press.

Pearce, W. B. (1994). *Interpersonal communication: Making social worlds*. New York: HarperCollins.

Pew Research Center for People and the Press. (2005, September 8). Huge racial divide over Katrina and its consequences. Retrieved June 1, 2006, from http://people-press.org/reports/pdf/255.pdf

Planalp, S. (1993). Communication, cognition, and emotion. *Communication Monographs*, 60, 3–9.

Putnam, L. L., & Holmer, M. (1992). Framing, reframing and issue development. In L. L. Putnam & M. E. Roloff (Eds.), *Communication and negotiation* (pp. 128–155). Newbury Park, CA: Sage.

Ross, L. (1977). The intuitive psychologist and his shortcomings: Distortions in the attribution process. In L. Berkowitz (Ed.), *Advances in experimental social psychology* (Vol. 10, pp. 173–220). New York: Academic Press.

Rothenberg, P. S. (1992). *Race, class, and gender in the United States*. New York: St. Martin's Press.

Ryan, E. B., Bourhis, R. Y., & Knops, U. (1991). Evaluative perceptions of patronizing speech addressed to elders. *Psychology and Aging*, 6, 442–450.

Samter, W., & Burleson, B. R. (1984). Cognitive and motivational influences on spontaneous comforting behavior. *Human Communication Research*, 11, 231–260.

Scollon, R., & Wong-Scollon, S. (1990). Athabaskan-English interethnic communication. In D. Carbaugh (Ed.), *Cultural communication and intercultural contact* (pp. 259–287). Hillsdale, NJ: Erlbaum.

Seligman, M. (1998). *Learned optimism*. New York: Simon & Schuster.

Shore, B. (1996). *Culture in mind: Cognition, culture and the problem of meaning*. New York: Oxford University Press.

Singh, D., & Bronstad, P. M. (2001). Female body odour is a potential cue to ovulation. *Proceedings of the Royal Society: Biological Science*, 268, 797–801.

Siu, W. L. W., & Finnegan, J. R. (2004, May). An exploratory study of the interaction of affect and cognition in message evaluation. Paper presented at the International Communication Association Convention, San Francisco, CA.

Smell report. (2006). Social Issues Research Centre, Oxford, UK. Retrieved March 18, 2006, from www.sirc.org/publik/smell_diffs.html

Smith, S. W., Kopfman, J. E., Lindsey, L., Massi, Y. J., & Morrison, K. (2004). Encouraging family discussion on the decision to donate organs: The role of the willingness to communicate scale. *Health Communication*. 16, 333–346.

Snyder, M. (1998). Self-fulfilling stereotypes. In P. S. Rothenberg (Ed.), *Race, class and gender in the U.S.: An integrated study* (pp. 452–457). New York: St. Martin's Press.

Spitzberg, B. (2001) The status of attribution theory *qua* theory in personal relationships. In V. Manusov & J. H. Harvey (Eds.), *Attribution, communication behavior and close relationships*. Cambridge: Cambridge University Press.

Stephan, C., & Stephan, W. (1992). Reducing intercultural anxiety through intercultural contact. *International Journal of Intercultural Relations*, 16, 89–106.

Ting-Toomey, S. (1999). *Communicating across cultures*. New York: Guilford.

U.S. National Research Council. (1989). *Improving risk communication*. Committee on risk perception and communication. Washington, DC: National Academy Press.

Weick, K. (1995). *Sensemaking in organizations*. Thousand Oaks, CA: Sage.

Wilson, D., & Nias, D. (1999). Beauty can't be beat. In J. A. DeVito & L. Guerrero, (Eds.), *The nonverbal communication reader: Classic and contemporary readings* (2nd ed., pp. 92–132). Prospect Heights, IL: Waveland.

Chapter 5

Active listening. (1997). *Public Management*, 79, 25–27.

Alberts, J., Yoshimura, C., Rabby, M., & Loschiavo, R. (2005). Mapping the topography of couples' everyday interaction. *Journal of Social and Personal Relationships*, 22(3), 299–322.

American Heritage Dictionary of the English Language. 4th ed, (2000) Boston: Houghton-Mifflin. Retrieved June 12, 2006, from www.bartleby.com/cgibin/texis/webinator/ahdsearch?search_type=enty&query=wise&db=ahd&submit=Search

Aries, E. (1996). *Men and women in interaction: Reconsidering the differences*. New York: Oxford University Press.

Austin, J. L. (1975). *How to do things with words* (2nd ed.). Cambridge, MA: Harvard University Press.

Aylor, B., & Dainton, M. (2004). Biological sex and psychological gender as predictors of routine and strategic relational maintenance. *Sex Roles: A Journal of Research*, 50, 689–697.

Baker, M. (1991). Gender and verbal communication in professional settings: A review of research. *Management Communication Quarterly*, 5, 36–63.

Bentley, S. C. (2000). Listening in the 21st century. *International Journal of Listening*, 14, 129–142.

Bippus, A. M., & Young, S. L. (2005). Owning your emotions: Reactions to expressions of self versus other-attributed positive and negative emotions. *Journal of Applied Communication Research*, 33, 26–45.

Bowen, S. P. (2003). Jewish and/or woman: Identity and communicative styles. In A. González, M. Houston, & V. Chen (Eds.), *Our voices: Essays in culture, ethnicity, and communication* (4th ed.). Los Angeles: Roxbury.

Boxer, D. (2002). Nagging: The familial conflict arena. *Journal of Pragmatics*, 34, 49–61.

Burrell, N. A., Donohue, W. A., & Allen, M. (1988). Gender-based perceptual biases in mediation. *Communication Research*, 15, 447–469.

Canary, D. J., & Emmers-Sommers, T. M. (1997). *Sex and gender differences in personal relationships*. New York: Guilford.

Canary, D. J., & Hause, K. S. (1993). Is there any reason to research sex difference in communication? *Communication Quarterly*, 41, 129–144.

Caughlin, J. P. (2002). The demand/withdraw pattern of communication as a predictor of marital satisfaction over time: Unresolved issues and future directions. *Human Communication Research*, 28, 49–85.

Chomsky, N. (1957). *Syntactic Structures*, The Hague/Paris: Mouton.

Coltri, L. S. (2004). *Conflict diagnosis and alternative dispute resolution*. Upper Saddle River, NJ: Prentice Hall.

Crystal, D. (2003). *The Cambridge encyclopedia of the English language*. New York: Cambridge University Press.

Dance, F. E. X., & Larson, C. E. (1976). *The functions of human communication*. New York: Holt, Rinehart, & Winston.

Eadie, W. F. (1982). Defensive communication revisited: A critical examination of Gibb's theory. *Southern Speech Communication Journal*. 47, 163–177.

Edwards, J. V. (2004). Foundations of bilingualism. In T. K. Bhatia & W. C. Ritchie (Eds.), *The handbook of bilingualism* (pp. 7–31). Malden, MA: Blackwell.

Ellis, A., & Beattie, G. (1986). The language channel. *The psychology of language.* New York: Guilford.

Fromkin, V., & Rodman, R. (1983). *An introduction to language.* New York: Holt, Rinehart, and Winston.

Gibb, J. R. (1961). Defensive communication. *Journal of Communication 11*(3), 141–148.

Gong, G. (2004). When Mississippi Chinese talk. In A. González, M. Houston, & V. Chen (Eds.), *Our voices: Essays in culture, ethnicity, and communication* (4th ed.). Los Angeles: Roxbury.

Halone, K. K., & Pecchioni, L. L. (2001). Relational listening: A grounded theoretical model. *Communication Reports, 14,* 59–71.

Hegarty, P., & Buechel, C. (2006). Androcentric reporting of gender differences in APA journals: 1965–2004. *Review of General Psychology, 10*(4), 377–389.

Hoijer, H. (1994). The Sapir-Whorf hypothesis. In L. Samovar & R. E. Porter (Eds.), *Intercultural communication: A reader* (pp. 194–200). Belmont, CA: Wadsworth.

Hudson, R. A. (1983*). Sociolinguistics.* London: Cambridge University Press.

Hyde, J. S. (2006). Gender similarities still rule. *American Psychologist, 61*(6), 641–642.

Jacobson, C. (2008). Some notes on gender-neutral language. Retrieved May 23, 2008, from www.english.upenn.edu/~cjacobso/gender.html

Kenneally, C. (2008, April 22). When language can hold the answer. *New York Times,* p. F1.

Kikoski, J. F., & Kikoski, C. K. (1999). *Reflexive communication in the culturally diverse workplace.* Westport, CT: Praeger.

Kim, M. S. (2002). *Non-Western perspectives on human communication.* Thousand Oaks, CA: Sage.

Knott, K., & Natalle, E. (1997). Sex differences, organizational level, and superiors' evaluations of managerial leadership. *Management Communication Quarterly, 10,* 523–540.

Koerner, F. F. K. (2000). Towards a "full pedigree" of the "Sapir-Whorf hypothesis." In M. Putz & M. H. Verspoor (Eds.), *Explorations in linguistic relativity* (pp. 1–23). Amsterdam: John Benjamins.

Kohonen, S. (2004). Turn-taking in conversation: Overlaps and interruptions in intercultural talk. *Cahiers, 10.1,* 15–32.

Krieger, L. (2004, February 26). Like, what dew you mean, tha-yt I hav-yvee an accent? *Detroit Free Press,* p. 16A.

Kubany, E. S., Bauer, G. B., Muraoka, M., Richard, D. C., & Read, P. (1995). Impact of labeled anger and blame in intimate relationships. *Journal of Social and Clinical Psychology, 14,* 53–60.

Labov, W. (1980). The social origins of sound change. In W. Labov (Ed.), *Locating language in time and space* (pp. 251–265). New York: Academic Press.

Labov, W. (Ed.). (2005). *Atlas of North American English.* New York: Walter De Gruyter.

Leaper, C., & Ayres, M. M. (2007). A meta-analytic review of gender variation in adults' language use: Talkativeness, affiliative speech, and assertive speech. *Personality and Social Psychology Review, 11*(4), 328–363.

Li, P., & Gleitman, L. (2002). Turning the tables: Language and spatial reasoning. *Cognition, 83,* 265–294.

Martin, J. N., Krizek, R. L., Nakayama, T. K., & Bradford, L. (1999). What do White people want to be called? A study of self-labels for White Americans. In T. K. Nakayama & J. N. Martin (Eds.), *Whiteness: The communication of social identity* (pp. 27–50). Thousand Oaks, CA: Sage.

Mehl, M. R., & Pennebaker, J. W. (2003). The sounds of social life: A psychometric analysis of students' daily social environments and natural conversations. *Journal of Personality and Social Psychology, 84,* 857–70.

Mey, J. L. (2001). *Pragmatics: An introduction* (2nd ed.). Oxford, UK: Blackwell Publishing.

Mulac, A., Bradac. J. J., Gibbons, P. (2001). Empirical support for the gender-as-culture hypothesis: An intercultural analysis of male/female language differences. *Human Communication Research, 27,* 121–152.

Nichols, M. P. (1995). *The lost art of listening.* New York: Guilford.

Nofsinger, R. (1999). *Everyday conversation.* Prospect Heights, IL: Waveland.

Orbe, M. P. (1998). *Constructing co-cultural theory: An explication of culture, power, and communication.* Thousand Oaks, CA: Sage.

Paramasivam, S. (2007). Managing disagreement while managing not to disagree: Polite disagreement in negotiation discourse. *Journal of Intercultural Communication Research, 36*(2), 91–116.

Pecchioni, L. L., & Halone, K. K. (2000). Relational listening II: Form and variation across social and personal relationships. *International Journal of Listening, 14,* 69–93.

Pennebaker, J. W., Mehl, M. R., & Niederhoffer, K. G. (2003). Psychological aspects of natural language use: Our words, our selves. *Annual Review of Psychology, 54,* 547–577.

Pennebaker, J. W., & Stone, L. D. (2003). Words of wisdom: Language use across the life span. *Journal of Personality and Social Psychology, 82,* 291–301.

Philips, S. U. (1990). Some sources of cultural variability in the regulation of talk. In D. Carbaugh (Ed.), *Cultural communication and intercultural contact* (pp. 329–344). Hillsdale, NJ: Erlbaum.

Piaget, J. (1952). *The origins of intelligence in children.* New York: International Universities Press.

Pinker, S. (2007). *The stuff of thought: Language as a window into human nature.* New York: Viking.

Pinto, D., & Raschio, R. (2007) A comparative study of requests in heritage speaker Spanish, L1 Spanish, and L1 English. *International Journal of Bilingualism, 11*(2), 135–155.

Preston, D. R. (2003). Where are the dialects of American English at anyhow? *American Speech, 78,* 235–254.

Purdy, M. W. (2000). Listening, culture and structures of consciousness: Ways of studying listening. *International Journal of Listening, 14,* 47–68.

Ramírez-Esparza, N., Gosling, S. D., Benet-Martínez, V., Potter, J. D., & Pennebaker, J. W. (2006). Do bilinguals have two personalities? A special case of cultural frame switching. *Journal of Research in Personality,40,* 99–120.

Reid, S. A., Keerie, N., & Palomares, N. A. (2003). Language, gender salience, and social influence. *Journal of Language and Social Psychology, 22,* 210–233.

Rose, C. (1995). Bargaining and gender. *Harvard Journal of Law and Public Policy, 18,* 547–65.

Rosenfeld, L. B., & Berko, R. (1990). *Communicating with competency.* Glenview, IL: Scott, Foresman/Little, Brown Higher Education.

Ruben, D. L. (2003). Help! My professor (or doctor or boss) doesn't talk English! In J. N. Martin, T. K. Nakayama, & L. A. Flores (Eds.), *Readings in intercultural communication* (2nd ed., pp. 127–138). Boston: McGraw-Hill.

Sacks, H., Schegloff, E., & Jefferson, G. (1978). A simplest systematics for the organization of turn-taking for conversation. In J. Schenkein (Ed.), *Studies in the organization of conversational interaction* (pp. 7–55). New York: Academic Press.

Sagrestano, L. M., Heavey, C. L., & Christensen, A. (1998). Theoretical approaches to understanding sex differences and similarities in conflict behavior. In D. J. Canary & K. Dindia (Eds.), *Sex differences and similarities in communication: Critical essays and empirical investigations on sex and gender in interaction* (pp. 287–302). Mahwah, NJ: Erlbaum.

Sbisa, M. (2002). Speech act in context, *Language & Communication, 22,* 421–436.

Schegloff, E. A. (2000) Overlapping talk and the organization of turn-taking for conversation, *Language in Society, 29,* 1–63.

Scheibel, D. (1995). Making waves with Burke: Surf Nazi culture and the rhetoric of localism. *Western Journal of Communication, 59*(4), 253–269.

Sellers, J. G., Woolsey, M. D., & Swann, J. B. (2007). Is silence more golden for women than men? Observers derogate effusive women and their quiet partners. *Sex Roles, 57*(7-8), 477–482.

Shutiva, C. (2004). Native American culture and communication through humor. In A. González, M. Houston, & V. Chen (Eds.), *Our voices: Essays in culture, ethnicity, and communication* (4th ed.). Los Angeles: Roxbury.

Weger, H., Jr. (2005). Disconfirming communication and self-verification in marriage: Associations among the demand/withdraw interaction pattern, feeling understood, and marital satisfaction. *Journal of Social and Personal Relationships, 22,* 19–31.

Wiest, L. R., Abernathy, T. V., Obenchain, K. M., & Major, E. M. (2006). Researcher study thyself: AERA participants' speaking times and turns by gender. *Equity & Excellence in Education, 39*(4), 313–323.

Wolfram, W., Adger, C. T., & Christian, D. (1999). *Dialects in schools and communities.* Mahwah, NJ: Erlbaum.

Wood, J. T. (2002). *Gendered lives: Communication, gender and cultures.* Belmont, CA: Wadsworth.

Wood, J. T., & Dindia, K. (1998). What's the differences? A dialogue about differences and similarities between men and women. In D. J. Canary & K. Dindia (Eds.), *Sex differences and similarities in communication: Critical essays and empirical investigations on sex and gender in interaction* (pp. 19–39). Mahwah, NJ: Erlbaum.

Chapter 6

Abu-Ghazzeh, T. M. (2000). Environmental messages in multiple family housing: Territory and personalization. *Landscape Research, 25,* 97–114.

Als, H. (1977). The newborn communicates. *Journal of Communication, 2,* 66–73.

Axtell, R. (1993). *Do's and taboos around the world.* New York: Wiley.

Becker, F. D. (1973). Study of special markers. *Journal of Personality and Social Psychology, 26,* 429–445.

Birdwhistell, R. L. (1970). *Kinesics and context.* Philadelphia: University of Pennsylvania Press.

Boone, R. T., & Cunningham, J. G. (1998). Children's decoding of emotion in expressive body movement: The development of cue attunement. *Developmental Psychology, 34,* 1007–1016.

Burgoon, J. K., Buller, D. B., & Woodall, W. G. (1996). *Nonverbal communication: The unspoken dialogue.* New York: Harper & Row.

Burgoon, J. K., & Guerrero, L. K. (1994). Nonverbal communication. In M. Burgoon, F. G. Hunsaker, & E. J. Dawson (Eds.), *Human communication* (pp. 122–171). Thousand Oaks, CA: Sage.

Burgoon, J. K., & Hale, J. L. (1988). Nonverbal expectancy violations: Model elaboration and application to immediacy behaviors. *Communication Monographs, 55,* 58–79.

Burgoon, J. K., & LePoire, B. A. (1993). Effects of communication expectancies, actual communication, and expectancy disconfirmation on evaluations of communicators and their communication behavior. *Human Communication Research, 20,* 67–96.

Capella, J. (1985). The management of conversations. In M. L. Knapp & G. R. Miller (Eds.), *Handbook of interpersonal communication* (pp. 393–435). Beverly Hills, CA: Sage.

Carvajal, D. (2006, February 7). Priming for the cameras in the name of research. *New York Times.* Retrieved February 23, 2006, from www.nytimes.com/2006/02/07/business/07hair.html?ex=1139979600&en=f5f94cb9d81a9fa8&ei=5070&emc=eta1

Chartrand T. L., & Bargh J. A. (1999). The chameleon effect: The perception-behavior link and social interaction. *Journal of Personality and Social Psychology, 76,* 893–910.

Chiang, L. H. (1993, October). *Beyond the language: Native Americans' nonverbal communication.* Paper presented at the Annual Meeting of the Midwest Association of Teachers of Educational Psychology, Anderson, IN: October 1–2.

Cicca, A. H., Step, M., & Turkstra, L. (2003, December 16). Show me what you mean: Nonverbal communication theory and application. *ASHA Leader, 34,* 4–5.

De Vito, J. A., & Hecht, M. L. (1990). Beginning perspectives. In J. A. De Vito & M. L. Hecht (Eds.), *The nonverbal communication reader* (pp. 3–17). Prospect Heights, IL: Waveland.

Dijksterhuis, A., & Smith, P. K. (2005). What do we do unconsciously? And how? *Journal of Consumer Psychology 15*(3), 225–229.

Duke, L. (2002). Get real! Cultural relevance and resistance to the mediated feminine ideal. *Psychology and Marketing, 19,* 211–234.

Eibl-Eibesfeld, I. (1972). Similarities and differences between cultures in expressive movement. In R. A. Hinde (Ed.), *Nonverbal communication* (pp. 297–314). Cambridge: Cambridge University Press.

Ekman, P. (2003). *Emotions revealed: Recognizing faces and feelings to improve communication and emotional life.* New York: Times Books.

Ekman, P., & Friesen, W. V. (1969). The repertoire of nonverbal behavior: Categories, origins, usage and coding. *Semiotica, 1,* 49–98.

Ekman, P., & Friesen, W. V. (1986). A new pan-cultural expression of emotion. *Motivation and Emotion, 10*(2), 159–168.

Elfenbein, H. A. (2007). Learning in emotion judgments: Teaching and the cross-cultural understanding of facial expressions. *Journal of Nonverbal Communication, 30,* 21–36.

Elfenbein, H. A., Maw, D. F., White, J., Tan, H. H., & Aik, V. C. (2006). Reading your counterpart: The benefit of emotion recognition accuracy for effectiveness in negotiation. *Journal of Nonverbal Behavior, 31,* 205–223.

Eskritt, M., & Lee, K. (2003) Do actions speak louder than words? Preschool children's use of the verbal-nonverbal consistency principle during inconsistent communication. *Journal of Nonverbal Behavior, 27,* 25–41.

Field, T. (2002). Infants' need for touch. *Human Development, 45,* 100–104.

Fussell, P. (1992). *Class: A guide through the American status system.* New York: Touchstone Books.

Givens, D. B. (2005). *The nonverbal dictionary of gestures, signs, and body language cues.* Spokane, WA: Center for Nonverbal Studies Press.

Grammer, K., Fink, B., Joller, A., & Thornhill, R. (2003). Darwinian aesthetics: Sexual selection and the biology of beauty. *Biological Reviews, 78,* 385–408.

Guerrero, L. K., & Andersen, P. A. (1991). The waxing and waning of relational intimacy: Touch as a function of relational stage, gender, and touch avoidance. *Journal of Social and Personal Relationships, 8,* 147–165.

Guerrero, L. K., & Andersen, P. A. (1994). Patterns of matching and initiation: Touch behavior and touch avoidance across romantic relationship stages. *Journal of Nonverbal Behavior, 18,* 137–153.

Guerrero, L. K., & Ebesu, A. S. (1993, May). *While at play: An observational analysis of children's touch during interpersonal interaction.* Paper presented at the annual conference of the International Communication Association, Washington, D.C.

Gundersen, D. F. (1990). Uniforms: Conspicuous invisibility. In J. A. Devito & M. L. Hecht (Eds.), *The nonverbal communication reader* (pp. 172–178). Prospect Heights, IL: Waveland.

Hall, E. T. (1966). *The hidden dimension.* New York: Doubleday.

Hall, E. T. (1983). *The dance of life.* Garden City, NY: Doubleday.

Hall, E. T., & Hall, M. R. (1987). *Hidden differences: Doing business with the Japanese.* Garden City, NY: Anchor.

Hall, E. T., & Hall, M. R. (1990). *Understanding cultural differences: Germans, French and Americans.* Yarmouth, ME: Intercultural Press.

Hanzal, A., Segrin, C., & Dorros, S. M. (2008). The role of marital status and age on men's and women's reactions to touch from a relational partner. *Journal of Nonverbal Behavior, 32,* 21–35.

Isaacson, L. A. (1998). Student dress codes. *ERIC Digest, 117.* Retrieved June 15, 2006, from http://eric.uoregon.edu/publications/digests/digest117.html

Johnson, A. G. (2001). *Privilege, power, and difference.* Boston: McGraw-Hill.

Jones, S. E., & LeBaron, C. D. (2002). Research on the relationship between verbal and nonverbal communication: Emerging integration. *Journal of Communication, 52,* 499–521.

Kemmer, S. (1992). Are we losing our touch? *Total Health, 14,* 46–49.

Knapp, M. L., & Hall, J. A. (1992). *Nonverbal communication in human interaction* (3rd ed.). New York: Holt, Rinehart and Winston.

Knapp, M. L., & Hall, J. A. (2001). *Nonverbal communication in human interaction.* Belmont, CA: Wadsworth.

Manusov, V. (1995). Reacting to changes in nonverbal behaviors: Relational satisfaction and adaptation patterns in romantic dyads. *Human Communication Research, 21,* 456–477.

Mast, M. S., & Hall, J. A., (2004). Who is the boss and who is not? Accuracy of judging status. *Journal of Nonverbal Behavior, 28,* 145–165.

Mehrabian, A. (1971). *Nonverbal communication.* Chicago: Aldine-Atherton.

Montpare, J. M., Goldstein, S. B., & Clausen, A. (1987). The identification of emotions from gait information. *Ethology and Sociobiology, 6,* 237–247.

Newport, F. (1999). Americans agree that being attractive is a plus in American society. *Gallup Poll Monthly, 408,* 45–49.

Parasuram, T. V. (2003, October 23). Sikh shot and injured in Arizona hate crime. *Sikh Times.* Retrieved February 24, 2006, from www.sikhtimes.com/news_052103a.html

Patterson, M. L. (1982). A sequential functional model of nonverbal exchange. *Psychological Bulletin, 89,* 231–249.

Patterson, M. L. (1983). *Nonverbal behavior.* New York: Springer.

Patterson, M. L. (2003). Commentary. Evolution and nonverbal behavior: Functions and mediating processes. *Journal of Nonverbal Behavior, 27,* 201–207.

Richards, V., Rollerson, B., & Phillips, J. (1991). Perceptions of submissiveness: Implications for victimization. *Journal of Psychology, 125*(4), 407–411.

Richeson, J. A., & Shelton, J. N. (2005). Brief report: Thin slices of racial bias. *Journal of Nonverbal Behavior, 29,* 75–86.

Schwartz, L. M., Foa, U. G., & Foa, E. B. (1983) Multichannel nonverbal communication: Evidence for combinatory rules. *Journal of Personality and Social Psychology, 45,* 274–281.

Segaloff, N. (2003, November 24). World War II on the air and my fellow Americans. Review. *Audio Books Today.* AudiobookToday.com

Segerstrale, U., & Molnár, P. (1997) (Eds.), *Nonverbal communication: Where nature meets culture* (pp. 27–46). Mahwah, NJ: Erlbaum.

Shelp, S. (2002). Gaydar: Visual detection of sexual orientation among gay and straight men. *Journal of Homosexuality, 44,* 1–14.

Tiedens, L., & Fragale, A. (2003). "Power moves: Complementarity in dominant and submissive nonverbal behavior." *Journal of Personality and Social Psychology, 84,* 558–568.

Young, I. M. (1990). *Throwing like a girl and other essays in feminist philosophy and social theory.* Bloomingdale, IN: Indiana University Press.

Wise, T. (2005, October 23). Opinions on NBA dress code are far from uniform. *Washington Post,* p. A01. Retrieved February 24, 2006, from www.washingtonpost.com/wp-dyn/content/article/2005/10/22/AR2005102201386.html

Wolburg, J. M. (2001). Preserving the moment, commodifying time, and improving upon the past: Insights into the depiction of time in American advertising. *Journal of Communication, 51,* 696–720.

Zezima, K. (2005, December 3). Military, police now more strict on tattoos. *The San Diego Union-Tribune.* Retrieved February 22, 2006, from www.signonsandiego.com/uniontrib/20051203/news_1n3tattoo.html

Chapter 7

Adler, P. (1975). The transitional experience: An alternative view of culture shock. *Journal of Humanistic Psychology, 15,* 13–23.

Alexie, S. (2003). *Ten little Indians.* New York: Grove Press.

Allen, B. (2003). *Difference matters: Communicating social identity.* Waveland Press.

Anzaldúa, G. (1999). *Borderlands/La frontera: The new mestiza.* San Francisco: Aunt Lute Books.

Bahk, M., & Jandt, F. E. (2004). Being white in America: Development of a scale. *Howard Journal of Communications, 15,* 57–68.

Bellah, R. N., Madsen, R., Sullivan, W. M., Swidler, A., & Tipton, S. M. (1996). *Habits of the heart: Individualism and commitment in American life.* Los Angeles: University of California Press.

Bennett, J. M. (1998). Transition shock: Putting culture shock in perspective. In M. J. Bennett (Ed.), *Basic concepts in intercultural communication: Selected readings* (pp. 215–224). Yarmouth, ME: Intercultural Press. First published in 1977, in N. C. Jain (Ed.), *International and Intercultural Communication Annual, 4,* 45–52.

Bercovitch, J., & Derouen, K. (2004). Mediation in internationalized ethnic conflicts, *Armed Forces & Society, 30,* 147–170.

Berry, J. W. (2005) Acculturation: Living successfully in two cultures. *International Journal of Intercultural Relations, 29,* 697–712.

Bhatia, S. (2008). 9/11 and the Indian diaspora: Narratives of race, place and immigrant identity. *Journal of Intercultural Studies, 29*(1), 21–39.

Blair, C., Brown, J. R., & Baxter, L. A. (1994). Disciplining the feminine. *Quarterly Journal of Speech, 80,* 383–409.

Blanco, T., Farrell, D., & Labaye, E. (2005, August 15). How France can win from offshoring. *The McKinsey Quarterly.* Retrieved June 15, 2006, from http://yaleglobal.yale.edu/display.article?id=6144

Bond, M. (1991). *Beyond the Chinese face.* Hong Kong: Oxford University Press.

Bond, M. (Ed.). (1996). *The handbook of Chinese psychology.* Hong Kong: Oxford University Press.

Broome, B. J. (1997). Designing a collective approach to peace: Interactive design and problem-solving workshops with Greek-Cypriot and Turkish Cypriot communities in Cyprus, *International Negotiation, 2,* 381–407.

Budelman, R. *Indian Cultural Tips.* Retrieved June 13, 2006, from www.stylusinc.com/business/india/americans_independant.htm

Chinese Culture Connection. (1987). Chinese values and the search for culture-free dimensions of culture. *Journal of Cross-Cultural Psychology, 18,* 143–164.

Clark-Ibanez, M. K., Felmlee, D. (2004). Interethnic relationships: The role of social network diversity. *Journal of Marriage and Family, 66,* 229–245.

Cowan, G. (2005). Interracial interactions of racially diverse university campuses. *Journal of Social Psychology, 14,* 49–63.

Dunbar, R. A. (1997). Bloody footprints: Reflections on growing up poor white. In M. Wray & A. Newitz (Eds.), *White trash: Race and class in America* (pp. 73–86). New York: Routledge.

Ewing, K. P. (2004). Migration, identity negotiation, and self-experience. In J. Friedman & S. Randeria, (Eds.), *Worlds on the move: Globalization, migration, and cultural security* (pp. 117–140). London: I. B. Tauris.

Fiebert, M. S., Nugent, D., Hershberger, S. L., & Kasdan, M. (2004). Dating and commitment choices as a function of ethnicity among American college students in California. *Psychological Reports, 94,* 1293–1300.

Finn, H. K. (2003). The case for cultural diplomacy. *Foreign Affairs, 82,* 15.

Flores, L. A. (1996). Creating discursive space through a rhetoric of difference: Chicana feminists craft a homeland. *Quarterly Journal of Speech, 82,* 142–156.

Gudykunst, W. B., & Lee, C. M. (2002). Cross-cultural communication theories. In W. B. Gudykunst & B. Mody (Eds.), *Handbook of international and intercultural communication* (2nd ed., pp. 25–50). Thousand Oaks, CA: Sage.

Hall, B. J. (1997). Culture, ethics and communication. In F. L. Casmir (Ed.), *Ethics in intercultural and international communication* (pp. 11–41). Mahwah, NJ: Erlbaum.

Hall, E. T., & Hall, M. (1990). *Understanding cultural differences: Germans, French and Americans*. Yarmouth, ME: Intercultural Press.

Halualani, R. T. (2008). How do multicultural university students define and make sense of intercultural contact? A qualitative study. *International Journal of Intercultural Relations, 32*, 1–16.

Hecht, M., Sedano, M., & Ribeau, S. (1993). Understanding culture, communication, and research: Application to Chicanos and Mexican Americans. *International Journal of Intercultural Relations, 17*, 157–165.

Hecht, M. L., Jackson R. L., II, & Ribeau, S. (2002). *African American Communication: Exploring identity and culture* (2nd ed.). Hillsdale, NJ: Erlbaum.

Hegde, R. S. (1998). Swinging the trapeze: The negotiation of identity among Asian Indian immigrant women in the United States. In D. V. Tanno & A. González (Eds.), *Communication of identity across cultures* (pp. 34–55). Thousand Oaks, CA: Sage.

Hegde, R. S. (2000). Hybrid revivals: Defining Asian Indian ethnicity through celebration. In A. González, M. Houston, V. Chen (Eds.), *Our voices: Essays in culture, ethnicity and communication* (pp. 133–138). Los Angeles: Roxbury.

Hemmingsen, J. (2002) Klamath talks begin. *Indian Country Today, 21*, A1.

Herbert, B. (2005, June 6). The mobility myth. *New York Times*. Retrieved October 7, 2005, from www.commondreams.org/views05/0606-27.htm

Ho, M. K. (1987). *Family therapy with ethnic minorities*. Newbury Park, CA: Sage.

Hofstede, G. (1997). *Cultures and organizations: Software of the mind* (Rev. ed.). New York: McGraw-Hill.

Hofstede, G. (1998). *Masculinity and femininity*. Thousand Oaks, CA: Sage.

Hofstede, G. (2001). *Culture's consequences* (2nd ed.). Thousand Oaks, CA: Sage.

Houston, M. (2004). When black women talk with white women: Why dialogues are difficult. In A. González, M. Houston, & V. Chen (Eds.), *Our voices: Essays in culture, ethnicity and communication* (4th ed.). Los Angeles, CA: Roxbury.

Hulse, E. (1996). Example of the English Puritans. *Reformation Today, 153*. Retrieved June 13, 2006, from www.puritansermons.com/banner/hulse1.htm

IIE (2007a). *Open Doors 2007: International students in the U.S.* Washington, DC: Institute of International Education. Retrieved April 7, 2008, from http://opendoors.iienetwork.org/?p=113119

IIE (2007b). *Open Doors 2007: American students studying abroad*. Washington, DC: Institute of International Education. Retrieved April 7, 2008, from open http://doors.iienetwork.org/?p=113744

Jarvis, J. (1995). *Euro Disneyland Paris cultural research project* (Report No. 2). Pittsburgh, PA: Robert Morris College.

Johnson, A. G. (2001). *Privilege, power and difference*. Thousand Oaks, CA: Sage.

Johnson, B. R., & Jacobson, C. K. (2005). Context in contact: An examination of social settings on Whites' attitudes toward interracial marriage. *Journal of Social Psychology, 68*, 387–399.

Jones, N. A., & Smith, A. S. (2001). The two or more races population. *Census 2000 Brief (U.S. Census Bureau Publication No. C2KBR/01-6)*. Washington, DC: U.S. Government Printing Office.

Jung, E., Hecht, M. L., & Wadsworth, B. C. (2007). The role of identity in international students' psychological well-being in the United States: A model of depression level, identity gaps, discrimination, and acculturation. *International Journal of Intercultural Relations, 31*, 605–624.

Kashima, E. S., & Loh, E. (2006) International students' acculturation: Effects of international, conational, and local ties and need for closure. *International Journal of Intercultural Relations, 30*, 471–486.

Kikoski, J. F., & Kikoski, C. K. (1999). *Reflexive communication in the culturally diverse workplace*. Westport, CT: Praeger.

Kim, Y. Y. (2005). Adapting to a new culture: An integrative communication theory. In W. B. Gudykunst (Ed.), *Theorizing about intercultural communication* (pp. 375–400). Thousand Oaks, CA: Sage.

Kivel, P. (1996). *Uprooting racism: How white people can work for racial justice*. Gabriola Islands, BC: New Society Publishers.

Kluckhohn, F., and Strodtbeck, F. (1961). *Variations in value orientations*. Chicago: Row, Peterson & Co.

Kohls, R. L. (2001). *Survival kit for overseas living* (4th ed.). Yarmouth, ME: Nicholas Brealey/Intercultural Press.

Lee, S. M., & Edmonston, B. (2005). New marriages, new families: U.S. racial and Hispanic intermarriage. *Population Bulletin, 60*, 3–36.

Lee, J. J., & Rice, C. (2007). Welcome to America? International student perceptions of discrimination, *Higher Education, 53*, 381–409.

Lin, C. (2006). Culture shock and social support: An investigation of a Chinese student organization on a U.S. campus. *Journal of Intercultural Communication Research, 35*(2), 117–137.

Loewen, J. W. (1995). *Lies my teacher told me*. New York: Simon & Schuster.

Martin, J. N., & Nakayama, T. K. (2008). *Experiencing intercultural communication: An introduction* (3rd ed.). Boston: McGraw-Hill.

Matsumoto, D. (2002). *The new Japan: Debunking seven cultural stereotypes*. Yarmouth, ME: Intercultural Press.

McGoldrick, M., Giordano, J., & Pearce, J. K. (Eds.). (1996). *Ethnicity and family therapy* (2nd ed.). New York: Guilford Press.

McKinnon, S. (2004, September 1). Spotted owl habitat plan ruffles feathers. *Arizona Republic*, B1.

Melmer, D. (2004). Buffalo and Lakota are kin. *Indian Country Today, 23*, B1.

Norris, F., (2007, December 3). Euro Disney. *New York Times*. Retrieved March 20, 2009, from http://norris.blogs.nytimes.com/2007/12/03/euro-disney/

Numbers. (2008, February 4). *Time*, 18.

Orbe, M. P. (1998). *Constructing co-cultural theory: An explication of culture, power, and communication*. Thousand Oaks, CA: Sage.

Passel, J. S., & Cohn, D. V. (2008, February 11). U.S. populations projections: 2005–2050. Retrieved March 20, 2009, from http://pewhispanic.org/files/reports/85.pdf

Porter, T. (2002). The words that come before all else. *Native Americas, 19*, 7–10.

Rabbi: My radio show pulled because of racism (2005, September 27). *The Associated Press*. Retrieved October 10, 2005, from www.newsmax.com/archives/ic/2005/9/22/173035.shtml

Riddle, D. (2000). Cultural approaches to innovation. *International Trade Forum, 2*, 23–26.

Root, M. P. P. (2001). *Love's revolution: Interracial marriage*. Philadelphia, PA: Temple University Press.

Rosenblatt, P. C., Karis, T. A., & Powell, R. D. (1996). *Multiracial couples: Black and white voices*. Thousand Oaks, CA: Sage.

Rosenstone, R. A. (2005). My wife, the Muslim. *Antioch Review, 63*, 234–246.

Schneider, S. C., & Barsoux, J. L. (2003). *Managing across cultures*. New York: Prentice Hall.

Shelden, R. G. (2004). The imprisonment crisis in America: An introduction. *Review of Policy Research, 21*, 5–13.

Shim, Y-J., Kim, M-S., & Martin, J. N. (2008) *Changing Korea: Understanding culture and communication*. New York: Peter Lang.

Snyder, M. (2001). Self-fulfilling stereotypes. In P. S. Rothenberg (Ed.), *Race, class & gender in the U.S.* (5th ed., pp. 511–517). New York: Worth.

Stewart, E. C., & Bennett, M. J. (1991). *American cultural patterns: A cross-cultural perspective*. Yarmouth, ME: Intercultural Press.

Taylor, P., Funk, C., & Craighill, P. (2006). *Guess who's coming to dinner*. Pew Research Center Social Trends Report. Washington, DC: Pew Research Center.

Tiger Woods on race. Media statement Retrieved June 13, 2006, from www.geocities.com/Colosseum/2396/tigerrace.html

Ting-Toomey, S. (1999). *Communicating across cultures*. New York: Guilford.

Tourism Highlights (2007 ed.). Retrieved April 7, 2008, from www.world-tourism.org/facts/eng/pdf/highlights/highlights_07_eng_hr.pdf

Triandis, H. (1995). *Individualism and collectivism*. Boulder, CO: Westview Press.

Trompenaars, F., & Hampden-Turner, C. (1997). *Riding the waves of culture: Understanding diversity in global business*. Boston: McGraw-Hill.

Ward, C. (2008). Thinking outside the Berry boxes: New perspectives on identity, acculturation and intercultural relations. *International Journal of Intercultural Relations, 32*, 105–114.

Wells, S. (2002). *The journey of man: A genetic odyssey*. Princeton, NJ: Princeton University Press.

Yamato, G. (2001). Something about the subject makes it hard to name. In M. L. Andersen & P. H. Collins (Eds.), *Race, class, and gender: An anthology* (4th ed., pp. 90–94). Belmont, CA: Wadsworth.

Zuni eagle aviary is a beautiful sign. (2002, July 31). [Editorial.] Retrieved March 20, 2009, from www.highbeam.com/doc/1P179291291.html

Chapter 8

Abbey, A. (1987). Misperceptions of friendly behavior as sexual interest: A survey of naturally occurring incidents. *Psychology of Women Quarterly, 11*, 173–194.

Abbey, A. (1988). Misperceptions as an antecedent of acquaintance rape: A consequence of ambiguity in communication between men and women. In A. Parrot & L. Bechhofer (Eds.), *Acquaintance rape: The hidden crime* (pp. 96–112). NY: John Wiley & Sons.

Aboud, F. E., & Mendelson, M. J. (1996). Determinants of friendship selection and quality: Developmental perspectives. In W. M. Bukowski, A. F. Newcomb, & W. W. Hartup (Eds.), *The company they keep: Friendship in childhood and adolescence* (pp. 87–112). New York: Cambridge University Press.

Affifi, W. A., & Faulkner, S. L. (2000). On just being friends: The frequency and impact of sexual activity in cross–sex friendships. *Journal of Social and Personal Relationships, 17*, 205–222.

Alberts, J., Yoshimura, C., Rabby, M., & Loschiavo, R. (2005). Mapping the topography of couples' everyday interaction. *Journal of Social and Personal Relationships, 22*, 299–322.

Allan, G. (1977). Class variation in friendship patterns. *British Journal of Sociology, 28*, 389–393.

Altman, I., & Taylor, D. A. (1973). *Social penetration: The development of interpersonal relationships*. New York: Holt, Rinehart & Winston.

Altman, I., & Taylor, D. (1987). Communication in interpersonal relationships: Social penetration theory. In M. E. Roloff and G. R. Miller (Eds.), *Interpersonal processes: New directions in communication research* (pp. 257–277). Newbury Park, CA: Sage.

Altman, I., Vinsel, A., & Brown, B. B. (1981). Dialectic conceptions in social psychology: An application to social penetration and privacy regulation. In L. Berkowitz (Ed.), *Advances in experimental social psychology* (Vol. 14, pp. 107–160). New York: Academic Press.

American Psychological Association. (1996). *Violence and the family: Report of the American Psychological Association presidential task force on violence and the family*. Retrieved June 15, 2006, from www.apa.org/pi/viol&fam.html

Andersen, P., Eloy, S. V., Guerrero, L. K., & Spitzberg, B. H. (1995). Romantic jealousy and relational satisfaction: A look at the impact of jealousy experience and expression. *Communication Reports, 8*, 77–85.

Anglin, K., & Holtzworth-Munroe, A. (1997). Comparing the responses of maritally violent and nonviolent spouses to problematic marital and nonmarital situations: Are the skills deficits of physically aggressive husbands and wives global? *Journal of Family Psychology, 11*, 301–313.

Argyle, M., & Henderson, M. (1984). The rules of friendship. *Journal of Social and Personal Relationships, 1*, 211–237.

Atkinson, B. (2005, January). The love breakthrough. *O, The Oprah Magazine*, 128–131, 163–164.

Atkinson, M. P., & Glass, B. L. (1985). Marital age, heterogamy and homogamy, 1900 to 1980. *Journal of Marriage and the Family* 47(3), 685–700.

Aune, K. S., & Comstock, J. (1991) Experience and expression of jealousy: Comparison between friends and romantics. *Psychological Reports*, 69, 315–319.

Baxter, L. A. (1982). Strategies for ending relationships: Two studies. *Western Journal of Speech Communication*, 46, 233–242.

Baxter, L. A. (1988). A dialectical perspective on communication strategies in relationship development. In S. W. Duck, D. F. Hay, S. E. Hobfoll, W. Ickes, & B. Montgomery (Eds.), *Handbook of personal relationships* (pp. 257–273). London: Wiley.

Baxter, L. A. (1991). Gender differences in the heterosexual relationship rules embedded in break-up accounts. *Journal of Social and Personal Relationships*, 3, 289–306.

Baxter, L. A., & Bullis, C. (1986). Turning points in developing romantic relationships. *Human Communication Research*, 12, 469–493.

Baxter, L. A., & Erbert, L. A. (1999). Perceptions of dialectical contradictions in turning points of development in heterosexual romantic relationships. *Journal of Social and Personal Relationships*, 16, 547–569.

Berg, J. H., & Piner, K. E. (1990). Social relationships and the lack of social relationships. In S. Duck & R. C. Silver (Eds.), *Personal relationships and social support* (pp. 140–158). London: Sage Publications.

Berger, C. R., & Calabrese, R. J. (1975). Some explorations in initial interaction and beyond: Toward a developmental theory of interpersonal communication. *Human Communication Theory*, 1, 99–112.

Berger, C. R., & Kellerman, N. (1994). Acquiring social information. In J. Daly & J. Wiemann (Eds.), *Strategic interpersonal communication* (pp. 1–31). Hillsdale, NJ: Lawrence Erlbaum.

Berscheid, E., & Reis, H. T. (1998). Attraction and close relationships. In D. Gilbert, S. Fiske, & G. Lindzey (Eds.), *Handbook of social psychology* (Vol. 2., 4th ed., pp. 193–281). New York: McGraw-Hill.

Blieszner, R., & Adams, R. G. (1992). *Adult friendship*. Newbury Park, CA: Sage.

Bok, S. *Lying: Moral choice in public and private life.* New York: Random House.

Bowker, A. (2004). Predicting friendship stability during early adolescence. *Journal of Early, Adolescence.* 24, 85–112.

Bramlett, M. D., & Mosher, W. D. (2002). Cohabitation, marriage, divorce, and remarriage in the United States. National Center for Health Statistics. *Vital Health Stat, 23*(22).

Buller, D. B., & Burgoon, J. K. (1996). Interpersonal deception theory. *Communication Theory*, 6, 203–242.

Bureau of Justice Statistics. (1995, August). *Special Report: Violence against women: Estimates from the Redesigned Survey* (NCJ-154348), p. 3.

Burgoon, J. K., Buller, D. B., Ebesu, A., & Rockwell, P. (1994). Interpersonal deception: 5. Accuracy in deception detection. *Communication Monographs*, 61, 303–325.

Burleson, B. R., & Samter, W. (1996). Similarity in the communication skills of young adults: Foundations of attraction, friendship, and relationship satisfaction. *Communication Reports*, 9, 127–137.

Buss, D. M. (1985). Human mate selection. *American Scientist*, 73, 47–51.

Buss, D. M. (1988). From vigilance to violence: Tactics of mate retention in American undergraduates. *Ethology and Sociobiology*, 9, 291–317.

Buss, D. M., Shackelford, T. K., Kirkpatrick, L. A., & Larsen, R. J. (2001). A half century of mate preferences: The cultural evolution of values. *Journal of Marriage and the Family*, 63, 491–503.

Byrne, D. (1997). An overview (and underview) of research and theory within the attraction paradigm. *Journal of Social and Personal Relationships*, 14, 417–431.

Canary, D. J., & Spitzberg, B. H. (1985). Loneliness and relationally competent communication. *Journal of Social and Personal Relationships*, 2, 387–402.

Canary, D. J., & Stafford, L. (1994). Maintaining relationships through strategic and routine interaction. In D. J. Canary & L. Stafford (Eds.), *Communication and relational maintenance* (pp. 3–22). San Diego: Academic Press.

Canary, D. J., Stafford, L., Hause, K. S., & Wallace, L. A. (1993). An inductive analysis of relational maintenance strategies: Comparisons among lovers, relatives, friends, and others. *Communication Research Reports*, 10, 5–14.

Cano, A., & O'Leary, K. D. (1997). Romantic jealousy and affairs: Research and implications for couples' therapy. *Journal of Sex and Marital Therapy*, 23, 249–275.

Cash, T. F., & Derlega, V. J. (1978). The matching hypothesis: Physical attractiveness among same-sex friends. *Personality and Social Psychology Bulletin*, 4, 240–243.

Cate, R. M., & Lloyd, S. A. (1992). *Courtship*. Newbury Park: Sage.

Cauffman, E., Feldman, S., Jensen, L., & Arnett, J. (2000). The (Un)acceptability of violence against peers and dates. *Journal of Adolescent Research*, 15, 652–673.

Centers for Disease Control and Prevention. (2002). Youth risk behavior surveillance—United States, 2001. In *CDC Surveillance Summaries*, June 28, 2002. *MMWR*, 51(SS-4), 5–6.

Chambers, V. J., Christiansen, J. R., & Kunz, P. R. (1983). Physiognomic homogamy: A test of physical similarity as a factor in mate selection process. *Social Biology*, 30, 151–157.

Cody, M. J. (1982). A typology of disengagement strategies and an examination of the role intimacy, reactions to inequity and relational problems play in strategy selection. *Communication Monographs*, 49, 148–170.

Commonwealth Fund. (1998, May). *Health concerns across a woman's lifespan: 1998 survey of women's health.*

Cordova, J. V., Jacobsen, N. S., Gottman, J. M., Rushe, R., & Cox, G. (1993). Negative reciprocity and communication in couples with a violent husband. *Journal of Abnormal Psychology*, 102, 559–564.

Dainton, M. A., Zelley, E., & Langan, E. (2003). Maintaining friendships throughout the lifespan. In D. J. Canary & M. Dainton (Eds.), *Maintaining relationships through communication* (pp. 79–102). Mahwah, NJ: Erlbaum.

Donaghue, N., & Fallon, B. J. (2003) Gender-role self-stereotyping and the relationship between equity and satisfaction in close relationships. *Sex Roles*, 48, 217–230.

Duck, S. (1991). *Understanding relationships*. New York: Guilford Press.

Duck, S. W. (1982). Social and cognitive features of the dissolution of commitment to relationships. In S. W. Duck (Ed.), *Personal relationships 4: Dissolving personal relationships*, (pp. 51–73). London: Academic Press.

Duck, S. W. (1988). *Relating to others*. Chicago: Dorsey Press.

Edgell, P. (2003). In rhetoric and practice: Defining the "good family" in local congregations. In M. Dillon (Ed.), *Handbook of the sociology of religion*. New York: Cambridge University Press.

Emmers-Sommers, T. M. (2004). The effect of communication quality and quantity indicators on intimacy and relational satisfaction. *Journal of Social and Personal Relationships, 21*(4), 399–411.

Essau, C. A., Conradt, J., & Petermann, F. (1999). Frequency and comorbidity of social phobia and fears in adolescents. *Behavior Research and Therapy*, 37, 831–843.

Fehr, B. (2000). The life cycle of friendship. In C. Hendrick & S. S. Hendrick (Eds.), *Close relationships: A source book* (pp. 71–82). Thousand Oaks: CA: Sage.

Felmlee, D. H. (1995). Fatal attractions: Affections and disaffections in intimate relationships. *Journal of Social and Personal Relationships*, 12, 295–311.

Ferraro, K. (1996). The dance of dependency: A geneology of domestic violence discourse. *Hypattia*, 11, 72–91.

Galassi, J. P., & Galassi, M. D. (1979). Modifications of heterosexual skills deficits. In A. S. Bellack & M. Hersen (Eds.), *Research and practice in social skills training* (pp. 131–188). New York: Plenum.

Gierveld, J., & Tilburg, T. (1995). Social relationships, integration and loneliness. In C. P. M. Knipscheer, J. Gierveld, T. Tilburg, & P. A. Dykstra (Eds.), *Living arrangements and social networks among older adults*. Amsterdam: VU University Press.

Goodwin, R., & Tang, D. (1991). Preferences for friends and close relationships partners: A cross-cultural comparison. *Journal of Social Psychology*, 131, 579–581.

Grotpeter, J. K., & Crick, N. R. (1996). Relational aggression, overt aggression, and friendship. *Child Development*, 67, 2328–2338.

Guerrero, L. K., & Afifi, W. A. (1999). Toward a goal-centered approach for understanding strategic communicative responses to jealousy. *Western Journal of Communication*, 63, 216–248.

Guerrero, L. K., & Andersen, P. A. (1998). Jealousy experience and expression in romantic relationships. In L. K. Guerrero & P. A. Andersen (Eds.), *Communication and emotion: Theory, research and application* (pp. 155–188). San Diego, CA: Academic Press.

Guerrero, L. K., Andersen, P. A., Afifi, W. A. (2007). *Close encounters: Communication in relationships*. Los Angeles: Sage.

Guerrero, L. K., Eloy, S. V., & Wabnik, A. I. (1993). Linking maintenance strategies to relationship development and disengagement: A reconceptualization. *Journal of Social and Personal Relationships*, 10, 273–283.

Haas, S. M., & Stafford, L. (1998). An initial examination of relationship maintenance behaviors in gay and lesbian relationships. *Journal of Social and Personal Relationships*, 15, 846–855.

Hays, R. B. (1988). Friendship. In S. W. Duck (Eds.), *Handbook of personal relationships* (pp. 391–408). New York: Wiley.

Hinsz, V. B. (1989). Facial resemblance in engaged and married couples. *Journal of Social and Personal Relationships*, 6, 223–229.

Holt-Lunstad, J., Birmingham, W., & Jones, B. Q. (2008) Is there something unique about marriage? The relative impact of marital status, relationship quality, and network support on ambulatory blood pressure and mental health. *Annals of Behavioral Medicine, 35,* 239–244.

Infante, D. A., Chandler, T.A., & Rudd, J. E. (1989). A test of an argumentative skill deficiency model of interspousal violence. *Communication Monographs*, 56, 163–177.

Janz, T. A. (2000). The evolution and diversity of relationships in Canadian families. *Canadian Journal of Higher Education*. Retrieved June 15, 2006, from www.lcc.gc.ca/research_project/00_diversity_1-en.asp

Johnson, A. J. (2000, July). A role theory approach to examining the maintenance of geographically close and long-distance friendships. Paper presented at the International Network on Personal Relationships Conference, Prescott, AZ.

Johnson, A. J., Wittenberg, E., Haigh, M., & Wigley, S. (2004). The process of relationship development and deterioration: Turning points in friendships that have terminated. *Communication Quarterly*, 52, 54–68.

Kalmijin, M. (1994). Assortative mating by cultural and economic occupational status. *American Journal of Sociology*, 100, 422–452.

Kelley, H. H., Berscheid, E., Christensen, A., Harvey, J., Huston, T., Levinger, G., McClintock, E., Peplau, L. A., & Peterson, D. (1983). *Close relationships*. San Francisco: Freeman.

Kenrick, D., & Trost, M. R. (1996). Evolutionary approaches to relationships. In S. Duck (Ed.), *Handbook of personal relationships* (2nd ed.). London: Wiley.

Kenrick, D. T., Sadalla, E. K., Groth, G., & Trost, M. R. (1990). Evolution, traits, and the stages of human courtships: Qualifying the parental investment model. *Journal of Personality*, 58, 97–116.

Kimmel, M. S. (2002). Male victims of domestic violence: A substantive and methodological research review. *Violence Against Women*, 8(11), 1332–1363.

Knapp, M. L. (1978). *Social intercourse: From greeting to goodbye*. Boston: Allyn & Bacon.

Knapp, M. L., & Vangelisti, A. (1997). *Interpersonal communication and relationships* (2nd ed.). Boston: Allyn & Bacon.

Knox, D., Schacht, C., Holt, J., & Turner, J. (1993). Sexual lies among university students. *College Student Journal*, 269–272.

Kowalski, R., Valentine, S., Wilkinson, R., Queen, A., & Sharpe, B. (2003). Lying, cheating, complaining, and other aversive interpersonal behaviors: A narrative examination of the dark side of relationships. *Journal of Social and Personal Relationships*, 20, 471–490.

Kramer, D., & Moore, M. (2001). Gender roles, romantic fiction and family therapy. *Family Therapy*, 12(24), 1–8.

Kurdek, L.A. (1991). The dissolution of gay and lesbian couples. *Journal of Social and Personal Relationships*, 8, 265–78.

Kurt, J. E., & Sherker, J. L. (2003). Relationship quality, trait similarity, and self-other agreement on personality ratings in college roommates *Journal of Personality* 71, 21–40.

LaFollette, H. (1996). *Personal relationships: Love, identity, and morality*. Cambridge, MA: Blackwell Publishers.

Lenski, T. (2006, September 11). Conflict and anger—Strategies to de-escalate and get conversation back on track. *Ezing @rticles*. Retrieved October 23, 2008, from http://ezinearticles.com/?Conflict-and-Anger-Strategies-to-De-Escalate-and-Get-Conversation-Back-on Track&id=296315.

Lim, G. Y., & Roloff, M. (1999). Attributing sexual consent. *Journal of Applied Communication Research*, 27, 1–23.

Lloyd, S. A. (1990). Conflict types and strategies in violent marriages. *Journal of Family Violence*, 5, 269–284.

Lloyd, S. A. (1999). The interpersonal and communication dynamics of wife battering. In X. Arriaga & S. Oskamp (Eds.), *Violence in intimate relationships* (pp. 91–111). Thousand Oaks, CA: Sage.

Lloyd, S. A., & Emery, B. C. (2000). The context and dynamics of intimate aggression against women. *Journal of Social and Personal Relationships*, 17(4-5), 503–521.

Mare, R. D. (1991). Five decades of educational assortative mating. *American Sociological Review*, 56, 15–32.

Marquardt, E., & Glenn, N. (2001). Hooking up, hanging out and hoping for Mr. Right: College women on mating and dating today. New York: Institute for American Values. Retrieved June 15, 2006, from www.Americanvalues.org/Hooking_up.pdf

McCormick, N. B., & Jones, J. J. (1989). Gender differences in nonverbal flirtation. *Journal of Sex Education and Therapy*, 15, 271–282.

McCornack, S. A., & Parks, M. R. (1986). Deception detection and relationship development: The other side of trust. In M. L. McLaughlin (Ed.), *Communication Yearbook 9*, 377–389. Newbury Park, CA: Sage.

Messman, S. J., Canary, D. J., & Hause, K. S. (2000). Motives to remain platonic, equity, and the use of maintenance strategies in opposite-sex friendships. *Journal of Social and Personal Relationships*, 17, 67–94.

Miller, R. S. (1997). We always hurt the ones we love: Aversive interactions in close relationships. In R. M. Kowalski (Ed.), *Aversive interpersonal behaviors* (pp. 12–29). New York: Plenum.

Miller, R. S. (2002). Suicidal and death ideation in older primary care patients with depression, anxiety, and at-risk. *American Journal of Geriatric Psychiatry*, 10, 417–427.

Mongeau, P. A., Ramirez, R., & Vorell, M. (2003). *Friends with benefits: An initial exploration of a sexual but not romantic relationship*. Paper presented at the Western States Communication Association. Salt Lake, UT.

MSNBC News. (2004, March 8). Lip-lock could mean lockup in Indonesia. Retrieved March 8, 2006, from www.msnbc.msn.com/id=/4478875/

Muehlenhard, C. L. (1989). Misinterpreted dating behaviors and the risk of date rape. In M. A. Pirog-Good & J. E. Stets (Eds.), *Violence in dating relationships: Emerging social issues* (pp. 241–256). New York: Praeger.

Muehlenhard, C. L., & Hollabough, L. C. (1988). Do women sometimes say no when they mean yes?: The prevalence and correlates of women's token resistance to sex. *Journal of Personality and Social Psychology*, 54, 872–879.

Muehlenhard, C. L., & Linton, M. A. (1987). Date rape and sexual aggression in dating: Incidence and risk factors. *Journal of Personality and Social Psychology*, 34, 186–196.

Muehlenhard, C. L., & McFalls, M. C. (1981). Dating initiation from a woman's perspective. *Behavior Therapy*, 14, 626–636.

Mulenhard, C. L., & Miller, E. N. (1988). Traditional and non-traditional men's responses to women's dating initiation. *Behavior Modification* 12(3), 385–403.

Mullen, P. E., & Maack, L. H. (1985). Jealousy, pathological jealousy, and aggression. In D. P. Farrington & J. Gunn (Eds.), *Aggression and dangerousness* (pp. 103–126). New York: Wiley.

Nardi, P. M. (1992). That's what friends are for: Friends as family in the gay and lesbian community. In K. Plummer (Ed.), *Modern homosexualities: Fragments of lesbian and gay experience* (pp. 108–120). New York: Routledge.

Noller, P., & Fitzpatrick, M. A. (1990). Marital communication in the eighties. *Journal of Marriage and the Family*, 52, 832–843.

O'Brien, E., & Foley, L. (1999). The dating game: An exercise illustrating the concepts of homogamy, heterogamy, hypergamy, and hypogamy. *Teaching Sociology*, 27(2), 145–149.

Owen, W. F. (1987). The verbal expression of love by women and men as a critical communication event in personal relationships. *Women's Studies in Communication*, 10, 15–24.

Paul, E. L., & Hayes, A. (2002). The causalities of "casual sex": A qualitative exploration of the phenomenology of college students' hookups. *Journal of Social and Personal Relationships*, 19, 639–661.

Paul, E. L., McManus, B., & Hayes, A. (2000). "Hookups": Characteristics and correlates of college students' spontaneous and anonymous sexual experiences. *The Journal of Sex Research*, 37, 76–88.

Pogrebin, L. C. (1992). The same and different: Crossing boundaries of color, culture, sexual preference, disability, and age. In W. B. Gudykunst, & Y. Y. Kim (Eds.), *Readings on communicating with strangers* (pp. 318–336). New York: McGraw-Hill.

Psarska, A. D. (1970). Jealousy factor in homicide in forensic material. *Polish Medical Journal*, 9, 1504–1510.

Rawlins, W. K. (1992). *Friendship matters*. New York: Aline de Guyter.

Reeder, H. (1996). *What Harry and Sally didn't tell you*. Unpublished doctoral dissertation, Arizona State University, Tempe.

Rennison, C. M., & Welchans, S. (2000). *Intimate Partner Violence Special Report*, NCJ 178247. Washington, DC: U.S. Department of Justice.

Rindfuss, R. R., & Stephen, E. H. (1990). Marital noncohabitation: Separation does not make the heart grow fonder. *Journal of Marriage and the Family*, 52, 259–270.

Root, M. P. (2001). *Love's revolution: Interracial marriage*. Philadelphia, PA: Temple University Press.

Rose, S. M. (1984). How friendships end: Patterns among young adults. *Journal of Social and Personal Relationships*, 1, 267–277.

Roth, M., & Parker, J. (2001). Affective and behavioral responses to friends who neglect their friends for dating partners: Influences of gender, jealousy and perspective. *Journal of Adolescence*, 24, 281–296.

Sabourin, T. C. (1996). The role of communication in verbal abuse between spouses. In D. D. Cahn & S. A. Lloyd (Eds.), *Family violence from a communication perspective* (pp. 199–217). Thousand Oaks, CA: Sage.

Sagarin, B. J., Rhoads, K. L., & Cialdini, R. B. (1998). Deceiver's distrust: Denigration as a consequence of undiscovered deception. *Personality and Social Psychology Bulletin*. 24, 1167–1176.

Sailer, S. (2003, March 14). *Interracial marriage gender gap grows*. United Press International (UPI). Retrieved June 28, 2004, from www.modelminority.com/article338.html

Schafer, R. B., & Keith, P. M. (1990). Matching by weight in married couples: A life cycle perspective. *Journal of Social Psychology* 130(5), 657–664.

Segrin, C., & Givertz, M. (2003). Methods of social skills training and development. In J. O. Green & B. R. Burleson (Eds.), *Handbook of communication and social interaction skills* (pp. 135–176). Mahwah, NJ: Erlbaum.

Shehan, C. L., Bock, E. W., & Lee, G. R., (1990). Religious heterogamy, religiosity, and marital happiness: The case of Catholics. *Journal of Marriage and the Family*, 52, 73–79.

Sias, P. M., & Cahill, D. J. (1998). From coworkers to friends: The development of peer friendships in the workplace. *Western Journal of Communication*, 62, 273–299.

Sollors, W. (Ed.). (2000). *Interracialism: Black and white intermarriage in American history, literature and law*. New York: Oxford University Press.

Spitzberg, B. (1998). Sexual coercion in courtship relationships. In B. Spitzberg & W. Cupach (Eds.), *The dark side of close relationships*. Hillsdale, NJ: Erlbaum.

Sprecher, S. (1998). Insiders' perspectives on reasons for attraction to a close other. *Social Psychology Quarterly*, 61, 287–300.

Sprecher, S., & Regan, P. (2002). Liking some things (in some people) more than others: Partner preferences in romantic relationships and friendships. *Journal of Social and Personal Relationships*. 19, 463–481.

Stafford, L. (2003). Maintaining romantic relationships: Summary and analysis of one research program. In D. Canary & K. Dindia (Eds.), *Maintaining relationships through communication* (pp. 51–78). Mahwah, NJ: Erlbaum.

Stiff, J. B., Kim, H. J., & Ramesh, C. N. (1989). *Truth biases and aroused suspicion in relational deception*. Paper presented at the annual meeting of the Interpersonal Communication Association (May), San Francisco, CA.

Surra, C. (1987). Reasons for changes in commitment: Variations by courtship type. *Journal of Social and Personal Relationships*, 4, 17–33.

Times Square Travels. (2004). Travel in Japan. Retrieved June 15, 2006, from www.taveltst.ca/index.php?tpl=vacation-guides_japan-guide_introduction

Tolhuizen, J. H. (1990). *Deception in developing dating relationships*. Paper presented at the Speech Communication Association Convention, Chicago, IL.

Trost, M. R., & Kenrick, D. T. (1993). An evolutionary perspective on interpersonal communication. In S. Petronio, J. K. Alberts, M. Hecht, & J. Buley (Eds.), *Contemporary perspectives on interpersonal communication* (pp. 120–124). Madison, WI: Brown & Benchmark.

Turner, R. E., Edgley, C., & Olmstead, G. (1975). Information control in conversations: Honesty is not always the best policy. *Kansas Journal of Sociology*, 11, 69–89.

U.S. Bureau of the Census. (1998, October 10) *Race of wife by race of husband, 1960, 1970, 1980, 1990, 1992*. Retrieved June 28, 2004, from www.census.gov/population/socdemo/race/interractab1.txt

Vangelisti, A. L. (1994). Family secrets: Forms, functions, and correlates. *Journal of Social and Personal Relationships*, 11(1), 113–135.

Vorauer, J., & Ratner, R. (1996). Who's going to make the first move? *Journal of Social and Personal Relationships*, 13, 483–506.

Weber, A. L. (1998). Losing, leaving and letting go: Coping with nonmarital breakups. In B. H. Spitzberg & W. R. Cupach (Eds.), *The dark side of close relationships* (pp. 267–306). Mawah, NJ: Erlbaum.

White, G. L. (1980) Physical attractiveness and courtship progress. *Personality and Social Psychology*, 39, 660–668.

White, G. L., & Mullen, P. E. (1989). *Jealousy*. New York: Guilford Press.

Willan, V. J., & Pollard, P. (2003). Likelihood of acquaintance rape as a function of males' sexual expectations, disappointment, and adherence to rape-conducive attitudes. *Journal of Social and Personal Relationships*, 20, 637–661.

World Travels. (2004). Kuwait travel guide. Retrieved March 16, 2006, from www.worldtravelguide.net/country/141/country_guide/Middle-East/Kuwait.html

Wright, D. E. (1999). *Personal relationships: An interdisciplinary approach*. Mountain View, CA: Mayfield Publishing.

Young, J. E. (1981). Cognitive therapy and loneliness. In G. Emery, S. D. Hollon, & R. C. Bedrosian (Eds.), *New directions in cognitive therapy: A casebook* (pp. 139–159). New York: Guilford Press.

Chapter 9

Adams, K., & Galanes, G. J. (2003). *Communicating in groups: Applications and skills.* Boston: McGraw-Hill.

Allen, T. H., & Plax, T. G. (2002). Exploring consequences of group communication in the classroom. In L. R. Frey (Ed.), *New directions in group communication* (pp. 219–234). Thousand Oaks, CA: Sage.

Alsop, R. (2003, September 9). Playing well with others. *Wall Street Journal* (Eastern Edition), p. R11.

Arrow, H., McGrath, J. E., & Berdahl, J. L. (2000). *Small groups as complex systems.* Thousand Oaks, CA: Sage.

Bantz, C. R. (1993). Cultural diversity and group cross-cultural team research. *Journal of Applied Communication Research, 21,* 1–20.

Barge, J. K. (1989). Leadership as medium: A leaderless group discussion model. *Communication Quarterly, 37,* 237–247.

Barnard, C. (1938). *The functions of an executive.* Cambridge, MA: Harvard University Press.

Barnlund, D. C., & Haiman, S. (1960). *The dynamics of discussion.* Boston: Houghton-Mifflin.

Benne, K. D., & Sheats, P. (1948). Functional roles of group members. *Journal of Social Issues, 4,* 41–49.

Bono, J. E., & Judge, T. A. (2004). Personality and transformational and transactional leadership: A meta-analysis. *Journal of Applied Psychology, 89(5),* 901–910.

Bormann, E. G. (1975). *Discussion and group methods* (2nd ed.). New York: Harper & Row.

Bowers, C. A., Pharmer, J. A., & Salas, E. (2000). When member homogeneity is needed in work teams: A meta-analysis. *Small Group Research, 31,* 305–327.

Broome, B. J., & Chen, M. (1992). Guidelines for computer-assisted problem solving: Meeting the challenges of complex issues, *Small Group Research, 23,* 216–236.

Broome, B. J., & Fulbright, L. (1995). A multistage influence model of barriers to group problem solving: A participant-generated agenda for small group research, *Small Group Research, 26,* 24–55.

Cady, S. H., & Valentine, J. (1999). Team innovation and perceptions of consideration: What difference does diversity make? *Small Group Research, 30,* 730–750.

Carwright, D. (1968). The nature of group cohesiveness. In D. Carwright & A. Zander (Eds.), *Group dynamics: Research and theory* (3rd ed., pp. 91–109). New York: Harper & Row.

Connaughton, S. L., & Shuffler, M. (2007). Multinational and multicultural distributed teams: A review and future agenda. *Small Group Research, 38(1),* 387–412.

Covey, S. R. (1989). *The seven habits of highly effective people: Restoring the character ethic.* New York: Simon and Schuster.

Cox, T. (1994). *Cultural diversity in organizations: Theory, research and practice.* San Francisco: Berrett-Kochler.

Cragan, J. F., & Wright, D. W. (1999). *Communication in small groups: Theory, process, skills* (5th ed.). Belmont, CA: Wadsworth.

Crown, D. F. (2007). The use of group and groupcentric individual goals for culturally heterogeneous and homogeneous task groups: An assessment of European work teams. *Small Group Research, 38(4),* 489–508.

Dennis, A. R., & Wixom, B. H. (2001–2002). Investigating the moderators of the group support systems use with meta-analysis. *Journal of Management Information Systems, 18(3),* 235–257.

Fisher, B. A. (1970). Decision emergence: Phases in group decision-making. *Speech Monographs, 37,* 53–66.

Fisher, B. A. (1980). *Small group decision making: Communication and the group process* (2nd ed.). New York: McGraw-Hill.

Foels, R., Driskell, J. E., Mullen, B., & Salas, E. (2000). The effects of democratic leadership on group member satisfaction: An integration. *Small Group Research, 31,* 676–701.

French, J. R., Jr., & Raven, B. H. (1959). The bases of social power. In D. Cartwright (Ed.), *Studies in social power* (pp. 150–167). Ann Arbor, MI: Institute for Social Research.

Frey, L. R. (1994). The call of the field: Studying communication in natural groups. In L. R. Frey (Ed.), *Group communication in context: Studies of natural groups* (pp. ix–xiv). Hillsdale, NJ: Erlbaum.

Gagné, M., & Zuckerman, M. (1999). Performance and learning goal orientations as moderators of social loafing and social facilitation. *Small Group Research, 30,* 524–541.

Gastil, J. (1994). A meta-analytic review of the productivity and satisfaction of democratic and autocratic leadership. *Small Group Research, 25,* 384–399.

Gokhale, A. (1995). Collaborative learning enhances critical thinking. *Journal of Technology Education, 7,* 22–30.

Gouran, D. S., Hirokawa, R., & Martz, A. (1986). A critical analysis of factors related to the decisional processes involved in the *Challenger* disaster. *Central States Speech Journal,* 119–135.

Grant, H. M., & Crutchfield, L. (2008). The hub of leadership: Lessons from the social sector. *Leader to Leader, 48,* 45–52.

Greenleaf, R. (1970/1991). *The servant as leader.* Indianapolis: The Robert K. Greenleaf Center, 1–37.

Greenleaf, R. K. (1977), *Servant leadership: A journey into the nature of legitimate power and greatness.* New York: Paulist Press.

Greenleaf, R. K. (2002). *Servant leadership: A journey into the nature of legitimate power and greatness.* 25th anniversary edition. New York: Paulist Press.

Groutage, H. (1999, October 10). Mother of slain student calls for tolerance. *Salt Lake Tribune,* p. A4.

Hargrove, R. (1998). *Mastering the art of creative collaboration.* New York: BusinessWeek Books.

Haslett, B. B., & Ruebush, J. (1999). What differences do individual differences in groups make? The effects of individuals, culture, and group composition. In L. R. Frey, D. S. Gouran, & M. S. Poole (Eds.), *The handbook of group communication theory and research* (pp. 115–138). Thousand Oaks, CA: Sage.

Henningsen, D. D., & Henningsen, M. L. M. (2006). Examining the symptoms of groupthink and retrospective sensemaking. *Small Group Research, 37(1),* 36–64.

Hirokawa, R. Y., & Salazar, A. J. (1999). Task-group communication and decision-making performance. In L. R. Frey, D. S. Gouran, & M. S. Poole (Eds.), *The handbook of group communication theory and research* (pp. 167–191). Thousand Oaks, CA: Sage.

Hobman, E. V., Bordia, P., Irmer, B., & Chang, A. (2002). The expression of conflict in computer-mediated and face-to-face groups, *Small Group Research, 33,* 439–465.

Hughes, L. (2003). How to be an effective team player. *Women in Business, 55,* 22.

Ilgen, D. R., Hollenbeck, J. R., Johnson, M., & Jundt, D. (2005). Teams in organizations: From input-process-output models to IMOI models. *Annual Review of Psychology, 56,* 517–543.

Janis, I. L. (1982). *Groupthink: Psychological study of policy decisions and fiascoes.* Boston: Houghton-Mifflin.

Judge, T. A., Bono, J. E., Ilies, R., & Gerhardt, M. W. (2002). Personality and leadership: A qualitative and quantitative review. *Journal of Applied Psychology, 87,* 765–780.

Judge, T. A., & Cable, D. M. (2004). The effect of physical height on workplace success and income: Preliminary test of a theoretical model. *Journal of Applied Psychology, 89,* 428–441.

Judge, T. A., Colbert, A. E., & Ilies, R. (2004). Intelligence and leadership: A quantitative review and test of theoretical propositions. *Journal of Applied Psychology, 89,* 542–552.

Jung, D. I., & Sosik, J. J. (2002). Transformational leadership in work groups: The role of empowerment, cohesiveness, and collective-efficacy on perceived group performance. *Small Group Research, 33,* 313–336.

Kent, M. V. (1994). The presence of others. In A. P. Hare, H. H. Blumberg, M. F. Davies, & M. V. Kent. *Small group research: A handbook* (pp. 81–106). Norwood, NJ: Ablex.

Keyton, J. (1999). Relational communication in groups. In L. R. Frey, D. S. Gouran, & M. S. Poole (Eds.), *Handbook of group communication theory and research* (pp. 199–222). Thousand Oaks, CA: Sage.

Keyton, J. (2000). Introduction: The relational side of groups. *Small Group Research, 34,* 387–396.

King, N., & Anderson, N. (1990). Innovation in working groups. In M. A. West & J. F. Farr (Eds.), *Innovation and creativity at work: Psychological and organizational strategies* (pp. 110–135). Chichester, UK: Wiley.

Klocke, U. (2007). How to improve decision making in small groups: Effects of dissent and training interventions. *Small Group Research, 38(3),* 437–468.

Knippenberg, D. van, De Dreu, C. K. W., & Homan, A. C. (2004). Work group diversity and group performance: An integrative model and research agenda. *Journal of Applied Psychology, 89(6),* 1008–1022.

Lewin, K., Lippit, R., & White, R. K. (1939). Patterns of aggressive behavior in experimentally created "social climates." *Journal of Social Psychology, 10,* 271–279.

Li, D. C. S. (2007). Computer-mediated communication and group decision making: A functional perspective. *Small Group Research 38(5),* 593–614.

Littlejohn, S. W. (2002). *Theories of human communication* (7th ed.). Belmont, CA: Wadsworth.

Littlejohn, S. W., & Jabusch, D. M. (1982). Communication competence: Model and application. *Journal of Applied Communication Research, 10,* 29–37.

Lowry, P. B., Roberts, T. L., Romano, N. C., Cheney, P. D., & Hightower R. T. (2006). The impact of group size and social presence on small-group communication: Does computer-mediated communication make a difference? *Small Group Research, 37(6),* 631–661.

MacNeil, A., & McClanahan, A. (2005). Shared leadership, The Connexions Project. Retrieved May 21, 2008, from http://cnx.org/content/m12923/latest/

Maznevski, M., & Chudoba, C. (2000). Bridging space over time: Global virtual team dynamics and effectiveness. *Organization Science, 11(5),* 473–492.

McLeod, P. L., Lobel, S. A., & Cox, T. H. (1996). Ethnic diversity and creativity in small groups. *Small Group Research, 27,* 248–264.

Meade, R. (1985). Experimental studies of authoritarian and democratic leadership in four cultures: American, Indian, Chinese and Chinese-American. *High School Journal, 68,* 293–295.

Mensch, G. O. (1993). A managerial tool for diagnosing structural readiness for breakthrough innovations in large bureaucracies (technocracies). In R. L. Kuhn (Ed.), *Generating creativity and innovation in large bureaucracies* (pp. 257–281). Westport, CT: Quorum.

Moore, R. M., III. (2000). Creativity of small groups and of persons working alone. *Journal of Social Psychology, 140,* 143–144.

Myers, S. A., & Goodboy, A. K. (2005). A study of grouphate in a course on small group communication. *Psychological Reports, 97(2),* 381–386.

Oetzel, J. G. (1998). Explaining individual communication processes in homogeneous and heterogeneous group through individual-collectivism and self-construal, *Human Communication Research, 25,* 202–224.

Oetzel, J. G. (2001). Self-construals, communication processes, and group outcomes in homogeneous and heterogeneous groups, *Small Group Research, 32*, 19–54.

Oetzel, J. G. (2005). Effective intercultural workgroup communication theory. In W. B. Gudykunst (Ed.), *Theorizing about intercultural communication* (pp. 351–371). Thousand Oaks, CA: Sage.

Paletz, S. B. F., Peng, K., Erez, M., & Maslach, C. (2004). Ethnic composition and its differential impact on group processes in diverse teams. *Small Group Research, 35*, 128–158.

Pavitt, C. (1999). Theorizing about the group communication-leadership relationship. In L. R. Frey, D. S. Gouran, & M. S. Poole (Eds.), *Handbook of group communication theory and research* (pp. 313–334). Thousand Oaks, CA: Sage.

Peterson, R. S., & Behfar, K. J. (2003). The dynamic relationship between performance feedback, trust, and conflict in groups: A longitudinal study. *Organizational Behavior and Human Decision Processes, 92*, 102–112.

Polzer, J. T., Milton, L. P., & Swann, W. B., Jr. (2002). Capitalizing on diversity: Interpersonal congruence in small work groups. *Administrative Science Quarterly, 47*, 296–324.

Poole, M. S. (1983). Decision development in small groups: A study of multiple sequences in decision-making. *Communication Monographs, 50*, 206–232.

Poole, M. S. (1999). Group communication theory. In L. R. Frey, D. S. Gouran, & M. S. Poole (Eds.), *Handbook of group communication theory and research* (pp. 37–70). Thousand Oaks, CA: Sage.

Propp, K. M. (1999). Collective information processing in groups. In L. R. Frey, D. S. Gouran & M. S. Poole (Eds.), *Handbook of group communication theory and research* (pp. 225–250). Thousand Oaks, CA: Sage.

Putnam, L. L., & Stohl, C. (1996). Bona fide groups: An alternative perspective for communication and small group decision-making. In R. Y. Hirokawa & M. S. Poole (Eds.), *Communication and group decision-making* (2nd ed., pp. 147–178). Thousand Oaks, CA: Sage.

Rauch, C. F., Jr., & Behling, O. (1984). Functionalism: Basis for alternative approach to the study of leadership. In J. G. Hunt, D.-M. H. Hosking, C. A. Schriesheim, & R. Stewart (Eds.), *Leaders and managers: International perspectives on managerial behavior and leadership* (pp. 45–62). New York: Pergamon.

Reeves, R., (2004, March). Enough of the 't'-word. *Management Today, 29.*

Riddle, B. L., Anderson, C. M., & Martin, M. M. (2000). Small group socialization scale: Development and validity. *Small Group Research, 31*, 554–572.

Rothwell, J. D. (1995). *In mixed company: Small group communication* (2nd ed.). Fort Worth, TX: Harcourt Brace.

Salazar, A. J. (1997). Communication effects in small group decision-making: Homogeneity and task as moderators of the communication performance relationship. *Western Journal of Communication, 61*, 35–65.

Sargent, L. D., & Sue-Chan, C. (2001). Does diversity affect group efficacy? *Small Group Research, 32*, 426–450.

Savič, B. S., & Pagon, M. (2008). Individual involvement in health care organizations: Differences between professional groups, leaders and employees. *Stress and Health, 24*, 71–84.

Schiller, S. Z., & Mandviwalla, M. (2007). Virtual team research: An analysis of theory use and a framework for theory appropriation. *Small Group Research, 38*(1), 12–59.

Schultz, B. G. (1999). Improving group communication performance. In L. R. Frey, D. S. Gouran, & M. S. Poole (Eds.), *Handbook of group communication theory and research* (pp. 371–394). Thousand Oaks, CA: Sage.

Schwartz, A., & Schwarz, C. (2007). The role of latent beliefs and group cohesion in predicting group decision support systems success. *Small Group Research, 38*(1), 195–229.

Scott, C. R. (1999). Communication technology and group communication. In L. R. Frey, D. S. Gouran, & M. S. Poole (Eds.), *The handbook of group communication theory research* (pp. 432–472). Thousand Oaks, CA: Sage.

Sell, J., Lovaglia, M. J., Mannix, E. A., Samuelson, C. D., & Wilson, R. K. (2004). Investigating conflict, power, and status within and among groups. *Small Group Research, 35*, 44–72.

Smith, P. G. (2001). Communication holds global teams together. *Machine Design, 73*, 70–73.

Sorensen, S. (1981, May). Grouphate. A paper presented at the International Communication Association, Minneapolis, MN.

Steinheider, B., & Wuestewald, T. (2008). From the bottom-up: Sharing leadership in a police agency. *Police Practice & Research, 9*(2), 145–163.

Stogdill, R. M. (1974). *Handbook of leadership: A survey of theory and research.* New York: Free Press.

Sunwolf & Seibold, D. R. (1999). The impact of formal procedure on group processes, members, and task outcomes. In L. R. Frey, D. S. Gouran, & M. S. Poole (Eds.), *Handbook of group communication theory and research* (pp. 394–431). Thousand Oaks, CA: Sage.

Valenti, M. A., & Rockett, R. (2008). The effects of demographic differences on forming intragroup relationships. *Small Group Research, 39*(2), 179–202.

Wellen, J. M., & Neale, M. (2006). Deviance, self-typicality and group cohesion: The corrosive effects of the bad apples on the barrel. *Small Group Research, 37*(2), 165–186.

Wheelan, S. A., Davidson, B., & Tilin, F. (2003). Group development across time: Reality or illusion? *Small Group Research, 34*, 223–245.

Chapter 10

Acker, J. (1990, June). Hierarchies, jobs, bodies: A theory of gendered organizations. *Gender & Society, 4*(2), 139–158.

Aeberhard-Hodges, J. (1996). Sexual harassment in employment: Recent judicial and arbitral trends. *International Labor Review, 135*(5), 499–533.

Alberts, J. K., Lutgen-Sandvik, P., & Tracy, S. J. (2005, May). *Bullying in the workplace: A case of escalated incivility.* Organizational Communication Division. The International Communication Association Convention, New York, NY.

American Management Association. (2005, May 18). 2005 electronic monitoring & surveillance survey: Many companies monitoring, recording, videotaping, and firing employees. Retrieved June 16, 2006, from www.amanet.org/press/amanews/ems05.htm

Arizona Republic. (2005, December 26). School chief understands need for customer service. p. 4.

Ashcraft, K. L., & Allen, B. J. (2003). The racial foundation of organizational communication. *Communication Theory, 13*, 5–38.

Babcock, L., & Laschever, S. (2003). *Women don't ask: Negotiation and the gender divide.* Princeton, NJ: Princeton University Press.

Barley, S. R., & Kunda, G. (1992). Design and devotion: Surges of rational and normative ideologies of control in managerial discourse. *Administrative Science Quarterly, 37*, 363–399.

Berger, C. (1979). Beyond initial interaction. In H. Giles & R. St. Clair (Eds.), *Language and psychology* (pp. 122–144). Oxford, UK: Basil Blackwell.

Bertalanffy, L. von. (1968). *General systems theory.* New York: Braziller.

Belous, R. (1989). *The contingent economy: The growth of the temporary, part-time and subcontracted workforce.* Washington, DC: The National Planning Association.

Blau, P. M., & Meyer, M. W. (1987). *Bureaucracy in modern society* (3rd ed). New York: Random House.

Brown, M. (1989, Winter). Ethics in organizations. *Issues in Ethics, 2*(1). Santa Clara University: Markkula Center for Applied Ethics. Retrieved March 15, 2006, from www.scu.edu/ethics/publications/iie/v2n1/homepage.html

Bullis, C., & Tompkins, P. K. (1989). The forest ranger revisited: A study of control practices and identification. *Communication Monographs, 56*, 287–306.

Casey, M. K. (1998). Communication, stress and burnout: Use of resource replacement strategies in response to conditional demands in community-based organizations. Unpublished doctoral dissertation, Michigan State University, East Lansing, MI.

Chambers, B., Moore, A. B., & Bachtel, D. (1998). Role conflict, role ambiguity and job satisfaction of county extension agents in the Georgia Cooperative Extension Service. *AERC Proceedings.* Retrieved September 15, 2006, from www.edst.educ.ubc.ca/aercd1998/98chambers.htm

Cheney, G. (1995). Democracy in the workplace: Theory and practice from the perspective of communication. *Journal of Applied Communication Research, 23*, 167–200.

Cheney, G., Christensen, L. T., Zorn, T. E., Jr., & Ganesh, S. (2004). *Organizational communication in an age of globalizations: Issues, reflections, practices.* Prospect Heights, IL: Waveland.

Chiles, A., & Zorn, T. (1995). Empowerment in organizations: Employees' perceptions of the influences on empowerment. *Journal of Applied Communication Research, 23*, 1–25.

Chilton, K., & Weidenbaum, M. (1994, November). *A new social contract for the American workplace: From paternalism to partnering.* St. Louis, MO: Center for the Study of American Business.

Conrad, C., & Poole, M. S. (2005). *Strategic organizational communication* (6th ed.). Belmont, CA: Wadsworth.

Conrad, C., & Witte, K. (1994). Is emotional expression repression oppression? *Communication Yearbook, 17* (pp. 417–428). Thousand Oaks: Sage.

Cummings, K. J., & Kreiss, K. (2008). Contingent workers and contingent health: Risks of a modern economy. *Journal of the American Medical Association, 299*(4), 448–450.

Daniels, T. D., Spiker, B. K., & Papa, M. J. (1996). *Perspectives on organizational communication* (4th ed.). Madison, WI: Brown & Benchmark.

Dansereau, F. D., & Markham, S. E. (1987). Superior–subordinate communication: Multiple levels of analysis. In F. Jablin, L. Putnam, K. Roberts, & L. Porter (Eds.), *Handbook of Organizational Communication* (pp. 343–386). Newbury Park, CA: Sage.

Deetz, S. (1992). *Democracy in an age of corporate colonization: Developments in communication and the politics of everyday life.* Albany, NY: SUNY Press.

DiTecco, D., Cwitco, G., Arsenault, A., & Andre, M. (1992). Operator stress and monitoring practices. *Applied Ergonomics 23*(1), 29–34.

Dockery, T. M., & Steiner, D. D. (1990). The role of the initial interaction in leader-member exchange. *Group and Organization Studies, 15*, 395–413.

Eisenberg, E., Goodall, H. L., & Trethewey, A. (2007). *Organizational communication: Balance, creativity and constraint.* Boston, MA: Bedford/St. Martin's.

Eisenberg, E. M., Monge, P. R., & Farace, R. V. (1984). Coorientation on communication rules in managerial dyads. *Human Communication Research, 11*, 261–271.

Equal Employment Opportunity Commission. (1980). Guidelines on discrimination because of sex (Sect. 1604.11). *Federal Register, 45*, 74676–74677.

Farace, R.V., Monge, P. R., & Russell, H. M. (1977). *Communicating and organizing.* Reading, MA: AddisonWesley.

Fischer, R., & Ury, W. (1981). *Getting to yes: Negotiating agreement without giving in.* New York: Hougton Mifflin.

Fishman, C. (2006). *The Wal-Mart effect.* NY: Penguin Press.

Follett, M. P. (1942). *Dynamic administration.* New York: Harper & Row.

Glisson, C., & Durick, M. (1988). Predictors of job satisfaction and organizational commitment in human service organizations. *Administrative Quarterly, 33*, 61–81.

Golembiewski, R. T., Boudreau, R. A., Sun, B. C., & Luo, H. (1998). Estimates of burnout in public agencies: Worldwide how many employees have which degrees of burnout, and with what consequences? *Public Administration Review, 58*, 59–65.

Gossett, L. (2001). The long-term impact of short-term workers. *Management Communication Quarterly, 15*(1), 115–120.

Graen, G., & Graen, J. (2006). *Sharing network leadership.* Greenwich, CT: Information Age Publishing.

Gruber, J. E., & Smith, M. D. (1995). Women's responses to sexual harassment: A multivariate analysis. *Basic and Applied Social Psychology, 17,* 543–562.

Harris, M. M. (1989). Reconsidering the employment interview: A review of recent literature and suggestions for future research. *Personnel Psychology, 42,* 691–726.

Hewlitt, S. (2003). *Creating a life.* NY: Hyperion.

Hewlitt, S. (2007). *Off-ramps and on-ramps: Keeping talented women on the road to success.* Harvard, MA: Harvard Business School Publishing.

Hochschild, A. (1983). *The managerial heart.* Berkeley: University of California Press.

Howard-Grenville, J. A. (2006). Inside the "black box": How organizational culture and subcultures inform interpretations and actions on environmental issues. *Organization & Environment, 19*(1), 46–73.

Igbaria, M., & Guimaraes, T. (1993). Antecedents and consequences of job satisfaction among information center employees. *Journal of Management Information Systems, 9*(4), 145–155.

Jablin, F. M. (1979). Superior-subordinate communication: The state of the art. *Psychological Bulletin, 86,* 1201–1222.

Jablin, F. M. (2001). Organizational entry, assimilation, and disengagement/exit. In F. M. Jablin & L. L. Putnam (Eds.), *The new handbook of organizational communication: Theory, research and methods* (pp. 732–818). Thousand Oaks, CA: Sage.

Jablin, F. M., & Krone, K. J. (1987). Organizational assimilation. In C. R. Berger & S. H. Chafee (Eds.), *Handbook of communication science* (pp. 711–746). Newbury Park, CA: Sage.

Jablin, F. M., & Sias, P. M. (2001). Communication competence. In F. M. Jablin & L. Putnam (Eds.), *The new handbook of organizational communication* (pp. 819–864). Thousand Oaks, CA: Sage.

James, G. (2007, March 3). *How to manage your boss.* BNET Business Network. Retrieved April 5, 2009, from www.bnet.com/2403-13056_23-57287.html

Jenner, L. (1994). Work-family programs: Looking beyond written programs. *HR Focus, 71,* 19–20.

Kirby, E. L., & Krone, K. J. (2002). "The policy exists but you can't really use it": Communication and the structuration of work-family polices. *Journal of Applied Communication Research, 30,* 50–77.

Koniarek, J., & Dudek, B. (1996). Social support as a barrier in the stress–burnout relationship. *International Journal of Stress Management, 3,* 99–106.

Kram, K.E., & Isabella, L.A. (1985). Mentoring alternatives: The role of peer relationships in career development. *Academy of Management Journal, 28,* 110–132.

Kreps, G. (1991). *Organizational communication: Theory and practice* (2nd ed.). New York: Longman.

Larson, J., Jr. (1989). The dynamic interplay between employees: Feedback-seeking strategies and supervisors' delivery of performance feedback. *Academy of Management Review, 14,* 408–422.

Lutgen-Sandvik, P., Tracy, S., & Alberts, J. (2005, February). *Burned by bullying in the American workplaces: A first time study of U.S. prevalence and delineation of bullying "degree."* Presented at the Western States Communication Convention, San Francisco, CA.

Martin, J. (2002). *Organizational culture: Mapping the terrain.* Thousand Oaks, CA: Sage.

Maslach, C. (2003). Job burnout: New directions in research and intervention. *Current Directions in Psychological Science, 12*(5), 189–192.

Maslach, C., & Leiter, M. (1997). *The truth about burnout: How organizations cause personal stress and what to do about it.* San Francisco: Josey-Bass.

McGrath J. E. (1976). Stress and behavior in organizations. In M. D. Dunnette (Ed.), *Handbook of industrial and organizational psychology.* Palo Alto, CA: Consulting Psychologists Press.

McNamara, C. (2008). *Field guide to leadership and supervision.* Minneapolis, MN: Authenticity Publishing.

Miller, K. (2009). *Organizational communication: Approaches and Processes* (5th ed.). Belmont, CA: Wadsworth.

Miller, V. D., & Jablin, F. (1991). Information seeking during organizational entry: Influence, tactics and a model of the process. *Academy of Management Review, 16,* 522–541.

Morgan, H., & Milliken, F. J. (1992). Keys to action: Understanding differences in organizations' responsiveness to work-and-family issues. *Human Resource Management, 31,* 227–248.

Myers, K. (2005). A burning desire: Assimilation into a fire department. *Management Communication Quarterly, 18*(3), 344–384.

Myers, K., & Oetzel, J. G. (2003). Exploring the dimensions of organizational assimilation: Creating and validating a measure. *Communication Quarterly, 51,* 436–455.

Murray, K. (2005, February). Improve staff communications. Retrieved September 5, 2005, from www.revisionsplus.com/Februaryarticle.doc Improve Staff Communications.

Putnam, L. L., Phillips, N., & Chapman, P. (1996). Metaphors of communication and organization. In S. R. Clegg, C. Hardy, & W. R. Nord (Eds.), *Handbook of organization studies* (pp. 375–408). London: Sage.

Rapoport, R., & Bailyn, L. (1996). *Relinking life and work.* New York: Ford Foundation.

Rawlins, W. K. (1994). Being there and growing apart: Sustaining friendships during adulthood. In D. Canary & L. Stafford, *Communication and relational maintenance* (pp. 275–294). San Diego, CA: Academic.

Richardsen, A. M., & Martinussen, M. (2004). The Maslach burnout inventory: Factorial validity and consistency across occupational groups in Norway. *Journal of Occupational and Organizational Psychology, 77,* 1–20.

Richmond, V. P., McCroskey, J. C., & Davis, L. M. (1986). The relationship of supervisor use of power and affinity-seeking strategies with subordinate satisfaction. *Communication Quarterly, 34,* 178–193.

Rizzo, J. R., House, R. J., & Lirtzman, S. L. (1970). Role conflict and ambiguity in complex organizations. *Administrative Science Quarterly, 15,* 150–163.

Roberts, B. S., & Mann, R. A. (2000, December 5). Sexual harassment in the workplace: A primer. Retrieved September 12, 2006, from www3.uakron.edu/lawrev/robert1.html

Roethlisberger, F. J. (1968). *Management and morale.* Cambridge, MA: Belknap Press.

Roy, D. F. (1995). Banana time: Job satisfaction and informal interaction. In S. R. Corman, S. P. Banks, C. R. Bantz, & M. E. Mayer (Eds.), *Foundations of Organizational Communication: A Reader* (pp. 111–120). White Plains, NY: Longman.

Rudman, L.A., Borgida, E., & Robertson, B. A. (1995). Suffering in silence: Procedural justice versus gender socialization issues in university sexual harassment grievance procedures. *Basic and Applied Social Psychology, 17,* 519–541.

Schor, J. B. (1992). *The overworked American: The unexpected decline of leisure.* New York: BasicBooks.

Scott, C., & Myers, K. (2005). The emotion of socialization and assimilation: Learning emotion management at the firehouse. *Journal of Applied Communication Research, 33*(1), 67–92.

Shuler, S., & Sypher, B. D. (2000). Seeking emotion labor: When managing the heart enhances the work experience. *Management Communication Quarterly, 14,* 50–89.

Sias, P. M. (2005). Workplace relationship quality and employee information experiences. *Communication Studies, 56*(4), 375–395.

Sias, P. M., & Cahill, D. J. (1998). From coworkers to friends: The development of peer friendships in the workplace. *Western Journal of Communication, 62,* 273–279.

Sias, P. M., & Jablin, F. M. (1995). Differential superior–subordinate relations: Perceptions of fairness, and coworker communication. *Human Communication Research, 22,* 5–38.

Sias, P. M., Smith, G., & Avdeyeva, T. (2003). Sex and sex-composition differences and similarities in peer workplace friendship development. *Communication Studies, 54,* 322–340.

Sigal, J., Braden-Maguire, J., Patt, I., Goodrich, C., & Perrino, C. S. (2003). Effect of coping response, setting, and social context on reactions to sexual harassment. *Sex Roles, 48*(3-4), 157–166.

Solomon, C. (1994). Work/family's failing grade: Why today's initiatives aren't enough. *Personnel Journal, 73*(5), 72–87.

Stanton, J. M., & Julian, A. L. (2002). The impact of electronic monitoring on quality and quantity of performance. *Computers in Human Behavior, 18*(1), 85–113.

Taylor, F. M. (1911). *The principles of scientific management.* New York: Harper & Row.

Taylor, J. R., & Van Every, J. F. (1993). *The vulnerable fortress: Bureaucratic organizations and management in the information age.* Toronto, Canada: University of Toronto Press.

Tompkins, P. K. (1982). *Communication as action: An introduction to rhetoric and communication.* Belmont, CA: Wadsworth.

Tracy, S. J. (2000). Becoming a character for commerce: Emotion labor, self-subordination and discursive construction of identity in a total institution. *Management Communication Quarterly, 14,* 90–128.

Tracy, S. J. (2005). Locking up emotion: Moving beyond dissonance for understanding emotion labor discomfort. *Communication Monographs, 72,* 261–238.

Trethewey, A., & Corman, S. (2001). Anticipating k-commerce: E-Commerce, knowledge management, and organizational communication. *Management Communication Quarterly, 14,* 619–628.

U.S. Department of Labor. (2008, October). Fact finding. *Report from the commission on the future of worker-management relations.* Washington, DC: Author Dunlop, J. T. Retrieved November 12, 2008, from www.dol.gov/_sec/media/reports/dunlop/summary/htm

U.S. General Accounting Office. (2000, June). *Contingent Workers: Income and benefits lag behind those of rest of workforce.* Washington, DC: Retrieved November 12, 2008, www.gao.gov/cgi-bin/getrpt?GAO/HEHS-00-76

Vault. (2003). Vault office romance survey. Retrieved March 10, 2006, from www.vault.com/nr/newsmain.jsp?nr_page=3dch_id=420d.article_id=16513021

Waldron, V. R. (1994). Once more, with feeling: Reconsidering the role of emotion in work. In S. Deetz (Ed.), *Communication yearbook, 17* (pp. 388–416). Thousand Oaks, CA: Sage.

Wayne, S. G., & Ferris, G. R. (1990). Influence tactics, affect and exchange quality in supervisor-subordinate interactions: A laboratory experiment and field study. *Journal of Applied Psychology, 75,* 487–499.

Westman, M., & Etzion, D. (2005). The crossover of work-family conflict from one spouse to the other. *Journal of Applied Social Psychology, 35*(9), 1936–1957.

Whetton, D. A., & Cameron, K. S. (2002). *Developing managerial skills* (6th ed.). Upper Saddle River, NJ: Prentice Hall.

Chapter 11

Aristotle. (1991). *On rhetoric: A theory of civic discourse* (G. A. Kennedy, Trans.). New York: Oxford University Press. (Original work written about 350 B.C.)

Associated Press. (2008, December 6). Judge's statement at O. J. Simpson sentencing. *International Business Times*. Retrieved January 6, 2009, from http://au.ibtimes.com/articles/20081205/judges-statement-at-o-j-simpson-sentencing_all.htm

Biesecker, B. (1992). Coming to terms with recent attempts to write women into the history of rhetoric. *Philosophy & Rhetoric, 25*, 140–162.

Bitzer, L. (1968). The rhetorical situation. *Philosophy and Rhetoric, 1*, 1–14.

Church of Jesus Christ of Latter-Day Saints. (2008, August 13). The divine institution of marriage. Retrieved January 6, 2009, from http://newsroom.lds.org/ldsnewsroom/eng/commentary/the-divine-institution-of-marriage

Conley, T. (1994). *Rhetoric in the European tradition*. Chicago: University of Chicago Press.

Crowley, S., & Hawhee, D. (1999). *Ancient rhetorics for contemporary students* (2nd ed.). Needham Heights, MA: Allyn & Bacon.

Darsey, J. (1981). From "commies" and "queers" to "gay is good." In J. Chesebro (Ed.), *Gayspeak: Gay male and lesbian communication* (pp. 224–247). New York: Pilgrim Press.

Darsey, J. (1991). From "gay is good" to the scourge of AIDS: The evolution of gay liberation rhetoric, 1977–1990. *Communication Studies, 42*, 43–66.

Darsey, J. (1994). Must we all be rhetorical theorists?: An anti-democratic inquiry. *Western Journal of Communication, 58*, 164–181.

Delgado, F. (1995). Chicano movement rhetoric: An ideographic interpretation. *Communication Quarterly, 43*, 446–455.

DeLuca, K. M. (1999). *Image politics: The new rhetoric of environmental activism*. New York: Guilford.

Dues, M., & Brown, M. (2004). *Boxing Plato's shadow: An introduction to the study of human communication*. Boston: McGraw-Hill.

Ehninger, D. (1967) On rhetoric and rhetorics. *Western Speech, 31*, 242–249.

Erdbrink. T. (2008, December 14). Woman blinded by spurned man invokes Islamic retribution. *Washington Post*, p. A1.

Harris, J. F. (2001, September 18). "Falwell apologizes for remarks." *Washington Post*, p. C4.

Infante, D. A., Rancer, A. S., & Womack, D. F. (1990). *Building communication theory*. Prospect Heights, IL: Waveland.

Johannesen, R. L. (1997). Diversity, freedom, and responsibility in tension. In J. M. Makau & R. C. Arnett (Eds.), *Communication ethics in an age of diversity* (pp. 157–186). Urbana: University of Illinois Press.

Kennedy, G. A. (1998). *Comparative rhetoric: An historical and cross-cultural introduction*. New York: Oxford University Press.

King, J. L. (2002). Cultural differences in the perceptions of sports mascots: A rhetorical study of Tim Giago's newspaper columns. In J. N. Martin, T. K. Nakayama, & L. A. Flores (Eds.), *Readings in intercultural communication: Experiences and contexts* (pp. 205–212). New York: McGraw-Hill.

Lu, X. (1998). *Rhetoric in ancient China, fifth to third century, B.C.E.: A comparison with classical Greek rhetoric*. Columbia: University of South Carolina Press.

Lucaites, J. L., Condit, C. M., & Caudill, S. (1999). *Contemporary rhetorical theory: A reader*. New York. Guilford.

Loving v. Virginia, 388 US 1 (1967).

Maffesoli, M. (1996). *The time of the tribes: The decline of individualism in mass society*. Thousand Oaks, CA: Sage.

Makau, J. M. (1997). Embracing diversity in the classroom. In J. M. Makau & R. C. Arnett (Eds.), *Communication ethics in an age of diversity* (pp. 48–67). Urbana: University of Illinois Press.

McGee, M. C. (1990). Text, context and the fragmentation of contemporary culture. *Western Journal of Speech Communication, 54*, 274–289.

Miller, L. (2008, December 6). Our mutual joy. *Newsweek*. Retrieved January 6, 2009, from www.newsweek.com/id/172653/pagee/1

Parker, M. (2008). Ironic opening: The interpretive challenge of the "Black Manifesto." *Quarterly Journal of Speech, 94*, 320–342.

Pew Research Center for People and the Press. (2005, September 8). Huge racial divide over Katrina and its consequences: Two-in-three critical of Bush's relief efforts. Retrieved June 26, 2006, from http://people-press.org/reports/pdf/255.pdf

Ryan, H. (2004, December 10). Jurors begin deliberating possible death sentence for Scott Peterson. CourtTV.com. Retrieved June 24, 2006, from www.courttv.com/trials/peterson/120904_ctv.html

Tucker, N. (2008, December 30). The possible dream: Louisiana's historic new congressman seems to surprise everyone but himself. *Washington Post*. Retrieved January 6, 2009, from www.washingtonpost.com/wp-dyn/content/article/2008/12/29/AR2008122902590_pf.html

Tumulty, K. (2006, March 27). The politics of fat. *Time*, 40–43.

Watts, E. K., & Orbe, M. P. (2002). The spectacular consumption of "true" African American culture: "Whassup" with the Budweiser guys? *Critical Studies in Media Communication, 19*, 1–20.

Chapter 12

Akhavan-Majid, R. (2004). Mass media reform in China: Toward a new analytical perspective. *Gazette: The International Journal for Communication Studies, 66*, 553–565.

American Academy of Pediatrics. (2002). Some things you should know about media violence and media literacy. Retrieved June 1, 2006, from www.aap.org/advocacy/childhealthmonth/media.htm

Anderson, C. A., & Bushman, B. J. (2002, March 29). The effects of media violence on society. *Science, 295*, 2377–2378. Retrieved May 1, 2006, from www.psychology.iastate.edu/faculty/caa/abstracts/2000-2004/02AB2.pdf

Aoyagi, C. (2004, July 2–15). TV networks' current fascination with Hawaii often doesn't translate into more roles for APAs. *Pacific Citizen, 139*, p. 1.

Are we stingy? Yes. (2004, December 30). *New York Times*. Retrieved May 10, 2006, from www.nytimes.com/2004/12/30/opinion/30thu2.html

Associated Press. (2008, December 23). Tina Fey voted AP entertainer of the year. *MSNBC*. Retrieved January 6, 2009, from www.msnbc.msn.com/id/28365871/

Aubin, B. (2004, March 1). Why Quebecers feel especially betrayed. *Macleans*. Retrieved May 10, 2006, from www.macleans.ca/topstories/politics/article.jsp?content=20040301_76248_76248

Bailyn, B., & Garrett, J. N., (Eds.). (1965). *Pamphlets of the American Revolution, 1750–1776*. Cambridge, MA: Belknap Press of Harvard University.

Berelson, B. (1971). *Content analysis in communication research*. New York: Hafner Publishing Co. Originally published 1952.

Billings, A. C., & Eastman, S. T. (2003). Framing identities: Gender, ethnic, and national parity in network announcing of the 2002 Olympics. *Journal of Communication, 53*, 569–586.

Bissell, K. L., & Zhou, P. (2004). Must-see TV or ESPN: Entertainment and sports media exposure and body-image distortion in college women. *Journal of Communication, 54*, 5–21.

Boorstin. D. J. (1965). *The Americans: The national experience*. New York: Random House.

Brown, J. D., & Schulze, L. (1995). The effects of race, gender, and fandom on audience interpretations of Madonna's music videos. In G. Dines & J. M. Humez (Eds.), *Gender, Race and Class in Media* (pp. 508–517). Thousand Oaks, CA: Sage Publications.

Bryant, J., & Miron, D. (2004). Theory and research in mass communication. *Journal of Communication, 54*, 662–704.

Cablevision. (2000, November 4). NBC to acquire Bravo from Cablevision Systems Corporation. Retrieved June 24, 2006, from www.cablevision.com/index.jhtml?id=2002_11_04

Cernetig, M. (2004, January 13). Radio-Canada satire strikes nerve. *Toronto Star*. Retrieved June 24, 2006, from www.ondespubliques.ca/index_f.php?page=96342876

Chalaby, J. K. (2003). Television for a new global order: Transnational television networks and the formation of global systems. *Gazette: The International Journal for Communication Studies, 65*, 457–472.

Chapman, J. (2005). *Comparative media history*. Malden, MA: Polity Press.

Cho, H., & Boster, F. J. (2008). Effect of gain versus loss frame antidrug ads on adolescents. *Journal of Communication, 58*, 428–446.

Cohen, J. (2002). Television viewing preferences: Programs, schedules, and the structure of viewing choices made by Israeli adults. *Journal of Broadcasting & Electronic Media, 46*, 204–221.

Dayan, D., & Katz, E. (1992). *Media events: The live broadcasting of history*. Cambridge, MA: Harvard University Press.

DeLuca, K. M., & Peeples, J. (2002). From public sphere to public screen: Democracy, activism, and the "violence" of Seattle. *Critical Studies in Media Communication, 19*, 125–151.

de Moraes, L. (2004, October 21). No more Miss America pageantry for ABC. *Washington Post*, p. C7. Retrieved June 24, 2006, from www.washingtonpost.com/wp-dyn/articles/A50114-2004Oct20.html

Dixon, T. L., & Linz, D. (2002). Television news, prejudicial pretrial publicity, and the depiction of race. *Journal of Broadcasting & Electronic Media, 46*, 112–136.

Durham, M. G. (2004). Constructing the "new ethnicities": Media, sexuality, and diaspora identity in the lives of South Asian immigrant girls. *Critical Studies in Media Communication, 21*, 140–161.

Fahmy, S. (2004). Picturing Afghan women: A content analysis of AP wire photographs during the Taliban regime and after the fall of the Taliban regime. *Gazette: The International Journal for Communication Studies, 66*, 91–112.

Federal Communications Commission. (2003, July 8). V-chip: Viewing television responsibly. Retrieved June 24, 2006, from www.fcc.gov/vchip/

Glaister, D. (2005, January 15). Wives or sluts? US viewers in love-hate match with TV hit. *Guardian*. Retrieved June 24, 2006, from www.guardian.co.uk/usa/story/0,12271,1391061,00.html

Hanke, R. (1990). Hegemonic masculinity in *thirtysomething*. *Critical Studies in Mass Communication, 7*, 231–248.

Hanke R. (1998). The "mock-macho" situation comedy: Hegemonic masculinity and its reiteration. *Western Journal of Communication, 62*, 74–93.

Jhally, S., & Lewis, J. (1992). *Enlightened racism: The Cosby show, audiences, and the myth of the American dream*. Boulder, CO: Westview Press.

Kennedy, M. G., O'Leary, A., Beck, V., Pollard, K., & Simpson, P. (2004). Increases in calls to the CDC National STD and AIDS Hotline following AIDS-related episodes in a soap opera. *Journal of Communication, 54*, 287–301.

Krauss, C. (2004, December 27). A twisted sitcom makes the Simpsons look like saints. *New York Times*, p. A4.

Law, C., & Labre, M. P. (2002). Cultural standards of attractiveness: A thirty-year look at changes in male images in magazines. *Journalism and Mass Communication Quarterly, 79*, 697–711.

Lazarsfeld, P. F., Berelson, B., & Gaudet, H. (1948). *The people's choice: How the voter makes up his mind in a presidential campaign*. New York: Columbia University Press.

Lemire, C. (2005, August 10). Even trashing "Deuce Bigalow" a tired cliché. MSNBC. Retrieved June 24, 2006, from http://msnbc.msn.com/id/8887672

Lowry, D. T., Nio, T. C. J., & Leitner, D. W. (2003). Setting the public fear agenda: A longitudinal analysis of network TV crime reporting, public perceptions of crime and FBI crime statistics. *Journal of Communication, 53*, 61–73.

McChesney, R. (1998). Making media democratic. *Boston Review, 23*, 4–10, 20. Retrieved June 24, 2006, from www.bostonreview.net/BR23.3/mcchesney.html

McQuail, D. (1987). *Mass communication theory: An introduction* (2nd ed.). Newbury Park, CA: Sage Publications.

Meyers, M. (2004). African American women and violence: Gender, race, and class in the news. *Critical Studies in Media Communication, 21*, 95–118.

Morgan, M., & Signorielli, N. (1990). Cultivation analysis: Conceptualization and methodology. In N. Signorielli & M. Morgan (Eds.), *Cultivation analysis: New directions in media effects research* (pp. 13–34). Newbury Park, CA: Sage Publications.

Nathanson, A. (2004). Factual and evaluative approaches to modifying children's responses to violent television. *Journal of Communication, 54,* 321–336.

Nielsen Media Research. (2005, September 29) Nielsen reports Americans watch TV at record levels. Retrieved June 26, 2006, from www.nielsenmedia.com/newsreleases/2005/AvgHoursMinutes92905.pdf

Olshan, J. (2008, October 13). Palin falls prey to Fey. *New York Post.* Retrieved January 6, 2009, from www.nypost.com/seven/10132008/news/politics/palin_falls_prey_to_fey_133371.htm

Peter, J. (2003). Country characteristics as contingent conditions of agenda setting: The moderating influence of polarized elite opinion. *Communication Research, 30,* 683–712.

Rainie, L. (2001). How Americans used the Internet after the terrorist attacks. Pew Internet and American Life Project. Washington, DC. Retrieved June 24, 2006, from www.denieuwereporter.nlwww.pewinternet.org/~/media/Files/Reports/2001PIP_Terror_Report.pdf.pdf

Romer, D., Jamieson, K., & Aday, S. (2003). Television news and the cultivation of fear of crime. *Journal of Communication, 53,* 88–104.

Saulsbury, S. (2004, June 23). Fuel for the camp fire. Box Office Mojo. Retrieved June 24, 2006, from www.boxofficemojo.com/reviews/?id=1348&p=.htm

Scott, D. K., Gobetz, R. H., & Chanslor, M. (2008). Chain versus independent television station ownership: Toward an investment model of commitment to local news quality. *Communication Studies, 59,* 84–98.

Shugart, H. (2008). Managing masculinities: The metrosexual moment. *Communication and Critical/Cultural Studies, 5,* 280–300.

Slater, M. D., Henry, K. L., Swaim, R. C., & Anderson, L. L. (2003). Violent media content and aggressiveness in adolescents: A downward spiral model. *Communication Research, 30,* 713–736.

Sproule, J. M. (1989). Progressive propaganda critics and the magic bullet myth. *Critical Studies in Mass Communication, 6,* 225–246.

Thomas, E. (2005, May 23). How a fire broke out: The story of a sensitive Newsweek report about alleged abuses at Guantánamo Bay and a surge of deadly unrest in the Islamic world. *Newsweek.* Retrieved June 24, 2006, from www.newsweek.com/id/52117

Trujillo, N. (1991). Hegemonic masculinity on the mound: Media representations of Nolan Ryan and American sports culture. *Critical Studies in Mass Communication, 8,* 290–308.

Tsfati, Y. (2007). Hostile media perceptions, presumed media influence, and minority alienation: The case of Arabs in Israel. *Journal of Communication, 57,* 632–651.

TV Parental Guidelines Monitoring Board. (n.d.) Understanding the tv ratings. Retrieved June 24, 2006, from www.tvguidelines.org/ratings.htm

Virilio, P. (2006). *Speed and politics.* (M. Polizotti,Trans.). Los Angeles: Semiotext(e).

Wardle, C., & West, E. (2004). The press as agents of nationalism in the Queen's Golden Jubilee: How British newspapers celebrated a media event. *European Journal of Communication, 19,* 195–219.

Washington State Department of Health. (n.d.) *Media literacy: fast facts.* Retrieved June 24, 2006, from http://depts.washington.edu/thmedia/view.cgi?section=medialiteracy&page=fastfacts

Woo, H. J., & Dominick, J. R. (2003). Acculturation, cultivation, and daytime TV talk shows. *Journalism & Mass Communication Quarterly, 80,* 109–127.

Chapter 13

Anderson, T. L., & Emmers-Sommer, T. M. (2006). Predictors of relationship satisfaction in online romantic relationships, *Communication Studies, 57*(2), 152–172.

Auter, P. J. (2007). Portable social groups: Willingness to communicate, interpersonal communication gratifications, and cell phone use among young adults, *International Journal of Mobile Communications, 5*(2) 139–156.

Baym, N. K., Zhang, Y. B., & Lin, M-C. (2004). Social interactions across media: Interpersonal communication on the Internet, telephone and face to face. *New Media & Society, 6*(3), 299–318.

BBC News. (2005, August 10). *S. Korean dies after games session.* Retrieved December 4, 2008, from http://newsvote.bbc.co.uk

Beer, D. (2008). Social network(ing) sites . . . revisiting the story so far: A response to danah boyd & Nicole Ellison. *Journal of Computer-Mediated Communication, 13,* 516–529.

Bimie, S. A. & Horvath, P. (2002). Psychological predictors of Internet social communication. *Journal of Computer-Mediated Communication, 7,* 1–25.

Boase, J. (2008). Personal networks and the personal communication system, *Information, Communication & Society, 11*(4), 490–508.

Bourdieu, P. (1986). The forms of capital. In J. G. Richardson (Eds.), *Handbook of theory and research for the sociology of education* (pp. 241–258). Westport, CT: Greenwood.

boyd, d. m. (2007a, June 24). Viewing American class divisions through Facebook and MySpace. [*Apophenia Blog Essay.*] Retrieved February 18, 2008, from www.danah.org/papers/essays/ClassDivisions.html

boyd, d. m. (2007b). Why youth (heart) social network sites: The role of networked publics in teenage social life. In D. Buckingham (Ed.), *Youth, identity, and digital media* (MacArthur Foundation Series on Digital Learning). Cambridge, MA: MIT Press.

boyd, d. m., & Ellision, N. B. (2007). Social network sites: Definition, history, and scholarship. *Journal of Computer-Mediated Communication, 13*(1), 210–230.

Boyd, J. (2003). The rhetorical construction of trust online. *Communication Theory, 13,* 392–410.

Carr, N. (2008, July/August). Is Google making us stupid? What the Internet is doing to our brains? *Atlantic, 302*(1), 56–63.

Carter, D. M. (2004). Living in virtual communities: Making friends online. *Journal of Urban Technology, 11,* 109–125.

Caspi, A., Chajut, E., & Saporta, K. (2008). Participation in class and in online discussions: Gender differences. *Computers & Education, 50,* 718–724.

Castells, M., Qiu, J. L., & Fernandez-Ardevol, M. (2006). *Mobile communication and society: A global perspective.* Cambridge, MA: MIT Press.

Center for On-Line Addiction. (2000). What is eBay addiction, compulsive on-line gambling, and other types of Internet addiction? Retrieved March 30, 2009, from www.netaddiction.com/net_compulsions.htm

Cheong, P., & Poon, J. (In press). Weaving webs of faith: Examining Internet use and religious communication among Chinese Protestant transmigrants. *Journal of International and Intercultural Communication.*

Cheong, P. H. (2008). The young and techless? Investigating Internet use and problem-solving behaviors of young adults in Singapore. *New Media & Society 10*(5), 771–791.

Cheong, P. H. Halavais, A., & Kwon, K. (2008). The chronicles of me: Understanding blogging as a religious practice. *Journal of Media and Religion, 7,* 107–131.

Chesebro, J. W., & Bonsall, D. G. (1989). *Computer-mediated communication: Human relationships in a computerized world.* Tuscaloosa: The University of Alabama Press.

Daft, R. L., & Lengel, R. H. (1984). Information richness: A new approach to managerial behavior and organization design. *Research in Organizational Behavior, 6,* 191–233.

Daft, R. L., & Lengel, R. H. (1986). A proposed integration among organizational information requirements, media richness, and structural design. *Management Science, 32*(5), 544–571.

Delgado, F. (2002). Mass-mediated communication. In J. N. Martin, T. K. Nakayama, & L. A. Flores (Eds.). *Readings in intercultural communication* (2nd ed., pp. 351–360). Boston: McGraw-Hill.

Demographics of Internet Users (2008, October). Retrieved March 30, 2009 from http://pewinternet.org/Data-Tools/Download-Data/~/media/Infographics/Trend%20Data/January%202009%20updates/Demographics%20of%20Internet%20Users%201%206%2009.jpg

DeRusha, J. (2007, May 14). Military bans MySpace, other web sites to soldiers. Retrieved February 18, 2008, from http://wcco.com/local/MySpace.Internet.Web.2.367379.html

Dijk, J. van, (2004). Divides in succession: Possession, skills, and use of new media for societal participation. In E. P. Bucy & J. E. Newhagen (Eds.), *Media access: Social and psychological dimensions of new technology use* (pp. 233–254). Mahwah, NJ: Erlbaum.

Ellison, N. B., Steinfeld, C., & Lampe, C. (2007). The benefits of Facebook "Friends:" Social capital and college students' use of online social network sites. *Journal of Computer-Mediated Communication, 12*(4), 1.

Emery, D. Urban Legends and Folklore Website. Available at http://urbanlegends.about.com/od/internet/a/current/netlore/htm.

Facenda, V. L. (2008, March 31). Chemistry.com reinforces formula with $40 M effort. *Brandweek, 10644318, 49*(13), 17.

Fallows, D. (2005). *How women and men use the Internet.* Washington, DC: Pew/Internet & American Life Project. Retrieved June 25, 2006, from www.pewinternet.org/pdfs/PIP_Women_and_Men_online.pdf

Fallows, D. (2008). Almost half of all Internet users now use search engines on a typical day. Pew Internet & American Life Project Data Memo. Retrieved March 30, 2009, from www.pewinternet.org/Reports/2008/Search-Engine-Use.aspx

Farrell, N. (2002, October 22). Second gamer dies after massive binge. Retrieved March 30, 2009, from www.vnunet.com/vnunet/news/2120472/second-gamer-dies-massive-binge

Fine, J. (2006, January 16). Old media's mobile future. *Business Week, 3960,* 20.

Finn, S., & Korukonda, A. R. (2004). Avoiding computers: Does personality play a role? In E. P. Bucy & J. E. Newhagen (Eds.), *Media access: Social and psychological dimensions of new technology use* (pp. 73–90). Mahwah, NJ: Erlbaum.

Fox, S. (2005, October 5). *Digital divisions.* Washington, DC: Pew/Internet & American Life Project. Retrieved March 30, 2009, from www.pewinternet.org/Reports/2005/Digital-Divisions.aspx

Fox, S. & Livingston, G. (2007). Latinos online. Pew Internet & American Life Project. Retrieved December 8, 2008, from www.pewinternet.org/pdfs/Latinos_Online_March_14_2007.pdf

Gergen, K. J. (2002). The challenge of absent-presence. In J. Katz & M. Aakhus (Eds.), *Perpetual contact: Mobile communication, private talk, public performance* (pp. 223–227). Cambridge, UK: Cambridge University Press.

Goggin, G. (2006). *Cell phone culture.* New York: Routledge.

Griffith, M. & Fox, S. (2007). Hobbyists online. Pew Internet & American Life Project. Retrieved March 29, 2009, from www.pewinternet.org/Reports/2007/Hobbyists-Online.aspx

Haines, L. (2008, June 19). Net addiction a "clinical disorder," says US shrink. *Register.* Retrieved December 8, 2008, from www.theregister.co.uk

Hargittai, E., & Hinnant, A. (2008). Digital inequality: Differences in young adults' use of the Internet. *Communication Research, 35*(5), 602–621.

Heaton, L. (2001). Preserving communication context: Virtual workspace and interpersonal space in Japanese CSCW. In C. Ess (Ed.), *Culture, technology, communication: Towards an intercultural global village* (pp. 213–240). Albany: State University of New York Press.

Henderson, S., & Gilding, M. (2004). "I've never clicked this much with anyone in my life": Trust and hyperpersonal communication in online friendships. *New Media & Society, 6,* 487–506.

Herring, S. C. (2004). Slouching toward the ordinary: Current trends in computer-mediated communication. *New Media & Society, 6,* 26–36.

Herring, S. C., Scheidt, L. A., Wright, E., & Bonus, S. (2005). Bridging the gap: A genre analysis of weblogs. *Information Technology & People, 18*(2), 142–171.

History of Wireless Technology. (n.d). Retrieved December 11, 2008, from http://wirelesshistory.org/fullscreen.htm

Horrigan, J. (2008a). Info on the go: Mobile access to data and information. Pew Research Center Publications (Pew Internet & American Life Project). Retrieved December 8, 2008, from www.pewinternet.org/pdfs/PIP_Mobile.Data.Access.pdf

Horrigan, J. (2008b). The Internet and consumer choice. Pew Research Center Publications (Pew Internet & American Life Project). Retrieved December 15, 2008, from www.pewinternet.org/pdfs/PIP_Online%20Shopping.pdf

Horrigan, J. C. (2008c). Adoption stalls for low-income Americans even as many broadband users opt for premium services that give them more speed. Pew Internet & American Life Project Report. Retrieved March 30, 2009, from www.pewinternet.org/Press-Releases/2008/55-of-adult-Americans-have-home-broadband-connections.aspx

Hutchinson, A. (2006, February). Mean, green, third world machine. *Popular Mechanics, 183,* 20.

Hwang, J. M., Cheong, P. H., & Feeley, T. H. (2008). Being young and feeling blue in Taiwan: Examining adolescent depressive mood and online and offline activities. Unpublished paper.

Jackson, L. A., Barbatsis, G., Biocca, F. A., von Eye, A., Zhao, Y., & Fitzgerald, H. E. (2004). Home Internet use in low-income families: Is access enough to eliminate the digital divide? In E. P. Bucy & J. E. Newhagen (Eds.), *Media access: Social and psychological dimensions of new technology use* (pp. 155–186). Mahwah, NJ: Erlbaum.

Jackson, L. A., Ervin, K. S., Gardner, P. D., & Schmitt, N. (2001). Gender and the Internet: Women communicating and men searching. *Sex Roles, 44,* 363–379.

James, G. (2003, March 1). Can't hide your prying eyes. *Computerworld, 38,* 35–37.

Jayson, S. (2008, June 2). Singles find love after 45. *USA Today,* Life Section p. 01d. Retrieved March 30, 2009, from www.usatoday.com/news/health/2008-06-01-late-life-marriage_N.htm

Jones, S., & Fox, S. (2009). Generations Online in 2009. Pew Internet & American Life Project Data Memo. Retrieved March 29, 2009, from www.pewinternet.org/~/media/Files/Reports/2009/PIP_Generations_2009.pdf

Jones, S., & Madden, M. (2002, September 15). *The Internet goes to college: How students are living in the future with today's technology.* Washington, DC: Pew/Internet & American Life Project. Retrieved March 30, 2009, from www.pewinternet.org/Reports/2002/The-Internet-Goes-to-College.aspx

Juan, S. (2006, September 22). Could you be addicted to the Internet? *Register.* Retrieved March 30, 2009, from www.theregister.co.uk/2006/09/22/the_odd_body_internet_addiction/

Jung, J-Y. (2008). Internet connectedness and its social origins: An ecological approach to postaccess digital divides. *Communication Studies, 59*(4), 322–339.

Katz, J., & Rice, R. (2002). *The social consequences of Internet use.* Cambridge, MA: MIT Press.

Katz, J. E. (2007). Mobile media and communication: Some important questions. *Communication Monographs, 74*(3), 389–394.

Kendall, L. (2002). *Hanging out in the virtual pub: Masculinities and relationships online.* Berkeley: University of California Press.

Keniston, K. (2001). Language, power and software. In C. Ess (Ed.), *Culture, technology, communication: Towards an intercultural global village* (pp. 283–306). Albany: State University of New York Press.

Kim, H., Kim, G. J., Park, H. W., & Rice, R. E. (2007). Configurations of relationships in different media: FtF, email, instant messenger, mobile phone, and SMS. *Journal of Computer-Mediated Communication, 12,* 1183–1207.

Kramarae, C. (1998). Feminist fictions of future technology. In S. G. Jones (Ed.), *Cybersociety 2.0: Revisiting computer-mediated communication and community* (pp. 100–128). Thousand Oaks, CA: Sage.

Krauss, A. (2008, February 20). Piggybacking on Facebook. *New York Times,* H0, p. 7.

Kraut, R., Kiesler, S., Mukhopadhya, T., & Scherlis, W. (1998). Social impact of the Internet: What does it mean? *Communications of the ACM, 41,* 21–22.

Lacy, S. (2005). America: Still the high-speed laggard. *Business Week Online.* Retrieved April 7, 2006, from http://biz.yahoo.com/special/broadband05_article1.html

Leggatt, H. (2007, April 17). More teens using legal online music download services. BizReport. Retrieved December 11, 2008, from www.bizreport.com/2007/04/more_teens_using_legal_online_music_download_services.html

Lenhart, A., Horrigan, J., Rainie, L., Allen, K., Boyce, A., Madden, M., & O'Grady, E. (2003, April 16). *The ever-shifting Internet population: A new look at Internet access and the digital divide.* Washington, DC: Pew/Internet & American Life Project. Retrieved March 30, 2009, from www.pewinternet.org/Reports/2003/The-EverShifting-Internet-Population-A-new-look-at-Internet-access-and-the-digital-divide.aspx

Lenhart, A., Jones, S., & MacGill, A. R. (2008). Adults and video games. Pew Internet & American Life Project Data Memo. Retrieved March 29, 2009, from www.pewinternet.org/Reports/2008/Adults-and-Video-Games.aspx

Lenhart, A., Kahne, J., Middaugh, E., Macgill, A. R., Evans, C., & Vitak, J. (2008). Teens, video games and civics. Pew Internet & American Life Project Report. Retrieved March 29, 2009, from www.pewinternet.org/Reports/2008/Teens-Video-Games-and-Civics.aspx

Lenhart, A., Madden, M., MacGill, A. R., & Smith, A. (2007). Teens and social media. Pew Internet & American Life Project. Retrieved July 5, 2009, from www.pewinternet.org/Reports/2007/Teens-and-Social-Media.aspx

Ling, R. (2007). *The mobile connection: The cell phone's impact on society.* San Francisco: Morgan Kaufmann.

Livingstone, S., & Helsper, E. (2007). Gradations in digital inclusion: Children, young people and the digital divide. *New Media & Society, 9*(4), 671–696.

Madden, M., & Jones, S. (2008). Networked workers. Pew Internet & American Life Project Report. Retrieved March 29, 2009, from www.pewinternet.org/Reports/2008/Networked-Workers.aspx

Madden, M., & Lenhart, A. (2006, March 5). *Online dating.* Washington, DC: Pew/Internet & American Life Project. Retrieved April 3, 2006, from www.pewinternet.org/pdfs/PIP_Online_Dating.pdf

Madden, M., & Rainie, L. (2003, December 22). *America's online pursuits: The changing picture of who's online and what they do.* Washington, DC: Pew/Internet & American Life Project. www.pewinternet.org

Mangla, I. S. (2008). Bye-bye love, bye-bye bank account. *Money, 37*(10), 18.

Marriot, M. (2006, March 31). Blacks turn to Internet highway, and digital divide starts to close. *New York Times,* p. A1.

Marwick, A. (2005, October). "I'm a lot more interesting than a Friendster profile:" Identity presentation, authenticity, and power in social networking services. Paper presented at Internet Research 6.0, Chicago.

McKenna, K. Y. A., Green, A. S., & Gleason, M. E. J. (2002). Relationship formation on the Internet: What's the big attraction? *Journal of Social Issues, 58,* 9–31.

Merryfield, M. (2003). Like a veil: Cross-cultural experiential learning online. *Contemporary Issues in Technology and Teacher Education, 3*(2), 146–171.

Nardi, B. A., Schiano, D. J., Gumbrecht, M., & Swartz, L. (2004). Why we blog. *Communications of the ACM, 47*(12), 41–46.

Nie, N. H., & Ebring, L. (2000, February 17). Internet and society: Preliminary report. Standford Institute of the Quantitative Study of Society (SIQSS). Palo Alto, CA, Stanford University. Retrieved June 24, 2006, from www.standford.edu/group/siqss/Press_Release/Preliminary_Report.pdf

Of Internet cafes and power cuts: Technology in emerging economies (2008, February 9). *Economist, 386*(8566), 75–78.

Osman, G., & Herring, S. (2007). Interaction, facilitation, and deep learning in cross-cultural chat: A case study. *Internet and Higher Education, 10,* 125–141.

Perils of modernity (2008, March 15). *Economist, 386*(8572), 73.

Rainie, L., Fox, S., Horrigan, J., Fallows, D., Lenhart, A., Madden, M., Cornfield, M., Carter-Sykes, C. (2005). Internet: The mainstreaming of online life. In *Trends 2005.* Washington, DC: Pew Research Center.

Rainie, L., & Smith, A. (2008). The Internet and the 2008 election. Pew Internet & American Life Project. Retrieved December 8, 2008, from www.pewinternet.org/Press-Releases/2008/The-internet-and-the-2008-election.aspx

Ramirez, A. (2007). The effect of anticipated future interaction and initial impression valence on relational communication in computer-mediated interaction. *Communication Studies, 58*(1), 53–70.

Ramirez, A., & Zhang, S. (2007). When online meets offline: The effect of modality switching on relational communication. *Communication Monographs, 74*(3), 287–310.

Rodgers, S., & Chen, W. (2005). Internet community group participation: Psychosocial benefits for women with breast cancer. *Journal of Computer-Mediated Communication, 10*(4), article 5. Retrieved March 30, 2009, from http://jcmc.indiana.edu/vol10/issue4/rodgers.html

Rogers, E. M. (2003). *Diffusion of innovations* (5th ed.). New York: Free Press.

Rojas, V., Straubhaar, J., Roychowdhury, D., & Okur, O. (2004). Communities, cultural capital, and the digital divide. In E. P. Bucy & J. E. Newhagen (Eds.), *Media access: Social and psychological dimensions of new technology use* (pp. 107–130). Mahwah, NJ: Erlbaum.

Rooksby, E. (2002). *E-mail and ethics: Style and ethical relations in computer-mediated communication.* New York: Routledge.

Rosen, L. D., Cheever, N. A., Cummings, C., & Felt, J. (2008). The impact of emotionality and self-disclosure on online dating versus traditional dating. *Computers in Human Behavior, 24,* 2124–2157.

Sawhney, H. (2007). Strategies for increasing the conceptual yield of new technologies research. *Communication Monographs, 74*(3), 395–401.

Scanlon, J. (2003, August). 7 ways to squelch the Net. *Wired,* 31.

Seagraves, L. (2004, May). Suing the pants off spammers. *Wired,* 114.

Selwyn, N. (2007). Hi-tech=Guy-tech? An exploration of undergraduate students' gendered perceptions of information and communication technologies. *Sex Roles, 56,* 525–536.

Serious trouble. (2007, December 8). *Economist,* (Technology Quarterly), pp. 3–4.

Short, J. A., Williams, E., & Christie, B. (1976). *The social psychology of telecommunications.* New York: John Wiley & Sons.

Siklos, R. (2006, October 19). A virtual world but real money. *New York Times.* Retrieved March 30, 2009, from http://query.nytimes.com/gst/fullpage.html?res=9907E2DA1F30F93AA25753C1A9609C8B63&sec=&spon=&pagewanted=2

Smith, G. G., Ferguson, D., & Caris, M. (2001). Teaching college courses online vs. face-to-face. *The Journal*: Technological horizons in education *28,* 18–26.

State of the Blogosphere/2008. (2008). Technocrati.com. Retrieved December 13, 2008, from http://technorati.com/blogging/state-of-the-blogosphere/

Stone, B. (2007, April 9). A call for manners in the world of nasty blogs. *New York Times.* Retrieved March 30, 2009, from www.nytimes.com/2007/04/09/technology/09blog.html

Thompson, L., & Ku, H-Y. (2005). Chinese graduate students' experiences and attitudes toward online leaning. *Educational Media International, 42*(1), 33–47.

Thurlow, C., Lengel, L., & Tomic, A. (2004). *Computer mediated communication: Social interaction and the Internet.* Thousand Oaks, CA: Sage.

Tong, S. T., Van Der Heide, B., Langwell, L., & Walther, J. B. (2008). Too much of a good thing? The relationship between number of friends and interpersonal impressions on Facebook. *Journal of Computer-Mediated Communication, 13,* 531–549.

Valkenburg, P. M., & Peter, J. (2007a). Online communication and adolescent well-being: Testing the stimulation versus the displacement hypothesis. *Journal of Computer-Mediated Communication, 12*(4), 1169–1182.

Valkenburg, P. M., & Peter, J. (2007b). Who visits online dating sites? Exploring some characteristics of online daters. *Cyberpsychology & Behavior, 10*(6), 849–852.

Walther, J. B. (1996). Computer-mediated communication: Impersonal, interpersonal, and hyper-personal interaction. *Communication Research, 23,* 3–43.

Walther, J. B., & Parks, M. R. (2002). Cues filtered out, cues filtered in: Computer-mediated communication and relationships. In M. L. Knapp & J. A. Daly (Eds.), *Handbook of interpersonal communication* (pp. 529–63). Thousand Oaks, CA: Sage.

Wang, H-Y., & Wang, Y-S. (2008). Gender differences in the perception and acceptance of online games. *British Journal of Educational Technology, 39*(5) 787–806.

Wheeler, D. (2001). New technologies, old culture: A look at women, gender and the Internet in Kuwait. In C. Ess (Ed.), *Culture, technology, communication: Towards an intercultural global village* (pp. 187–212). Albany: State University of New York Press.

Whitty, M. T. (2007). Revealing the "real" me, searching for the "actual" you: Presentations of self on an Internet dating site. *Computers in Human Behavior, 24,* 1707–1723.

Wood, A. F., & Smith, M. J. (2005). *Online communication: Linking technology, identity and culture* (2nd ed.). Mahwah, NJ: Lawrence Erlbaum Associates, pp. 10–15.

Wray, R. (2007, June 14). China overtaking US for fast Internet access as Africa gets left behind. Guardian: guardian.co.uk. Retrieved March 30, 2009, from www.guardian.co.uk/money/2007/jun/14/internetphonesbroadband.digitalmedia

Zywica, J., & Danowski, J. (2008). The faces of Facebookers: Investigating social enhancement and social compensation hypotheses: Predicting Facebook and offline popularity from sociability and self-esteem, and mapping the meaning of popularity with semantic networks. *Journal of Computer-Mediated Communication, 14,* 1–34.

Chapter 14

Ayres, J. (1996). Speech preparation processes and speech apprehension. *Communication Education, 45,* 228–235.

Beaver, H. D. (2005, June). Nobody knows you're nervous. *ABA Banking Journal, 97,* 60.

Behnke, R., & Sawyer, C. (1999). Milestones of anticipatory public speaking anxiety. *Communication Education, 48,* 165–173.

Behnke, R., & Sawyer, C. (2004). Public speaking anxiety as a function of sensitization and habituation processes. *Communication Education, 53,* 164–173.

Boswell, J. (1995). *Same-sex unions in pre-modern Europe.* New York: Vintage.

Bruce, T. J., & Saeed, S. A. (1999). Social anxiety disorder: A common underrecognized mental disorder. *American Family Physician, 60,* 2311–2320.

Bureau of Justice Statistics. (2006, April 18). Crime characteristics. Retrieved June 26, 2006, from www.ojp.usdoj.gov/bjs/cvict_c.htm

CBS. (2008, December 30). Streisand: Perfection is imperfection. *The Early Show.* Retrieved on January 5, 2009, from www.cbsnews.com/stories/2008/12/30/earlyshow/leisure/music/main4691743.shtml

Chauncey, G. (2004). *Why marriage: The history shaping today's debate over gay equality.* Cambridge, MA: Perseus Books.

Cott, N. F. (2002). *Public vows: A history of marriage and the nation.* Cambridge, MA: Harvard University Press.

Gayle, B. M. (2004). Transformations in a civil discourse public speaking class: Speakers' and listeners' attitude change. *Communication Education, 53,* 174–185.

Katz, B. (2008, March 24). Public speaking matters—Listen to our president. *Los Angeles Times.* Retrieved January 7, 2009, from www.latimes.com/news/nationworld/nation/ny-opkat245624217mar24,0,1714387.story

Levasseur, D. G., Dean, K. W., & Pfaff, J. (2004). Speech pedagogy beyond the basics: A study of instructional methods in the advanced public speaking course. *Communication Education. 53,* 234–252.

Lucas, S. E. (2004). *The art of public speaking* (8th ed.). Boston: McGraw-Hill.

McKerrow, R. E., Gronbeck, B. E., Ehninger, D., & Monroe, A. H. (2003). *Principles of public speaking* (15th ed.). Boston: Allyn & Bacon.

Miller, A. N. (2002). An exploration of Kenyan public speaking patterns with implications for the American introductory public speaking course. *Communication Education, 51,* 168–182.

O'Hair, D., Stewart, R., & Rubenstein, H. (2004). *A speaker's guidebook* (2nd ed.). Boston: Bedford/St. Martin's.

Osterman, R. (2005, May 23). "Soft skills" top list of what area employers desire. *Sacramento Bee,* p. D1.

Pew Forum on Religion and Public Life. (2008, December 18). Many Americans say other faiths can lead to eternal life. Retrieved January 7, 2009, from http://pewresearch.org/pubs/1062/many-americans-say-other-faiths-can-lead-to-eternal-life

Sanow, A. (2005, March 3). How I overcame the fear of public speaking. Retrieved June 26, 2006, from www.expertclick.com/NewsReleaseWire/default.cfm?Action=ReleaseDetail&ID=8372&NRWid=1698

Schneier, F., & Welkowitz, L. (1996). *The hidden face of shyness.* New York. Avon Books.

Sprague, J., & Stuart, D. (2005). *The speaker's handbook.* Belmont, CA: Wadsworth/Thomson.

Tulchin, A. A. (2007). Same-sex couples creating households in Old Regime France: The uses of the *affrèrement. Journal of Modern History, 79,* 613–647.

U.S. Bureau of Labor Statistics. (2007, May). Table 788. Individuals employed in science and engineering (S&E) occupations as share of workforce by state and other areas: 2007. *National Occupational Employment and Wage Estimates.* Retrieved April 17, 2009, from www.census.gov/compendia/statab/tables/09s0788.pdf

U.S. Census Bureau. (2003, February 25). Census 2000. Table 5: Detailed list of languages spoken at home for the population 5 years and over by state. Retrieved March 27, 2009, from www.census.gov/population/www.cen2000/briefs/phc-t20/tab05.pdf

Vaznis, J. (2008, December 10). Bright sign for tech in Mass.: Science, math pupils near top internationally. *Boston Globe.* Retrieved January 7, 2009, from www.boston.com/news/local/massachusetts/articles/2008/12/10/bright_sign_for_tech_in_mass/

Von Drehle, D. (2004, May 24–30). Culture clash: Geography, technology and strategy have nurtured a political split. *Washington Post National Weekly Edition,* pp. 6–7.

Webster, D. (1989). "Bunker Hill Monument Oration (1825)." In James Andrews and David Zarefsky (Eds.), *American voices: Significant speeches in American history, 1640–1945* (pp. 125–138). New York: Longman.

Yook, E. L. (2004). Any questions? Knowing the audience through question types. *Communication Teacher, 18,* 91–93.

Credits

Text Credits

Chapter 1 p. 3, From "Prospective associations of co-rumination with friendship and emotional adjustment," July 16, 2007, New-Medical.Net, www.news-medical.net Reprinted by permission; p. 4, From "Careers in Communication: An update," by A. D. Wolvin, *JACA: Journal of the Association for Communication Administration.* Copyright 1998 by Association for Communication Administration. Reproduced with permission of Association for Communication Administration in the format Textbook and Other Book via Copyright Clearance Center; p. 8, From "A World of Eloquence in an Upturned Palm," by John Tierney, *The New York Times,* August 28, 2007. © 2007 The New York Times. All rights reserved. Used by permission and protected by the Copyright Laws of the United States. The printing, copying, redistribution, or retransmission of the Material without express written permission is prohibited; p. 22, From "Employers scrutinize Facebook profiles," by Kate Maternowski, *The Badger Herald,* February 1, 2006, http://badgerherald.com Reprinted by permission.

Chapter 2 p. 34, "Origins of Classical Rhetoric: Greek or Egyptian?" from www.physics.wustl.edu © 1997 Mark Alford. Reprinted by permission of Mark Alford.

Chapter 3 p. 58, From "Women's Pay: Why the Gap Remains a Chasm," by Aaron Bernstein. Reprinted from June 14, 2004 issue of *BusinessWeek,* by special permission, copyright © 2004 by The McGraw-Hill Companies, Inc.; p. 70, From "DNA Is Only One Way to Spell Identity," by W. Ralph Eubanks as appeared in *The Washington Post,* January 1, 2006. Reprinted by permission of the author; p. 75, Reprinted by permission of Waveland Press, Inc. from Barbara J. Allen, *Difference Matters: Communicating Social Identity* (Long Grove, IL: Waveland Press, Inc., 2004). All rights reserved.

Chapter 4 p. 91, From "The Smell Report: Sex Differences," by Kate Fox, Social Issues Research Centre, www.sirc.org. Reprinted by permission; p. 92, From "Hearing Colors, Tasting Shapes," by S. Vilayanur, V. S. Ramachandran & E. M. Hubbard, *Scientific American,* May 2003. Copyright © 2003 Scientific American, Inc. All rights reserved.

Chapter 5 p.107, Words of the Year reprinted with permission of the American Dialect Society, www.americandialect.org; p. 116, Adapted from Pseudodictionary.com. Reprinted by permission of H.D. Fowler. Copyright © 2009 H.D. Fowler; p. 126, From "'Nappy-Headed Ho' Top Politically incorrect Phrase for 2007 Closely Followed by 'Ho-Ho-Ho' and 'Carbon Footprint Stomping'", *The Global Language Monitor,* March 21, 2008, www.languagemonitor.com. Reprinted by permission of Paul J. J. Payack, The Global Language Monitor; p. 129, From "Mind Your (Terror) Language," by Khody Akhavi, *Asia Times Online,* May 21, 2008. Reprinted by permission of Asia Times Online (www.atimes.com).

Chapter 6 p. 145, Etiquette for the world traveler. Courtesy Vayama; p. 151, From "Looking to Avoid Aggressive Drivers? Check Those Bumpers." by Shankar Vendantam, *The Washington Post,* June 16, 2008. © 2008 The Washington Post. Reprinted with Permission.

Chapter 7 p. 167 top, Allison Nafziger Travel Blog. Reprinted by permission of Allison Nafziger; p. 167 bottom, From "U. S. Populations Projections: 2005–2050," by J. S. Passel and D. V. Cohn, Washington, DC: Pew Hispanic Center, p. 9, www.pewhispanic.org. Reprinted by permission; p. 173, From *English usage Among Hispanics in the United States,* by S. Hakimzadeh & D. Cohn, 2007, Washington, DC: Pew Hispanic Center, www.pewhispanic.org. Reprinted by permission; p. 181, From "Zuni Eagle Aviary Is a Beautiful Sign". This editorial first appeared in *Indian Country Today,* July 31, 2002, http://indiancountry.com. Reprinted by permission; p. 187, From "TV Reality Not Often Spoke of: Race," by Eric Deggans, *St. Petersburg Times,* October 24, 2004. Reprinted by permission of St. Petersburg Times.

Chapter 8 Table 8.1, p. 198, From Mark L. Knapp & Anita L. Vangelisti, *Interpersonal Communication And Human Relationships, 2/e.* Published by Allyn and Bacon/Merrill Education, Boston, MA. Copyright © 1992 by Pearson Education. Adapted by permission of the publisher; p. 202, From P. Mongeau, A. Ramirez, & M. Vorell (2003). *Sexual cross-sex friendship: Friends with benefits relationships.* Paper presented to the Western States Communication Association, Salt Lake City, UT. Reprinted by permission of the authors; Table 8.3, p. 205, From *Maintaining Relationships Through Communication: Relational, Contextual, and Cultural Variations* by D. Canary & M. Dainton. Copyright 2002 by Taylor & Francis Group LLC–Books.

Reproduced with permission of Taylor & Francis Group LLC–Books in the format Textbook and Other Book via Copyright Clearance Center; Table 8.4, p. 206, From J. Alberts, C. Yoshimura, M. Rabby and R. Loschiavo (2005), "Mapping the topography of couples' everyday interaction," *Journal of Social and Personal Relationships,* 22, pp. 299–322.

Chapter 9 p. 226, This is a condensed version of "Enough of the T-word," by Richard Reeves as first published in *Management Today,* March 2004. Reproduced from *Management Today* magazine with permission of the copyright owner, Haymarket Business Publications Limited; p. 246, Excerpted from "Is Collaboration the Future of Invention?" by P. Willis for CNN.com, April 7, 2008. Reprinted by permission.

Chapter 10 p. 264, From "150 Typical Job Interview Questions," copyright by Quintessential Careers. The original article can be found at www.quintcareers.com/interview_question_database/interview_questions.html. Reprinted with permission; p. 271, From "Improve Staff Communications," by Katherine Murray, www.revisionsplus.com/February article.doc. Reprinted by permission of the author; p. 278, From "Hollywood to script outsourcing saga," by C. Rajghatta, *Times News Network,* August 19, 2005, http://economictimes.indiatimes.com. The Times of India. Copyright 2008, Bennett, Coleman & Co. Ltd. All Rights Reserved. Reprinted by permission; p. 281, From "Blackberry rollout stalled over work/life balance debate," by Darren Pauli, *Computerworld,* December 13, 2007, www.pcworld.idg.com.au. Published by IDG Communications. Reprinted by permission of Copyright Agency Limited; p. 282, From *Big in Japan: Man works himself to death, company compensates wife,* by M. Firestone, December 6, 2007, www.gadling.com. Reprinted by permission of Matthew D. Firestone; p. 286, From Brown, M. (Winter 1989). "Ethics in organizations." *Issues in Ethics,* 2(1). Santa Clara University: Markkula Center for Applied Ethics. Reprinted with permission of The Markkula Center for Applied Ethics at Santa Clara University, www.scu.edu/ethics.

Chapter 11 p. 293, From "The Divine Institution of Marriage," August 13, 2008, http://newsroom.lds.org. Official Online Newsroom of the Church of Jesus Christ of Latter-day Saints. © 2008 Intellectual Reserve, Inc. Reprinted by permission of the Church of Jesus Christ of Latter-day Saints; From "Our Mutual Joy" by Lisa Miller, *Newsweek,* December 15, 2008. © 2008 Newsweek, Inc. All rights reserved. Used by permission and protected by the Copyright Laws of the United States. The printing, copying, redistribution, or retransmission of the Material without express written permission is prohibited; p. 304, From "The Possible Dream: Louisiana's Historic New Congressman Seems to Surprise Everyone but Himself," by N. Tucker, *The Washington Post,* December 30, 2008. Copyright © 2008, The Washington Post. Reprinted with Permission; p. 309, From "Judge's statement at O. J. Simpson sentencing," *International Business Times* (AP), December 6, 2008, au.ibtimes.com. Used with permission of The Associated Press Copyright © 2009. All rights reserved.

Chapter 12 p. 327, From "Tina Fey voted AP Entertainer of the Year," The Associated Press, December 23 2008. Used with permission of The Associated Press. Copyright © 2009. All rights reserved.

Chapter 13 p. 350, From "With Friends Like These...," by Tom Hodgkinson, *The Guardian,* January 14, 2008, www.guardian.co.uk. Copyright Guardian News & Media Ltd 2008. Reprinted by permission; p. 365, From "Putting Your Best Cyberface Forward," by Stephanie Rosenbloom, *The New York Times,* January 3, 2008. © 2008 The New York Times. All rights reserved. Used by permission and protected by the Copyright Laws of the United States. The printing, copying, or retransmission of the Material without express written permission is prohibited; p. 366, Excerpt posted by Steven Rothberg, CollegeRecruiter.com on September 26, 2008. Courtesy of CollegeRecruiter.com job board; p. 370, From "Romance on the Internet," *The Police Notebook,* University of Oklahoma Department of Public Safety, www.ou.edu. Reprinted by permission; Table 13.5, p. 375, From Pew Internet and American Life Project, www.pewinternet.org. Used by permission; p. 379, "The Ten Commandments of Computer Ethics," by the Computer Ethics Institute retrieved from http://cpsr.org. Reprinted by permission of the Computer Ethics Institute and CPSR.

Chapter 14 p. 387, From "Public speaking matters—listen to our president," by Bob Katz, *Los Angeles Times,* March 24, 2008, www.latimes.com. Copyright © 2008, Los Angeles Times. Reprinted by permission; p. 407, From "PowerPoint Is Evil," by Edward Tufte as appeared in *Wired Magazine,* September 2003. Reprinted by permission, from Edward R. Tufte, *The Cognitive Style of PowerPoint* (Cheshire, Connecticut, Graphics Press, 2003).

Photo Credits

Chapter 1 p. xx, © 2009 iStockphoto/urbancow; p. 3, Index Open/PhotosToGo; p. 2, © Kes/www.CartoonStock.com; p. 6, Photos.com; p. 8 bottom, © PhotoStock-Israel/Alamy; p. 9, Eye-Wire/PhotoDisc/Getty Images Royalty Free; p. 11 top, Index Open/PhotosToGo; p. 15, Francis Specker/Landov; p. 16, © Tomas Van Houtryve/Corbis; p. 18, Index Open/PhotosToGo; p. 19, © David J. Green - lifestyle 2/Alamy; p. 24, © Michael Newman/PhotoEdit Inc.

Chapter 2 p. 30, © 2009 Creatas/Jupiterimages; p. 32, BananaStock/Super Stock Royalty Free; p. 35 left, Bettmann/Corbis; p. 35 right, © Shahidul Alam/AUW/Drik/Majority World/The Image Works; p. 38, Library of Congress; p. 39, Scott J. Ferrell/Congressional Quarterly/Getty Images; p. 40, Gary Conner/Phototake NYC; p. 42 left, Spencer Grant/PhotoEdit; p. 42 right, © Peter Hvizdak/The Image Works; p. 43 left, Eurelios/Phototake NYC; p. 43 right, Robert W. Ginn, Photo Edit; p. 44, Richard Olsenius/National Geographic/Getty Images; p. 45, Mark D. Phillips/South Brooklyn Internet Inc.; p. 47 middle, Spencer Grant/PhotoEdit; p. 47 bottom, Courtesy of Dr. Dana Cloud; p. 49, Christopher Robbins/Digital Vision/Getty Images Royalty Free.

Chapter 3 p. 54, © 2009 iStockphoto/double; p. 56, Photos.com; p. 57, © Peter Turnley/Corbis; p. 59, Ulrich Perrey/dpa/Corbis; p. 60, Index Open/PhotosToGo; p. 61, ZITS Partnership, King Features Syndicate; p. 62, Ian Waldie/Reportage/Getty Images; p. 64, Photos.com; p. 66 left, Photos.com; p. 66 middle, Photos.com; p. 66 right, Photos.com; p. 66 bottom, Photos.com; p. 67 top, © Joan Vicent Cantó Roig/iStock Photo; p. 67 bottom, Larry Gatz/Image Bank/Getty Images; p. 72, © Maya Barnes Johansen/The Image Works; p. 74, © Purestock/Alamy Royalty Free.

Chapter 4 p. 80, © 2009 iStockphoto/4x6; p. 82 top, © Alex Hallatt/www.CartoonStock.com; p. 82 middle, © René Mansi/iStockPhoto; p. 85, Index Open/PhotosToGo; p. 87, Photodisc/Getty Images Royalty Free; p. 88, Marc Romanelli/Getty; p. 89, Image 100/Alamy Royatly Free; p. 93 top, Index Open/PhotosToGo; p. 93 bottom, Index Open/PhotosToGo; p. 94, © John Birdsall/The Image Works; p. 96, AP Images/Chen xiaogen-maginechina; p. 101, © Radius Images/Alamy Royalty Free.

Chapter 5 p. 104, © 2009 Blend/Jupiterimages; p. 106 top, Index Open/PhotosToGo; p. 109 middle, © Robert Thompson/www.CartoonStock.com; p. 109 bottom, Photos.com; p. 110, Photos.com; p. 111, Index Open/PhotosToGo; p. 112, Index Open/PhotosToGo; p. 114, © New Line Cinema/Topham/The Image Works; p. 116, Courtesy of Matthew T. Campbell and Dr. Greg Plumb, East Central University; p. 119, Index Open/PhotosToGo; p. 132 top left, Photos.com; p. 132 top right, Photos.com; p. 132 middle right, Photos.com; p. 132 bottom right, Photos.com; p. 132 bottom left, Photos.com; p. 120, Photos.com; p. 128, Index Open/PhotosToGo.

Chapter 6 p. 138, © 2009 Polka Dot/Jupiterimages; p. 140 top, Index Open/PhotosToGo; p. 140 bottom, Getty Images/Altrendo Images; p. 141, © Steve Skjold/Alamy; p. 144, Photos.com; p. 145, © Icon Sports Media Inc. (Icon SMI) All Rights Reserved, supplied by Newscom; p. 146, © Paul Piebinga/iStockPhoto; p. 150 top left, Photos.com; p. 150 middle right, Photos.com; p. 150 middle left, Photos.com; p. 150 bottom right, © Dennis MacDonald/PhotoEdit Inc.; p. 153, Photos.com; p. 155 middle, © RGJ Richard Jolley/www.CartoonStock.com; p. 155 bottom, Photos.com; p. 157, Getty Images; p. 159, SABA Press Photos, Inc./Corbis.

Chapter 7 p. 164, © Steven Sutton/Corbis Sports/Duomo/CORBIS; p. 168 top, © Roger Bamber/Alamy; p. 168 bottom, Courtesy of Peter Stalker; p. 169 top, AP Images/Rick Rycroft; p. 171 middle, © Bob Daemmrich/The Image Works; p. 171 bottom, © Jack Hollingsworth/Blend Images/Corbis Royalty Free; p. 172 top left, © Peter Turnley/CORBIS; p. 172 top right, Sebastian Bolesch/Das Fotoarchiv; p. 172 bottom left, Peter Turnley/CORBIS; p. 172 bottom right, KRISTIN MOSHER/Danita Delimont; p. 174, Frederick M. Brown/Agence France Presse/Getty Images; p. 179, Blend Images/Getty Images Royalty Free; p. 181, Index Open/PhotosToGo; p. 184, Photos.com; p. 186, AP Images/Tony Dejak.

Chapter 8 p. 192, © 2009 iStockphoto/DanielBendjy; p. 194 top, Thomas Northcut/Lifesize/Getty Images Royalty Free; p. 195, Stewart Cohen/Index Open/PhotosToGo; p. 199, Index Open/PhotosToGo; p. 201, Index Open/PhotosToGo; p. 204 top, Index Open/PhotosToGo; p. 204 bottom, UPI

Photo/Landov; p. 205, Photos.com; p. 206, Index Open/PhotosToGo; p. 207, © Noel Ford/www.CartoonStock.com; p. 208, Photodisc/Getty Images Royalty Free; p. 211, PhotoAlto/Laurence Mouton/Getty Images Royalty Free; p. 216, George Doyle/Stockbyte/Getty Images Royalty Free; p. 218, Tara Moore/Stone/Getty Images.

Chapter 9 p. 222, © 2009 Pixland/Jupiterimages; p. 224, © Andrew Toos/www.CartoonStock.com; p. 227, © moodboard/Corbis Royalty Free; p. 229, Tom Merton/OJO Images/Getty Images Royalty Free; p. 231, Copyright © 2009 Arizona Board of Regents. Used with permission; p. 233, NBC/Courtesy, Everett Collection; p. 234, Photo by Dan Sears; p. 236, Andy Lyons/Getty Images; p. 237 left, Library of Congress; p. 237 middle, © Photos 12/Alamy; p. 237 right, Mark Richards/PhotoEdit; p. 241 top, Billy E. Barnes/PhotoEdit; p. 241 bottom, © James Marshall/The Image Works; p. 243, George Tames/The New York Times/Redux; p. 245, © Davis Barber/PhotoEdit Inc.; p. 250, © Bob Daemmrich/The Image Works.

Chapter 10 p. 254, © 2009 Comstock/Jupiterimages; p. 256, Otto Pohl/The New York Times/Redux; p. 257, © JIM YOUNG/Reuters/Corbis; p. 260, Carin Baer/© AMC/Courtesy: Everett Collection; p. 261, Photo Courtesy of US Army (photo of Teddy Wade); p. 262, Mary Haggerty/The New York Times/Redux; p. 264, Dynamic Graphics/Jupiter Images Royalty Free; p. 266, Index Open/PhotosToGo; p. 268, 20th Century Fox /Redin, Van/The Kobal Collection; p. 273, Dennis McDonald/PhotoEdit; p. 275, © Jim Sizemore/www.CartoonStock.com; p. 279, Mario Tama/Getty Images; p. 282, Index Open/PhotosToGo; p. 283, Jim Varney/Photo Researchers; p. 284, Index Open/PhotosToGo; p. 286 left, Photos.com; p. 286 middle, Photos.com; p. 286 right, Photos.com.

Chapter 11 p. 290, © Wally McNamee/CORBIS; p. 292, © Corbis Royalty Free/SuperStock Royalty Free; p. 293, © John Nordell/The Image Works; p. 300, Bob Parent/Hulton Archive/Getty Images; p. 301, Phil Sears/The New York Times/Redux; p. 304, AP Images/Alex Brandon; p. 305, Fred Conrad/The New York Times/Redux; p. 306 top, Susan Van Etten/PhotoEdit; p. 306 middle, AP Images; p. 306 bottom, AP Images; p. 307, AP Images//Charles Dharapak; p. 308, © Fran/www.CartoonStock.com; p. 310, © Frank Trapper/Corbis; p. 313a, Jake Price/The New York Times/Redux; p. 313b, © Ralf-Finn Hestoft/Corbis; p. 313c, Prentice Hall High School; p. 313d, Nancy Siesel/The New York Times/Redux; p. 314, Library of Congress.

Chapter 12 p. 318, © 2009 Ralph Orlowski/Getty Images News/Getty Images; p. 320, Enigma/Alamy; p. 322, Michael Kamber/The New York Times/Redux; p. 323, Jochen Tack/Alamy; p. 326, Dana Edelson/© NBC/Courtesy: Everett Collection; p. 328, AP Images; p. 330, Courtesy of the authors François Avard & Jean-François Mercier, and the producers Fabienne Larouche & Michel Trudeau from Aetios Productions inc.; p. 331, ARUNAS KLUPSAS/Photolibrary; p. 336, Digital Vision/Getty Images Royalty Free; p. 338, Sean Locke/Digital Planet Design/iStockPhoto; p. 343 top, AP Images/Chris Weeks; p. 343 bottom, © David Brown/www.CartoonStock.com; p. 345, New Stock/Alamy.

Chapter 13 p. 348, © 2009 Comstock/Jupiterimages; p. 350 bottom, Imago/ZUMA Press; p. 354, Index Open/PhotosToGo; p. 358 a, Photos.com; p. 358 b, Photos.com; p. 358 c, Photos.com; p. 358 d, Photos.com; p. 358 e, Corbis Royalty Free/SuperStock Royalty Free; p. 360, Photos.com; p. 363, © vario images GmbH & Co.KG/Alamy; p. 368, © JUPITERIMAGES/PHOTOS.COM/Alamy Royalty Free; p. 369, Jerry King/www.CartoonStock.com; p. 370, Index Open/PhotosToGo; p. 372 bottom, Photo by Lance Cpl. Katina J. Johnson, Courtesy of United State Marine Corps; p. 379, Vanessa Vick/The New York Times/Redux.

Chapter 14 p. 384, © 2009 Comstock/Jupiterimages; p. 386, CBS Photo Archive/Getty Images; p. 388, Toastmasters International; p. 389 top, Photos.com; p. 389 middle, Michael Newman/PhotoEdit; p. 389 bottom, K. Shamsi-Basha/The Image Works; p. 390, UPI Photo/Ken James via Newscom; p. 391, © Robert Thompson/www.CartoonStock.com; p. 393, © Bob Daemmrich/The Image Works; p. 394, Donna Alberico/The New York Times/Redux; p. 396, Index Open/PhotosToGo; p. 399, Michael Newman/PhotoEdit; p. 403, © Bob Daemmrich/The Image Works; p. 406, Michael Newman/PhotoEdit; p. 409, © Syracuse Newspapers/Michelle Gabel/The Image Works; p. 411 middle, Scott Cunningham/PH Merrill Publishing.

Index